TRUST AND CORPORATION PROBLEMS

By

HENRY R. SEAGER

and

CHARLES A. GULICK

ARNO PRESS
A New York Times Company
New York / 1973

Reprint Edition 1973 by Arno Press Inc.

Reprinted from a copy in The Newark Public Library

BIG BUSINESS: Economic Power in a Free Society
ISBN for complete set: 0-405-05070-4
See last pages of this volume for titles.

Manufactured in the United States of America

Library of Congress Cataloging in Publication Data

Seager, Henry Rogers, 1870-1930.
Trust and corporation problems.

(Big business: economic power in a free society)
Reprint of the ed. published by Harper, New York.
Bibliography: p.
1. Trusts, Industrial--United States. 2. Corporation law--United States. I. Gulick, Charles Adams, 1896- joint author. II. Title. III. Series.
HD2785.S4 1973 338.8'5'0973 73-2534
ISBN 0-405-05112-3

TRUST AND CORPORATION

PROBLEMS

TRUST AND CORPORATION PROBLEMS

By

HENRY R. SEAGER

Columbia University

and

CHARLES A. GULICK, Jr.

University of California

Harper & Brothers Publishers

NEW YORK AND LONDON

TRUST AND CORPORATION
PROBLEMS

PRINTED IN THE U.S.A.

Third Printing

F-E

CONTENTS

CONTENTS

PREFACE

The purpose of this book is to discuss the combination or trust problem as it has developed in the United States and other countries. Since the organization of business enterprises as corporations has been an essential condition to the formation of trusts, some consideration of the corporation problem has been included. The chapter headings which precede indicate sufficiently the topics which are treated and the proportionate attention that is given to the economic and legal aspects of the subject.

In the United States as elsewhere the combination movement has resulted from the efforts of business men to throw off the restraints and avoid the wastes of unregulated competition. It is one of our conclusions that even after all of the economies of large-scale production have been realized, there remain wastes and losses that can be avoided only through the exercise of sufficient control over prices to maintain them at profitable levels and over outputs to secure the highest attainable regularity in the operation of plants. The combination movement is thus a natural and indeed inevitable business development, which is not in and of itself opposed to the public interest. Every improvement in the means of communication and in transportation facilities widens the field over which combinations may operate. If there lies before the world, as we all hope, a long period of international peace during which international trade will expand to vaster proportions than have yet been attained, then international combinations are bound to multiply.

While combinations, going even to the length of monopolistic control over outputs and prices, have strong economic justification, they may operate to the serious disadvantage of independent producers and of consumers. Unless the public welfare is to be sacrificed either their formation must be prevented or they must be subjected to a certain amount of control and regulation.

When first confronted by the combination movement, American opinion strongly favored prevention. Even when creating machinery for the regulation of the railroads, through the Interstate Commerce Act of 1887, Congress felt impelled to insert an antipooling clause. Nor did our legislators except the railroads from the prohibitions and penalties of the more drastic Antitrust Act of 1890. It was not until after the country had experienced the advantages of centralized control under government administration during the Great War that the Transportation Act of 1920 removed the earlier restraints upon combination in the railroad field and substituted the policy of encouragement, subject to regulation through the Interstate Commerce Commission. There has been as yet no similar relaxation of the prohibitions on industrial combinations in general, but exceptions have been made of particular branches, like farming and foreign trade. Reflecting this more tolerant attitude, the Supreme Court, in interpreting the antitrust acts, has refused to condemn an industrial combination like the United States Steel Corporation merely because its size involves the potential danger of monopolistic control of an industry.

The crux of the trust problem lies in the question whether a country like the United States, which has shown itself vacillating in its policies and inefficient in its administration, can be depended upon to exercise the control and restraint that are necessary to prevent industrial combinations from oppressing independent producers and exploiting consumers. Unless it can, the case is strong for the continuance of anticombination laws and policies. By suppressing combinations, we may prevent the most rational and efficient organization of our national industries, but that may be better in the long run than permitting oppressive combinations to develop. If the policy of suppression is decided upon, the antitrust laws should be strengthened to condemn unequivocally even potential monopolistic control of an industry.

The alternative to a policy of repression is the development of adequate and efficient administrative machinery for control and regulation. Essential to the successful operation of such machinery are enforced publicity as regards all important agreements and operations and prevention of all unfair and oppressive policies toward competitors. In the Federal Trade Commission, created in 1914, we have an agency which might be developed into a regulative body for industrial combinations comparable with the Interstate Commerce Commission for the railroads. Experience alone can determine how far regulation once embarked upon should be carried, but it is quite clear that without the help of such an investigating body the courts are ill-equipped to determine when prices are unfair and unreasonable. Moreover, if we delegate to an enlarged and strengthened Federal Trade Commission the task of determining when the prices charged by industrial combinations are unreasonable and therefore unlawful, we must face the probability that we will soon be forced by the logic of events to give this commission the power to decide what prices would be reasonable and therefore permissible.

The following pages trace the variable policies which the United States has pursued in its handling of the trust problem, compare them with the policies adopted by other leading countries and supply material for an intelligent discussion of the relative advantages of repression and of regulation at our present stage of political and economic development. We have conceived it to be our chief task to present an accurate and adequate account of the facts of the corporation and combination situation, and of the arguments for and against policies that are being tried or that have been proposed. Our own opinions and conclusions are expressed freely, but we have endeavored not to present them dogmatically nor to ignore the objections that may be urged against them.

As teachers directing courses on these problems, we have necessarily had in mind the kind of treatise we should ourselves like to have for class use. But we hope the book will be found interesting and suggestive also by public men and business executives to whom Trust and Corporation Problems have long since ceased to have merely an academic interest.

It would be impossible to list all of the fellow economists, public officials, business managers and executives, and students who have helped us in various ways in the preparation of this volume. To the general expression of our deep appreciation for the assistance of each and everyone of these coworkers, we wish to add our special thanks to Professor George W. Stocking for reading the greater part of the proof, to Professor James W. Angell for reading the chapters on German policies, to Dr. W. H. S. Stevens and Mr. O. B. Johnson of the Federal Trade Commission, and to Paul Kosok, Malcolm McComb, Myrtle Hosang, Milton Redford, Elizabeth Brandt, Carmen Haider and Irma Rittenhouse for assistance in collecting material, verifying references, reading proof, preparing the index, and doing many other tasks that have hastened the completion of our undertaking.

Henry R. Seager,
Charles A. Gulick, Jr.

TRUST AND CORPORATION PROBLEMS

CHAPTER I

INTRODUCTION

THE term "trust," as used in this book, signifies *an industrial combination, not a legal nor a natural monopoly, which seeks to escape the restraints and avoid the wastes of competition by absorbing, controlling, or forcing out of business its would-be competitors, or by acting in concert with them in fixing prices or regulating outputs.* The word thus embraces all combinations in the industrial field which enjoy or seek to enjoy the advantages of monopoly except those based upon some legal privilege, like a franchise or a patent, or those which are monopolies by nature. There is difference of opinion as to the industries embraced in this last class, but it is generally agreed that it includes all the so-called public-service industries—that is, water companies, gas and electric-light companies, street-railway companies, telephone companies, and, in the national field, telegraph and railway companies. These will receive no special attention in this book.

Trusts, as broadly defined, have tempered business competition from an early period, but it is only within the last fifty years that they have assumed such proportions as to constitute a special problem. The first trust of national significance in the United States was the Standard Oil Trust, organized in 1879 and reorganized in 1882. The plan adopted by this combination of vesting control of the combined properties in a board of trustees was the circumstance which caused the term "trust" to acquire its present significance. Judicial decisions holding the trust *form* of organization unlawful caused it to be abandoned in the early 'nineties. The trust *name,* however, has remained the distinctive American designation of what in other countries are called monopolistic industrial combinations.

The following forms of trusts may be distinguished: (1)

Simple Agreements; (2) Pools; (3) Trade Associations; (4) Trusts Proper; (5) Holding Companies; (6) Outright Consolidations. The last three alone are often thought of when the trust movement is mentioned. Simple agreements and pools have usually been secret in the United States and have always been transitory. Trade associations are generally free from any monopolistic purpose. Nevertheless agreements and pools are usually and trade associations are sometimes trusts, in accordance with our definition, and therefore merit attention. As is brought out in the sections which follow, the combinations that have at different periods been most in evidence in the United States have assumed forms determined not only by economic but also by legal considerations.

Of all forms of combination, Simple Agreements are the most numerous and most varied. There is scarcely a branch of business in which they do not serve to modify somewhat the stress of unbridled competition. In retail trade it is not unusual for local dealers, for example coal and ice dealers, to agree as to the prices to be charged. Such agreements may be tacit, experience having convinced the rival dealers that price-cutting was bad business policy, or formal, the result of a conference and definite pledge. As a rule such agreements are kept secret, as consumers are only too apt to regard them as inimical to their interests.

Instead of relating to prices, the agreement may concern the volume of goods to be produced or sold or the localities in which sales are to be made by each party to the agreement. Farmers sometimes join together in withholding their crops from the market in the hope that they may in this way secure higher prices. Even among newsboys, some understanding as to the corner on which each boy shall offer his wares is not unusual. It may seem exaggeration to describe all such agreements as entailing some degree of monopoly, but a little thought will convince the reader that even the haphazard and constantly changing agreements in regard to the division of territory on the part of newsboys introduces some slight element of monopoly on the side of the sellers. This slight element, which in the case of newsboys may be of no perceptible disadvantage to the buyers, since the price of newspapers is fixed by higher powers, may expand into an important influence on prices. When a sufficient number of producers or dealers join in agreements in regard to the fields they are respectively to cover to affect prices, we have, however, something more than a simple agreement. Such agreements are really examples of the "market pools" discussed in the next section.

Where agreements as to prices, outputs, or territories to be covered are entered into by big business men, they are often styled "gentlemen's agreements" to emphasize the fact that strict adherence to them rests on the honor of the parties to the agreement. Gentlemen's agreements, like those implicitly resulting from the "Gary dinners" in the steel industry,[1] have played an important rôle in the combination movement in the United States in part because, with the law prohibiting combinations in restraint of trade and monopolies, it has been impossible to accomplish the same purpose through legally enforceable contracts.

Though very widespread, simple agreements as to prices, outputs, or division of territory do not usually involve any very serious hardship upon consumers. This is because an agreement which caused extortionate prices to be demanded would contain in itself the seeds of its own destruction. On the one hand, consumers, conscious of being mulcted, would be apt to seek redress by invoking the law against restraint of trade and monopoly. On the other, the high profits enjoyed would be a temptation to the parties to the agreement to break it by granting secret concessions in price to enlarge the volume of their sales and to others to enter the industry as competitors. Experience of the instability of unreasonable agreements causes business men who continue to temper their competition by this means to curb their cupidity, with the result that the long-run influence of simple agreements on prices is less unfavorable to the interests of consumers than might be expected.

It was largely because of the instability of simple agree-

[1] See *infra*, pp. 245, 246.

ments that business men who sought to lessen the severity of competition devised the more refined form of combination known as Pools. These are agreements of a more formal character which have as their essential element the combining, or "pooling," of some common factor with a view to controlling supplies and fixing or influencing prices. The common factor combined may be the output of the plants concerned (or, in the case of transportation companies, the traffic), the market to be supplied, patents essential to some stage of the process of production, or the gross or net returns from the businesses affected. Accordingly, we have as the principal forms of pools: (1) output pools; (2) market pools; (3) patent pools; and (4) earnings pools.[1]

Output pools are much more important practically than the other three types, and assume a great variety of forms. Simplest of all are agreements as to the volume of goods each party to the understanding will offer for sale during an ensuing period, coupled with some stipulation as to the minimum prices to be charged. Such pools are not very satisfactory, since market conditions may change and larger or smaller outputs than were contemplated may become advisable. More refined are agreements as to the percentage of the total volume of goods sold by the parties to the agreement to which each party shall be entitled as his allotment. Such agreements are nearly always coupled with some understanding as to prices and often with machinery for imposing agreed forfeits on members of the pool exceeding their allotments, the proceeds being shared *pro rata* among those who have not come up to theirs. To facilitate the collection of such forfeits a frequent device is a proportionate contribution by each member of the pool to a common fund, such contribution being liable to attachment until forfeits imposed shall have been paid. The most developed form of output pool, little used in this country because condemned by the law, but

[1] This classification is less elaborate than that proposed by W. H. S. Stevens in his valuable article, "A Classification of Pools and Associations Based on American Experience," *American Economic Review*, vol. iii (September, 1913), pp. 545-575, but is thought to include all of the important examples which he describes.

very common in Europe under the name of the *cartel,* is the combination which disposes of the agreed aggregate outputs of all of the members through a common selling agent or company in which each has a proportionate interest. This has the obvious advantage of direct control of prices supplemented by indirect control of supplies, while at the same time it leaves the members quite free, except as regards prices and the amounts which they shall produce, in the management of their individual properties. This form of combination is believed by many students to afford to business men all or nearly all of the advantages which they can hope to derive from combined action. We shall discuss it more fully in Chapters VII and XXIV.

Market, patent, and earnings pools have been important usually as supplements to other forms of combination. Thus at different times there have been international pooling agreements between the leading manufacturers and sellers of powder, tobacco, and steel products that limited each member to an agreed portion of the world market. These were important chiefly because of the dominant influence already enjoyed by the members in their respective fields.[1] Similarly, patent pools, like that giving rise to the so-called Bathtub Trust,[2] have been important because of the monopoly inherent in the patents controlled.

As officially defined by the American Trade Association Executives, a Trade Association is "an organization of producers or distributors of a commodity or service upon a mutual basis for the purpose of promoting the business of its branch of industry or commerce and improving its service to the public."[3] Although limited usually to forms of cooperation that are free from any suspicion of monopoly, such associations have at times developed into monopolistic com-

[1] Cf. Stevens, *ibid.*, p. 570; *Report of the Commissioner of Corporations on the Tobacco Industry,* part i, Exhibits I and II, pp. 431 *et seq*; Liefmann, *International Cartels, Combines and Trusts,* pp. 42-66.

[2] Cf. Ripley, *Trusts, Pools and Corporations,* revised edition, pp. 606-634.

[3] Quoted in the U. S. Department of Commerce Report, *Trade Association Activities,* 1923, p. 1.

binations ranging from gentlemen's agreements to outright pools. As this implies, there is no sharp logical distinction between monopolistic trade associations and these other forms. They have become such an important phase of the combination movement, however, that we have given them separate treatment in Chapter XVI.

By Trusts Proper in these pages we mean trusts after the model of the Standard Oil combination of 1882, which is described at length in Chapter V. The vogue which this form of combination enjoyed during the 'eighties was due to the fact that it seemed a legal method of securing the advantages of the close-knit pool—control of outputs and of prices, through a unified selling organization, coupled with as complete independence of management of the different properties combined as might be deemed advisable—after the courts had held that pooling contracts were unenforceable. The decisions of the courts in the early 'nineties, reviewed in Chapter V, deprived trust organizers of this refuge for their combinations and led to the development of the holding company.

The Holding Company is a corporation which combines the business and properties of other corporations through ownership of all or a controlling majority of their capital stock. Its advantages in a country like the United States, where so much of the business carried on is already in corporate form, are obvious. First, the acquisition of the businesses to be combined may usually be secured both more easily and more cheaply by the purchase of all or a majority of their capital stock than by the outright purchase of the businesses themselves. Secondly, the corporate businesses acquired, although completely controlled, may yet be permitted to retain the semblance of independent existence. This has sometimes made it possible for a combination to advertise and sell the products of some of its controlled plants as "independent," and thus retain customers who would not knowingly buy from itself. Also it permits operation of the different corporations by different boards of directors and different managers, who may be stimulated into as eager competition to "show results" as though they were in fact independent of one another. Thirdly, the businesses and properties combined may be rearranged into new corporate units to an almost indefinite extent or the individual corporations may be dissolved and the holding company may become an outright consolidation.

In the United States the holding company was made possible by the deliberate amendment of the corporation law of New Jersey in 1889 to permit this form of combination and the subsequent modification of the corporation laws of other states in the same direction. Such wide use of it was made by the combinations which aroused most public opposition that a strong movement developed to have the holding company declared unlawful. In 1913 this bore fruit in New Jersey in an amendment to the corporation law of that state [1] which prohibited the combining of competing corporations in holding companies. This condemnation by public opinion and the dissolution of some of the most conspicuous of the holding companies, like the Northern Securities Company and the Standard Oil Company of New Jersey, made trust organizers for a time chary of this form of combination. Outright consolidation is still somewhat less liable to legal attack, whatever its merits in other respects.

Outright Consolidations may come about by the acquisition by one business of another, when it is said to be the result of a "merger," or by the fusing together of two or more businesses into a new business organization or new corporation, when it is said to be an "amalgamation." Outright consolidation implies that complete unity of ownership and control is secured by the merger or amalgamation and that not even the semblance of divided management or responsibility is retained. It thus has all of the advantages and disadvantages of centralized, unified control. The policy as to output, prices, and treatment of competitors may be clear cut and definite; the capacity for efficient organization of the central authority may extend its influence into every department;

[1] Chapter 18, Laws of 1913, approved February 19, 1913, but repealed in 1917. Cf. Chapter XVII.

and there need be no hesitation nor delay in inaugurating new business policies. Under capable management these advantages permit of the indefinite expansion of a consolidated company, rivals being either brought into the combination, limited to a restricted portion of the market, or forced out of business altogether. But the centralized control, which enables the business organizer of commanding capacity to infuse his energy and ability into every department of a rapidly expanding enterprise, has certain disadvantages. Expansion, if carried too far, may render the business unwieldy. The "master's eye," of which Adam Smith wrote, cannot continue to oversee every department. As the business grows, more and more responsibility will of necessity be transferred to hired managers. The task of the directing mind gradually changes from that of directing the business to that of directing the subordinates who direct it. Many an able business man who directs a growing business in masterly fashion so long as it is possible for him to keep in touch with the operations of every department, fails when consolidation and expansion are carried so far that he is forced to rely entirely on the supervision of subordinates. Others have the capacity and adaptability to meet this test, but the consolidations that grow up under their direction are confronted by a further danger. The period of highest efficiency of a business man is limited at best to but a few years. The greater the capacity of the individual or individuals under whose guidance a great consolidation has been effected and carried on successfully, the greater the difficulty of securing men of equal ability to succeed them when old age or death forces their retirement. This is the principal reason for the checkered fortunes of many American consolidations. Everything has depended on the capacity and integrity of purpose of the man or men at the top, and inevitably when these men have been changed, the success of the business has been affected, sometimes disastrously.[1]

In the development of the trusts an essential rôle has been

[1] The development of business management as a special profession has tended to lessen this danger. Cf. *infra,* pp. 660, 661.

played by the business corporation. Private enterprises might enlarge the scale of their operations by forming partnerships with their business rivals, but in a country as large and complex as the United States these could never secure more than a local and temporary control of any branch of business. It was by substituting for private or partnership ownership and control corporate ownership and control that American business men prepared the way for the trust movement. Even the original trusts, combined through trust agreements rather than by means of charters of incorporation, were dependent for their existence on the fact that most of the properties to be brought under the control of a board of trustees were already organized as corporations. This was shown by the fact that the dissolution of these early trusts was brought about, not by attacking the trust agreements directly, but by securing the revocation of the charters of corporations that had entered into them. The dissolution of the constituent corporations inevitably involved the dissolution of the trusts which combined them. Even more significant was the decision of these early trust organizers that the only way effectively to continue their combinations in existence was to substitute for the discredited trust agreement a charter of incorporation from some state, like New Jersey, which not only permitted but encouraged the organization of corporations with unlimited capital and with power to own and control the shares of stock of other corporations. Thus underlying the trust problem is the more fundamental corporation problem. In recognition of this dependence of the American trust on the American business corporation, we proceed in the next three chapters to a consideration of business corporations.

CHAPTER II

BUSINESS CORPORATIONS IN THE UNITED STATES

A corporation may be defined as *a voluntary association endowed with autonomy and continuity of existence through a government-granted license or charter.* Business corporations have the further characteristics that they exist for designated purposes and that participation in them is secured through ownership of transferable shares of stock. Each one of these aspects deserves special consideration.

The incorporation of a business enterprise is a *voluntary* procedure. Business men sometimes complain that the burdens imposed on corporations, especially in the form of taxes, are becoming too onerous. They seem to forget that they are under no obligation to organize their businesses as corporations, and that if they do so, because of the substantial privileges which the law grants corporations, they should be willing also to accept the obligations which the law imposes.

The grant of the charter, which gives the corporation its legal being, though at one time dependent on royal whim or favor, is now universally controlled by the lawmaking power. In the United States, charters of incorporation may be granted by each of the forty-eight states, by the governing authorities of the territories and insular possessions, and by Congress either in its national capacity or as the legislative authority for the District of Columbia. Even if the charter-granting policies of these fifty-four different authorities were fixed and unalterable, their multiplicity would inevitably result in confusion, since business corporations organized by lawful authority in any part of the United States may usually do business in any other part. As a matter of fact their charter-granting policies have been subject to constant modification, and in consequence the corporation situation in the United States today is little short of chaotic.

One tendency, however, all incorporation policies have shared. They have become more and more liberal with the passing of the years, until at present nearly all authorities permit the incorporation of ordinary business undertakings under general laws and regulations. All that is now required in most jurisdictions of those who desire to incorporate a business is that they fill out an application in proper form and send it with the prescribed fees to the Secretary of State or other appropriate officer. The charter is returned, as the application is made, by mail, and little personal responsibility in connection with it attaches to the incorporators.

The continuity of existence which corporations enjoy varies under different laws. In nearly half of the states it is still true that corporations have perpetual life. In the other states, where they are chartered for a limited term of years, provision is uniformly made for the easy renewal of the charter, so that such limitation is not of serious practical consequence.

In applying for a charter to the appropriate authority, the incorporators must indicate the nature of the business in which the corporation is to engage. Such statement is reproduced in the charter and thereafter limits the field within which the corporation may lawfully act. Any action by a corporation not authorized, expressly or by implication, by its charter is *ultra vires*—that is, in excess of the corporation's powers, and may result in the imposition of penalties ranging from the invalidation of the contract to which the corporation sought to be a party to the forfeiture of its charter. Organizers of corporations in the United States largely escape this limitation by applying for all-embracing or "blanket" charters, but it nevertheless has played an important rôle in checking certain tendencies in corporate development.

The device of representing the property or capital of a corporation as "shares" in an aggregate total issue of shares and allowing these shares to be transferable, so that participation in the corporation may pass from person to person, without any interruption of its activities, was first utilized by the so-called joint-stock companies, which attained their highest development in Europe in the seventeenth and eighteenth centuries. As perfected in the corporation it gives elasticity to corporate enterprise without interfering seriously with its stability. Through the agency of stock markets, individual business men may acquire or divest themselves of stock holdings in corporations almost at will. Ordinarily, this shifting about of stockholders has little effect on the business policy of the corporation, since a majority of the shares remains in the same hands. Only when serious dissensions arise among the stockholders are changes in the ownership of shares likely to result in a change of management. Disturbing as such changes in control necessarily are, they more often than not are a means of ousting corrupt or inefficient officers and thus serve in the long run to promote the best interests of the corporations affected.

In addition to the characteristics already considered, there are two others which, though not essential to the idea of a business corporation, are so commonly present and so important that they merit consideration. American corporation laws usually grant to stockholders the privilege of *limited liability* for the debts of the corporation of which they are part owners. Historically, this is the principal distinction between joint-stock companies and corporations. Stockholders in the former bore the same relation to it as partners in a partnership and were liable to the full extent of their resources for any debts it might contract. Unlike partners, however, they might transfer their interest and liability by selling their stock, without thereby forcing the dissolution of the joint-stock company. By gradual stages, limited liability has been substituted in corporations for this old full liability. Under the National Bank Acts the liability of stockholders in national banks is limited to an amount equal to the par value of the shares of stock which they hold, in addition to whatever they may have paid for such shares when they were subscribed for or purchased. The most common provision as regards ordinary business corporations is that the stockholders are liable only for unpaid balances of the sums originally subscribed for the stock of which they are owners. If the stock is full-paid and non-assessable, no further liability attaches to the stockholders, even if the corporation becomes bankrupt. As the usual practice in launching American business corporations is to issue only full-paid stock, "limited liability" in connection with American corporations as a rule means no liability at all beyond the risk of losing what one has already paid for the stock of which he is the owner. Such limited liability is one of the most important privileges which investors in corporate enterprises enjoy. Its introduction was a chief cause of the enormous multiplication and expansion of American business corporations described hereafter and, though all corporations do not enjoy this privilege, it is so well-nigh universal in the United States that it is commonly thought of as one of their most essential characteristics.

The other non-essential characteristic is the requirement that a corporation must be for the promotion of some public interest. Historically this was an important principle, since strict adherence to it long prevented any large development of corporations. Legally it may still be invoked when the penalty for *ultra vires* acts is under consideration. Practically, however, since the introduction of general incorporation acts, it has lost its significance. American legislatures take the position virtually that it is for business men themselves to decide whether or not the corporate form of organization is suited to their particular enterprises. The question whether substitution of a corporation for a private firm or partnership will really advantage the public is not definitely raised. It is rather taken for granted that in this connection public interest and private interest coincide. The history of American corporations abounds in instances to prove that this assumption is unwarranted. As our next chapter shows, the public interest has all too often been sacrificed by the wide extension of the privilege of incorporating business enterprises. The grants of limited liability, continuity of existence, etc., have been continued but the safe-guarding restraints on these grants have largely been removed.

Adam Smith's discussion of joint-stock companies still constitutes an excellent starting point for a study of the corporation movement. When he published the *Wealth of Nations* in 1776 the incorporation of a joint-stock company was still a sufficiently unusual proceeding to call for special remark. No one at that time believed that the privilege of incorporating an undertaking should be lightly given. It was looked upon as a species of governmental interference with the normal course of industry—something warranted only when some great and certain public benefit was likely to result.

Adam Smith begins his discussion [1] by referring to a list of fifty-five joint-stock trading companies which had been established in the different countries of Europe since the year 1600, and all of which, according to the Abbé Morellet, had failed. The reason for these failures he finds in the fact that "the only trades which it seems possible for a joint-stock company to carry on successfully, without an exclusive privilege, are those of which all the operations are capable of being reduced to what is called a routine, or to such a uniformity of method as admits of little or no variation." His argument in support of this view is familiar. "The directors of [joint-stock] companies," he says, "being the managers rather of other people's money than of their own, it cannot well be expected that they should watch over it with the same anxious vigilance with which the partners in a private copartnery frequently watch over their own. Like the stewards of a rich man, they are apt to consider attention to small matters as not for their master's honor, and very easily give themselves a dispensation from having it. Negligence and profusion, therefore, must always prevail, more or less, in the management of the affairs of such a company."

The only businesses which he considered adapted to the corporate form of organization were: "first, the banking trade; secondly, the trade of insurance from fire, and from sea risk and capture in time of war; thirdly, the trade of making and maintaining a navigable cut or canal; and, fourthly, the similar trade of bringing water for the supply of a great city." Thus, according to his view, the only ventures likely to prove

[1] *Wealth of Nations,* bk. v., chap. i, pt. iii, art. 1.

successful under the corporate form of organization—assuming that the privilege of incorporation be extended to them—are banks, insurance companies, canals, and municipal water companies.

But he was far from thinking that every business which was likely to succeed as a corporation should be allowed to become one. For, as he goes on to say:

> To establish a joint-stock company, however, for any undertaking, merely because such a company might be capable of managing it successfully; or to exempt a particular set of dealers from some of the general laws which take place with regard to all their neighbors, merely because they might be capable of thriving if they had such an exemption, would certainly not be reasonable. To render such an establishment perfectly reasonable, with the circumstance of being reducible to strict rule and method, two other circumstances ought to concur. First, it ought to appear with the clearest evidence, that the undertaking is of greater and more general utility than the greater part of common trades; and secondly, that it requires a greater capital than can easily be collected into a private copartnery. If a moderate capital were sufficient, the great utility of the undertaking would not be a sufficient reason for establishing a joint-stock company; because, in this case, the demand for what it was to produce, would readily and easily be supplied by private adventurers. In the four trades above mentioned, both those circumstances concur.

Adam Smith, accordingly, would have subjected would-be corporations to a searching scrutiny before giving them the privileges they sought. Unless it was clearly apparent that the capital required could not be secured under another form of organization and that they promised to be of "greater and more general utility than the greater part of common trades," he would have denied them corporate charters. It seems highly probable that with these opinions he would have sympathized with those who think that limits—both lower and upper—should be placed upon the capitalization which any corporation should be permitted to have.

Notwithstanding Adam Smith's view that, in the absence of exclusive privileges, corporations could succeed only in banking, insurance, building and operating canals and supplying cities with water, there were, of course, many corporations in other fields of enterprise in his day. The great trading companies like the East India Company and the Hudson Bay Company were no exceptions to his rule, as they enjoyed exclusive privileges. He himself mentions others, however, that appear to resemble our present-day competitive corporations. Among these the English Copper Company, the Lead Smelting Company, and the Glass Grinding Company have a distinctly modern sound. As to the success of these, Adam Smith expresses himself somewhat skeptically, especially as the Mine Adventurers Company of an earlier period had been a complete failure, and the stock of the British Linen Company, the only other corporation of which he speaks, was selling considerably below par. Thus his narrow limiting of the field open to successful corporate enterprise was not based on theory alone, but upon a study of experience.

It is a familiar story how the industrial revolution, with its introduction of the factory system and of production on a larger scale than had before been dreamed of, opened a vast new field to corporate enterprise. For some time public opinion continued to look upon the grant of a charter of incorporation as an unusual privilege to be jealously guarded. In the United Kingdom charters were granted only by special Act of Parliament until 1844, when a general incorporation act was passed. This first act did not grant limited liability to stockholders in corporations organized under it, however, and it was not until 1855 that this privilege, which had been given to several special act corporations earlier, was extended to all business corporations. The first general act of incorporation in the United States including the grant of limited liability to shareholders was the New York law of 1811,[1] which permitted the organization of corporations with capital of not more than $100,000 for a period of not more than twenty years for certain designated manufacturing purposes by simply filing a certificate in proper form with the Secretary of State. Few corporations appear to have been organized under this law, and it was not until forty years later that organizations under general laws became the rule, the legislatures in many of the states having been deprived by consti-

[1] Gerstenberg, *Materials of Corporation Finance,* pp. 31-33.

tutional amendment (*e.g.*, Iowa, 1846) of the right to organize corporations by special acts.

The change from granting charters only through special legislative acts to that of prohibiting such special incorporating acts and issuing charters under general laws was revolutionary, but when made seemed justified by sound reasons of public policy. As the tendency to seek incorporation spread, the special act system proved to be a fruitful source of legislative corruption. Business men with political influence or willing to employ corrupt lobbyists could obtain charters; others were unable to do so. This was resented as unfair and undemocratic. Moreover, the time required to pass incorporating acts threatened to divert the attention of the legislature from matters of much more public importance. The plan of enacting general incorporating laws which prescribed the conditions under which charters of incorporation might be secured was an obvious remedy for these evils. Even states which still permitted incorporating by special act passed such measures, so that about the time that the first English act was passed similar acts became common in this country. Before the outbreak of the Civil War most of the states had general incorporation laws under which ordinary business enterprises might obtain charters giving all the privileges that have been enumerated, including that of limited liability.

In the United States, as in Europe, banks were among the first businesses to be incorporated. Thus the Bank of North America was chartered in Philadelphia in 1781. Three years later the Massachusetts Bank and the Bank of New York were chartered by those respective states. The way was thus prepared for the incorporation by Act of Congress of the First United States Bank in 1791.

Next to banks the corporations that were most prominent during the first four decades of our national history were stage companies, turnpike companies, canal companies, water companies, and insurance companies. Our experience, therefore, confirmed in the main the accuracy of Adam Smith's reasoning as to the types of business which are adapted to the corporate form of organization.

After 1830, railroad companies began to appear in the lists of corporations in different states, and during the next three decades they took first place. About the time of the Civil War, gas companies also began to be organized. Since the Civil War, manufacturing corporations have become more and more numerous.

While this spread of corporate enterprise has been influenced by the principles which Adam Smith laid down—that is, has been concerned mainly with businesses requiring large capital whose management could be reduced to definite rules—it is clear that corporations now embrace all kinds of businesses. Not only is manufacturing of every sort now conducted through them, but trade, farming, newspaper and magazine publishing, and, in short, every species of business, is so conducted.

The aspect which Adam Smith overlooked was that, when the incorporation policy of a government permits, a business man or group of business men may incorporate their business and still run it as their own. The withdrawal of the business from the "master's eye" is not, therefore, the necessary result of incorporating it. If he retains all the stock, or a majority of the stock, in his own control, the master may continue to run it as *his* business after incorporation as before. It is just this that has happened on an enormous scale in the United States as incorporation laws have become more and more liberal. Not only businesses specially adapted to the corporate form of organization have been incorporated, but all kinds of businesses, irrespective of their special characteristics, have been involved in a general movement toward incorporation that has been controlled by no sound principles of public policy and has been allowed to pass all reasonable bounds.

It is one result of the wide-open corporation policy adopted by so many American states that no satisfactory record is available of the number of charters of incorporation that have been issued by the different states. Records are of course kept by the state officials charged with the issue of such charters, but few states publish them in a way that permits of comparison with other states.

A casual examination of the current records of the incorporating activity of any state emphasizes the fact that the multiplication of corporations is not a proof of increasing concentration in business or of an increase in the average amount of capital required for the successful conduct of business. Small corporations are quite as numerous as large corporations.

At the time of writing, the incorporation laws of Delaware happen to be among the most liberal from the point of view of the advantages offered incorporators and the moderation of the taxes imposed. This would tend to attract to that state incorporators from all parts of the country and cause the proportion of large corporations to be unduly great. Though this tendency is discernible, the proportion of small-scale enterprises which incorporate even in Delaware is also striking. In January, 1929, 673 charters of incorporation for ordinary businesses [1] were issued. Four hundred and fifty-seven of the corporations created, or 68 per cent, had no-par stock, and 216, or 32 per cent, par stock only. This affords clear evidence of the marked preference promoters have developed for no-par stock. Analyzing the 326 of the no-par stock corporations which had no-par common only, we find that 28 of them, or 8 per cent, had 200 shares or less; 237, or 73 per cent, from 200 to 100,000 shares, and 61, or 19 per cent, more than 100,000 shares each. Of the 216 with par stock only, 43, or 20 per cent, had capitalizations of $20,000 or less; 155, or 71 per cent, capitalizations of $20,000 to $1,000,000; and 18, or 8 per cent, of $1,000,000 and over, the largest being capitalized for $75,000,000. Thus even in Delaware, with the strong appeal which its liberal law and moderate corporation taxes make to promoters of big business enterprises all over the country, and especially in the near-by financial centers, New York and Philadelphia, small corporations are numerous.

More clearly indicative of the present tendency to incorporate small as well as large business enterprises are the char-

[1] Not including banking, insurance, or public-service industries, for each of which in Delaware, as in other states, special incorporation laws have been passed adapted to their particular requirements.

ters currently issued by the state of New York. In January, 1929, 2,757 certificates of incorporation of stock companies were filed at Albany, an average of more than one hundred a day for the twenty-six business days in that month.[1] New York took the lead in permitting the issue of no-par stock through an amendment to her corporation law adopted in 1912. Assuming that the same proportions held for the 2,757 charters granted in January as for the 1,848 granted on sixteen days of the month selected at random as samples, 808, or 29 per cent, of this January crop of new corporations had no-par stock, and 1,949, or 71 per cent, par stock only. Of the corporations with no-par stock, 719, or 89 per cent, had common stock only; 89, or 11 per cent, no-par common with par, or in one instance no-par, preferred. The predominance of small enterprises is shown by the fact that 610, or 85 per cent, of the corporations with no-par common stock only had 200 shares or less, and only 109, or 15 per cent, over 200 shares. The same thing appears even more strikingly as regards the corporations with par stock only. Of the 1,949 in this group, 1,521, or 78 per cent, had a nominal capital of only $20,000 or less. Included among these were 1,057 corporations, or 54 per cent of the total, with capitalizations of $10,000 or less, of which 431, or 22 per cent of the total, had capitalizations of $5,000 or less. Thus it appears that four-fifths of the corporations currently granted charters by the state of New York, the center of big business, are small enterprises whose capital of $20,000 or less could readily be provided by hundreds of thousands of the individual business men in the state. The advantage so often claimed for corporations, that they permit the assembling from numerous investors of the large aggregations of capital required in modern large-scale operations, applies at most only to the 164 corporations, 8 per cent of the total, with nominal capitals of over $50,000. That only seven of the corporations had capitals of over $1,000,000 affords convincing proof that only

[1] This was a somewhat higher average than for preceding years, but an average of 2,000 charters a month had been maintained since 1925, when the total for the year was 24,703 charters. In 1928 a total of 26,817 was granted.

in exceptional circumstances do really large business enterprises accept the restrictions and the relatively heavy tax burdens with which the state of New York conditions the privilege of incorporation under its laws. As the relative prominence of large corporations among those currently chartered by Delaware indicates, it is to her and to the other states actively competing for the business of selling corporate charters, that the promoters of large enterprises and combinations go for the limited liability charters essential to the realization of their plans.

With each decade during the last fifty years an increasing proportion of the wealth of the United States has been brought under corporate control. In some fields, especially transportation, insurance, and banking, the corporate form of organization has almost entirely superseded other forms. According to a census estimate the total wealth of the United States in 1922 was $320,804,000,000. For the same year the Census Bureau found $35,365,000,000 invested in transportation industries, practically all under corporate control. This was nearly 11 per cent of the total wealth of the country. In manufacturing and mining, corporate control has not yet entirely crowded out individual ownership, but it is moving rapidly in that direction. In 1919, the latest year for which the census gives information on this point, 87.7 per cent of the value of the products of manufacturing industry was credited to corporations. The total capital invested in manufacturing in that year was given as $44,466,593,771. Assuming that the same percentage applying to the products of manufactures applied to the capital engaged in manufacture, $39,000,000,000 of this sum was controlled by corporations. Allowing for some expansion during the next three years, this would indicate that at least $40,000,000,000, or 12.5 per cent of the total wealth of the country in 1922, was controlled by manufacturing corporations. In 1919 the census credited 93.6 per cent of the value of the products of our mining industries to corporations. The total capital of the mining industries in that year was found to be $7,225,446,992. If we may assume that the above percentage applies to this total it follows that approximately $6,750,000,000, or at least 2 per cent of our national wealth in 1922, was controlled by mining corporations. Considering the prominence of corporations in other lines of business activity and that in the three lines referred to corporations controlled 25.5 per cent of the total national wealth, it is not surprising that other investigations applying the inventory method to the problem led to the conclusion that nearly one-third of all of the wealth in the United States was controlled by corporations in 1922. Thus the Federal Trade Commission made a supplementary investigation of the total national wealth in the country in 1922, and the proportion of the wealth that was controlled by corporations. It concluded that the total wealth in that year was not less than $353,000,000,000, or $32,000,000,000 more than was estimated by the Census Bureau. It placed the wealth controlled by corporations at $102,000,000,000, on the basis of the returns which it collected from them, and the business community's valuation of that wealth, based on the total market value of all outstanding corporate securities, at $98,500,000,000. When it is added that the Commission estimated that the value of real estate in that year totaled $230,000,000,000, and thus constituted 65 per cent of the national wealth, and when it is recalled that most real estate consists of the farms and homes of non-corporate owners, the extent to which corporations have come to dominate American business begins to be appreciated. Allowing for the rapid progress of the incorporation movement since 1922, we believe that no exaggeration is involved in the statement that more than four-fifths of American business enterprise is now carried on by corporations.

The reasons for this enormous development of corporate business are the advantages which corporations enjoy under present corporation laws and the absence of serious obstacles to the enjoyment of these advantages. Charges for incorporation and taxes on business corporations are moderate and the supervision to which they are subjected negligible in most of the states. A summary statement of these advantages, most of which have already been considered, will serve to introduce a discussion of the nature of the corporation and its relation to the state in the next chapter.

The advantages which American business corporations enjoy are:

(1) Autonomy, which includes the right to sue or to be sued in the corporate name, the right to own and control property and the right to enter into legally binding contracts;

(2) Continuity of existence, going to the point, under the laws of twenty-three of the states, including Delaware, of perpetual life;

(3) Limited liability of shareholders;

(4) Flexibility of management;

(5) Easy transfer of shares of stock and through them of ownership and control;

(6) Elasticity of capital;

(7) Release of shareholders and other beneficiaries from the responsibilities of management.

To these the liberalization of corporation laws has added in many states:

(8) Moderate fees for incorporation;

(9) All-embracing or blanket charters under which almost any conceivable development of the original corporate purpose becomes possible;

(10) Opportunity afforded ambitious business men to command the capital of minority investors without surrendering control over the business.

Putting all of these advantages together, we have a situation in which business men who incorporate their enterprises retain practically all of the rights and privileges which they enjoyed as individual enterprisers or partners, and gain important new rights and privileges. Under these circumstances the question now presented to American business men is not "why incorporate?" but "why not incorporate?" Their answer is given in the statistics of corporate organizations presented above. That incorporation promotes the interests of many business men is undoubted. In the succeeding chapters we consider respects in which it has failed to serve equally the interests of the public.

CHAPTER III

NATURE OF THE CORPORATION AND ITS RELATION TO THE STATE

One reason why American corporation laws are not more uniform is that there has been no universally accepted theory of the nature of corporations and of their true relation to the state for the guidance of American legislatures and courts.[1] To the layman, who has given little thought to the subject, the idea of the corporation seems simple enough. It is an association of individuals clothed with certain collective rights and with certain collective responsibilities. But this description applies equally well to other associations, like partnerships. As the corporation has developed from the partnership it will aid toward an understanding of its nature to consider how these two forms of association differ.

The differences emphasized by legal writers are:

(1) The corporation is a legal person, whereas the partnership is not;

(2) The shares carrying with them participation in the corporation may change hands without affecting it, whereas a change of partners dissolves the firm;

(3) Shareholders are not usually personally liable for the debts of the corporation, whereas partners are for the firm debts;

(4) Only the legally constituted officers of the corporation may act for it, whereas partners are each other's agents in respect to the firm business;

(5) Corporations must be formally created by the grant of a charter, whereas partnerships require no special sanction for their existence.

Not all of the above differences are equally important.

[1] Cf. Freund, E., *The Legal Nature of Corporations,* to which the authors are indebted for a part of the analysis which follows.

Thus in many states, midway between ordinary partnerships and ordinary corporations, the law provides for limited liability partnerships, on the one hand, and unlimited liability corporations or joint-stock companies, on the other. Moreover, the enactment of general corporation laws has made the task of securing a charter so easy that the fact that such a charter is necessary to the existence of a corporation has largely lost its significance. The special characteristics that remain are that a corporation is a distinct person in the eyes of the law and that its existence continues however much the personnel of its shareholders may change.

Historically, the last characteristic—that is, continuity of existence—may almost be said to have been the cause of the first. The early English jurists seem to have been unable to think of an association as a continuing entity distinct from its members without personifying it. Thus Blackstone in trying to explain the nature of a corporation declared that it was "an artificial person created for preserving in perpetual succession certain rights, which, being conferred on natural persons only would fail in process of time." Accepting this view of the corporation, Chief Justice Marshall formulated a definition in the Dartmouth College Case [1] which has been frequently quoted since: "A corporation is an artificial being, invisible, intangible, and existing only in contemplation of the law. Being a mere creature of the law, it possesses only those properties which the charter of its creation confers upon it, either expressly or as incidental to its existence."

The theory that the corporation is an "artificial person, existing only in contemplation of law," is usually described as the "fiction theory" and, like other legal fictions, has given rise to no little confusion. Corporation lawyers have shown great ingenuity in making use of it, sometimes to claim for the corporations they represent the rights and immunities enjoyed by natural persons on the ground that corporations, too, are persons, and at others to set up their artificiality to relieve them from the moral responsibilities imposed upon natural persons. In trying to deal with them as persons and,

[1] 4 Wheat. 518, 636 (1819).

at the same time, to adhere to the theory that they are only artificial persons, the courts, too, have registered decisions which were not always in accord with the common sense of the situation. An illustration drawn from litigation affecting some of the early trusts will serve to explain why the fiction theory has fallen into deserved disrepute.

The corporations which formed the American Sugar and Standard Oil trusts were attacked on the ground that they had exceeded their corporate powers. Their counsel attempted to defend them and escape the threatened forfeiture of their charters for the commission of *ultra vires* acts by a resort to the fiction theory. The facts in regard to these trusts were that the stockholders, who controlled the constituent corporations, joined together in a trust agreement, lodged control of their corporations in the hands of trustees by exchanging their stock certificates for trust certificates, and thereby enabled these trustees to administer their business and property as a single enterprise. The defense set up when the Attorney General of New York attacked the North River Sugar Refining Company for being a party to the "Sugar Trust" [1] was that that corporation was not a party to the agreement. The government was challenged to show any resolution of the directors or of the stockholders that connected the corporation with the arrangement. It was the stockholders as individuals, it was contended, who, acting within their legal rights, had exchanged their stock certificates for trust certificates and thus transferred to trustees the right to vote their stock. As an artificial person the corporation had taken no action. It was, therefore, obvious that it could not be guilty of *ultra vires* acts.

Not satisfied with this defense, the attorneys for the corporation went even further. Chief Justice Marshall's definition was cited in support of the view that as an artificial person created by law and clothed only with the powers which the law conveyed, a corporation as such could not exceed its corporate powers. As a creature of law it could do only the

[1] People of State of New York *v.* the North River Sugar Refining Company, 121 N. Y. 582 (1890).

things that the law permitted it to do. If the acts complained of were unlawful acts, they could not, therefore, be condemned as acts of the corporation. They must be attacked as the acts of individuals and the punishment must be meted out to individuals. To deprive the corporation of its charter because of acts which it, as a creature of the law, could not do, was denounced as an obvious piece of injustice. In support of this view numerous decisions of the United States Supreme Court were cited to the effect that "the objection to a contract [that is *ultra vires* of the corporation charged with making it] is not merely that the corporation ought not to have made it, but that it could not make it."[1] According to this argument the only remedy in the Sugar Trust case would have been to attack the trust directly, instead of indirectly through the corporations that were parties to it. Fortunately, the court refused to be diverted by this extreme application of the fiction theory, but held that a corporation might be guilty of *ultra vires* acts and that it was liable to forfeiture of its charter when, as in this case, those acts were clearly opposed to public policy.

As this illustration indicates, the tendency of the theory that a corporation is an "artificial person" distinct from the shareholders who compose it, is to relieve such shareholders from the obligations and restraints to which they should be subject.

The reaction from the fiction theory of the corporation has been in two directions. Certain jurists of a sociological turn of mind have proposed to substitute the "organic theory." Instead of describing the corporation as a fictitious person, they characterize it as a real person. They maintain that, in addition to physical organisms, there are organisms of higher forms made up of associated organisms of lower forms. Such are the family, the club, the nation, society as a whole. One of these higher organisms is presented by the corporation. From this point of view the corporation is not a creature of the law. It comes into existence spontaneously, and the law merely gives it a legal sanction. The principal objection to

[1] Central Transportation Co. *v.* Pullman's Palace Car Co., 139 U. S. 24, 48 *et seq.* (1891).

this solution of the difficulty is that it puts too severe a strain upon the imagination. The view that society is an organism has been made fairly familiar, but it cannot be said to have been accepted by any very large number of sociologists. There seems even less reason for maintaining that such loose and fortuitous organizations as business corporations have a real organic unity.

The other theory that has largely displaced the fiction theory among American jurists is known as the "representation theory." It holds that the entity we call a corporation is merely an association of individuals having a common purpose. For convenience it may be designated as a "legal person," but this fiction must not be allowed to obscure the fact that in reality it is not a person at all, but an association of persons who enjoy certain privileges and have certain responsibilities determined by the powers granted in the charter. Corporate action is merely the collective action of the members of the association conforming to the provisions of the charter. Corporate will is the expression of the collective will determined in accordance with rules prescribed in the charter. As it is impossible, in the nature of the case, that there should be complete unanimity of opinion as to every act and every decision to be made by the corporation, provision is necessary by which the corporation should be *represented* in some practical way by persons empowered to act for it and to express its decisions. The most general provision of this sort is that directors shall be chosen by majority vote of the shareholders. The majority *represents* the corporation. Other provisions define the powers and duties of these directors and other officers. So far as their powers go, they in turn *represent* the corporation. Thus the corporation itself is the association of individuals interested in it as shareholders. It has continuing life because an association may persist even though its members are constantly changing. As an association it may enter into contracts and other legal relations with individuals, other corporations, and even with its own members as individuals. The latter retain their separate and distinct individuality in all other relations of life, although as shareholders their interests are merged in those of the association. Finally, as an association of individuals the corporation has moral and legal obligations as much as the individuals who compose it. They enjoy certain collective privileges and immunities; correlative with these are collective obligations and responsibilities. They cannot evade these by setting up the claim that the corporation is a fictitious person. So far as it *is* at all it is real, and they are part and parcel of it so far as they share in its benefits. As was well said in the decision in the North River Sugar Refining Company case: [1] "The state gave the franchise, the charter, not to the impalpable, intangible, and almost nebulous fiction of our thought, but to the corporators, the individuals, the acting and living men, to be used by them, to redound to their benefit, to strengthen their hands and add energy to their capital. If it is taken away, it is taken from them as individuals and corporators, and the legal fiction disappears. The benefit is theirs, the punishment is theirs, and both must attend and depend upon their conduct." Equally clear was the view taken by the Supreme Court of Ohio in the similar Standard Oil Trust case. It declared: [2]

> On a question of this kind, the fact must constantly be kept in view that the metaphysical entity [the corporation] has no thought or will of its own; that every act ascribed to it emanates from, and is the act of the individuals personated by it, and that it can no more do an act or refrain from doing it, contrary to the will of these natural persons than a house could be said to act independently of the will of its owner; and where an act is ascribed to it, it must be understood to be the act of the persons associated as a corporation.

The great merit of the representation theory is that it does away at once with all metaphysical sophistries in regard to the nature of the corporation. It is not artificial, but real. It is not a person, in any but a highly figurative sense, but an association of persons. It is not limited in its acts by the provisions of its charter, but may do things which exceed its corporate powers, and when it does it is liable to have its privileges withdrawn from it on the ground of *ultra vires*.

[1] 121 New York 582 (1890).
[2] 49 Ohio 137 (1892).

Finally, it substitutes for the "soulless corporation" an association of living beings who can be held accountable for the acts which they perform collectively as strictly as for the acts which they perform in their individual capacities. It is believed that this conception satisfies all the requirements of juristic reasoning as well as of common sense—and it certainly furnishes a basis for a discussion of the trust problem that is far superior to that to be deduced from the fiction theory that so long held sway.

Though legal definitions of corporations have not always been clarifying, there has never been any wavering in judicial decisions as to the purpose for which corporations are created. The reason and excuse for their existence in the eyes of the law are that they advance the public interest. Before the advent of general incorporation laws, this aspect of the relation of the corporation to the state was more universally recognized than it is today. The early English corporations, like the East India Company, were chartered to undertake the promotion of great national interests which the state hesitated, for some reason, to undertake for itself. These corporations were clothed with powers commensurate with the magnitude of the tasks entrusted to them. The right of taxation, the right of eminent domain, and even the police power were conferred on the East India Company, and before it was actually taken over by the British government in 1858 it had become practically a government department. Gradually from incorporating only great and usually monopolistic undertakings, governments, especially in the United States, came to view the incorporation even of small competitive enterprises as advantageous. Scandals in connection with the methods used to secure the enactment of special acts of incorporation led, as we have seen, to the substitution of general corporation laws, under which in all of the states charters may now be secured for any lawful purpose at a minimum of trouble and expense. Thus by gradual stages, and almost unconsciously, to incorporate a private business enterprise has ceased to be looked upon—outside of the courts—as a privilege and has come to be considered a right.

One factor in the changed attitude of public opinion in reference to the proper relation between the state and the corporation which it creates was the view early taken by our federal courts (1819) and consistently adhered to since, that a charter of incorporation is in the nature of a contract between the state and the incorporators and that therefore states are precluded from altering or amending charters of incorporation—unless they expressly reserve this power—by the 10th section of Article I of the Federal Constitution, which provides that "No State shall . . . pass any . . . law impairing the obligation of contracts." According to this view a charter of incorporation is a binding agreement between the incorporators of a company and the state which creates it, rather than a grant of privileges to them by the state. This obviously implies a parity of rights between the associated incorporators and the state, and readily merges into the view that incorporation is itself a right rather than a privilege.

The anomalous situation created by the famous Dartmouth College decision alluded to previously could not continue. It was necessary that corporations be subject to regulation and control by the states which created them to prevent them from developing in directions opposed to the public interest. To recover the right to complete control nearly all of the states have, either by constitutional amendment or by general statute, expressly reserved to the legislature the right to alter or amend the charters of all corporations that might thereafter be created. Thus the right to "alter and amend" has been made in nearly all American jurisdictions a part of the "inviolable contract" into which a state is held to enter when it grants a charter of incorporation.

Unsatisfactory as was the method by which the courts sought to protect the vested interests of those who had embarked their capital in corporate enterprises in the Dartmouth College decision, the end sought was clearly desirable and important. If corporations are to render the useful service of which they are capable, they must be protected from unjust and oppressive exactions on the part of shifting and sometimes irresponsible legislatures. This end is now secured by extending to corporations other constitutional guaranties against the abuse of governmental powers. Through judicial decisions, extending over a considerable period of years, the following principles have now become firmly established.

(1) Corporations are not "citizens" in the sense in which that word is used in Section 2 of Article IV of the Federal Constitution, which provides that "The citizens of each State shall be entitled to all privileges and immunities of citizens in the several States." The states may thus impose restrictions upon "foreign" corporations—that is, corporations organized outside of the state, from which domestic corporations are exempt.[1]

(2) Corporations are, however, "persons" in the sense in which this word is used in Section 1 of the Fourteenth Amendment of the Federal Constitution, which provides that "No State shall deny to any person within its jurisdiction the equal protection of the laws" and "No State shall deprive any person of property without due process of law." These phrases protect corporations from unfair discrimination after they are once admitted within the jurisdiction of a state and from deprivation of their property without just compensation. In practice this protection to corporate property means that the courts will annul any law or regulation which imposes unjust or discriminatory burdens on corporations or which makes the rates which they may charge for their services so low as to prevent them from enjoying a reasonable return on their investment. Just what constitutes a "reasonable return" is a matter for judicial determination in the light of all of the facts as to risk, depreciation, etc., in each concrete case. As most of the state constitutions contain similar guaranties of property rights,[2] corporate as well as personal, there is little ground for complaint on the part of those interested in corporations that corporate interests are not at least as adequately safeguarded as are those of individuals.

[1] Paul *v.* Virginia, 8 Wall 168 (1868).

[2] Thus the New York constitution provides (Art. I., Sec. 6): "No person shall be . . . deprived of life, liberty, or property without due process of law; nor shall private property be taken for a public use without just compensation."

The other important powers which the state may exert over corporations—besides that to amend the charter where that is reserved—are the police power and the taxing power.

In the exercise of its police power, with a view to the regulation of corporations, the state has been accorded sweeping powers of control over corporations whose businesses are "affected with a public interest." Just what businesses these are cannot be determined in advance, but the tendency is to give this phrase broader and broader connotation. Public utilities ("special franchise corporations") are all affected with a public interest. In Munn *v.* Illinois [1] the Supreme Court of the United States held that the business of storing grain in elevators along the line of a railroad was affected with a public interest to an extent justifying the regulation of storage charges by the state legislature. From this case it may be inferred that any business concerned with a necessary of life which displays some of the characteristics of a monopoly is affected with a public interest. In the police power, as these examples indicate, the state has a powerful weapon to enable it to regulate such corporations as are thought to require regulation.

Finally, the taxing power applies to corporations in the same sweeping way that it does to individuals, and while in interpreting it the courts have sometimes been misled by the fiction theory into applying rules to corporations that apply properly only to physical persons, on the whole the efforts of legislatures to impose burdens on corporate property and corporate income have been loyally seconded by the courts. They have upheld a great variety of taxes under the head of franchise taxes, and it has been more the fault of the legislatures and the tax assessors than of the courts if corporations have not paid adequately for the privileges that they have enjoyed.

So far as powers go, each state is thus amply able to regulate and control not only the corporations which it itself creates, but also foreign corporations. It can impose such limitations as it chooses upon the charter of incorporation.

[1] 94 U. S. 113 (1876).

It can amend that charter after it has been granted if, as in most of the states, this power has been reserved, subject only to the limitations which restrain all its acts where property rights are concerned. It can condemn and acquire the property or franchise of a corporation for a public purpose on payment of reasonable compensation. Under its police power it may regulate the charges of corporations "affected with a public interest." Finally, it may, if it chooses, in the exercise of its taxing power, secure for itself all but a reasonable return on capital invested in the form of a franchise tax. The causes that give rise to the corporation problem are not to be found in any limitation in the powers of the states over corporations, but in their failure to exercise those powers with sole reference to the promotion of the public interest. How private interests and the selfish interests of individual states in the revenue they can derive through incorporating companies to carry on business in other jurisdictions have served to give an unfortunate direction to American corporation legislation is brought out in the next chapter.

CHAPTER IV

DEVELOPMENT OF AMERICAN CORPORATION LAWS

The responsiveness of American legislative bodies to special interests and their failure to safeguard the wider public interests, which it should be their chief business to protect, has been shown nowhere more strikingly than in connection with legislation with reference to corporations. Attention has already been called to the abuses that arose during the first half of the last century when the incorporation of each company required a special legislative act. The reaction from these abuses registered itself not only in general incorporating acts, but in amendments to the constitutions of most of the states, depriving the legislatures of their power to create corporations by special enactment. Constitutional limitation on this power of the legislature is now found in the constitutions of all but five of the states (Connecticut, Massachusetts, New Hampshire, Rhode Island, and Vermont), either in the absolute prohibition of the creation of corporations except under the general law (nineteen) or in the limitation of special-act corporations to public corporations, charitable corporations, banking and insurance corporations, public-utility companies, and others of a distinctive character. In few of the states are industrial corporations excepted from the requirement that they must be organized under the general law.

The first general incorporation laws that were enacted contained many restrictions designed to protect the public interest. As time went on, however, these restrictions were relaxed in one state after another. Three circumstances have contributed to this result.

First has been the persistent desire of business men to secure liberal charters of incorporation and the absence of any widespread appreciation of the need of limiting charters if the public interest was to be safeguarded. Representatives of the business interests have been returned to the legislatures and have readily yielded to the demands of lobbyists appearing for would-be incorporators that the laws should be made more liberal in this direction or in that. Thus corporation laws have been framed with more and more regard to the desires of those seeking charters and with less and less to the interests of others than the promoters and incorporators immediately concerned.

A second circumstance has been the discovery by some of the smaller states that by modifying the corporation law to suit the views of corporation promoters, substantial revenues might be derived from incorporation fees and franchise taxes. New Jersey was the pioneer in this new field of state enterprise. From 1889, when she altered her corporation law to permit holding companies, until 1913, when, under the leadership of the late President, then Governor, Wilson, she passed her so-called "Seven Sister Acts," her deliberate policy was to shape her corporation laws so that they would offer the greatest possible attraction to organizers of giant corporations. Her success is indicated by the fact that of the 318 trusts enumerated in a comprehensive list prepared in 1904 [1] 170, including all of the larger ones, had obtained their charters of incorporation from New Jersey. The large revenue which she received from incorporation fees and franchise taxes induced other states with limited resources to enter into competition for a share of this profitable business. Delaware, Maine, South Dakota, and, more recently, Nevada and Florida, have made themselves especially conspicuous by their attempts to best New Jersey in this new field of state enterprise.

A third circumstance has been the pressure which the states willing to liberalize their corporation laws "for revenue only" have been able to bring to bear on more conservative states. The latter saw their business men going to New Jersey or other liberal charter-granting states to incorporate enterprises

[1] Moody, *Truth About the Trusts*.

to be carried on, not in those states, but within their own limits. They might have checked this tendency by imposing onerous restrictions on "foreign" corporations, but a way less likely to rouse opposition was to introduce into their own corporation laws the provisions which made the laws of New Jersey and her imitators attractive. Thus states whose only motive was the quite legitimate desire to have corporate enterprises that were to be carried on within their borders incorporated under their own laws were drawn into the competition to liberalize the corporation laws. The movement to let down the bars thus became nation wide and, as we shall see, few of the earlier restrictions designed to limit the privilege of incorporation to cases where this was clearly in the public interest survived.

Passing from a general characterization of American corporation laws to a detailed description of what these laws provide in the fifty-four lawmaking and charter-granting jurisdictions of the country is as bewildering as passing from open country into a jungle. For our purpose it will suffice to indicate only the more common provisions and requirements of the corporation laws of the forty-eight states as of January 1, 1929, and to emphasize the respects in which they fail adequately to protect the public interest.[1]

The provisions of the corporation laws of most of the states are very liberal as regards the process by which ordinary business corporations may be organized. All but four of the states—Kansas, Tennessee, Utah, and West Virginia—permit incorporation by as few as three persons, the exceptions specifying "five or more"; five states—Georgia, Mississippi, Pennsylvania, South Carolina, and Washington—are satisfied with "two or more"; and three states—Arizona, Iowa, and Nebraska—say "any number." In Iowa the courts have held that "any number" may be interpreted to mean a single person. In all of the states, transfer of the stock by the incorporators after the corporation has been properly launched

[1] Cf. Parker, John S., *Corporation Manual, 1929*. For the tabulation of the legal provisions, which follows, the authors are indebted to Mr. Collis Stocking.

has no effect upon the continuity of its existence. The result is that the requirement of a certain number of incorporators is a formality easily complied with. Many trust companies regularly supply clerks to act as dummy incorporators. Stock certificates may be issued to these dummies for the minimum number of shares required by the law, and immediately assigned back by them to the real promoter or promoters of the corporation, who may thus actually control all of the stock during every stage of its organization, without having their names appear in connection with it.

All of the incorporators may now, in most of the states, be non-residents, the requirement that one or more must be residents having been retained in the laws of only eleven states. The ease with which such a restriction may be met by the employment of a dummy makes it an inconvenience rather than an effective means of regulation. Nearly two-thirds of the states have similarly relaxed the requirement that at least one of the directors must be a resident, this having served merely as an invitation to the employment of a dummy director to succeed the dummy incorporator. In both connections state incorporation laws have developed in a direction which tends to make each state the incorporator not merely of its own business enterprises, but of enterprises to be carried on in any part of the country or even of the world and not merely by its own business men, but by Americans or even aliens who are willing to pay the prescribed charges for the privilege of incorporation.

As regards the purposes for which a business corporation may be organized, "any lawful business" is the phrase used in thirty-three of the state laws, exceptions then being made of banking, insurance, and public utilities. It is also usually added that the purposes must be set forth with "reasonable definiteness" in the charter. This has served as an incentive to corporation promoters to enumerate in their applications all of the purposes which their imaginations can suggest, so that any possible development of the business which may be desired at a later time will be included among its corporate purposes. The broad charters which have resulted from this tendency often conceal rather than explain the true nature of the business which is to be undertaken. It has been said, with some exaggeration, that under its charter the United States Steel Corporation may do everything but coin money. Certainly the risk it runs of being guilty of *ultra vires* acts has been reduced to a minimum.

Only ten states provide for the minimum amount of capital with which a corporation may begin business, the remaining thirty-eight having no requirement. The highest minimum, required by Minnesota, is $10,000. New Jersey, Delaware, and four other states require $2,000, Ohio only $500.

More important than prescriptions in regard to the minimum capital are those in regard to the minimum amount that must be "paid in" before a corporation may begin business. Six states, including Florida and Nevada, prescribe a minimum of $500; six, including Delaware and New Jersey, of $1,000; four, 10 per cent of the subscribed capital; one, 20 per cent; and six, larger proportions ranging up to 50 per cent, prescribed by the law of Texas. Twenty-five of the states, including Massachusetts and New York, have no requirement expressed in the law.

All but two of the states—New Hampshire and Tennessee—require a statement of the number and par value of the shares of stock, but in forty of the states the par value may be any amount which the incorporators choose.

No-par value stock was introduced into the law of New York in 1912. Forty-one of the states now permit no-par-value shares. Those not yet permitting no-par stock are: Iowa, Montana, Nebraska, North Dakota, Oklahoma, South Dakota, and Wyoming.

It is usually said to be one of the characteristics of corporations that they enjoy perpetual life. As a matter of fact, perpetual charters are granted by only twenty-three of the states, including, of course, New Jersey, Delaware, and Nevada, but also Massachusetts and New York. In six of the states—Illinois, Louisiana, Missouri, Nebraska, Ohio, and Oklahoma—the statutes are obscure. In the nineteen other states which limit the lives of their corporations, provision is made for the renewal of the charter at little trouble and expense. These states are Arizona, California, Colorado, Georgia, Idaho, Indiana, Iowa, Kansas, North Dakota, Oklahoma, Michigan, Minnesota, Montana, Mississippi, New Mexico, Texas, Utah, Washington, West Virginia, and Wyoming, and their limitations range from twenty (Colorado) to one hundred (Utah) years. All but thirteen of the states require that the duration be stated in the articles of incorporation. With the right to "alter and amend" the charter of a corporation reserved to the legislature, limitations upon the lives of corporations have no special significance except that they make it somewhat easier to render corporations subject to changes in the corporation law. A corporation which seeks renewal of its charter must accept without demur whatever new conditions the law prescribes. Similar conditions imposed upon existing corporations in the exercise of the right to alter or amend corporate charters might be successfully opposed on the ground that they involved the taking of property without due process of law.

There has been much discussion of the question whether corporations should be allowed to own or acquire shares of stock in other corporations. As already stated, New Jersey amended her corporation law in 1889 to permit intercorporate holdings of stock, and in consequence of this and other liberal provisions became the "mother of the trusts" which were organized during the next few years. Most of the states have followed New Jersey's example either by expressly authorizing intercorporate stockholdings (thirty-nine states) or by acquiescing in the rule laid down by the courts that "where there is no statutory provision against the holding of stock in other corporations and the state officials allow the insertion of a provision allowing such a power [in the articles of incorporation], it is valid." The power is expressly limited in Georgia, Illinois, and Massachusetts, and was so limited from 1913 to 1917 in New Jersey.

The tendency of American corporation laws to remove all restrictions that might be distasteful to incorporators that has been indicated above, shows itself with equal clearness as regards minor provisions. The answer to the question as to the consideration for which stock may be issued has, in most jurisdictions, come to be "whatever the incorporators are willing to accept." Thirty-eight of the states and territories now permit the issue of stock for "services" or "labor" as well as for property, while seven ignore the question, although notoriously the services usually rewarded in this way are those of promoters and underwriters, whose only interest in the corporation is often what they can make out of it during its period of incubation.

The incorporators may also decide as to the classes of stock to be issued, and are given wide latitude as to the issue of bonds. In several states (*e.g.,* Delaware) the privilege of voting may be extended to bondholders as well as to stockholders. In thirty-eight states the charter decides. In eight states all stocks appear to be given voting power. California expressly provides this.

Nearly all of the corporation laws require meetings of the stockholders to be held at least once a year, but all of them, also, permit stockholders to vote by proxy. The result is, as is well known, that comparatively few stockholders ever attend the meetings of their corporations. The great majority content themselves with filling out proxy forms supplied by the officers in control, or, when there is dissatisfaction with the management, forms supplied by committees organized to oppose them.

Twenty-two of the states, including New Jersey and New York, require their corporations to hold their annual meetings within their limits, and a smaller number, including New Jersey and Nevada, require them to have offices within the state. This facilitates the collection of corporation taxes, but in the case of large corporations encourages rather than discourages absentee voting on the part of stockholders and unhampered control by boards of directors.

All of the states, except Minnesota, require annual reports, but these are usually merely for purposes of taxation and calculated to throw little light on the financial operations of corporations for the information of stockholders and the public. Annual reports that are really informing are becoming more and more common on the part of American corporations, but this has come about less through legal requirements, except in the case of public-service corporations, than through the influence of stock-exchange authorities and of public opinion as voiced by the financial press.

Most of the states make the dissolution of corporations, with the concurrence of two-thirds of the stock, as easy as their organization, so that incorporators may, when their plans miscarry, easily divest themselves of any long continued liability.

The differences between the states that make a business of issuing charters and those that still view incorporation as a privilege to be safeguarded and not merely to be sold, appear more in the attitude taken toward would-be incorporators than in the provisions of the corporation laws.

New Jersey was the pioneer in the business, and until led by public criticism to change her policy, openly advertised the advantages of her laws. Prior to 1913 the Secretary of State supplied to any inquirer an excellent treatise on the New Jersey law, emphasizing the liberality of its provisions, and at the same time turned over the inquiry to a trust company which entered vigorously upon the correspondence, sending forms for proxies, etc., and offering to secure the desired charter at a minimum of trouble and expense. The New Jersey law required that the corporation must place in a conspicuous position before its home office, which must be in the state, the name of the company. At the entrances of several New Jersey trust companies there are hundreds of such names. Discrimination against New Jersey corporations by other states, which may object to provisions in her corporation law or to her methods, is discouraged by the requirement that foreign corporations doing business in New Jersey must pay the same taxes, fines, penalties, licenses, fees, and other obligations as are required of New Jersey corporations in the states of their origin.

In response to a request for information, the Secretary of State of Delaware sends an annotated version of the corporation law of that State. In addition he sends a list of trust companies that act as agents for Delaware corporations. These companies are given the name and address of the applicant and several of them begin at once soliciting business. In the preface to the pamphlet which was at one time sent out by the state the advantages of incorporating in Delaware were clearly set forth, and it was asserted that "no State has on its statute books more complete and liberal corporation laws than these." These advantages, as officially described, are:

Corporations may conduct business in this or any state or foreign country.

Stockholders' and Directors' meetings may be held out of the State if desired.

Original stock and transfer Ledgers may be kept out of the State, if duplicates of such books be kept at the principal office in this state.

Stock fully paid up is non-assessable, and full paid non-assessable stock can be issued for property, labor and services.

No stock or bonds issued can be taxed by this state, when the same are owned by non-residents of this state or foreign corporations.

State tax is about one-half of that under laws of other states, offering proper security to stockholders.

Delaware corporations may confer upon the holders of bonds or debentures the power to vote to the same extent and in the same manner as stockholders.

The corporation law of Delaware was deliberately amended in 1899 for the purpose of attracting business away from New Jersey. Its "advantages" are clearly thought of, even by state officials, not from the viewpoint of protecting the interests of the creditors or even of the shareholders in corporations, but from that of attracting corporation organizers.

The responses from Delaware trust companies that were called forth by an inquiry sent to the Secretary of State by one of the authors in January, 1929, were numerous. The following extracts indicate how simple incorporation under the Delaware law has become and how quickly a charter may be secured. One company writes:

To facilitate the business, save time and, if desired, to prevent publicity in obtaining your Charter, we will furnish the three Incorporators from this office, who will attend to the filing of the original Certificate of Incorporation, the recording of the certified copy and will then meet in our office and hold the first meeting of Incorporators, and elect your selected Directors, who can meet in your City, elect Officers and proceed with the business of your Company. These services are generally included in our quoted fee. If we furnish the above service, you need only send us the form of Certificate of Incorporation with your approval, information for By-Laws, names of Directors to be elected and remittance covering cost.

We will be glad to send you Minutes of First Meeting of Incorporators, Waiver, Proxies, By-Laws, etc., and Minutes of First Meeting of Directors, including Waiver of Notice, Secretary's Oath and Vendor's Agreement, if you desire same.

If you incorporate your company in Delaware, appoint us your resident agent, and will advise us of the business you will engage in, we will, without any addition to our registration fee, prepare a special Charter for your approval.

Another explains:

We enclose herewith, a Memoranda (*Sic!*) for Preparing Organization Papers, which, when returned to this office together with check, will enable us to prepare charter for you, have our people sign same as incorporators, if you so desire, attend to the necessary filing and recording, hold the First Meeting of Incorporators at this office, adopt By-Laws in accordance with your instructions, authorize the issue of stock and elect the permanent Board of Directors. Books and papers can then be forwarded to you complete up to the First Meeting of Directors, which meeting may be held at a time and place to suit your convenience. The company can be completely organized two days after receipt of your prepared memo.

A third promises:

If you will fill in the blanks in this form and return it with certified check or bank draft to cover the total expense, we will prepare the papers, furnish the incorporators, incorporate the company, elect the directors, adopt the by-laws, prepare the minute book and forward the records to you within from 24 to 48 hours.

As we pass to the newer west the methods of soliciting corporation business followed by some of the states are even more frankly commercial. Until recently, in answer to an inquiry, the Secretary of State of South Dakota would send to the would-be incorporator a pamphlet edition of the corporation law of that state which displayed prominently on its cover page the words:

"No annual reports required to be filed in the office of the Secretary of State. No annual franchise tax. No taxes whatever, except upon taxable property owned by the corporation within the state."

The name of the inquirer was then brought to the attention not only of South Dakota trust companies, but also of the Librarian of the state Supreme Court. That obliging gentleman wrote to one of the authors on the *official stationery of the Supreme Court* that for a fee of ten dollars for the first year and five dollars a year thereafter he would secure the charter and act as resident incorporator, director, and agent, and maintain the domiciliary office in the state. He added: "I will furnish you my power of attorney or any stockholder you may designate to represent me at all meetings of the stockholders and directors. You can have one share of stock issued in my name and I will assign it back to the company for your protection." Could courtesy be carried further or service rendered more reasonably?

A characteristic of incorporation under the laws of South Dakota seems to be swiftness as well as cheapness. "In nineteen cases out of twenty," wrote the president of another South Dakota trust company, "we are able to get the charter into the mails within ten hours after the application is received here."

Having found its divorce mill so profitable, Nevada has recently entered the field to draw away from Delaware a part of its lucrative incorporating business. As in other states, the name of the inquirer is brought by the Secretary of State to the attention of trust companies engaged in the business of procuring charters. One of these supplies a pamphlet containing the Nevada Corporation Act, in full, with a convenient index-digest, forms to be filled out by the would-be incorporator, and an exposition of the advantages offered by the Nevada law in comparison with those offered by the law of Delaware. The advantages of the Nevada law are set forth as follows:

(1) No Blue Sky law; (2) No Necessity of trips to Nevada to hold corporate meetings; (3) No State tax (only $5.00 filing fee, yearly, for

list of officers); (4) No Annual reports; (5) No Stockholders' liability; (6) No Resident Directors required; (7) No Delay in Organization (our home office completes the organization of the company the same day as instructions are received, including issuance of stock certificates); (8) No Taxation of non-residents' stock; (9) No State inheritance tax; (10) No Difficulty in conducting your corporate affairs as you wish them conducted; (11) No High valuation of non-par stock (for purposes of filing non-par stock is valued at $1; most states value it at $100); (12) No time limit in the charter; may be perpetual.

The services offered by this particular company, which acts for attorneys only, include: (1) preparation, examination, and filing of articles of incorporation; (2) furnishing incorporators and directors; (3) holding incorporators' and directors' meetings; (4) preparation of minutes of meetings; (5) preparation of by-laws; (6) issuance of stock at time of incorporation; (7) advice and consultation; (8) all other services necessary to turn back to the attorney a company complete from the Nevada end; (9) maintaining for the company its Nevada office in strict compliance with statutory requirements; (10) furnishing the company with notice as to all requirements to be met.

In emphasizing its high ethical standards it declares: "Our services being available to attorneys only, and our incorporating fees solely with them, no embarrassment whatsoever should ever arise in the fees charged clients by the attorney." Which seems to mean so long as you pay our fees, you may charge your own clients whatever you like!

The comparative table of charges under the Delaware and Nevada laws, which is a feature of the pamphlet, shows how systematically the Nevada legislature, in drafting its law, underbid the lawmakers of Delaware and justified the claim that charters could be bought from it more cheaply than from any other state. Thus for a corporation with a capitalization of $10,000,000 the Nevada organization tax in 1928 was $550, the Delaware tax $600, the New Jersey tax $2,000, and the New York tax $5,000. For the more popular no-par form of capitalization, the Nevada tax for a corporation with 1,000,000 no-par shares was only $100, whereas the Delaware tax was $2,550, the New Jersey tax $10,000, and the New York tax $50,000. Added to this were the further attractions that Nevada has no annual franchise tax, beyond the five-dollar filing fee in connection with the requirement that a list of the corporate officers must be filed each year with the Secretary of State, and no inheritance taxes. Only the remoteness of Nevada from the business centers of the country, and misgivings in regard to the permanency of its recently adopted policies toward corporations, will prevent it from attracting the charter-selling business away from Delaware as Delaware attracted it away from New Jersey after the seven-sister legislation of 1913. Could anything demonstrate more strikingly the way in which we permit the national public interest to be sacrificed to special local interests than that our present standards in regard to the privileges and obligations of American corporations are determined largely by the sordid competition for revenue between the state in the Union which is next to the smallest in area and the state which is smallest in population?

It would be unprofitable, until we have considered the incorporation policies of other countries, to take up the question of remedies for the evils that have been disclosed. We may, however, conclude this survey by calling attention to the more conspicuous omissions in the corporation laws of the principal charter-granting states:

(1) They encourage the use of dummy incorporators and dummy directors, by failing to impose adequate personal responsibility on incorporators and directors.

(2) They make no effort to cause the nominal and the actual capital of a corporation to correspond, either when the corporation is first launched or afterwards, and, by permitting no-par stock, provide no indication even of the nominal capitalization.

(3) They impose no adequate restrictions on the activities of unscrupulous promoters, with the result that in most states the main reliance for the protection of innocent investors is the Post Office Department's enforcement of the law against using the mails to defraud.

(4) They do not require adequate annual reports.

(5) They impose no adequate restraint on the issue of bonds and permit the issue of non-voting stock without the protection afforded to bonds.

(6) They permit holding companies, with their inevitable tendency to diffuse responsibility and confuse the interests to be protected.

(7) Though they incorporate businesses to be carried on all over the United States, their guiding motive is too often not the best interests of the whole country, but "revenue only."

These are the principal corporation evils to be remedied as a step toward a solution of the broader trust problem to which we shall now direct our attention.

CHAPTER V

AMERICAN TRUST MOVEMENT, 1879-1929

THE trust movement began in the United States with the organization of the first Standard Oil Trust in 1879 and ended as a movement in 1903. There were two distinct phases: 1879 to 1896 was the period of the trust proper; 1897 to 1903, that of the holding company and giant consolidation. Since 1903 trusts have been occasionally organized, but at no time in such number as to constitute a movement. In the following treatment we have therefore divided the story into three parts: first period, 1879-1896; second period, 1897-1903; third period, 1904-1929.

FIRST PERIOD, 1879-1896

Most of the combinations of this period were organized by the manufacturers and other business men immediately affected, and owed little or nothing to the activity of professional promoters or underwriters. The first Standard Oil Trust was soon superseded by the better known Standard Oil Trust Agreement of January 2, 1882. Since this served as a model for the other trusts of the period, it merits detailed description.

The agreement was assented to by all the stockholders and members of fourteen corporations and limited partnerships, by some forty-six individuals, and by a majority of the stockholders and members of some twenty-six additional corporations and limited partnerships. The properties and businesses combined under one management in this trust represented over 90 per cent of the oil-refining capacity of the country and an almost equal proportion of the pipe-lines for the transportation of oil.

The plan of organization was simple. As a first step, a "fair valuation" was made of the property and assets of the various corporations and associations to be combined. On this basis trust certificates having a par value of $100 each were issued in exchange for their property, assets, or shares of stock to the owners of the businesses by nine trustees, who thus acquired complete control of the combined assets. Each trustee was elected for three years and the group was divided into three classes, so that normally there would be three vacancies to be filled each year at the annual meeting of the holders of trust certificates. It was further agreed that the trust should remain in operation until twenty-one years after the death of the last survivor of the original nine trustees, but that it might be dissolved at any time after one year by a vote of 90 per cent of the outstanding trust certificates, or at any time after ten years by a two-thirds vote. An incidental purpose of the trust, which was only partially achieved, was to combine all the constituent companies and associations in each of the states into a single corporation to be known as the "Standard Oil Company" of the appropriate state. The shares of stock of these Standard Oil companies were to be retained by the trustees, trust certificates continuing to represent the interests in them of the parties to the agreement. These trust certificates were transferable like shares of stock in a corporation. The arrangement thus had most of the advantages which actual incorporation would have secured and yet avoided the publicity[1] and amenability to governmental control which incorporation would have entailed.

Under its novel form of organization the Standard Oil Trust realized to the full the anticipations of its organizers. The business was systematized, economies were introduced in all departments, and the production and price of refined oil were controlled over the greater part of the United States. When the trust was formally dissolved in 1892, some 972,500 trust certificates were outstanding, but the assets of the combination were worth considerably more than the $97,250,000, represented by the face value of these certificates.

[1] The details of this second trust agreement first became known to the public through the trust investigation of the New York Senate in 1888. The earlier trust agreement was only brought to light in connection with the government's dissolution suit commenced in 1906.

Following the example of the Standard Oil Trust, similar trusts were organized in other important branches of manufacturing. The Cotton-seed Oil Trust (1884), the Linseed Oil Trust (1885), the National Lead Trust, the Distillers and Cattle Feeders, or Whisky Trust, and the Sugar Refineries Company or Sugar Trust (1887) were the most important of these imitators. During this same period, other combinations, organized as single corporations or holding companies, were also launched. Among these the Diamond Match Company (1889), the American Tobacco Company (1890), the United States Rubber Company (1892), the General Electric Company (1892), and the United States Leather Company (1893) were the most important.

This first period of the trust movement was brought to a close, not by the lack of success of these early combinations, since several of them, besides the Standard Oil Trust, were highly successful, but through the condemnation of the trust form of organization as unlawful by the courts and through the business depression which began in 1893. The first trust to be prosecuted was the Cotton-seed Oil Trust, which the state of Louisiana attacked as an illegal combination in 1887. More important in establishing the unlawfulness of the "trusts" were the dissolution suits started by the Attorneys General of New York and Ohio to forfeit the charters of constituent members of the Sugar and Standard Oil Trusts in 1889 and 1890. These suits were both based on the common law and had no connection with the antitrust acts which were passed by several of the states and by Congress in this same period.

The New York prosecution was against the North River Sugar Refining Company, all of the shares of stock of which had been transferred by the stockholders to the trustees of the Sugar Trust. The questions to be decided in this case, as defined by the New York Court of Appeals in rendering its decision,[1] were: "first, has the defendant corporation exceeded or abused its powers, and, second, does that excess or abuse threaten or harm the public?" Reference has already been

[1] 24 N. E. 834 (1890).

made to the argument by which the attorneys for the corporation sought to draw a distinction between the act of the stockholders and the act of the corporation and to the decision of the court that where, as in this case, the result of the stockholders' action was to make the corporation "an integral part and constituent element of a combination which possesses over it an absolute control, which has absorbed most of its corporate functions and dictates the extent and manner and terms of its entire business activity. . . . We must shut our eyes in wilful blindness if we fail to see both corporate neglect and corporate action." On the question whether the abuse of power of which the corporation was found guilty justified forfeiture of the charter the court was equally emphatic. "It is quite clear," it declared, "that the effect of the defendant's action was to divest itself of the essential and vital elements of its franchise by placing them in trust . . . and to give away to an irresponsible board its entire independence and self-control. . . . But graver still," it continues, "is the illegal action substituted for the conduct which the State has a right to expect and require. It has helped to create an anomalous trust which is, in substance and effect, a partnership of twenty corporations. . . . It is a violation of law for corporations to enter into a partnership." On these grounds the decision declared the charter of the North River Sugar Refining Company forfeited and ordered the liquidation of that corporation. Having found a sufficient basis for its decision in the fact that it was contrary to law and to public policy for a corporation to enter into a partnership with other corporations, the court expressly declined to venture "into the wider discussion over monopolies and competition and restraint of trade and the problems of political economy" which had been urged upon it in the brief of the Attorney General. The decision, therefore, condemned the form of the combination as inappropriate for a New York corporation, but did not consider the lawfulness of the combination itself. This point must be borne in mind in passing judgment on the measures which were at once taken by the organizers of the Sugar Trust to continue the combination in full and effective operation as a New Jersey holding company.

The issues in the suit against the Standard Oil Company of Ohio, begun by the Attorney General of that state in 1890, were identical with those in the New York case, but the decision rendered by the Ohio Supreme Court [1] went somewhat further. The evidence showed, according to the court, that: "The Standard Oil Company of Ohio was required to transfer all of its property, assets and business to a new company to be organized in the state; and this was to be accomplished by the obligation imposed on its members and stockholders, all of whom are parties to the agreement, to authorize and require the directors and managers to make the transfer. The property and assets of the corporation could only be transferred by a corporate act, and the agreement could not in this respect be carried into effect, other than by such corporate act; and clearly indicates that the purpose of the stockholders of the defendant, in becoming a party to it, was to affect their property and business as a corporation; in other words, was to act in their corporate and not in their individual, capacity." Having thus determined that the entry of the Ohio Standard Oil Company into the trust was through corporate action and having pointed out that such action was clearly *ultra vires*, the court went on to justify punishment of the delinquent corporation on the following grounds: "The law requires that a corporation should be controlled and managed by its directors in the interest of its own stockholders, and conformable to the purpose for which it was created by the laws of its state. By this agreement . . . the defendant is controlled and managed by the Standard Oil Trust, an association with its principal place of business in New York City, and organized for a purpose contrary to the policy of our laws. Its object was to establish a virtual monopoly of the business of producing petroleum, and of manufacturing, refining and dealing in it and all its products, throughout the entire country, and by which it might not merely control the production but the price at its pleasure. All such associations are contrary to the policy

[1] 30 N. E. 279 (1892).

of our state and void." The action of the Standard Oil Company of Ohio was thus condemned, not merely on the formal ground that it was unlawful for an Ohio corporation to enter into a trust, but because the monopolistic combination resulting from the trust agreement was itself opposed to public policy and unlawful.

The reasoning of the court clearly justified forfeiture of the charter of the offending corporation. This was not actually required in the decree, however, partly because of the operation of the statute of limitations. Instead, the Standard Oil Company of Ohio was directed to withdraw from the trust and enjoined from permitting the transfer of its stock to the trustees or the administration of its affairs by them. In the circumstances the trustees decided not only to release the Standard Oil Company from any relations to the trust, but to dissolve the trust itself, by transferring its property and obligations to themselves as a board of "liquidating trustees."

The view that was taken by the courts of New York and Ohio that it was unlawful for corporations to become members of trusts and that such action justified forfeiture of the corporate charter, was accepted as authoritative all over the country. One by one all of the other trusts dissolved and substituted some other method of combination for that which had been condemned.

Doubtless it was the expectation of the prosecuting officers and the intention of the courts that the forfeiture suits that have just been described should result in the breaking up of the monopolistic combinations that had been organized as trusts and the restoration of a condition of free competition in the branches of production affected. The actual outcome, as implied above, was quite otherwise. In 1889 the state of New Jersey opportunely amended her corporation law to permit "the directors of any company incorporated [thereunder] . . . [to] purchase . . . the stock of any company or companies owning, mining, manufacturing, or producing materials, or other property necessary for their business, and issue stock to the amount of the value thereof in payment therefor."[1] Thus the way was prepared for the holding company. Not only the Sugar Trust, reorganized as the American Sugar Refining Company in 1891, but most of the other early trusts, found shelter under the protecting wings of New Jersey.

All that was necessary to transform a trust into a holding company was to procure a charter of incorporation from New Jersey, providing for the requisite capitalization, and to permit the holders of trust certificates to exchange them for stock certificates in the new company. The trustees of the dissolving trust would naturally become the directors of the new corporation and in their dual capacity could vote to dissolve the trust and destroy the trust certificates. Of course where the courts had already interfered to forfeit the charter of one of the constituent corporations combined in a trust, as in the case of the North River Sugar Refining Company, it would be necessary to organize another company to acquire the property of the defunct corporation or else to arrange to have the holding company itself acquire this property and hold it for the benefit of its shareholders along with the stocks in the other corporations which might enter into the combination. Under either plan the transfer of control from the former board of trustees to the new board of directors could be effected without a single day's interruption in the management of the business or a single change in the personnel of those intrusted with such management.

The holding company was so obviously a device for accomplishing exactly the same purposes which the courts had held could not be accomplished through the trust form of organization that there was some doubt as to its legality. This doubt was all the greater because at the very time when this litigation was in progress the states and Congress were passing antitrust acts which added not a little to the stringency of the common-law condemnation of combinations in restraint of trade and monopolies. Doubtless this uncertainty as to the legal fate of this new device for effecting a combination

[1] Chap. cclxv, sec. 4, p. 414, of Acts of 1889.

was one of the circumstances which deterred the organizers of the Standard Oil Trust from attempting to substitute any formal organization for that which they were directed to give up. Instead they depended upon the good faith of the parties interested to secure the harmonious management of the twenty-odd corporations with assets in excess of $100,000,000 which had come to be controlled by that trust. This could hardly have been done, however, had not the nine trustees together controlled a clear majority of the trust certificates. In dissolving the trust each certificate-holder was given his proportionate share in the stocks and assets of each of the different corporations and associations which were combined in the trust. Thus the nine trustees were able, as individuals, so long as they could agree on the lines of policy to be followed, to administer the vast business as effectively as they had before as a regularly constituted board. Harmony of action was further facilitated by the failure of the holders of trust certificates to present them for exchange for the fractional shares of stock in the twenty different corporations to which, under the terms of the liquidation, they were entitled. Mr. John D. Rockefeller, Sr., who held 256,854 of the 972,500 Standard Oil Trust Certificates which were outstanding at the time that the suit was decided, exchanged them for a proportionate allotment of the stocks of the different corporations. His example was followed by the other large holders, so that by the end of the year 494,619 certificates had been exchanged and control of a clear majority of the shares of each of the twenty corporations controlling the aggregate property of the trust had passed to the trustees individually. No serious effort appears to have been made, however, by the liquidating trustees to induce the smaller holders of trust certificates to make a similar exchange. On the contrary, the refusal to pay dividends on fractional shares of stock served to discourage such exchange. The 477,881 certificates which had not yet been exchanged at the end of 1892, were still outstanding at the end of 1896. The result was that the original nine trustees controlled a majority of the shares of the Standard Oil companies as individuals and the rest as "liquidating trustees" for the Standard Oil Trust. This situation was so anomalous that the Attorney General of Ohio, in November, 1897, began a proceeding against the Standard Oil Company officers for contempt of court in failing to carry out in good faith the decree entered against the company in 1892.

Partly to escape this litigation and partly because ten years' trial seemed to have proved the invulnerability of the New Jersey holding-company device, the directors of the Standard Oil combination secured an amendment to the charter of the Standard Oil Company of New Jersey by which its capitalization was increased in June, 1899, from $10,000,000 to $110,000,000, $10,000,000 of which was to be preferred stock and to be liquidated within a short period. The one million shares of common stock were to be exchanged at par for the old trust certificates and on an equitable basis for the shares of the twenty Standard Oil corporations which had passed into private hands. Thus the Standard Oil combination was also finally metamorphosed into a New Jersey holding company.

During the years following the decisions causing the dissolution of the early trusts and the enactment of the anti-trust acts, the trust movement came almost to a standstill. Thus in the years 1894 and 1896 no single combination of importance was organized, and of the four combinations launched in 1895, the only one of national significance, the American Spirits Manufacturing Company, was merely a reorganization of the ill-starred Whisky Trust. This virtual suspension of the trust movement is usually ascribed to the business depression of this period, and doubtless that had a good deal to do with it. It is interesting to recall, however, that up to that time the most widely accepted explanation of the trust movement was that it was the last resort of harassed manufacturers rendered desperate by a long era of falling prices. If this was the chief incentive to trust organization before 1893, it should have operated with intensified force during the three following years. That so few manufacturers were willing to hazard the plants in which their fortunes were invested to great combinations must be ascribed chiefly to misgivings as to the fate of these combinations when attacked as being in violation of the federal Antitrust Act which became law July 2, 1890.

The applicability of this law to manufacturing combinations organized under New Jersey charters was first tested in the case of the United States *v.* E. C. Knight Company[1] decided by the U. S. Supreme Court on January 21, 1895. The issue in this case was whether the acquisition of the shares of stock of four competing Pennsylvania sugar-refining companies, and, therefore, of control over their output of sugar by the American Sugar Refining Company, involved a violation of the Antitrust Act. The Supreme Court decided that it did not, on the ground that the federal Antitrust Act, as indeed the power of Congress under the Constitution, was limited to combinations in restraint of *commerce among the several states or with foreign nations,* and that the business of refining sugar was not commerce in the constitutional sense. A few extracts from the opinion which Chief Justice Fuller submitted in support of the decision of the majority of the court in this momentous case will serve to explain why it was interpreted by the business community as relieving manufacturing and mining combinations from any danger of successful attack under this federal statute. The evidence showed clearly that the American Sugar Refining Company, upon acquiring the four Philadelphia refineries, would control more than 95 per cent of the production of refined sugar in the United States and thus enjoy a virtual monopoly of the business.

Doubtless [said the Chief Justice] the power to control the manufacture of a given thing involves in a certain sense the control of its disposition, but this is a secondary and not the primary sense; and although the exercise of that power may result in bringing the operation of commerce into play, it does not control it, and affects it only incidentally and indirectly. Commerce succeeds to manufacture, and is not a part of it. . . .

Contracts, combinations, or conspiracies to control domestic enterprise in manufacture, agriculture, mining, production in all its forms, or to raise or lower prices or wages, might unquestionably tend to restrain external

[1] 156 U. S. 1 (1895). Reprinted in Ripley, *Trusts, Pools and Corporations,* pp. 506-533.

as well as domestic trade, but the restraint would be an indirect result, however inevitable and whatever its extent, and such result would not necessarily determine the object of the contract, combination or conspiracy.

Limiting thus the scope of the act, the Chief Justice concluded that "the contracts and acts of the defendants related exclusively to the acquisition of the Philadelphia refineries and the business of sugar refining in Pennsylvania and bore no direct relation to commerce between the states or with foreign nations." [1] This narrow interpretation was given official confirmation and support in statements to Congress by both President Cleveland and Attorney General Olney that the federal law was ineffective and that the remedy must be sought in state action.

Thus the danger of effective Congressional interference with the trust movement seemed entirely removed. There remained some uncertainty as to what might result from the antitrust legislation of the states. But as time went on and the futility of the spasmodic efforts that were made by a few of the states to enforce their antitrust acts became apparent, this danger, too, ceased to have any terrors for the would-be trust organizer. This apparent removal of the legal barriers to the organization of combinations as New Jersey holding companies or outright consolidations did not lead at once to a resumption of the trust movement because of the continuance of the business depression and the uncertainty as to the outcome of the election of 1896. It will be recalled that the years of depression and falling prices had led the Democrats headed by Bryan to advocate the free coinage of silver. The election of McKinley was hailed by the business community as a triumph for "sound money." Incidentally, it assured the revision of the tariff upward, which was also favored by American manufacturers. Only after the Dingley bill became a law in the late summer of 1897 was the way clear for the second

[1] Although controlling, this important decision was not unanimous. Justice Harlan dissented vigorously on grounds which showed a clear understanding of the economics of the situation, and forecast the interpretation of the act which was subsequently accepted by a majority of the court. Cf. Chapter XVIII, pp. 377, 378.

trust movement. The fervor with which it was entered upon and the gigantic proportions which it soon assumed make it one of the most significant chapters in the business history of the United States.

SECOND PERIOD, 1897-1903

The organization of trusts which occurred during the years from 1879 to 1896 barely attained to the dignity of a movement. Altogether there were not more than twelve important combinations formed during the entire period, and their total capital was well under $1,000,000,000. The contrast between the spasmodic and irregular formation of trusts in these years and the second rust movement that set in after the return of prosperity in 1897 was very striking. Its progress is indicated in any list of the important industrial combinations to which the dates of their organization are appended.

The first official survey of industrial combinations in the United States was that made in connection with the manufacturing census of 1900. This showed that in the previous year there were in active operation in the United States some 185 manufacturing combinations with a combined capital outstanding (including $216,412,759 in bonds) equal at par to $3,093,095,868. The total capital credited to all manufacturing industries in the same year was $8,975,000,000, so that the trusts had come to control, roughly speaking, one-third of the manufacturing capital of the country. In the list of 185 trusts there were 73 whose capitalization equaled or exceeded $10,000,000. Of these only 18 were organized before 1897. In that year 2 were added; in 1898, 11; in 1899, 36; and in the first six months of 1900 the remaining 6.

Following the census of 1900 several investigations of the number and capitalization of the trusts were made by students of the problem. Of these the most comprehensive was that contained in Moody's *Truth about the Trusts* published in 1904. This showed that on January 1 of that year there were in active operation 305 industrial combinations with a combined capital outstanding of $6,717,791,533. In addition, 13 important industrial combinations with a combined capital of $528,551,000 were in process of reorganization. There were in existence, in 1904, therefore, according to this computation, 318 industrial combinations with a total capital of $7,246,-342,533. As many mining companies were included in this list, the total capitalization is not comparable with the total capital credited by the census to manufacturing industries in this year, which was $12,676,000,000. Making full allowance for industrial combinations in the mining field, however, it appears that by 1904 the trusts controlled fully two-fifths of the manufacturing capital of the country. Eliminating from the Moody list combinations which lacked the characteristics of trusts, as we have defined them, the capitalization controlled by trusts appears in that year to have been not far from $5,000,000,000. Even more significant than this aggregate figure were the size and degree of monopolistic control attained by some of the trusts in the particular branches of production with which they were concerned. Thus, 10 of those in Moody's list had capitalizations of $100,000,000 or over, 30 of $50,000,000 or over, and 129 of $10,000,000 or over. As regards monopolistic control, 26 controlled 80 per cent or more of the aggregate production in their fields, 57, 60 per cent or more, and 78, 50 per cent or more. It was this ascendancy of individual trusts and the fear that a similar ascendancy might be secured by other combinations that alarmed the country and reinvigorated the antitrust movement.

Of the 318 trusts listed by Moody, 82, with a capitalization of $1,196,700,000, were organized before January 1, 1898, and 234, with a capitalization of over $6,000,000,000, between that date and January 1, 1904. Of these 318 combinations, 125 had capitalizations of $10,000,000 or more. Twenty-two, or less than one-fifth of these, were organized before January 1, 1897. Of the remaining 101, only 3 were organized in 1897, and only 7 in 1898.[1] On the other hand, in 1899, 32, or as many as had been organized in all of the preceding years together, were launched. There ensued a breathing space in 1900, when 5 were organized, but the movement soon got under way again, 20 being organized in 1901 and 27 in 1902.

[1] Definite dates of the organization of two are not given.

Seven were organized in 1903, but the movement had spent itself. Since that year there have been numerous reorganizations, and recently a large number of mergers and combinations, but it would be an exaggeration to characterize these developments as constituting a trust movement.

Reviewing the financial literature of these fevered years, it is not difficult to understand the forces behind this second trust movement. From the autumn of 1896 until the close of 1902 general business in the United States was almost continuously prosperous.[1] Crops were good and were marketed at advancing prices. The triumph of the opponents of "free silver" in 1896, and their more decisive victory in 1900, stimulated confidence. Our foreign-trade balances attained such proportions that the European financial press began to speak of the "American invasion" and even of the "American peril."

Upon this foundation of general business prosperity security markets displayed a buoyancy they had not shown since 1892. The Spanish War in 1898 delayed somewhat the flotation of combinations projected in that year, but only, as has been shown, to increase the number launched in 1899. A small panic on December 18 gave warning that the issue of new securities was proceeding at too rapid a pace, but the caution which checked flotations during the first ten months of 1900 was thrown to the winds when McKinley was reëlected by enhanced majorities in November. There followed a wild outburst of speculative activity of which the promoters of new combinations were only too ready to take advantage. In February and March, 1901, Mr. Morgan and his associates launched the billion-dollar Steel Trust and found the public so eager to take the shares of this gigantic combination that it was necessary to call for only $25,000,000 of the $200,000,000 which the underwriters had agreed to furnish, and this with 200 per cent profits was later returned to them.

The six months' orgy of speculation was brought to a dramatic close on May 9, when the stock market was thrown

[1] For a more detailed account of this period cf. Mitchell, *Business Cycles*, edition of 1913, pp. 63-68, and Noyes, *Forty Years of American Finance*, Chapter XII.

into a panic by the discovery that rival factions contending for control of the Northern Pacific Railroad had created a corner in that stock. Though confidence was in some measure restored before the end of the month, public enthusiasm was cooled. Evidence began to accumulate that the rosy predictions as to the earnings of the new combinations were not to be realized. Thus the attempt of the Amalgamated Copper Company to hold the price of copper at seventeen cents broke down in December of that year. The price of its stock, which had been 130 in June, fell to 60½. Other trusts showed similar if less extreme losses for those who had taken their securities at the boom prices of earlier years. Even trusts that had prospered were sympathetically affected. American Sugar Refining Common fell from 153 to 103½ from June to December.

Business was prosperous in 1902, but the stock market remained inactive. During the year the total number of shares sold was only about two-thirds the number marketed in 1901. Combinations continued to be launched, but the revelations which began to leak out with reference to some of them, and notably the United States Shipbuilding Company, which was a disastrous and disgraceful failure culminating in bankruptcy in July, 1903, barely one year after it was organized,[1] shattered whatever confidence the public still felt in the trusts. Even the great prestige of the Morgan firm was unable to make the launching of the giant shipping trust, the International Mercantile Marine Company, in the autumn of 1902, successful. The extent to which the public had lost its confidence in the industrial combinations was shown by the prices at which their shares came to be quoted in 1903. In October of that year, according to a calculation in the *Wall Street Journal,* the securities of the one hundred principal trusts showed a shrinkage from the top prices quoted in 1899 and 1900 of $1,750,000,000, or 47 per cent of their total par value of $3,690,000,000. The trust movement as a movement was over.

The motives which actuated the participants in this second

[1] Cf. Chapter XII.

trust movement may be inferred from the foregoing sketch. On the side of the owners of the manufacturing and other enterprises was a violent distaste for competition, the "death of trade" as it had come to be styled, engendered by the falling prices and business depression from 1893 to 1896. They were easily persuaded that combination offered them a means of escape from their difficulties, particularly as the three most widely heralded trusts of the earlier period, the Standard Oil, the American Sugar, and the American Tobacco, had continued to prosper and pay dividends while American business generally was prostrated. Assured by their legal advisers that the antitrust acts were no real barrier to the realization of similar successes in their different lines, American manufacturers stood ready to strike hands and substitute combination for competition from one end of the country to the other.

This favorable attitude of business men would have resulted in the launching of numerous trusts after 1897, but to explain the veritable furore for combination that developed we must give due credit to the professional promoter. Business men who have been active competitors do not easily put aside the dislike and suspicion to which competition too often gives rise to join their properties and abilities in friendly coöperation. It is true that most of the earlier trusts were organized without the aid of the promoter. One man or a group of men in the business discerned the advantages of combination and persuaded or coerced competitors to join in the move. But this method took time and could be successful in only a relatively few instances. The sensational progress of the second trust movement was possible only because a group of shrewd, plausible, and aggressive promoters was at hand to make fullest use of the favorable business situation.

The rôle of the promoter differs with every undertaking to be fostered, but in essentials it is always the same. He must have the imagination and the insight necessary for devising a workable plan. He must then persuade the business men concerned of the merits of his proposal and induce a sufficient number of them to join with him to insure its success. Finally he must have affiliations with banking interests willing to back his project to the extent of providing whatever money may be needed to buy out important business men who cannot otherwise be brought in and to provide working capital until the new enterprise is a going concern.

In connection with the combinations of the period 1897 to 1902, the usual method pursued by promoters was first to secure financial backing. In fact, this was so important that not infrequently, as in the case of the United States Steel Corporation, the promotion was actually engineered by the financial firm which took a leading part in the subsequent underwriting. Having the assurance of financial support, if a promising combination could be brought about, the promoter next approached the business men to be brought in. The initial proposal to them would usually be that they turn over their properties and business to the new corporation to be organized in exchange for a fair proportionate share of the stock of such corporation. If the promoter was of the higher type and all the important firms that he desired to combine could be induced to agree to the plan, the allotment of stock might be based on appraisals made by the same accountants, so that each would get his exact proportionate share as so determined. Additional stock would, of course, be needed to reward the promoter for his services and to secure from the underwriters any working capital that might be required. In exceptional cases all of these details might be agreed to openly and freely by all of the parties to the undertaking, so that each would know exactly what everyone else was getting and in exchange for what contribution.

Usually the promoters found it easier to deal independently with each business man to be brought in, giving each the impression that he was getting specially favorable terms, while making the terms to all such that the promoter himself and the underwriters on whom he so vitally depended would be amply rewarded. This might result in a good deal of bitter feeling after the promotion was completed, but would obviate the necessity of inducing all those concerned to agree in advance to all of the complex details to be determined.

A favorite method, which became more and more usual as

the movement progressed, was to issue preferred stock, usually 7-per-cent cumulative,[1] equal to the estimated value of the properties and businesses to be taken in and a bonus in common stock determined by the exigencies of each separate bargain. This meant inevitably over-capitalization. Since the promoter and underwriters were usually the ones to determine how large the capitalization should be, and since they usually expected to sell their allotments of securities before the ability of the trust to earn dividends on its outstanding stock could be determined by actual experience, there was little check on such over-capitalization and it was pushed in many instances to a point that involved grave consequences to investors.

The last influence encouraging the trust movement was the buoyant optimism of speculators and investors in this period. If it was easy to persuade business men to combine, it was even easier for a time to persuade the public that the combinations would be a success. In the three years 1899, 1901, and 1902, seventy-nine giant trusts with capitalizations aggregating more than $4,000,000,000, that is, over $50.000,000 each on the average, were launched, and it was only in the last of these years that the investing public revolted and refused any longer to absorb the new securities that were offered in such unprecedented volume. How violent the public's reaction became when its suspicions were thoroughly aroused has already been indicated.

In addition to the reaction inevitable after a period of excessive speculation, there were more fundamental and abiding reasons for the suspension of the trust movement in 1903. But for them it might have been resumed again when business and speculative conditions were once more favorable.

First and most obvious was the fact that the combination movement had gone far toward its attainable goal in a country as large as the United States. A substantial proportion of the large-scale manufacturing and mining industries of the country had been drawn together into combinations of a

[1] Preferred stock is stock entitled to dividends out of earnings before dividends may be paid to common stock and with a first claim on assets in case of liquidation. "Cumulative" means accumulating as a prior claim year after year until paid.

more or less permanent character. Small-scale industries, unless confined to local markets and protected from outside competition by high freight charges, cannot easily be combined, for the obvious reason that there are too many conflicting interests to be reconciled and too much danger of new sources of competition to render the combination of any particular value to its members. These considerations set a certain, if elastic, limit to the combination movement, and by 1903 that limit had been reached in most fields of enterprise in the United States.

A second reason, which was for some time influential in preventing any general resumption of the trust movement after 1903, was the more determined and successful efforts of the federal government to make the Antitrust Act of 1890 effective. On February 14, 1903, the Bureau of Corporations was created on the initiative of President Roosevelt and began the investigations into the Standard Oil, American Tobacco, and other trusts that enabled the Department of Justice to push to a successful conclusion the dissolution suits which it was already contemplating. Meantime the suit against the Northern Securities Company, organized to combine two of the transcontinental railroad systems, was being actively prosecuted. The decision which dissolved this corporation on March 14, 1904, showed conclusively that a New Jersey holding-company charter was no protection to a combination in restraint of interstate commerce. It was still doubtful whether manufacturing or mining combinations would fall under a like condemnation, but the confidence of corporation lawyers in their immunity was thoroughly shaken. Conservative business men could no longer view combinations as safe from legal attack, and therefore only the strongest assurance of lowered costs and increased profits could induce them to venture their properties in such questionable undertakings.

THIRD PERIOD, 1904-1929

As implied by the foregoing statements, the chief development in the American combination movement in the last twenty-five years has been a reorganization of the earlier trusts to comply with the requirements of the antitrust laws, as these have gradually acquired definiteness through judicial decisions. In succeeding chapters detailed accounts are given of the reorganizations of leading trusts, some of them, like those of the Standard Oil and American Tobacco combinations in 1911, necessitated by adverse court decisions; others, like that of the International Harvester combination in 1918, the result of acquiescence in consent degrees dictated by the Attorney General. Few forced dissolutions have occurred since 1920 when the Supreme Court decided not to dissolve the Steel Trust on grounds interpreted to mean that so long as a business organization controlled not more than 50 per cent of its branches and refrained from unfair or oppressive policies toward its competitors and from agreements with them to control outputs or fix prices, it would not be deemed in violation of the antitrust laws. In fact ever since the important dissolutions of 1911, the managers of big business enterprises have disclaimed any ambition to enjoy monopolistic advantages as vigorously as the promoters of the trusts during the earlier years claimed such advantages for the combinations for which they sought the favor of the investing public.

The reorganization of American business enterprises has been hastened since 1914 by the activities of the Federal Trade Commission created in that year. The investigations and "cease and desist" orders of that body have gradually become our most important means of securing law enforcement and occupy a correspondingly large place in any account of recent happenings.[1]

Most of the new combinations that have been organized since 1904 are concerned with industries that hardly existed when the Sherman law was passed. The principal as regards their size and their prominence in their respective branches of production are:

(1) General Motors Company, organized with a New Jersey charter in 1908 and reorganized with a Delaware charter in 1916;

[1] Cf. Chapters XXII and XXIII.

(2) Allied Chemical and Dye Corporation, organized with a New York charter in 1920;
(3) Radio Corporation of America, organized with a Delaware charter in 1919;
(4) Aluminum Company of America, organized under a Pennsylvania charter in 1907 and reorganized in 1927;
(5) Paramount-Famous-Lasky Corporation, organized in 1916 and reorganized under the above name in 1927 with a New York charter.

Although it has grown enormously in the twenty-one years since its creation until its assets now exceed $1,000,000,000 and its net earnings ($272,000,000 in 1928) compare with those of the U. S. Steel Corporation, the General Motors Company has at no period dominated the automobile industry. Its success, free from any suspicion of attempts to limit output or control prices, appears to justify the claim of its officers that it illustrates how economy and efficiency may be increased by combining "Decentralized Operations and Responsibilities with Coördinated Control." [1]

The Allied Chemical and Dye Corporation was a child of the war, during which the United States seized German patents and formulæ for the manufacture of dyes, in which that country enjoyed before 1914 almost a world monopoly. Acquisition of these patents from the government and the discovery of new processes and formulæ on its own initiative have enabled this company to expand rapidly until in 1928 it showed net earnings of just under $30,000,000 and an accumulated surplus of $182,000,000. It probably owes any monopolistic power which it possesses under the protection of high import duties on dyes to its control over patents and secret processes. In June, 1929, this company was confronted by a formidable rival when an American branch of the German dye trust was launched through the aid of American bankers.

The Radio Corporation of America is the latest child of the revolutionary inventions that have contributed so much to recent progress all over the world. Though it owes its pre-

[1] Title of paper presented at meeting of American Management Association, February, 1927, by Donaldson Brown, vice-president of the corporation.

dominance in its industry in part to patents that have not yet expired, it also seems to be true as regards its service as a means of long-distance communication that it presents some of the characteristics that have caused the telegraph and telephone businesses to be classed as natural monopolies. In any event, its future development presents so many novel problems and possibilities that it would obviously be improper to classify it as an ordinary manufacturing combination.

The Aluminum Company of America is another industry of recent development owing its predominance until recently to unexpired patents and at present to its acquisition of all the known important deposits of bauxite on the North American continent. This company was enjoined by a consent decree entered on June 7, 1912,[1] from continuing certain restrictive agreements and practices that were objected to by the Attorney General and is currently the subject of a complaint charging unfair methods of competition that is in course of trial by the Federal Trade Commission.[2] It is impossible to judge the merits of this complaint until the trial has been concluded.

The last of the combinations mentioned, the Paramount-Famous-Lasky Corporation, is the largest of several motion-picture companies which were accused by the Federal Trade Commission of attempting by restrictive agreements and the acquisition of motion-picture houses to monopolize the industry and ordered under date of July 9, 1927, to cease and desist from such practices.[3] Following this adverse ruling, representatives of the motion-picture industry met in New York with a member of the Federal Trade Commission and agreed upon a code of rules to govern the future relations between producers, distributors, and exhibitors. These rules were divided into four groups, the first of which was approved by the Commission; the second "received and accepted"; the third disapproved; and the fourth held in abeyance.[4] The

[1] *Decrees and Judgments in Federal Anti-Trust Cases,* p. 341.

[2] Complaint No. 1335. Cf. *Annual Report of Federal Trade Commission for 1928,* p. 160.

[3] Cf. *Annual Report of Federal Trade Commission for 1928,* p. 137.

[4] *Ibid.,* pp. 6-8.

extent to which the government now depends on this new method of securing compliance with the law, called "the trade practice conference," is discussed in Chapter XXIII.

While the number of new monopolistic industrial combinations organized during the last twenty-five years has been insignificant, a new form of combination, the Trade Association, has become very widespread as a means of promoting coöperative relations among business men in the same branch of manufacturing, mining, or trade. At present more than a thousand trade associations are in actual operation in the United States. Their activities are so important and diversified that we have devoted a special chapter to their consideration.[1] On the basis of the above survey of the facts of the American trust movement, we turn in the next chapter to a brief review of conflicting opinions in regard to the advantages and disadvantages of monopolistic combinations.

[1] Chapter XVI.

CHAPTER VI

CONFLICTING THEORIES IN REGARD TO THE ADVANTAGES AND DISADVANTAGES OF TRUSTS

NOTWITHSTANDING the fact that the operation and policies of the big American industrial combinations have been eagerly studied for more than a generation, there is still great difference of opinion as to their advantages and disadvantages. In this chapter we shall consider this problem primarily from the point of view of business men, leaving for later consideration the broader social interests involved.

The most obvious advantage which business men may derive from the different forms of combination that have been described is ability to hold the prices for their services or goods at levels which afford monopoly profits. Unrestrained competition has a tendency to force prices down to the level fixed by the expenses of production of representative firms.[1] It is a wearing process and the desire of business men to escape from it and enter the haven of monopoly is easily understandable. A familiar illustration is the situation of rival coal or ice dealers in a small town. There may be only two such dealers. Unrestrained competition implies that each will constantly be reaching out for the customers of the other by offering the product at a slightly lower price. The only limit to this process, so long as competition is persisted in, is the expense of production including the wage of management of the weaker competitor. If the competitors are equally able they may divide the market about equally between them, their competition assuring to consumers the lowest prices that will suffice to induce the dealers to remain in the business. But if there are only two dealers, the chance of obtaining higher prices by means of a simple agreement will be exceedingly

[1] Cf. Seager, *Principles of Economics,* Third Edition, 1923, chap. xi, especially section 106, and chaps. vi, vii, xii, and xiii, for a fuller discussion of this point.

tempting. The semblance of competition, even its reality as regards aggressive efforts to secure more customers, may be maintained, but a uniform price schedule may be adhered to that will afford substantial monopoly profits to both. Pools, trusts proper, holding companies, and outright consolidations offer the same lure of monopoly profits in the more complex and extended fields to which they apply, as does the simple agreement in the field of retail trade. If through them prices can be advanced to or held at levels above the expenses of production, including a proper wage of management, the business man's advantage from them is evident.

Desire for monopoly profit, the most obvious motive for organizing trusts, is, at the same time, the motive which most arouses the suspicion and antagonism of the public. If combining means exacting from the public higher prices than would result from unhampered competition, there is a clear opposition between the interests of the business men who organize trusts and of the public which depends upon them for the commodities or services which they control. Under these circumstances, the government, representing the public interest, is fully warranted in enacting and enforcing antitrust acts, and the only satisfactory solutions of the trust problem are their abolition or the rigid regulation of their price policies.

But there is more behind the trust movement than greed for monopoly profits. Competition is not merely a wearing process; it is also in many respects a wasteful process. Many business men disclaim any desire for monopoly profits and yet defend trusts on the ground that they make possible attainment of the economies and efficiencies of combination, on the one hand, and avoidance of the wastes of competition, on the other.

There has been a good deal of confusion in discussing the claims made for trusts from the viewpoint of economy and efficiency because the important distinction between the advantages of large-scale production and the further advantages of control by a monopolistic combination has not always been held clearly in view. To avoid this confusion it will be helpful to begin our analysis with a brief consideration of the advantages of large-scale production.

In each branch of business there appears to be a size of producing unit and a scale of operations which under average business management make for maximum economy and efficiency.[1] In the farming industry in the United States, for example, the truck farm, the dairy farm, or the wheat farm which pays best is one which is not too large to be rather rigidly supervised by the owner. Improvements in agricultural methods and the introduction of power machinery have, of course, tended to increase the area of land that can be most advantageously farmed as a unit, but, the country over, the small farm of twenty to three hundred acres has shown remarkable persistency as the representative farm. Similarly, in artistic and professional work, where constant attention to matters of detail or personal contact between the worker and the customer or client to be served is essential to success, the scale of the producing unit has remained small.

Very different has been the tendency in manufacturing industries. There the bringing together under one supervision of elaborate and costly complexes of machinery, operated by hundreds and even thousands of hired workers specializing on different processes, has become essential to economical production. For the "master's eye," a variety of devices which automatically record the speed and efficiency of the worker and, therefore, penalize the "slacker," have been introduced. Moreover, the use of power machinery itself sets the pace in many manufacturing plants, and spinners, weavers, and other operatives must conform to it under penalty of being discharged. To insure still further the largest possible outputs through hired workers directed by hired superintendents, methods of wage payment have been devised, like the piece wage and the premium or bonus system, which cause remuneration to vary with the work accomplished. Finally, so-called "scientific management" has been developed to reduce to rule and system the selection of workers for different tasks, and their guidance and supervision in the performance of those

[1] Cf. Seager, *Principles of Economics,* sections 93 and 94.

tasks, so that they may expend their efforts even more efficiently, though working for an employer, than they could if carrying on a similar enterprise entirely for themselves.

With the aid of power machinery and of these devices for securing efficient service from employees, the modern manufacturer finds it profitable to enlarge the scale of his operations to an extent that it is difficult to limit. In connection with the sugar-refining industry, for example, it is said that the smallest plant that can be equipped for really economical production involves an outlay of $3,000,000. In the iron and steel industry an indefinitely larger outlay is necessary to maximum economy. Blast furnaces and finishing mills must be in close proximity and under the same management if costly reheating of the metal is to be avoided. Not merely one rolling mill, but several, must be aggregated under the same management or the expense of changing rolls to turn out different sizes of product must be incurred. The outlays for raw materials and for transportation from the point of origin to the point of use are such substantial items that ownership and operation of ore and coal mines and limestone quarries, of coke ovens, of steamships and of railroads, give the large producer an advantage over the smaller rival, whose supplies are less regular and certain and whose costs vary with the changing prices of ore and coke. Investigations by the United States Bureau of Corporations [1] seem to show that the largest six iron and steel producers in the country, each with an investment of over $50,000,000, can produce more cheaply per ton of output than the smaller competing plants. The investigation failed to show, however, that the United States Steel Corporation with its investment of more than $1,000,000,000 can produce more cheaply than the larger of its competitors, like the Bethlehem Steel Company.[2] When a certain point is reached, it appears to be the case in the iron and steel industry as in other manufacturing industries that all of the possible economies resulting from enlarging the scale of opera-

[1] *Report of the Commissioner of Corporations on the Steel Industry,* part iii, *Cost of Production* (1913).

[2] No comparison of the costs of the different companies among themselves is made, so positive evidence is lacking in the published report.

tions and size of plant will be secured. Further enlargement beyond this point will serve merely to make the business more unwieldy and cumbersome, and, therefore, to reduce somewhat its efficiency. And this point of maximum efficiency appears, moreover, even in the iron and steel industry, to be reached long before the producing unit has attained a scale or size that carries with it monopolistic control of the business. If such monopolistic control, through a trust, has advantages from the point of view of efficient production, they must be other than those usually thought of as pertaining to large-scale production.

To make quite clear what the independent advantages enjoyed by trusts are, it will be well to summarize those which may be credited to large-scale production. The principal are:

(1) It permits the economical utilization of expensive machinery and other equipment, which the small-scale producer could not afford because he could not keep them continuously busy.

(2) It permits the economical grouping together of related plants, like blast furnaces and rolling mills, thus saving transportation and other expenses of handling, reheating, etc.

(3) It makes possible the securing of raw materials at lower or steadier prices, through long-time contracts on advantageous terms or through the ownership of the sources of supply of such materials.

(4) It permits a utilization of by-products, which would not be profitable for the small-scale producer with his smaller output of the waste materials from which such products are made.

(5) It permits a more minute subdivision and specialization of labor, applying even to the executive departments of the business, and thus a better distribution of the varied talents and capacities required.

(6) It permits larger expenditures to discover and test out new processes through experimental departments, which the small-scale producer could not afford to maintain, and thus is favorable to steady improvement in the technique of production.

The extent to which these advantages will be utilized depends very largely on the enterprise, judgment, and shrewdness of the master mind or minds which direct the business. If this directing intelligence displays unusual executive capacity [1]—that is, capacity to pick out the very ablest men to direct each department and to keep these men up to their best work all of the time, the business may grow and prosper to an almost indefinite extent. But, as already pointed out, the ablest executives are mortal. Large-scale enterprises which owe their expansion to the unique capacity of an individual are always in a somewhat precarious situation. When that individual dies or retires, it may be impossible to replace him with a man of the same talent, and the enterprise which he directed with ease may prove a veritable white elephant to his successor. Moreover, actual genius for business administration is exceedingly rare. Most business men, even successful men, have limited talents. This fact and the fact that geniuses must pass from the scene like ordinary mortals and rarely leave geniuses in their places, put limits on the size of manufacturing plant and scale of operations that is in the long run advantageous. These considerations serve to confirm the conclusion that for manufacturing industry, as for farming, the concentration of ownership and direction that will prove advantageous as a means of realizing the economies of large-scale production, stops short of monopolistic control of the branch of production under consideration.

A more precise way of describing the fact that there are distinct limits beyond which it is uneconomical to enlarge the scale of operations in farming and manufacturing is to say that these businesses become subject, after they have attained a certain size, to a law of increasing expense. A truck gardener, for example, finds it advantageous to acquire more land and enlarge the scale of his operations up to the point where he can utilize fully all of the best implements and most im-

[1] Executive capacity has been defined by someone as "ability to make others do your work better than you could do it yourself," but it is more than this. The good executive secures the efficient performance not only of work he might do himself, but also of work which he is entirely incompetent to perform.

proved processes, but as he does so he experiences the disadvantages of depending upon hired labor rather than upon his own more intelligently directed efforts. Up to a certain point his expenses per unit of product fall and his profits increase, not only because of the larger volume of his sales, but because the margin of profit is greater. When that point is passed, however, he finds himself over-expanded. The day is not long enough to enable him to keep track of all of the operations that need his personal attention if they are to be well done. Consequently, further enlargement means rising unit expenses, and before long smaller profits, notwithstanding his larger output and sales. If he is an intelligent producer he will curtail his operations when he finds himself in this situation and bring his business back to the scale which experience teaches him that he can handle most successfully.

Variations of climate and other conditions make exact calculations of normal expenses difficult for the truck gardener. Greater precision is possible in manufacturing. In the making of cotton goods, for example, the same principle of unit expenses diminishing up to a certain point, and then increasing as the scale of operations is enlarged, is encountered, and its influence can be more certainly traced. It would, of course, require careful study of each branch of this business by competent experts to decide just what size of plant is most economical in each given situation, but it is obvious from the way this business expands, not by the indefinite enlargement of old plants or the indefinite concentration of groups of plants under one management, but by the continuous launching of new companies and the construction of new plants, none of them exceeding a certain size, that concentration pays only up to a certain point and not beyond it.

In these businesses, taken as illustrations, and thousands of others like them, the unit of production affording the best results remains relatively small. There are hundreds of truck farmers supplying the needs of every city and thousands of manufacturers of the cheaper grades of cotton goods for the world market. It is situations such as these that economists have in mind when they speak of competition as a leveling and steadying influence. Each of the hundreds of competitors seeks to expand his sales until he is able to dispose of the volume of goods which experience teaches him he can turn out at lowest unit expense. The easiest way to do this is by selling at lower prices and the only certain limit to such lowering of prices is the expenses of production, including a fair wage of management. But as each producer attains his goal, a market for the volume of goods he can turn out at lowest unit expense, his desire for further expansion gives way to a desire for a higher margin of profit. So far as he is concerned there is no further tendency toward lower prices. If the market broadens, he takes advantage of the situation to demand higher prices. An enlargement of production comes from new competitors who are attracted into the industry by the high margin of profit which it affords. In such situations competition is a leveling influence because it tends to establish the same price for the same quality of goods for all competitors supplying the same market. It is a steadying influence because it tends to hold prices at the level that will just cover the expenses of production, including a fair wage of management, of representative firms. On the whole the best interests of the industrial community are served in such businesses by having competition free and unhampered. This assures to consumers the lowest prices compatible with proper regard for the interests of producers.

In coming to the above conclusion we must not ignore the fact that free and unhampered competition in truck farming and small-scale businesses results in serious wastes and losses. Truck farmers and small manufacturers frequently misjudge the requirements of the market. When high prices prevail for particular products, the absence of any restraint on competition too often results in over-investment of capital in the lines of production concerned. Presently a volume of products begins to come upon the market in excess of consumers' requirements at remunerative prices. Prices fall and some of the competitors are forced into bankruptcy, to their own loss and indirectly to the loss of the community. Moreover, active competition in production means also active competition in selling. Between producer and consumer a large class of middlemen must be maintained, whose service might be rendered much more cheaply and efficiently if production were controlled and the disposal of the entire product were attended to systematically and intelligently by a single organization. Competitive advertising and competitive selling through numerous traveling and local agents add substantially and often wastefully to the original expenses of production.

In connection with businesses in which the small producer is able to show lowest unit costs, desire to avoid these wastes and losses of unregulated production and competitive selling leads not to combination among the producers as such, but to various plans for the collection and dissemination of information of common concern through the government or other agencies, and for coöperative marketing of the product. The government's crop reports and the fruit exchanges of California and Oregon are familiar illustrations.

If these wastes and losses are relatively small and if the producers who experience them are numerous and widely separated, they must, except for these plans, be borne as part of the price that must be paid for efficient production. The larger they become and the fewer the producers concerned, as in branches of manufacturing where the advantages of large-scale production have caused a high degree of concentration, the stronger the inducement to avoid them through combination. It is right here, in the opinion of defenders of the trusts, that we have the true explanation and the true justification of their existence.

The statement that manufacturing becomes subject to a law of increasing expense after concentration has reached a certain point rests on analysis of only one side of the problem that confronts the business man. It is probably true as far as it goes, but it ignores the fact that marketing products is just as essential to business success as making them. If production, in the narrow sense, covered the whole problem, manufacturers in all lines, like farmers, would concentrate their attention on ways in which they could produce most cheaply. The scale of operations in each branch of manufacturing would be that which experience showed to result in lowest unit expenses, and the expenses of representative firms would fix the prices at which all their products would be regularly sold. But to produce cheaply is not enough. To find customers who will buy is quite as essential if the business is to escape bankruptcy. In most branches of farming the production that results in lowest unit expenses is on such a small scale that the task of marketing the product falls to middlemen. They organize markets for wheat, corn, and other staple products, and farmers usually accept the resulting prices as factors in the situation that are beyond their control. Branches of manufacturing which find small-scale production economical also rely on middlemen for the marketing of their products. But more and more branches of manufacturing find large-scale production preferable. When the scale of operations reaches a certain point, the efficient organization of the selling side of the business becomes too important to be left to middlemen. The manufacturer becomes his own distributor. With this change competition among manufacturers enters upon a much more aggressive stage.

It is generally agreed that the circumstances which make the railroad business a natural monopoly are that in it the advantages of large-scale operations and concentrated management persist beyond any assignable limit, and that among its expenses of production, fixed charges, interest on the investment in roadbed, bridges, tunnels, terminals, etc., so preponderate that competition, when attempted, is always of a violent and destructive character.[1] Deterred only by the need of recovering operating expenses from any given quantity of traffic, railroad managers, when engaged in "rate wars," are led to reduce rates to levels that would be ruinous if long maintained. Consequently, competition in this industry inevitably leads to combination. Uniform rate schedules sanctioned and supervised by a governmental commission alone give efficiency and stability to the railroad business.

Though outlay for plant, machinery, and other necessary equipment probably attains the relative importance in no

[1] Cf. Seager, *Principles of Economics*, chaps. xxiii and xxiv.

branch of manufacturing that it does in railroading, it is evident that it is vastly more important in some branches than in others. In the manufacture of cotton cloth the outlay for building and machinery is not great, especially if power is produced from coal, in comparison with the outlay for labor, materials, and fuel. If trade is dull, a shut-down is not disastrous to the manufacturer, because interest on the relatively inexpensive fixed plant is not such a large item. In iron and steel manufacturing the fixed investment is relatively much larger. It includes mines and railroads as well as mills, and in every department labor-saving machinery has been so perfected that interest on the investment in such machinery and on other features of the fixed plant constitutes a chief item of expense. A shut-down under these circumstances means much heavier loss to the manufacturer than under those presented in cotton manufacturing. It follows that competition among iron and steel manufacturers has much more of the character of competition among railroads than of that which regulates the price of cotton goods in the world market. If trade is depressed, to avoid the heavy loss resulting from a shut-down, the iron and steel manufacturer will cut his prices far below what would ordinarily be a profitable level. His problem is not to make profits, but to curtail losses. If he can get any return over and above his operating expenses he will be better off than if he gets no return at all toward interest on his investment, which will continue whether his plant is running or is idle. On the other hand, if trade is booming, the very heavy outlays necessary to efficient production serve as a bar to added investment in the industry until the margin of profit has become very high or the guaranty of continued prosperity is very certain. It is for these reasons that the iron and steel industry in the period when it was actively competitive was accurately characterized by Mr. Carnegie as "either prince or pauper." Its profits in boom times were immensely large. In periods of depression losses were so great, especially for the less efficient plants which were compelled at such times to shut down, that bankruptcies were common.

The basis of the advantage claimed for the monopolistic trust as contrasted with the large-scale enterprise is made clear by the above description. The scale of operations contemplated is already vast, involving immense investments in plant, machinery, and other fixed forms. In many branches of manufacturing such degree of concentration is clearly required if lowest unit expenses are to be achieved. As a result the field is occupied by a dozen, a score, or at most half a hundred giant competitors each as aggressively concerned with the marketing of his product as with its manufacture. It is maintained that when this stage is reached competition becomes so wasteful and destructive that it threatens disaster to all competitors alike. As in the railroad industry, so in manufacturing carried on on this gigantic scale, it is claimed that competition knows no limits. In periods of depression it becomes a struggle which forces rivals to shut down because prices are too low even to cover operating expenses, and then to become bankrupt because fixed charges so soon eat up any surplus that may have been accumulated. The competitor who is strong enough to survive in such an encounter rapidly gains in strength, because he alone is ready and able to take fullest advantage of rising prices and expanding sales when prosperity returns, but his success is really at the expense of his own customers as well as of his rivals. A monopolistic combination, it is urged, is able to check a depression before it goes to an extreme by curtailing production somewhat in all plants, by shutting down entirely plants which can profitably be altered or repaired during the dull season, and by refraining from cutting prices below operating expenses. By conserving the capital invested in the industry by these means, the trust maintains itself in a position to meet the demands of expanding trade when the depression is over, and it is as much to its long-run interest as to the interest of its customers to prevent prices from advancing to an unreasonable extent, in order that competitors may not be drawn into the industry. Avoiding disastrous losses during depressions, it will, if wisely managed, it is maintained, also refrain from exacting unreasonable profits during periods of prosperity.

Its aim should be to steady prices and by so doing make more uniform the volume of products which can be marketed. Avoiding the wastes of competition, it will be able to sell its products at lower prices year in and year out than can competing manufacturers, and still make larger aggregate profits than they could command.

It will be noted that attainment of this result does not call for an outright consolidation of competing business firms or corporations. All that is required is such degree of combination as will result in effective control over supplies and prices. Plants may continue under independent operation. The combination may be only for a term of years. Thus well-organized production and selling pools, like the cartels so common in Germany, satisfy the requirements of the argument as well as the holding company or consolidation types of trust that have been more familiar in this country.

In addition to the enormous savings that will result, according to the argument of trust defenders, from steadying prices by limiting outputs in periods of depression, and expanding them rapidly in periods of active demand, there are other savings that are claimed for the trusts. Of these the most important is the avoidance of the wastes of competitive advertising and competitive selling which now play such a conspicuous part in the distribution of widely-used articles. That the expense of marketing products, where competition is active, adds unduly to the expense of production under modern conditions is very generally conceded. In many branches of production, business men expect to spend regularly as much in finding customers for their products and securing payment for them as in manufacturing them. Opinions differ, however, as to the extent to which this outlay can safely be curtailed by a monopolistic combination. Even when competition in the sale of the particular product concerned has been restrained, there will remain competition between that product and other products which gratify the same or similar wants. An anthracite-coal combination, even if it could control all of the anthracite coal output of the country, would still have to reckon with the competition of bituminous coal and coke and even of fuel oil in communities where oil-burners have come into use. There is not quite the same danger of competition of substitute products to a "sugar trust" or a "steel trust," but no monopolistic combination, no matter how firmly intrenched in its own line, could safely adopt the policy of waiting for purchasers to come forward on their own unaided initiative to buy its products. How extensive are the possible savings that may be effected by a trust in this direction will be a question for consideration as we pass now to a study of typical trusts. We shall also consider why, if selling pools carry a combination as far as is necessary to secure the principal advantages that may be claimed for monopolistic control, they have played such an inconspicuous rôle in the American trust movement.

CHAPTER VII

THE ADDYSTON PIPE COMBINATION AND OTHER POOLS

Pools were the earliest effective form of combination resorted to by American business men and are the form for which they would perhaps still show a preference, as have the business men of Germany, if the law left them free to follow their inclinations.

Agreements dating back to 1861 in the cordage industry were gradually strengthened into a formal pool in 1878.[1] In the same period and in the 'eighties pools were organized in the salt, whisky, coal, and other industries. They became very common in the iron and steel industry in the 'nineties. In nearly all cases the formation of these pools was preceded by a period of severe competition and falling prices. Consequently, their immediate purpose was most commonly restraints on competition that would serve to restore prices to a profitable level. This purpose was too often displaced in the case of successful pools by the further purpose of exacting monopoly profits from defenseless consumers. Pools have thus come to signify in the public mind "unconscionable monopolies," whereas a more accurate characterization, if we consider their origin, would be "means for avoiding the wastes and losses resulting from unrestrained competition." The examples that follow have been chosen partly because fairly full accounts of them are accessible to students, but chiefly because they are believed to be typical.

The Michigan Salt Association was a well-organized pool in an industry in which the disadvantages of unrestrained competition are specially marked.[2] The salt field of Michigan

[1] Dewing, *Corporate Promotions and Reorganizations,* p. 114.

[2] Excellent accounts of the series of combinations in this industry are given in Jenks' article on "The Michigan Salt Association," reprinted in Ripley's

began production from wells in and about Saginaw in 1860. At that time most of the salt of the country came from central New York, though Ohio was also beginning to be an important source of supply. In all three fields production was either through mining rock salt, which was never very pure and was expensive to refine, or through pumping up the brine found at a considerable depth underground and refining it in pans and vats made for the purpose. In connection with the last process, which was the one most commonly used, the principal items of expense were for the pumping plant and the refining apparatus. The cost of operation was small because most of the wells were operated in connection with sawmills which furnished fuel in the form of sawdust and other waste products for running the pumps at no expense, and materials for making the barrels for packing the salt at very slight expense. The salt-well operator was thus in somewhat the same situation as the railroad operator. Rather than shut down he could afford to sell his salt at any price that would cover his small operating expenses, though such a price, if maintained, would in the end spell ruin to the industry. Furthermore, salt is a very cheap commodity, selling in Saginaw, at the time the association was organized in 1876, for about a dollar a barrel of 280 pounds and for as little as fifty cents a barrel in periods of active competition since. The freight charge to markets at any considerable distance from the source of supply thus becomes the principal item of expense, and to overcome this disadvantage in markets where the competition of other fields is encountered, individual producers seeking an outlet for their outputs may be tempted to cut prices to a minimum. Another element in the situation is the inelasticity of the demand for a commodity like salt. It is so cheap that all classes consume all they desire, and lowering of the price cannot, therefore, stimulate demand appreciably, at any rate for domestic use. Add to these considerations the speculative character of the industry growing out of the uncertainty as

Trusts, Pools and Corporations, pp. 1-21, and in Dewing, *Corporate Promotions and Reorganizations,* chap. viii.

to the quality and permanence of the deposits and we can appreciate the force of the appeal sent to manufacturers to attend the meeting which resulted in the organization of the Michigan Salt Association in January, 1876. It read: [1]

> Salt has depreciated in value, dropped steadily down, until today it has no market price on the Saginaw river, and is quoted at only $1.27 in Chicago, and $1.00 in Toledo. That the experience of '75 will be that of each succeeding year, unless something is done to check the general demoralization, cannot be gainsaid. The oldest manufacturers of the Syracuse, Kanawha, and Ohio districts, tell us that their experience, dating back forty years in some cases, has *always* been this: *"Organized we have prospered. Unorganized we have not."* This is the experience which we have been buying and paying dearly for. . . . The trouble lies in the *marketing* of the product. Each man has taken care of (or attempted to) his own product. . . . The other salt districts of the United States are now organized, and are ready to treat with us. . . . But we must first be organized. They cannot treat with individuals.

The association which was organized as a result of this meeting to put a stop to reckless competition and place the industry on a more stable basis was given a capital of $200,000, of which only $16,000 ($2 for each $25 share) was paid in. It was managed by a board of nineteen directors, of whom no more than one could be from the same firm, and was to expire by limitation unless renewed at the end of five years. As a matter of fact, it was renewed and remained in successful operation for more than twenty-five years.

The success of this pool was due to the efficiency and conservatism of the management, aided by certain unusual features in the organization. Under the by-laws shares of stock were to be held only by manufacturers of salt and in the proportion of one share for each barrel of their average daily capacity. On becoming a member each manufacturer was required to enter into a contract to deliver his entire product to the association or to lease his plant to it. There were also provisions insuring the quality of the product and binding the association to advance money on the salt produced, so that the manufacturer would be relieved of any financial inducement to dispose of his product privately. At the same time

[1] Quoted in Ripley, *Trusts, Pools and Corporations,* p. 6.

any manufacturer was permitted to market his own product on paying a fine of ten cents a barrel to the association for salt so disposed of. Given control of the bulk of the supply of salt produced in the Michigan field, the association was in a position to market it advantageously. It was deterred at the same time from attempting to advance prices unduly by the competition from other fields and by the absence of any restriction on the output of its members. The old cutthroat competition gave place to intelligent coöperation in improving methods of manufacture, standardizing the different grades offered for sale, and extending the market. Prices were gradually lowered rather than raised [1] so that the benefits of these economies were shared with consumers.

Unfortunately, the success of the Michigan Salt Association in handling the product of the Michigan field inspired a group of New York manufacturers with the ambition to organize a more comprehensive trust which should control the entire salt industry of the country. The National Salt Company was organized in 1899 to control the principal New York wells. In 1900 it entered into contracts to take the bulk of the product of the Ohio and Michigan fields and thus controlled for a time 73 per cent of the evaporated salt produced east of the Rocky Mountains.[2] For two years it was able to maintain prices at a highly profitable level. This apparent success led to the organization in 1901 of the International Salt Company with an even more ambitious program. Before this new combination was fairly launched, however, the National Company, which it was to take over, found itself in financial difficulties. By advancing prices it had stimulated production to such an extent that it was unable to dispose of the product of its subsidiaries. Prices broke badly in 1902 and the National Company became bankrupt. The International Company acquired its assets, but was not able to achieve even the temporary success of its predecessor. There could hardly be a more striking illustration of the benefits to be derived from a

[1] Cf. Tables II and III of prices from 1860 to 1887 in Ripley's *Trusts, Pools and Corporations*, pp. 15-17.

[2] Dewing, *Corporate Promotions and Reorganizations*, p. 211.

well-managed pool which seeks to avoid the wastes of competition and of the perversion of these benefits so soon as greed for monopoly profits becomes the dominant motive, than is afforded by the history of these successive combinations in the American salt industry.

The motive for combination among manufacturers of standard iron and steel products was nearly as strong as among salt manufacturers. By the late 'eighties concentration, impelled by the economies to be effected through enlarging the scale of production, had been carried so far in these industries that the number of independent firms and corporations engaged in each branch was no longer a serious obstacle to combination. The Steel Rail Pool, entered into on August 2, 1887, represented more than 90 per cent of the steel-rail output of the country, although it numbered only fifteen members.[1] The numbers included in the Wire Nail Pool of 1895 and the Steel Billet Pool of 1896 were considerably larger, but the Structural Steel Association of 1897[2] needed to include only ten members, and the Steel Plate Association of 1900[3] only eleven, to secure substantial control over their respective branches of production. As the most stable and successful of these combinations the Steel Rail Pool merits brief description.

Added to the high degree of concentration attained and the preponderance of fixed over operating expenses in an industry using expensive and largely automatic machinery, there was another urgent reason why steel-rail makers should combine. Their chief customers were the railroads, many of them more powerful financially and better organized to strike hard bargains than the manufacturers themselves. In the period before the Interstate Commerce Commission became an effective regulative body, the railroads had, in discrimination in freight rates, a powerful weapon for inducing rail manufacturers to supply them with cheap rails. Under these condi-

[1] Cf. *Report of the Commissioner of Corporations on the Steel Industry*, vol. i, pp. 68 *et seq.*, for an account of this and other steel pools.

[2] Stevens, *Industrial Combinations and Trusts*, pp. 211-219.

[3] *Ibid.*, pp. 219-225.

tions competition in the sale of rails partook of the nature of a struggle for existence. In periods of depression, rather than shut down, manufacturers would take orders at cost or even below cost. In periods of expansion those who had survived would recoup themselves at the expense of the railroads, but the seesaw up and down was satisfactory to neither side in the contest. Manufacturers much preferred a stable price on which they could base their calculations of expense and profit. The railroads also preferred a uniform price and more coöperative relations with the manufacturers designed to effect improvements in the quality of the product. Formally organized in 1887, the Steel Rail Pool was frequently dissolved and renewed thereafter, with the result that a uniform price of $28 a ton for standard steel rails was maintained continuously, except for a brief period of price-slashing in 1897 [1] after the disruption of the pool and before its reorganization, for over twenty years, to the certain advantage of the manufacturers and without any demonstrable disadvantage to the railroads or the public, since the price, considering the whole period, appears to have been as reasonable as would have been secured under any system.

In the formal agreement of 1887 no provision appears in reference to prices, although some understanding as to prices was doubtless reached. The pool was concerned solely with the tonnage of steel rails, weighing fifty pounds and upward to the yard, to be manufactured and sold by the members, and with their respective proportions of this tonnage.

The machinery for controlling tonnage and allotments was simple. A board of control consisting of three members designated in the agreement was given general supervision. To it the members were required to make monthly reports of sales and shipments, and by it, with the written consent of 75 per cent of the total allotments agreed upon, the tonnage for the year might be increased. It was the Board's duty to call meetings of the pool members from time to time on its own initiative or at the written request of any three members. Finally

[1] Standard rails were sold for as little as $15 a ton in this year, a price that would have been ruinous if maintained.

it was empowered to levy assessments on the members in proportion to their allotments to cover its expenses.

The tentative allotment for 1888 was fixed at 800,000 tons, of which the fourteen active manufacturers were entitled to shares varying from 13.5 per cent for the two Carnegie companies to 1.4 per cent for the Worcester Steel Works.[1] In addition, the board of control was to assign 250,000 tons more "to whom it [might] deem equitable in the adjustment of any differences that [might] arise." Furthermore, it was directed to see to it that the allotments assigned aggregated not less than 200,000 tons above the total sales reported to the board each month by the members, so that there might always be a working margin for the negotiation of new contracts. There was also the usual provision in connection with output pools—that is, that at the beginning of each quarter the board should cancel parts of allotments which the members concerned might be unable to fill and assign such canceled tonnage to other members at its discretion.

As so organized the pool was continued until 1893. Dissolved in this year, it was soon renewed and remained in operation until January, 1897. Its dissolution in this year of depression was followed by a fierce struggle for the small tonnage for which the railroads cared to contract, a return to pre-pool conditions which soon caused the manufacturers to settle their differences and reëstablish the combination. As we show in Chapter XIV, there is fairly conclusive evidence that the rail and other steel pools continued until 1904, and, in less formal fashion, until 1906. Except for the fact that rail prices have been "pegged" during most of the intervening years, evidence of pool action, if any pools have existed, since 1906, is lacking.

The secrecy which has characterized pooling agreements in the United States since the enactment of the Antitrust Act in 1890 has led to abuses that probably would not have developed had this country followed Germany in tolerating combinations in restraint of trade. One of the most notorious exam-

[1] For some reason the Springfield Iron Company, although appearing as a regular member, was not given any allotment.

ples of such abuses was the pool dissolved by decree of the United States Supreme Court in 1899, of which the Addyston Pipe and Steel Company of Cincinnati was a member.

The Associated Pipe Works [1] was a combination of six pipe manufacturers located in Ohio, Kentucky, Tennessee, and Alabama, organized in December, 1894, for two years. Its general purpose was to control prices in all that portion of the United States lying south of Virginia and west of Pennsylvania, known as "bonus territory," through secret understandings as to outputs and collusive bids. It was able to succeed in this purpose because the six companies controlled about two-thirds of the pipe-manufacturing capacity of this section and were protected from outside competition by freight charges, which for a commodity like iron pipe are an important item of expense. Designated cities in this territory were assigned outright to the nearest member. For example, a part of the agreement read: "The Addyston Pipe and Steel Company shall handle the business of the gas and water companies of Cincinnati, Ohio, and Covington and Newport, Kentucky, and pay the bonus hereafter mentioned, the balance of the parties to this agreement shall bid on such work such reasonable prices as they shall dictate." Under the original agreement the bonuses, which ranged from $1 a ton in Eastern territory, where competition was a factor, to $4 in the far West, were paid to an auditor who kept a record of all shipments and apportioned the bonuses among the members entitled to receive them. The system of fixing bonuses in advance proving unsatisfactory, a board was organized in May, 1895, which thereafter determined the prices to be charged for different contracts and awarded the task of supplying the pipe to the member bidding the lowest price for the privilege, the bonus being the difference between the price charged the purchaser and the price resulting from such secret bidding. Under this new system the bonuses averaged $7 to

[1] The salient facts in reference to this pool are disclosed in the argument of the Assistant Attorney General in the dissolution suit and in the decision of the United States Supreme Court reprinted in Ripley, *Trusts, Pools and Corporations,* pp. 78-96 and 533-546. Cf. also Stevens, *Industrial Combinations and Trusts,* pp. 205-209.

$8 in the following year, and at least one of the companies found it more profitable to sell its pipe in "free" territory—that is, territory not covered by the agreement—and add its share of the bonuses to the profits it was able to make in this way. The most flagrant aspect of this arrangement was the hypocritical bids put in by companies which knew in advance that a lower bid was to be made by the member to which the work had already been awarded. For example, an order for pipe by the Knoxville Woolen Mills having been secretly assigned to the Chattanooga Company, that company put in a bid of $22 per ton and at the same time wired other members of the pool, "Please protect!" The Howard Harrison Company thereupon put in a bid of $22.24 a ton, with the usual "trusting that we will be favored with your order." A little later the Chattanooga Company bid $24.80 a ton on an Omaha contract that had already been assigned to the Howard Harrison Company at $23.40, adding, "We are in a position to give you prompt shipment on this pipe and trust this time we will be favored with your order." Lying and cheating of the public inevitably led to lying and cheating among the members themselves to an extent that makes the inner history of this pool a depressing chapter in the record of American business.

Another reason for giving prominence to the Associated Pipe Works is that its prosecution by the government led to the second decision of the United States Supreme Court applying the Antitrust Act to an industrial combination.[1] The chief significance of this decision was that it helped to dispel the uncertainty created by that in the Knight case as to what, if anything, the Antitrust Act would restrain. The court held that, though the members of the pool manufactured pipe, their agreement was concerned with the buying and selling of that commodity across state lines, which was clearly interstate commerce. The case was therefore to be distinguished from the Knight case, and the arrangement fell clearly within the condemnation of the statute.[2] Since this decision was

[1] Addyston Pipe and Steel Co. et al. *v.* U. S., 175 U. S. 211 (1899).

[2] For a more detailed treatment of the legal aspects of this pool see Chapter XVIII, pp. 383, 384.

unanimous and its reasoning unassailable, it marks the beginning of the effort on the part of the Supreme Court to apply the Antitrust Act positively and constructively to the regulation of business methods and conditions.

A study of the many other pools that have been organized in different branches of American business would merely confirm the conclusions suggested by the above description. Such pools have usually been formed after periods of active competition which have forced prices below, at times far below, remunerative levels. The indispensable condition to their existence is concentration of production in a comparatively small number of plants, so that the competitors are not too numerous to be brought together into an effective coöperative organization. A condition almost as necessary is heavy fixed expenses, which cause competition to take on that life-and-death character with which railroad-rate wars have made us familiar. Though usually honestly approved by the business men who have from time to time organized them, they have been under the shadow of condemnation by the common law and later by the antitrust acts. This has compelled them to resort to secrecy, with results that have very properly discredited them in American public opinion. Notwithstanding the flagrant abuses of which American pools have been guilty, many business men believe that, if they had enjoyed the same legal protection as did the similar cartels in Germany and at the same time had been compelled to make public their agreements and operations, they would have demonstrated that in certain industries they were capable of rendering valuable services not only to their members, but to the whole industrial community.

CHAPTER VIII

THE STANDARD OIL TRUST

AMONG the "romances of trade," few are more absorbing than the story of the rise and progress of the Standard Oil Company. In this chapter it will be possible to deal only with the portions of this story which help to an understanding of the combination movement as a whole.[1]

The petroleum industry dates from the boring of the first oil well—"Drake's Folly"—at Titusville, Pennsylvania, in August, 1859. Drake's success led to something of the same sort of a furore for oil that had been aroused for gold in California ten years earlier. It was not long before the region was flooded with oil—much more oil than could possibly be stored and refined with the limited facilities for handling the product that were at first available. The price of crude petroleum, which had been $20 a barrel in January, 1860, was forced down by this excess production to ten cents a barrel before the close of 1861. Thus at the very outset was the importance of facilities for storing and transporting, as well as for refining, petroleum, if enormous waste was to be avoided, impressed upon those who interested themselves in the industry. The history of the next few years was the history of feverish activity, not only in boring new wells, but in constructing storage tanks, refineries, branch railroads, and pipe lines to handle and market the product economically.

The first thought of the pioneers in the industry was that

[1] The most comprehensive account of the early career of the Standard Oil Trust is Ida Tarbell's *The History of the Standard Oil Company,* 2 vols. (1904, reprinted, 1925). This is supplemented by G. H. Montague's more tolerant *The Rise and Progress of the Standard Oil Company* (1903), and the reports of the U. S. Bureau of Corporations on *The Transportation of Petroleum* (1906) and *The Petroleum Industry,* parts i and ii (1907). The reports of the Federal Trade Commission on *Pipe Line Transportation of Petroleum* (1916), *The Pacific Coast Petroleum Industry* (1921), and *Petroleum Industry: Prices, Profits and Competition* (1928) throw light on conditions in the industry since the trust was formally dissolved in 1911.

it would pay best to build the oil refineries in close proximity to the oil wells, and some of the largest early refineries were so built. To this, however, the very inadequate means of transporting the needed equipment into the region offered a serious obstacle. Everything required except the crude oil was so much cheaper in the near-by cities that refineries were started in Pittsburgh and Cleveland only a few months after they were started in Titusville itself, and in a few years they were also started in the seaboard cities, Philadelphia, New York, Brooklyn, and even Baltimore and Boston.

Next to the finding of oil in 1859, the most important event in the development of the industry was the demonstration by a man by the name of Van Syckel in 1864 that the crude oil could be successfully conveyed in pipes for considerable distances, even over elevations. Pipes soon displaced all other means of shipping oil from the wells to the railways, and with the aid of connecting storage tanks served to reduce greatly the waste of oil that had characterized the industry down to that time. A little later the tank car came into use and the lines along which the further perfection of the transportation side of the industry was to proceed were clearly indicated.

Mr. John D. Rockefeller first interested himself in oil refining in 1862, when, with his partner in a successful produce commission business in Cleveland, he advanced $4,000 to Mr. Samuel Andrews to enable him to erect an improved refinery.

This oil refinery prospered and in 1865 Rockefeller, then twenty-six years of age, determined to devote all of his time and ability to its further development. The firm name at this period was Rockefeller and Andrews. As methods of refining were perfected, the small plants of the early 'sixties were displaced by more costly establishments. Following this trend Rockefeller and Andrews combined in 1867 with two other firms, in which Mr. William Rockefeller was already interested, and organized the firm of Rockefeller, Andrews and Flagler. The continued success of their business led them in 1870 to organize it as a corporation, the Standard Oil Company of Ohio, with a capital of $1,000,000. The fifth director of this company, besides the men mentioned, was Mr. Stephen V. Harkness.

Miss Tarbell in her *History* ascribes the remarkable success of the Rockefeller refineries from 1865 to 1870 to railway rebates. There seems to be no positive evidence that the original organizers of the Standard received rebates at this time, but there was a general impression among their competitors that they did so. Some of these competitors even testified that they themselves obtained rebates from the railroads by merely protesting their belief that Rockefeller, Andrews and Flagler were getting them. Certainly rebates were in the air. It was the usual practice of the railroads to make special rates to their large shippers to keep them from resorting to rival lines. If the Rockefeller firm did not benefit by this practice it would be a matter for a good deal of surprise in the light of the proficiency they later displayed in playing railroads off against one another. At the same time it is quite probable, as Mr. Montague maintains, that the principal cause of the rapid evolution of a $4,000 partnership into a $1,000,000 corporation in the short period of eight years was the remarkable energy, foresight, and ability with which advantage was taken of an unusually favorable opportunity. The oil industry as a whole was growing at this period by leaps and bounds. All those who brought brains, energy, and confidence in the future to the adventure succeeded and succeeded greatly. In 1870 the Standard Oil Company was simply one of several large refineries that had grown up from nothing within the decade since oil was first discovered. Its output of refined oil was only a small fraction of the total output of the country, and its future seemed no more assured than that of other refineries in Cleveland, in the oil region, in Pittsburgh and elsewhere.

To understand the progress of the oil industry after the Standard Oil Company was organized it is necessary to have in mind a clear picture of the transportation situation. The oil region from which nearly all the raw material was still obtained was confined to the strip of territory not over fifty miles in length which borders upon Oil Creek in Northwestern Pennsylvania. This region was by this time entered by three railroads. The Pennsylvania conveyed oil from Oil City to Pittsburgh, a distance of eighty miles, and thence to Philadelphia, three hundred miles farther. It was the earliest road to enter the region and afforded the shortest route to the seaboard. The Atlantic and Great Western and the Erie, which were operated practically as one road, reached Oil City from the north and conveyed oil to New York, a distance of five hundred and fifty miles. Finally the New York Central and the Lake Shore and Michigan Southern, which were also closely affiliated, connected Oil City with New York *via* Cleveland, a distance of seven hundred and forty miles. As regards the Eastern market, therefore, the Cleveland refiners were the least favorably situated of all. They had to haul their raw material nearly one hundred and fifty miles, and even then were farther removed from the seaboard with their refined product than their competitors either in the oil region or in Pittsburgh. This disadvantage was partly offset by their command of the cheap water route afforded by Lake Erie and the Erie Canal and by their proximity to the growing Western market.

By 1871 all three of the great railway systems concerned with the oil traffic, the Pennsylvania, the Erie, and the Central, had completed connections through to Chicago and were engaged in a fierce struggle for Western freight. It was the custom of the traffic managers of the three roads at this period to meet annually to agree upon rates. But the rates that were agreed upon in December were regularly broken before August. Discriminations in the form of rebates to large shippers were very generally given and the roads were in a situation in which they were ready to welcome any plan which would assure to all of them a reasonable share of a remunerative traffic.

It was at this juncture that the notorious South (or "Southern") Improvement Company was organized. The charter of this company was granted by the legislature of Pennsylvania in 1870 along with three or four other charters, and it has never become known whether or not the use to which it was finally put was that originally contemplated. Its terms were of the broad and sweeping character that we have since learned to associate with a New Jersey charter. Among other things, it gave power "to construct and operate any work or works, public or private, designed to include, increase, facilitate or develop, trade, travel, or the transportation of freight, live-stock, passengers or any traffic by land or water, from or to any part of the United States." There is clear evidence that the plan of utilizing this charter as a means of consolidating the oil-refining business of the country originated in Pittsburgh rather than in Cleveland. In fact, both Rockefeller and Flagler later testified that they never believed in the plan. However that may be, they appear to have been convinced that it was a plan from which the Standard Oil Company could not afford to hold aloof. On January 2, 1872, the South Improvement Company was launched as an active organization. Its 2,000 shares of stock were so divided that 900 shares went to five men interested or about to be interested in the Standard Oil Company (*i.e.,* 180 shares each to the two Rockefellers, Flagler, O. H. Payne, and J. H. Bostwick); 475 shares each went to A. F. Waring and to W. G. Warden, representing (respectively) the largest refining interests in Pittsburgh and Philadelphia; and the remaining 150 shares to several small refiners in these two cities.

The plan of the organizers was to get preferential rates from the five railroads interested in the oil traffic, which would give them a virtual monopoly of the business of refining and shipping to the seaboard. In return they proposed to act as "eveners" between the roads and to assure to each a stipulated share of the combined traffic at remunerative rates. The task of inducing the officials of the five railroads (including the Atlantic and Great Western and the Lake Shore and Michigan Southern) to enter into the arrangement appears to have been easy. In describing this phase of the plan to a committee of Congress a few months later, Mr. Warden, the secretary of the company, said the railroads objected to granting the rebates asked for unless all the refiners were included in the arrangement. They appear to have been satisfied, however, with the general assurance that all "would be taken in." On January 18 the Pennsylvania Railroad signed the agreement in regard to rates and rebates, and before the end of the month all of the other roads had signed and the plan was ready to go into operation.

The following table shows the rates and rebates called for in the contract:

Crude petroleum	*Rate per barrel*	*Rebate per barrel*
From any common point (in the oil region) To		
Cleveland	$.80	$.40
Pittsburgh	.80	.40
New York	2.56	1.06
Refined petroleum		
Pittsburgh to New York	2.00	.50
Cleveland to New York	2.00	.50

So far as this table shows, the plan was not unlike any other arrangement by which a favored shipper was given a rebate. Its peculiarity was that *the rebates called for were to be paid to the South Improvement Company, not only on its own shipments, but also on those of other shippers.* That is to say, the South Improvement Company, in which the Standard Oil Company was so largely interested, was to receive, in addition to the return of one-half of the freight rate that it was called upon to pay on the shipments of crude oil to Cleveland and Pittsburgh which it made for its members, a gift of one-half of the freight rates paid by their Cleveland and Pittsburgh competitors. In return for this extraordinary concession, the South Improvement Company undertook to distribute the oil traffic among the three railroad systems, so that 45 per cent of that moving east should go over the Pennsylvania, and 27½ per cent each over the Erie and the Central. The westbound traffic was to be divided equally among the roads. To give a semblance of equity to the arrangement each road reserved the right to grant the same privileges to any other shipper who could furnish a like amount of traffic as the South Improvement Company, but at the same time promised, so "far as it legally [might] to maintain the business of the [South Improvement Company] against loss or injury by competition . . . and to lower or raise the gross rates of transportation . . . for such times and to such extent as [might] be necessary to overcome the competition. . . . The rebates and drawbacks to be varied *pari passu* with the gross rates." [1] From this it appears clearly that it was not intended that any other shipper should be able "to furnish a like amount of traffic."

Just what the promoters of the enterprise meant by their declaration that other refiners would be "taken in" was soon made plain. On January 1, the day before the stock of the South Improvement Company was distributed among the subscribers, the Standard Oil Company increased its capital from $1,000,000 to $2,500,000. During the next three months the directors were busily engaged in persuading competing refineries in Cleveland to sell out to the Standard. Miss Tarbell offers abundant evidence to show that the chief inducement that was held out to the other refiners was that, if they did not sell out while they could, they would be forced out of the business. Many who did not sell out testified on the witness stand subsequently that they had been given to understand that the Standard had an arrangement with the railroads by which it could dominate the oil business at Cleveland, and that on applying to railroad officials they were put off with evasive replies, coupled usually with advice to sell to the Standard. Miss Tarbell also gives evidence to show that the terms offered were distinctly unfavorable to the sellers. That this was true in some cases is highly probable, but on the other hand the offer of the Standard appears usually to have been Standard stock in exchange for the actual value of the tangible property of the companies to be absorbed. Those who accepted this offer in preference to cash, which was also offered, and retained their Standard Oil stock, certainly had little to complain of as regards the financial out-

[1] Article 4 of Agreement with the Pennsylvania R. R.

come. The arguments in favor of selling out which were advanced at this time were convincing to some twenty of the twenty-six refining companies which were doing business in Cleveland in January, 1872. In a few short weeks the Standard increased its refining capacity by this move from 1,500 barrels a day to 10,000 barrels a day, and thus gained control over about one-fifth of the refining capacity of the country. Thus the South Improvement Company scheme, even though it never went into operation, proved an efficient aid toward the purpose which its promoters had in view—that is, the consolidation of all the refineries in the country. In Pittsburgh and Philadelphia similar efforts to combine the local refineries appear to have been made, but with less signal success than in Cleveland.

While these changes were occurring in Cleveland, Pittsburgh, and Philadelphia, news of the South Improvement Company "conspiracy," as it was at once styled, reached the oil region. The new rates, through some blunder, were announced prematurely, and as they represented a marked advance over the prevailing rates, the conviction that some combination had been effected became general. Miss Tarbell has described in truly dramatic style the struggle between the oil-producers, the refiners, and the railroads which followed in February and March, 1872.[1]

The producers found an embargo on all shipments an effective weapon, but also appealed to Congress, to the legislature of Pennsylvania, and to the courts. So great was the popular indignation as more and more of the details of the plan became matters of common knowledge, that the railroads at the end of March capitulated. They formally repudiated their contract with the South Improvement Company and instead agreed with the Oil Producers Union that a uniform rate of $1.50 a barrel from any point in the oil region or from Cleveland or Pittsburgh to New York should be charged, and a rate of 50 cents a barrel from the oil region to Cleveland or Pittsburgh, these rates to be maintained on "a basis of perfect equality to all shippers, producers and re-

[1] "The Oil War of 1872," *ibid.*, vol. i, chap. iii.

finers, and that no rebates, drawbacks, or other arrangements of any character shall be made or allowed that will give any party the slightest difference in rates or discrimination of any character whatever."

Meantime the pressure brought to bear upon the legislature of Pennsylvania led it, toward the end of March, to revoke the now useless charter of the South Improvement Company, and in April a Congressional investigation occurred which confirmed all the worst suspicions of the oil producers as to the sinister nature of the arrangement that they had successfully opposed.

The rates agreed upon in March, 1872, were very unfavorable to the refiners in both Cleveland and Pittsburgh. Apparently this was neutralized by the willingness of both the Pennsylvania and the Central to return to the old custom of granting rebates. But neither the refiners nor the railroads enjoyed the resumption of the secret and underhanded methods of the past. In August, 1872, the refiners were induced to enter into a loose association, the National Refiners Association, which was a first step in the direction of the Standard Oil Trust. This association controlled some four-fifths of the refining capacity of the country, but the bond of self-interest which held it together proved to be too weak, and in less than a year it was disbanded.

The Standard Oil Company also, in this period, strengthened its position in the oil region by acquiring an interest in the pipe lines upon which the crude-oil producers were coming more and more to depend. At the same time it took steps to supply itself with nearly all of the tank cars and other special equipment that was needed in connection with the transportation of its products. Its growing ascendency over the New York Central and Erie Railroads was shown by the fact that early in 1874 it purchased the oil yard of the former in New York and leased that of the latter in Weehawken, New Jersey. Some time in 1873 it began again to receive rebates, and in 1874 the situation was so unsatisfactory that another serious rate war was threatened.

At this juncture the railroads themselves evolved a plan

which they hoped would put the oil business upon a more stable and profitable basis. Experience had taught them the futility of an arrangement which discriminated against the powerful refining interests of Cleveland and Pittsburgh. No pledge was sufficiently binding to prevent the railroads from violating such an agreement soon after it was made. The new plan was to discriminate against refineries in the oil region. The arrangement was simple enough in principle, although somewhat complicated in its actual operation. On all refined oil shipped from either the oil region, Cleveland, or Pittsburgh to Eastern points uniform rates were to be charged (*i.e.* $2.10 a barrel to Boston, $2 to New York, etc.). From these rates Cleveland and Pittsburgh refiners were to be allowed a rebate equal to the rail freight from the mouth of the pipe to the refining point of 35 cents a barrel on the crude oil that went to the production of the refined.[1] Under this plan the railroads practically agreed to carry the crude oil, which they later carried in refined form to the seaboard, from the wells to the refineries in Cleveland and Pittsburgh free. It deprived the oil region of any advantage it derived from its nearness to the oil wells, but at the same time left it all the disadvantages connected with its distance from the markets in which the other materials and equipment needed in the business had to be purchased.

The disadvantage under which the refiners of the oil region labored in consequence of this new freight policy of the railroads was increased by the growing ascendency of the Standard Oil Company in the field of pipe-line transportation.

Early in 1874 the firm of Vandergrift & Forman, which controlled more pipes than any other company, was reorganized as the United Pipe-line Company with six officials of the Standard among its nine directors. In the following year this company absorbed all the important pipe lines in the region except those controlled by the Empire Transportation Company, a corporation closely affiliated with the Pennsyl-

[1] Fourteen barrels of crude was considered equivalent to ten barrels of refined.

vania Railroad, and the Columbia Conduit Company, a protégé of the Baltimore and Ohio Railroad.

At the same time that the plan described above "for treating all refiners alike"—to quote the language of the "Rutter Circular," through which it was officially announced, September 9, 1874—was being worked out, the Standard Oil Company was secretly extending its influence by buying up competing plants in Pittsburgh, Philadelphia and Brooklyn. The last and most important purchase was that of Charles Pratt & Son, of Brooklyn, consummated on October 15, 1874. In the following March the Standard increased its capital to $3,500,000, presumably in connection with these earlier acquisitions. This extension was important chiefly because it gave the Standard influential representatives in all the other important refining centers of the country and had much to do with the successful organization of the second national association of refiners, the "Central Association," in the spring of 1875. Another important result of the purchase of these refineries was the addition of several capable and far-seeing business men to the Standard group, including Mr. Henry H. Rogers, who only two years before had led the opposition of the New York refiners to the South Improvement Company scheme. The spring of 1875 really marks the beginning of the Standard Oil Trust, as the alliance then formed only grew stronger with the different plans of organization that were successively tried during the ensuing years.

The rate arrangement into which the railways entered in September, 1874, broke down because it made no provision for an evener to attend to the division of traffic between the three railroads concerned. It was particularly unsatisfactory to the Pennsylvania because under it the Standard was drawing more and more of the oil business to the north for the benefit of the Central and the Erie. The end came in the summer of 1875, when the Erie accused the Pennsylvania of granting rebates to the Empire Transportation Company, through whose pipes most of the latter's oil traffic came, and proceeded to negotiate independently for as large a share of the oil traffic as it could get. The arrangement finally made with the Standard Oil Company was that its traffic should be divided equally between the Central and the Erie, that it should guarantee that the Erie's share under this plan of distribution should be not less than 27 per cent of the whole oil traffic, and that in return it should receive from both roads a rebate of 10 per cent on all its shipments. Just what arrangement the Pennsylvania Railroad made with the Empire Transportation Company and with the independent refineries on its lines is not known, but its concessions must have been, at least for the time being, satisfactory. On these terms the oil industry was continued through the latter half of 1875 and all of 1876.

Apparently the Pennsylvania Railroad resolved at this time to make a last stand against the Standard Oil Company. With its aid in 1877 the Empire Transportation Company began to acquire and build refineries in Philadelphia and New Jersey. News of this move was equivalent to a call to arms to the Standard Oil Company and its allies, the New York Central and Erie Railroads. The latter immediately commenced a rate war against the Pennsylvania, and on March 18, 1877, the Standard did its part by ceasing to send any of its freight over that road. The struggle continued all through the summer of 1877. At one time the Pennsylvania was carrying oil for the Empire Transportation Company at a loss, and the latter was virtually giving away refined oil in markets that had been controlled by the Standard. Such a struggle could not last. The advantages were from the first with the Standard with its perfected organization, its large measure of control over the pipe lines of the oil region, and its allies, the Central and Erie Railroads. On October 17, 1877, the Pennsylvania Railroad abandoned the struggle, the Standard Oil Company on its side agreeing to take over for $3,000,000 the Empire Transportation Company.

The traffic agreement that was entered into at this time gave the Standard Oil Company a substantial advantage in the business of transporting oil. It was to act as evener between the different roads and to see that 63 per cent of the oil traffic went to New York City and 37 per cent to Philadelphia and Baltimore; of the traffic going to New York City, the New York Central, the Erie, and the Pennsylvania were each to have a third; of the traffic going to Philadelphia and Baltimore the Pennsylvania was to have 70 per cent and the Baltimore and Ohio 30 per cent; finally the Standard Oil Company guaranteed that the Pennsylvania's share of the traffic should amount to at least 2,000,000 barrels annually. In return the Standard was to get a rebate, or "commission," as it was called, of 10 per cent on all of its shipments.

The Standard's position now seemed impregnable, and was so in fact so far as control over rail shipments was concerned. Its next serious difficulty was in connection with the development of the pipe line as a substitute for the railroad even for long-distance transportation. In all the various struggles that had thus far taken place but little consideration had been given to the producers of the raw material. Naturally they watched with alarm the gradual consolidation of the pipe lines, upon which they so vitally depended, under the control of the refiners to whom they must sell their oil, and the growing intimacy of the relations of these same refiners and the railroads. Two ways of opposing these developments suggested themselves. One was an appeal to the legislature and the courts for protection; the other the construction of a pipe line which the producers themselves should own that would give them an independent outlet to the seaboard, where at least transportation by water was open on equal terms to all. During the year 1878 both these remedies were tried. The officers of the Standard Oil Company were indicted for conspiracy in Pennsylvania, and two pipe-line companies, the Seaboard Pipe-line Company and the Equitable Petroleum Company, later succeeded by the Tide Water Pipe Company, were organized. The fate of the suits against the officers of the Standard Oil Company and the corporations that they controlled was similar to that of most of the litigation in which the Standard Oil Company has been involved. For one reason or another they never came to trial.

The effort to secure relief through an independent pipe line was more successful. On June 1, 1879, the Tide Water

Pipe Company began transporting oil in its own pipes a distance of 109 miles over an elevation of 2,600 feet from Bradford to Williamsport, Pennsylvania, and thence by rail to Philadelphia, 250 miles farther, over the Philadelphia and Reading. The Standard railroads were at once stirred to activity. On June 5th they agreed to lower their rates on crude oil shipped by the Standard Oil Company from the oil region to the seaboard to 20 cents a barrel, the rate to other shippers being 30 cents instead of $1.15 as theretofore. This was a reduction of about 75 per cent. In August the rates were lowered to 15 and 25 cents, respectively. While the struggle thus inaugurated between the railroads and the first pipe line of any considerable length was in progress, the Standard Oil Company, convinced of the superiority of pipe-line transportation even for great distances, prepared with its usual vigor to gain control over this new branch of the business. On the one hand, it entered upon an aggressive campaign to secure the Tide Water Pipe Company and, on the other, to lay pipe lines of its own that would make it independent of the railroads. In both directions it was successful. Although it was unable to acquire complete control of the Tide Water Company, it acquired about one-third of that company's stock, and in October, 1883, it induced the remaining stockholders to enter into an agreement by which the Tide Water Company was to have 11½ per cent of the oil traffic conveyed in pipes from the oil region to the seaboard by both companies and to be guaranteed an annual profit of $500,000 for fifteen years, on condition that it allowed the Standard Oil Company to control its charges. On these terms the Tide Water Company became virtually a subsidiary of the Standard Oil Company.

In carrying out the other part of its policy the Standard Oil Company soon had pipe lines connecting its refineries at Cleveland, Buffalo, and Pittsburgh with the oil region, and lines under construction to Philadelphia and Bayonne, New Jersey. To develop this new department of the business, a new corporation, the National Transit Company, was organized in 1881 under a Pennsylvania charter. On April 1, 1884, the Standard's United Pipe Lines Company was merged with this new corporation, the combined capital of the two being $31,000,000.

In order to carry the pipe lines to Bayonne, New Jersey, it was necessary to cross the tracks of the Pennsylvania Railroad. For this purpose a new traffic arrangement was entered into with that road under which the road was guaranteed 26 per cent of "all petroleum brought to the Atlantic seaboard by all existing carriers, whether rail or pipe" and payment for the same in accordance with a sliding scale that was very advantageous to it. Thus by the summer of 1884 the Standard Oil Company controlled long-distance pipe-line transportation as completely as it had controlled local pipe-line transportation before the Tide Water Pipe Company was started five years before.

While this struggle for control over long-distance pipe-line transportation was in progress the Central Association of 1875 was superseded by the first Standard Oil Trust of 1879 and this in turn by the reorganized and enlarged Standard Oil Trust of 1882, which has already been described. The dominance of this trust was not again seriously threatened through competition. Its significant later history has, therefore, been concerned with the legislation, the governmental investigations, and the judicial decisions which finally culminated in its dissolution by order of the United States Supreme Court in May, 1911.

When questioned by the Hepburn Committee in 1879 as to the reasons for the dominance of the Standard Oil Company, Mr. William H. Vanderbilt said: "I never came in contact with any class of men as smart or as able as they are in their business, and I think that a great deal of their advantage is to be attributed to that. They never could have got in the position they are in now without a great deal of ability, and one man would hardly have been able to have done it. It is a combination of men. I don't believe that by any legislative enactment or anything else through any of the States or all of the States, you can keep such men down. They will be on top all of the time. You see if they are not." This tribute to the founders of the Standard Oil Trust was doubtless deserved. Such men could not be kept down. The company which they organized in 1870 was certain to be one of the leading refineries in the United States. But what made it the nucleus of a great, monopolistic trust was not the ability of its organizers to refine and sell oil cheaper than their competitors, but their ability to transport it cheaper. Railway rebates and pipe lines were the means by which this combination first obtained, and then for so many years retained, its virtual monopoly over the petroleum industry of the country.

That advantages in the field of transportation were a principal factor in its rapid progress from 1870 to 1882 has been indicated by the foregoing sketch. Conceding everything that may be claimed in regard to the superior ability and foresight of Mr. Rockefeller and his early associates, it remains true that it was the lower rates that they were able to get from the railroads that enabled them to build up the trust. The combination of all the leading refineries in Cleveland, which they were able to effect in the early months of 1872, was not due to any sudden enthusiasm for the economies of combination, but to dread of the exclusive advantages which those interested in the South Improvement Company had secured from the railroads. From that time until the capitulation of the Pennsylvania Railroad in October, 1877, competition in the oil business was a struggle between rival railway systems, each fostering, by means of special rebates, the refiners from which it drew its traffic. The treaty of peace which concluded this last great struggle involving the railroads and which added the Empire Transportation Company to the Standard Oil group, provided for an exclusive rebate to the Standard Oil Company, a rebate which was especially advantageous to it because made specific as the railroads lowered their rates in their efforts to defeat the Tide Water Pipe project from 1879 to 1883. And while alliance with the railways was rendering the trust master of the oil business at the seaboard, the help of the railways was enabling it to make profits where its competitors could make none all through the central West. Special rates given by the Lake Shore gave it an advantage in markets north and west of

Cleveland. That other railroads were also granting it special rates can hardly be doubted in the light of known facts as to the railway-rate situation at this period. These special advantages enabled it to wear out its competitors and absorb them or drive them entirely out of business. Finally, when convinced that pipe lines must displace the railways as carriers of crude oil, the comparative ease and dispatch with which the Standard was able to construct the pipe lines it required was due to the ascendency it had by this time gained over the railroads in consequence of the vast traffic which it controlled. Instead of opposing fiercely its pipe-line projects as they did those of the independent refiners, the railroads tamely acquiesced in them.

That the combination built up by means of these advantages in transportation was efficiently managed no one can question. That through it many economies in the refining and marketing of petroleum products were realized is undoubted. But so long as competitors were debarred from enjoying the low transportation charges which the Standard secured, there was no way by which their capacities as producers in the narrow sense could be measured against those of the trust. This combination cannot, therefore, be explained or defended as the offspring of normal business evolution. It was an artificial creation resulting from the monopolizing ambition of a remarkably able, far-sighted, and determined group of men who attained their end through a use of means that are now universally condemned as unfair.

It had been frequently asserted by Standard Oil officials that when the Interstate Commerce Act was passed they had promptly abandoned the practice of seeking special advantages from the railroads and thereafter conducted their business in strict conformity to the law. The absence of any prosecutions involving the Standard Oil Trust, except those relating to rates on tank-car and barrel shipments, where no definite rules had yet been laid down by the Interstate Commerce Commission, long served to substantiate this claim. It was not, in fact, until the Bureau of Corporations was created in 1903 on the initiative of President Roosevelt, and until the

PRINCIPAL TRUNK PIPE LINES IN AND FROM THE APPALACHIAN, LIMA-INDIANA, ILLINOIS AND MID-CONTINENT OIL FIELDS, 1904.

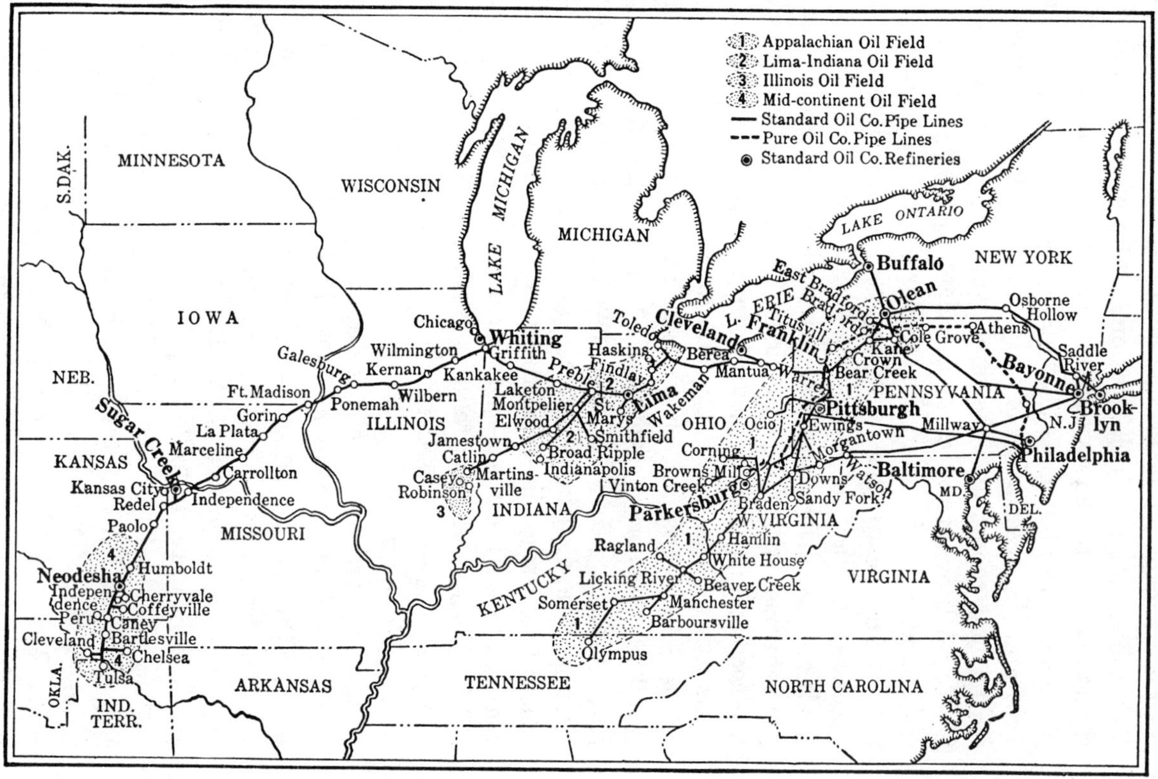

results of its investigation into the *Transportation of Petroleum* were made public in the report bearing this title, in 1906, that the extent to which the domination of the Standard Oil Company still rested on advantages as regards railroad transportation was appreciated. This investigation was begun in 1904 and the description of the petroleum industry contained in the first report and the later volumes on *The Petroleum Industry,* brought out in 1907, relate to that year.

In order to understand the significance of the advantageous rate arrangements that were enjoyed by the Standard, it is necessary to have in mind the location not only of the oil fields and the principal markets, but also of the pipe lines and the refineries which it controlled. These facts are shown on the accompanying map, taken from the Bureau's report.

As this map indicates, by 1904 the original or Appalachian oil field had expanded enormously from the original "oil region" of the early 'seventies. At the same time the new Lima-Indiana field had been developed and the still newer Illinois, Mid-Continent, Texas, and California fields. The amounts of crude oil—from these fields and the Western fields not shown on the map—consumed in 1904 by the Standard Oil Company and other refiners appear in Table I.

The map also shows the Standard's control of the indispensable pipe lines by which nearly all of the crude oil was transported from the wells to the refineries. Its only serious rival in this department in 1904, the Pure Oil Company, had only 550 miles of pipe, as compared with 40,000 operated by the Standard, and handled barely 10 per cent of the oil even from the Appalachian field. In the newer fields all of the trunk lines were controlled by the Standard.

The Standard's refinery at Bayonne, New Jersey, was the largest in the United States, while that at Philadelphia was a close second. The crude oil for these refineries and the four others located on New York Harbor—one other in New Jersey and three on Long Island—came principally from the original, or Appalachian, and the Lima fields. Oil piped all the way from Indian Territory, 1,500 miles, and brought in tank steamers from Texas, was, however, also used. In 1904 these seaboard refineries, including the one at Baltimore, used about equal quantities of oil from the Appalachian and Lima fields, and a small quantity of Texas crude—about 10 per cent of the total. Together they refined about two-thirds of the total amount of crude oil used by the Standard.

TABLE I

CONSUMPTION OF CRUDE OIL OF EACH FIELD BY STANDARD AND INDEPENDENT REFINERIES, 1904.
(Barrels of 42 gallons)

Kind of Crude	Consumption by all refineries	Consumption by Standard and Affiliated refineries	Consumption by Independent refineries	Standard's proportion Per Cent
Appalachian	27,628,000	22,253,000	5,375,000	80.5
Lima-Indiana	24,230,000	22,908,000	1,322,000	94.5
Mid-Continent	1,056,600	1,046,000	10,600	99.1
Colorado and Wyoming	440,000	435,000	5,000	98.9
California	4,167,000	3,317,000	850,000	79.6
Southeastern Texas and Louisiana	7,847,000	5,284,000	2,563,000	67.3
Corsicana	800,000	455,000	345,000	56.9
Total	66,168,600[a]	55,698,000	10,470,600	84.2

[a] This total, based on estimates for the separate fields, is a little less than the amount reported by the Bureau of the Census for 1904 (66,982,862 barrels).

The second large group of Standard refineries was in the Appalachian field and included the refineries at Parkersburg, West Virginia, at Pittsburgh and Franklin, Pennsylvania, and at Olean and Buffalo, New York. These used Appalachian crude almost exclusively.

The Standard had only one refinery in the Lima field, that at Lima, Ohio, but the Cleveland refinery was not far away and also used Lima oil exclusively.

The Standard's refinery at Whiting was the third largest in the United States and consumed more crude oil—all drawn from the Lima field—than the seven refineries in the Appalachian and Lima fields taken together.

Finally, the Standard had two refineries in the Mid-Continent field, at Neodesha, Kansas, and at Sugar Creek, Missouri (near Kansas City and opened in November, 1904), and one in California at Richmond, near San Francisco. It also controlled, through purchase of their entire product, the two refineries in Colorado and two or more refineries in Texas.

Through these various refineries the Standard owned or controlled nearly 90 per cent of the refined oil which was produced in the United States. Its own production in 1904 was given as 20,500,000 barrels, and of this nearly 60 per cent, drawn almost entirely from the seven seaboard refineries, was exported. From the point of view of production for the domestic market, the Whiting refinery led in 1904 with nearly 33 per cent of the total. Next came the following refineries: Bayonne, 9.4 per cent; Franklin, 8.9; Philadelphia, 8; Lima, 6.6; Baltimore, 5.2; and Buffalo and Olean, 5 each. Together these eight refineries turned out over four-fifths of the refined oil marketed by the Standard in the United States, or about seven-tenths of the total domestic consumption.

In order to understand clearly the advantages which the Standard derived from its control over pipe lines and in connection with the transportation of oil generally, it is necessary to bear in mind that oil is a cheap commodity, and that, therefore, the cost of transportation is one of the chief items in its expense of production. At the period investigated, Pennsylvania crude was worth only from three to four cents a gallon. Lima crude was worth only from two to three cents; Kansas and Texas crude under one cent. Refined illuminating oil at the refineries was worth only from three to seven cents. Thus a difference in transportation rates of half a cent a gallon might mean all the difference between a reasonable profit and a loss. Freight rates are usually quoted at so many cents a hundred pounds, and the standard weight of refined oil is about 6.4 pounds to the gallon. A difference in rates of eight cents per hundred pounds thus amounts to a difference of one-half cent a gallon, and may suffice to drive out the competitor who does not enjoy the lower rate, while the favored shipper continues to market his product at a profit.

The advantage which the Standard Oil derived from its control over pipe lines is apparent from a study of the foregoing map. By their means the Standard and the Tide Water Pipe Company, which it controlled, were able to prevent the successful operation of competing refineries on the Atlantic seaboard, except by the Pure Oil Company, which had its own pipes. The Standard did this by maintaining rates for pipage which were virtually prohibitive. Its charge for carrying oil from Western Pennsylvania to the seaboard was forty-five cents a barrel, the same charge as was made by the railroads. According to an estimate of the Bureau of Corporations, a rate of ten cents a barrel would have been remunerative. To be sure, the Standard refineries themselves paid the higher rate, but of course what they lost the Standard's pipe-line company gained, so that the arrangement amounted merely to transferring money from one pocket to another.

The great profit earned by the pipe lines might be expected to attract capital into this field of investment. It did so in two instances, but in only one of them did a real competitor of the Standard result. But who, having followed the experiences of the Tide Water Pipe Company and the United States Pipe Line Company, would have wished to hazard his capital in a similar enterprise? The investment called for was enormously great because refineries to take care of the oil had to be erected, as well as the pipe line to transport it, since, unless a large volume of oil was handled from the start, the cost of transportation per barrel would be even higher than the forty-five cents charged by the Standard and the railways. Finally, the would-be competitor of the Standard would have found the task of building up a market for his product more serious than any other part of the undertaking. Like the Pure Oil Company, he would have been very apt to find Europe his easiest outlet, and in Europe he would have encountered competition on the part of refiners in other parts of the world as well as on the part of the Standard. When all of these conditions are considered, the strength of the position of the Standard at the seaboard begins to be appreciated. Laws had, to be sure, by this time been passed by Pennsylvania and New Jersey declaring pipe-line companies common carriers, but in the absence of any attempt on the part of these states or of the United States to require that their charges be reasonable, these had accomplished nothing. So long as the Standard was not actually required to manage its piping business as a common carrier, it was in little danger of losing its hold on seaboard markets.

The same advantages that came to it from its ownership of long-distance pipe-lines came to it in lesser degree from its ownership of the shorter, "gathering," pipe-lines upon which the crude-oil producers depended. Largely by their means it had gained control over the price of crude oil as well as over the price of refined and had been able to benefit by its virtual monopoly of buying power in its dealings with producers in somewhat the same way as it benefited by a virtual monopoly of selling capacity in its dealings with consumers. Just as it announced through its agents the prices it would charge for its products, so it announced through the Seep Purchasing Agency, the organization through which it conducted its purchases, the prices it would pay for crude oil, and these prices were necessarily the market prices so long as it was the only important purchaser.

It was the conclusion of the Commissioner of Corporations, from his investigation in 1904, that "the Standard Oil Company has habitually received from the railroads and is now receiving, secret rates and other unjust discriminations." [1] A brief consideration of the situation as regards two important portions of the country will serve to show that this charge did not lack substantial foundation.

The refined-oil requirements of northern New York and western New England were most conveniently supplied by rail shipments from the refineries in the Appalachian field. To supply this market the Standard had a refinery at Olean, New York, just over the Pennsylvania line, while the refineries of its competitors were all located in Pennsylvania. It was found by the Bureau that the Standard was receiving from the Pennsylvania Railroad a secret rate of nine cents a barrel on tank-car shipments from Olean to Rochester. The Penn-

[1] *Report on the Transportation of Petroleum*, p. xxi.

sylvania published no rate, but the Erie's published rate for a similar haul was 10½ cents per cwt., or about four times as great. Much of this oil was shipped on to Norwood, New York, at a discriminatory state rate from Rochester of nine cents per cwt., and thence at very low tank-car rates over the Rutland Railroad to Burlington. From here the Standard enjoyed very low rates, not known to its competitors, to other Vermont points. The total rate for the Standard through this combination was only 15.34 cents per cwt. from Olean to Burlington, while the lowest combination of rates open to its competitors figured out, according to the Bureau, 33 cents. The difference was thus quite sufficient to enable the Standard to dominate this portion of the New England market. Some of these arrangements, though unfair, were not in violation of the law. Some of them, however, clearly involved discrimination in interstate commerce. For its part in these arrangements favorable to the Standard, the New York Central was successfully prosecuted and required to pay a fine of $15,000.

Another case of unfair discrimination that received much more attention was that connected with shipments of refined oil to the Southwestern market, of which St. Louis was the distributing center. This market was supplied by the Standard through its large refinery at Whiting, Indiana. Investigations by the Bureau showed that the Standard was receiving a secret rate of six cents per cwt. on its shipments from Whiting to East St. Louis from three railroads, although the open rate was eighteen cents. One of these railroads, the Chicago and Alton, billed the shipments of the Standard at the eighteen-cent rate, but collected only six cents. Since the Standard Oil Company shipped 204,000,000 pounds of refined oil to East St. Louis in 1904 alone, its saving from this arrangement was substantial. Suit was brought against the Standard Oil Company of Indiana for its part in this violation of the Interstate Commerce Act, and after a trial in which every phase of the transaction was carefully examined, the company was found guilty and a fine of $29,000,000 was imposed by Judge Landis. The case was, of course, appealed, and the verdict was set aside, not so much on the ground that the company was innocent, as on that that the fine was out of all reason for a company whose capital was only $25,000,000. If the court had viewed the Indiana Company (as it in fact was) as merely an administrative department of the Standard Oil Company of New Jersey with its hundreds of millions of assets, this fine might not have seemed so unreasonable. It is more significant of the real merits of the contentions of the government that the railroads concerned changed their secret rate of six cents to an open rate of ten cents.

The above and numerous other examples of unfair rates were exposed in May, 1906. "Within three months after that date," to quote from a later *Statement of the Commissioner of Corporations in Answer to Allegations of the Standard Oil Company* (December 30, 1907), "every such rate criticized by the Bureau as illegal had been canceled by the railroads making the said rates. This voluntary action of the railroads themselves more than justified the conclusion of the Bureau that there had been in existence for a long time a system of railway discrimination in favor of the Standard Oil Company in almost every section of the country."

Advantages in the domain of transportation were undoubtedly the principal means by which the Standard Oil Company first obtained and later retained its domination over the petroleum industry. It was also charged with other unfair practices by the Bureau of Corporations. Among these the most important was lowering prices to an extent ruinous to competitors in competitive markets, while maintaining them at highly remunerative levels in other parts of the country, and thus forcing competitors out of business, whenever they had the temerity to try to wrest a part of the market from the Trust. That this was the policy of the Standard appears to have been abundantly established.[1]

[1] The Bureau summarizes its findings as follows:

"The Standard discriminates greatly in fixing prices in different sections and in different towns, charging extortionate prices where there is no competition, and cutting prices sharply where competition is active. In some cases net prices in one locality in a single state, after deducting freight, have been almost double the net prices in another locality in that state." It also

Even more reprehensible from a moral point of view was the organized system of espionage and bribery of the employees of the railroads and of its competitors by which the Standard kept itself informed in regard to every aspect of the business of the few independents who succeeded in maintaining a precarious standing in the industry.

The clearest evidence of the monopolistic control which the Standard maintained over the oil industry was the enormous profits which it was able to earn after its business was firmly established. According to careful estimates of the Bureau of Corporations its annual earnings from 1882 to 1896 averaged about 19 per cent on its constantly expanding investment. During the next ten years, 1897 to 1906, its total earnings amounted to the huge sum of $800,000,000. The dividend policy of the trust was always conservative, but during the twenty-four years 1882 to 1906 it disbursed in dividends a total of over $550,000,000, or an average of $22,000,000 a year. At the time of its dissolution in 1911 it was regularly paying $40,000,000 a year to its shareholders. That the source of these huge profits was monopolistic control over the industry was indicated by the fact that the Trust was able to widen the margin between the prices it paid for crude oil and the prices it received for kerosene at the same time that its utilization of by-products was increasingly profitable. Thus, according to the calculations of the Bureau of Corporations, the margin to cover the expenses of refining and afford a profit in 1898 was 5.3 cents. In 1903, the year of largest profits, the margin was increased to 7.1 cents or by 1.8 cents. The profits that year were $81,000,000. The following year prices averaged a little lower, but the margin was still 1.5 cents wider than in 1898. Since the production in that year totaled 1,400,000,000 gallons, this meant an addition of $21,000,000 to earnings.

When it is recalled that during this entire period a sub-

charges that: "The Standard has sold illuminating oil and other petroleum products in the foreign trade much cheaper than in the domestic trade, the difference having become inordinately great since 1902."—(*Report on the Petroleum Industry,* vol. ii, "Prices and Profits," pp. 1 and 2.)

stantial majority of its stock was owned by nine individuals and their descendants, and that more than one-fourth belonged to a single individual, John D. Rockefeller, Sr., it will be appreciated what an influential factor toward the concentration of the wealth of the country into a few hands this most successful of the trusts became.

The most important result of the searching investigation and reports of the Bureau of Corporations was the prosecution of the Standard Oil Company of New Jersey as an unlawful trust begun by the Attorney General of the United States, Mr. Moody, on November 15, 1906. Owing to circumstances entirely beyond the control of the government, the case dragged along for five tedious years, but on May 15, 1911, a unanimous decision was finally handed down affirming the decree of the lower court that the trust must be dissolved.

That the history of the Standard Oil Company revealed an intent and purpose to restrain trade and create a monopoly was held by the court to be proved by the following considerations:

(a) Because of the way in which the New Jersey corporation was organized and its business extended, "not as a result of normal methods of industrial development, but by new means of combination which were resorted to in order that greater power might be added than would otherwise have arisen had normal methods been followed."[1]

(b) Because of the conduct of the persons who dominated the trust, including "the acquisition here and there . . . of every efficient means by which competition could have been asserted, the slow but resistless methods . . . by which means of transportation were absorbed and brought under control, the system of marketing . . . by which the country was divided into districts and the trade in each district in oil was turned over to a designated corporation within the combination and all others were excluded."[1]

Considering that the trust had been in full and successful operation for ten years before the Antitrust Act of 1890 was passed, and that twenty-one years more elapsed before this

[1] 221 U. S. 75-77 (1911).

decision was rendered, this sweeping condemnation by a unanimous court came as a welcome if somewhat tardy assertion of the authority of Congress over combinations engaged in interstate commerce.

Less satisfactory than the decision that the Standard Oil Company of New Jersey must be dissolved was the method of dissolution approved in the final decree. It was exactly the same method which the original trust had itself voluntarily chosen in 1892 when the Standard Oil Company of Ohio was ordered to withdraw from it by the Ohio courts—that is, a *pro rata* distribution of shares in all of the thirty-three corporations whose stock was held by the New Jersey holding company to each and all of the shareholders of that company. The result was that a controlling interest in every one of these corporations passed to the small group of men who all along had constituted the real strength of the combination. So long as these men retained enough shares to constitute a majority and continued to act as a unit, any real competition among these companies was not to be expected. All of these gentlemen believed firmly in the superiority of combination—or coöperation, as they preferred to style it—over competition. A dissolution that permitted them to retain control of the Standard Oil subsidiary companies was, at least at first, only a paper dissolution, just as was that of the Standard Oil Trust decided upon in 1892.

To the cynically minded an illuminating aspect of the dissolution of the Standard Oil Company was the effect it had upon the value of its shares. When the dissolution decree was issued the stock was selling at about $600. There followed a period of uncertainty until the distribution of the shares of the thirty-three constituent companies had been effected. The inevitable consequence of such a distribution without any public appraisal of the assets of these different companies—and the Standard Oil Company had never divulged anything about its business that it was not compelled to—was that the small shareholders knew little of the value of the scraps of paper to which they became entitled. There began an active period of speculation in these shares, blind-pool speculation so far as the outside public was concerned, shrewd investment-buying on the part of the inner circle. Nearly all of the shares went up at first. Some continued to go up, while others reacted. The net result was that shares of the New Jersey holding company, some of which were long withheld from exchange for shares of the subsidiary companies, began to advance, and by March 17, 1917, were quoted at 2,390 bid. Thus, superficially considered, one consequence of the dissolution of this trust was to enhance the value of its shares nearly fourfold during the six years which followed the announcement of the dissolution decree! Whatever the other influences that brought about this astounding result, it is clear that the method of dissolution adopted failed for some time to alter conditions in the oil industry in ways that were of any perceptible disadvantage to those interested in the constituent properties of the trust.

The conclusion that seems warranted from this brief study of the Standard Oil Trust during the period from its organization until its formal dissolution in 1911 is that the principal sources of its monopolistic control over the oil-refining industry were advantages in the field of transportation. It was through specially favorable freight rates and control of pipe lines that it was first able to establish its domination. Until 1906 it continued to enjoy specially favorable freight rates, and even in 1914, notwithstanding the formal dissolution of 1911, the Standard Oil group, which continued to control the Standard Oil subsidiary companies and other companies that had been organized, still controlled most of the important pipe lines and thus still had substantial advantages over would-be competitors in the transportation field.

CHAPTER IX

THE AMERICAN PETROLEUM INDUSTRY, 1911-1929

In 1906 the Interstate Commerce Act was amended to declare pipe lines, except those concerned with water and gas, common carriers and make them subject to regulation by the Interstate Commerce Commission. The constitutionality of this amendment was not finally upheld by the Supreme Court until 1914.[1] The Interstate Commerce Commission and the Federal Trade Commission have since investigated the business and policies of the pipe-line companies in the different fields, with a view to determining whether the rates charged are reasonable and whether all shippers are accorded equal treatment. On the basis of its investigation a *Report on Pipe Line Transportation of Petroleum* in the Mid-Continent field was issued by the Federal Trade Commission in 1916. This shows at some length the phenomenal development of the Mid-Continent field during the ten years, 1904 to 1914. In 1904 this field was credited with barely 1,000,000 of the 66,000,000 barrels of crude oil consumed by all American refineries. In 1914 its production of crude oil totaled almost 98,000,000 barrels, which was nearly 37 per cent of the total crude-oil production of the country. As the 100,000,000-odd barrels which were produced in California in the same year were of lower grade and used chiefly as fuel oil, the Mid-Continent production supplied nearly one-half of the 191,429,000 barrels of crude which were converted into refined products in 1914. Even more striking is the fact that by that year 37½ per cent of all the crude oil conveyed in pipes to refineries east of the Mississippi was drawn from the Mid-Continent field.

Storage tanks and pipe lines to handle this rapidly growing volume of oil called for large investments. The *Report* es-

[1] 234 U. S. 548 (1914).

timates that the pipe-line property of the five large interstate systems operating in the Mid-Continent field represented a net investment in 1913 of nearly $44,000,000. As we should expect, the Standard Oil group had not been backward in extending its influence in this field. Two of the largest of the five pipe lines were Standard Oil lines and a third was said to be controlled by Standard Oil capitalists. The largest of these, the Prairie Pipe Line Company, was the only one constructed to carry oil east of the Mississippi. The two large independent lines, the Texas Company's line and the Gulf Pipe Line Company, conveyed the product south to points on the Gulf of Mexico.

As a result of its study of the whole pipe-line situation in this comparatively new but already highly important oil field, the Trade Commission came to the following conclusions: [1]

(1) There is generally a large difference between the cost of pipe-line transportation and pipe-line tariff rates, while the independent shipper cannot use railroads instead because their rates are still higher.

(2) The pipe-line companies generally require large minimum shipments, which makes it impracticable for small producers or refiners to ship crude oil by pipe line.

(3) The price of the crude oil delivered at the refineries is to a large extent made up of the transportation charge.

(4) The cost of pipe-line construction is so great that small concerns cannot build lines from the Mid-Continent field to the large consuming and distributing markets.

(5) Lower pipe-line rates and small minimum shipments are necessary to enable small concerns to compete with large refineries affiliated with pipe-line companies.

The investigation thus confirmed the impression that in the field of pipe-line transportation the Standard Oil group still had a substantial advantage as regards markets east of the Mississippi and that the inability of small producers to own pipe-lines or to get moderate rates on small shipments from the pipe-line companies was one factor contributing to the persistent concentration of most of the oil business in the Standard Oil group and its chief American competitors at that period, the Texas, Gulf, and Pure Oil companies.

[1] *Report on Pipe Line Transportation of Petroleum,* 1916, p. 4.

Since 1914 the production, transportation, refining, and sale of petroleum products have ceased to be dominated, at least to the same extent, by the Standard Oil companies, and there is evidence that the Standard companies themselves are no longer as harmonious and "coöperative" in their relations as was the case during the years immediately following dissolution. As the original leaders have died or withdrawn from business, their holdings have become more and more widely diffused.[1] According to information collected by the Federal Trade Commission and submitted to the United States Senate[2] on December 12, 1927, most of the holdings of John D. Rockefeller, Sr., had by 1926 passed to his children, and especially to his son, John D. Rockefeller, Jr., and to the numerous foundations he had endowed. Thus John D. Rockefeller, Jr., was credited with being the largest single stockholder in seven of the Standard Oil companies, holding from 23.6 to 10.6 per cent of their respective voting securities, while the Rockefeller Foundation was the largest single stockholder in four additional companies, holding from 23.7 to 5.1 per cent of their stock, and the General Education Board in one with 25.8 per cent of its stock. The diffusion of the shares of the other leaders in the industry has been even greater. Through being dealt in on the stock exchanges of the country, distributed through employee stock-ownership plans, and sold as a result of the liquidation of estates, the former concentrated control of the thirty-three Standard Oil companies and their subsidiaries, with their enormously increased capitalization, has disappeared. In fact, there is strong evidence that the leading companies of the Standard Oil group, the Standard Oil Company of New Jersey, the Standard Oil Company of Indiana, and the Standard Oil Company of California, are developing into strongly integrated companies, each control-

[1] The contest at the annual meeting of the Standard Oil Company of Indiana in March, 1929, which resulted in the defeat of Col. R. W. Stewart and his withdrawal from the company, afforded proof that control by the original Standard Oil group rested on confidence in their leadership rather than on ownership by them of a majority of the voting shares.

[2] *Petroleum Industry: Prices, Profits and Competition.* Senate Document, No. 61, 70th Congress, 1st Session, 1928, p. 70.

ling sources of crude oil as well as pipe lines and refineries and not hesitating to invade, in the marketing of their products, territory formerly assigned exclusively to some other member of the group.[1]

Equally important with the gradual breaking up of the Standard Oil group into separate companies, no doubt friendly in most of their relations but no longer subject to unified control, has been the entry of new capital into the oil business, often strongly hostile to Standard Oil domination and not less aggressive in its policies. This has come about through the enormous expansion of the industry as a whole and the shifting of the centers of production from the East to the West. The annual production of crude oil barely doubled from 1881 to 1891 and increased less than 28 per cent from 1891 to 1901. By contrast from 1901 to 1911, the year of dissolution of the Standard Oil combination, the increase was 218 per cent; from 1911 to 1921, 114 per cent; and from 1921 to 1928, 91 per cent. Comparing the absolute figures for total production, which give a clearer idea of the revolutionary changes in the industry in recent years, the output of crude oil in 1901 was under 70,000,000 barrels. By 1911 the total output had increased to over 220,000,000 barrels, and in 1928 the total reached the stupendous figure of 902,000,000 barrels, with the prospect of an even larger total for 1929. What this has meant for the expansion of the industry may be brought out in another way. During the fifty-two years from the birth of the industry in 1859 to the dissolution of the Standard combination in 1911, the total output of crude oil by the United States is estimated at 2,377,866,000 barrels. During the seventeen years from 1911 to the close of 1928, the total output was 8,866,068,000 barrels, or more than three and a half times as much for a period less than one-third as long.

The following table shows the production by the twelve leading producing states from 1899 to 1928 inclusive.

[1] Detailed information as to these developments is given in Senate Document, No. 61, 1928, chaps. iii-v.

Table II

PRODUCTION OF CRUDE PETROLEUM BY STATES, 1899–1928.
(IN 1,000 BARRELS OF 42 U. S. GALLONS)

Years	California	Oklahoma	Texas	Arkansas	Kansas	Wyoming	Louisiana
1899	2,642	....	669	....	70	6	....
1904	29,649	1,367	22,241	....	4,251	12	2,959
1909	55,472	47,859	9,534	....	1,264	20	3,060
1914	99,775	73,632	20,068	....	3,104	3,560	14,309
1919	101,183	86,911	79,366	....	33,048	13,172	17,188
1924	228,933	173,538	134,522	46,028	28,836	39,498	21,124
1925	230,148	176,760	142,618	74,749	38,284	29,217	20,013
1926	224,673	179,195	166,916	58,332	41,498	25,776	23,201
1927	230,751	276,022	220,031	40,411	41,944	20,984	24,331
1928	231,983	247,501	255,354	32,138	38,155	21,403	22,863

Years	Illinois	Pennsylvania	Ohio	Kentucky	West Virginia	All Others	Total
1899	....	13,054	21,142	18	13,911	5,559	57,071
1904	....	11,126	18,877	998	12,645	12,956[a]	117,081
1909	30,898	9,299	10,633	639	10,745	3,748	183,171
1914	21,920	8,170	8,536	503	9,680	2,506	265,763
1919	11,960	8,137	7,736	9,278	8,327	2,061	378,367
1924	8,081	7,486	6,811	7,407	5,920	5,756	713,940
1925	7,856	7,824	7,168	6,764	5,776	16,823	764,000
1926	7,760	8,961	7,272	6,274	5,964	15,070	770,874
1927	6,873	9,642	7,542	6,590	6,033	9,975	901,129
1928	6,475	9,914	7,105	7,350	5,746	16,013	902,000

[a] In 1904, Indiana, which began production in 1889, attained its maximum output of 11,339,000 barrels. Since 1912 the wells of this state have averaged less than 1,000,000 barrels per annum.

A careful study of this table should disabuse the reader's mind of the view that since the aggregate output of crude oil has increased in nearly every year since 1859, there is no danger within the near future of exhaustion of the country's sources of supply. Of the twelve states included in the list (and the combined production from other states during the last twenty years has only twice exceeded 2 per cent of the total and may therefore be disregarded) all but one, Texas, had passed their periods of maximum production.[1] In the case of the newer producers, like Oklahoma,[2] California, Kansas, and Wyoming, the discovery of new fields may disprove this assertion, but in the case of the older oil-producing states east of the Mississippi intensive exploitation over so many years makes the discovery of any important new sources of supply highly improbable. The extent to which the future of the American oil industry depends on continued production from the Western fields is shown by the fact that of all the crude oil produced during the last five years (1924-1928), 77 per cent has come from the wells of California, Oklahoma, and Texas, their combined output rising from 75 per cent of the total in 1924 to 81 per cent in 1928. The well-nigh unanimous opinion of experts that production in these states is near the peak and must rapidly decline in the future, coupled with the fact that there is no unexplored region left where the geological formation offers any strong prospect of oil, are the bases for the pessimistic view taken by so many oil men as to the future of the oil industry in this country.

According to estimates of the Federal Trade Commission, the Standard Oil companies' proportion of the total production of crude oil for the United States increased from 16 per cent in 1889 to 33.5 per cent in 1898.[3] From this highest point it declined to only 11 per cent in 1906. It increased somewhat in the succeeding years to 21.3 per cent in 1919. In 1924 it was 24 per cent.[4]

The decline in recent years in the Standard Oil companies' proportion of the business of transporting oil through pipe lines and of refining it has been even more significant. Thus, in 1904, they were credited with transporting from 80 to 90 per cent of the total crude oil handled by pipe lines in that

[1] California produced 262,876,000 barrels in 1923, an amount not since attained; Louisiana's maximum of 35,714,000 barrels was attained in 1920.

[2] Oklahoma's production was restrained in 1928 by agreement among the producers, and is therefore quite likely to attain a new maximum before a real decline begins.

[3] Cf. Stocking, *The Oil Industry and the Competitive System,* p. 60 *et seq.*

[4] Senate Document, No. 61, 1928, p. 27.

year. In 1920, according to the Interstate Commerce Commission, the Standard companies owned only 68 per cent of the interstate pipe lines of the country and transported only a slightly larger proportion of the crude oil handled. By 1926 their ownership had increased to 72 per cent.[1]

In 1904 the Standard companies consumed 84 per cent of the crude oil run to refineries, a proportion that held substantially up to the time of dissolution in 1911. At the close of 1921 there were 479 completed refineries in the country with a daily reported capacity of 2,164,050 barrels of crude oil. Of this capacity only 45 per cent was credited to Standard refineries, but because of their more active operation they probably turned out about 50 per cent of the refined petroleum products of the country during the succeeding year. This proportion has been maintained with little variation since.

While the evidence thus shows that the Standard Oil companies are no longer operated as a unit and that they now control not more than one-half of the oil-refining business of the country, it also seems to be true that competition in the oil industry is tempered by the conviction that lowering prices to wrest markets from other refiners is not good business policy. The statements of leaders of the industry that the oil business is highly competitive[2] are confirmed by the latest investigation of the Federal Trade Commission as regards the aggressive efforts of the leading producers, each to outstrip the other. On the other hand it found that "price competition is generally only sporadic, local or temporary."[3] The truth seems to be that the nine giant independent companies which, with the eleven giant Standard companies, control the transporting and refining branches of the Ameri-

[1] *Ibid.*, p. 35.

[2] In 1920, in addressing the American Petroleum Institute, Mr. Henry L. Doheny, a leading independent producer, declared: "The oil business of this country is now, and has been for a long time, a highly competitive business; in fact, too much so for the public good." Similarly, in December, 1922, in an address before the same body, the late Mr. A. C. Bedford, chairman of the board of the Standard Oil Company of New Jersey, said: "The oil industry remains essentially a free industry. Its very nature prevents monopolization or group control." Quoted by Stocking, *op. cit.*, pp. 54 and 55.

[3] Senate Document, No. 61, 1928, p. xx.

can petroleum industry[1] still accept the leadership of the Standard group in connection with the prices to be paid for crude oil and the prices to be charged for refined products, not because of any formal agreement to do so, but from the conviction that unrestrained competition in reference to prices would be disadvantageous for all concerned. The situation which the Federal Trade Commission found in existence in 1915 seems to have been maintained to date, or at least until quite recently. It said: [2]

"The various Standard companies, with relatively unimportant exceptions, in announcing their tank-wagon price of gasoline in any locality, practically fix the price that prevails." The United States Fuel Administration reached the same conclusion in 1919, declaring: [3] "Thus each Standard company, in establishing values and prices sets the pace for all." In its study of *The Advance in the Price of Petroleum Products* [4] the Federal Trade Commission in 1920 said again: "Price initiative today seems to be left generally to the Standard companies and competition is apparently more directed to developing facilities for getting business than to seeking to obtain it by underselling." While still adhering to this view in its report published in 1928 it adds that "no recent evidence was found of any understanding, agreement, or manipulation among large oil companies to raise or depress prices of refined products." [5] With competition confined in most markets to a few giant companies, and those companies dominated by business men who consider competition in prices poor business policy, acceptance of the leadership of one of these companies in price-making becomes a matter of course. The

[1] Each of these twenty companies had invested capital in 1926 in excess of $100,000,000. Of the total combined capital of slightly under $6,000,000,000 the ten Standard companies of that year held 60.5 per cent. The subsequent acquisition by the Standard of Indiana of the Pan-American Petroleum and Transport Co., one of the ten former independents, raised this proportion to 64.4 per cent.—Senate Document, No. 61, 1928, p. 61.

[2] Report on *The Price of Gasoline in 1915,* Washington, 1917, pp. 5-6. Quoted in Stocking, *op. cit.*, p. 80.

[3] Report of the United States Fuel Administration, *Prices and Marketing Practices Covering the Distribution of Gasoline and Kerosene throughout the United States,* p. 13.

[4] P. 53.

[5] Senate Document, No. 61, 1928, p. xix.

prestige of the Standard group and its older and more highly developed organization adequately account for its continued leadership.

While the prices paid for crude oil and the prices charged for gasoline by the big companies usually move together or are quickly harmonized when changes are made, those prices necessarily vary in accordance with the relations between the demand and supply for petroleum products. In recent years the constantly increasing demand for gasoline has been the driving influence shaping the development of the industry. But for it, the prices of petroleum products must have fallen to much lower levels had new sources of supply been opened up as rapidly as they have been since 1911. However, but for it, there would have been less incentive to develop these new sources of supply. One of the most interesting results of the steady increase in the demand for gasoline has been improvements in methods of distillation which have greatly increased the proportion of gasoline recovered from each barrel of crude oil refined. The following table shows this and other changes in the volume of petroleum products during the last twenty-nine years.

As shown by this table, the amount of crude oil produced in the United States increased from 57,071,000 barrels in 1899 to 902,000,000 barrels in 1928, or 1,480 per cent. The proportion of crude oil run to stills, which fell as low in 1904 as 57 per cent, when the crude oil output temporarily ran far ahead of the refinery capacity of the country, exceeded 90 per cent in 1928, when even the heaviest oil could be forced to give up a part of its gasoline content by the "cracking" process.

The increase in gasoline recovery from only 12.8 per cent in 1899 to 41.3 per cent in 1928 has contributed largely to the phenomenal increase in gasoline production from 6,689,000 barrels in the former year to 377,183,000 barrels in the latter, an increase in the twenty-nine years of 5,538 per cent.

Equally significant has been the marked decline in the relative recovery of kerosene from 57.7 per cent of the crude refined in 1899 to only 6.5 per cent in 1928. In consequence of this decline its production increased during these twenty-

TABLE

ANNUAL PRODUCTION OF CRUDE OIL, CRUDE OIL RUN TO THE STILLS, AND PRO
PERCENTAGE RECOVERY OF THE FOUR PRINCIPAL PRO

Year	Crude oil produced in United States		Crude oil run to stills		Gasoline		
	Thousand barrels	Index numbers	Thousand barrels	Index numbers	Thousand barrels	Index numbers	Percentage of crude oil run to stills
1899	57,071	100	51,905	100	6,689	100	12.8
1904	117,081	205	66,905	129	6,929	104	10.3
1909	183,171	321	120,714	233	12,857	192	10.6
1914	265,763	466	191,429	369	35,714	534	18.6
1919	378,367	663	361,520	697	94,235	1,409	26.0
1924	713,940	1,251	643,719[a]	1,240	213,326	3,189	33.1
1925	763,743	1,338	739,920[a]	1,426	259,601	3,875	35.0
1926	770,874	1,350	779,264[a]	1,501	299,734	4,481	38.5
1927	901,129	1,579	828,514[a]	1,596	330,567	4,943	39.9
1928	902,000	1,580	912,831[a]	1,758	377,183	5,638	41.3

[a] Includes foreign crude as follows: 1924, 45,765,000 barrels; 1925, 41,338,000 barrels.

six years only from 29,976,000 to 60,156,000 barrels, or little more than 100 per cent. Partly accounting for this relative decline was a great falling off in the domestic demand for kerosene for illuminating purposes, because of the remarkable progress of electric lighting in all sections of the country.

Next in significance to the increase in the output of gasoline has been that in the output of gas and fuel oils. In 1899 only 7,262,000 barrels of the crude oil run to stills, or 13.9 per cent, was left as a residue, available as gas or fuel oil. In 1928 the residue was 425,755,000 barrels, or 46.6 per cent of the crude oil sent to refineries, making the increase for the twenty-nine years 5,763 per cent. Adding to the residue from the distilling process the crude oil used as gas or fuel oil direct from the wells in 1928, 64,053,000 barrels, gives a total output

III

DUCTION OF THE PRINCIPAL PETROLEUM PRODUCTS IN THOUSANDS OF BARRELS; DUCTS, FROM THE CRUDE RUN TO THE STILLS, 1899–1928

Kerosene			Lubricating oil			Gas and fuel oils		
Thousand barrels	Index numbers	Percentage of crude oil run to stills	Thousand barrels	Index numbers	Percentage of crude oil run to stills	Thousand barrels	Index numbers	Percentage of crude oil run to stills
29,976	100	57.7	4,047	100	7.7	7,262	100	13.9
32,310	108	48.2	7,500	185	11.2	8,571	118	12.8
39,881	133	33.0	12,786	316	10.5	40,524	558	39.4
46,071	154	24.0	12,310	304	6.4	88,905	1,224	46.4
55,753	186	15.4	20,161	498	5.5	181,602	2,501	50.2
60,126	200	9.3	27,498	679	4.3	320,475	4.413	49.7
59,689	199	8.1	31,055	765	4.2	364,991	5,009	49.2
61,768	206	7.9	32,293	798	4.1	365,195	5,028	46.9
56,114	187	6.7	31,721	783	3.8	392,342	5,402	47.4
60,156	200	6.5	34,659	856	3.8	425,755	5,863	46.6

barrels; 1926, 44,963,000 barrels; 1927, 48,701,000 barrels; and 1928, 74,884,000

of gas and fuel oil for that year of 489,808,000 barrels or 54 per cent of the crude output. In 1899 the corresponding proportion of the crude-oil output used as gas and fuel oil was less than 22 per cent. This great increase in the proportion of the country's output of crude oil used mainly as fuel in competition with our superabundant coal seems at first thought a deplorable waste. But it must be noted that most of this oil is a by-product in connection with the manufacture of gasoline, and that the proportion "wasted" is becoming every year less. Also an increasing proportion of so-called "fuel and gas oil" is used not as fuel merely, but as a source of motive power in railroad and ocean transportation. Finally, the perfection of the Diesel engine, which uses fuel oil as a direct motive power, affords promise that in coming years the heavy oils that have been looked upon as our least valuable petroleum product may in the near future take rank as our chief source of motive power, not only for land and ocean transportation, but also for airplanes and dirigibles.

Until the recent past, the aspect of the American petroleum industry that has been most prominent in the public mind has been the tendency toward trust control. Efforts to break up the Standard Oil monopoly and to put a stop to unfair and oppressive methods have so absorbed the attention and energy of federal and state authorities, that an even more fundamental aspect, the rapid exhaustion of our petroleum resources due in part to the wasteful processes of exploitation that have been not only permitted but encouraged by our antitrust laws, has received little consideration.

If we desire to conserve this limited resource, what seems to be called for is not a policy of free and unrestrained competition, but a policy of unified control and regulation. This appears to be particularly the case as regards the initial stage of the business, the production of crude oil. A full discussion of this point would require the combined knowledge of the geologist and the petroleum engineer, but certain aspects of it, and those the most vital, may be easily comprehended by the layman. Petroleum exists in subterranean pools lying at varying depths and overlaid by varying formations, but always presenting certain characteristics. They are always subject to great pressure. Floating upon them there is always a larger or smaller volume of oil vapor or "natural gas," which if tapped first in the process of exploitation will escape or "blow off" into the atmosphere, but which, if left undisturbed while the lower levels of the oil pool are tapped, will force part of the oil to the surface and to that extent save the exploiter the expense of pumping. The very first desideratum in connection with the exploitation of an oil pool is, therefore, that the natural gas suspended above it shall not be drawn off until its pressure has been utilized to the fullest possible extent as a means of forcing the oil to the surface. But this means that when a new pool has been discovered and before the natural conditions underground have been seriously disturbed, the situation should be carefully explored by competent geologists and engineers to ascertain the limits of the oil pool and to decide upon a program for tapping it at its lower levels with just the number of wells that is calculated to insure maximum recovery. To this end the pool must be studied and treated as a unit. Since the natural gas is itself a valuable product second only in importance to the oil, a second desideratum is that a full equipment of tanks, pipes, and other receiving and storing apparatus shall be provided for it as well as for the oil, before they are allowed to come to the surface. Still a third desideratum is that the methods of exploitation used shall not permit the flooding of the oil pool by a watercourse at some other level in the formation. These three conditions to economical and efficient exploitation of a newly discovered oil deposit are almost certain to be disregarded if free play is given to competition controlled only by the ordinary rules of fair dealing and of established property rights. Divided ownership of acres on the surface may permit dozens, hundreds, even thousands of individuals to sink wells to the new pool before any one of them has the requisite knowledge of the underground conditions that will be encountered. If some of these wells tap the cloud of oil vapor, or natural gas, overhanging the pool, the gas will be allowed to escape into the atmosphere, a complete loss not only in itself, but, what is quite as serious, a wanton waste of the source of power which would have aided greatly the economical recovery of the oil that lies below it and which without its aid must be laboriously and expensively pumped after the gas pressure has exhausted itself. For these reasons the technical subcommittee of the American Petroleum Institute Gas Conservation Committee reported on December 2, 1927, that: "The data [which it had collected] show finally that many, probably most, of the best methods for gas utilization can be practiced advantageously only when they can be applied systematically to a whole field; that competitive drilling in individual fields almost inevitably leads to gas waste and lessened ultimate oil production; and that either complete coöperation or unit operation is the ideal operating condition for the conservation of both gas and oil." [1]

The history of the exploitation of our petroleum resources is the story of successive mistakes in permitting vast volumes of natural gas to escape into the atmosphere, when through more wisely directed methods it might have cheapened and increased greatly our recovery of oil and served itself as a highly valuable addition to our natural wealth. Notwithstanding all of the experience gained in the exploitation of the Appalachian and other Eastern oil fields, methods of exploitation continued to be so wasteful that a competent engineer,[2] after careful study of the available information, came to the conclusion that down to 1913, 425,000,000,000 cubic feet of gas, worth as much as all the oil produced from the field up to that time, had been allowed to go to waste in the Mid-Continent field.

The losses resulting from permitting water to flood oil sands through ignorant or careless methods of exploitation have been quite as serious. In fact, one writer declares that "underground water is the greatest single cause of waste in oil production, and has come to be regarded by the oil operator as the greatest possible source of financial loss." [3] In some cases, as this writer goes on to explain, "practically entire pools have been drowned out." These losses through flooding could also be avoided to a large extent, if oil pools were carefully explored before exploitation, and if the sinking of wells and their operation were directed with a view to obtaining a maximum of oil with a minimum of waste.

Estimates as to the proportion of the oil that is never recovered from the different oil fields that have been exploited and then abandoned are necessarily rough guesses. Mr. J. O. Lewis, an experienced petroleum engineer who investigated this aspect for the Bureau of Mines,[4] put the proportion at

[1] Appendix "B" of *Report of Committee of Nine to Federal Oil Conservation Board,* January 28, 1928.

[2] Blatchley, *Waste of Oil and Gas in the Mid-Continent Fields,* United States Bureau of Mines, 1913, p. 47.

[3] Stocking, *op. cit.,* p. 185 *et seq.*

[4] *Methods for Increasing the Recovery from Oil Sands,* Bureau of Mines Bulletin No. 148, p. 28, Washington, 1917.

from 80 to 90 per cent. That the *preventable* losses constitute a substantial percentage of, perhaps as much again as, the oil recovered, is generally agreed.

Demonstration that competitive methods of producing crude oil are necessarily highly wasteful methods is by no means an argument for giving free play to the forces of combination and monopoly. The Standard Oil Trust, when at the height of its power, contributed little to the elimination of these wastes, since it considered it good business policy to leave to others the risks and losses connected with crude-oil production. If a remedy is to be found for these wastes, it must be not merely through relaxation of the antitrust laws to permit coöperation in the exploitation of our oil resources, but through governmental regulation and supervision of the methods of exploitation dictated by the desire, not for maximum financial returns in the present, but for a maximum recovery of our limited and rapidly wasting oil resources over a period of years. To "the principle of robbery, the aim of each producer to drain the largest possible underground area in the shortest length of time, before the oil is secured by a competitor," which is the necessary law of exploitation under the competitive system,[1] must be opposed the principle of conservation.

Realization that waste has become a more menacing evil than monopoly has led during the last few years to important steps in the direction of conservation. In its latest report on the oil industry,[2] the Federal Trade Commission gives evidence of what has been accomplished. Among the executives of the leading refining companies it found the conviction still widespread that "the only way to cut down the production of crude is to cut the price."[3] Though at times efficacious, this method is naturally not liked by the producers of crude, who lose heavily on their investment when prices

[1] Stocking, *op. cit.*, p. 140 *et seq.*

[2] *Petroleum Industry: Prices, Profits and Competition.* Transmitted to the Senate, December 12, 1927, and published as Senate Document, No. 61, 70th Congress 1st Session, 1928.

[3] Statement of Mr. D. W. Moffitt of the Mid-Continent Petroleum Corporation.

are severely cut. In several districts they have successfully united to control production and thus carry the industry through threatened crises of overproduction. In the Salt Creek field in Wyoming crude dropped from an average of $1.40 a barrel in the first six months of 1922 to $.70 in August, from which it was brought back to $1.05 in December by a concerted movement to limit the output to 25 to 35 per cent of the capacity of the 600 to 700 wells in operation. This was continued during 1923 to the great advantage of the local community and without detriment to the country, since the limitation meant a curtailment of only a few per cent in the total supply. A similar curtailment was effected in the Panhandle Field of Texas in 1926, the method there being to suspend drilling operations by mutual agreement among the big operators until the market had absorbed the excess production. As it is more largely dependent on crude petroleum for its prosperity than any of the other producing states, Oklahoma, as we might expect, has gone farther than any other in controlling production through coöperation. The legislature has enacted an oil and gas conservation law which makes it the duty of the state corporation commission, when the production of any oil field exceeds the capacity of the local pipe lines and storage tanks, to see that the runs from the different leases are prorated equitably among the different producers, so that the volume of production is curbed and no oil is allowed to go to waste. In accordance with this policy, production has been repeatedly curtailed in the Seminole and other fields, since it was first made effective in 1926. On February 5th, 1929, the Oklahoma operators met at Tulsa and agreed to try to hold down the crude production of the state to a maximum of 650,000 barrels a day, which was 78,000 barrels less than the daily production of the preceding two weeks, the curtailment to become effective on and after February 14. The curtailment relates to flush production only. The Greater Seminole Area was to reduce its production 18 per cent; the St. Louis Pool, 20 per cent; and the Maud Pool 23 per cent. An umpire, who had previously served in a similar capacity and enjoyed the full confidence of the operators, was chosen to make this program effective.

While Oklahoma was thus adjusting her production to market requirements the American Petroleum Institute, in session at St. Louis, was passing resolutions in support of state legislation to curb waste and encourage coöperation to control production in the general interest, and the legislature of Texas was considering a law that would empower the State Railroad Commission to deal effectively with this problem. As finally passed and made immediately operative on March 29, this law [1] expressly prohibited "waste" in the production, transportation, storing or using of natural gas or crude petroleum. Waste is defined to include permitting natural gas to escape into the air (except as may be necessary in the drilling or operation of a well), drowning with water any valuable oil or gas stratum, wasteful burning of natural gas, etc. Although merely an extension of a policy of conservation to which the state was already committed, this bill was opposed by the operators in the newest oil region of the state, the West Texas field, at their convention at San Angelo, on January 25, 1929. Unless Texas operators are willing to coöperate, curtailment by the operators of Oklahoma must fail of its purpose. Thus the question of conservation transcends state lines.

In recognition of the national importance of the problem President Coolidge appointed a Federal Conservation Board on December 19, 1924, consisting of the members of his Cabinet chiefly concerned with it—the Secretaries of War, Navy, Interior, and Commerce. This board submitted three reports to President Coolidge, Part I in September, 1926, Part II in January, 1928, and Part III on March 3, 1929, which were later published by the Department of the Interior. In its first report the board presents an interesting survey of the petroleum industry, not only of the United States, but of the world, and brings out clearly the fact that while the most urgent current problem in the United States is overproduction, just behind it lurks the certainty that in a few

[1] Chapter 313 of Session Laws, Regular Session of 1929, p. 694.

years the country will have passed the peak of its output of crude oil and will be confronted with the necessity of depending more and more on foreign sources of supply or upon substitute fuel oils. This certainty is again emphasized in the last report, which points out that while in 1927 we produced 72 per cent of the world's output, each of our three principal producing states individually bringing more oil to the surface than the three leading foreign producing countries, Venezuela, Russia and Mexico, combined, competent oil geologists credited us with only 18 per cent of the world's known oil resources. The high development of our industry is causing us to realize rapidly on our limited oil inheritance, while the rest of the world is only just beginning to draw on this resource.

To emphasize the advantages of coöperation in the exploitation of a new pool, the board, in its first report, contrasts instances of coöperative control and reckless competition, as follows: [1]

> The Reagan County, Texas, field . . . was controlled by two companies which coöperated rather than competed, with resulting conservative rates of development, spacing of wells, and holding back of production during times of greatest over-production. The decline in the Reagan Country has not yet begun—two and one-half years after its discovery—so that it serves in a way as a reserve to be drawn on when its output is needed by the country and the price compensates the owners.

Very different was the case of the Santa Fé Springs field in California!

> In this small but highly productive field, forty-five operating companies competed, drilling more wells than necessary, letting loose an unneeded flood of oil on the market, with resultant disaster to the price structure, and creating conditions of increased operating costs. The total losses attributed to this competitive struggle in a single field are estimated as in excess of $200,000,000, but even greater perhaps than this economic waste, involving a loss to the industry, is the loss to the country involved in the dissipation of gas pressure, leaving in the upper sands oil that might well have been recovered to an amount equal to that actually taken out under the rush methods of competitive drilling and producing.

The Board considers that the most promising remedy for

[1] *Report of the Federal Oil Conservation Board,* Part I, p. 18.

this situation is a modification of state laws to recognize and protect the common property right of adjoining owners in the oil and gas underlying the areas they control. Under such a plan a producer drawing oil and gas from the common reservoir "should be required to recognize the right of the neighbor to so much of the oil as is withdrawn from underneath his property less a reasonable allowance for the cost of production, the hazard of the undertaking, and a reasonable profit on the undertaking."[1] Such recognition that an oil pool is not the individual but the common property of those controlling the land area which it underlies would tend to substitute for competitive and wasteful exploitation coöperation and conservation. Having laid down the principle which, in its judgment, should guide public policy, the Board appointed a committee of nine experts, of which four were experienced oil men and one a professor of law, to study the problem and report concrete recommendations. The findings of this committee were made public by Secretary Work, chairman of the Board on February 6, 1928.[2]

The first important conclusion of the Committee of Nine is that the change in the law applying to land areas overlying oil pools, so that the surface owner would be entitled only the oil and gas actually underlying his property, as suggested by the Board, is "wholly impracticable." They point out that there is no way of measuring oil and gas still in the ground or determining just what surface area it underlay before it was brought to the surface. They are quite emphatic in the opinion that "the only practical law governing the right to recover oil is that which now exists."

On the other hand, they are hopeful of worth-while results through legalizing and encouraging the coöperative method of exploiting oil pools. To this end their positive recommendations are as follows:

(1) Federal legislation which shall (a) unequivocally declare that agreements for the coöperative development and operation of single pools

[1] Report, *op. cit.*, p. 15.

[2] Mimeographed release by Federal Oil Conservation Board, Department of Interior Building, Washington, D. C.

are not in violation of the federal antitrust laws, and (b) permit, under suitable safeguards, the making, in times of over-production, of agreements between oil producers for the curtailment of production.

(2) Similar legislation by the various oil-producing states.

(3) Immediate further study into the matter of the waste of natural gas, in order that legislation may be formulated which will forbid such waste as fully as may be done without working injustice and unreasonable hardship.

(4) Legislation by Congress granting the Secretary of the Interior authority to join and to permit lessees from the Government to join in agreements for the coöperative development and operation of single pools.

As a further recommendation aiming at conservation it urged action by Congress changing the law requiring the Secretary of the Interior to offer for lease annually not less than one hundred thousand (100,000) acres of the Osage Indian lands. This last recommendation was the first to bear fruit. At the very close of its last session, the 70th Congress enacted a law which became operative on March 3, 1929, which reduced the mandatory acreage to be offered annually for lease to 25,000 acres.

In its third report the Conservation Board includes as Appendix I the report of the Committee of Nine and supplements it with a report on the legal aspects of the situation by a committee of the American Bar Association which it prints as Appendix II. This contains definite drafts of bills for enactment by the various states, one legalizing voluntary coöperative agreements among producers to promote conservation and exempting them from the state antitrust laws, the other providing for compulsory unit and coöperative development and operation in the public interest through the exercise of the police power. While not formally indorsing these recommendations, the board quotes with apparent approval the following statement of the Bar Association's committee:

We are convinced that the American petroleum industry will never find its proper place in our economic structure until it solves the problems that arise from the competitive drilling and operation of oil and gas pools. Whether that is to be accomplished by voluntary action in the industry or by the compulsion of law is yet to be determined. After an extended inquiry into the two possibilities, we have reached the conclusion that, by force of circumstances entirely beyond the control of the industry, comprehensive voluntary action is improbable if not impossible. Upon the basis of this conviction your committee proposes one compulsory measure.

As in connection with the production of crude oil, so in connection with the transportation branch of the industry, unified development and control of facilities seems to make for maximum economy and efficiency. In declaring pipe-line companies common carriers and subjecting their rate schedules to the control of the Interstate Commerce Commission, Congress has recognized the inevitable tendency of pipe lines to develop as large, semi-monopolistic organizations and has taken steps to apply the remedy that we are finding fairly efficacious in dealing with the parallel problem presented by the railroads. The publicity given to pipe-line rate schedules since 1914, and the liability they are now under to be set aside if found unfair or unreasonable, have no doubt contributed to the elimination of the abuses that used to be complained of. Only one case against pipe-line companies has thus far been passed upon by the Interstate Commerce Commission,[1] and in that the commission contented itself with ordering that the companies concerned lower their requirements as to minimum shipments of crude oil from 100,000 to 10,000 barrels. The evidence presented was held *not* to show that the rates charged were unfair and unreasonable under all the circumstances of risk, including the inevitable ultimate exhaustion of the field and writing off of the entire investment. The latest investigation of the Federal Trade Commission fails also to indicate unfairness in the present charges for pipe-line transportation or that independents are discriminated against. In fact, it reveals evidence that leading pipe-line companies are now anxious to secure all the traffic which independent producers can give them. It is equally favorable in its findings as to the absence of discrimination in rates on the part of the railroads.[2]

The advantages of operation under unified control are less

[1] *In re* Complaint of Brundred Bros. *et al. v.* Prairie Pipe Line Co. *et al.*, decided April 15, 1922.

[2] Senate Document, No. 61, 1928, pp. 42 and 45.

conspicuous in connection with the refining branch of the oil industry, but here, too, the economies that can be attained by enlarging the scale of operations are substantial until a very high degree of concentration has been reached, and the savings that result from locating refineries of the size requisite to supply each market at the points most convenient to such market are also important. From the social point of view another consideration is that only through pooling all improved methods, whether patented or otherwise, can the most efficient means of recovering the maximum amount of gasoline, kerosene, and lubricating oils from each barrel of crude oil be employed by all refiners. The Department of Justice began on June 25, 1924, an action against five of the leading oil companies (including the Texas Company and the Standard companies of New Jersey and of Indiana) which had pooled patents they controlled covering improved ("cracking") processes for recovering gasoline and licensed some forty-four smaller companies to use them on the payment of royalties. Restrictive provisions in the license contracts of the patent pool were attacked as involving unlawful restraint of trade. As we go to press the decision of the lower court is announced upholding the government's contentions. If this is affirmed by the Supreme Court and if as a result of the action the pool should be dissolved and use of the new processes be again limited to the owners of the patents, the public will be more injured than benefited by the proceeding.

An important part of the task of the Federal Oil Conservation Board was to make a study of the oil reserves still available in the United States. On the basis of estimates by the most competent oil geologists it came to the conclusion that "the reserves of oil available by flowing and pumping wells from present production and proven fields amount to about 4,500,000,000 barrels."[1] At the present rate of production this is only five years' supply. Of course this does not mean that oil geologists believe that our petroleum resources will be exhausted in five years. New sources of supply will un-

[1] *Op. cit.*, part i, p. 8.

doubtedly be discovered, but the unexplored areas are few and far between so that not even the most optimistic expect the new pools that may be found in the next ten years to replace the pools developed in the last ten. Also as our supplies begin to show signs of exhaustion costs will rise and we will draw more and more oil from Mexico and South America, conserving our own resources proportionately. What it does mean is that we are within a few years of the time when peak production of this enormously valuable resource will have been passed and we will be compelled to readjust ourselves to steadily, probably rapidly, dwindling supplies.

Realization of this prospect first registered itself in the notorious naval oil reserve leases negotiated during the Harding administration. Warned by this false start, President Coolidge appointed the Federal Oil Conservation Board in 1924, and the wide distribution of its reports has contributed greatly to the education of the public in regard to the true situation. After expressing satisfaction that the volume of "shut-in production"—that is, oil discovered but allowed to remain undisturbed, is now greater than at any previous period, the Board in its last report registered its conviction that "storage of oil underground, where nature placed it, is regarded as the best method because it is cheapest and safest." [1] Clear recognition of this principle marks a turning point in our national policy. President Hoover was so impressed by its truth that one of his first important acts after his inauguration was the issuance of an order effective on March 12, 1929, suspending all sales and leases of oil lands owned or controlled by the Federal government except those actually entered upon or made mandatory by Act of Congress. As some 10 per cent of the country's current production of crude oil comes from leased government or Indian oil lands, this constitutes an important practical step toward the conservation of our oil resources. Even greater will be its moral effect in stimulating oil producers by voluntary coöperation to restrict their drilling operations and control supplies, when as at present production is so clearly running ahead of the country's

[1] *Third Report of Federal Oil Conservation Board,* March 3, 1929, p. 3.

requirements. Whatever the value of unrestricted competition under ordinary conditions to regulate business relations, it is the almost universal conclusion of students of the petroleum industry that, as regards crude-oil production, the national interest will be best served by permitting combination or coöperation to be carried at least far enough to insure unified operation of every oil pool. If this conclusion leads Congress and the states to relax their antitrust laws as they apply to this industry, the reckless waste of the past may yet give place to a rational policy of conservation while there is still something left to conserve.

CHAPTER X

THE AMERICAN TOBACCO TRUST

THE Tobacco Trust was not so important from the point of view of capitalization or significance of product as a number of other combinations. It merits detailed analysis, however, as an example of the business methods of early consolidations and as a further test of the efficacy of dissolution decrees as a solution of the trust problem.

The course of the combination movement in the tobacco industry was affected materially by two of its outstanding characteristics—separation into distinct branches such as cigarettes, snuff, plug and cigars—and the varying adaptability of these branches to machine processes. The former made it possible to accomplish unification by stages, obviously an easier maneuver than its antipode; the latter established limits which largely determined the degree of combination possible in these respective branches. The only branch in which the trust failed to achieve a practical monopoly was cigar manufacture, the one to which machinery was not successfully applied on any extensive scale until nearly a decade after the dissolution decree.

Prior to 1890 competition flourished in all branches of the tobacco trade. Indeed, the competition between the original constituents of the trust, cigarette manufacturers primarily, was characterized in the decision of the Supreme Court as "fierce and abnormal," [1] and this situation and the decline in profits which resulted from it were important factors in impelling combination. Other factors were the invention of certain patented machines important to the manufacture of cigarettes, the control of the best of these patents by a few men, the concentration of cigarette-making in a few factories,

[1] 221 U. S. 157 (1911).

and the rapid extension of the popularity of cigarettes.[1] After three abortive attempts at amalgamation in 1887, 1888, and 1889 the first unit of the trust, the American Tobacco Company of 1890, was formed by the fusion of W. Duke, Sons & Company, Allen & Ginter, Kinney Tobacco Company, W. S. Kimball Company, and Goodwin & Company. The combination started with a capitalization of $25,000,000. The constituent companies had produced just short of 90 per cent of the country's total output of cigarettes. Although all of them designated their businesses as the manufacture of cigarettes and smoking-tobacco, their proportion of the country's business in the latter was quite small, *viz.*, 7.9 per cent in 1890. They were not engaged in any other branches of the industry.

From the outset a policy of expansion was adopted. In its second year the cigarette trust acquired four additional concerns which gave it an interest in all the important branches of the tobacco business. The most important of these was the National Tobacco Works at Louisville, secured for $600,000 cash and $800,000 in common and $400,000 in preferred stock. The output of this concern was confined to plug; the others produced cheroots, snuff, smoking, and fine cut. Although its sales of plug in 1891 were only 2.7 per cent of the production of the United States, the combination had secured as a part of the National Works a number of brands, including "Piper Heidsieck," "Newsboy," and "Battle Ax," which were already well established and on the way to the great popularity which they later achieved. Within a short time further activities made it clear that the plug branch was the next in which it was intended to effect a combination.

In view of the present low esteem into which the art of tobacco-chewing has fallen and the consequent decrease in plug business, a question may arise as to the cause of the difference in the accuracy of the prognostications of the leaders in the industry with reference to cigarettes and plug. But a little investigation reveals the fact that on the basis of

[1] *Report of the Commissioner of Corporations on the Tobacco Industry,* part i, 1909, p. 63. This publication will be cited hereafter as the *U. S. Report on the Tobacco Industry.*

the immediately antecedent history of the industry the leaders were entirely justified in the action they took. Between 1880 and 1891 the production of plug and twist had increased from 90,000,000 to 166,000,000 pounds, or about 85 per cent, and those weights represented approximately a third of all the tobacco manufactured. Moreover, manufacturers of those products were exceedingly prosperous. It is true that the rate of increase was greater in the other branches, but there was certainly nothing in the situation to presage the revolution in consumers' tastes which caused the output of plug within the next decade to remain almost constant, ranging between 148,000,000 and 189,000,000 pounds, with an average closer to the smaller figure.[1] At any rate, the American Tobacco entered into a vigorous campaign to secure domination of the plug field.

The precise methods adopted by the cigarette trust in thus extending its control will be set forth in more detail in a subsequent discussion of its competitive practices; at this point it is necessary to point out, however, that control of the cigarette business not only provided large profits with which to finance an expansion program, but also furnished a basis for inducing, or coercing, dealers, who were practically compelled to handle the trust's cigarettes, to handle also its plug. As might be expected, the established concerns did not propose to be dislodged or engulfed by the newcomer without a struggle, and consequently the "plug war" raged for several years at costs which the combatants could ill afford. Between 1891 and 1898 the trust increased its percentage of the country's output of plug from 2.7 to 23. In the latter year the more important independents, with the exception of Liggett & Myers, capitulated, and this company too was brought in in the spring of 1899. Meanwhile a new corporation, the Continental Tobacco Company with a capitalization at the outset of $62,000,000 had been chartered in December, 1898, to conduct the plug business. For the plug properties the Ameri-

[1] Cf. *U. S. Report on the Tobacco Industry,* part i, pp. 53 and 364. On the latter page some additional minor reasons for the decrease in plug production will be found.

can Tobacco Company transferred to the Continental it received less than half of the common and preferred stocks of the latter, a proportion still further reduced when Liggett & Myers was absorbed. But in spite of this the plug combination was completely dominated by the cigarette-trust interests from the beginning, for J. B. Duke was president of both concerns and the majority of the directors of the Continental were American Tobacco men.

The reason for the delay in acquiring the Liggett & Myers concern is worthy of note, since it involved a serious threat to the maintenance of the American's position in cigarettes as well as an obstacle to its procurement of dominance of plug. In June of 1898 a group of financiers and tobacco men, including Thomas F. Ryan, W. Bourke Cockran, William H. Butler, and George P. Butler, formed a syndicate for the purpose of acquiring tobacco businesses and establishing a new tobacco company. P. A. B. Widener, Frank Tilford, Anthony N. Brady, and Thomas Dolan subsequently joined the group. Its first step was to purchase for $800,000 cash the only important independent cigarette-producer remaining in the country, the National Cigarette and Tobacco Company. Next, it organized the Union Tobacco Company of America, transferred to it the National, and received the former's stock in exchange. Then the Union acquired control of Blackwell's Durham Tobacco Company, producer of one of the most important brands of smoking-tobacco. Finally, the promoters of the Union secured an option on a controlling interest of Liggett & Myers's stock. Thus in virtual control of the chief independent plug producer, the only important cigarette independent, and a popular brand of smoking-tobacco, the interests behind the Union were in a position to exact from the American and Continental a very high price for their holdings or to force a fight which would be far from one-sided. The combination preferred not to fight, for two excellent reasons: it had lost a great deal of money in the "plug war," and it could make good use of the financial resources and of the abilities of the Union men in carrying further its plans for completely dominating the industry. Consequently, in April,

1899, arrangements were consummated by which the Union Tobacco Company was transferred to the American Tobacco Company and Liggett & Myers became a part of the Continental. The cigarette and smoking-tobacco business of Liggett & Myers was sold by the Continental to the American for $50,000 cash.

Subsequently, in 1899, the Continental acquired control of the R. J. Reynolds Tobacco Company of Winston, North Carolina. This move was particularly significant in that it gave the trust a preponderant position in the production of the "flat plug" which was the most popular type of chewing tobacco in the South. The total of thirteen concerns which were added between 1897 and 1900 to the plug business of the combination advanced its percentage of the total output from 23 in 1898 to 56.3 in 1899, 62 in 1900, and 67.7 in 1901. This advance continued steadily until 1905, when the combination produced 80.7 of the total. From that year until the dissolution its percentage ranged between 80 and 85.

Although it is correct to conclude from the foregoing paragraphs that the heaviest battalions of the tobacco combination were directed between 1891 and 1898 to the prosecution of the "plug war," it would not be correct to infer further that it disregarded opportunities more thoroughly to intrench itself in the cigarette field or to extend its activities into other salients. The necessity for doing the former would not seem great because of the high proportion of the cigarette business held by the original constituents of the American Tobacco Company, but competitors developed sufficient strength to convince the leaders of the combine of the wisdom of buying them before they became too troublesome. Steps were taken, moreover, to perfect control over cigarette machines and to expand into the so-called "all-tobacco" cigarette business. A number of the concerns taken over during this period were engaged in the production of smoking-tobacco and snuff, the Gail & Ax and the Marburg concerns of Baltimore almost entirely confining themselves to those products. Their output added to that of the original five raised the trust's control of smoking from 7.9 in 1890 to 21.9 per cent in 1892, near which it remained until 1898, when it advanced to 26.9. Incidental to the formation of the plug combine sufficient smoking business was procured to bring about an increase to 54.3 per cent of the total output in 1899. From that time until 1910 control was steadily extended until it reached 76.2 per cent. The smoking business was largely kept as a part of the operations of the American Tobacco Company, no separate corporation similar to the Continental or the American Snuff Company being created.

The last-named combination was organized in 1900 to take over the business accumulated in that branch during the developments described above. As late as 1898 the part of the snuff business in the hands of the trust was only 6.1 per cent, and the only action toward combination had been taken by a group entirely independent of it, the Atlantic Snuff Company. This concern was created January 25, 1898, to include W. E. Garrett & Sons of Philadelphia, Stewart Ralph Snuff Company of Philadelphia and Clarksville, Tennessee, Bruton & Condon of Nashville, and Dental Snuff Company of Lynchburg, Virginia. It produced 46.5 per cent of the total output of the United States. The Continental plug combine had included among its original members two concerns which made snuff: Daniel Scotten and Company of Detroit and P. Lorillard Company of Jersey City, the latter being far more important. As a result of these and some minor acquisitions the combined output of the snuff subsidiaries of the American and Continental in 1899 was brought up to 32.4 per cent. The stage was now set for a price war between the two combinations, and during 1899 this was carried on with great vigor. But as we have grown to expect, the combatants concluded that there were no profits in such tactics. Consequently, in the first months of 1900, an agreement was perfected by which the new American Snuff Company took over the businesses in that branch of the American, Continental, Lorillard, and Atlantic Companies, and in addition that of the George W. Helme Company, the largest manufacturer outside of the two combinations. In 1901, the first full year of the new trust's operations, it produced 80.2 per cent of the snuff output of the United States. Four years later it secured the last large independent concern, Weyman & Brother of Pittsburgh, so that in 1906 its control had advanced to 96 per cent. This proportion it maintained without significant fluctuation until the dissolution decree of 1911.

To this point the process of combination in the various branches of the industry has proceeded unchecked. In the only important division remaining, cigars, similar efforts were fruitless, chiefly for the reason already stated that until about 1917 the problem of developing an effective machine for making them withstood the best efforts of inventive genius. It is true that machines were utilized earlier in the manufacture of stogies and cheroots, but for decades it was generally held in the industry that the only "good" cigars were those made by hand. Under such conditions, with only a small outlay of capital required in order to enter the business and no marked advantage in costs from large-scale operation, the great majority of the "factories" remained small. But the value of the annual production of cigars was 50 per cent or more greater than that of all the other manufactures of tobacco combined,[1] so that there was the best of reasons for the combination's persistent efforts to extend its control over that branch. It had entered the field in a small way as early as 1891 by the acquisition of the manufacturer of "Virginia Cheroots," but for the next eight years its energies were expended in the efforts in other branches previously recorded. As a preliminary maneuver in the cigar campaign the American Tobacco Company secured control of the United States Cigar Machine and Manufacturing Company in 1899. In the same year it also took over control of the Banner Cheroot Company and organized the Porto Rican-American Tobacco Company.

The organization of the American Cigar Company in 1901 was effected by the transfer to it of the cigar properties and leaf plants of the American Tobacco Company, including the recently acquired Powell, Smith & Company cigar factories at New York, Kingston, and Poughkeepsie, and the invest-

[1] *U. S. Report on the Tobacco Industry,* part i, p. 149.

ment in it by the Continental of $3,500,000 in exchange for approximately 35 per cent of the stock (all of one class) of the new concern. Throughout 1901 other properties were acquired in rapid succession. The most important of these was the Havana-American Company, itself a combination of eight concerns, which operated ten factories making Havana and high-grade domestic cigars, and had an interest in the large retail and wholesale tobacco business of J. and B. Moss of Chicago. Among the others may be mentioned Harburger, Homan & Company, manufacturer of the popular George W. Childs cigar; Brown Brothers Company of Detroit; and Barlow, Rogers & Company of Binghamton, New York. In subsequent years before the dissolution three cigar-machine companies and more than a score of other concerns ranging in their activities from leaf growing and curing to retail distribution of tobacco products were secured. Several of these had from one to a half-dozen subsidiaries.

Despite these efforts to integrate the cigar branch, extensive advertising, price-cutting, premiums to consumers, liberal "deals" offered to distributors, and other sales-boosting devices, the combination never came within hailing distance of a monopoly position in cigars. In 1898, the year before the drive for control began, it produced 2.2 per cent of the output of the United States. In 1901 with the organization of the American Cigar Company it had advanced to 10.9, and in 1903 to 16.4, but by this time the realization that a great deal of money was being lost in this branch checked the intensity of the campaign for control. The change in tactics was promptly reflected by a loss in relative importance to 13.9 per cent of total output in 1904. During the following six years before dissolution the trust's proportion fluctuated between 13 and 14.7 per cent.

An interesting by-product of the combination's entrance into the cigar field was a change of policy in the retail distribution of its products. Although there had been instances in which it continued the retail business of a former competitor acquired primarily because the competitor was a manufacturer, the established policy was to avoid such ventures. Because of the lack of other advantages in the cigar branch it was felt that the establishment of stores which would particularly stress the new company's products would aid in establishing control. And at this juncture opportunity seemed to have gone out of its way to knock at the trust's door, for in spite of a rapidly expanding business the independently chartered United Cigar Stores Company of New Jersey was in such a weak financial position that for the trifling sum of $46,000 the trust obtained control of it. Thereupon it promptly embarked upon the policies of acquiring the most advantageous sites for its stores, regardless of expense, and of distributing coupons and premiums to its customers that have made it as well known throughout the land as the most popular brands of the product it sells.

Notwithstanding certain advantages in tracing the development of control in each of the major branches of the tobacco industry as we have done in the preceding pages, such procedure has the disadvantage of obscuring the relationships between the various constituents of the combination. Therefore, it seems expedient at this point to postpone consideration of monopolistic tendencies in foreign trade and in some adjuncts to the tobacco business, such as the manufacture of licorice paste and tin foil, in order to describe the changes in organization and financial structure which accompanied the developments already set forth.

The original capitalization of the American Tobacco Company of 1890, $25,000,000, was divided into two-fifths preferred stock and three-fifths common. In the following year an additional $4,000,000 of preferred and $6,000,000 of common were authorized for the purpose of acquiring properties, but only $1,935,000 of the former and $2,900,000 of the latter were actually issued. This brought the total issue to $29,835,000, at which figure, except for script subsequently redeemed in cash, it stood until 1898, when it became $35,000,000. In the following year the common shareholders received a 100-percent common stock dividend of $21,000,000 and the Union Tobacco interests received $12,500,000 in common. The total issue thus attained, $68,500,000 ($54,500,000 common and

$14,000,000 preferred), remained unchanged as long as the company maintained a separate existence.

The initial issue of securities in 1898 by the Continental Tobacco Company (the plug trust) was $62,290,700 in stock divided almost evenly between common and preferred. Within a few months the total was raised to $97,690,700 to absorb Liggett & Myers. Except for $1,581,100 in gold debenture bonds issued in 1900 and redeemed in 1905, there were no further changes in the Continental's capitalization.

The community, not to say identity, of interests between the American and Continental companies was more firmly established by the creation on June 5, 1901, of the Consolidated Tobacco Company. This New Jersey corporation, though chartered to manufacture tobacco as well as to hold the securities of other concerns, functioned solely in the latter capacity. Within three and a half months after its organization the Consolidated held 98 per cent of the common stock of the Continental and 90 per cent of the common of the American Tobacco, an arrangement effected by the exchange of the 4-per-cent gold bonds of the new concern for the said stocks. The original issue of stock by the Consolidated was $30,000,000, all of one class, and paid for in cash. A subsequent increase of $10,000,000 was also paid for in cash and distributed pro rata to the original holders. The purposes of so narrowly limiting the total stock issue seem to have been at least two, *viz.*, to concentrate even more closely in the hands of a few "insiders" the control of the combination, and to divert into the pockets of these same individuals the greatly increased profits which they had reason to believe would shortly accrue to the combination. The large percentages of the common stock of the older companies acquired by the new gave to the latter complete control of them. The majority of the stock of the Consolidated was held by six men: J. B. Duke, A. N. Brady, O. H. Payne, T. F. Ryan, P. A. B. Widener, and W. C. Whitney. Prior to the organization of the holding company they had jointly voted only a small minority of the stocks of the older concerns. The change in their control is obvious.

But even more important than control were profits, and on this score, too, the insiders had ample opportunity for self-congratulation. On the face of it their offer to the stockholders of the American Tobacco of $200 in 4-per-cent bonds for $100 in stock which was paying only 6 per cent was more than fair. Since the Continental had never paid a penny of dividends on its common and had sold as low as $20 for a $100 share, the offer of $100 in bonds for $100 in its stock seemed even more advantageous to the shareholders. The factor which the majority of them doubtless overlooked was that, just before the organization of the Consolidated, Congress had reduced the relatively heavy Spanish war tax of 12 cents a pound on manufactured tobacco and snuff to 9.6 cents. The increase of the tax from 6 to 12 cents during the war had been largely transferred to the consumer in higher prices, though not without some difficulty and loss at first. But prices for all sorts of package goods, into which category most tobacco products fall, rapidly become conventionalized or customary prices, so that a higher price for them, once established, is much easier to maintain than prices for other types of products. Moreover, monopolistic control adds to the ease of maintaining prices. As it turned out, the combination was able to maintain its prices practically without deviation after the tax-reduction just mentioned as well as after a later one in 1902, which restored the pre-war schedule. The common stocks of the American Tobacco and Continental paid, respectively, 10 and 13 per cent in 1902, and 12 and 16 in 1903, making possible a 20-per-cent dividend in both those years on the stock of the Consolidated. The results as regards earnings were even more striking. During the three and a half years before the next reorganization the Consolidated accumulated a surplus of $17,000,000, while paying $6,000,000 in dividends, and acquired an equity in the surplus of $7,000,000 accumulated by the American and Continental companies which it controlled. Naturally, opinions will differ widely as to the ethics of these transactions. Upon the facts just stated and others indicating deliberate manipulation of the securities of the combination we are inclined to feel that the dominant group in the combination showed a sad lack of appreciation of the obligation resting upon directors and officials to protect the interests of shareholders.[1]

In a little over three years from the date of its organization the Consolidated was discarded as a device for unifying the tobacco interests and a new American Tobacco Company was organized to take over the assets of the old American Tobacco, the Continental, and the Consolidated. Although the official statements of the cause of this move stressed the "increased security and simplification of the whole investment and business as well as economy of management,"[2] the low price of Consolidated bonds and the Supreme Court decision adjudging the Northern Securities holding company illegal under the Sherman Act were doubtless important motivating factors.

As a result of a series of complicated rearrangements of the securities of the three concerns the small clique which had dominated the Consolidated acquired even more complete control of the new American Tobacco Company of 1904,[3] a position it retained until the dissolution.

The excursions of the Tobacco Trust into the fields of foreign trade and of branches of manufacture collateral to tobacco remain for treatment. The latter may be disposed of briefly by pointing out that by 1911 subsidiaries of the combination produced approximately 95 per cent of the country's total output of licorice paste, used primarily in plug; that another subsidiary manufactured the cloth and made the bags in which certain brands of smoking were sold; that another made the wooden boxes in which plug was customarily shipped; and still others made the pasteboard cartons, tin

[1] Cf. Jacobstein, M., *The Tobacco Industry in the United States,* pp. 133-134, for additional evidence on this point. Mr. Jacobstein concludes that the shareholders were "fleeced."

[2] *U. S. Report on the Tobacco Industry,* part i, p. 129.

[3] The new company had $40,242,400 of common stock, of which $40,000,000 was exchanged share for share for Consolidated common and the $242,400 for outstanding common stock of the old American and Continental companies. It had also $78,389,100 non-voting preferred stock and $136,360,600 bonds.

boxes, tin foil packages, and other containers in which cigarettes and other products were packed.

The first venture into foreign markets was made in 1894, when the original American Tobacco Company acquired the cigarette business of Hyde, Todman & Company in New South Wales. Cigarette companies were organized in two other provinces of Australia in the same year, and in the following year one New Zealand and two Canadian cigarette concerns were purchased. For the next few years nothing was done outside the continental United States, but in 1899 there was a revival of foreign activities. Those connected with the development of the American Cigar Company centering in Porto Rico and Cuba have already been mentioned. The acquisition in 1899 of Murai Brothers Company, cigarette manufacturers of Japan, signalized entry into the Oriental field. The reason for this purchase was desire to avoid the new Japanese tariff, but the success of the move was only short-lived, for Japan took over the tobacco business as a state monopoly in 1904. The last of these relatively minor acquisitions was that of the George H. Jasmatzi Company (Ltd.), a large cigarette-manufacturing concern of Dresden, Germany, in 1901. But all of the foregoing were subsequently brought into the major combination in foreign business which grew out of the American trust's invasion of the British Isles in 1901.

For several years prior to the date just mentioned the proceeds from the British business had been highly unsatisfactory, and since the British tariff on tobacco was believed to be primarily responsible for this situation, leaders in the trust decided to use a part of the cash derived from the sale of Consolidated stock to establish subsidiaries in Great Britain. Within a few months they had purchased practically all of the stock of Ogden's, (Ltd.), one of the most important tobacco producers in that country. Fearful of the competition of the American giant, thirteen British tobacco concerns organized themselves into the Imperial Tobacco Company, made the most strenuous efforts to retain their trade, and promised large bonuses to dealers who would refrain from handling the American combine's products for a number of years. The trust immediately retaliated with an offer to dealers to distribute all of its profits for the next four years among those who purchased from it, and in addition to divide a lump sum of £200,000 a year among such dealers. There was, however, no insistence that British dealers refrain from purchasing from British manufacturers. Obviously, there were no profits in such arrangements as the foregoing, and consequently, about a year after the date of the acquisition of Ogden's, an agreement was reached by which that concern became a part of the Imperial, the latter was assured control of British business, the American combination was left in control of its native field of operations, and a new British-American Tobacco company was created to handle the distribution of tobacco products in markets not reserved in the manner just stated. This last concern took over the Australian, Canadian, Japanese, German, and other subsidiaries of the parent companies in foreign markets. The Imperial, although barred from manufacturing tobacco in the United States, reserved the right to purchase and treat tobacco leaf in this country. The arrangements thus perfected remained in effect until 1911. Meanwhile the activities of the British-American Company had been extended into the furthermost parts of the earth. At the present time it continues to do a world-wide business but the American interest in it has dropped from an original two-thirds to less than one-fourth.[1]

The degrees of control of the various branches of the tobacco trade acquired from time to time by the trust, indicated above, are presented in summary form in Table IV.

Next in importance to the degrees of control attained by the combination are the means by which they were acquired and the effects of the success of the trust upon the growers of leaf tobacco, the various middlemen in the industry, and the consumers of tobacco products. In the matter of competitive methods we have found no evidence upon which to qual-

[1] Fitzgerald, P., *Industrial Combinations in England,* p. 145.

ify in the slightest degree the judgment of the United States Supreme Court that the history of the combination is replete with the doing of acts which are "demonstrative of the existence from the beginning of a purpose to acquire dominion and control of the tobacco trade, not by the mere exertion of

TABLE IV

TOBACCO COMBINATION'S PROPORTION OF ANNUAL OUTPUT BY BRANCHES, 1890–1910[1]

Year	Plug	Smoking	Fine cut	Snuff	Cigarette	Little cigars	Cigars
	Per cent	Per cent	Per cent	Per cent	Per cent	Per cent	Per cent
1890		7.9					
91	2.7	18.0	3.3	3.6	88.9		
92	3.5	21.9	4.1	4.0	87.9		
93	5.9	21.7	4.7	4.7	85.3		
94	5.6	20.6	4.3	3.4	86.5		
95	12.4	22.5	4.3	3.9	87.3		
96	20.1	20.7	4.5	5.6	83.4		
97	20.9	22.7	4.6	4.8	80.0		
98	23.0	26.9	6.0	6.1	88.3	48.7	2.2
99	56.3	54.3	48.5	32.4	94.7	54.7	4.0
1900	62.0	59.2	50.5	78.0	92.7	60.6	4.8
01	67.7	57.8	48.1	80.2	89.9	73.3	10.9
02	71.2	66.3	73.7	85.9	84.6	71.8	14.3
03	76.9	67.1	77.6	89.4	83.9	67.9	16.4
04	78.2	69.2	80.4	90.6	87.7	79.2	13.9
05	80.7	68.7	81.7	93.8	84.7	78.3	13.3
06	81.8	70.6	80.9	96.0	82.5	81.3	14.7
07	80.5	72.4	81.4	95.7	81.7	90.8	14.5
08	81.9	73.6	79.2	95.7	81.8	88.7	13.0
09	83.3	75.3	80.1	96.1	83.6	89.0	13.1
10	84.9	76.2	79.7	96.5	86.1	91.4	14.4

the ordinary right to contract and to trade, but by methods devised in order to monopolize the trade by driving competitors out of business, which were ruthlessly carried out upon the assumption that to work upon the fears or play upon the

[1] *U. S. Report on the Tobacco Industry,* part iii, 1915, pp. 49, 84, 127, 138, 153, 181, and 192.

cupidity of competitors would make success possible."[1] The specific items in the program thus condemned included:

(1) Local price-cutting, a device sufficiently explained in our discussion of the Standard Oil combination.

(2) Fighting brands. In a sense this device is only a part of the preceding one, but it is worth special attention because of its extensive use. As the term indicates, the combination used certain brands as instruments for destroying competitors. The most notorious of these was "Battle Ax" plug, a product which was given away literally by the hundredweight during the "plug war." The losses involved in such methods ran into hundreds of thousands of dollars, but their ultimate success in all branches but cigars has already been described.

(3) Bogus independent concerns. Because of hostility to the trust on the part of labor unions and a large section of the consuming public, a number of concerns advertised their goods as "not made by the trust." In several instances the trust acquired control of such concerns and continued the advertisements. The frequency of the general practice is attested by the large number of instances of it cited by the Bureau of Corporations.[2]

(4) Factor's agreements or consignment agreements. By the terms of these contracts jobbers were offered special rebates or discounts in return for handling trust products exclusively, or, in some instances, for boycotting certain independents.

(5) Brand imitation. This self-explanatory device was used against the United States Tobacco Company's "Union Leader." The trust for a time distributed its "Central Union" free to dealers in order that they might undersell "Union Leader."

(6) Coupon and premium systems. Since tobacco products sell at customary prices, such plans as these are an obviously effective method of price-cutting.

[1] 221. U. S. 181, 182 (1911).

[2] Cf. *U. S. Report on the Tobacco Industry,* part i, pp. 13, 21, 90, 91, 110, 111, 225, 231; part ii, pp. 175, 196, 200, 203, 208, 222, 267.

(7) Abstention from competition agreements. It was the regular practice to require a competitor who had been bought out or otherwise acquired to agree not to compete for a long period of years.

(8) Utilization of the immense profits of the early cigarette combination in financing these methods and in buying up competitors. This was perhaps more potent than any of the foregoing methods. These cash resources were at once the bludgeon by which a competitor was subdued and the net by which he was drawn into the combination. Without them it seems highly improbable that so large a measure of concentration would have been achieved.

The results of the organization of the trust to tobacco-growers, middlemen, and consumers of tobacco products are reflected chiefly in the sets of prices involved. With the relatively unimportant exceptions of the Porto Rican and Cuban leaf companies already mentioned the trust made no attempt to produce its chief raw material. To the extent to which it monopolized the manufacturing business, however, it obviously strengthened its bargaining power with the growers. The degree to which it utilized this power to depress prices for leaf is a matter of considerable dispute. The great majority of growers were convinced they were being victimized and there is some evidence to support their view. The Bureau of Corporations held that one result of the formation of the original cigarette combine was to reduce the number of leaf-buyers in the different markets, with the consequent result of materially lowering the average price of leaf used primarily for cigarettes.[1] Testimony before the federal courts demonstrated that in 1902, when the Imperial Tobacco Company was really competing with the American for leaf in Virginia and the Carolinas, prices were high notwithstanding a large crop. Later in the year, when this competition ceased, prices fell below cost of production and in spite of declining production did not reach the average for 1902 until 1907.[2] Letters

[1] *U. S. Report on the Tobacco Industry,* part ii, 1911, p. 97.

[2] U. S. *v.* American Tobacco Company and others, *Brief for the U. S.,* pp. 214, 215, before the Supreme Court, October term, 1910.

from the American agent of the Imperial to its home office demonstrate the intention of the two trusts of "working amicably regarding the leaf purchases," and of "encouraging farmers to grow a big crop next year." [1]

But it seems to us that other evidence presented by the Bureau of Corporations makes its conclusion on the combine's domination of the price of cigarette leaf extremely questionable if, indeed, it does not overthrow it. In the first place, the increased taxes on cigarettes, which were advanced from fifty cents to one dollar and subsequently to one dollar and fifty cents per 1,000 in 1897 and 1898, greatly decreased output, lowered the demand for cigarette leaf, and probably depressed prices. Even prior to this certain states had prohibited or made more difficult the sale of cigarettes. Between 1895 and 1900 there was a decided swing in popular taste toward Turkish cigarettes. During the period 1895-98 the selling prices of all leaf tobacco for all purposes were low so that some other factor at work in the branches not dominated as yet by the combination might easily have operated in the one branch it did control. Finally, for a later period, 1901 to 1907, the Bureau's figures show that of a 40-cent increase in manufacturing costs per 1,000 cigarettes, 27 resulted from increased leaf costs.[2] When we turn to the other branches which subsequently came under the control of the trust we find that in the plug branch a "marked decrease in the profits after 1908 was due almost entirely to the increase in costs which was brought about by high prices for leaf tobacco"; that for the same period profits in fine-cut chewing "decreased very considerably" for the same reason; and that an increase from 14.1 to 18.1 cents in the manufacturing costs per pound of the smoking business was likewise explained.[3] For the remaining branch controlled by the trust, snuff, the Bureau notes as the primary cause of a drop in profits in 1907 and 1908 the "effective organization of the growers of dark leaf." [4]

[1] *Ibid.*, p. 217.

[2] *U. S. Report on the Tobacco Industry,* part ii, p. 316; part iii, pp. 150, 149, 164.

[3] *Ibid.*, part iii, pp. 59, 131, 90.

[4] *Ibid.*, part ii. p. 269.

From these facts it seems to us only fair to conclude that, although there were doubtless instances in which the growers of particular types of leaf or growers in given localities were paid lower prices than unrestrained competition would have established, the extent and effectiveness of the trust's power to dictate prices to the producers of its chief raw material have been "greatly exaggerated."

On the other hand, there can be no doubt that the jobbers' margins on tobacco products were substantially reduced by the trust. The figures of the Bureau of Corporations show conclusively that although there were practically no changes in the prices of tobacco products to consumers between 1901 and the middle of 1910, prices to jobbers were raised materially.[1] To some extent this cutting of jobbers' margins was justified by the practice of the trust in taking over more and more completely the task of pushing its products by extensive advertising and other means.

It is from the point of view of the consumer, however, that the organization of the trust and its management along the lines adopted seem most unfortunate. As control was extended over the various products the power to dictate prices for all except cigars became almost complete. Few small producers had the temerity to engage in a price war with the combination, the ruthlessness of whose methods made such opposition suicidal. The power of the trust was most perfectly demonstrated by the manner in which it turned to its own advantage the increases and decreases in taxes during and after the Spanish War. Temporarily there was a decline in consumption of certain products as a result of price increases sufficient to pass on practically the entire tax to consumers, but the decline was soon checked, and when the taxes were reduced in 1901 and 1902 prices were not. In other words, the combination was strong enough to reap for itself the advantage of a legislative measure designed to relieve consumers of tobacco. It is true that in 1910 a tax increase was largely shouldered by the trust, but by this time it was in such bad repute that it seems probable that its leaders

[1] *Ibid.*, part iii, pp. 8, 71, 80, 101, 111, 171, 190.

were chary of further antagonizing the public. Moreover, the increase was very small in comparison with those of 1897 and 1898. If there were anything in the record to indicate that the action in 1902 was only an attempt to recoup previous losses resulting from the existence of customary or conventional prices for tobacco products, or that it was in any way justified, our conclusion on the relations of the trust and the consuming public might be questioned; but we are convinced that there is no satisfactory evidence that the leaders in the group were any more alive to their obligations to the public than they were to their obligations to their shareholders.

The degree of control over prices to consumers exercised by the combination might be expected to result in extraordinary profits; and so it did. The most superficial examination of the dividends paid to holders of common stock at various stages will yield this general impression in spite of certain exceptions, but conclusions based on even the most careful study of dividend records understate the case because of gross over-capitalization. At every stage of the growth of the combination an excessive valuation was placed upon "good will." The Bureau of Corporations estimated the over-valuation of this item in the original capitalization of $25,000,000 of the cigarette trust at $12,500,000. Similarly, it found an over-valuation of good will in the organization of the Continental Tobacco Company of $54,194,170 in an aggregate capitalization of $97,690,700. Even in the reorganization of 1904 the Bureau considered that an additional over-valuation of good will to the extent of $36,553,017 had been made. Now it goes without saying that in such a business as tobacco good will is an extremely important asset, and estimates in regard to its value are unreliable, but the enormous sums indicated above leave no doubt of gross over-capitalization in connection with this item.[1]

An examination of the earnings statements of the combination reveals the necessity for revisions there, too, since it was its practice to deduct therefrom all interest on borrowed

[1] Cf. *ibid.*, part ii, pp. 5-13.

money, including that on its debentures, as well as certain depreciation and premium redemption funds. The Bureau of Corporations report demonstrates that deductions for the last accounts were excessive.[1] Although the first practice is quite common, so that objection may be made to the Bureau's adjustments, the items are in most years so small as to have no material effect on the rates of earnings. In the following table the revised total assets, revised earnings, and rates of earnings for the combination are set forth.

TABLE V

ASSETS, EARNINGS, AND RATES OF EARNINGS OF THE TOBACCO COMBINATION IN DIRECT BUSINESS, 1890–1908.[a]

Year	Assets	Earnings	Rate of earnings (per cent)
1890	13,881,533	2,511,180	18.0
1891	20,665,528	4,396,794	21.2
1892	22,528,030	4,739,301	21.0
1893	23,503,197	4,334,467	18.4
1894	25,265,295	5,065,493	20.0
1895	26,925,082	3,816,520	14.1
1896	27,515,859	3,412,899	12.4
1897	29,067,623	3,996,115	13.7
1898	29,046,777	3,584,785	12.3
1899	78,933,426	6,708,942	8.4
1900	95,518,453	10,433,179	10.9
1901	115,073,923	15,077,103	13.1
1902	138,017,587	16,890,684	12.2
1903	141,648,479	23,168,517	16.4
1904	146,094,737	24,496,154	16.8
1905	156,067,538	29,147,044	18.7
1906	165,430,916	34,103,627	20.6
1907	173,945,062	33,152,021	19.1
1908	181,783,353	35,325,138	19.4

[a] Compiled from the *U. S. Report on the Tobacco Industry*, part ii, pp. 305 and 308. Data were not collected by the Bureau in sufficient detail to make possible the calculation of the items for 1909 and 1910. See part iii, p. 363 of its *Report*. It should be noted that certain "miscellaneous investments" of the trust in securities, loans, etc., are not included above, following the classification of the Bureau.

[1] Cf. *ibid.*, part ii, pp. 141-145, 153-158.

The drop in the rate of earnings from 1895 to 1898 reflects the losses from the "plug war"; that in 1899 the effects of the increased prices following the second advance in taxes plus the fact that because of delays in perfecting the organization several of the branches of the Continental contributed only a portion of a year's earnings to it. As soon as a substantial degree of control was established in all the branches, however, rates rapidly advanced. If further proof of the relation between degree of control and profits be necessary, conclusive demonstration is found in a comparison of the snuff and cigar branches. The former represents the greatest degree of maintained control by the trust of any branch; the latter represents the least. The detailed facts on control and profits are presented in Table VI below.

Organized as it was in the height of the agitation against trusts and ruthless as it was in the methods by which it destroyed its competitors, the tobacco combination was the object of numerous investigations and prosecutions. An early instance of this sort was an inquiry into its affairs by a committee of the New York state legislature which was engaged in investigating a number of trusts. At about the same time indictments were returned against the officers and directors of the American Tobacco Company, but so far as we have been able to ascertain nothing came of them.[1]

An early prosecution in Missouri resulted in a victory for the trust in 1903 as the Supreme Court of that state ruled the Continental Tobacco Company to be within the law.[2] A New Jersey court held that it was within the rights of the combination to impose upon a jobber, as a condition of getting its goods, that he do not deal in those of independents.[3] The Massachusetts courts prohibited such restrictions but permitted "exclusive" sales to jobbers who carried only its products,[4] apparently a distinction without a difference. In the

[1] *Literary Digest,* vol. xiv, p. 453; 44 N. Y. S. 336 (1897). Although in the decision just cited a demurrer to the indictments was dismissed, there is no further reference in the printed court reports to them.

[2] 177 Mo. 1, 29, 44 (1903); 75 S. W. 737, 745 (1903).

[3] Cited in Jacobstein, *op. cit.,* p. 130.

[4] Cf. 188 Mass. 229 (1905) and 191 Mass. 545 (1906).

case of E. Locker *v.* The American Tobacco Company a New York court upheld the trust's right to refuse to sell to whomsoever it saw fit.[1] As the outcome of these suits demonstrated, the trust had little to fear from the state antitrust laws or state courts. Much the same might be said for the federal courts as long as the actions brought hinged on restrictive covenants involved in sales. Thus the Eighth Circuit Court

TABLE VI

PERCENTAGE OF CONTROL OVER AND PROFITS IN THE SNUFF AND CIGAR BRANCHES OF THE COMBINATION, 1898–1910.[a]

Year	Snuff		Cigars	
	Per cent of total output	Per cent of profits	Per cent of total output	Per cent of profits
1898	6.1		2.2	
1899	32.4		4.0	
1900	78.0	18.2	4.8	
1901	80.2	26.3	10.9	2.1
1902	85.9	33.7	14.3	−13.6[b]
1903	89.4	37.1	16.4	− 5.7[b]
1904	90.6	41.5	13.9	− 3.5[b]
1905	93.8	41.8	13.3	6.3
1906	96.0	45.9	14.7	11.0
1907	95.7	44.0	14.5	9.8
1908	95.7	43.7	13.0	1.9
1909	96.1	43.8	13.1	5.5
1910	96.5	44.9	14.4	6.6

[a] Compiled from *U. S. Report on the Tobacco Industry,* part iii, pp. 138, 142, 192, 195. The "profits" of this table differ from the "earnings" of the preceding one in that they are computed by comparing the margin of the net price less tax per pound of the product above the cost per pound with that cost. They are used because they are available through 1910. The data on "earnings" through 1908, appear in part ii, pp. 268 and 289. The same differences between branches appear.

[b] Loss, due to unusually heavy advertising expenses.

of Appeals, in a suit brought against the Continental Tobacco Company, held that "the restriction of their own trade by the defendants to those purchasers who declined to deal in the goods of their competitors was not violative of the antitrust

[1] 106 N. Y. S. 115, 120 (1907); 195 N. Y. 565 (1909).

act."[1] On the other hand, the MacAndrews & Forbes Company and the J. S. Young Company, the licorice trust, were indicted under the Sherman Act and convicted.[2]

All these actions were insignificant compared with that undertaken on July 19, 1907, when suit was instituted in the Federal Circuit Court for the southern district of New York alleging violations of the Sherman Act by the whole combination, twenty-nine individuals, sixty-five American corporations, and two British corporations being named. In view of the record, the conclusions of the judges in this court are nothing short of astonishing. One justice held that the government had made no case and that the bill should be dismissed. In general terms the decision of the other three was a victory for the prosecution, since most of the American corporate defenders were found guilty of participation in combinations in restraint of trade and were enjoined from further continuance as parties to such contracts, but the bill was dismissed as to all the individuals, three American subsidiary concerns, the United Cigar Stores Company, and both the British companies, and the court stated that it had found no "persuasive evidence" of increased prices to consumers, or unfair competition, or improper practices! The basis for the judgment of guilt was the nature of the contracts involved and that alone.[3] Since the decision was highly unsatisfactory to both parties at interest, an appeal was taken to the Supreme Court.

The facts before the court were essentially those set forth in this chapter. In marked contrast with the interpretation of the district court, it held in an unusually detailed review of the evidence that the intent of the combination to destroy competitors was "ruthlessly" carried out by working upon their fears or playing upon their cupidity. Furthermore, the court found in the changing methods of acquiring control of competitors an "ever-present manifestation . . . of a conscious wrong-doing," and in the "constantly recurring stipulations" binding such competitors not to engage again in com-

[1] 125 Fed. 454, 455 (1903).

[2] 149 Fed. 823 (1906); 212 U. S. 585 (1908).

[3] 164 Fed. 728, 702 (1908).

petition for long periods in the future a proof of illegal combination. "Indeed," the court continues, "there comes inevitably to the mind the conviction that it was the danger which it was deemed would arise to individual liberty and the public well-being from acts like those which this record exhibits, which led the legislative mind to conceive and to enact the Anti-Trust Act. . . ."[1] Consequently, it condemned the "elaborate arguments advanced to affix a different complexion to the case" as "wholly devoid of merit."

The remedy found necessary to meet the situation disclosed was a dissolution of the combination and a "re-creating, out of the elements now composing it, a new condition which shall be honestly in harmony with and not repugnant to the law." For this purpose the case was remanded to the lower court with directions to work out an effective plan of dissolution.

As may well be surmised, a judicial decree which would at once untangle the meshes of the tobacco combination, restore *bona fide* competitive conditions, and in the process do no injury to the purchasing public or to those innocently involved in the situation must itself be of a complicated nature. Under the procedure adopted the American Tobacco Company drew up a plan of dissolution, criticisms and amendments from various sources were heard and in part adopted, and, on November 16, 1911, a decree, worked out with the assistance and approval of the Attorney General, Mr. Wickersham, and acceptable to the Supreme Court, was issued.

The first step in reorganization was the distribution of the assets of the trust among fourteen designated corporations. The United Cigar Stores Company was maintained in full efficiency and with assets unimpaired. The tin-foil business of the Conley Foil Company was divided between itself and its chief subsidiary, the Johnston Tin Foil and Metal Company. The licorice trust was resolved into two concerns, the new MacAndrews & Forbes Company and the J. S. Young Company. The snuff properties were split between three

[1] 221 U. S. 181, 182, 183, 187 (1911). It should be noted that the court did not consider here the legality of isolated contracts involving future abstention from competition; it was the "constantly recurring" and combined effect of a number of such contracts which it condemned.

concerns, one continuing to bear the name of the American Snuff Company, the others designated as the George W. Helme Company and the Weyman-Bruton Company. Two concerns in foreign trade were to be severed from the trust's influence, *viz.*, the Porto Rican-American Tobacco Company and the British-American Tobacco Company. As is quite obvious, the bulk of the tobacco business controlled by the trust, that is, the cigarette, plug, and smoking-tobacco branches, has hardly been touched to this point. Since the disappearance of the Continental in the reorganization of 1904 these lines had been directly under the control of the American Tobacco Company. Under the reorganization of 1911 it was decreed that four concerns should fall heir to this business. One was to continue as the American Tobacco Company; the others were Liggett & Myers, P. Lorillard, and R. J. Reynolds. All of them except Reynolds were to receive such assets as to enable them to do a general tobacco manufacturing business on a large scale. The Reynolds concern had succeeded in retaining a certain degree of autonomy even in the combination, and, as events later to be narrated will demonstrate, has continued since 1911 to play a unique rôle in the tobacco industry.

As regards the distribution of assets among these companies, there was every appearance of a division which would leave no individual concern in a dominating position with regard to the production of any particular product. On the other hand, an examination of the details of the breaking up of the trust's business raises serious questions concerning the probable effectiveness of the decree. The cigarette business was so divided that the American Tobacco Company retained 33.15 per cent in value of the country's total production; Lorillard, 26.02 per cent; and Liggett & Myers, 21.03—leaving only 19.8 per cent for all other concerns. In the smoking branch the American received 40.53 per cent in value of the total; Lorillard, 18.88 per cent; Liggett & Myers 16.47 per cent; and Reynolds 2.73 per cent. The aggregate 21.39 per cent remaining for all other companies was only slightly more than half that in the hands of the American alone. The plug business was distributed by allotting 37.84 per cent in value to Liggett & Myers, 22.98 per cent to the American, 15.49 per cent to R. J. Reynolds and 4.64 per cent to Lorillard. Again the independents are left with about half the business of the most important concern, and slightly less than that of the second, *viz.*, 19.05 per cent. In little cigars the division gave Lorillard 40.95 per cent control of the country's total, Liggett & Myers 38.69 per cent, and American Tobacco 13.41 per cent. The insignificant 6.95 per cent remaining was thus about half of the American's share, less than one-sixth of Liggett & Myers', and about one-seventh of Lorillard's. Snuff addicts, if interested in ascertaining the facts, would have discovered 7.82 per cent of the value of the output in that branch handled by independents, and from three to four times that much in the hands of each of the three successor companies in the snuff business. But it still seems true that if these major successor concerns honestly desired to compete with one another, the assets were so distributed as to make it feasible. Were the securities so distributed as to make it probable?

In general terms the plan of distribution followed that already discussed in the oil case—that is, the securities of the new concerns were distributed among the stockholders of the American Tobacco Company of 1904 to the extent that that concern had any claim upon such securities. In the case of the R. J. Reynolds Tobacco Company, for example, the American Tobacco held about two-thirds of its stock. Under the decree the American had to divest itself of these shares, but it did so by giving them to its stockholders as a dividend. The same procedure was followed with the securities of the licorice, tin-foil, and snuff subsidiaries, as well as those of the British-American Tobacco Company and the United Cigar Stores corporation. The transactions with Liggett & Myers and Lorillard were slightly more complicated, for here the American Tobacco first transferred part of its assets in factories, brands, etc., to the new concerns, receiving in exchange all the bonds, and common and preferred stock, of the latter, and then passed these on to holders of the securities of the

American by sale and exchange. It was provided that no one of the twenty-nine individual defendants might acquire for three years after the date of the decree any stock or equitable interest in stock of any one of the fourteen companies, except the British-American, in excess of the amount to which he was entitled under the terms of the decree. This was qualified by the exception that any one of the twenty-nine might within the three years acquire stock from another or others of the group or from the estate of one of them who had died. With the purpose of further decentralizing control, full voting rights were given to the preferred stocks of the chief successor companies. The net result of these changes was to reduce the aggregate voting power of the twenty-nine individual defendants from about 56 per cent in the combine to 35 per cent on the average in the successor companies on the date of the decree. Their control over the three major concerns, American Tobacco, Liggett & Myers, and P. Lorillard was 35.16, 40.76, and 40.76, respectively. Obviously, this group, so long as its members acted together, could continue to dominate the successor companies unless the widely scattered stockholders who constituted the majority evinced a most improbable spirit of coöperation.

It remains necessary to note certain injunctive provisions designed to prevent the continuance or revival of an illegal combination in the tobacco industry. Among these were the following:

(1) No one of the defendants, their officers, directors, servants, agents, or employees might cause the conveyance of the properties, business, etc., of any of the fourteen corporations to any other one of the group, or centralize control by establishing voting trustees or any similar device.

(2) Expressed or implied agreements relating to the management of the successor companies, prices, terms of sale, transportation, and manufacture of tobacco products, and division of business were prohibited.

(3) Joint clerical forces or officers were prohibited.

(4) With a few stated exceptions, no one of the fourteen successor concerns might hold the stock of any other corporation any part of whose stock was held by any other one of the fourteen.

(5) Each successor company was prohibited from doing business under

any other name than its own or the name of a subsidiary, and in the latter case the products of the subsidiary bearing the manufacturer's name and sold in the United States were required to indicate the control.

(6) Refusals to sell a jobber a particular product unless he purchased some other were prohibited except in so-called "combination orders" in which one product is sold at a reduced price on the condition that a stated quantity of another product be purchased.

(7) The British-American Tobacco Company and the Imperial Tobacco Company were prohibited from acting as agents for each other, from employing a common agent, and from employing a common agent with any of the successor companies for the purchase of tobacco leaf.

In addition to the foregoing permanent restraints each of the fourteen companies was enjoined for five years from having any common officer or director with any other of the corporations, from retaining or employing any common agent for purchasing leaf or other raw material or for selling products, and from directly or indirectly acquiring any stock, purchasing or acquiring any factories, plants, brands, or business, or making loans or otherwise extending financial aid to any other member of the group.[1] Finally, the court retained jurisdiction of the cause for the purpose of making such further orders or decrees, if any, which might become necessary for carrying out the mandate of the Supreme Court.

The abysmal character of the differences of opinion on the efficacy of the dissolution may be most effectively epitomized by quoting two of the present members of the Supreme Court. In his message to Congress of December 5, 1911, President Taft stated that "not in the history of American law has a decree more effective for such a purpose been entered by a court than that against the Tobacco Trust."[2] Mr. Brandeis, on the other hand, was of the opinion that "the decision of the U. S. Circuit Court approving the plan submitted by the American Tobacco Company is in effect a nullification not

[1] The distinction, if any, between this limited prohibition of acquisitions of factories, business, etc., and the permanent injunction noted above against "conveyance" of such assets seems to lie in the fact that the limited prohibition was against the corporations, the permanent against individuals. Cf. *Decrees and Judgments in Federal Anti-Trust Cases,* pp. 187 and 189.

[2] *Congressional Record,* vol. xlviii, p. 23.

only of the Sherman Law, but of the decision of the Supreme Court of the United States."[1]

Previously Mr. Brandeis and Mr. Felix Levy, representing a number of independent interests in the growing, manufacturing, and selling of tobacco, had filed with the circuit court a brief protesting against the form of decree originally proposed by the trust.[2] This presents in cogent form the objections to dividing up the assets of this monopolistic combination among so few companies and leaving control of large blocks of the stock of these companies in the hands of the very individuals who had dominated the combination before its dissolution. In the final decree the court included most of the specific prohibitions of unfair methods requested by Messrs. Brandeis and Levy, but disregarded their principal objections to the plan of dissolution finally adopted. Decision in regard to the validity of these objections and the real effect of the dissolution belongs to the history of the American tobacco industry since 1911.

[1] *World Today* for December, 1911, p. 1440.

[2] The most convenient sources for the complete text of this brief are the *Hearing before the Committee on Interstate Commerce on the Control of Corporations, Persons, and Firms engaged in Interstate Commerce,* pp. 315-322, U. S. Senate, 62d Congress, 2d Session, 1911-1912, and W. H. S. Stevens, *Industrial Combinations and Trusts,* pp. 485-498. Mr. Levy's oral argument supporting the objections to the decree is printed in the *Hearing* just cited at p. 340 and in Stevens's book at p. 498.

CHAPTER XI

THE AMERICAN TOBACCO INDUSTRY, 1911-1929 [1]

IN CONSIDERING the developments in the tobacco industry of recent years we have been impressed with the dependence of the individual investigator upon the reports of the Federal Trade Commission or other governmental agencies for the information necessary to a conclusion. American business activity has become so complex that the private individual is almost helpless without such assistance. Even the trade and financial journals, numerous as they are, prove much less valuable for our purposes than might be hoped. The facts in which we are interested are just the ones which such journals refrain from publishing. But when we turn to the three reports made by the Federal Trade Commission on the tobacco industry since the dissolution, we are also disappointed. As regards developments with reference to the extent to which the twenty-nine individuals named in the dissolution suit and their successors have retained a dominant position in the industry, we are given no adequate information. As regards the extent to which the four successor companies in the cigarette, plug, and smoking-tobacco branches and the three successor snuff concerns continued to dominate those branches after the dissolution, we have, however, important evidence. The table on the following page indicates how little the control of the successor companies had changed down to 1913.

Official statistics on the exact proportions of the various branches controlled by successor companies are not available since 1913, but that they continue to dominate the tobacco business of the United States is conclusively demonstrated by the data at hand. In the first place we may note that in 1919

[1] In the preparation of this chapter we have been materially aided by an unpublished manuscript on *The History of the American Tobacco Industry, 1911-1929,* by Mr. Reavis Cox.

more than 60 per cent of the leaf used in the manufacture of tobacco products, exclusive of cigars, intended for domestic consumption or export by American manufacturers, was purchased by the seven successor companies mentioned above.[1] Figures on the degree of control over tobacco products exercised by these concerns also support our generalization, although there have been important changes in the relative positions of certain members of the group.

TABLE VII

CONTROL OF THE SPECIFIED BRANCHES OF THE TOBACCO INDUSTRY BY THE COMBINATION IN 1910 AND BY SUCCESSOR COMPANIES IN 1913[a]

Branch	Proportion manufactured by the Combination in 1910[b]	Proportion manufactured by the successor companies in 1913
	(Per cent)	(Per cent)
Plug	84.5	84.7
Smoking	76.1	73.4
Fine-cut	79.7	77.2
Snuff	96.5	97.3
Cigarettes	83.9	90.7
Little cigars	91.4	91.0

[a] *U. S. Report on the Tobacco Industry*, part iii, p. 11.

[b] Exclusive of quantities manufactured and held for export in bonded warehouses.

Most noteworthy of these changes has been the rise of the R. J. Reynolds Company in the cigarette and smoking-tobacco fields. It was not given any of the combination's business in the former branch by the dissolution, and only 3.4 per cent of the latter. In 1912 it sold nearly 9 per cent of the country's total of smoking. The following year it introduced the "Camel" brand of cigarettes, selling two-tenths of 1 per cent of the total, and advanced its proportion of smoking to a little over 10 per cent. Estimates from private sources, such as the investment house of Charles D. Barney & Company, which

[1] *Federal Trade Commission Report on the Tobacco Industry*, 1920, 1921 edition, p. 51; 1922 edition, p. 54.

specializes in tobacco securities and issues an *Annual Review* on the industry, placed the output of "Camels" in 1924 at approximately one-half of the total cigarette production of the United States.[1] In the smoking field Reynolds's "Prince Albert" brand has been extremely popular, though no accurate data on its relative importance could be secured from the company or from any other source. Whether or not changes have taken place to increase or decrease the 20-per-cent control of the plug business held by Reynolds in 1912 and 1913 is unknown for the same reason.

In the survey just cited the business of the American Tobacco for 1921 in the cigarette, smoking-tobacco, and plug branches was estimated at 20, 26, and 16 per cent, respectively, of the national total. If accurate, these percentages represent a severe loss in cigarette business and a slight loss in the other two branches since the years just following the dissolution. In 1912 the percentages were 36, 29, and 20; and in 1913, 35, 28, and 18. Five years later, however, an estimate published in *Standard Corporation Records* credited the American Company with about one-third of the national total in the cigarette and smoking branches and about one-quarter of the plug. In other words, this successor concern had almost regained the position of 1912 and 1913 in the former two products and bettered the position of those years materially in the last.[2]

Liggett & Myers produced in 1912 approximately 37 per cent of the output of the country in cigarettes, 16 per cent of the smoking tobacco, and 38 per cent of the plug. In 1913 these percentages remained practically constant at 34, 17, and 39, respectively. Although the company is engaged in all lines of tobacco production except snuff and large cigars, we have been able to secure even approximately accurate information on its position for only the cigarette branch. Its three chief brands, "Chesterfield," "Fatima," and "Piedmont," ranked second, fourth, and fifth in sales in the United States in 1926.[3]

[1] Barney, *The Tobacco Industry,* 1924, p. 36.

[2] *Standard Corporation Records,* Annual Report Section, A 41, revised May 2, 1927.

[3] *Ibid.,* L 29, revised January 26, 1928.

In 1927 the company claimed to have sold 28,000,000,000 "Chesterfields" alone. Since the total consumption for the United States that year was only 97,000,000,000 and since Liggett & Myers sell six other brands of cigarettes, two of which at least are quite popular, it seems that it must have sold at least one-third of the national total.[1] Although 1927 data for all companies are not available, it has been estimated that in 1926 the three firms of Reynolds, American, and Liggett & Myers jointly produced 90 per cent of the cigarettes sold in the United States.

The final member of the Big Four, P. Lorillard & Company, held its strongest positions in the little cigar and fine-cut chewing branches in the years immediately following the dissolution, though its percentages in the cigarette and smoking fields were substantial. For all the divisions except cigarettes we have failed to secure data on the company's position, and even for that one they are not adequate. The decline in popularity of Turkish cigarettes caused Lorillard to lose ground in that branch materially. In an endeavor to regain these losses the company introduced early in April, 1926, a new blended brand, "Old Gold," and pushed it by one of the most ambitious advertising campaigns ever seen in this country. It is interesting to note, however, that in financing this campaign it was necessary for the company to suspend dividend payments and float an issue of gold debentures in the sum of $15,000,-000. The results from the point of view of sales seemed quite satisfactory during 1927 and early 1928, for they advanced from an average of 12,000,000 a day in July to 20,000,000 a day in November, 1927, and to 30,000,000 a day in April of

[1] The percentages of national output of various branches given by companies for 1912 and 1913 in the foregoing paragraphs have been computed from data in volume iii of the *U. S. Report on the Tobacco Industry.* Nowhere in the three volumes were outputs by individual companies and branches given for these years, but *total output* for the United States, *aggregate output* for all the successor companies, and *sales* in pounds or other measures for each company were given. Our percentages represent the proportion of the *sales* of individual companies to the national *output*. Of course, sales and output are not the same, but the sum of the sales of the successor companies as a group was always very nearly identical with the aggregate output of these successor companies, so that the error involved in our computation is negligible.

1928. But the net earnings available for dividends tell a very different story. From $5,641,431 in 1925 they fell to $4,117,198 in 1926, to $2,490,787 in 1927, and to $1,817,428 in 1928.[1]

Somewhat less reliable estimates of cigarette sales than those from Charles D. Barney & Company and the *Standard Corporation Records* appeared during the course of the brief "price war" in the spring of 1928. These estimates set the daily sales of "Camels" at 125,000,000, of "Lucky Strikes" at between 90,000,000 and 100,000,000, of "Chesterfields" at 90,000,000, and of "Old Golds" at 30,000,000. As is well known, there is considerable fluctuation in these daily sales figures from month to month. Moreover, on the basis of a 365-day year, these estimates would figure out sales for the four brands above for 1928 totaling 122,000,000,000, whereas the total sales of all cigarettes were just short of 106,000,000,000. But assuming the approximate accuracy of the relative positions of the companies as indicated by these estimates, and making allowance for the few billions of other brands sold, we conclude that in 1928 the percentages of total cigarette sales of the four leading brands were not far from the following: "Camel," 35 per cent; "Chesterfield," 25 per cent; "Lucky Strike," 26 per cent; "Old Gold," 8 per cent.[2]

The emphasis placed upon the cigarette branch of the industry in the foregoing discussion is justified by common knowledge of the shift of consumers' tastes from other forms, particularly since the World War, but a few figures are even more convincing than observation. In the last year of the combination 350,481,000 pounds of leaf tobacco were used for snuff and manufactured tobacco, 136,462,000 pounds for cigars, and 31,099,000 for small cigarettes—*i.e.,* those weighing not more than three pounds to the thousand. In 1918 cigarettes exceeded cigars in consumption of leaf with a total of 177,168,000 pounds to 158,346,000 pounds, but the other branches

[1] Barney, *The Tobacco Industry, Annual Review,* 1928, p. 19; *Barron's,* February 18, 1929, p. 11.

[2] Cf. *New York Evening Post,* April 23, 1928. More recent statements in the *U. S. Tobacco Journal,* December 29, 1928, p. 9, claiming 11,000,000,000 sales for "Old Golds" in 1928 would advance their percentage to between 10 and 11.

still used more than twice the total of cigarettes, *viz.,* 369,081,000 pounds. In 1927 cigarettes had not only far outstripped cigars with a consumption of 290,368,000 to 151,049,000 pounds of tobacco, but also had finally exceeded the total, 278,482,000, used in manufactured tobacco and snuff.[1] In percentage terms the foregoing figures mean that cigars required approximately 26 per cent of the leaf used in manufacturing tobacco products in 1910 and 21 per cent in 1927; that manufactured tobacco and snuff dropped from 67 per cent in 1910 to only 39 per cent in 1927; and that cigarettes advanced from 6 per cent in 1910 to 40 per cent seventeen years later.

In the snuff branch it will be recalled that 1910 found the trust with 96.5 per cent of the output in its hands and that this was divided into almost precisely equal parts among the three successor companies. In 1913 these three jointly produced 96.1 per cent of the total, the division among themselves remaining practically unaltered. Reliable data for degrees of control held by the companies in subsequent years have not been found, and their officials prefer not to supply them. That there has been a marked change in their relative positions, however, is easily demonstrable. The book value of the net investment of the United States Tobacco Company increased from $8,660,671 in 1912 to $30,413,615 in 1927, and of the George W. Helme Company from $8,550,727 to $18,190,605 in the same period, whereas that of the American Snuff increased only $4,506,780—*i.e.,* from $18,872,482 to $23,379,262.[2]

Some indication of the nature and character of the competition that developed in the snuff branch may be found in the details of the cease and desist order entered by the Federal Trade Commission against the American Snuff Company on June 30, 1927, in which the Commission held as established by evidence that the company was making, publishing, and circulating written and oral statements or representations that

[1] Data from *Annual Reports* of the Commissioner of Internal Revenue.

[2] Cf. *The Corporation Service* (*Moody's Manual*), 1913, with *Poor's,* Industrial Section, 1928.

its competitors' snuff products are made of trash, inferior tobacco, cigar stubs, old tobacco chews, and tobacco stems; that they contain opium, copperas, glass, hair, dirt, or similar substances; that they will cause blindness and tuberculosis; that they will destroy the teeth, cause pyorrhea, bleeding of gums, or other maladies, etc., etc.[1]

Further evidence of the preponderant position of the successor companies in the various branches of the industry is simply cumulative of that offered above. Consequently, it may be argued that the advantages conferred by the distribution of assets in 1911 upon these concerns have made it impossible for a new company to achieve a position of any significance in any branch formerly dominated by the trust. Certainly none of them have done it. It may be argued, on the contrary, that the rise of the Reynolds concern from a position of producing two-tenths of 1 per cent of the cigarettes in 1913 to something like 50 per cent of them in 1924 is conclusive proof of a free field in the most important branch of the industry. And the increase in the book value of its net investment from $15,844,573 in 1912 to $150,265,321 in 1927 is a buttress for that argument which cannot easily be demolished. Finally, the fluctuating percentages of cigarette output produced by the individual members of the Big Four and the even more noticeable fluctuations in the percentage of the total represented by particular brands do not seem consistent with monopolistic domination.

But this brings us back to the points raised above concerning the restoration of price competition and the difficulties thereof. In his excellent study of trusts published in 1921 Professor Eliot Jones seems to find no evidence to amend the analysis of the Bureau of Corporations on the factors of conventional price and of legal regulation of the size and weight of units of tobacco products. Consequently, he concludes that "without further legislation permitting smaller differences in the size of the package than one-quarter of an ounce, or permitting all tobacco products to be packed and stamped in wholesale quantities, no real competition in prices was to be

[1] F. T. C. *Annual Report,* 1928, p. 69.

expected." [1] Since he made that comment, however, considerable evidence has accumulated to indicate that with the exception of the R. J. Reynolds Company the former members of the trust are willing to go to considerable lengths to prevent *bona fide* price competition in the sale of their products even when conditions are permissive. In its report on *Prices of Tobacco Products* the Federal Trade Commission stated:

> From evidence gathered in response to a Senate resolution adopted August 9, 1921, asking information on the tobacco situation the commission here reports its conclusion that since April, 1921, the American Tobacco Co., P. Lorillard Co., and to a less extent Liggett & Myers Tobacco Co., have each been engaged in conspiracies with numerous sectional and local jobbers' associations to keep up the prices of tobacco products in the United States through price agreements and intimidation.
>
> . . . . .
>
> While the evidence indicates that in some localities agreements to keep up the price of tobacco products originated with the jobbers, and in others were rather the result of the stand taken by the manufacturers, it is clear that the movement could not have developed so successfully on a practically nation-wide scale, as it did, except for the fact, shown by the evidence, that the above-named manufacturers fostered and aided these agreements and actively coöperated with the jobbers in carrying them out.

On subsequent pages of the report the Commission added that the Tobacco Products Corporation, Bloch Brothers Tobacco Company, and Scotten-Dillon Company were also active in the price-fixing campaign. Furthermore, the Commission characterized as unwarranted attempts to justify the maintenance of prices in 1921 at the high levels established in 1919 and 1920 because of the fact that a good part of the finished products of 1921 was manufactured from leaf purchased eighteen months before at extremely high prices. The view of the Commission here is based on the accounting practice of the industry, by which the new unused leaf on hand is included in arriving at the average inventory price at which leaf is currently charged into factory costs. Since prices paid for leaf in 1920 were low, a point to which we shall return, consistent use of the accounting methods employed to justify

[1] *Trust Problem in the United States,* pp. 473-474.

high prices in 1919 and 1920 should result in justifying lower prices in 1921.[1]

The evidence supporting the conclusions just summarized prompted the Federal Trade Commission to issue during 1922 and 1923 some thirty complaints against a number of manufacturers, as individual concerns, one manufacturers' association, and fifteen jobbers' associations, alleging unfair methods of competition in general and a conspiracy to maintain resale prices in particular. Most of these were subsequently dismissed as a result of the altered attitude toward such issues displayed by the appointees to the Commission of Presidents Harding and Coolidge, but one involving the American Tobacco Company and a dealers' association of Philadelphia was taken into court. In an opinion later characterized by the Supreme Court as "of uncertain intendment" and "not satisfactory as an exposition of the law" the Circuit Court of Appeals, Second Circuit, held for the company. In spite of the comment just quoted the Supreme Court affirmed the decision because it preferred to adhere to the rule of noninterference with a decision resting upon "appreciation of circumstances which admit of different interpretations."[2] The unsatisfactory nature of such a decision needs no comment. On the decision of the lower court we find ourselves in thorough accord with the comments of the Commission:

> . . . the lower court appears to hold that the commission's finding of price agreement between the jobbers and the manufacturer was not supported by evidence; that it is lawful for the manufacturer to aid and abet jobbers in making effective their illegal price agreement; that it is not unlawful for a jobbing association to agree to fix prices and prevent members and nonmembers who do not observe the agreed price from procuring goods; that it is not an unfair method of competition for a manufacturer to join with a jobbers' association in compelling observance of prices illegally agreed upon; that it is unlawful for jobbers to sell goods at prices satisfactory to themselves and which, in the past, have sustained their business, though such prices may be lower than those agreed upon by the members of the association of competing jobbers; and, conversely, that it is fair competition for jobbers to combine to coerce competitors into charging prices which they have agreed upon as satisfactory to them-

[1] Federal Trade Commission, *Prices of Tobacco Products,* 1922, pp. 6, 7, 10.

[2] 9 Fed. (2d) 570 (1925); 274 U. S. 544 (1927).

selves; that a combination in restraint of interstate commerce in violation of the Sherman Act is not also an unfair method of competition; that it is not to the interest of the public to prevent jobbers from agreeing upon prices at which they will sell and from agreeing to prevent those who will not observe their prices from getting the goods.[1]

The continued predominance of the seven chief successor companies as purchasers of leaf for domestic manufacture has been brought out. Furthermore, it should be noted that six other purchasing units, the Imperial Tobacco Company, the British-American Company, the French and Italian monopolies, the International Planters Corporation, and the Universal Leaf Tobacco Company, bought an aggregate of upward of 30 per cent of the 1919 crop of export and manufacturing tobaccos, these constituting about 85 per cent of the entire production. The thirteen concerns together then purchased approximately 75 per cent of the export and manufacturing tobacco crop. Even this understates the concentration since the "Big Four" American manufacturers jointly purchased seven times the quantity needed by the three snuff concerns, and one of the British companies took over 15 per cent of the crop. When attention is directed to particular grades of tobacco we find that 90 per cent of the burley crop was acquired by six concerns, that 64 per cent of the dark-fired went to the French and Italian monopolies, the snuff companies and one British manufacturer, and that 47 per cent of the bright Southern was sold to the two British concerns, and 20 per cent more to three of the successor companies.

Since these facts were fairly well known to leaf-growers, it was a foregone conclusion that they would protest against the situation that developed in 1919 and became worse in 1920, under which they found themselves receiving prices only a third to a half of those paid in 1918 and at the opening of the market in 1919, although prices for tobacco products had dropped not at all. The volume and vigor of these protests were sufficient to call forth resolutions by the House of Representatives in 1920 and by the Senate in 1921 directing the investigations by the Federal Trade Commission which

[1] Federal Trade Commission, *Annual Report,* 1926, pp. 31-32.

have been cited above. The conclusions of the Commission may best be stated in its own words:

> While no conclusive evidence was found of collusion to depress the prices paid to the growers of the 1920 leaf, it appears that a few large buyers had a dominant position and each purchased only a certain percentage of the offerings; that common buying agencies were used, and that secret purchases were made through independent dealers while the ultimate purchasers held off the market, or practically so.[1]

In the earlier investigation the same facts which underlay the conclusions just stated had forced the Commission to the further judgment that the successor companies as well as the Imperial and British-American concerns had violated both the spirit and the letter of the dissolution decree. Consequently it recommended:

> 1. That the provision relating to the use of common agencies by the defendant companies, in the purchase of leaf tobacco, which expired by limitation November, 1916, be revived and made permanent.
>
> 2. That the provision relating to the defendant companies doing business under any other than their own corporate name or that of a subsidiary corporation controlled by them be made specific so as to include the purchase of leaf tobacco through agencies not disclosed to the trade.

As a partial remedy for some other features of the situation the Commission further recommended that a federal system of grading leaf tobacco be established by the Department of Agriculture.[2] On the first two recommendations nothing was done because the Department of Justice convinced itself that the practices had been abandoned.[3] In conformity with the third the Department of Agriculture issued in 1925 a *Type Classification of American-grown Tobacco.*

Meanwhile the growers had taken active steps to meet the situation outlined above by the organization of coöperative marketing associations. The most important of these were the Burley Tobacco Growers Coöperative Association, Dark Tobacco Growers Coöperative Association, and the (Tri-State) Tobacco Growers Coöperative Association. For vary-

[1] *Prices of Tobacco Products,* 1922, p. 9.

[2] Federal Trade Commission, *Report on the Tobacco Industry,* 1920, 1921 edition, p. 162; 1922 edition, p. 165.

[3] Letter from Assistant Attorney General W. J. Donovan, April 13, 1928.

ing lengths of time these associations were quite successful, but fairly early in the history of the last named a group of its members and some others began to complain that the remnants of the old trust were discriminating against the coöperatives and utilizing every conceivable method to discredit and ruin them. Again the Senate ordered an investigation, but the resolution was so worded as to enable the Commission to confine it almost entirely to the activities of the American and Imperial Companies on the one side and the Tri-State Association on the other. The report, styled *The American Tobacco Company and the Imperial Tobacco Company,* was a practically complete exoneration of the companies named and a rather thoroughgoing condemnation of the Tri-State Coöperative. And there seems little doubt that the affairs of the Tri-State Association had been conducted in such a fashion as to merit severe censure.[1] On the other hand, the Commission noted that "the apparent success of the burley association and of organizations of growers in other regions would indicate that coöperative marketing of leaf tobacco is generally successful."

Nearly three years later the Commission's report on *Cooperative Marketing* revealed the fact that the two other major coöperative associations had failed, as had two additional smaller associations. Among the causes found for these failures were: mismanagement, delays in paying for crops, mistakes in grading leaf, extraordinarily large crops, changes in consumers' tastes, and internal dissensions. It should be noted that the Commission found no "illegal opposition or interference" with the associations.[2] Although the report on the American and Imperial Companies was interpreted in many quarters as a "whitewashing" for them by the Commission, subsequent developments would indicate that the failure of the coöperatives resulted from causes other than the opposition of the large manufacturers.

But whatever the merits of this particular phase of the controversies involving the tobacco companies, the foregoing

[1] Cf. editorial in New York *Times,* January 14, 1927.
[2] Cf. pp. 306-316 of the report.

facts force us to two general conclusions: first, the form of the decree of 1911 was unsatisfactory; and, second, events since that date have demonstrated that to a considerable extent it has proved ineffective in restoring the degree of free and open competition relied upon by economists for the maintenance of fair prices. There remain for consideration, however, the questions of the desirability of attempting to restore that degree of competition and of the probability of the rise of a new combination in the tobacco industry. Our answer to the former appears in our final chapter. To the latter we can answer here that there are at least two influences at work which would indicate a possible new combination in the offing, one technological, the other organizational.

Interestingly enough, the technical factor tending toward a new combination has appeared in the one branch of the industry which the old trust found it impossible to subjugate: cigars. The reason for this failure it will be recalled was the inability of its inventors to devise a satisfactory cigar-making machine, although generous subsidies were provided. Beginning in 1898 under the leadership of Rufus L. Patterson, an associate of the late J. B. Duke, experiments costing upward of $7,000,000 and extending over a period of twenty years were finally rewarded by a machine which seems to be demonstrating its effectiveness in spite of the dictum of a considerable group of die-hards in the business that "good" cigars can be made only by hand. Evidence of the tendency toward concentration appears in Tables VIII and IX.

These data are supplemented, and, in a sense, corrected by figures in Charles D. Barney & Company's *Annual Review* of the tobacco industry for 1927, in which it is shown that at the end of 1925 there were only 8,533 cigar factories in operation, that 281, or 3.3 per cent, of these manufactured 71 per cent of the total output of cigars, and that these 281 factories were owned by about 20 corporations.[1] Though little positive evidence is available for the three succeeding years on the concentration of ownership, that little indicates that the

[1] P. 17.

TABLE VIII

CIGAR FACTORIES CLASSIFIED BY ANNUAL PRODUCTION[a]

Output—cigars	Number of factories in operation during						
	1921	1922	1923	1924	1925	1926	1927
Under 500,000	13,149	10,775	9,282	8,755	9,789	9,281	8,470
500,000 to 1,000,000	510	471	420	339	282	281	243
1,000,000 to 2,000,000	324	273	284	240	213	196	167
2,000,000 to 3,000,000	147	140	136	113	106	89	88
3,000,000 to 4,000,000	76	77	108	74	65	61	44
4,000,000 to 5,000,000	73	67	56	59	50	53	43
5,000,000 to 10,000,000	178	169	177	166	152	147	123
10,000,000 to 20,000,000	85	84	96	77	77	74	69
20,000,000 to 40,000,000	25	42	34	39	34	42	37
Over 40,000,000	11	7	12	15	18	23	28
Total	14,578	12,105	10,605	9,877	10,786	10,247	9,312

TABLE IX

CIGAR FACTORIES CLASSIFIED BY ANNUAL PRODUCTION[a]

Output—cigars	Per cent of total cigars manufactured during						
	1921	1922	1923	1924	1925	1926	1927
Under 500,000	13.7	11.19	12.42	10.59	10.15	8.00	6.96
500,000 to 1,000,000	5.3	5.00	4.25	3.63	3.12	3.01	2.61
1,000,000 to 2,000,000	6,8	5.81	5.78	5.10	4.72	4.34	3.70
2,000,000 to 3,000,000	5.3	5.14	4.80	4.14	4.04	3.37	3.36
3,000,000 to 4,000,000	3.9	3.96	5.40	3.88	3.53	3.26	2.37
4,000,000 to 5,000,000	4.9	4.49	3.60	3.98	3.43	3.64	2.93
5,000,000 to 10,000,000	18.4	17.52	17.98	17.80	16.98	15.61	13.27
10,000,000 to 20,000,000	16.0	16.68	18.48	15.71	16.53	15.45	15.00
20,000,000 to 40,000,000	10.0	18.46	13.22	16.04	15.66	18.35	16.58
Over 40,000,000	15.7	11.75	14.07	19.13	21.84	24.97	33.22
Total	100.00	100.00	100.00	100.00	100.00	100.00	100.00

[a] From *Annual Reports* of the Commissioner of Internal Revenue.

process is continuing. During these three years the preceding tables show clearly the rapidly increasing predominance of the largest producing units—*i.e.,* those making the most use of machines.

Obviously the "machine age" has at last extended its domination to the cigar industry. As usual, the small manufacturer is losing ground, and for the usual reasons. The cigar machines cost about $8,000 each and operate most economically in units of four or more. If the present tendencies continue, there is every reason for believing that in a very short while practically all cigars retailing at fifteen cents or less each will be manufactured by machines. And this class now constitutes about 97 per cent of the total of large cigars. Technologically, then, the cigar industry is, or shortly will be, in the situation which made possible the first combination in the cigarette branch.

Moreover, there are indications of something more than willingness on the part of certain of the major concerns to join interests. The Consolidated Cigar Company, recipient in 1926 of the largest earnings of any cigar concern in the country, has been charged by the Federal Trade Commission with acquiring illegally the stock of two of its competitors, the "44" Cigar Company and the G.H.P. Cigar Company, the alleged effect of said acquisition being to lessen competition, restrain commerce, and create a monopoly.[1] In the early summer of 1927 there were persistent rumors in financial and tobacco-trade circles in New York that the Consolidated was engaged in merger negotiations with the Union and United Tobacco Company discussed later. Of a more positive character was the action of the Porto Rican-American Cigar Company in acquiring control of the Congress Cigar Company.

Another movement toward a new combination in tobacco, and one not confined to a single branch, centered around the so-called Whelan and Schulte groups. Mr. George J. Whelan and Mr. David A. Schulte, leading figures in these groups, are best known in the trade through their connection with the United Cigar Stores and the Schulte Retail Stores, respectively, the two largest retail tobacco chain-store systems in the country. Early in 1926 the Whelan interests organized

[1] *Annual Report,* 1928, p. 171.

the Union and United Tobacco Company. Toward the close of that year a "close working arrangement" between the United and the Schulte chains was brought about through the new Union and United concern.[1] The latter has also created a manufacturing subsidiary, the Union Tobacco Company. In addition to the popularly priced "Three Castles" ("Three Kings") and "Herbert Tareyton" cigarettes, this company took over from the American Tobacco Company several higher-priced brands which it had leased for a while from the Tobacco Products Corporation.

By this time the situation appears complicated, but further details bring further complications. "Three Castles" is the chief brand of W. D. and H. O. Willis Tobacco Company, the chief manufacturing unit of the Imperial Tobacco Company of England. Tobacco Products Corporation was organized in 1912 as a holding company for a number of small concerns. For a time it functioned as an operating concern, but in 1923 returned to holding-company status. Its chief source of income was dividends from its large block of United Cigar Stores common stock.

Meanwhile, other moves designed to strengthen the position of the Whelan-Schulte group have been made. Early in 1928 one of their affiliated concerns, the Union Cigar Company, acquired control of Otto Eisenlohr & Brothers, one of the larger cigar manufacturers of the country. In October, 1928, D. A. Schulte became president of the Eisenlohr company and W. T. Posey, president of the United Cigar Stores of America, became chairman of its board of directors. At the time of these changes it was rumored that steps would be taken to assume control of other tobacco companies through the agency of Eisenlohr, and subsequently at least one cigar concern has been thus acquired. Other rumors, guesses, and conjectures concerning the activities of the United-Schulte group in bringing about a new tobacco combination have been current in financial circles for two or more years. The outcome of these maneuvers, announced in June, 1929, was in some respects rather surprising. A new concern, the United Stores

[1] New York *Herald Tribune*, December 7, 1926.

Corporation, was chartered in Delaware to acquire by exchange of stock the capital stocks of the United Cigar Stores Company of America, the Tobacco Products Corporation and the Union Tobacco Company. It is expected to acquire from United Cigars its interests in the chain drug-store field. Mr. G. K. Morrow, president of the Gold Dust Corporation, is slated to become president of the new corporation and among its directors are to be leading figures in four food products companies. Furthermore it is rumored that the arrangements involve the practical retirement of George Whelan from active participation in the industry. Consequently it still remains to be seen whether or not the merger develops into a "tobacco trust."[1]

[1] Cf. *San Francisco Call and Post,* June 6, 1929, and *Barron's Weekly,* June 17, 1929.

CHAPTER XII

THE UNITED STATES SHIPBUILDING COMPANY

Success did not always reward the efforts of promoters and underwriters to combine the plants of rival manufacturers, even in the period when the trust movement was at its height. A classic example of failure, at the expense not of the public, but of the so-called "insiders," is afforded by the United States Shipbuilding Company.[1]

The thought that a combination of shipbuilding plants would be financially advantageous took form in the mind of Mr. John W. Young some time in 1896 or '97. On the basis of an understanding that the Newport News Shipyard, with which he had had some previous connection, would enter a combination, he secured an option on the more important yard of Cramp & Sons, in Philadelphia. Nothing came of this first project, but in the early autumn of 1899 Young made the acquaintance of Mr. Lewis Nixon, from whom he secured, with the assistance of Colonel John J. McCook of the law firm of Alexander & Green, an option on the Crescent Shipyard, the yard of Samuel L. Moore & Sons, and other property which he controlled. About the same time he obtained options also on the Union Iron Works at San Francisco and on several

[1] Because of the prominence of the men connected with this combination, its failure within less than a year after its organization, and the complicated litigation to which this gave rise, the accounts of its promotion and reorganization in the contemporary financial papers are unusually full. The episode has been described at length by Dr. Arthur S. Dewing in his *Corporate Promotions and Reorganizations,* Chapters XVII and XVIII. A somewhat exaggerated account of the causes of the failure is contained in the report of the receiver of the United States Shipbuilding Company, James Smith, Jr., filed October 31, 1903, and reprinted in abridged form and with valuable explanatory and bibliographical notes as Chapter XII of Ripley's *Trusts, Pools and Corporations.* We have found the files of the New York *Times* and New York *Tribune* for the years 1901 to 1904 the best supplementary sources of information. Certain events connected with the promotion and underwriting are described by L. W. Sammis of the New York *Sun* in a paper contributed to the *Annals of the American Academy of Political and Social Science,* vol. xxiv (1904) pp. 241-270.

smaller Atlantic-coast yards. H. W. Poor & Company agreed to undertake the marketing of the securities of the combination and by May 7, 1901, a prospectus had been drawn up and was about to be issued announcing the formation of the "United States Shipbuilding Company," with a capital of $65,000,000, one-half preferred and one-half common, and inviting subscriptions at $100 per share of preferred plus a share of common stock. Already in this prospectus exaggerated estimates of the value of the yards to be included and of the earnings to be expected were made on the basis of letters supplied by Lewis Nixon, who was to have been president of the combination, and Admiral Bowles, who was represented as having made a careful appraisal of the yards and calculation of the savings that would result from their unified operation. Unfortunately for this second attempt, the Northern Pacific corner, occurring on May 9, the very date borne by the prospectus, so disturbed business confidence that the bankers abandoned the project.

Still confident that a successful combination could be effected, Young next went to Paris, where he interested certain French financiers in the project of placing some of the securities in the shipbuilding combination abroad, should a practicable plan be worked out. Returning to New York in the winter of 1901-1902, he made the acquaintance of Mr. Daniel Leroy Dresser, president of the Trust Company of the Republic, which had just opened its doors (March 31, 1902) with a capital of $1,000,000, surplus of $500,000, and expanding deposits which were not yet fully employed in the business on which it expected to specialize, loaning money on raw cotton and to manufacturers and merchants, like Dresser himself, interested in the drygoods trade. Through Young, Nixon, and McCook, Dresser was persuaded that participation in the launching of the shipbuilding combination would prove both profitable to his Trust Company and creditable to himself, as its head. Young secured renewal of the options on most of the shipyards which he hoped to combine, including Crescent Shipyard Company, Samuel L. Moore & Sons Company, Union Iron Works Company, Harlan & Hollingsworth Company, Bath Iron Works, Hyde Windlass Company, and the Eastern Shipbuilding Company, but not the more important Cramp & Sons or Newport News yards, and under date of April 19, 1902, a "private and confidential" prospectus of the United States Shipbuilding Company was printed announcing the Trust Company of the Republic as "Bankers" and Alexander & Green as "counsel." In place of the $65,000,000 capitalization in stock formerly proposed, this prospectus announced that the stock would be limited to $10,000,000 preferred and $10,000,000 common, but that there would be an issue of $16,000,000 5-per-cent sinking-fund gold bonds, of which $5,500,000 would be given in part payment for the plants to be taken in, $1,500,000 retained in the treasury of the company, and the remaining $9,000,000 sold to the underwriters at 90, with a bonus of $2,500,000 in each class of stock. Convinced that the combination would be a financial success and that the public would eagerly buy the bonds at the price, 97½, at which it was proposed to offer them, Dresser presented the project to the board of directors of the Trust Company of the Republic, and secured their authorization to subscribe, on behalf of the company, for $3,000,000 of the bonds to be issued. He testified later that he was assured by Young and McCook that arrangements had been made for floating the remaining $6,000,000 abroad, and certainly paper commitments for the underwriting of $4,250,000 of the bonds in Paris were actually secured by Young through a syndicate headed by a Baron P. Calvert-Rogniat. Because of the preparations for the coronation ceremonies then in progress, no serious attempt was made to organize a syndicate to market part of the issue in London. Instead, Dresser was later persuaded to add the remaining $1,750,000, that it was necessary to sell, to the $3,000,000 for which his Trust Company was already obligated. He did this the more readily because he had experienced little difficulty in getting subscriptions to the underwriting on the generous terms offered.

Before the bonds were actually tendered to the public the underwriters appear to have realized that the combination, with the Cramp and Newport News yards left out, might not prove attractive to investors. Dresser subsequently testified that he was lunching with Nixon on June 11 when Mr. Charles M. Schwab came to their table and, after some preliminary conversation, asked, "Why don't you buy the Bethlehem plant?" The Bethlehem Steel Company was a property which had been acquired by the syndicate, headed by J. P. Morgan and Company, which had launched the United States Steel Corporation the year before. It was well equipped to manufacture steel plates and the other forms of steel required in the shipbuilding industry. In fact, one reason alleged for the decision of the syndicate not to include it in the United States Steel combination was that it was one of the three companies, the Carnegie Company and the Midvale Company being the others, which were organized to manufacture armor plate for battleships, and that a combination of two of these companies might put an end to this profitable business by causing Congress to equip one of the navy yards to manufacture armor plates to meet the government's requirements.

Whether the proposal came from Schwab or the other side, the purchase had such obvious advantages to the projected combination that Dresser, Nixon, McCook and the others interested eagerly fell in with it. The economies to be realized by combining shipyards scattered all the way from New York to San Francisco and from the Delaware River to Maine were debatable. There could be no question, however, of the savings that would result from including with them a well-organized and efficiently managed steel plant which could assure them a continuous flow of the materials they required and, on the other hand, could be assured a steady market, at remunerative prices, for its products. Nixon and Dresser at once began negotiating with Schwab over the terms on which the Bethlehem plant might be acquired. More cautious and experienced men, with such an important negotiation pending, would have postponed any public offering of securities until the terms of purchase had been settled, so that a prospectus covering the whole undertaking could be issued. As a matter of fact, a verbal agreement with Mr. Schwab appears to have been reached on the very day, June 14, when a prospectus was printed in the financial papers offering the United States Shipbuilding bonds to the public and describing the proposed capitalization without any reference to the changes that were to be made to permit the Bethlehem purchase. This prospectus was worse than premature. It was grossly inaccurate and misleading in important particulars. It listed as "directors" some ten prominent men, when, as a matter of fact, the company had not been incorporated. Only four of those named ever became directors, and several of the others declared that the use of their names was entirely unauthorized. Furthermore, it reproduced from the earlier prospectus the false and exaggerated statements as to the value of the properties to be combined and their probable earnings at the same time that it declared that the present promotion had no connection with that of the previous year.

Whether because of its growing distrust of new promotions, or because of the careless way in which these bonds were offered, before the company had even been incorporated or its composition determined, the investing public received the tender coldly. Instead of taking the whole issue or even the $4,750,000 of the bonds that it was proposed to sell in the United States, it took only $490,000. This made it doubly important that the French syndicate take the bonds for which it had subscribed. It was in this situation that a cable was dispatched to Young, apparently by Dresser, stating that the offer of the bonds in the United States had been a "success." On the strength of this assurance, as he afterward declared, Baron Calvert-Rogniat paid over to Young $25,000. This was the only money ever actually paid by the French underwriters, who repudiated their obligation as soon as they learned that the sale of the bonds in the United States had really been an almost complete failure. They asserted that the basis on which they had made their subscriptions was representations by Young that all of the bonds would be eagerly taken in New York, so that their obligation would prove merely nominal. When questioned subsequently as to whether he had made inquiry as to the financial responsibility of the French underwriters, Young stated that he considered that to be the business of the Trust Company of the Republic, a striking illustration of his attitude toward his responsibilities as promoter.

As an offset to this disappointing and, as it later proved, disastrous failure to find purchasers for the shipbuilding bonds, the negotiations to acquire for the Shipbuilding Company the valuable Bethlehem plant proceeded quickly after the initial conversation between Dresser, Nixon, and Schwab on June 11. In this transaction Schwab exhibited the skill in bargaining for which he is famous, and Dresser and Nixon the compliance of men offered a possible means of escape from impending disaster. The Bethlehem Steel Company's 300,000 shares of stock had been acquired by the Morgan syndicate on August 16, 1901, at $24 a share, or for the aggregate sum of $7,200,000. The company when acquired for the shipbuilding combination had a bonded debt of $8,851,000, calling for interest payments of $517,550 a year. Schwab's first offer was to sell the stock for $9,000,000 cash plus some share of the common and preferred stock of the combination. It was evident at once that the Shipbuilding Company was in no position to pay cash. Dresser and Nixon finally offered, instead, $10,000,000 in 5-per-cent bonds to be a direct lien on the Bethlehem plant and other property, and a second lien on the properties of the United States Shipbuilding Company, and $9,000,000 in each class of shipbuilding stock. After cabled communication with J. P. Morgan, who was in Europe, Schwab agreed on condition that the stock offer be increased to $10,000,000 in each class, of which $2,500,000 in each class was to go to the Morgan syndicate as profits on the Bethlehem stock purchase. This stock Schwab later acquired for $75,000. After a general verbal understanding was reached, Mr. Max Pam, Schwab's attorney and associate in the operation, was called in to draw up a legally binding agreement. Mr. Pam later justified the unusual provisions of this agreement on the ground that he felt bound to protect his client, Schwab, against any untoward contingencies. The provisions, described hereafter, did this so completely that it is difficult to understand how Dresser and Nixon were persuaded to agree on their side, except on the theory that by July 2, when the contract was formally signed, they were ready to accept anything that promised to lighten the task that confronted them of finding purchasers for the shipbuilding bonds.

Meanwhile the United States Shipbuilding Company had been incorporated under the laws of New Jersey on June 17 by three clerks of the Corporation Trust Company who subscribed collectively for fifteen shares of the preferred and fifteen shares of the common stock and who on June 24 held their first meeting and elected as directors other clerks of the Corporation Trust Company, Frederick K. Seward, to serve for one year, Raymond Newman to serve for two years, and Louis B. Dailey to serve for three years. Howard K. Wood, one of the dummy incorporators, assigned to each of the dummy directors the necessary qualifying shares out of his five shares of common stock. On the same day the dummy directors of this corporation, whose capitalization was still only $3,000, none of it apparently actually paid in, solemnly received an offer from the promoter, Young, setting forth in detail the terms on which he was prepared to turn over to the company the shipbuilding and Bethlehem plants that were to be taken in. To take advantage of this offer they increased the capitalization of the company from the $20,000,000 announced in the circular of April 19 to $45,000,000, $20,000,000 in preferred and $25,000,000 in common stock. They then solemnly voted:

> Whereas, in the judgment of this Board the value of the properties . . . offered . . . is at least the par value of the stocks and bonds of this Company proposed to be issued therefor, to wit, the sum of $70,997,000, and said properties are necessary for the business of this company;
>
> Resolved, that said offer be and the same is hereby accepted.

The Shipbuilding properties were taken in on terms usual in such transactions, payments to be made in cash, bonds, and stock, with the added provision in the case of some of the plants that designated officers of the companies acquired should continue in the employ of the United States Shipbuilding Company for stated periods at designated salaries. The acquisition of the Bethlehem plant, however, was coupled with the following extraordinary provisions:

(1) The 300,000 shares of stock acquired were to be deposited with the New York Security and Trust Company under a mortgage or deed of trust which should be a first lien upon the stock and, subject to the priority of the mortgage to secure the $16,000,000 United States Shipbuilding Company bonds, a lien upon the property and plants covered by this $16,000,000 mortgage.

(2) The holders of the $10,000,000 Bethlehem bonds were to have the same voting power in the United States Shipbuilding Company, as though these were $10,000,000 in stock.

(3) As additional security the single bond of the Bethlehem Steel Company for $10,000,000 was to be deposited with the New York Security and Trust Company carrying 5 per cent interest, conditioned on the due payment of principal and interest of the other issue of $10,000,000 in bonds to be made over to Mr. Schwab.

(4) To insure the business success of the Bethlehem Company, the United States Shipbuilding Company was required to enter into a formal agreement: (a) that dividends should be paid on the stock of the Bethlehem Company at the annual rate of three dollars per share, "aggregating an annual dividend contribution of $900,000, and for that purpose [it should] supply and furnish said Bethlehem Steel Company . . . business and . . . means of earning to enable it to pay said annual dividends . . . or advance sufficient money . . . to make such annual dividend payments." (b) That the Bethlehem Company should be "protected in keeping on hand and maintaining cash or cash assets of not less than $4,000,000 cash value over and above its current business liabilities."

(5) To make doubly sure that, whatever might happen to the parent company, the Bethlehem property should be preserved intact, it was finally provided "that so long as any of said $10,000,000 bonds are outstanding said Bethlehem Steel Company shall always remain an independent and distinct corporation, and shall not be merged in or consolidated . . .

unless requested or consented to by the holders of not less than 75 per cent of said outstanding bonds."

An analysis of these provisions shows clearly the purpose aimed at by Pam in his desire "to protect his client." While Schwab nominally sold the Bethlehem plant to the United States Shipbuilding Company, he really retained complete control of it and at the same time acquired control of the Shipbuilding Company itself! By giving the $10,000,000 bonds the same voting power as stock, the organizers turned over to Schwab and his associates $30,000,000, or a clear majority of the total of $55,000,000 of voting securities. According to the terms of the mortgage securing the $10,000,000 bonds the New York Security and Trust Company, acting for Schwab, was to name three of the seven directors, while the directors of the Shipbuilding Company, also acting for Schwab, as things were arranged, named the other four. Schwab continued to control the Bethlehem Company as though it were his own private property, and at the same time was able, so far as he chose, also to control the policies of the United States Shipbuilding Company. This made the provisions guaranteeing dividends and unimpaired working capital quite superfluous, but their inclusion illustrates the thoroughness with which Pam saw to it that his client should receive everything, while he parted with nothing, so long as his $10,000,000 in bonds remained unpaid.

In the report of the receiver, which was submitted October 31, 1903, Schwab is severely criticized for his part in this transaction, but it would seem that the blame attaches rather to the promoter, John W. Young, to the underwriters, headed by Daniel Le Roy Dresser and his close associate in all these transactions, Lewis Nixon, and all the others who acted on behalf of the United States Shipbuilding Company, but seemed so culpably indifferent to its real interests. Schwab drove a hard bargain, but through it all he was the one participant who was to receive not a dollar of immediate profit from the organization of the combination. On the contrary, he was compelled to furnish the money to pay the Morgan syndicate for the Bethlehem stock. Having paid more than seven million dollars to acquire this stock, he could urge justification from a business point of view for imposing conditions that would preserve and even strengthen Bethlehem as a separate organization until the success of the shipbuilding combination was assured. The most significant aspect of the transaction is the illustration it affords of the way in which, under the corporation law of New Jersey (and the same is true of the laws of the other leading charter-granting states), a corporation with millions of nominal assets may be launched by men no one of whom is financially responsible or even more than dimly aware of the significance of the resolutions passed or of the property interests involved. In this instance no one of the men chiefly concerned had any great interest in the success over a term of years of the United States Shipbuilding Company. Young, the original promoter, expected to profit by receiving $140,500 of the cash for which the $9,000,000 bonds were to be sold and by marketing his share of the bonds and stock. Dresser was interested in the underwriting and sale of the bonds and agreed to Schwab's terms because he believed that acquisition of the Bethlehem would make the bonds attractive and enable him at least to minimize his loss and that of his Trust Company. Nixon sold the shipbuilding properties he controlled for $900,000 cash, $1,337,-000 in bonds, and over $2,000,000 in each class of stock. If the bonds could have been marketed at 90, as everyone confidently expected even after the public offering had failed, the arrangement would have been highly advantageous to him, whatever the ultimate value of the stock. The other shipyard owners were also more than repaid for their properties by the cash and bonds turned over to them, assuming the bonds to be worth at least 90, and therefore were little concerned over the long-run prospects of the new company. Finally, as has been indicated, Schwab parted with nothing to the United States Shipbuilding Company and was in a position to withdraw the Bethlehem property without serious loss at any time he became convinced that this was to his financial advantage. Launched primarily as a means of permitting the promoter, the underwriters, and the venders of the constituent properties to make a profit from it, whatever its own ultimate fate, the United States Shipbuilding Company was almost predestined to end in a receivership. We must now describe the means by which Dresser and Nixon secured the money needed to pay for the properties to be acquired during the first weeks of August, the later stages of the underwriting, the causes of the failure of the company within less than a year after its inception, and the reorganization that followed.

With the failure of the public offering of the Shipbuilding bonds, and the unwillingness of the French underwriters to make good their pledge to take the $4,250,000 of these bonds which had been assigned to them, the burden of actually providing the money indispensable to the organization of the combination fell almost entirely on Dresser, his faithful associate, Nixon, and the Trust Company of the Republic. Both men, on the basis of the statements sent them from Paris by Young, confidently believed that the French payments were only delayed. Mr. C. B. Alexander, of the law firm of Alexander & Green, joined Young in Paris in July, and, while he was unable to secure any payments, he did obtain the personal notes of the underwriters due on October 6, which he considered good. Schwab had made it one of the conditions of the sale of the Bethlehem stock that "said Shipbuilding Company shall have been duly purchased and become possessed of the property and assets or the capital stock, or both, of said 'Subsidiary Companies.'" All of the $8,100,000 that was to have been paid for the $9,000,000 bonds was not actually required as purchase money, but the minimum amount necessary to satisfy the shipyard owners was $6,000,000 and in addition $1,500,000 was to be placed in the treasury of the Shipbuilding Company as working capital. The bonds being unsalable, Dresser's only recourse to supplement receipts from the participants in the American underwriting was to secure loans on the basis of the bonds and the unpaid underwriting subscriptions. In this situation Dresser, with Nixon as indorser, proceeded to borrow from the Trust Company of the Republic and from other financial institutions on the guaranty of that company, the amount needed. When their ability to secure loans on their own credit was exhausted, they appealed for aid to Schwab's counsel, Pam, Schwab himself having gone to Europe. According to contemporary accounts, Pam joined them in asking Mr. George W. Perkins, who represented J. P. Morgan & Company in the absence of Mr. Morgan, for a loan of $2,500,000 on the security of Shipbuilding bonds and the French underwriting. This was refused, but Perkins finally agreed to loan $700,000 to each of three designated trust companies with the understanding that they would in turn loan it to Dresser on the proposed security. The companies named by Dresser were the Knickerbocker, the Manhattan, and the Trust Company of the Republic. The Manhattan Trust Company refused to accept the deposit on the proposed terms, but the other companies did so, and Dresser was later able to negotiate a similar loan from the New York Security and Trust Company, of which both Schwab and Perkins were directors. By these means the necessary $6,000,000 were assembled by August 11, $3,672,187.50 on the promissory notes of Dresser indorsed by Nixon either from the Trust Company of the Republic or from other trust companies on its guaranty, and the remaining $2,327,812.50 from the American underwriters, including $250,000 subscribed by the Trust Company of the Republic itself. Payment having been made to the shipyard owners and their plants having been acquired, the Bethlehem transfer was effected on the following day, August 12. At the same time the Trust Company of the Republic credited the United States Shipbuilding Company with the needed $1,500,000 working capital. As the Shipbuilding Company soon had to draw on this credit balance, and the Trust Company was short of funds, Dresser and Nixon had to borrow on August 30 and September 4 and 5 the $1,500,000 from New York banks on their notes secured by Shipbuilding bonds and guaranteed by the Trust Company of the Republic.

The shipbuilding combination having been launched with Nixon as its president, Dresser himself went to Paris in September to try to collect the notes representing the French underwriting. He soon convinced himself that these were valueless and so cabled the Trust Company of the Republic early in October. Meantime his associates on the executive committee of the company had become alarmed over the situation. Mr. Stuyvesant Fish, chairman of the committee, called upon Nixon in Dresser's absence to take care of the $4,000,000 odd notes of which he was indorser. Nixon explained that he had acted entirely under Dresser's directions and could do nothing except make over for the protection of the company the shipbuilding securities left in his control by Young, the promoter. A syndicate was then organized headed by Mr. George R. Sheldon, which took over from the Trust Company of the Republic $5,500,000 of the Shipbuilding bonds together with $2,750,000 preferred stock and $5,500,000 common stock as a bonus, paying for the bonds at the rate of 75 and agreeing to share with the Trust Company any profit over and above their expenses on their resale prior to January 29, 1904, when the syndicate was to be dissolved. While there were undoubtedly other motives leading to the organization of this syndicate besides expectation of profit from the sale of the shipbuilding securities, it nevertheless indicates how confident careful business men still were, in October, 1902, that the shipbuilding combination, after weathering its early difficulties, would prove successful. It was, in fact, only through the investigations into the financial standing of the different companies which the Sheldon Syndicate itself inaugurated, after it had taken over the securities, that the gross disparity between the claims as to value of plants and earning capacity made in the prospectus and the actual facts became known.

While the action of the Sheldon Syndicate saved the Trust Company of the Republic from bankruptcy, it did not save it from crushing loss in consequence of its connection with the shipbuilding flotation. In his annual report for 1903, State Bank Examiner Kilborn described the conditions he found when he made his examination in the autumn of that year. Dresser and Nixon appeared as borrowers from the company on their personal notes of $1,750,000, while the Trust Company had guaranteed their loans from other banks and trust companies to the extent of $2,000,000 more—all on the basis of United States Shipbuilding securities. The loan to Dresser was ten times the amount permitted to an officer of the company under the New York law. Vigorous measures were taken, and within a few months, through money supplied by the Sheldon Syndicate, and by Dresser and his friends, all of the notes were taken up. But when the account was balanced it appeared that the Trust Company had lost through the shipbuilding operation almost $900,000, or its entire surplus of $500,000 and nearly one-half of its capital. It was so discredited in the financial community that its directors decided that it would be better to reorganize under another name. As the Commonwealth Trust Company under more conservative management it in time regained its lost prestige.

The principal loser in connection with the shipbuilding operation was Daniel Leroy Dresser himself. He had been so confident that the Trust Company of the Republic would make large profits from the underwriting and its other business that he invested more than $500,000 in the stock of the Trust Company, thereby weakening his own financial position at a period when credit was difficult to obtain. In the suit for $3,000,000 damages, which he brought on April 26, 1905, against the Mercantile Trust Company, the law firm of Alexander & Green, and others, for losses in connection with the shipbuilding underwriting suffered by himself and the Trust Company of the Republic, he charged that he had been grossly deceived by John W. Young, John J. McCook, and others in regard to several different aspects of the undertaking, and that his credit had suffered with that of the Trust Company of the Republic to an extent that caused the bankruptcy of Dresser & Company with very heavy loss to himself and his creditors. This suit dragged on for several years, but was finally settled out of court in 1908 by the payment to Dresser of $200,000. On March 16 of the same year he was arrested on the charge of larceny, brought by John W. Young, who claimed that the shipbuilding securities belonging to him had been taken by Dresser and never accounted for. He was soon released under the statute of limitations. Although Dresser was discharged from bankruptcy in 1907 on paying $1,000,000 to his creditors whose claims aggregated $1,400,000, he never succeeded in restoring his fortunes. On July 10, 1915, after writing his lawyer that "the nervous strain has become so great that I can bear it no longer," he committed suicide in his fraternity house in New York, a victim of his own imprudence and the excesses of high finance, in which he had become involved.

The Shipbuilding fiasco was not without its political aspect. Among those who had participated in the American underwriting was Governor Benjamin Odell, who took $188,000 of the bonds at the issue price of 90, together with 500 shares each of the preferred and common stock. On March 9, 1904, these bonds were sold at auction at 26 and the stock at $50 for the lot of 500 shares of preferred and $10 for the lot of 500 shares of common. Having established his loss by this means, the Governor brought suit to recover against the underwriting syndicate, now represented by the Commonwealth Trust Company, on August 17, 1904. This suit was dropped in April, 1905, on the payment by the defendants, as stated in the New York *Tribune* for February 4, 1906, of $75,000. Similar suits were brought by other subscribers to the underwriting, but were unsuccessful.

While suits and countersuits to the number of a score or more were being pressed in the courts for several years after the Shipbuilding Company was organized, that company itself was dissolved and its assets distributed with unusual dispatch. As already stated, it was forced into the hands of a receiver within one year after its organization. The causes of the failure were inadequate working capital for the constituent companies, excessive fixed charges in relation to earnings and the unwillingness of Schwab to allow the profits of the Bethlehem Company, which were substantial, to be used to pay interest and other charges falling more properly on the earnings of the shipbuilding plants. In the report of the receiver and Mr. Dewing's chapters already referred to, full accounts are given of these different factors. It will suffice for our purpose to summarize the more important aspects.

In the prospectus put out when the bonds were offered to

the public in June, 1902, the combined working capital credited to the constituent shipbuilding companies was $5,000,000. A report made as of July 31, 1902, scaled this down to $3,278,798.48. More careful scrutiny of the actual situation after the shipbuilding combination was organized as a going concern in the fall of 1902 showed that even this smaller sum was largely illusory. The yards were found to have debts in excess of $2,000,000. For example, the Crescent Shipyard Company, instead of having a surplus, had an actual deficit of over $400,000. Even worse, the Union Iron Works, supposed by Nixon to have a surplus, most of it working capital, of over $1,000,000, showed instead an actual deficit of $1,400,000. As a consequence the shipbuilding plants, instead of turning in revenue to the parent company, were from the outset eager claimants for financial assistance. During the year ending June 30, 1903, the parent company was forced to advance to the shipbuilding plants over $1,000,000 of its treasury surplus and received back in earnings less than $61,000.

Added to the advances that were required by the shipbuilding plants were the overhead expenses and fixed charges that must be met. Although Nixon was nominal president, he had only limited control. The plants had been leased back to the old companies and their officers were still directing their policies, but not always in the interest of economy and efficiency. Moreover, Max Pam, Schwab's representative, was made chairman of the board on September 22, 1902, at a salary of $18,000, and friction between him and Nixon became so acute in the ensuing months that Nixon resigned the presidency in June, 1903. The fixed charges amounted in round figures to $1,225,000, $725,000 interest on the outstanding Shipbuilding bonds, and $500,000 interest on the Bethlehem bonds.

While the earnings of the shipbuilding plants were far below the estimates when the combination was organized—that is, as calculated for the receiver only $833,458.74 for the year ending July 31, 1903, instead of the estimated $2,225,000—the earnings of the Bethlehem Company exceeded substantially the estimate of $1,500,000, amounting for the same year to more than $2,000,000. If Bethlehem had really been controlled by the United States Shipbuilding Company and its earnings expended as the interests of the parent company demanded, failure might have been avoided. Instead, as the facts about the financial situation and earning capacity of the shipbuilding plants became known, Schwab appears to have decided that a reorganization was essential if his interests were to be protected. At their meeting April 7, 1903, the executive committee of the Shipbuilding Company, dominated by Schwab's representatives, authorized the Bethlehem Company to make expenditures for improvements aggregating $2,802,000, although the financial situation of the Shipbuilding Company was rapidly becoming desperate. When this resolution came before the full board on April 14, Nixon demanded that it be amended so as to provide clearly that such expenditures should be contingent on the payment of the $900,000 dividends on the Bethlehem stock, in accordance with the guaranty of the Shipbuilding Company. His protest was disregarded and the resolution was approved without any provision for dividends. From that date until June 22, it was impossible for Nixon to get together a quorum of either the executive committee or the board of directors of the United States Shipbuilding Company, and he later testified that Schwab told him that he had instructed certain members not to attend meetings. In desperation he addressed an eleventh-hour appeal, under date of June 27, 1903, to Mr. E. M. McIlvain, the president of the Bethlehem Company, demanding that that company pay over to the Shipbuilding Company before June 30 not less than $362,500 on account of dividends, to enable that company to pay the interest on its own bonds due on July 1. No attention was paid to this demand and the Shipbuilding Company was forced to default payment.

The receiver appointed to take over control of the Shipbuilding Company was James Smith, Jr., prominent as a New Jersey politician, rather than as a financier. He employed as his counsel Mr. Samuel Untermeyer, whose remarkable gift for effective presentation is illustrated in the receiver's report of October 31, 1903.

Meantime the leading members of the Sheldon Syndicate had constituted themselves a reorganization committee, with Max Pam as a member, and had submitted, on May 25, a plan of reorganization that would have been highly advantageous to Schwab. This was vigorously opposed by Untermeyer representing an independent Bondholders' Protective Committee, headed by Mr. Roland R. Conklin, as well as the receiver after the latter's appointment. In the report of October 31 the receiver recommended the sale of the Crescent and Harlan and Hollingsworth yards and the filing of a suit against the Bethlehem Company to procure the appointment of a receiver for it, who should operate it for the benefit of the Shipbuilding Company. There ensued several months of litigation and conference, in the course of which the receiver was won over to a somewhat different view of the situation from that maintained by his counsel, Untermeyer. While he was unwilling to accept the plan of the reorganization committee, he gave out an interview which appeared in the financial papers of January 29, 1904, in which he is quoted as saying: "Mr. Schwab has everything that is worth anything in the company in the Bethlehem plant. He wants to get it back, and why shouldn't he? He paid $7,500,000 for it, and since he bought it $4,000,000 of profit was accumulated, so that the plant is worth $11,500,000." This called forth a sharp rejoinder from Untermeyer. While he complimented Smith for his conduct as receiver, he insisted that the holders of the Shipbuilding bonds had a first claim on Bethlehem as well as on the other plants. In regard to Bethlehem's withholding its earnings from the parent company he said: "Why should the people to whom these earnings belong permit them to be withheld by sheer brute force? It is the most brazen and shameless exhibition in financial history. It is almost a crime to tolerate such an outrage." A few days before, the receiver had addressed a letter to the reorganization committee, which appears in the circular which it caused to be published on February 4. In it he says that he had "for some time past been considering a modification of the plan of reorganization of the United States Shipbuilding Company, which would be likely to be acceptable to both classes of bondholders." In reality this plan appears to have been agreed to in conference by the representatives of the two sides before it was announced and in consequence there was no serious opposition to it, especially as the reorganization committee controlled the Bethlehem bonds and $12,000,000, or over 80 per cent, of the outstanding Shipbuilding bonds.

The plan adopted for reorganizing the Shipbuilding and Bethlehem companies was simple but drastic. A new company, the Bethlehem Company of the present day, was to be organized with a capital of $15,000,000 preferred stock, $15,000,000 common stock, and $3,000,000 of ten-year 6 per cent bonds. The holders of the $14,500,000 Shipbuilding bonds on which $725,000 interest was overdue were to receive pro rata $6,000,000 of the preferred stock, $9,000,000 of the common stock, and $420,000 cash to cover their contingent expenses. The holders of the $10,000,000 Bethlehem bonds on which $500,000 interest remained unpaid were to receive $9,000,000 of the preferred stock, $6,000,000 of the common stock, and $630,000 cash for contingent expenses. Each group was to have the privilege of subscribing for $1,500,000 of the 6 per cent bonds at 87½ and an underwriting syndicate was organized to take any bonds not subscribed for. The cash redemption price finally put upon the Shipbuilding bonds by the reorganization committee and approved by the court was $156.25 for each $1,000 bond. The preferred and common stockholders of the United States Shipbuilding Company received nothing, and the former mortgages, except the underlying mortgages on the Bethlehem property, were cancelled, so that the new company started off in full control of all the assets of the old companies free and clear of other encumbrances.

The brief career of the United States Shipbuilding Company illustrated all of the different ways in which advantage may be taken of the lax provisions of the corporation law of an American state to offer the public securities far in excess of any tangible value or earning power behind them. There was the unscrupulous promoter intent on immediate personal profit and ready grossly to misrepresent the value of the properties which he combined. There were the unscrupulous owners of these properties eager to get more for them than they knew them to be worth. There was the over-sanguine underwriter, dazzled by the prospect of large profits and willing to risk the funds belonging to the trust company he controlled without verification of the many misleading and untruthful statements that were made to him. Once committed, the underwriter and his associates ran true to type. They were entirely unwilling to draw back, while yet there was time, and confess their error in ever supporting such an unsound project. But they did not hesitate to resort to the most reckless and questionable methods to carry it out. There was even the naïve reliance on the French underwriting backed by the myth of the unlimited savings of French peasants, once available for Russian bonds and now represented as avid for American industrial securities, and the demonstration of the willingness of reputable, or at any rate titled, Frenchmen to lend their names to enterprises of which they knew little in the hope of getting something for nothing. Finally there was the refusal of one of the participants to sacrifice his own financial interest to save the company which he controlled from bankruptcy, and the reorganization which allowed nothing to the holders of the stock, whether preferred or common. The one striking dissimilarity between this flotation and others equally unsound that occurred in the same period was that in this case the public responded so feebly to the exaggerated promises of the prospectus that practically the entire loss fell upon the underwriter and his associates and the promoter. Under the laws of the United Kingdom or of Germany such a promotion would have rendered the participants liable to severe criminal penalties. Although the details of the operation were given unusual publicity, no change resulted in the corporation laws of New Jersey or any other state in consequence. This restatement of the story will serve little purpose if it does not increase interest in the proposals for reforming our American corporation laws, which are presented in Chapter XXVII.

CHAPTER XIII

THE UNITED STATES STEEL CORPORATION

THE United States Steel Corporation is an even better example than the tobacco trust of a "combination of combinations." In order to comprehend how it developed it is necessary to recall some of the earlier history of the steel industry. Prior to 1898 steel was an actively competitive industry. Although there had been numerous gentlemen's agreements and pools controlling a large part of the production of steel rails, billets, wire nails, and other products at various earlier periods, one of their outstanding characteristics was the frequency with which they collapsed. In the late 'nineties, however, combination began with a rush, so that within three years something more than half of the industry was in the hands of less than a dozen concerns. The most important of the consolidations, the year of organization, and the security issues authorized at the time of organization are shown in Tables X and XI below.

All these concerns may be grouped into two general categories on the basis of products: those manufacturing crude, semifinished, and heavy-finished products, and those manufacturing lighter and more highly finished goods. The second group bought most of its steel from the first, so that there was for a time little or no competition between the groups. Of the companies which later entered the United States Steel Corporation, the Federal, Carnegie, and National were in the first group; the other concerns were concentrating on more highly finished goods.

From the standpoint of financial backing there were three chief groups in the subsequent Corporation subsidiaries: Mr. Carnegie behind his own company; Mr. J. P. Morgan behind the Federal, the American Bridge, and the National Tube; and Judge W. H. Moore behind the National Steel Company, and

TABLE X

LEADING CONSOLIDATIONS IN THE IRON AND STEEL INDUSTRY 1898–1900[a]

A. Consolidations later merged into the United States Steel Corporation[b]

Name and year of organization	Preferred stock	Common stock	Bonds
1898			
American Steel and Wire Co. of Illinois[c]	$ 12,000,000	$ 12,000,000	....
Federal Steel Co.	100,000,000	100,000,000	$ 30,217,179
American Tin Plate Co.	20,000,000	30,000,000	273,000
1899			
American Steel and Wire Co. of New Jersey	40,000,000	50,000,000	130,656
American Steel Hoop Co.	14,000,000	19,000,000	....
National Steel Co.	27,000,000	32,000,000	2,561,000
National Tube Co.	40,000,000	40,000,000	....
1900			
American Bridge Co.	35,000,000	35,000,000	156,000
American Sheet Steel Co.	26,000,000	26,000,000	2,000,000
Carnegie Co. of New Jersey[d]	....	160,000,000	185,081,813[e]
Shelby Steel Tube Co.	6,000,000	9,000,000	....
Total	$320,000,000	$513,000,000	$220,419,648

[a] *Report of the Commissioner of Corporations on the Steel Industry*, part i, pp. 80–81.

[b] As noted in the text, in most cases practically all of the authorized securities were actually issued. The most conspicuous exceptions in this list were the Federal Steel Co., which issued rather less than $100,000,000 of stock; the American Bridge Co., which issued originally about $30,500,000 of each class; and the American Tin Plate Co., which retained in its treasury about $2,000,000 preferred and $2,000,000 common stock.

[c] This Illinois company was in 1899 merged into the New Jersey concern of the same name.

[d] This company was a consolidation of interests, most of which were previously affiliated and not competing.

[e] Including, in addition to the $160,000,000 bond issue of the Carnegie Company of New Jersey, $25,081,813 of underlying indebtedness, this including purchase-money obligations, and not merely bonds.

TABLE XI

LEADING CONSOLIDATIONS IN THE IRON AND STEEL INDUSTRY 1898–1900
(*Continued*)

B. Consolidations not subsequently merged into the United States Steel Corporation[a]

Name and year of organization	Preferred stock	Common stock	Bonds
1899			
American Car and Foundry Co.	$ 30,000,000	$ 30,000,000	....
American Iron and Steel Mfg. Co.	3,000,000	17,000,000	....
Empire Steel and Iron Co.	5,000,000	5,000,000	....
National Enameling and Stamping Co.	10,000,000	20,000,000	$ 600,000
Pressed Steel Car Co.	12,500,000	12,500,000	....
Republic Iron and Steel Co.	25,000,000	30,000,000	....
Sloss Sheffield Steel and Iron Co.	10,000,000	10,000,000	3,835,000
U. S. Cast-Iron Pipe and Foundry Co.	15,000,000	15,000,000	....
Virginia Iron, Coal and Coke Co.	....	10,000,000	10,000,000
1900			
Crucible Steel Company of America	25,000,000	25,000,000	....
Total	$135,500,000	$174,500,000	$14,435,000

[a] Several of the concerns in this group had not issued the full amount of their capitalization. The most conspicuous instances were the National Enameling and Stamping Co., which had issued about $21,700,000 of its stock; the Sloss Sheffield Steel and Iron Co., the issued stock of which was $14,200,000; and the Republic Iron and Steel Co., which retained in its treasury about $7,500,000 of its stock.

the Plate, Sheet and Hoop combinations. The financial connections of the Moore concerns were an important cause of the purchase from the National Steel Company, a primary concern, of the crude and semifinished products which the other three secondary companies needed. This result did not work out in the case of the Morgan companies because the secondary concerns were so far from the Federal that they found it more advantageous to buy from Carnegie. The American Steel and Wire Company, which was not affiliated with any of the financial groups mentioned, bought most of its "raw" material from the Federal. The degree of dependence involved in this relationship and the possibilities of profit offered by other arrangements were such that early in 1900 the Steel and Wire Company began to plan to make pig iron and steel. The National Tube (Morgan) also was intent on becoming independent from the Carnegie. Confronted with this probable loss of market, the obvious procedure for the primary group was to enter into the field of highly finished goods, and this they promptly planned to do. Otherwise stated, both groups were endeavoring to "integrate" their companies—that is, they were working to control their product from the raw material of iron ore and coking coal to the finished product and to secure all the advantages of large-scale production. As a matter of fact, integration had been one of the ends in view in connection with the organization of several of the companies listed above, but experience seemed to be showing that from their organizers' point of view the process had not gone far enough.

Other causes of these early combinations, in the opinion of the federal Commissioner of Corporations, were the desires to restrict competition and to secure large profits from the creation of great quantities of inflated securities.[1] Of course not all the causes operated in every case. In the Carnegie Company, for example, promoters' profits from excessive security issues played no part, and in the Plate and Sheet Companies there was no attempt at integration. The latter two concerns were excellent examples of the desire to restrain competition, and the chief reason for their organization at this particular time was stated to be the intense competition that existed in those lines in 1897 and at least part of 1898.

But as suggested above, the hoped-for elimination or radical reduction of competition was not secured. When the

[1] *Report of the Commissioner of Corporations on the Steel Industry,* part i, p. 82.

National Tube Company decided to cease purchasing crude steel from the Carnegie Company, Carnegie announced his intention of erecting at Conneaut Harbor the finest tube works in the world. Moreover, Carnegie was said to have plans for constructing a railroad from Pittsburgh to the Atlantic seaboard which would probably have seriously cut into the receipts of the Pennsylvania Railroad, dominated by Morgan. Consequently, it seemed likely that a most serious trade war was in the making, so much so that the daily newspapers and the trade journals were speaking of an impending "battle of the giants." The federal government later contended in its suit against the Corporation that the competition of 1897 and 1898 was "destructive" only of excessive profits and cited the cost and price figures from the Carnegie Company, the minutes of the Carnegie Company, the annual report for 1897 of the Illinois Steel Company, and the personal testimony of officials of four small companies in proof thereof.[1] The Corporation replied that the Carnegie costs really did not include depreciation and replacement charges and that consequently its alleged profits were nonexistent. Moreover, Judge Gary testified that the Illinois Company's annual report was so far from showing the real situation that papers for a petition in bankruptcy were actually drawn up though not filed.[2] Whatever may be the truth touching this argument the fact remains that the competition of 1897 hastened a number of combinations, and that the specter of its repetition in 1900 caused considerable alarm among steel producers.

The relative abilities of the recent combinations to live through a fight of the size and character that threatened can be briefly stated. The Carnegie Company was just about impregnable. It had no watered stock, possessed ample cash resources, and the finest organization of practical steel-makers in the country. The Moore concerns, at the other extreme, had been so heavily over-capitalized, and their backing was so distinctly speculative, that the beginning of hostilities

[1] U. S. *v.* U. S. Steel. *Brief for U. S.* before District Court of N. J., p. 221 *et seq.*, and *Brief for U. S. before* U. S. Supreme Court, vol. i, p. 18 *et seq.*

[2] *Brief for U. S. Steel Corporation* before U. S. Supreme Court, p. 80 *et seq.*

would have had a disastrous effect upon the value of their securities on the market. The Morgan companies, Federal National Tube, and American Bridge, were not so heavily over-capitalized as the Moore companies and had, of course, excellent financial support. The Morgan interests, however, had extensive investments elsewhere, especially in railroads, so that they were not at all eager for a fight. Particularly were all the others desirous of avoiding a contest with Carnegie, a point emphasized by Gary as the "opinion of a great many different people" when he told the Stanley Committee that " . . . it is not at all certain that if the old management or the management which was in force at one time had continued, the Carnegie Company would not have driven entirely out of business every steel company in the United States." [1] It must be noted, however, that the financiers saw an opportunity for great gain in the situation if it could be turned in the proper direction. The public was now buying securities in great volume, so that if a new combination could be formed it might be possible to avert the impending war and reap another crop of promoters' profits. Obviously the new combination would definitely limit competition.

These financial considerations to some of the interested individuals were less impelling than the opportunity they believed they saw for achieving a thoroughly integrated concern. Among these were Gary, at the time president of the Federal Steel Company, and C. M. Schwab, chief lieutenant of Carnegie. Since Gary had for some time been convinced that the Federal needed to be converted into what he called a more "rounded-out proposition," he had frequently urged the acquisition of the Carnegie upon Morgan. Early in 1899 Mr. H. C. Frick, at that time Carnegie's partner, approached Gary with a proposition that the Federal buy the Carnegie Company. The negotiations got so far as the drawing up of memoranda assigning values to the Carnegie property, but finally came to nothing. One explanation of their failure was

[1] *Hearings before the Committee on Investigation of the U. S. Steel Corporation*, H. R. No. 1127, 62nd Congress, 2nd Session, 1911, vol. i, p. 220. Hereafter this document will be cited as the *Stanley Hearings*.

that Frick refused to agree that the whole Carnegie organization, including himself, should go with the bargain. Another explanation was that no agreement could be reached on the financial arrangements. The Carnegie partners had agreed on a price of $250,000,000 for their properties and the approximately one-fourth interest in the H. C. Frick Coke Company owned by the Carnegie Company, payment to be one-half in cash and one-half in fifty-year, 5-per-cent gold bonds. The Federal interests, it is claimed, refused this because they had hoped to pay a considerable part of the bill in stock.[1] Later in the same year W. H. Moore, together with Frick and Mr. Henry Phipps of the Carnegie firm, secured an option on Carnegie's entire holdings in the industry, including slightly more than one-half of the Carnegie Company and slightly more than one-fourth of the Frick Coke Company. The price to be paid Carnegie for his holdings was $157,950,000. For the purposes of this transaction the Carnegie concern was valued at $250,000,000 and the Frick Coke Company at $70,000,000. According to the story current at the time, the Mellon interests of Pittsburgh offered to put up half the sum necessary to secure Carnegie's properties, but Frick could not persuade Morgan to advance the remainder, roughly $80,000,000.[2] Not all of the details concerning this Moore-Frick-Phipps option were agreed upon by the principal individuals concerned, but from it and the earlier negotiations between Frick and Gary some notion may be secured as to what Morgan considered unfavorable terms upon which to secure the Carnegie properties. Thus the matter stood in the closing months of 1900.

But in December of that year, at a dinner at which Morgan was a guest and Schwab the chief speaker, the latter presented an argument for a new combination which would control its product from ore to finished articles, secure all the advantages of the most advanced technical organization, and expand its

[1] Cf. Tarbell, Ida M., *Life of Elbert H. Gary,* p. 107, and Bridge, J. H., *Inside History of the Carnegie Steel Company,* p. 300.

[2] Cf. the testimony of W. C. Temple to the Stanley Committee of Congress in 1911, *Stanley Hearings,* vol. iii, p. 1724.

activities into the international market. Possibly the address fired Morgan's imagination; possibly he had become convinced of the necessity of preventing a steel war; possibly Gary had at last brought him around to the view that the Federal Steel Company was not the "rounded-out proposition" they had both hoped to construct. At any rate, only a few days later, he requested Schwab to ascertain the terms on which Carnegie would sell. Since the latter was really anxious to retire from the steel business and devote the remainder of his life to various philanthropic projects, he made a price that Morgan accepted. At the time Carnegie believed that the Carnegie Steel Company, which since the spring of 1900 had included the Frick Coke Company, was sold to the United States Steel Corporation for $420,000,000 in securities, of which his personal share was $213,000,000. As a matter of fact the Corporation paid $492,006,160 in securities. It will be recalled that the previous year the aggregate price of the Carnegie and Frick Companies had been set at $320,000,000 and that in 1899 the price made to the Federal for the Carnegie Company and one-fourth of the Frick Company was only $250,000,000. The very great difference in these figures forces the Bureau of Corporations to the conclusion that Morgan had raised his price in order to eliminate Carnegie.[1]

Thus it is seen that the three major considerations which had led to the earlier combinations also played a decisive part in the "combination of combinations," but it is interesting to note that Gary later testified that the "dominating factor" in his action at the time was his interest in the development of an extensive export trade.[2] All three of the motives were realized in what must have been a highly satisfactory fashion to the Corporation's organizers. Among its assets were enormous quantities of the raw materials of the industry, railway and steamship lines in which to transport them, and the coking plants, blast furnaces, rolling mills, etc., necessary for the manufacture of every sort of iron and steel product. Com-

[1] *Report of the Commissioner of Corporations on the Steel Industry*, part i, p. 163.

[2] *Stanley Hearings*, vol. i, p. 104.

petition was certainly lessened by the combination into one concern of more than half the steel business of the country. Promoters' profits realized by the banking syndicate were computed to have been about $62,500,000, a net amount realized on the sale of 649,987 shares of preferred stock and 649,988 shares of common after deducting $25,000,000 cash capital provided the Corporation by the syndicate and $3,000,000 spent for various purposes during the organization by the syndicate.[1]

The number of shares received by the syndicate immediately arouses the suspicion that here, as in earlier combinations, the security issue was greatly inflated. Later investigations have justified this opinion beyond reasonable doubt. The most trustworthy attempt to measure the amount of this inflation is that of the Bureau of Corporations. According to its calculation[2] the total capitalization with which the Steel Corporation was launched was $1,402,846,817. The total investment in tangible property alone shown by the Bureau's historical analysis was $676,000,000, indicating an excess capitalization, part of which might of course be credited to good will, of $726,846,817. The total value indicated by the market prices of the securities prior to organization of the Corporation was found to be $793,000,000, indicating an excess capitalization of $609,846,817. Finally the total value of tangible property as estimated by the departments of the business was $682,000,000, leaving an excess of $720,846,817, part of which again might be credited to good will.

Additional evidence of the purpose of the organizers to dominate the steel industry was shown by their acquisition for the Corporation of properties assuring control over the essential raw materials upon which it depended, particularly coking coal and iron ore. In the original syndicate agreement of February 26, 1901, relative to the organization of the steel combination it was proposed to include the following concerns: Carnegie, Federal, National Steel, National Tube,

[1] *Report of the Commissioner of Corporations on the Steel Industry,* part i, p. 244.

[2] Part i, p. 239.

American Steel and Wire of New Jersey, and the Sheet, Hoop, and Tin Plate trusts. But by the time the underwriting agreement of April 1 was drawn up the plans had been expanded to include a number of others of which the Lake Superior Consolidated Iron Mines, the Bessemer Steamship Company, and the American Bridge Company were the most important. The ore holdings of the first-named concern were estimated in 1901 at from 300,000,000 to over 400,000,000 tons and probably constituted 40 per cent of the Corporation's ore resources at the time organization was completed.[1] Among the other acquisitions at this time were a one-sixth interest in the Pittsburgh Steamship Company and in the Oliver Iron Mining Company (the other five-sixths of both had been secured in the purchase of Carnegie). The ore properties brought in with the Oliver concern were less extensive than those of the Lake Superior Company, but were extremely valuable because of their high quality.

The next important addition to the new combination was the Shelby Steel Tube Company, made in the summer of 1901. This concern manufactured drawn or seamless tubing and controlled so large a portion of that product that for a time it might fairly have been termed a trust. The National Tube at first manufactured different types of tubing, but later went into the seamless field and cut into the business of the Shelby heavily. The purpose of acquiring the Shelby was to eliminate its competition and to secure certain patents.

In November of 1901 the Corporation added to the large quantities of coke properties that had been acquired with the Carnegie Company 50,000 acres of coking and fuel-coal property in the Pocahontas coal region, and thus in the judgment of its officers brought its estimated tonnage of the former to an aggregate equal at the rate of consumption in 1901 to sixty years' supply. Notwithstanding this official view, more coke properties were bought and leased in practically every year covered by the Bureau of Corporation's reports. Some of these

[1] Curiously enough, these ore properties seem to have been overlooked in the earlier plans. Cf. G. Harvey, *Henry Clay Frick, The Man,* pp. 261-267, for an interesting and amusing account of the details of the transaction.

properties were brought in by transactions primarily designed to secure manufacturing establishments, as will appear shortly, but those involving the Hecla Coke Company, the Colonial Coke Company tract, and numerous others that added thousands of acres of coking coal land, lend support to the idea that domination of the steel industry was being sought.

For well over a year after the absorption of Shelby Tube no other manufacturing company of importance was taken into the Corporation, but in November of 1902, almost simultaneously with the news of the merger of the Union and Sharon Steel Companies, came the further announcement that United States Steel had absorbed the new Union Steel, as the merger was designated. Though a small concern as compared with the major components of the trust, the Union was well integrated. Not only did it have valuable ore property in the Lake Superior district and long-term contracts for other ore, but also it had acquired large tracts of coking and steam coal land in the Connellsville region and elsewhere, limestone property near the Sharon plant, and railroad terminal property. To these raw material assets it had added blast furnaces and rod, sheet, wire and pipe mills, and open hearth furnaces were under construction. Thus equipped and under the forceful direction of H. C. Frick, one of its chief backers, the Union was generally believed to be in a position to provide real competition for the Corporation.

Again some eighteen months elapsed before another major acquisition of a manufacturing concern was made. This time it was the Clairton Steel Company, controlled by the Crucible Steel Company. For a considerable period the Clairton had been losing money; in fact, it was in the hands of receivers at the time of its transfer in May, 1904. Why, then, was it desired? In the first place, there was considerable valuable equipment in blast furnaces, open-hearth furnaces, and mills of various sorts. The cause of the company's difficulties was apparently its need for several millions of working capital that the Crucible was not in a position to supply. But among the assets of the Clairton were ore properties in the Mesabi range with an estimated deposit of 4,000,000 tons and a lease on another 3,500,000 tons in that region, 20,000 acres of ore land in the Marquette range, and 2,644 acres of coking-coal land in Fayette County, Pennsylvania. There seems little doubt that on these last properties the attentions of the directors of the trust were centered.

Moreover, the Corporation picked up small parcels of ore land not attached to any steel concern at every opportunity. Among these minor transactions were the acquisition of the Wick mine in 1902, the Arcturus in 1904, and the Whiteside mining lease in 1905. Somewhat larger operations involved the leasing of the properties of the Chemung Iron Company in 1903 and the Canisteo Mining Company in 1905. The deposits held by these concerns were estimated at 70,000,000 and 100,000,000 tons, respectively. Opinions have differed sharply as to whether these acquisitions were dictated by keen business prudence or were a reflection of a desire and intent to monopolize. The Bureau of Corporations was convinced that the second alternative provided the correct explanation. In reaching this conclusion its investigators were strongly influenced by certain events in 1907, particularly the Hill ore leases, to which we shall return. At this point, however, we wish to introduce an incident in the early financial history of the Corporation upon which there is by now little or no conflict of judgments—*viz.,* the so-called bond-conversion plan.

This rearrangement of the Corporation's securities seems to have originated in the realization by its directors of the unfortunate result on the stock-market status of their securities of the company's enormous capitalization. The plan did not pretend to eliminate any "water," the existence of which was officially denied, but it evidently was hoped that it would exert some stabilizing influence, at least on the preferred stock. Conservative investors regarded that stock as decidedly speculative in spite of the 7-per-cent dividends it was paying, so that the distribution of it by the banking interests who held it in large quantities was hampered and delayed. If a considerable block of it could be converted into 5-per-cent bonds there would be a saving to the Corporation in the difference between the rates, and at the same time the stock would be placed in a firmer position. A third reason for the operation was the belief of the directors that the time was opportune for increasing the productive capacity of the Corporation's plants, and for this additional capital was necessary. To attain these purposes the directors decided to issue $250,000,000 of 5-per-cent 10-60 year sinking-fund gold bonds of which $200,000,000 were to be exchanged for preferred stock at par and $50,000,000 sold for cash at par.

The acrimonious controversies to which this bond conversion plan gave rise, the circumstances which compelled the directors to discontinue it, after 1,500,000 shares of preferred had been exchanged for bonds and only $20,000,000 bonds had been sold for cash, the balance remaining in the treasury for subsequent use, and the conclusive demonstration it afforded that at that period the Corporation's policies were directed more by financiers than by experienced steel manufacturers, are brought out in easily accessible sources.[1] Since there are other evidences of this financial control to which we give attention, we omit further details of this operation and merely record our concurrence with the view now generally held that the plan was essentially unwise.

As suggested above, the most important of all the ore leases made by the Corporation was that effected in January, 1907, with the Great Northern Railway interests and most frequently referred to as the "Hill" lease. For some time prior to this date the Great Northern had been acquiring small parcels of ore land until it controlled some 65,000 acres containing hundreds of millions of tons of ore. Although the Corporation leased only 60 per cent approximately of these lands, its ore was estimated to be increased by 500,000,000 tons or more. The most interesting aspect of the transaction was the precise terms upon which it was made. The Corporation was required to pay royalties upon a minimum tonnage in 1907 of 750,000 tons and this minimum was to increase 750,000 tons each year until in 1917 it reached 8,250,000 tons, where

[1] For a detailed discussion of the scheme cf. W. Z. Ripley's *Trusts, Pools and Corporations,* revised edition, pp. 228-268.

it was to remain for the duration of the leases. Since the Great Northern itself held only part of the ore leased to the Corporation in fee, it was agreed that the term of the new lease should run with respect to fee ore until all merchantable ore containing 49 per cent or more of iron should have been shipped, and, with respect to leaseholds during the term of those leases, less three months. The Corporation reserved the right to cancel the lease on January 1, 1915, on two years' notice. The royalty on dried ore containing less than 49 per cent of iron was a flat rate of $1.10 a ton, but from 49 per cent up there was a sliding scale ranging from $1.168 a ton. As a matter of fact, ore of 59 per cent iron content was the standard unit for computing royalties, and for it a royalty of $1.65 a ton, including freight and dockage charges, was agreed upon for the year 1907. Since the freight and dockage from the Mesabi range to Lake Superior had been 80 cents a ton for some time the base rate of royalty was 85 cents. But it must be noted that this was for 1907 only; for every succeeding year of the duration of the lease the rate was to increase 3.4 cents on all grades of ore of 49 per cent and over.[1] Finally, the lessee agreed to ship all the ore mined over the railroad of the lessor.

According to Gary's testimony in the anti-trust suit involving the Corporation there was considerable disagreement among the directors on the wisdom of this lease, and certain additional facts go far toward making this disagreement understandable. In the first place, the Corporation had at least a thirty years' (and possibly a fifty years') supply of ore. Moreover, the average rate of royalty paid for Mesabi range properties at this time was about 44 cents a ton. Since there is no evidence that the Hill ores were of extraordinarily good grade, the difference between 44 and 85 cents plus the annual increases of 3.4 cents demonstrate the willingness of a majority of the directors to commit the Corporation not only to extremely high royalties, but also to advancing royalties irre-

[1] It will be noted that 3.4 cents is 4 per cent of 85 cents; in other words the Corporation agreed to buy the ore in the ground at 85 cents a ton and to add 4 per cent simple interest on this purchase price until the ore was taken out and paid for.

spective of the trend of ore prices. It furthermore seems to demonstrate a conviction that that trend would be or could be made to be upward. For this combination of facts the Bureau of Corporations could find only one "reasonable explanation," namely, "that it was designed to prevent this ore from falling into the hands of competitors of the Corporation." [1]

As time went on the disadvantages of the lease became more and more pronounced, so that early in 1911 there were rumors in the trade papers that it would be canceled. At the same time there were other rumors that the federal Department of Justice was considering the filing of Sherman Act proceedings against the Corporation. Which of these considerations was more important we cannot be positive, but what is certain is that the finance committee of the Corporation on October 17, 1911, voted to cancel the lease. This action was ratified by the board of directors on October 26, the very day on which the government filed suit.

But the most important event of the year 1907 in the history of the Steel Trust was the acquisition of the Tennessee Coal, Iron and Railroad Company. Unfortunately for those interested in a clear statement of the causes and results of this acquisition, it is the center of perhaps the most acrimonious in a long list of disputes involving the Corporation. During the course of subsequent Congressional investigations and court proceedings involving it competent witnesses under oath flatly contradicted the testimony of preceding witnesses, they were in turn flatly contradicted by subsequent witnesses, and a former President of the United States was accused by a Congressional committee of "having the wool pulled over his eyes." Briefly stated, the opposing views are about as follows. The Corporation had had a number of earlier opportunities to purchase the Tennessee Company, but had consistently rejected them because of the metallurgical difficulties experienced by the latter concern in utilizing its vast potential ore resources as a consequence of their high phosphorus content, and because of the criticisms that might be made that the

[1] *Report,* part i, p. 322.

combination was attempting to secure a "corner" of the iron of the country. A reversal of these judgments was made only for the purpose of aiding in the alleviation of the financial panic of 1907 and only after a conference with President Roosevelt in which he stated that he saw no basis in public policy for objecting to the transaction. On the other hand, it was contended that the developments of 1906 and 1907 in both the technological and financial position of the Tennessee Company had forced the trust to the realization that a new competitor had arisen which must be crushed or absorbed, and that with the help of the Morgan banking house an unfair advantage was taken of the panic to secure the second result.

On a number of important points there was, of course, substantial agreement among the individuals who contradicted one another on others. For example, it was generally accepted that the natural resources controlled by the Tennessee Coal and Iron were in quantity second only to those of the Steel Corporation. Moreover, these resources had been placed by nature in such close proximity that it seemed as though there had been a definite plan to lay out ideal conditions for the development of a great steel center. The properties of the Tennessee, located chiefly near Birmingham, Alabama, included, according to estimates of 1906, 700,000,000 tons of ore and 2,000,000,000 tons of coal. A large part of the ore was self-fluxing and about half of the coal was of an excellent coking quality. As if this were not enough, there were large quantities of limestone and dolomite also included in the holdings and within a few miles of the ore and coal. But as suggested above, the ore was of non-Bessemer grade; that is, it contained too much phosphorus to be converted into steel by the Bessemer process. Other difficulties of a technical sort and some seemingly poor management had prevented the Tennessee from becoming the success it should have been.

In 1906 a new syndicate took over the concern with the idea of rehabilitating it, and in the next eighteen months spent some $8,000,000 for that purpose. One measure of the syndicate's success was an order in 1907 from E. H. Harriman for 160,000 tons of open-hearth rails, and another may be found in the comments in the trade and other papers on the superiority of this type of rail over the Bessemer still in common use. A much less favorable aspect of the situation appears, however, in Miss Tarbell's statement that some time in 1907 an expert appraisal of the Tennessee plant revealed the necessity for an additional $20,000,000 investment to make it a paying proposition.[1] In this uncertain state of the internal affairs of the company it became for a time the center of the brief but severe panic of 1907.

As is well known, the spectacular collapse in that year of the Knickerbocker Trust Company of New York caused great uneasiness for the safety of other concerns. During October matters grew steadily worse. The national banking system proved so completely inadequate for meeting the situation that in many localities banks limited narrowly the sums depositors might draw within a stated period of time. In New York City there were nightly meetings of bankers at the home of J. P. Morgan that frequently lasted till daybreak. A run on the Trust Company of America that forced it to pay out $13,500,000 on October 23 and $70,000,000 in a week was met without bankrupting that institution, but on November 1 intimations of a most disquieting nature were brought to Morgan concerning the financial position of Moore & Schley, prominent stockbrokers. According to the subsequent testimony of Mr. L. C. Ledyard, attorney for Colonel O. H. Payne, this firm was on the verge of bankruptcy because of the fact that it had hypothecated large quantities of Tennessee Coal and Iron stock—a majority, in fact—with banks and trust companies as part of the collateral for loans aggregating $38,000,000. Pressure was apparently being put on Moore & Schley to meet these obligations, or at least substitute some other collateral for Tennessee stock, which most of the creditors considered unsatisfactory collateral in the existing emergency.

Colonel Payne, it should be noted, was a member of the syndicate which had acquired the Tennessee in 1906. As a friend of the imperiled concern he had already given to its

[1] *Life of Elbert H. Gary*, p. 198.

members millions of current securities in exchange for those now being questioned, but as the situation became more serious he was forced to the conclusion that unless the Steel Corporation would purchase the Tennessee stock at a price which would relieve the brokers a smash was inevitable. When Ledyard, on Payne's direct or indirect instructions, went to Morgan with this story, the latter was greatly concerned and immediately laid the matter before Gary and Frick. According to their biographers, neither believed that the Tennessee stock was worth more than $60 and neither wanted to purchase it at any price. Conferences continued during Saturday and Sunday, November 2 and 3, during which a number of proposals for meeting the situation were made and rejected. Sunday evening the finance committee of the Corporation finally decided to make the purchase, but Gary insisted that before it was completed it was necessary to consult President Roosevelt for the reason that, "If we do this without consulting the administration . . . a bill in equity might stop the sale, and in that case more harm than good would be done. He cannot say that we may or may not purchase, but we ought to know his attitude, since he has a general direction of the law department of the United States." [1] After further debating, Gary and Frick were agreed upon as emissaries to the President.

When they reached the White House the President's secretary at first refused to announce them on the ground that Roosevelt saw no one before ten, but since the New York Stock Exchange opened at that hour they were particularly anxious to secure an answer earlier. And according to the usual version of the incident Roosevelt left his breakfast table in time to hear the trust's representatives and to give them the answer they wanted at the time they wanted it. Before formulating his final judgment, however, he called in Secretary of State Root, the Attorney General being out of the city. Root's opinion was that though the President was unable to declare the proposed transaction legal or illegal, he might with propriety express his view of the public policy

[1] Tarbell, *op. cit.*, p. 200.

involved. Thereupon Roosevelt dictated a letter to Attorney General Bonaparte outlining the situation and concluding with the statement: " . . . I felt it no duty of mine to interpose any objection." As his later statements showed, he had been convinced that the emergency demanded prompt action and that the proposal of Gary and Frick was a salutary one. In this judgment he was supported by the majority of business men, bankers, and financial writers.[1]

By the terms of the agreement as consummated United States Steel second-mortgage bonds bearing 5 per cent interest were exchanged for Tennessee stock at 84 for the bonds and 100 for the stock. Otherwise stated, $11,904.76 par value of bonds were given for $10,000 par value of stock. Of a total of $30,500,000 common stock the Corporation acquired all but $220,000 for a little over $35,000,000 in bonds (at par) and cash. The general impression was that a bargain had been secured.

As previously indicated, however, there were many who believed that the bargain had not only been a hard one, but also an unfair one. Perhaps the most important members of this group were the Congressmen who signed the majority report of the Stanley Committee of the House of Representatives. Among other things this majority apparently believed that the Steel Corporation was seriously alarmed over the prospect of competition from the Tennessee Company, that it took advantage of the financial situation of 1907 to exert pressure on the holders of Tennessee stock, that the story concerning Moore & Schley's holdings of that stock was a pure fabrication since it was Schley individually who was in trouble, that Gary and Frick misrepresented the facts to Roosevelt, that Roosevelt acted hastily and unwisely, and that the vaunted relief brought to the situation by the transaction was almost entirely illusory. Because of the violently contradictory accounts of the leading figures in the negotiations,

[1] For a sympathetic treatment of the episode cf. Tarbell, *Life of Elbert H. Gary;* Harvey, *Henry Clay Frick, the Man; The Commercial and Financial Chronicle* issues of November 1907; and the minority report of O. H. Young in the final *Report of the Stanley Committee,* House Report 1127, 62nd Congress, 2nd Session.

notwithstanding the fact that most of them were given under oath, it seems a hopeless task for us to attempt at this date to establish the truth. Of two conclusions, however, we can be positive: first, if the officers of the Corporation were motivated solely or even primarily by a desire to stabilize the industrial situation, they displayed a considerable degree of disregard for the interests of their shareholders; second, the acquisition of the Tennessee Company was used effectively by those who urged a prosecution of the steel combination under the Sherman Act.

Since 1907 there have been no purchases or leases of manufacturing or raw material properties comparable in importance to those described above. Before the last of them had been completed, however, the increase in business in the Middle West had so far outstripped the capacities of the Corporation's mills in the Chicago district that it was decided to build a new steel center at the southern end of Lake Michigan. Real estate was purchased for this purpose in 1905 and construction was soon under way to transform a desolate expanse of sand dunes into the city of Gary, Indiana.[1] During the next few years the annual reports of the Corporation show appropriations aggregating upward of $40,000,000 for this development, "provided entirely from surplus net profits." With the exception of a few minor issues of bonds and notes the Corporation has uniformly financed its other enormous increases in physical properties without adding to its capital liabilities. (The amount of common stock outstanding remained constant from 1901 to 1927; the preferred has remained constant from the date of the bond conversion plan until the present; and the outstanding bonds, notes, etc., after some fluctuations, have shown since 1912 a steady tendency to decrease.) In other words, it has plowed back large sums from its earnings into the business. That this has been the policy has been well known; the sums involved and the significance of the policy merit somewhat detailed analysis.

In December, 1926, the board of directors of the Corporation voted to recommend an increase of 40 per cent in the common

[1] *Annual Report,* 1905, p. 25.

stock. In justifying this recommendation the annual report for 1926 presented this statement: [1]

In the period from April 1, 1901, to December 31, 1926, after providing for depletion and depreciation arising from exhaustion of natural resources and deterioration of improvements, including the writing off of property abandoned, making payment of interest on bonded and other debt, and setting aside reserves for contingencies, the net profits earned totaled the aggregate sum of ....$2,345,308,723.

Of this there were distributed in Cash the following dividends on the Capital Stock:

On preferred stock, 180¼%..............	$672,929,461	
On common stock, 131¼%..............	667,125,176	
		$1,340,054,637
Balance of surplus earned..........		$1,005,254,086

Now, as pointed out earlier, the original capitalization of the Steel Trust was at least double the value of its tangible assets. Even after making a generous allowance for good will there can be no doubt that the entire common-stock issue represented only prospective profits, or "water." Despite this, dividends aggregating 131¼ per cent were paid on this common stock in twenty-five years, at the same time that the Corporation had built up out of earnings not otherwise appropriated an earned surplus of $1,005,254,086. This surplus was almost exactly double the original common issue of $508,-302,500. Since it has, in one way or another, been turned back into the business, it has not only put tangible assets behind every dollar of the original common capitalization, but also has justified the 40-per-cent stock dividend of July 1, 1927, and helped to make possible the current earnings in excess of 7 per cent on the expanded common-stock capitalization. Without attempting to bring down to date the elaborate analyses of the investment and earnings of the steel combination made by the Bureau of Corporations,[2] we submit that the foregoing data are ample justification for the con-

[1] P. 6.

[2] *Report on the Steel Industry,* part i, chaps. ii, vi, and vii. As we have previously stated, such studies are outside the scope of the powers and resources of private investigators.

clusion that earnings of United States Steel have been since 1901 materially in excess of those usual in a competitive manufacturing industry. That they have continued to be so is indicated by the annual report for 1928 which shows an increase in undivided surplus of almost $130,000,000 since 1926.[1]

On the basis of these continued high profits the stockholders ratified, on April 15, 1929, a proposal by the directors looking forward to the immediate redemption of the entire bonded indebtedness of the Corporation proper (*i.e.,* not including bonds of subsidiaries or mining royalty notes). To effect this the authorized common stock was increased from $753,321,000 to $1,250,000,000. On the following day the directors offered to shareholders the right to purchase 1,016,605 shares of common, only about one-fifth of the authorized increase, at $140 each in the ratio of one new share for each seven held. On this basis the proceeds of the new issue, $142,324,700, would not quite pay for the $134,830,000 of the fifty-year bonds outstanding, since the great majority of them were callable at 115. According to the newspaper accounts, however, the directors not only called the fifty-year issue for payment on September 1, 1929, but indicated an intention to call the outstanding $136,550,000 of the 10-60 year bonds on November 1. The opinion of the financial writers at this time (April 20, 1929) is that the funds necessary for the completion of the bond retirement will be taken from surplus. And although one of these writers expressed the view that "the steel melon turned out to be more of a lemon," a more significant aspect of the arrangements appears in their striking contrast to the bond conversion scheme of 1902-1903. In that case the directors proposed to saddle the Corporation with an additional $250,000,000 in bonds and the fixed charges attached thereto. The 1929 plans will eliminate the bonded indebtedness of the Corporation as such. The advantages of the simplified capitalization and of the removal of the incubus of such a large part of the fixed charges are obvious. Consequently, the plan

[1] Cf. *Annual Reports,* 1926 and 1928, p. 19.

will probably be as cordially approved as its predecessor was condemned.

The fact remains, however, that these advantages to shareholders have been attained in no small measure through the exaction from consumers of steel of excessive prices. As is to be expected, Corporation spokesmen deny most vigorously that excessive prices have been charged. They insist that the chief effect of the policy of the Corporation upon the prices of steel has been to stabilize them, and that this stabilization of prices has resulted in a more stabilized industry with a lower long-run average of prices than would otherwise have been true. The statistical evidence on this point is inadequate to support the sweeping generalizations too frequently based upon it, for the reason that with the exception of a very few steel products the data are not available for years prior to 1898. The figures we have, however, indicate strongly that a considerable degree of price stabilization has been secured since 1901. Furthermore, one investigator [1] at least has directed his inquiries into these data specifically to the questions that interest us here:—price stabilization and industrial stabilization.

In his study of price stabilization Professor Berglund analyzed the prices of a group of finished steel products from 1898 to 1922, of steel billets from 1886 to 1922, and of steel rails from 1880 to 1922. In all cases his data were grouped in three chronological periods: the earliest year in his series to 1901, 1902-1914 and 1915-1922. The average price of finished steel, billets, and rails in each of the periods was computed, and the highest annual average price and the lowest annual average price of each product in each period was ascertained. A comparison of these data revealed some annual average which represented the greatest deviation from the average for the period and this deviation was computed as the "per cent of greatest variation from periodic mean." Similar comparisons were made between the periodic averages and the highest monthly average, the lowest monthly average, the average of

[1] Professor A. Berglund in the *Quarterly Journal of Economics,* vol. xxxviii, pp. 1-30, and 607-630.

the highest monthly prices for each year, and the average of lowest monthly prices for each year in the respective periods. The results of these computations convinced Professor Berglund, as they will any one, we think, that "after the organization of the United States Steel Corporation and prior to the outbreak of the World War, there was a pronounced reduction in extreme fluctuations of prices."

The best known feature of this stabilization process is, of course, its effect on rail prices. In the period 1880 to 1901 the monthly average price per ton of standard Bessemer rails had ranged from $85 to $16.50. For the next fifteen years they sold for $28 a ton without a deviation, except perhaps on a rush order. During the period 1915-1922 steel prices again fluctuated to a marked degree, but even at this time there was clear evidence of a desire to prevent a runaway market, particularly in certain products. So marked, indeed, was this restraining influence on rail prices that for a time rails sold for $20 less a ton than the pig iron from which they were made! But efforts within the industry were not sufficient, so that it became necessary for a time for the government to fix steel prices along with those of numerous other products. Then came the post-armistice slump in business activity, the revival carrying on into 1920, and the severe depression of 1921. During these movements steel prices oscillated materially. Since 1922, however, they have remained more nearly constant, and, as might have been expected, the price of rails has been steadiest of all, having been "pegged" at $43 since October, 1922.[1]

But granting the stabilization of prices there remain the probably more important questions of the stabilization of production and employment. In checking the claims made by leaders in the industry that price stabilization carried with it industrial stabilization, Professor Berglund found available somewhat more complete data on production than he had on prices. His measure of variations in production was the deviation of each year's total from a five-year moving average

[1] Cf. *Iron Age* January 1, 1914, with January 3, 1929, for tables and charts showing iron and steel prices in detail.

within each of two periods:—1887-1901 and 1902-1922 for pig iron, steel ingots, and rolled iron and steel; 1880-1901 and 1902-1922 for rails. For pig, ingots and rolled iron and steel the computations show that " . . . the percentages of average deviation for the years succeeding the organization of the United States Steel Corporation are materially greater than the corresponding percentages for the period from 1887 to 1901, inclusive. The extreme variations are even more pronounced." Moreover, it should be noted that these greater deviations between 1902 and 1922 were not the result of war-time disturbances, since a division of this period into two sections, 1902-1914 and 1915-1922, shows slightly greater average deviations in the former than in the latter. For rails the differences in the percentages of average deviation were not so pronounced in the periods before and after the organization of the Corporation. It should be noted, however, that for the period during which rail prices were absolutely fixed (April 1901 to May 1916) fluctuations in production were very pronounced.[1] We have continued Professor Berglund's computations through 1927 without finding any reason to amend his conclusions.

Attempts to compare fluctuations in steel employment, the most important aspect of the stabilization of business, for the periods before and after the formation of the Corporation, are even worse handicapped than are such attempts with reference to prices and output. Berglund abandoned such efforts and presented simply the deviations from a five-year moving average of the average employment a year provided by United States Steel alone. He found the average percentage of deviation to be materially lower than similar percentages in production.[2] There is, however, the suggestion of another possibility of checking the results achieved in the statement of the Commissioner of Labor in his *Report on Conditions of Employment in the Iron and Steel Industry in the United States* that "in 1909 the steel works and rolling

[1] *Quarterly Journal of Economics,* vol. xxxviii, pp. 614-622.

[2] Eight and nine-tenths per cent for the period 1902-1922 as against 13.5 for pig iron, 14.7 for ingots, 14.9 for rolled iron and steel, and 14.9 for rails.

mills had relatively the largest fluctuation in the size of the labor force of any of the large manufacturing industries."[1] The basis for this statement was a comparison of the figures presented in the census reports on the maximum and minimum amount of employment provided by months in the manufacturing industries of the United States. These industries were listed in the order of their importance as measured by total average wage-earners and the fluctuations in employment were measured by a computation of the percentage which the minimum employment was of the maximum. We have extended this comparison to cover every manufacturing census year from 1904 to 1925 for the ten most important industries. The rank of the steel works and rolling mills among these ten in providing regular employment is as follows:[2]

Year	Rank	Year	Rank
1904	8	1921	9
1909	10	1923	5
1914	9	1925	5
1919	10		

For a number of reasons conclusions based on the foregoing tabulation must be drawn with care. There are, of course, many industries employing smaller numbers of employees whose fluctuations in employment are greater than those in steel. Moreover, steel is probably more susceptible to changes in general business conditions than any other major industry, so much so, in fact, that it has frequently been used as a "business barometer." Again, the evidence indicates that since the organization of the Corporation recovery in production from recessions has been more prompt than in earlier years. To the extent that drastic reductions in output to permit the maintenance of stable prices result in prompt recoveries, and thus in shortening periods of trade depression, price stabiliza-

[1] Vol. iii, p. 205 (note).

[2] *Census of Manufactures,* 1905, pp. lxxviii, 26 *et seq.; Thirteenth Census of the U. S.,* 1910, vol. viii, p. 277; *Abstract of the Census of Manufactures,* 1914, pp. 436, 466 *et seq.; Abstract of the Census of Manufactures,* 1919, pp. 19, 404 *et seq.; Biennial Census of Manufactures,* 1921, pp. 19, 1274 *et seq.; Biennial Census of Manufactures,* 1923, pp. 24, 1136 *et seq.; Biennial Census of Manufactures,* 1925, pp. 10, 1208 *et seq.*

tion may bring about industrial stabilization. As stated above, however, the statistical evidence is not of sufficiently conclusive character to justify positive pronouncements of any sort. If the foregoing discussion avails no more than to offset some of the pontifical utterances that have emanated from both Corporation and outside sources at various times, it will have served its purpose. At any rate, evidence to be presented in the next chapter on the methods of price-making in the steel industry should go far to disabuse the reader of any idea that stabilization of industry has been the chief aim in the stabilization of prices.

CHAPTER XIV

THE UNITED STATES STEEL CORPORATION

(Continued)

As brought out in an earlier chapter, the steel industry was one of the first in which pools were developed. During the intense competition of 1897, most of them collapsed, as they had in previous periods of stress. An exception was the Structural Steel Pool formed in January, 1897, to include Carnegie Steel, A. and P. Roberts, and the Universal Construction Company, all later in the Corporation. The minutes of the Carnegie Company for October 22, 1900, show Schwab outlining a project for "dividing the plate business and maintaining the price," and those for November 13, 1900, contain his report that "we have finally concluded the agreement on plates." [1] This agreement provided for the fixing of prices, apportionment of sales, etc. It included the Carnegie Company, Illinois Steel Company, and American Steel and Wire, all subsequent Corporation subsidiaries. Before the district court of New Jersey the federal government charged the Corporation with participation in other pools, particularly that in rails. The Corporation denied the existence of formal agreements, but admitted that some of its subsidiaries were parties to "tacit understandings" with other concerns prior to the formation of the Corporation and on until late in 1904. Mr. Corey, at that time president of the Corporation, testified to the existence of a friendly relationship among the producers of steel rails in accordance with which each one was supposed to manufacture a certain amount each year, whereby the prices of rails were generally uniform.[2]

The date mentioned above as the termination of the sub-

[1] Quoted in the *Brief for the U. S. before the District Court of New Jersey* in U. S. *v.* U. S. Steel, part ii, pp. 122, 123.

[2] *Ibid.*, part ii, pp. 128, 139.

sidiaries' "tacit understandings" was set by a letter written by Corey at Gary's direction instructing the presidents of the subsidiaries to withdraw from all pools and combinations and "everything of that kind that might be regarded as illegal."[1] Additional light on the matter, however, was provided by the "commissioner" or manager of the Plate, Structural Steel, and Shafting pools, W. C. Temple, who testified that Corey's letter caused the collapse of the pools mentioned. This is some indication that there was more than a "tacit understanding" between the Corporation subsidiaries and other companies. More interesting were the further statements of Temple that after the Plate and Structural pools were dissolved he acted as "the intermediary by which information as to the output and capacity was disseminated" for two years or a little less; that former members "presented their reports to me just as they did before"; that meetings were still held, though of a less formal character; that in his opinion the group worked together just as harmoniously as it had before the formal dissolution in 1904; that "as a general proposition" the subsidiaries of the Corporation formerly in the pools continued to send representatives to the meetings after the dissolution; and that these meetings were fully as effective in steadying prices and preventing destructive competition as the agreements prior to 1904.[2]

From the foregoing evidence it seems clear that a number of the Corporation subsidiaries were more or less active members of pools or their equivalents until some time in 1906. From then until late in 1907 there is little or no evidence of concerted action on prices except the fact that the price of rails remained constant. The first part of 1907 was an exceedingly prosperous time for the Corporation, its reported earnings for the second quarter of $45,500,000 being the highest reached until that time, and those of the third quarter, $43,800,000, exceeding all prior to the record set in the preceding quarter. But the fourth quarter showed a drop to

[1] U. S. *v.* U. S. Steel, *Brief for the Corporation before the U. S. Supreme Court,* p. 207.

[2] *Stanley Hearings,* vol. iii, pp. 1732-1739.

$32,500,000, and the first quarter of 1908 a continued fall to $18,000,000. It will be recalled that the panic of 1907 occurred early in the last quarter of that year, and that for a time the banking system was thoroughly disrupted and all sorts of businesses handicapped or worse. The effect of earlier fluctuations in business activity had earned for steel the sobriquet of "prince or pauper," since some of the companies adopted during depressions the policy of taking orders at almost any price in order to keep their mills running and their organizations as nearly intact as possible, with most disastrous results to some of their competitors. Without doubt these conditions in the industry prompted the revival of coöperation embodied in the famous "Gary dinners."

In Gary's language their purpose was "to maintain to a reasonable extent the equilibrium of business, to prevent utter demoralization of business and destructive competition." [1] The precise methods by which this end was to be attained are well stated in the recent biography of Gary by Miss Ida M. Tarbell: "At the first of the Gary dinners, given November 20 [1907], and at others which followed in 1908, he had urged upon his guests, who represented fully 90 per cent of the industry, that they coöperate in holding prices where they were." Again, J. H. Reed is quoted as stating that Mr. Gary "exhorted us like a Methodist preacher at a camp meeting." Miss Tarbell goes on to state that, although Gary's guests, "almost to a man, had always held and practiced the exact opposite of this doctrine" of maintaining prices during depressions, "they now rallied to his exhortations and agreed that they would follow his leadership in the troubled period which they saw before them." [2] It must be noted that there is no record of any exchange of correspondence agreeing to this policy, no signing of a formal statement, as in the old pools, although Gary did testify to the Stanley Committee that since the panic of 1907 the steel people had been "in quite frequent intercourse, furnishing one to all the others information in regard

[1] *Stanley Hearings,* vol. i, p. 264.
[2] Tarbell, *op. cit.*, pp. 205, 206, 210, 211.

to exactly what he was doing."[1] The usual procedure at the dinners seems to have been for Gary to set forth the prospective policy of the Corporation, to "exhort" his guests to fall in line, and then to ask for expressions of opinion from them. So far as we have records of the speeches at these dinners, and for some the record is practically a stenographic report, there seems to have been no difference of opinion concerning the proper course to be followed. The dinners were given at irregular intervals for some fifteen months or more. The reasons ascribed for their discontinuance vary considerably, but it seems likely that doubts concerning their legality affected the final decision. At any rate, the government believed them illegal and included them as a reason for filing its dissolution suit.

The last of the methods of making prices to be discussed here persisted more nearly to the present time than any other —the so-called "Pittsburgh-plus" scheme. Stated as simply as possible, this was a method of establishing steel prices so that the delivered price of steel was quoted to a customer as the Pittsburgh price plus the exact freight from Pittsburgh to the delivery point. In its operation it meant that a customer in a town fifty miles from Chicago would pay, not Chicago manufacturing costs, plus a profit, plus freight from Chicago, but Pittsburgh costs, plus profit, plus the freight from Pittsburgh. Exactly how long the plan operated is not certain, but at any rate it was well established prior to the organization of the Corporation. At an even earlier date there existed a Pittsburgh zone-plus plan under which the country was divided into freight zones from Pittsburgh as a focal point, and in each of which there was a flat zone price. This plan was disrupted by a customer who ascertained a way station in the zone next to his and closer to Pittsburgh which happened to have the same freight rate as the through rate to the customer's home. Then he ordered the steel for delivery at the way station from the steel company, and made an arrangement with the railway not to leave the steel at the way station, but to bring it on to the place he really wanted it. A

[1] *Stanley Hearings,* vol. i, p. 195.

few experiences of this sort caused the steel companies to drop the Pittsburgh zone-plus plan and adopt Pittsburgh plus.

The question naturally arises: who set the Pittsburgh base price? Part of the answer is in the foregoing sections—*i.e.*, the prices which a great part of the trade followed were set by pools or by the pronouncements at the Gary dinners. After the latter were discontinued the Steel Corporation continued through the daily press and the trade journals to give the greatest publicity to its prices, and a very large portion of the trade saw fit to follow these prices closely. For any number of reasons, such as rush delivery, there were opportunities for getting more than the base price at times, and reasons for taking less at others, but as has been shown, a remarkable degree of stabilization of prices over a period of time was secured. The contribution of Pittsburgh plus was primarily to aid in maintaining uniformity of prices at a given time. When the Steel Corporation announced a Pittsburgh price, everyone in the trade knew that that meant the price in Oshkosh would be the Pittsburgh price plus the freight from Pittsburgh to Oshkosh, wherever the steel might be manufactured. The net result was to reduce price competition to the vanishing point, but since salesmen continued to compete for business this situation was deemed not to constitute a violation of the antitrust laws.

But in the meanwhile technical processes had reached the stage where rolled-steel products, the basis of the modern skyscraper, the automobile, the bridge, the railroad, and the farm implement, to mention a few of their uses, were thoroughly standardized as to physical qualities. The result of this standardization was, of course, to reduce competition in physical qualities to a low estate, for every producer knew the standard specifications for the product and realized that since they were standard there could be little use in talking "quality" to rolled-steel purchasers.

From the viewpoint of the immediate purchaser of rolled steel the situation had obvious advantages. Since quality was standardized and prices were uniform at a given time and stable over considerable periods, any farm-machinery manufacturer, for example, knew rather closely what his competitors could do in setting a price to the consuming public. The result of all these factors to Professor Commons' mind is summarized in his statement that "uniformity of prices through standardization, stabilization, and publicity gets by the Supreme Court, satisfies the immediate consumers, and soaks the ultimate consumers."[1]

An entirely different interpretation of the origin and purpose of Pittsburgh plus is set forth in Miss Tarbell's *Life* of Judge Gary. After explaining that Philadelphia was at one time the center of the iron industry of the country before steel became more important, Miss Tarbell goes on to show why Pittsburgh became more prominent:

> Steel could be made cheaper there than anywhere else; it became the base for prices in all the territory which it served. Steel makers at other points quoted their prices plus the freight from Pittsburgh—it was their protection against their big rival. It was the only practical way of developing the steel industry in new territories. Buyers in the territory might pay more, but they were willing to do this because in the long run they believed their own industry would so develop that it could go on its own in prices. . . . As time went on, the new steel centers did develop, thus Chicago had come to a point by 1918 when it could satisfy, or nearly satisfy, all the demands of its natural territory. Consumers began to complain about "Pittsburgh Plus."[2]

Here the practice is pictured as a sort of protective tariff under which the infants of the industry may develop to maturity. The costs of a plant at Youngstown, say, were higher than those of competing plants at Pittsburgh, but since the freight from Pittsburgh to Milwaukee was more than that from Youngstown, the Youngstown plant could meet the Pittsburgh base price plus freight and recoup itself on the freight margin for its deficiencies in position, management, lack of integration, or whatever factors explained the difference in cost. On the other assumptions, that Youngstown costs were equal to or even less than those in Pittsburgh, it was still claimed that at least in the beginning Pittsburgh plus

[1] *American Economic Review,* September, 1924, p. 509. The article in which this quotation appears has been drawn upon freely in the text.

[2] Tarbell, *op. cit.,* p. 322.

was necessary, for the newer plants would not be able to meet all the demand in their immediate vicinity, and consequently prices must be set at a point which would permit Pittsburgh to furnish that part of the demand the newer mills were not yet able to meet—that is, at "Pittsburgh plus."

But it seemed that as in our experience with the tariff, the steel "infants" failed to reach maturity, or at least that stage of maturity where they could dispense with the pap of Pittsburgh plus. Therefore, as Miss Tarbell says, "consumers began to complain." In fact, the Western Association of Rolled Steel Manufacturers was urgent enough in its complaints to engage a lawyer, Mr. John S. Miller, of Chicago, to secure the abolition of this plan, which it claimed was discriminatory in its operations. We have Miss Tarbell's word for it that Miller went directly to Gary in his capacity as president of the American Iron and Steel Institute (for Pittsburgh plus, it must be remembered, was not solely a Corporation affair), that there was considerable correspondence, and that finally Gary proposed that they take the whole question to the Federal Trade Commission with the hope of securing coöperation and assistance from that body. But there is no doubt that even if Gary had not taken this step the situation would have been brought to the attention of the Commission. In fact, another organization, the "Western Association of Rolled Steel Consumers for Opposing the Practice of Pittsburgh Plus" in its very title made clear its purpose. Moreover, concerted action through their governors, legislatures, or attorney generals was taken by thirty-two states to secure the abolition of Pittsburgh plus. Possibly because of the widespread nature of the complaints Gary's hope of "coöperation" was not fulfilled, for the Commission chose to act as a prosecuting body, and, from his point of view, made a bad matter worse by centering the prosecution on the Corporation instead of on the industry or the group, including independents, of whom the Western Association of Rolled Steel Manufacturers had complained. In this position, more or less forced to fight, the Corporation rested its defense of Pittsburgh plus on two chief points. It is interesting to note that these points resolve themselves into arguments of economic theory on the so-called "law of supply and demand," and the nature of a market.

First, the Corporation advanced the contention summarized above that Pittsburgh was a point of surplus production and that Chicago and other cities were points of deficit production—*i.e.,* not sufficient for local needs—so that the Pittsburgh plus price was the "natural" price fixed by demand and supply. The second argument was that each point of delivery is a separate market for steel; that all producers competed freely at these points; that the Corporation charged the prices thus competitively determined; and that any apparent discrimination resulted from the operation of the law of supply and demand.

These arguments received at the hands of the Commission no shorter shrift than they deserved. It is obvious that Pittsburgh plus did not permit the free competition the Corporation claimed, for even if there was competition at delivery points between steel *producers,* which is extremely doubtful, there was none at production points between steel *consumers.* The result may be most easily visualized by noting the situation in a town halfway freightwise between Chicago and Pittsburgh in 1920, when steel was at $40 a ton in Pittsburgh and the freight between the cities was $7.60. The price of steel delivered at this midway town was $43.80, whether the steel was made in Pittsburgh or Chicago. The same steel delivered in Chicago was $47.60, the Pittsburgh-plus price. But it must be noted that if the steel were shipped from Chicago there was a deduction of the freight paid of $3.80, so that the net to the mill was $40, as it was to the Pittsburgh mill. The mill at Chicago was getting $7.60 a ton net more for steel delivered in Chicago than for steel shipped halfway to Pittsburgh. According to Judge Gary the manufacturing costs in the Chicago mills of the Corporation in 1918 were only about 80 per cent of those of Corporation mills in Pittsburgh. Not only was the Chicago consumer not getting the benefit of the lower costs; he was actually being discriminated against. The competitive market and the free play of supply and demand which the Corporation insisted upon as causing Pittsburgh plus did not exist. In addition to being accessible to both sellers and buyers, a competitive market is characterized by trade in a standardized commodity. Pittsburgh plus made this impossible, for by it the steel companies refused to sell at prices f. o. b. mill; they insisted on a delivered price. In other words, this was not a market for steel, but a market for steel plus variable quantities of freight. The discriminations which resulted were ample justification for the order of the Federal Trade Commission to the Corporation and most of its subsidiaries to "cease and desist" from Pittsburgh plus. Moreover, a review of the evidence on pools, Gary dinners, and Pittsburgh plus gives strong support to the claim that the methods of making prices adopted by the Corporation and the industry at large have been through a good part of its history exactly the reverse of the method which many students agree is the surest guaranty of fairness—full and free competition.

Of even more importance, however, than the justification for the specific order of the Federal Trade Commission suggested by the foregoing facts is the justification they afford for the existence of such an administrative body as the Commission. In its opinion in the dissolution suit the District Court of New Jersey said:

> It is also just to say that in giving timely notice of its purposes to change them [prices], and in giving publicity to its prices, in adhering to them, it will be seen on reflection that the Steel Corporation has adopted a policy of price publicity and adherence, somewhat analogous to the freight rate stability followed by the railroads under the directions of the Interstate Commerce Commission, which published their rates and only changed them on notice.[1]

A little further reflection will convince anyone of the essential difference in the cases. The Interstate Commerce Commission has *prevented* discriminations in freight rates. Pittsburgh plus *resulted* in discriminations in steel prices. The moral is obvious. And to the credit of Gary and others in the steel industry it must be remembered that they as in-

[1] 223 Fed. 92 (1915).

dividuals recognized for many years the need of governmental supervision and strict governmental supervision.

Judge Gary's position was perhaps best stated before the Stanley Committee:

"I realize as fully, I think, as this committee that it is very important to consider how the people shall be protected against imposition or oppression as the possible result of great aggregations of capital, whether in the possession of corporations or individuals. I believe that is a very important question, and personally I believe that the Sherman Act does not meet and will never fully prevent that. I believe *we must come to enforced publicity and governmental control, even as to prices,* and, so far as I am concerned, speaking for our company, so far as I have the right, I would be very glad if we had some place where we could go, to a responsible governmental authority, and say to them, 'Here are our facts and figures, here is our property, here our cost of production; now you tell us what we have the right to do and *what prices we have the right to charge.*' I know this is a very extreme view, and I know that the railroads objected to it for a long time; but whether the mere standpoint of making the most money is concerned or not, whether it is the wise thing, I believe it is the necessary thing, and it seems to me corporations have no right to disregard these public questions and these public interests."

"Your idea then," said Martin Littleton of the committee, "is that coöperation is bound to take the place of competition and that coöperation requires strict governmental supervision?"

"That is a very good statement," replied the Judge.[1]

Several times subsequently Gary made similar statements, one of the most interesting being that before the meeting of the American Iron and Steel Institute on October 23, 1925. After reviewing the efforts of the Corporation to stabilize the industry he went on to say:

As a suggestion for consideration by the iron and steel industry, which is large and influential, would it be advisable to make another effort to stabilize the business? Suppose the Department of Justice would be willing to participate. If meetings should occasionally be held by the manufacturers for the discussion of business on the lines pursued in 1907 and a representative of the Department of Justice should be designated by the Attorney General to attend and listen, and whenever necessary and appropriate to advise concerning the law, what would be the effect upon the steel business, and perhaps other lines? Possibly this could be accomplished.[2]

[1] Quoted in Tarbell, *op. cit.,* pp. 231-232.
[2] Pamphlet report of Gary's speech, p. 24.

To restate the case, then, certain leaders in the steel industry have become convinced that competition in steel degenerates into "destructive" competition just as truly as competition between the railroads in the 'seventies became "cutthroat" competition. They are also convinced that the work of the Interstate Commerce Commission has on the whole been an excellent thing for the railroads. Consequently, they are willing and desirous that some means be found of preventing destructive competition and that that means be unquestionably legal. Obviously the issue becomes one of the proper safeguarding of the public interest and the development of the machinery to do this safeguarding.[1]

Meanwhile there had developed an appreciable sentiment that the methods utilized by the Corporation in limiting destructive competition were neither legal nor in the public interest. Miss Tarbell records a conversation between Roosevelt and Gary as far back as 1904, in which the President intimated broadly that the Corporation would have to take its turn at being investigated. At this time Gary promised that in the event an investigation was decided upon there would be complete coöperation from his side. Within a few months the head of the recently created Bureau of Corporations came to Gary to begin an examination of the trust. There is every evidence that he received the thoroughgoing coöperation that had been promised. For several years the investigation went on, but very little publicity was given it, and as late as the summer of 1911 the members of the Stanley Committee were engaged in somewhat of a controversy with the Secretary of Commerce and Labor because of the lack of coöperation of the Bureau of Corporations with the committee.[2] As stated in the preceding chapter, the acquisition of the Tennessee Company gave some impetus to the demand for a prosecution. Added to these factors were the condemnation of the Corporation by the American Federation of Labor in 1909 as the "greatest enemy" of organized labor, and the

[1] The functioning of the Federal Trade Commission in this respect is discussed in Chapters XXI, XXII, and XXIII.

[2] Cf. *New York Times*, June 2, 1911, p. 1.

complaints by its president, Mr. Gompers, to the Attorney General that were tantamount to a demand for dissolution; the strength and courage of a number of journalists and magazines who were busily engaged in uncovering all the defects they could find in "Big Business"; and the reports of the "Pittsburgh Survey." But the deciding factor that impelled the Taft administration to bring suit against the Corporation seems to have been political pressure. In the latter part of Roosevelt's term his political opponents were more or less directly charging that his personal friendship for Gary was preventing Sherman Act proceedings against "the biggest trust of all." Attempts for earlier Congressional investigating committees had been blocked by the Republican majority, and of course the Democrats raised the cry of favoritism. When that majority disappeared from the House in the middle of Taft's administration it was commonly believed that investigations would soon be instituted. There was some excuse for postponing new suits until after the Supreme Court announced its decisions in the Oil and Tobacco Trust cases, but when the government won those and still there was no action from the Department of Justice against steel, the criticisms from Democratic leaders and from substantial sections of the press grew stronger. Charges that the administration was shielding the steel combine were broadcast; demands that Attorney General Wickersham be impeached were made. Still nothing was done. And then the Stanley Committee began its hearings on the Steel Corporation. Within a few months the government filed suit against the Corporation and a number of its subsidiaries as unlawful monopolies.

In its briefs and in its evidence the government undertook to show that the earlier combinations which later became parts of the Corporation were not the result of "natural growth," but artificial combinations, one of whose chief purposes was the restriction of competition, and that the organization of the Corporation was a further attempt to restrict competition. Moreover, it was claimed that the Corporation had actually attained a preponderant position in the trade, so that it unduly restrained competition, particularly price competition.

From the testimony of their own officials and from trade statistics of output there was no difficulty in establishing the facts that such companies as American Tin Plate, American Sheet Steel, American Steel and Wire of New Jersey, and the National Tube hoped to limit competition and that they acquired 75 per cent or more of the output of their respective products at the time of their organization.[1] A number of the constituents of the Corporation, moreover, were before its organization active competitors, so that in their combination the government saw further proof of illegality.

Intent to monopolize was obviously difficult to establish in the face of denials from those who were accused of harboring such intent, but the previously described activities of the Corporation in buying and leasing ore lands and in taking over the Tennessee Coal, Iron and Railroad Company were construed by the Department of Justice as indicative of such intent.

In the matter of prices the government contended that after the organization of many of the earlier combinations and again after the formation of the Corporation prices rose and subsequently displayed a degree of constancy inconsistent with the existence of a competitive market. Particular attention was called to the fact that the price of Bessemer steel rails remained fixed at $28 a ton from May, 1901, to 1916. During the period 1867 to 1900 there had been no two consecutive years in which the prices of rails had been the same. In less than sixty days after the formation of the Corporation they were "pegged."

Finally, the government devoted considerable attention to such factors as the size of the Corporation's capital as compared with that of its competitors; its proportion of the total production of iron and steel in the United States; its proportion of ore reserves; and opinion evidence on the Corporation's power. All of these were submitted as demonstrating pre-

[1] Cf. the *Report of the Commissioner of Corporations on the Steel Industry*, part i, pp. 90 *et seq.*

ponderant position and domination which resulted in an undue restraint upon trade.

The Corporation contended that the government was entirely erroneous in its interpretation of the combination movement in the steel industry, since there was no attempt to secure a monopoly, since the combinations resulted from the process of integration that had been going on for years in the industry, since in so far as there was any restriction of competition it was restriction of a "destructive" type of competition injurious in the long run to consumers as well as producers; and that, consequently, there was no "undue" restraint of trade. On the charge of elevating and controlling prices the Corporation made the general answer that the rises were sufficiently explained by improvements in business at the date, cited by the government. On the price of rails it made the specific answer that the railroads were really responsible for the stabilized price, and went on to claim that about 1900 the Pennsylvania Railroad adopted the plan of buying rails for a year at a time and dividing its order between a number of mills, with some reference to the freight tonnage these mills gave to the Pennsylvania. Other railroads began to follow this plan, so that soon a very large part of all rail orders for any year was being booked in the closing months of the preceding year. It was further claimed that having the Pennsylvania agree to a certain price practically set the price for the other roads, and that buying a year's supply at a time set the price for that period.[1] On the other hand, Mr. James Gayley, at one time a partner in the old Carnegie Company and later the head of the Corporation's ore department, testified before a Congressional committee that this plan of the Pennsylvania's began about 1885, or sixteen years before the remarkable stabilization of rail prices occurred.[2] Moreover, the government submitted an extract from the minutes of the executive committee of the Corporation which proves that Gary and Corey were appointed a special com-

[1] U. S. *v.* U. S. Steel, *Brief for the Corporation before the U. S. Supreme Court,* p. 211 *et seq.*

[2] *Stanley Hearings,* vol. i, p. 308.

mittee to consider the price of rails, that their report was a recommendation "that the price of rails for 1908 be fixed at $28 f.o.b. mills," and that on motion the report was approved and adopted.[1] Similar extracts were cited for other years and other commodities. The exact language of the minutes is interesting and affords some light on the topic of the method by which prices were established, but it also indicates that the Corporation's explanation lacks a good deal of being satisfactory.

The charges of "preponderant position" and monopoly were met by the contention that mere size was no offense against the law, and by the presentation of figures showing the changes in the proportion of the country's production of iron and steel made by Corporation subsidiaries. These data are brought down to date in Table XII below. They afford conclusive proof that the Corporation has at no time had a monopoly of the steel business of the country.

Finally, the Corporation offered as additional refutation of the charge of unduly restraining competition the testimony of a considerable number of its competitors that there was competition and keen competition, but that it was competition of the fairest sort.

As might have been expected from its magnitude and importance, the case dragged through the courts for years. Literally hundreds of witnesses were examined and thousands of pages of testimony recorded. On June 3, 1915, the four judges of the District Court of New Jersey unanimously decided to dismiss the bill and to refuse to order the dissolution of the Corporation, though they disagreed as to the reasons for the refusal. The lengthy opinion of Judge Buffington summarizes a considerable portion of the evidence and shows a complete conversion to the Corporation's contention that the purpose of its organizers was integration. In fact, except for the statement that the object and effect of the Gary dinners was illegal, the opinion might have been written by the defendant's attorneys. Judge McPherson concurred with Judge

[1] U. S. *v.* U. S. Steel, *Government Exhibits,* vol. ii, pp. 607-608.

Buffington. The other two judges, Woolley and Hunt, though agreeing that dissolution was not necessary, concluded that "the organizers of the Corporation (1) intended to create a monopoly and to restrain trade, and (2) combined with others and attempted to monopolize trade, within the meaning of the act, and that the *Corporation* (1) neither attempted nor possessed the power alone to do the unlawful things intended

TABLE XII

PERCENTAGE OF PRODUCTION OF LEADING IRON AND STEEL PRODUCTS BY THE UNITED STATES STEEL CORPORATION FROM 1901–1927[a]

Year	Production of pig iron	Production of steel ingots and steel castings	Production of all kinds of finished rolled products
1901	43.2	65.7	50.1
1902	44.8	65.2	51.3
1903	40.4	63.1	51.2
1904	44.7	60.7	47.8
1905	44.2	60.0	47.4
1906	44.5	57.8	48.2
1907	44.3	57.1	48.5
1908	43.5	55.9	47.1
1909	45.0	55.8	48.9
1910	43.3	54.3	48.1
1911	45.4	53.9	45.7
1912	47.7	54.1	48.5
1913	45.5	53.2	47.8
1914	43.1	50.3	44.1
1915	45.6	50.9	44.6
1916	44.7	48.9	44.4
1917	40.5	45.0	42.0
1918	40.8	44.0	41.7
1919	44.0	49.6	44.6
1920	39.4	45.8	41.6
1921	52.0	55.4	50.5
1922	44.2	45.2	42.9
1923	41.4	45.2	42.9
1924	40.4	43.4	40.2
1925	40.3	41.6	38.4
1926	39.9	42.0	38.9
1927	37.7	41.1	37.7

[a] *Annual Statistical Report of the American Iron and Steel Institute* for 1928.

by its formation, but (2) that it unlawfully combined with others to restrain trade by controlling prices."[1]

The government appealed the case to the Supreme Court, where it was argued March, 1917. The justices who took part in the case were evenly divided, so that a reargument was ordered. In a few weeks war was declared. Therefore the government decided to postpone the case until the termination of hostilities. The Corporation's attorneys protested strongly against this course, but the government refused to accede on the ground that public policy demanded concentration on the prosecution of the war, and that if dissolution were ordered its financing might interfere with federal loans.[2]

In the decision handed down March 1, 1920, two justices did not participate, three voted for the dissolution of the trust, and four for the dismissal of the bill, thus upholding the lower court. Among other interesting points the majority decision held that the formation of an industrial combination with the expectation of achieving a monopoly is not enough to make it a monopoly within the meaning of the Sherman Act; that such a combination, short of monopoly, is not objectionable merely because of its size or merely because of a power to restrain competition, if not exerted; and that the fact that a combination for a long period persuaded and joined with its competitors in efforts, sometimes successful, sometimes not, to fix and maintain prices in violation of the antitrust act does not warrant present relief against said combination, if the illegal practices were transient in purpose and effect, were abandoned before the suit was begun because of a conviction of their futility and not from fear of prosecution, were not resumed, and if no intention to resume them or dangerous probability of their resumption is shown by the evidence. Furthermore, the majority members of the court seemed greatly impressed by the testimony of the business competitors. As pointed out above, this testimony was to the effect that the Corporation's competition was "genuine, direct, and vigorous." In the language of the opinion the Corporation

[1] 223 Fed. 178 (1915).

[2] Cf. Tarbell, *op. cit.*, pp. 264 and 317.

"resorted to none of the brutalities or tyrannies that the cases illustrate of other combinations. It did not secure freight rebates; it did not increase its profits by reducing the wages of its employees—whatever it did was not at the expense of labor; it did not increase its profits by lowering the quality of its products, nor create an artificial scarcity of them; it did not oppress or coerce its competitors—its competition, though vigorous, was fair; it did not undersell its competitors in some localities by reducing its prices there below those maintained elsewhere, or require its customers to enter into contracts limiting their purchases or restricting them in resale prices; it did not obtain customers by secret rebates or departures from its published prices; there was no evidence that it attempted to crush its competitors or drive them out of the market, nor did it take customers from its competitors by unfair means, and in its competition it seemed to make no difference between large and small competitors."[1]

In referring to the government's attempts to prove the intent of the Corporation to monopolize the steel business of the country by the citation of its acquisition of control over certain companies subsequent to the formation of the Corporation the majority opinion made this comment:

There is, however, an important circumstance in connection with [the acquisition of] the Tennessee Company which is worthy to be noted. It was submitted to President Roosevelt and he gave it his approval. His approval, of course, did not make it legal, but it gives assurance of its legality, and we know from his earnestness in the public welfare he would have approved of nothing that had even a tendency to its detriment . . . it would seem a distempered view of purchase and result to regard them as violations of the law.[2]

If the opinion as a whole brought pleasure and satisfaction to the chief figures in the Corporation, this section probably amused them. Although Roosevelt and Gary were the best of friends, a number of the directors of the Corporation were bitter in their condemnation of the "trust-buster." Indeed, this feeling was so intense that at one time a resolution was offered at a meeting of the directors instructing Gary "to make no more visits to the White House."[3] To have a man they had at one time considered a most dangerous enemy to business thus brought forward for their defense must have

[1] 251 U. S. 440, 441 (1920).
[2] 251 U. S. 446, 447 (1920).
[3] Tarbell, *op. cit.,* p. 183.

introduced an element of hilarity into whatever celebration there was over the victory.

But the most important factor in saving the Corporation from dissolution was summed up by the majority in the final paragraph of its opinion:

> In conclusion we are unable to see that the public interest will be served by yielding to the contention of the Government respecting the dissolution of the company or the separation from it of some of its subsidiaries; and we do see in a contrary conclusion a risk of injury to the public interest, including a material disturbance of, and, it may be serious detriment to, the foreign trade. And in submission to the policy of the law and its fortifying prohibitions the public interest is of paramount regard.[1]

In other words, the "rule of reason" becomes under this interpretation the "rule of business expediency."

In a vigorous dissenting opinion, in which Justices Pitney and Clarke concurred, Justice Day stated that the record left no fair room for doubt that the Corporation and its subsidiaries named in the bill were formed in violation of the Sherman Act; that the Corporation had within its control the domination of the trade and the ability to fix prices and restrain the free flow of commerce upon a scale heretofore unapproached in the history of corporate organization in this country; and that if the Sherman Act were to retain its efficacy "there must be a decree undoing so far as is possible that which has been achieved in open, notorious, and continued violation of its provisions."[2] Justice Day went on to attack the principle of interpretation just suggested in the following language:

> I know of no public policy which sanctions a violation of the law, nor of any inconvenience to trade, domestic or foreign, which should have the effect of placing combinations, which have been able thus to organize one of the greatest industries of the country in defiance of law, in an impregnable position above the control of the law forbidding such combinations. Such a conclusion does violence to the policy which the law was intended to enforce, runs counter to the decisions of the court, and necessarily results in a practical nullification of the act itself.[3]

[1] 251 U. S. 457 (1920).
[2] 251 U. S. 460 (1920).
[3] 251 U. S. 463 (1920).

In view of the facts that of the two justices who did not participate, Justice McReynolds had aided at an earlier time in preparing the government's case against the Corporation, and Justice Brandeis had as a citizen expressed the opinion that the Corporation was an uneconomic and illegal, and, in its labor policy, an unsocial combination, it is not at all impossible that the final decision did not represent the opinion of a majority of the court. When the opinions of the eleven justices of the two courts which heard the case are examined in some detail we find that seven of the eleven agreed that the Gary dinners were illegal, five of them believed the organizers of the Corporation acted illegally in forming it; but only three were willing to go the length of ordering its dissolution. Differences of opinion of such a degree on such fundamental aspects of the case must lead even the most casual observer to question the efficacy of our methods of safeguarding the public from possible undue exercise of the power inherent in such an industrial combination as the Steel Corporation. Just what restraint is exercised by the Sherman Antitrust Law as here interpreted? If we are to abandon any attempts to check "good" trusts by dissolving them, what remedy shall we seek for protection against "Gary dinners" and other forms of coöperation that may react to the disadvantage of consumers? If the claim of many business men, that heretofore governmental concern with such questions has been too much in the spirit of "interference," is justified, can we evolve a system that will embody more of the coöperation Judge Gary wished? To these and similar queries some suggested answers will be found in subsequent chapters.

CHAPTER XV

OTHER TYPICAL TRUSTS: THE INTERNATIONAL HARVESTER COMPANY AND THE UNITED SHOE MACHINERY CORPORATION

A. The International Harvester Company

PRIOR to the formation of the International Harvester Company in 1902, the farm-implement manufacturing business, in common with many other businesses, had demonstrated a tendency toward concentration. In 1850 the making of farm implements was still to a considerable extent in the hands of the village blacksmith, but factory industry was well begun and soon was producing the great majority of the implements as they themselves were undergoing the metamorphosis from hand tools to machines. In the following summary of the census data for the last half of the nineteenth century the general trend toward concentration is apparent: [1]

TABLE XIII

TENDENCY TOWARD CONCENTRATION IN AGRICULTURAL IMPLEMENT FACTORIES, 1849–1899.

Year	Number of establishments	Average capital invested	Average number of wage-earners	Average value of product
1849	1,333	$ 2,674	4.4	$ 5,133
1859	2,116	6,222	8.0	9,845
1869	2,076	16,780	12.1	25,080
1879	1,943	31,966	20.3	35,327
1889	910	159,686	42.6	89,310
1899	715	220,571	65.1	141,549

[1] The table in the text is computed from data on the growth of the manufacture of agricultural implements in the Bureau of Corporations' report, *The International Harvester Company*, p. 43.

The chief reasons for this tendency were two: the fact so common in manufacturing that increasing the output lowers the expenses per unit of production—*i.e.,* the making of farm implements is an industry of "diminishing expense" in the jargon of economic writers; and second, the methods of marketing which developed. The first of these factors has been demonstrated many times in this industry and others, and, consequently, may be taken for granted. The second probably requires a brief explanation.

When the first agricultural implements of a machine type were offered for sale their makers found most of their prospective customers lacking in sufficient cash to buy outright. Moreover, credit at satisfactory terms for farmers was very rare in the new Western communities which provided the best market. Consequently, implement manufacturers, and particularly harvester manufacturers, whose machines were fairly expensive, found themselves practically compelled to sell on long-time credit. The most common practice was for the farmer to pay for his harvester from the proceeds of two or three crops, so that the credit was extended over a period ranging from fifteen to thirty months. Though there was a great amount of direct canvassing of farmers by salesmen representing the manufacturer, the machines were usually delivered and payments received by a local retail dealer who acted as the producer's agent. The development of this system soon called for the establishment of large warehouses and general agencies at various points in order to meet the demands of the local retailers promptly and to exercise some supervision over the extension of credit to farmers. Finally, it was found necessary to maintain a staff of mechanical experts in the field more or less all of the time to assist farmers in assembling the more complicated types of machines which had been shipped in sections, and to make repairs. Thus a sales-and-maintenance organization of considerable size became necessary unless the manufacturer was content to restrict his activities to a narrow area. Obviously, the expense of such an organization was to a considerable extent a "fixed charge" on the business which it was desirable to spread over as great a volume of sales as possible. Moreover, an increased volume of sales meant the more intensive use of the manufacturing establishments, with a consequent lowering of expenses of production per unit of product. As long as patents continued valid a particular firm's tendency toward expansion was in some degree confined to increasing the production of the articles for which it held the best patents, but as these patents lapsed and became common property the desire to utilize the sales organization more completely expressed itself in the development of "full line" activities by more and more firms. In other words, manufacturers found that to sell one line of goods it was necessary to build up a sales organization which was working only a part of the time. In order to maintain the organization and utilize its full time it seemed necessary to sell a number of lines. The importance of the impediment which the patent situation presented to this development may easily be exaggerated, but it should not be overlooked.

Until 1890 the tendency toward concentration did not involve any important examples of combination. In that year, however, a charter was secured from Illinois for the "American Harvester Company," a concern into which it was proposed to draw some twenty manufacturers of harvester machinery, including the McCormick, Deering, Walter A. Wood, Johnston, Adriance-Platt, Milwaukee, Champion, Plano, Aultman-Miller, and Whitman & Barnes companies. The combination got as far as electing a board of directors and officers and sending out printed contract forms to retailers, but finally collapsed because some of the members decided that other plants were being included at excessive valuations which not only were prejudicial to their particular interests, but also threatened the financial success of the whole undertaking.[1]

From 1890 until 1902 conditions in the harvester business were definitely competitive, except for a period in 1900 during which there seems to have been a gentlemen's agreement between the McCormick and Deering companies which possibly included one or more of their competitors. In fact, competi-

[1] Cf. Commissioner of Corporations, *The International Harvester Company*, pp. 57-59.

tion during the 'nineties was characterized as "fierce" by Cyrus H. McCormick when testifying in the suit of the State of Missouri against the International Harvester Company. Agents' methods of doing business, described in detail by other witnesses, appear frequently to have bordered on sharp practices.[1] Consequently, it was to be expected that the organizers of the International Harvester Company would offer the nature of the competition as a reason for desiring to combine, and in this Missouri suit it was contended that the "real and only purpose" of the combination was to avoid ruinous and wasteful competition.[2] Subsequently, additional reasons were offered in defense of the combination, including:

(1) The necessity of securing larger capital.
(2) The desirability of securing a "full line" in order to utilize the sales force more adequately.
(3) The desirability of fostering foreign trade.

In summarizing its conclusions on the motives leading to the combination, the Bureau of Corporations discounted the factor of foreign-trade promotion, largely on the grounds that before 1902 American harvesters were being sold all over the world and that the company's witnesses themselves seemed to bring this factor in as an afterthought. The possibility of securing economies in selling through combination was admitted by the Bureau, but the International Harvester Company's claim that competition was ruinous was not admitted and considerable evidence was adduced to show that with one exception the concerns which went into the combination for the five years prior to 1902 made good profits. Finally, the Bureau concluded that "the principal motive for the formation of the International Harvester Co. was to eliminate competition and to secure a dominant position in the trade."[3]

The degree to which this chief motive was attained may be judged from the fact that in 1902 the combination con-

[1] Commissioner of Corporations, *The International Harvester Company,* pp. 59-61, quoting the court record.

[2] Quoted in *Brief for the U. S. in International Harvester* v. *the U. S.* before the U. S. Supreme Court, October term, 1916, p. 144.

[3] Commissioner of Corporations, *The International Harvester Company,* pp. 62, 63, 70.

trolled about 85 per cent of the total production of harvesting machines in the United States. The concerns included in the original merger were: McCormick Harvesting Machine Company, Deering Harvester Company, Warder, Bushnell & Glessner Company (Champion brand), Plano Manufacturing Company, and Milwaukee Harvester Company. The only important manufacturers of harvesting machines not included were a few companies in New York state whose production was largely for foreign markets. But as has been true of other combinations, this one did not maintain its position, so that its 85 per cent control in 1902 dropped to about 80 in 1911, to about 64 in 1918, and remained practically constant at the last figure until at least 1923.[1] Even the last figure, of course, insured a dominating position in the manufacture of harvesting machines.

To this point the Harvester combination has seemed to conform fairly closely to the usual pattern of such combinations, but an important difference must now be noted. The proportion of the International Harvester Company's tangible assets plus working capital to its capitalization of $120,000,000 at the time of organization was about 90 per cent. Though the company claimed to possess a valuable asset in good will it did not enter a good-will item in its formal statement of assets. There seems little room for doubt that a fair valuation of good will would have covered the difference between tangible assets and capitalization.[2] A combination which did not extensively water its stock in this period is so conspicuous that its virtue should not be overlooked.

Another respect in which the International Harvester Company differed from trusts previously considered was that as originally organized it did not follow the fashion then prevalent of taking a New Jersey holding company charter; the property of the constituent concerns was held outright by the

[1] Cf. U. S. *v.* International Harvester Co., *Brief for the U. S. before the District Court of the U. S., District of Minnesota, third division,* filed October, 1924, pp. 48-56, with *Report of the Federal Trade Commission on the High Prices of Farm Implements,* p. 679.

[2] Commissioner of Corporations, *The International Harvester Company,* p. 133.

new company and stock issued for their total assets, including factories, inventories, and bills receivable. The relative importance of the constituents is indicated by the fact that after more than a year's delay the distribution of the $120,000,000 stock was finally made according to the following percentages:

TABLE XIV

DISTRIBUTION OF STOCK OF INTERNATIONAL HARVESTER COMPANY

McCormick interests	42.6
Deering "	34.4
Champion "	3.8
Plano "	5.2
J. P. Morgan & Co.	13.4
Total	99.4

It will be noted that the foregoing percentages total only 99.4 and that the Milwaukee interests are not included. The former discrepancy results from using only the first decimal; the latter requires a more detailed explanation of the negotiations which preceded the organization of the combination. During the course of a suit against the company for violating the antitrust law of Missouri[1] its officers had testified that there were no conferences or understandings among the chief stockholders and officers prior to July 28, 1902, and that G. W. Perkins, acting for the Morgan banking house, had conducted negotiations with the companies separately. The Bureau of Corporations convinced itself that these statements were not accurate; that the old companies had discussed plans for a combination for some time; and, particularly of interest here, that the McCormick people had secured an option on the Milwaukee Company which they subsequently transferred to J. P. Morgan & Company. At the actual date of the merger, then, after this option had been exercised, the Morgan house held all the shares of the Milwaukee Company except eight to qualify directors,[2] and a part of its share of the combination's stock was in payment for that company. In addition it re-

[1] Cf. pp. 360, 361 *infra*.

[2] Commissioner of Corporations, *The International Harvester Company*, pp. 72, 76, 69.

ceived $10,000,000 in stock in exchange for raising that sum to serve as cash capital for the new concern and a commission of $2,957,142.86. The peculiarity of the last item is explained by the fact that though a commission of $3,000,000 had originally been agreed upon, it became necessary during the progress of the adjustments to issue to the Champion and Plano interests an additional amount of $150,000 in stock which had not originally been contemplated. Since the two chief companies in the merger, McCormick and Deering, and the promoters were determined to restrict the total issue to $120,000,000, they agreed to contribute this $150,000 from their original allotments. Morgan's share was $42,857.14 and reduced the commission to the figure stated.[1]

Before all of these complications had been resolved, however, the Harvester Company effected a change in its organization of considerable importance. It acquired all the stock of the Milwaukee Harvester Company (of which it already held the property), changed the name of this subsidiary to the "International Harvester Company of America," and transferred to it practically all of its warehouses and other facilities for selling machines. From that time the actual selling was done by this "America" Company, as it was called. Since the capital of the selling company was only $1,000,000, it would not be subject to as heavy taxes in some states as the producing company. Moreover, as the Milwaukee Company, it possessed licenses to do business in a number of states, whereas the combination might have had trouble in some states to secure licenses because of antitrust laws. Financially and legally the arrangement seemed a good one for the company.

As was pointed out above, the profits realized by the components of the harvester trust for the five years prior to their amalgamation had been good, though not remarkably so. The available figures since that date indicate that the same generalization remains true for most years when the organization as a whole is considered. The Bureau of Corporations computed the company's earnings on "net assets, exclusive

[1] *Ibid.*, pp. 85, 86.

of good will," at the following percentages for the years indicated: [1]

TABLE XV

PROFITS ON NET ASSETS

Year	Per cent	Year	Per cent
1903	0.73	1908	8.73
1904	5.34	1909	13.43
1905	7.01	1910	12.77
1906	6.74	1911	11.51
1907	7.31	Average	8.47

For the years 1913-1918 the Federal Trade Commission computed the International Harvester Company's profits on its "investment," defined as "the actual cash or its equivalent invested either by stockholders or others in the entire business of the company, including any subsidiary companies." On January 27, 1913, the International Harvester Company had been divided into two concerns, the International Harvester Company of New Jersey, and the International Harvester Corporation. To the latter were transferred the transportation companies, the foreign plants, and the domestic plants engaged exclusively in manufacturing the so-called "new lines" —*i.e.*, wagons, manure-spreaders, and a number of other articles not made by the original companies in 1902. These companies and their accounts were recombined in 1918, so that for that year profits cannot be shown separately.[2]

On the basis of the figures given in Table XVI, the Federal Trade Commission held that for this period the average return was "something more than adequate" and that for certain years it was excessive. For twenty-one other companies the Commission found the average profit for 1913-1918 to be only 10.03 per cent as against the International's 12.48.

In attacking these conclusions the Harvester Company contended that the comparison was not a fair one, since, though the comparison purported to be one on implement business only, the Harvester Company's figures included profits from

[1] Commissioner of Corporations, *The International Harvester Company,* p. 238. The item for 1903 is really for fifteen months, including last quarter of 1902.

[2] *Report of the Federal Trade Commission on the Causes of the High Prices of Farm Implements,* p. 103.

TABLE XVI

PROFITS ON INVESTMENT

Year	International Harvester Co. of N. J.	International Harvester Corporation	Combined
	Per cent	Per cent	Per cent
1913	13.64	7.79	10.67
1914	10.35	4.69	7.60
1915	11.08	4.46	7.84
1916	13.36	7.74	10.62
1917	28.21	10.11	18.59
1918	....	....	19.59
Average	15.03	6.96	12.48[a]

[a] The combined average omitting 1918 is 11 per cent.

its steel, lumber, and fiber subsidiaries. Deducting these, the company claimed its average profit on the implement business from 1913 to 1918, inclusive, was 10.5 per cent, or only .47 of 1 per cent more than the average profits of its twenty-one competitors as reported by the Federal Trade Commission. Furthermore, the company called attention to the fact that these percentages were computed before the deduction of certain charges such as taxes, interest, war losses in Russia and elsewhere. Finally, it claimed that the "average return on the capital during the entire life of the Harvester Company has been only 6.75 per cent."[1]

Profits on particular implements and for separate companies in the combination are presented in detail in the two government publications cited most frequently above. Two points are particularly significant. In the earlier report of the Bureau of Corporations it was stated, reiterated, and emphasized that profits in harvesting machine lines, which were practically monopolized, were much greater than those in more competitive lines. In the Federal Trade Commission's

[1] U. S. *v.* International Harvester Company in the District Court of the United States, District of Minnesota, third division; *Brief for Defendants* (No. 624), pp. 117, 119, 121.

study great stress was laid upon the profits of the Wisconsin Steel Company, ranging from 11 to 119 per cent and averaging 56 per cent during the period 1913 to 1918.[1]

The International Harvester Company objected vigorously to this last statement on three grounds. First, the Trade Commission assigned no part of the working capital to the Wisconsin Steel Company's business. Second, it reduced the value of the investment in its iron mines by $5,500,000, as the company believed without warrant. Third, the period selected was such as to include a large inventory profit resulting from the general rise in prices which was subsequently wiped out.[2]

The questions of accounting involved in the controversy over profits just outlined make any decision open to question, but on the whole it seems that the generalization made above for an earlier period, *viz.*, that they have been good though not remarkably so, may be allowed to stand for the whole period. Although in certain years profits in some departments were undoubtedly excessive, there have been others in which there were none, so that even in an individual department the charge of excessive profits seems without substantial warrant when a period of years is considered.

To this point in our discussion the International Harvester Company seems on most counts to qualify as what President Roosevelt termed a "good" trust. One criterion not yet applied, and one which Roosevelt would have stressed, is the competitive methods of the combination. From time to time it has been charged with deceptive or unfair practices, the more important of which were:

(1) The maintenance of pretended competition in the earlier years of the organization.

(2) The allotment of its brands of harvesting machines in

[1] Cf. Commissioner of Corporations, *The International Harvester Company*, p. 255, and *Report of the Federal Trade Commission on the Causes of the High Prices of Farm Implements*, pp. 670-675.

[2] U. S. *v.* International Harvester Company in the District Court of the U. S., District of Minnesota, third division. *Defendant's Statement of the Case* (No. 624), pp. 191, 192.

such a manner as to secure an undue proportion of the dealers.

(3) Attempted coercion of dealers to secure exclusive handling of some of the company's lines.

(4) Full-line forcing.

(5) "Suggested" retail price lists.

(6) Special and discriminatory prices and terms.

(7) Misrepresentations by salesmen regarding competitors.

Agents of the Bureau of Corporations interrogated over 800 retail dealers in some 600 towns scattered through 27 states concerning these competitive methods, with the result that 25 per cent of the dealers seemed favorable to the company, 20 per cent were noncommittal, and 55 per cent were unfavorable. On the basis of these and other data the Bureau concluded that some of the most objectionable methods had been eliminated or greatly reduced a number of years before its investigation, but that there was still ample ground for complaint and that the preponderant size of the International Harvester Company made the practices even more objectionable.[1] The prevalence of these practices and the size of the combination made a judicial review of the situation inevitable sooner or later, and to this phase we will now turn our attention.

Since the first legal action against the Harvester combination, brought by the state of Missouri, is discussed in detail elsewhere,[2] we confine ourselves here to the federal litigation.

Plans for prosecution under the Sherman Act which were being considered by Attorney General Wickersham in the fall of 1911 were temporarily held up by the action of the Harvester Company in attempting to arrange with the Attorney General a plan of dissolution which would satisfy the government. The company proposed to sell the Champion and Osborne plants and all its lines of harvesting machines except the McCormick and the Deering. Partly on the advice of the

[1] Commissioner of Corporations, *The International Harvester Company*, pp. 290, 291, 326.

[2] Cf. pp. 360, 361, *infra*.

Bureau of Corporations, the Attorney General refused to accede to any plan which did not separate the McCormick and Deering interests in stockholding as well as in plants and brands. Since the company refused to separate these two major constituents, the government filed suit on April 30, 1912, in the District Court of the United States for the District of Minnesota. The defendants were charged with being an unlawful combination and a monopoly. Dissolution of the combination and a plan for restoring competitive conditions were requested.

On August 12, 1914, the decision of the District Court held that "the International Harvester Company was from the beginning in violation of the first and second sections of the Sherman law—and that all the defendant subsidiary companies became from time to time parties to the illegal combination, and the defendant companies are combined to monopolize a part of the inter-state and foreign trade."[1] In a brief concurring opinion Judge Hook stated that the combination "still maintains a substantial dominance" which was illegal when secured and was still illegal at the time the opinion was written. Judge Sanborn, in a dissenting opinion, held that the company should not be dissolved because at the time the suit was filed and for seven years before that time it was not unduly restraining trade or threatening to do so. However, the majority ordered a dissolution into at least three substantially equal and independent corporations, a plan for such dissolution being required from the company within ninety days, under penalty of a receivership. On October 3, 1914, the court amended its decree by substituting for the requirement of a division into three corporations a division "into such number of parts of separate and distinct ownership as may be necessary to restore competitive conditions and bring about a new situation in harmony with law."[2] In spite of ordering the combination's dissolution the court did not specifically uphold a number of the government's

[1] 214 Fed., 987, 1001 (1914).

[2] *Decrees and Judgments in Federal Anti-Trust Cases,* p. 340.

charges and did specifically exonerate the International Harvester Company from the charges of over-capitalization and of misconduct in its business methods, stating that "in the main" its conduct "has been honorable, clean and fair." [1]

The Harvester Company appealed to the Supreme Court, where the case was argued in 1915, again in 1917, and then placed on the calendar for reargument. But in January, 1918, the government requested a continuance of this case and a number of other antitrust cases on the ground that if reorganizations were ordered their financing would interfere with the government's financial operations in prosecuting the war with Germany. By this time the International Harvester Corporation, separated from the original combination in 1913 to carry on the export business, had suffered heavy losses, so that the two companies were anxious to recombine. Moreover, since it seemed that the war was to continue for an indefinite time, the Harvester Company faced an indefinite postponement of the antitrust case. With the suit still pending the difficulties of recombining the two companies were obviously augmented. Consequently, the International Harvester Company negotiated an agreement with the then Attorney General, Thomas Watt Gregory, whereby the case before the Supreme Court was to be dismissed and a consent decree from the District Court of Minnesota was to be arranged. The chief provisions of the decree, filed November 2, 1918, were as follows:

1. The company was to sell the Champion plant at Springfield, Ohio, and the Osborne harvester plant at Auburn, New York.

2. The company was also to sell the Osborne, Milwaukee, and Champion lines of harvesting machines to some "responsible manufacturer of agricultural implements in the United States."

3. The company was to have only one agent or representative in any city or town in the United States after December 31, 1919.

[1] 214 Fed. 1002 (1914).

4. The United States reserved the right to further relief in case competitive conditions were not restored by a stipulated date (finally determined as November 2, 1920).[1]

In the meantime (May 13, 1918) the Senate of the United States had authorized the Federal Trade Commission to make an investigation of the causes of the high prices of agricultural implements, the existence of unfair methods of competition or combinations, and the relation of the prices farmers had to pay for their implements to their profits. Under the powers granted by the act creating it the Commission decided somewhat later to include in the report called for a section on the manner in which the decree of November 2, 1918, was being carried out.[2] Briefly stated, its conclusions were:

1. The decree as drawn was inadequate to restore competition in harvesting machines because
   a. The brands and plants to be sold had been constantly decreasing in importance as compared with those retained;
   b. The costs of two of the three brands sold were in excess of the two retained and were showing a tendency to increase this excess;
   c. The costs of the McCormick and Deering machines were extremely low as compared with the costs of other machines;
   d. The Wisconsin Steel Company was not detached from the McCormick and Deering interests;
   e. The McCormick and Deering interests were not separated.
2. The decree should be so amended as to separate the Deering from the McCormick plants and brands, to separate the Wisconsin Steel Company from both of them,

[1] *Final decree International Harvester Case, District Court of the United States for the District of Minnesota,* pp. 5, 6, 7.

[2] It should be noted that the International Harvester Company considered this action by the Commission as wholly unwarranted and, in fact, as "not authorized by any law of the United States." *Answer to Supplemental Petition,* p. 21, in U. S. *v.* International Harvester Company (No. 624) in District Court of the U. S., District of Minnesota, third division. The company seems in error in the statement just quoted.

and to prevent common ownership of stock of any of them.[1]

Largely on the basis of this Federal Trade Commission report the government on July 17, 1923, filed a supplemental petition in the United States District Court of Minnesota claiming that the 1918 decree had proved ineffective, so that the International Harvester Company was still unlawfully monopolizing and restraining interstate commerce, and praying for a further decree which would separate it into at least three separate, distinct, and independent corporations. In its arguments the government followed closely those of the Federal Trade Commission just summarized, particularly stressing the low costs and high profits of the International Harvester Company as the means by which it dominated the industry and prevented effective competition.

In their answer the defendants denied that the Osborne, Milwaukee, and Champion lines were insignificant, questioned the accuracy of the costs and profits data presented by the government, and developed at length the changes in the farm-implement business which they claimed made the harvester lines much less important than they had been in 1902. Moreover, they produced a great deal of evidence from dealers and competitors to show that they had carried out the provision of the 1918 decree which restrained them from having more than one dealer in a town, and that this had had a marked effect in making conditions truly competitive. This evidence they contended was sufficient to throw out the government's request for dissolution.

As is most commonly the situation in these antitrust cases, there seems to be a great deal of truth in the contentions of both parties. The government's contention that the sale of the two plants and the three lines of harvesters as provided in the 1918 decree could not have any great effect in altering the situation one way or the other seems to be true, but the obvious observation is that the government should not have assented to the arrangement. The disagreement over costs

[1] *Report of the Federal Trade Commission on the Causes of High Prices of Farm Implements,* 1920, pp. 669, 680.

and profits is a highly involved accounting controversy, in which the contentions of the company seem to us largely justified. Moreover, it will be recalled that the combination was not over-capitalized and that with the possible exception of two or three years its profits certainly have not been excessive. The defendants were able to show that in a number of respects the costs data on which the government relied were not strictly comparable, and that some of the conclusions drawn on the relation between cost margin and monopolistic power were open to serious question. It should be noted, however, that just to the extent the International Harvester Company is able to demonstrate a lack of advantage in costs it cuts from under its feet the chief economic justification for its existence. Finally, the defendants seemed to score heavily on the effect on competition of their adherence to the one dealer to a town provision of the 1918 decree.

The judges before whom the cause was pleaded were compelled, of course, to reach some definite decision without such conditions and qualifications as are found above, but in this cause, if one may judge from the tone of the opinions, they had little difficulty in formulating the most positive answers to the questions at issue. It is some consolation to mere economists to note, however, that two of them decided that the Harvester Company was all right, and the other that it was nearly all wrong. In the opinion of the majority the evidence not only failed to prove that since the sale of the Osborne, Champion, and Milwaukee lines the International Harvester Company had unduly monopolized or restrained interstate commerce in harvesting machines, but, on the contrary, said evidence "conclusively proves that it has not done and is not doing so, that competition in the manufacture and sale of harvesting machines and their appurtenances in interstate commerce in the United States has been and is free and untrammeled," and that "it cannot and does not control or dictate the prices of the harvesting machines and their appurtenances which it and its competitors make and sell." Further on the court laid down the proposition that "The purpose of preventing undue restraint of trade is to prevent unreasonably high prices to the purchasers and users of the articles traded in," and went on to say that "The evidence in this case satisfies us that these objects have been successfully attained under the decree of November 2, 1918."

In his dissenting opinion Judge Stone stated that the consent decree of 1918 "has entirely failed to restore genuine competitive conditions. . . . Competition which depends upon the sufferance of one of the competitors is a complete sham. This evidence convinces me that the International has such advantages in resources, organization, selling mediums, production costs, ownership and manufacture of raw material (steel) and in volume and spread of business as to be able completely to dominate this business. Also, that it does so control, and dominate by regulating prices. The International fixes prices for its own harvesting machinery and the other manufacturers prudently govern their prices thereby." [1]

The Supreme Court affirmed the decision of the lower court by a unanimous vote of the six justices who sat. They were convinced by the evidence that competitive conditions had been restored by the consent decree and stressed the importance of the limitation of the International to one dealer in a locality in securing that result. The steel decision was relied upon as a precedent. It is interesting to note the grounds on which the court refused to be guided by the report of the Federal Trade Commission on the prices of farm implements.[2] The opinion stated that ". . . the government relies in large measure upon various statements and tabulations contained in the report of the Federal Trade Commission, which was introduced in evidence over the objection of the International Company. But it is entirely plain that to treat the statements in this report—based upon an *ex parte* investigation and formulated in the manner hereinabove set forth—as constituting in themselves substantive evidence upon the questions of fact here involved, violates the fundamental rules of evidence entitling the parties to a trial of issues of fact, not upon hearsay, but upon the testimony of persons having first-hand knowledge

[1] 10 Fed. (2d) 827, 828, 829 (1925).

[2] 274 U. S. 693 (1927).

of the facts, who are produced as witnesses and are subject to the test of cross-examination."[1]

The final outcome of this litigation was a reassertion by the Supreme Court of the moderate position it had taken when it refused to dissolve the Steel Corporation in 1920. In the absence of proof of unfair methods of competition or serious injury to the public, the court again refused to dissolve a corporation merely because of its possession of potential monopoly power. From the business standpoint the principal result has been that in accordance with the consent decree of 1918 the International Harvester Company has been compelled to combine into one its two chief lines, the Deering and McCormick, and handle them through a single agent in each American community.

B. The United Shoe Machinery Corporation

The second of the combinations selected for brief treatment in this chapter is the United Shoe Machinery Company of New Jersey, organized in 1899. For many years prior to this date the transition from hand to machine methods of manufacturing shoes had been going on, and within the shoe-machinery manufacturing industry itself a considerable degree of combination had taken place.[2] Largely as a result of this tendency there were by 1898 three or four large concerns which together produced upwards of 70 per cent of the machines used in the so-called bottoming-room in which the soles of the shoes were prepared and attached to the uppers. The principal machines used here, the lasting, welting, outsole-stitching, heeling, and metallic fastening machines were essential to the whole process. In 1898 the Consolidated and McKay Lasting Machine Company produced about 60 per cent of the lasting machines made in the United States; the Goodyear Shoe Machinery Company produced about 80 per cent of the welting and outsole-stitching machines and about 10 per cent of the lasting machines; and the McKay Shoe Machinery Com-

[1] 274 U. S. 703 (1927).

[2] *Hearings before the U. S. Senate Committee on Interstate Commerce on Control of Corporations*, 1912, vol. ii, p. 2112.

pany made about 70 per cent of the heeling machines and 80 per cent of the metallic fastening machines.[1]

The leading figure in the Consolidated and McKay Company, S. W. Winslow, and in the Goodyear Company, E. P. Howe, decided sometime in the middle 'nineties that the time was ripe for a further degree of combination. In 1897 formal negotiations were begun, and on February 8, 1899, the Goodyear Company sent out the following letter to its stockholders:

> The great advantages to be secured by the control in one corporation, both in the United States and in foreign countries, of the efficient types of shoe machinery, have been for several years recognized by the officers of the principal shoe-machinery companies. For more than a year your directors and large stockholders have been in negotiation to accomplish this end.
>
> After a thorough investigation of the financial condition and the business of the shoe-machinery companies named below, the organization of a corporation has been effected under the laws of the State of New Jersey, to be known as United Shoe Machinery Company.
>
> The United Shoe Machinery Company has already contracted for more than a majority of the capital stock of Goodyear Shoe Machinery Company, Consolidated and McKay Lasting Machine Company, McKay Shoe Machinery Company, Goodyear Shoe Machinery Company of Canada, International Goodyear Shoe Machinery Company, Eppler Welt Machine Company, International Welt Machine Company, Davey Pegging Machine Company, besides stocks in other shoe-machinery companies, letters patent, and other property.
>
> The United Company will also from time to time acquire other shoe-machinery properties, either by direct ownership or by purchase of shares of their stock.[2]

The intention stated in the last paragraph of the foregoing letter was so well carried out that more than fifty concerns had been brought into the combination within a decade.[3]

Reserving for later discussion the effect of this combination on the free working of competition, we should emphasize at the outset the difference between the Shoe Machinery Trust and the others discussed. Any particular product, a machine, for example, might or might not be patented. In case it was

[1] 227 U. S. 215 (1913).
[2] 247 U. S. 41-42 (1918).
[3] 247 U. S. 86 (1918).

patented the company which produced it had, of course, a complete and legalized monopoly of it. Since some other company might also produce a machine of the same type,—that is, for doing the same work,—on which that company also held a patent, it is clear that a patent on a lasting machine, although it secured a legal monopoly on that particular machine, did not give the owner a monopoly on lasting machines in general. The monopoly could be secured in entirety only by combining all the manufacturers of lasting machines into one concern. A quasi monopoly might be established by the acquisition of something less than all the production. Throughout the controversy which developed shortly after the organization of the combination, the United Shoe Machinery Company insisted that to the extent it had a monopoly that monopoly rested upon rights guaranteed in the patent laws, upon the excellence of its products, and upon its service to shoe manufacturers. The contrary view is that the original combination was a violation of the Sherman Act, and that its business methods, particularly the so-called "tying" clauses in the leases under which the company put out its machines, have carried it to a position of dominance far beyond that which its patent rights are sufficient to sustain. The relations of our patent laws to our antitrust policy constitute, therefore, the chief interest for this study in the history of the United Shoe Machinery Corporation. With this in mind we return to that history.

In form the new concern was a typical New Jersey holding company which began business with an issued capital stock of $17,318,425.[1] In 1902 the Goodyear Shoe Machinery Company took out a new charter in Maine as the United Shoe Machinery Company of Maine. Since that time it has functioned as a selling and leasing department for the original New Jersey company in certain states from which the New Jersey company was barred by a statutory provision prohibiting the issuance of a license to a foreign corporation whose capitalization was as great as that of the New Jersey com-

[1] *Petition,* p. 78, in U. S. *v.* United Shoe Machinery Company of New Jersey, and others, 1911.

pany.[1] In 1905 a new holding company with a capitalization of $50,000,000, called the United Shoe Machinery Corporation, was organized. It held 98½ per cent of the stock of the New Jersey Company, and according to the federal Department of Justice was organized for the purpose of facilitating the distribution of some accumulated profits of the New Jersey Company and of securing "better facilities for destroying competition, and restraining and monopolizing interstate and foreign trade and commerce in shoe machinery. . . ."[2] The company denies the latter half of the explanation and states that the most important purpose was the desire to alter certain of the powers granted to the original company in its 1899 charter.[3] In 1917 the old "Company" was merged with the "Corporation."

The letter quoted above, which was sent out by the Goodyear Company to its stockholders at the time of the combination, did not specify precisely what would be the "great advantages" secured by the control of "the efficient types of shoe machinery" in "one corporation," and as a matter of fact there had been a prior proposal for a "working agreement" or "harmonious arrangement" rather than a merger. This idea was overruled by E. P. Howe of the Goodyear Company because he had "a sort of indefinite idea that it might be deemed to be a combination in restraint of trade."[4] It should be noted, however, that two of the reasons the Bureau of Corporations' investigations usually disclosed for combination, *viz.*, integration and the desire to secure promoter's profits, were not involved.[5] The company itself has stated that the purpose of the combination was to reduce the cost of production of the machines, to improve the quality of the service furnished without increasing its cost to the shoe manufac-

[1] In Equity No. 4517. The United States *v.* United Shoe Machinery Company and others in the District Court of the U. S. for Eastern District of Missouri. *Brief for U. S.*, p. 6.

[2] *Petition,* p. 75, in U. S. *v.* United Shoe Machinery Company of New Jersey and others, 1911. 234 Fed. 129 (1916).

[3] Conversation with Mr. H. G. Donham, vice-president of the company, in May, 1926.

[4] 247 U. S. 77 (1918).

[5] 222 Fed. 363 (1915).

turers, and to give to each manufacturer who might wish it an opportunity to get from a single company the machines needed in the bottoming-room. It specifically denied any intent to destroy competition.[1] As far as the original combination of 1899 was concerned, excluding the leasing system, which was not involved, Justice Holmes of the Supreme Court said in 1913: "On the face of it the combination was simply an effort after greater efficiency." [2]

The opposite view that the original combination was formed for the purpose of limiting competition is not without support, however. The language of the letter to the stockholders quoted above concerning the control by "one corporation" of the efficient types of shoe machinery can be so interpreted without doing it violence. Moreover, the president of the combination testified that "After the formation of the United Company it was manufacturing *every single lasting machine* that was being put out in the United States except the Seaver machine; and in 1900 we acquired the Seaver Company." [3] Both Winslow and Howe, the original proponents of combination, testified that the Goodyear and Eppler Companies were sharply competitive prior to the combination in the welting, outsole-stitching, and at least two auxiliary machines.[4] But the most convincing evidence of the continued intent to monopolize the manufacture of bottoming-room machines is seen by some students in the so-called "Plant episode." The evidence in regard to this episode from individuals who were in a position to know the facts is so contradictory that some points must remain in doubt. Those on which there is more or less agreement are as follows.

After some years of experimentation Thomas G. Plant of Boston, on May 1, 1910, canceled his leases on a number of the United Company's machines then in use in his shoe factory, replaced them with his own machines, and advertised

[1] United Shoe Machinery Company, *The Story of Three Partners* (pamphlet), pp. 15-17.

[2] 227 U. S. 217 (1913).

[3] 247 U. S. 81 (1918). Italics in original, Justice Clarke quoting Mr. Winslow.

[4] 247 U. S. 82 (1918).

his readiness to supply other shoe manufacturers with his machines. On June 16, 1910, negotiations were begun with the United Company looking toward a sale of Plant's property to the United Company. These negotiations were broken off on July 5. A series of suits was filed by the United against Plant on July 28, August 11, August 13, and September 3, alleging breach of contract on the canceled leases and infringement of patents. On September 22, at four in the morning, Plant agreed to sell his entire property, including his shoe factory, his shoe machinery, patents, etc., for $6,000,000, half in cash and half in the United Company's common stock at twice its par value of $25 a share.[1]

The details of this transaction have remained to this day a matter of acrimonious dispute. C. H. Jones, a shoe manufacturer of Boston, told a Senate Committee in 1911 that he had been in touch with Plant for some time during his work on the machines; that Plant intended to put his machines into factories, not simply force them on the United Company; that he had secured a promise from Plant to permit a group of shoe manufacturers to make an offer on the financing of his machines before he made final arrangements with some New York capitalists (as Plant preferred to do); that the arrangement with the capitalists fell through; that Jones arranged a meeting of shoe manufacturers interested in Plant's machines; that they agreed to pay $1,600,000 for half of Plant's holdings at eight o'clock one evening; that during that night Plant effected the sale to the United Company; and that when reproached for not giving the manufacturers one more day in which to raise the cash required, Plant replied that the pressure on him to pay a debt of $140,000 the next day was so great that he had to close the deal immediately. Jones further testified that Plant told him that he believed the pressure to pay up his loans originated with the United Shoe Machinery Company.[2]

The other side of the story is that Plant was not a com-

[1] 247 U. S. 87, 88 (1918). 222 Fed. 378 (1915).

[2] *Hearings before the U. S. Senate Committee on Interstate Commerce o the Control of Corporations,* 1912, p. 2256 *et seq.*

petitor in any real sense; that he was not prepared to supply machines; that his real intention all along was to force the United Company to buy his patents; that he set the negotiations on foot; that he was at one time under an obligation to pay a shoe manufacturer $250,000 if the said manufacturer effected a sale for him; that he offered and later had to pay a 5-per-cent commission to a second intermediary; that his machines at the time of sale were still in an experimental stage, since they had not been successful in his own factory; and that the United Company had never directly or indirectly attempted to damage Plant's credit standing or to put pressure on him to pay his debts.[1]

In discussing this episode with complete approval of the United Company's actions, Judge Dodge of the United States Circuit Court stated that "the patents acquired were the controlling feature of the purchase." On the same page of his opinion, however, he stated that the United Company refused to listen to Plant's proposals until he offered to include the shoe-manufacturing business in the sale, and that his efforts to sell his machines and his patents by themselves "were wholly ineffectual."[2] When the matter came before the Supreme Court of the United States it held, by a margin of one vote, that the real reason for the Plant sale was that the patent situation was in a deadlock, since both parties were afraid to proceed with improvements for fear of infringing on the patents of the other, and that if their differences had not been adjusted there would have been "a stop in the development of shoe machinery in these lines." The court went on to say that in these facts it saw sufficient reason for the purchase of the Plant property without having recourse to the idea that the United Company was forcing a monopoly.[3]

The "service" item in the company's statement of the purposes of its organizers referred to the fact that the manu-

[1] 222 Fed. 376, 377 (1915). *Closing argument for Defendants* (*U. S. M. Co.*) *by F. P. Fish before District Court of Massachusetts,* June 5, 1914, p. 48.

[2] 222 Fed. 379 (1915). Mr. H. G. Donham, vice-president of the U. S. M. Co., told the writers that the patents were the controlling feature and that his company did not want Plant's shoe business.

[3] 247 U. S. 48-52 (1918).

facturers of shoe machinery maintained a group of road men whose task it was to keep the machines of the company in good repair. Since the majority of the machines were leased, not sold, to the manufacturers of shoes, this aided the shoemaker in maintaining production without employing a force of specialized mechanics, and brought in more continuous royalties to the manufacturer of the machines. If all the machines in a single shoe factory's bottoming-room were leased from the same company, or better, from the United's point of view, if all the bottoming-room machines in a shoe-manufacturing town were leased from a single company, a considerable degree of duplication in service might be eliminated.

The final item in the company's statement of its purposes, the desire to give every manufacturer who wished it the opportunity to secure from a single company all the machines needed in the bottoming-room, has been compared to the convenience of a department store. That there is a considerable degree of convenience in such an arrangement cannot be denied, but if the convenience becomes compulsory—an aspect to be discussed later—it becomes objectionable.

The remaining factor in the situation, which has rarely been stressed in discussions and which was not even mentioned in the United Company's pamphlet quoted above on the purposes of its organizers, seems to the writers of great significance and of more validity as a justification of the combination than some of the reasons given. This factor was the patent situation. Despite the fact that a number of combinations had taken place before 1899 in which the desire to acquire patent rights was the impelling motive, there were suits in quantity over such patents. In 1899 litigation was pending between the Consolidated and McKay Company and the Goodyear Company over some lasting machines, each concern claiming that the others infringed its patents. Similar litigation concerning welting-machine patents was pending between the Eppler and Goodyear companies. Obviously, a consolidation of the disputants would end such controversies. But much more important than the termination of more or less petty legal squabbles were the possibilities of accelerating technological progress. Machines for making shoes had by this time reached the stage where progress was most likely to result from constant tinkering and improving upon working models. In numerous cases a great improvement in one machine could be effected by the application to it of some feature of another. If by combinations and mergers common use of the best features of a number of sets of patents could be achieved, the whole shoe industry, as well as the shoe-machinery industry, would be benefited. Moreover, a stimulus to further invention and improvement might be given, since the fear of infringement would be removed. It is possible, of course, that a mutual leasing of patent privileges would have been a better method of securing the end in view, but the advocate of a merger had something of a case.[1]

The degree of control of shoe-machinery manufacture secured and maintained by the United Company is a matter of dispute. A proportion as high as from 70 to 80 per cent of the chief bottoming-room machines in 1899 is indicated by the available data. Attempts at more specific statements were made by the government in its suits. The results are summarized in Table XVII on the next page.

The competitive methods by which this monopolistic position was secured and maintained have been attacked as oppressive, coercive, intimidating, and threatening; but the District Court of Massachusetts failed to find any support for these charges in the evidence it heard, and exonerated the United Company.[2] Whether this exoneration should have included the "tying" clauses in the company's leases is a question open to considerable difference of opinion.

But more important than the company's competitive methods is the influence which it has exerted upon the progress of the industry. The importance of the patent situation has been brought out in discussing the causes of the original combination and of the Plant sale. The company claims that it spends every year thousands of dollars in improving and per-

[1] Cf. 222 Fed. 367 (1915). The company does not admit the validity of our suggestion of the patent situation as a justification of the 1899 combination.

[2] 222 Fed. 357, 380-385 (1915).

TABLE XVII

BOTTOMING MACHINES IN USE, 1911 AND 1920[a]

Machines	1911				1920			
	Manufactured by United Shoe Machinery Co.		Manufactured by all others		Manufactured by United Shoe Machinery Co.		Manufactured by all others	
	No.	Per cent	No.	Per cent	No.	Per cent	No.	Per cent
Pulling-over machine	1,632	100.0	None	......	2,441	100.0	None	.....
Lasting machine	7,496	99.9	7	.1	8,499	99.5	48	.5
Standard screw machine	409	100.0	None	......	280	100.0	None	.....
Pegging machine	146	100.0	None	......	23	95.9	1	4.1
Tacking machine	3,488	99.8	6	.2	7,937	99.9	11	.1
Welt-sewing machine	2,527	94.7	142	5.3	2,609	95.1	135	4.9
Outsole-stitching machine	2,676	78.0	758	22.0	2,906	80.9	689	19.1
Loose-nailing machine	1,835	98.8	24	1.2	2,026	99.7	6	.3
Heeling machine	2,019	99.2	17	.8	2,086	95.0	110	5.0
Slugging machine	1,876	98.8	23	1.2	1,718	99.4	12	.6
McKay sewing machine	898	99.2	8	.8	711	68.5	326	31.5

[a] 1911 figures from *Brief for U. S. (No. 207)* p. 150, before Supreme Court of U. S., October term, 1917, in U. S. *v.* United Shoe Machinery Co. *et al.* 1920 figures from *Brief for U. S. (No. 119)*, p. 99, before Supreme Court of U. S., October term, 1921, in United Shoe Machinery Co. *et al. v.* U. S. Percentages computed by the authors.

fecting its machines and in developing new ones, and that the shoe manufacturers who hold United machines on lease are promptly given the benefit of every advance made, even to the extent of having their old model machines replaced without charge by a newly invented one. Furthermore, the United Company states that the result of this policy has been to leave the shoe manufacturer his full time for the manufacturing of shoes, safe in the certainty that it is no longer necessary for him to investigate the claims of every itinerant inventor, since the United Company is making progress as rapidly as could reasonably be expected. In these claims the company has found support from a number of manufacturers.[1]

On the other hand, it has been stated that improvements of an important character have been much less frequent since the combination was formed; that only minor changes in old machines, primarily with the purpose of reviving the patents, are made; and that the United Company has really choked off invention. The members of the Shoe Manufacturers' Alliance, making in 1911 40 per cent of all the shoes manufactured in the United States, were strongly of the opinion that the United Company's methods constituted a bar to technical progress.[2] The weight of the evidence convinces the writers that this position was justified.

To this point only incidental reference has been made to the best-advertised aspect of the business of the United Shoe Machinery Company—its "tying" leases. For many years prior to the combination the general practice of shoe-machinery manufacturers had been to lease, not sell, their products. There is considerable evidence to prove that the majority of shoe manufacturers favored leases rather than outright sales because they believed the leases more economical and because they gave the small manufacturer a much better chance. The machines were complicated and expensive. The capital outlay for a complete set of machines for a small factory turning out only a few hundred pairs of shoes a day was prohibitive for many who wished to enter the industry. Moreover, under the leasing system the manufacturer of machines maintained a force of road men who were available on short notice for repair and adjustment work. The testimony of a number of small manufacturers on the convenience

[1] *Hearings before U. S. Senate Committee on Interstate Commerce on Control of Corporations,* 1912, vol. ii, p. 2159.

[2] *Ibid.,* pp. 2116, 2117, 2266, 2267. In Equity No. 4617. In District Court of the U. S. for Eastern District of Missouri. U. S. *v.* United Shoe Machinery Co. and Others. *Brief for U. S.,* p. 276.

and value of this service to them leaves no doubt of its importance.

The basis of the protests against the system lay in what many manufacturers believed to be a perversion of the leases by the United Company—*viz.,* in the introduction of "tying" clauses. The idea that the United Company invented the "tying" clauses is a mistake, for they had been used by predecessors of the combination, but there is no question that they were greatly developed and extended by it after 1899. The forms of these leases were so varied and the possibilities so numerous that almost any general statement is certain to have an appreciable number of exceptions. First, it must be noted that the United Company has always been willing to sell a considerable portion of its products, slightly over 50 per cent, for example, in 1906. These were what it termed general-department machines. If a general-department machine was sold outright there were no restrictions on its use, but if it was leased the lessee was required to use it only in connection with special-department machines leased from the United Company.

The special-department machines were never sold. The leases under which the company put them out, however, seem to have been of a number of forms. A very few were always leased with no restrictions; others were leased only under restrictions which compelled the lessee to use them only with others of the special-department machines; still others were put out under two types of leases, one in which they were tied to other machines, and a second in which there was no such "tying." In this second "independent" form the royalties were higher, at least until about the time the Clayton Act was passed, and in most, if not all, there was an initial payment required at the time of installation which was not required of the man who signed a lease containing the "tying" clauses.[1]

But here fresh complications appear. It might be inferred

[1] Cf. the memorandum of April 25, 1906, from Louis D. Brandeis to the judiciary committee of the Massachusetts legislature, quoted in *Hearings before the U. S. Senate Committee on Interstate Commerce on the Control of Corporations,* 1912, p. 1974.

from the foregoing statement that an "initial payment" form of lease never carried a "tying" clause, and as a matter of fact the terms "independent" and "initial payment" and "unrestricted" were used as more or less synonymous terms. The truth is, however, that a considerable number of the "initial payment" leases contained "tying" clauses.[1] Finally, it should be noted that the restrictive leases for the most important and practically indispensable bottoming-room machines all contained one or more of the "tying" clauses. The net result of the clauses was to insure that a manufacturer who took one of these machines practically had to take a number of others.

At least ten clauses have been protested against from time to time. The most objectionable of them were the "restricted use," "exclusive use," and "cancellation of all leases" clauses. The restricted-use clause under which lasting machines were leased provided, (1) that such lasting machines could not be used on any *welted* foot-wear which had been or was to be welted in whole or in part on a welt-sewing or sole-stitching machine not leased from the United Company; (2) that they could not be used on any *turned* footwear, the soles of which had been or were to be attached to their uppers by a turn-sewing machine not leased from the United Company; (3) that they could not be used on any footwear which had been or was to be in whole or in part pulled-over, slugged, heel-seat nailed, or otherwise partly made by the aid of a pulling-over or "metallic" machine not leased from the United Company. In addition to lasting machines this clause was used for a very wide range of other machines, limiting each to use only on shoes on which certain other operations were performed by United Company machines.

On the face of it the foregoing clauses seem to make it clear that if a manufacturer wished to use a United lasting machine he absolutely had to take a number of other machines. This is not the case, however, for, as stated above, he might have

[1] For a list of such "independent" leases which actually contain "tying" clauses, see *Brief for the U. S. upon reargument,* pp. 223-228, in United Shoe Machinery *et al v.* U. S. before the Supreme Court of the U. S., October term, 1921, No. 119.

taken a so-called "unrestricted" lease which did not contain this particular clause. The United Company stresses this point in its defense. The answer to that defense is simple. For a number of years the manufacturer who took such an unrestricted lease had to pay 10 per cent higher royalties than if he took the other form, and in addition had to make an initial payment of $300 on each lasting machine. The higher royalties on most machines were abandoned, but the initial payments were retained. The range of these initial payments was at least from $25 to $1,000, with the majority of them included in a range of $200 to $500. But such figures mean little without some knowledge of the aggregate sum which a manufacturer who took only initial-payment leases would be required to pay in order to maintain a specified output and retain the maximum amount of independence. The United Company contended that this sum was not sufficiently large to add substantially to the manufacturers' costs, particularly if it was distributed over a period of years as it should be. But it must be remembered that these initial payments were in addition to the royalties and other charges, and that the man who took the initial-payment form of lease paid the same royalties (for a time 10 per cent higher) as those paid by the competitor who accepted the restricted leases. Moreover, it seems that the company's conclusions rested upon the theoretical capacity of its machines. During the litigation subsequently discussed the government was able to show that in the actual operation of their factories manufacturers used substantially more of a number of different types of machines than the theoretical capacity computation would indicate as necessary. Furthermore, the computations of the government based on the United machines actually in use by the Commonwealth Shoe and Leather Company indicated that the leasing of them on initial-payment leases would have cost $92,930 more than leasing them on the restricted basis. Similar computations for the equipment of the Thomas G. Plant Company indicated an additional cost of $206,005. The respective capacities of these concerns were 6,000 and 12,000 pairs of shoes daily. For larger concerns, such as the International Shoe

Company of St. Louis with an output of 50,000 pairs a day in 1920, these initial payments would mount to staggering figures. Finally, it should be noted that according to the testimony of the president of the United Company the percentages of machines held on unrestricted leases decreased between 1905 and 1911.

In the face of these facts the attempts of spokesmen for the trust to prove that the initial payments and extra royalties were not "prohibitive" and did not force manufacturers to use restricted leases are far from convincing. The plain intent and purpose of the restrictive-use clause was to force the shoe manufacturer to use only United machinery in his bottoming-room. The alleged freedom of action offered in the alternative leases was really no freedom at all.[1]

The purpose of the exclusive-use clause is clear enough from its name. If a shoe manufacturer leased a single machine of a given type from the United Company, his lease compelled him to use United Company machines only for that type of work. If the manufacturer introduced a competitor's pulling-over machine, for example, in any one of twenty factories he might operate, the United Company reserved the right to cancel all his leases for that machine in all his factories. In some instances failure to use one machine exclusively might cause the loss of it and some other machine as well. That is, the "tying" principle was sometimes involved in this clause whose primary purpose was to force the manufacturer to use only United machines for certain jobs.

But a much more thoroughgoing use of this "tying" principle is found in the "cancellation of all leases" clause. This permitted the company to cancel *all* the leases of a particular lessee for a breach of *any* clause in *any* lease. Not only was the arrangement as sweeping as could be devised; it had the additional effectiveness of being contained in every single one of the United Company's restricted leases. Of course, a manu-

[1] Cf. the *Brief for the U. S.*, p. 169, in U. S. *v.* United Shoe Machinery of New Jersey, and others, in district court of U. S. for District of Massachusetts, in Equity, No. 301, with the *Brief for the U. S.*, pp. 295-301, 371, in U. S. *v.* United Shoe Machinery Company and Others, District Court for Eastern District of Missouri. In Equity No. 4617.

facturer had to sign a restricted lease for only a small number of machines since he had the option of signing an unrestricted lease on most of them; but as brought out above, this privilege was more illusory than real. The psychological threat carried in this clause cannot be appreciated by one who has not studied the leases in some detail. A Senate committee's report published in 1912 printed in detail a large number of leases, though apparently not all those in use at that time. They fill eighty pages of fine type. Although probably few manufacturers signed each one of the leases exhibited, many signed a large number of them. In case such a manufacturer wished to adopt a competitor's machine, he faced the prospect of taking off a couple of weeks to ascertain, with the aid of a first-class lawyer, whether or not he would thereby make himself liable to a wholesale cancellation of his United leases. This may not be compulsion technically, but we are unable to see that its practical results differ from compulsion.[1]

The amount of opposition to these clauses in the first years of the trust's operations is not clear. In May, 1906, however, it took the tangible form of the introduction into the Massachusetts legislature of a bill by Mr. Long of Framingham to prohibit the "tying" leases. Partly as a result of the expressed wishes of certain shoe manufacturers, action was deferred until the next year, but the measure then became law (1907). Obviously it affected only sales made in Massachusetts. The United Company met the situation by attaching a rider to all leases entered into with Massachusetts lessees which provided that "any and all agreements, stipulations, provisions, and conditions hereinbefore printed in this instrument which are in violation of the provisions of Chapter 469 of the Acts of the General Court of Massachusetts for the year 1907, if

[1] Cf. *Hearings before the U. S. Senate Committee on Interstate Commerce on Control of Corporations,* 1912, vol. ii, pp. 2170-2250; and *Brief for the U. S.,* p. 90, in U. S. *v.* United Shoe Machinery Co. and Others in the District Court of the U. S. for the Eastern District of Missouri. In Equity No. 4617.

The exact language of all the restrictive clauses, with comments on them, will be found in the brief just cited, p. 76 *et seq.,* and in the *Brief for the U. S. upon reargument,* pp. 14-24, 88 *et seq.,* in the case of the United Shoe Machinery Corporation *et al.* *v.* U. S. before the Supreme Court of the U. S., October term, 1921. No. 119.

there are any such, are hereby stricken out before execution and are not agreed to nor made a part of this contract."[1]

The practical results of this legislation seem to have been nil. The manufacturers were not willing to risk the loss of all their machines leased from the United Company under a clause, not listed above, which gave the lessor the right to terminate any lease at any time simply by notifying the lessee that the lease was thereby terminated.

The opposition continued to grow, however, until in 1911 manufacturers producing well over 50 per cent of the country's shoes were formally on record as opposed to the "tying clauses."[2]

The validity of these criticisms of its leases has never been admitted in the slightest degree by the United Company. It contends to this day that they were economically and legally sound. The first item in its defense, or explanation, is that the leasing system was inherited from its predecessors, even to the "tying" clauses. These predecessors found that leases were better than outright sales because they permitted a man with limited capital to enter the shoemaking business, and they tied some of their machines together because they believed that the functions they performed were so closely related that unless this were done poor workmanship, damaged machines, loss of revenue, and loss of reputation were sure to follow. This latter contention, an economic argument, of course, was particularly true of the welting and outsole-stitching machines put out by the Goodyear Shoe Machinery Company. Any shoe machine must be so constructed that its operation will not damage work done by preceding machines or hinder work to be done by subsequent machines. In principle this situation does not differ from that in any factory, but the United Company claims that there exists such an extraordinary degree of relationship between some shoe machines that they have to be tied together, or, as its spokesmen frequently say, "operated in teams."

[1] *Journal of Political Economy,* vol. xxi, pp. 945-946.

[2] *Hearings before the U. S. Senate Committee on Interstate Commerce on the Control of Corporations,* 1912, p. 2121.

Now no one is going to deny the economic advantages of proper coördination of machinery—they are too well demonstrated—but if the disadvantages of using competitors' machines were as disastrous as the United Company would have us believe, then why was it not content to permit these unfortunate consequences to bring customers into line rather than adopt the methods it did? We entirely agree with the United Company that it is a good thing for all the shoemaking machinery used in the country to be as completely synchronized and standardized as possible, but at the same time we feel sure that it is neither wise nor safe to approve the use by a private corporation of such methods as were embodied in these leases.

The company's legal justification for the "tying" clauses rested upon the patent law. As its attorneys interpreted that law it gave to the patentee for seventeen years an absolute monopoly and power of restraint. Consequently, they held that there was no trade in patented articles to which the public was entitled, and no trade which a court could hold, on grounds of public policy, should remain free and untrammeled; and furthermore that to use the expression "suppression or restraint of trade" with respect to patented articles was to misdescribe the situation and misrepresent the facts. The patentee had for the duration of the patent the exclusive right to make, use, and vend the articles patented. On the machines it did not care to sell the United Company might share the use, that is, lease them, and it claimed the right to lease them on such terms as it saw fit. The question raised by this reasoning is clear: does the issuance of letters patent render their holder immune from prosecution under the Sherman Act for restraint of trade?

At the time the federal government filed its first suits against certain individuals in the United Company and against the company itself in 1911 the status of court decisions seemed to favor the latter's position. As far back as 1896 it had been held in the Button-fastener case that the manufacturer of a machine for attaching buttons to shoes was within his patent-law rights in making it a condition of sale of his patented machine that it be used only with a non-patented metallic staple which the purchaser of the machine agreed to buy only from the manufacturer of the machines.[1] In 1902 the Supreme Court upheld a license contract of the National Harrow Company, owner of certain patents on harrows, in which the licensee agreed to maintain prices fixed in the license and to refrain from manufacturing any other type of float-spring-tooth harrow than that authorized in the license. The case is particularly in point here since the licensee, a Mr. Bement, urged in his defense that he was not liable for damages for breaching such a contract because the contract itself was in violation of the Sherman law. Despite the facts that the contracts were evidently in restraint of trade and that they affected interstate commerce, the court held them legal, stating that "the general rule is absolute freedom in the use or sale of rights under the patent laws of the United States. The very object of these laws is monopoly, and the rule is, with few exceptions, that any conditions which are not in their very nature illegal with regard to this kind of property, imposed by the patentee and agreed to by the licensee for the right to manufacture or use or sell the article, will be upheld by the courts."[2] Six years later the Supreme Court held in the Paper-bag Patent case that the owner of a patent might hold it out of use and prevent others from using it for the duration of the patent.[3]

Before the United Company's case came to trial its position was further reinforced by the decision in Henry *v.* A. B. Dick Company. The facts were similar to those in the Button-fastener case and the effect of the decision was the same—*viz.,* to uphold the right under the patent law of the manufacturer of patented mimeograph machines to attach to these machines a license restriction compelling purchasers to use with them only stencil paper, ink, and other supplies made by the manufacturer of the machines. The decision emphasized the point that the court was dealing with a "constitutional and statutory

[1] 77 Fed. 288 (1896).
[2] 186 U. S. 91 (1902).
[3] 210 U. S. 405 (1908).

monopoly," and pointed out that if Congress had acted unwisely in failing to impose limitations on a patentee's exclusive rights, it was the task of Congress to remedy that omission.[1]

In the criminal case brought against the president of the company and others there was no adjudication of the leases, since the United States District Court of Massachusetts construed the indictments as confined to the original combination of February 7, 1899. This court held the original combination valid in 1912 and was sustained by the Supreme Court in 1913.[2]

The leases were the vital point in the case brought against the United Company under the Sherman Act. The defense followed the lines suggested above and relied largely upon the cases we have discussed. These arguments seemed conclusive to the United States District Court of Massachusetts and so it held the original combination, the later acquisitions, and the leases to be legal.[3] The decision was presented in three sections, Judge Brown devoting his attention almost solely to the leases. In approving them, he relied largely upon the Dick case,[4] stating that "the patentee's right embraces the lesser right of permitting others to use upon such terms as the patentee chooses to prescribe."

In presenting its case the United States contended that the ownership of patents did not create an exemption from the antitrust laws nor did it confer the right to insist upon such "tying" clauses as the United Company used. It pointed out that even in the Button-fastener case, in which the doctrine of the Dick case originated, the court stated that it was "not at all prepared to say that there are no limitations upon a patentee's power of contract with reference to the use of his invention by others," and that "Neither the patentee, nor the machine involving his invention, nor a license for use, can be exempted from the liabilities and regulations which, in the public interest, attach to all persons and property under the

[1] 224 U. S. 1, 35 (1912).
[2] 195 Fed. 593-595 (1912); 227 U. S. 218 (1913).
[3] 222 Fed. 349 (1915).
[4] 222 Fed. 397, 399 (1915).

general laws of the land." [1] Other cases were cited to substantiate the point that the right to contract concerning a patent is not derived from the patent itself, but from the general law, and therefore that the patentee's rights are governed by that law. The government further attempted to distinguish between the case at bar and both Bement *v.* National Harrow Company and the Dick case on the ground that in the latter cases there were only contracts between particular parties, not a system of contracts together constituting a far-reaching scheme for restraining trade. For positive support of its position the prosecution relied upon such cases as United Shoe Machinery Co. *v.* La Chapelle, 212 Mass. 467; Blount Manufacturing Co. *v.* Yale and Towne Manufacturing Co., 166 Fed. 555; and U. S. *v.* Standard Sanitary Manufacturing Co., 191 Fed. 172 and 226 U. S. 20.

In the last-named case the so-called "Bathtub Trust" had perfected a scheme whereby the owners of several patents for applying an enamel glaze to bathtubs and other articles had assigned those patents to one Wayman, who was authorized to license manufacturers to use the patents. The licenses involved a scheme for maintaining prices. Jobbers were brought into the scheme and agreed to maintain resale prices and not to handle products of a manufacturer outside the group of licensees, under severe penalties. This plan was condemned unanimously by the Supreme Court as a perversion of patent rights.

Although these arguments did not prevail with the District Court of Massachusetts, the government considered its position materially strengthened before the case was settled by the Supreme Court. During the interim that court had expressly overruled the Button-fastener and Dick decisions in its determination of the case of Motion Picture Patents Company *v.* Universal Film Manufacturing Company *et al.* The former concern sold motion-picture projecting machines with the stipulations on a plate attached to the machines that first, they should be used solely with films leased from a manufacturer licensed by the Motion Picture Patents Company, and

[1] 77 Fed. 292-293 (1896).

second, that the purchaser agreed in advance to abide by "other terms to be fixed by the Motion Picture Patents Company." The Supreme Court held that the rights which the Motion Picture Patents Company attempted to establish by this notice were not covered by the patent law, since "the exclusive right granted in every patent must be limited to the invention described in the claims of the patent," and that consequently "it is not competent for the owner of a patent by notice attached to its machine to, in effect, extend the scope of its patent monopoly by restricting the use of it to materials necessary in its operation, but which are no part of the patented invention." The court furthermore condemned the stipulation of terms to be fixed after the sale as a "perfect instrument of favoritism and oppression." [1]

On the basis of the reasoning already summarized plus the reversal of the case upon which the lower court had relied in sustaining the United Company's leases, the government contended that the Supreme Court could not affirm that decision. But the court did exactly that. It held that the leases were "simply bargains" and that "the conditions were within the lessor's patent rights, and not violate of the Anti-trust Act." [2] It construed the Motion Picture case, and other similar decisions not discussed above, as applying only when an article has been sold. Since these shoe machines were leased, not sold, the United Company retained the title to them and was within its legal rights in imposing the lease forms it used.[3] Two justices did not sit on the case and three dissented, two of the latter writing vigorous opinions voicing the grounds for their dissent.

The practical effect of this decision was, of course, to restore the situation established by the Button-fastener and National Harrow cases. On its metallic-fastening machines the United Company issued a lease requiring all materials used in the machine to be purchased from it. In the opinion of the writers there was a sound reason for such a restriction in this

[1] 243 U. S. 506, 515, 516 (1917).
[2] 247 U. S. 66, 33 (1918).
[3] 247 U. S. 58 (1918).

particular case, since improperly-fitting material might easily damage the company's machines, but the court laid down a general proposition which made it easy for the owner of any patented article to extend his control over other unpatented articles used with the patented one by going through the farce of leasing it for 999 years instead of selling it. Such a perversion of the patent law to escape the penalties of the Sherman Act (the highest court having sanctioned it) called for legislative action. As a matter of fact Congress had already supplied the remedy four years earlier, but after this litigation was begun, by passing the Clayton Act.

A more detailed discussion of that act will be found elsewhere; [1] here it is sufficient to notice that its third section was aimed directly at just such "tying" contracts as those we have been discussing, and that it specifically prohibited all such arrangements covering commodities "whether patented or unpatented" when their effect might be "to substantially lessen competition or tend to create a monopoly in any line of commerce."

As soon as the Clayton bill became law the United Company altered its leases by substituting for them "temporary loan agreements" which did not contain the objectionable clauses. Since they were "temporary," and since the lessor reserved in them the right to terminate them and substitute another form for them which the lessee must accept or relinquish his machines within thirty days, it is perfectly apparent that the company's intention was to restore the "tying" clauses in the event that it was able to win the litigation which was certain to arise.

This time the case brought against the United Company originated in Missouri on application by the United States for a temporary injunction restraining the use of the objectionable clauses. This was granted November 9, 1915. On June 6, 1916, the District Court of Eastern Missouri denied the motion of the defendants to dismiss the case, and on March 31, 1920, decided the case against the company. This decision was affirmed April 17, 1922, by a seven to one vote

[1] See Chapter XX.

of the United States Supreme Court, Justice McKenna dissenting and Justice Brandeis not sitting. The exact language of the court was, "That although there was no specific agreement not to use machinery of a competitor, the practical effect of these restrictive provisions, thus tied together, was to prevent such use and necessarily to lessen competition and to tend to create monopoly, in violation of § 3 of the Clayton Act." [1]

We have included the United Shoe Machinery Corporation among the combinations to which we have given special attention because the prolonged litigation in which it was involved brings out clearly the difficulty of reconciling the patent law and the antitrust laws. The fact that in the end it was necessary for Congress to enact the special legislation of 1914 to prevent the use of patent rights to serve as a cloak for maintaining a monopolistic combination suggests the need of a modification of the patent law itself. In one of the cases reviewed the Supreme Court expressly upheld the right of a patentee to withhold the patent from use should he so desire. In our opinion the American patent law should be amended to provide that the patent rights should lapse when a patentee fails to make use of the patent within a period of, say, seven years. As regards the effect of the decision of 1922 upon the dominant position of the United Company in the shoe-machinery manufacturing industry, no perceptible change appears as yet to have occurred.

[1] 258 U. S. 452 (1922).

CHAPTER XVI

TRADE ASSOCIATIONS IN THE UNITED STATES

SINCE the close, about 1903, of the most important period of active trust organization, the trade association [1] has come to the fore as a method of avoiding certain of the restraints and wastes of competition. As will be shown, the activities of trade associations are extensive in scope. By no means all of them are directed toward the limitation of competition, but fundamentally the predilection of trade associations is for coöperation. In his recent book on *Trade Associations* and in a brief summary of their history written for the Department of Commerce, Mr. E. H. Naylor advances the opinion that "trouble" of some sort was the most frequent reason for their organization, particularly the difficulties experienced during periods of business depression. The study of the National Industrial Conference Board comes to the conclusion, however, that the movement has "received its chief impetus under the influence of prosperous conditions and profit-making opportunities." [2] The conclusion seems justified that the reasons for the organization of trade associations have been various.

The membership of a trade association consists of manufacturers, jobbers, wholesalers, retailers, or, in rare cases, combinations of these groups. It differs from a local manufacturers' association and from such an organization as a chamber of commerce in that the latter two include a variety of industries or businesses, whereas the trade association confines itself to one industry or a closely related group of industries. Typical examples of such associations are The American Association of Creamery Butter Manufacturers, the American Iron and Steel Institute, the Bicycle Manufacturers Association, the Fire Extinguisher Exchange, the United States Potash

[1] For definition, cf. ch. 1, p. 5, *supra*.

[2] Cf. Naylor, *Trade Associations*, pp. 7, 8, with National Industrial Conference Board, *Trade Associations*, pp. 7, 9.

Producers Association, and the Writing Paper Manufacturers Association.

Although the trade association has recently attracted more attention than formerly, it should not be supposed that it is a twentieth-century phenomenon; on the contrary, the movement has been more or less active in this country since the Civil War. The earlier American associations appear to have been in the majority of cases quite restricted in the range of their activities, often being almost indistinguishable from the pools and agreements discussed in an earlier chapter whose chief object was the enhancement of prices by restriction of output or other devices. The duration of most of them was very brief, for, as with the ordinary pools, a chief characteristic was lack of cohesiveness.

In the late 'eighties and 'nineties a modification in trade association activities began to develop; a shift from obviously restrictive practices to what later was termed "coöperative competition." The passage of the Sherman Antitrust Act in 1890 doubtless was of considerable significance in this shift, but probably equally important was a changing conception among the members of the associations of what should be the range of their activities. Generally speaking, the tendency was to expand the functions of the associations into fields which were less restrictive and more constructive.

About 1911 began what is for us the most significant of all the developments in trade associations: the so-called open-price or open-competition movement. As defined by Professor M. N. Nelson in his monograph on the subject, an open-price association is "an organization which provides a medium for the exchange of business information among members of a given industry whereby they may arrive at an intimate acquaintance with competitive conditions as they exist among themselves and in the whole industry." [1] The individual to whom credit is given for the origination of this plan was Mr.

[1] Cf. Nelson, M. N., *Open Price Associations*, pp. 24, 9. This definition appears to us to be more satisfactory than the briefer one adopted in the report of the Federal Trade Commission; viz., an "open-price trade association" is one "distributing or exchanging price information." Cf. *Open-Price Trade Associations*, p. 36.

A. J. Eddy, a Chicago lawyer, under whose personal guidance and supervision twenty-two such associations were formed. By 1921 there were nearly one hundred other associations reputed to be doing open-price work.[1] In that year an adverse decision of the United States Supreme Court on the activities of one [2] of them put a temporary check on trade associations in general. Subsequent decisions [3] have been interpreted as qualifying the condemnation of price-exchanging activities, and within the limitations laid down the exchange of price and other information has been resumed. Even by 1927, however, price-exchanging had not regained the scope established in 1921.[4]

Trade associations proper, which might or might not be engaged in open-price work, received a tremendous impetus during the war of 1914-18. Since the government found it impossible to secure under the arrangements existing prior to our entry into that war the necessary degree of coöperation with industry and business, a policy of encouraging agreements and coöperation among business men was inaugurated. Well before the signing of the Armistice business men were made to feel that the government much preferred to deal with them as members of associations than as individuals. Moreover, the government adopted the price-fixing policy which it had always held as anathema when undertaken by private individuals. Of course, price-fixing by individuals and price-fixing by government are two distinct things, but such a wide variety of forms of group action had been encouraged that Mr. Charles E. Hughes felt justified in stating that "The war has compelled coöperation and the Government, under this compulsion, has fostered what it previously denounced as criminal." [5] As a result of this reversal of attitude associations of all sorts multiplied with great rapidity. Just how many there were

[1] Nelson, *op. cit.*, pp. 207-210.

[2] The American Hardwood Manufacturers Association. 257 U. S. 377 (1921). For a detailed discussion of these and other trade association cases see Chapter XXI, pp. 453-467, *infra*.

[3] The Maple Flooring Manufacturers Association and Cement Manufacturers Protective Association cases. 268 U. S. 563 and 268 U. S. 588 (1925).

[4] *Open-Price Trade Associations,* pp. 15, 40.

[5] *New York Times,* December 1, 1918, section 1, p. 19.

at the close of hostilities will probably never be known. A contemporary estimate of 5,500 was probably too high. At any rate, the National Industrial Conference Board study indicated a 1925 total of only about 1,000.[1] The chief explanation of the divergent estimates is lack of agreement in defining what a trade association is. The 1927 revision of the Department of Commerce publication just cited states that there are "perhaps a thousand organizations that may properly be classed as trade associations" in the United States.[2]

In geographical extent the associations vary widely. A considerable number are national in their scope, such as the National Paper Trade Association, with subdivisions designated as the New England Paper Merchants Association, the Northwestern Paper Merchants Association, and the Pacific Coast Paper Trade Association. At the other extreme is the Brooklyn Hardware Dealers Association, and in between are the Paint and Oil Club of New England and the Kansas Book Dealers Association.

In view of the wide range of industries in which associations have developed and their varied geographical extent, it is to be expected that their activities also are quite diverse. In general, these activities may be loosely classified as restrictive and constructive. Since the former have frequently resulted in legal proceedings designed to stop them, it seems more logical to discuss them in Chapter XXI.

The more constructive aspects of the work of trade associations have been described at length in a number of publications, the most convenient of which is that of the federal Department of Commerce: *Trade Association Activities.* In the revision of 1927 trade association activities were classified as follows: (1) Statistics, (2) Cost Accounting, (3) Industrial Research, (4) Commercial Research, (5) Simplified Practice, (6) Industrial Standardization, (7) Public Relations, (8)

[1] Cf. Hunt, E. E., in the *Outlook,* vol. cxxx, p. 352, with National Industrial Conference Board, *Trade Associations,* p. 326. Estimates by Mr. E. H. Naylor in 1921 set the total at about 1,000, but subsequently (1923) he raised this to 1,800. Cf. his *Trade Associations,* p. 13, with his article in the Department of Commerce volume, *Trade Association Activities,* 1923 edition, p. 304.

[2] *Trade Association Activities,* 1927, p. 86.

Trade Relations, (9) Credit, (10) Insurance, (11) Employer-employee Relations, and (12) Traffic and Transportation. Of these activities simplified practice, industrial standardization and statistics have received the most widespread attention, a prominence justified by their importance. Five others in the list, cost accounting, industrial research, commercial research, trade relations, and credit, also seem to us to merit fairly detailed treatment. The remainder may be dismissed more briefly.

"Public relations" is the term by which is designated the activity of a trade association in attempting to secure public appreciation and better understanding of the nature and problems of particular industries. The most usual method employed is advertising. A recent example is the action taken by the candy trade to offset the advice proffered by the American Tobacco Company to "reach for a Lucky instead of a sweet" and thus preserve that "girlish figure." After condemning the cigarette advertisement as unfair competition, the candy producers published advertisements emphasizing the food rather than the fattening qualities of candy.

The "insurance" activities of trade associations present four aspects: educational campaigns among the members, constructive research into insurance legislation, the reduction of waste, and the provision of actual coverage. The Department of Commerce publication previously cited gives evidence that these activities are proving highly beneficial.

Under the head of "employer-employee relations" trade associations carry on a large number of personnel activities ranging from methods of selecting and training employees to "welfare." Although more than one trade association executive has issued warnings against the participation of associations as such in industrial controversies, there is evidence that some of them have considered their chief function in this field to be the smashing of trade unions.

The "traffic and transportation" service bureaus of trade associations function as the medium for expressing the joint wishes of the members in such matters as rates, freight classification, car supply, etc. Examples of the more successful of these bureaus are those of the National Automobile Chamber of Commerce, the Pacific Coast Shippers' Association, and the Silk Association of America.

The significance of "standardization" in a mechanized world needs no detailed treatment. The ten-year old proprietor of a bicycle knows that its parts have to fit, not approximately but exactly, and that there are great advantages in having those parts easily replaceable at the nearest shop. Nor need we concern ourselves with the jeremiads of the social philosophers, from John Ruskin to Bertrand Russell, who have viewed with alarm the prospects of man himself becoming standardized. We are committed to a mechanized civilization and no Ghandi is likely to turn us back. This being the case, it may be possible that the cure for standardization is more standardization, which will further increase output, shorten hours, and permit more general enjoyment of its products. Most observers are inclined to believe that this is the trend and that trade associations are performing an invaluable service in furthering it. In addition to working toward uniformity of dimensions of parts and quality specifications for materials and equipment, standardization involves uniformity of nomenclature, of methods of tests to determine standards of quality and performance, and of ratings of machinery and apparatus. An interesting aspect of the movement in recent years has been the encouragement and aid given it by the federal government.

Closely allied to standardization is simplification or "simplified practice," defined by the Department of Commerce as "the collective effort of an industry to reduce waste in the production and distribution of its products, through eliminating unnecessary varieties in sizes, dimensions, grades, or qualities." [1] At the time of the report just cited 243 trade associations had promulgated and accepted 60 simplified practice recommendations. The work of the division of simplified practice of the Department of Commerce has been of substantial aid in securing these results. As one might expect, the procedure followed in establishing simplified practice has itself been "standardized." Moreover, it seems that the god

[1] *Trade Association Activities,* 1927, p. 75.

of standardization, once created, immediately begins to receive the homage of his creators, for we find it stated that the procedure "if followed closely, usually secures the results sought!"[1] In general terms this procedure requires some preliminary presentation to interested concerns of the advantages of simplified practice, a careful survey of the existing varieties of products in the industry, a conference at which recommendations are made concerning eliminations, the circularization of these recommendations to the trade with a request for formal acceptance of them, a propaganda campaign to secure acceptances, publication in the Department of Commerce's series on simplified practice of the recommendations, and periodic resurveys upon which to base constructive revisions of practices. The most important of these steps is the survey by which the facts are developed. Its chief purpose is to determine the varieties to be eliminated; haphazard selection of these has generally brought failure to the whole plan.

Among the conspicuous successes secured by the program are the reduction of the varieties of paving-brick from 66 to 4, of sheet steel from 1,819 to 261, of range boilers from 130 to 13, and of invoice, inquiry, and purchase order forms from 4,500 to 3. That the financial savings resulting from these changes have been material goes without saying, but the frequent attempts to reduce them to dollars-and-cents estimates are of dubious value. Our scepticism in this matter is not lessened by the discovery that on page 81 of *Trade Association Activities* "the sheet-steel industry" estimates an annual saving of $8,000,000 from simplification, whereas on page 82 the "leaders" of this same industry are content with the much more modest claim of an annual saving of $2,400,000!

The desirability of the more widespread use of "cost accounting" systems is taken for granted. Moreover, individual firms in the same industry or business should utilize uniform systems because of the advantages from both private and public viewpoints. It is perfectly possible to work out a "best" system for the lumber industry, though that may be quite different from the "best" system for retail clothing mer-

[1] *Trade Association Activities,* p. 76.

chants, and once it is demonstrated as the most advantageous, a concerted effort on the part of a trade association to secure its adoption throughout the business is legal and wise. Our experience with the railroads has demonstrated that to the extent public supervision of business seems necessary a uniform accounting system makes that supervision more intelligent and useful. The difficulty arises when the trade association goes past the installation of a uniform system of accounting among its members and fosters the adoption of uniform costs or uniform elements in cost. Some years ago one of the writers had occasion to interview several job printers in Austin, Texas, on a publishing contract. All of them produced a small book from which they jotted down most of the cost items, and on all the lists these items were the same. Subsequently he ascertained that this booklet was compiled by a price list committee of the United Typothetæ of America, that it was revised from time to time, and that it contained average production costs on a wide range of possible jobs and precise items for use in computing costs. The Federal Trade Commission charged the United Typothetæ with advocating or suggesting uniform percentages of profit as well as using uniform cost items and forced a change in these practices.[1]

The Woven Label Manufacturers Association was ordered dissolved in 1917 partly because its members had set up for certain common processes a fictitious and arbitrary set of costs which were used in determining total costs and selling prices.[2]

The foregoing specific instances reflect an all-too-common notion among trade association members that a primary purpose of cost-accounting is to raise prices to some level which will enable inefficient producers to remain in business. Doubtless proper accounting will tend to eliminate selling below costs, but it should also tend to eliminate some concerns. Emphasis on the former tendency and experience to date confirm the Trade Commission's conclusion that uniform cost

[1] *Federal Trade Commission Decisions*, vol. vi, p. 345. Hereafter references to these decisions will be cited as follows: 6 F. T. C. D. 345 (1923).

[2] U. S. *v.* Kluge, *et al.*. *Decrees and Judgments in Federal Anti-Trust Cases*, p. 631 (1917).

accounting is one of the constructive activities of trade associations most likely to lead to uneconomic and illegal abuses.[1]

The "credit" bureau function of a trade association, when confined to the "sole purpose of furnishing credit information" has been certified as legal in several recent decrees of the federal courts.[2] The economic basis for such activities is unquestionable. Without entering into a discussion of the relative validity of the various explanations of the business cycle now current, it can be safely stated that sound credit relations are vital to the maintenance of business stability. Since unwarranted extensions or restrictions of credit rest all too frequently upon ignorance, organized efforts to dispel that ignorance are commendable. Unfortunately, some associations have not been content to collect data on their customers' average purchases, the periods at which the heaviest and lightest volume of purchases may be expected, and the promptness of payment, but have agreed that in case certain standards set by the association are not met the defaulting concern will not be extended credit by any member of the association. Competition in credit terms may be as important as competition in price, and in principle an agreement on credit terms is as illegal as agreements on price. In the Tile Manufacturers Credit Association case just cited the court perpetually enjoined the defendants from "combining, conspiring or agreeing, expressly or impliedly, directly or indirectly . . . to refuse to sell to any persons or corporations because of any unpaid account or accounts," or "to formulate and establish or to retain in effect any requirements, circumstances, or conditions, non-conformity or non-compliance with which shall exclude any customer or customers from securing credit or shall impose any limitations or conditions whatsoever upon the credit granted." Any individual remained free, of course, to extend credit on any basis not otherwise illegal, and, as stated above,

[1] *Open-Price Trade Associations,* p. 175 *et seq.*

[2] U. S. *v.* Tile Manufacturers Credit Association, U. S. District Court, S. D. Ohio. In Equity No. 201; decree of November 26, 1923.

U. S. *v.* Gypsum Industries Association, U. S. District Court, S. D. New York. In Equity No. E. 25-215; decree of January 3, 1923. Reprinted in National Industrial Conference Board, *Trade Associations,* pp. 350-358.

the association was specifically guaranteed in the decree the right to perform the usual functions of a "credit" bureau.

Trade association activities in "industrial and commercial research" rarely lend themselves to the sort of publicity given to standardization and simplification. Moreover, it is more than improbable that such activities would result in an illegal restraint of trade, so that in a sense a discussion of them has no place in a book on trusts. On the other hand, it is impossible to exaggerate their potential possibilities, at least in their industrial aspect. The chief plans adopted by trade associations in furthering industrial research have been summarized by the Department of Commerce about as follows:

(1) Coöperation with government laboratories through the maintenance therein of research associates. This coöperation has been developed to the greatest extent with the Bureau of Standards.

(2) Arrangements with commercial laboratories by which members of their organizations have been placed at the disposal of the association.

(3) Establishment of fellowships at educational institutions. Practically every major university in the country has accepted one or more of these fellowships.

(4) Development of laboratories owned and operated by the associations. Among these may be mentioned the Electrical and Gas Refrigeration Trade Extension Bureau, The American Institute of Baking, and the National Canners Association.

So-called commercial research, concerned with problems of distribution, has not reached the stage of development attained by its industrial counterpart. And unfortunately, there is considerable evidence to indicate that the community benefits from it to date are far more questionable, for its emphasis seems all too frequently to rest upon additional stimuli to greater consumer demand, regardless of needs, and to "conspicuous expenditure." Since it is well known that the costs of distributing a product in many cases exceed its costs of manufacture, the opportunities of commercial research are boundless. As time goes on there is reason to expect that these opportunities will be more thoroughly appreciated and acted upon..

By "trade relations" as a field of association work is meant primarily the adjustment of disagreements and the mitigation or elimination of abuses. In the transmission of goods from manufacturer to jobber to retailer it is inevitable that honest disagreements should arise and that a small minority of the individuals in the trade should resort to practices positively dishonest. Among the abuses most frequently complained of may be listed the following: unjust returns of merchandise, failures to deliver promptly, misrepresentations of merchandise by salesmen, unreasonable cancellations, delivery of merchandise not in accordance with samples or specifications, acceptance of orders which cannot be delivered, etc. In meeting these difficulties trade associations have followed three chief methods: the adoption of "codes of ethics," encouragement of commercial arbitration, and the establishment of trade relations committees. Although the principle of the codes of ethics is excellent, it remains true that most of them are of too general a character to be of particular significance and that many of the associations are too weak to exercise any real enforcement powers. Worse than these limitations even is the not uncommon practice of using the code as a cloak for unfair and illegal methods.[1] An obvious remedy for the weakness of many of the codes and the associations formulating them is to couple the code with an agreement to settle differences by commercial arbitration. In some cases such an agreement is a condition of membership in the association. The delay and expense of court settlements are largely avoided by arbitration, and in the numerous instances where a technical knowledge of the industry is important, if not vital, to a judgment on the merits of a case, the parties to it are more likely to be satisfied with the action of arbitrators from the trade. By 1927 more than 200 national trade associations had either established arbitration machinery or were actively inter-

[1] Cf. Jones, F. D., *Trade Association Activities and the Law*, p. 43, where it is pointed out that this intrinsically laudable idea "has repeatedly been grossly abused."

ested in its development. But since membership in an association is usually confined to one functional group, that is, to either manufacturers, or jobbers, or retailers, and since disputes most frequently occur across these lines, it has proved expedient to establish trade relations committees. In the food and grocery business eight individual trade associations have created trade relations committees. The chairmen of these eight committees act as a joint trade relations committee for the entire industry.[1]

The collection and dissemination of trade "statistics" is considered by many trade association executives to be the most important and the most valuable function of their organizations. For this and the additional reason that it has been the center of considerable litigation in recent years it deserves more extended treatment than other phases have received.

The actual data included in a trade association's statistical work may include figures on production, costs, stocks of raw materials and finished products on hand, employment, wages, shipments, orders, cancellations, prices, and other items. Obviously, the particular items selected will vary from industry to industry. The figures generally considered "essential" are those for production, shipments, stocks, new orders, and unfilled orders. To be of any real use association statistics should include 50 per cent or more of the industry's normal output and 70 per cent is desirable to secure data of a thoroughly representative character.

In collecting, compiling, and disseminating trade data to their members the trade associations have inevitably encountered on a small scale the sort of difficulties met in the federal census. It has been necessary, for example, to work out precise definitions so that "new orders" and "shipments" shall mean the same thing to all the reporting concerns. The frequency of reports is a matter deserving particular attention. Although the data should be as recent as possible, the members who provide them should not be made to feel that the frequency of making out reports has become a nuisance. A middle course must be steered between reducing the figures to

[1] *Trade Association Activities,* 1927, p. 115.

largely unintelligible summaries and averages and presenting them in such detail as to reveal individual business transactions. Price statistics are particularly troublesome because of obvious legal issues. Any semblance of an agreement concerning them must be scrupulously avoided. It is equally important to publish all sales data, not simply those covering the "best" sales. In condemning the latter practice the Department of Commerce says, "Such a method of reporting sales is manipulation of the market, a suppression of truth for the purpose of creating a false impression, an unlawful method of accomplishing an unlawful object."[1]

But despite these possible pitfalls the advantages of exchanging business statistics have appealed so strongly to trade associations that well over one hundred were engaged in it in 1927. And the advantages, of course, are by no means necessarily confined to the members of the association. From the time we first became acquainted with the concept of the business cycle there has been a steadily growing emphasis on the value of the dissemination of business facts as a method of controlling it. The success of certain concerns, the American Radiator Company and the Dennison Manufacturing Company, for example, in meeting periods of depression by the intelligent use of business statistics demonstrates what might be expected from *a priori* reasoning. Since many individual concerns are not able to finance alone the collection of all the facts they would like to have, and since they want detailed information on their own industries in addition to that on the general state of business, it seems that joint collection of the facts is a perfectly normal and desirable function of a trade association. The method of disseminating these data is discussed more at length in connection with the application of the antitrust acts to trade associations by the United States Supreme Court.[2]

Despite the repeated statement by economists that really free competition exists only when all the traders in a market have perfect knowledge of the conditions of supply and de-

[1] *Trade Association Activities,* p. 34.
[2] Cf. ch. xxi, pp. 453-467, *infra.*

mand, and despite the lip service of most business men to the ideal of free competition, there has been a marked hesitancy on the part of these same business men to exchange trade information. This hesitancy rests upon the fear of in some way aiding a competitor to get business which the donor of the information thinks should come to him, and upon the fear that the public or the courts will construe this trading of information as an evidence of collusion for the purpose of restraining trade and enhancing prices. As a result the sort of competition which actually has existed has been far from the ideal of the *laissez faire* economists. It has been hampered rather than free, unintelligent rather than informed. On the basis of partial or erroneous information manufacturers have frequently extended production when they should have restricted it, applied for additional credit when they should have been paying off their obligations, and have otherwise defeated their own best interests.

Moreover, the development in more and more industries of extremely expensive tools of production, involving the burden of a high percentage of fixed charges which each manufacturer wishes to distribute over as large an output as possible, has accentuated the tendency inherent in all competition to become cutthroat competition. When the railroad managements realized what cutthroat competition meant they organized to stop it, a measure which at first met with legislative disapproval, but which now, after almost forty years, stands endorsed by Congress. Numerous lines of industry have been for some time more or less in the same predicament faced by the railroads. They had to continue to extend the mechanization of their plants or fall behind in the race for efficiency. If they installed newer and bigger and better machines they found themselves haunted by a "specter of overhead costs" which forced overproduction and price-cutting. Agreements to restrict production or fix prices are illegal as well as exceedingly difficult to maintain. What was needed was some method of informing each unit of the business or industry of the exact situation in that line with the hope that the intelligence of even the most incompetent member of the group would be equal to the task of interpreting and applying the information supplied in such a way as to prevent overproduction and cutthroat competition. And, as noted in the introductory sections of this chapter, the "open-price" or "open-competition" plan was formulated to meet this need. Although an association of lumber manufacturers in Laurel, Mississippi, seems to have worked out a scheme independently, Mr. A. J. Eddy, as stated above, is entitled to recognition as the originator and chief proponent of the system. The point of view with which Eddy approached his problem is epitomized in the caption across the top of the title page of his book: "Competition is War and 'War is Hell.'" The title of the book, *The New Competition,* indicates his idea much more accurately than the term "open-price movement," which is now more common. The chief objection to the latter term is that it seems to restrict the functions of the type of association Mr. Eddy had in mind more than he intended, and more than, as a matter of practice, they are restricted.

The essentials of open competition consist of a system of reports of business facts by the members of the group to a central office, the dissemination of this information to the members, and meetings at which these reports and any other matters of interest are discussed. In addition, the "Eddy" associations [1] attach considerable importance to the maintenance of cordial relations among their members, the absence of secrecy at their meetings or in their operations, the nonexistence of penalties of any kind in connection with their activities, and the freedom of members to quote at all times such prices and terms as they see fit.[2] In working out the details of its operation any particular association which had adopted the principles of open-price work or coöperative competition would be sure to differ in certain respects from other associations. Obvious examples suggest themselves. The

[1] Until his death Mr. Eddy acted as counsel and adviser to a number of associations. This work has been continued by his successor, Mr. Wm. J. Mathews. Nelson, *op. cit.,* p. 69.

[2] Nelson, *op. cit.,* p. 19.

members of one association may agree to report their sales in such detail as to include the name of the purchaser and the exact terms of the transaction and to require the secretary to send out all these data to all members. The members of another may report only total sales for an agreed period and require its secretary to omit all names in sending out his summaries of the reports. Price information may be disseminated by the interchange of price lists which will not be altered without notice, instead of by reporting actual transactions to the secretary. Manufacturers who regularly carry considerable quantities of their products in their warehouses may wish to exchange data on stocks on hand, whereas the manufacturer who produces primarily to individual order may be more enlightened by reports of current and of unfilled orders.

But from all these differences of detail one item of similarity stands out conspicuously. The nature of competition is altered by such an arrangement. As a matter of fact, there are some who believe that when a group of men in the same line know each other's stocks, orders, costs, shipments, bids, contracts, cancellations, and a variety of other items, competition has been "altered" out of existence. And that is the question for us here. Is this "new" competition that "free" competition which theoretical economists have so freely assumed in writing their treatises? Or is it simply the ogre of monopoly, attired in a different garb, but still up to its old tricks of restricting output and raising prices? Or may it possibly be an intelligent method of meeting a difficult situation, more real than "free" competition and less dangerous than monopoly? With the qualifications stated in the next few pages we are inclined to the third view. Our reasons for this conclusion will be found in the remaining sections of this chapter and in Chapters XXI and XXVIII.

Spokesmen for the associations, as for the Steel Trust, contend that the chief purposes of the exchange of these business facts in general and of price data in particular are the elimination of cutthroat competition and the stabilization of industry. Doubts concerning the validity of such contentions were partly responsible for the Senate resolution of 1925 authorizing the

Trade Commission to investigate the activities of open-price associations. Incidentally to its main task the Commission developed the facts that practically all the open-price work is being carried on by associations which are well-developed trade associations, and that approximately 20 per cent of the commodities for which the Bureau of Labor publishes wholesale prices are affected by open-price activities.[1]

Since the products sold by members of open-price associations enter primarily wholesale markets so that the prices which these members desire to stabilize are wholesale prices, an obvious measure of the success of such efforts is the relative stability of wholesale prices of commodities in lines in which associations are operating and wholesale prices in lines in which they are not. On the basis of such comparisons the Commission was able to reach only negative conclusions; "that is, if open-price associations effectively stabilize prices, that effect is brought about in other ways by equally important factors, whatever they may be, so that the open-price commodities show no greater stability, or no more undue stability, as the case may be, than other commodities. In fact they appear to show a trifle less constancy in their movements from month to month." Among the other factors, the Commission considered as most important price leadership by some dominant concern or group.[2] Disappointing as these results are in their inconclusiveness, it would be captious to criticize them too severely, for the examination of the files of all or even a significant proportion of the members of some ninety open-price groups is a task which seems beyond the resources even of a government bureau. Moreover, the detailed studies made of five large lumber-trade associations and of certain other groups were again of an inconclusive character, so that the desirability of detailed studies for all the associations seemed at least questionable.

In other respects, however, the findings of the Commission are particularly significant. For example, many of the associations which began with great emphasis on price and sta-

[1] *Open-Price Trade Associations*, pp. 59, 69.

[2] *Ibid.*, pp. 357, 92-103, 121.

tistical work have subsequently abandoned it and among these are a number that started or resumed such activities after the Supreme Court decisions of 1925 previously mentioned. In general the association members seem to have decided that the work did not pay for itself, but with particular reference to price data an important reason was the discovery that unscrupulous members were attempting to exploit the reports by making falsified and/or incomplete returns. In explaining its discontinuance of price-reporting one association wrote the Commission as follows: "Gradually some members began either padding their reports, or making false reports, or not making any reports, thinking that they could confuse things and that they were smarter than the other fellow, and that they could profit by his having information that was not correct." [1] Unfortunately this attitude has occasionally been reflected in a different fashion by association secretaries who juggled their reports in such a way as to influence members to a certain course of action. Obviously the value of fact-exchanging both to association members and to the purchasing public is largely if not completely destroyed by such departures from accuracy and objectivity.

On the assumption that price data are honestly exchanged, however, there remain grounds for questioning our inclusion of the practice in our rather sweeping approval in earlier paragraphs of the exchange of business facts in general among ostensible competitors. As we pointed out with reference to the steel industry, stabilization of production and employment is much more important from the public viewpoint than the stabilization of prices. Consequently, we are greatly interested to note that the Commission found that "prices for open-price associations are much more stable than output." [2] Granting the validity of its suggestion that this is "true for manufacturers generally," it still seems clear that the more important aspects of stabilization have been inadequately, if at all, secured by open-price work. And this conclusion receives considerable support from a second finding of the Commission that, "it does not appear that industries with open-price asso-

[1] *Open-Price Trade Associations,* p. 136. [2] *Ibid.,* p. 357.

ciations are better in respect to stability or regularity of operation than those that merely have trade statistics; indeed, the comparison, though on too narrow a basis, is more in favor of the latter." [1]

Closely touching the consumers' interests in efficient distribution of goods are the further conclusions of the Commission that "In trade-association circles, emphasis on seeking profits instead of volume of business is current and conspicuous," and that "Emphasis on restriction of output, though, of course, on its face without any element of concert or agreement, is the central idea of the theory back of a good deal of trade-association work." [2] The second of these is obviously a means to the first and both represent a protest against the tendency of individual manufacturers to seek volume by national advertising, high-pressure salesmanship, and similar methods which have tended to obscure the costs of attaining that volume. As a result business men have complained of "profitless prosperity," the public has complained of waste and inefficiency in distribution, and both seem in large measure to be correct. In a society which interprets progress as a multiplication of material instruments of want gratification there would seem no excuse for any limitation on the production of such instruments; but, on the other hand, the evidence is accumulating that not only are we losing our appreciation of non-material satisfactions, but also that, disregarding æsthetic phases, we have overreached ourselves in the material aspect alone. Therefore it may be that trade-association activities directed toward restricting output are temporarily socially desirable. That they must be carried through with due regard to the general interest goes without saying. Meanwhile the writers are inclined to take a more positive position than that reflected in the Trade Commission's query on the desirability of beginning the stabilization of prices with raw rather than finished products. As its report states, "Whatever stabilization of prices has been effected by trade associations of manufacturers has probably contributed to unsatisfactory conditions in agriculture." [3] The Capper-Volstead Act discussed

[1] *Open-Price Trade Associations,* p. 358. [2] *Ibid.,* p. 365. [3] *Ibid.,* p. 366.

in Chapter XX was a step in the right direction. Whether or not the farm-relief legislation of 1929 will also be beneficial remains to be seen. In our judgment the stabilization of prices for raw products should have been accomplished first because the reverse process means a waste of those raw products and a further aggravation of the farm problem. Since the much greater ease of joint action by manufacturers than by farmers has brought about the situation now existing, we can only hope that the efforts now being made may prove successful and that the producers of raw materials may ultimately reap the benefits of stabilization, even though by a wrong-end-to process.

The legal issues involved in open-price work constitute a part of the "Judicial Interpretation of the Antitrust Acts." Consequently, we have reserved a discussion of the important court decisions involving this aspect of trade association activities to Chapter XXI.

To give a clearer picture of the diversified activities of trade associations, we will now describe briefly the work of three outstanding organizations: the Institute of American Meat Packers, the Portland Cement Association and the National Coal Association.

The Institute of American Meat Packers, though only ten years old under that name, is one of the most important trade associations in the United States. The facts that the industry with which it is concerned supplies products consumed by nearly every individual in the country, and that it ranks first among American industries in the total volume of its sales, would justify a description of this association; but in addition there are the more cogent reasons that behind it lies the history of the so-called "Beef Trust" and that the work of the Institute is of an especially representative character.

As implied, the Institute is a reorganization effected in 1919 of an earlier association, the American Meat Packers Association. This earlier group was constituted in 1906 at a time when the industry was under fire from the federal government and from private sources for violations of the Antitrust Act and for operating its packing houses in an unsanitary, not to say filthy, fashion. As is well known, the pure food and drug and meat inspection legislation grew out of the investigations of this period. Among the most important purposes of the 1906 association were the general advancement of the interests of the industry and the maintenance of standards, particularly in the latter respect, by coöperation with the federal Department of Agriculture in the enforcement of the meat-inspection law. In the opinion of a recent writer on the industry excellent work was done in these respects and in establishing a sense of unity among the packers.[1] Reserving for later treatment the question of the legality of the "unity" achieved, by the association or otherwise, we return to the Institute of American Meat Packers.

The reorganization of the packers' association was effected at a time when the industry was again under fire. The preliminary summaries of the Federal Trade Commission report of 1918-20 had been very unfavorable and a number of regulatory bills of a most sweeping character were before Congress. Consequently, it was felt by leaders among the packers that a shift of emphasis in the work of the association from the betterment of conditions in the industry to improvement of relations with the public would be desirable.[2] Needless to say the new group proposed to fight the pending legislation.

The membership (260) of the Institute of American Meat Packers is practically identical with a list of the principal meat-packing concerns in the country. Its purposes are declared to be:

(a) To secure coöperation among the meat packers of the United States in lawfully furthering and protecting the interests and general welfare of the industry;

(b) To afford a means of coöperation with the federal and state governments in all matters of general concern to the industry;

(c) To promote and foster domestic and foreign trade in American meat products;

[1] Clemen, R. A., *American Live Stock and Meat Industry,* p. 802.

[2] Cf. the address of the retiring president of the old association at the first convention of the new in 1919. *National Provisioner,* September 20, 1919, p. 133.

(d) To promote the mutual improvement of its members and the study of the arts and sciences connected with the meat-packing industry;

(e) To inform and interest the American public as to the economic worth of the meat-packing industry;

(f) To encourage coöperation with live-stock producers and distributors of meat-food products.[1]

The dues paid by members of the Institute engaged in slaughtering operations vary with production: one cent for each head of cattle slaughtered (calves exempted), and one-fifth of a cent for each hog. Other members pay a fixed sum, twenty-five dollars a year. Voting rights, however, are allotted on the "one member, one vote" system.

In 1923 the association expanded its activities along the lines of an "Institute Plan." In the words of the chairman of the "Plan Commission" the "Plan" itself " . . . provides for the ultimate development of a structure and organization which shall be a combined trade association, as the Institute now is; an industrial museum, of which the Institute already has developed certain meager beginnings; an industrial research institute, and a technical educational institution."[2] The most significant results have been accomplished in the first, third, and fourth items of this program. As a trade association, the Institute represents the industry in trade, governmental, and public relations. Numerous departments and committees perform a variety of functions, including the provision to members of advice on accounting problems, preparation of publicity on meat as a food, its costs, methods of preparing it, etc., and joint purchase of certain supplies other than live stock in order to effect savings.

The chief research laboratory is maintained at the University of Chicago, where continuous study of the processes of curing meat and of the prevention of spoilage is being made. In coöperation with the Tanners Council of America research on the curing of hides has been carried on in the latter's laboratory at the University of Cincinnati. By concentrating the research in the Institute's laboratories considerable dupli-

[1] The Institute of American Meat Packers, *The Packing Industry,* p. 4, quoted there from the constitution of the association.

[2] *Ibid.,* p. 17.

cation of individual effort has been eliminated and material saving effected.

The original project for the educational institution purposed to provide "broad but specialized" collegiate education for young men intending to enter the packing industry, to furnish special training to intermediate sub-executives of promise already in the industry, and to conduct a continuation school for plant employees and junior office help. The most important center for accomplishing these purposes is the Institute of Meat Packing conducted coöperatively with the University of Chicago. Similar arrangements have been perfected with educational institutions located in other packing-house communities.

The accomplishments of the Institute have to some extent been indicated in the foregoing. Leaders in the industry feel satisfied that the Institute has been highly successful in securing a greater degree of coöperation within the trade among the four groups interested, producers of live stock, commission men, packers, and retailers; in providing information to the consuming public on the business and correcting certain misapprehensions in the public mind; in decreasing losses in the handling of live stock; in standardizing containers of meat products and reducing costs; in improving methods of foreign trade; etc. For most, if not all, of these claims the support of a former Secretary of Agriculture and of the Department of Commerce may be cited.[1]

As in many other lines of business, there is no single trade association in the cement industry; the Department of Commerce publication previously cited discusses briefly the Portland Cement Association, the Cement Manufacturers Protective Association, the American Concrete Institute, and the Concrete Products Association. The first two of these together carry on most of the activities listed in our general description of such associations; the third is really a technical body devoted to the better use of concrete; the fourth is concerned with the development of methods and markets in the field of

[1] Cf. an address by Henry C. Wallace printed in *The Packing Industry*, p. 37 *et seq.*, and *Trade Association Activities*, 1927, p. 228.

concrete building units. The "Protective Association" carries on many of the activities of an open-price or open-competition association, and as such was prosecuted in the federal courts for violating the Sherman Act. The details of the charges and the importance of the association's exoneration as effecting another step in the judicial interpretation of that statute are reserved for discussion in Chapter XXI. For the purposes of the present chapter the Portland Cement Association is the most significant of the four.

This last-named organization is described by the Department of Commerce as "unique among the large trade associations in that it is concerned solely with promoting the use of a standardized product meeting uniform specifications."[1] The Department report goes on to say that "Matters affecting trade practices are not touched upon. . . ." For a number of reasons these statements appear to us to be so sweeping as to result in a misrepresentation of the facts. In the first place, the organization came into being in 1902 as the result of a meeting of cement manufacturers called "to discuss and find a solution, if possible, for 'the present methods of handling the subject of sacks, which are almost universally unsatisfactory,'" and these "sack troubles" have been frequently discussed at later meetings of the association.[2] Moreover, the association includes in its headquarters organization a "Bureau of Accident Prevention and Insurance" and a division of "Uniform Cost Accounting."[3] In following up the work of the former the accident-prevention committee announced at the May, 1927, meeting of the association that on June 1, 1927, "the greatest concerted safety drive ever made by a whole industry will be opened."[4] Again, one of the association's earliest actions was the appointment of a committee on "uniform contracts," and it has amended its constitution to include in its statement of its purposes the discussion of methods of "conducting the

[1] *Trade Association Activities,* 1927, p. 152.

[2] Lesley, R. W., *et al., History of the Portland Cement Industry in the United States,* pp. 196, 199, 203.

[3] *Ibid.,* p. 230.

[4] *Concrete,* June, 1927, p. 120.

business."[1] These bureaus, committees, etc., we find it impossible to reconcile with the Department of Commerce's description, though it remains true that that description does characterize the activities deemed most important by the association.

For the accomplishment of these primary tasks of increasing sales and of improving the quality of cement the association employs more than five hundred individuals in its central office, district offices, laboratories, and in the field. The national headquarters, located in Chicago and called the "General Office," is organized into a dozen bureaus or divisions, among which may be mentioned the advertising, cement products, editorial, road, statistical, and extension bureaus. The last of these contains five sub-bureaus designated as educational, farm, lecture, library, and trade coöperation bureaus.[2]

The organization was supported by a membership in January, 1929, of eighty-five cement manufacturers. From the date of its organization to that of its last convention in Chicago, November, 1928, the association members have jointly produced between 90 and 95 per cent of the cement output of the country. The financial resources of the organization are the members' "general" dues, paid since 1910 in proportion to production, and "special" dues authorized in 1916 for emergency situations.[3]

The extensive laboratory research engaged in under the direction of the group was concentrated from 1915 to about June 1, 1926, inclusive, in the Lewis Institute of Chicago under the terms of a contract with the Institute. This contract was discontinued in 1926 when the association moved into its new building in Chicago, and since that date almost all the research has been carried on in its own laboratories, although some is done in collaboration with the Bureau of Standards. The following titles of bulletins or circulars issued by the "Structural Materials Research Laboratory," by no means a complete list, indicate the nature of the research:

[1] Lesley, *op. cit.*, pp. 203, 212.
[2] *Ibid.*, p. 230.
[3] *Ibid.*, pp. 222, 231.

(1) Effect of Curing Condition on the Wear and Strength of Concrete, (2) Effect of Fineness of Cement, (3) Modulus of Elasticity of Concrete, (4) Effect of Storage of Cement, and (5) Effect of Hydrated Lime and Other Powdered Admixtures in Concrete. The magnitude of the work may be estimated from the fact that in its own laboratory the association is making some 45,000 tests a year. The appropriation to finance these experiments was $150,000 in 1926.

But the available data indicate that the most expensive part of the organization's activities has been for some time its coöperative advertising program. For years the industry has been advocating "concrete for permanence" by means of the dissemination of leaflets, bulletins, moving pictures, etc. The value of the distribution of upward of 3,000,000 pieces of propaganda literature a year during recent years might be questioned, but not so the work which justified the statement that at the close of 1914, "Some 260 farm journals, representing more than 6,000,000 circulation, were using regular stories on the farm uses of concrete, text and illustrations for which were furnished by the Association's Publicity Bureau."[1] The success of these efforts perhaps prompted the inauguration of a national advertising campaign in December, 1915. At first the emphasis was on the use of farm papers. In 1918, for example, advertising was placed in 10 weekly and monthly magazines, 23 trade and professional papers and 59 farm journals, at a total cost of $119,059.70. In June, 1920, the campaign was suspended, but at the December meeting of that year it was voted to modify it by giving preference to newspapers, and a program was drawn up for 1921 involving the use of 172 leading newspapers, 41 farm papers, 53 trade and professional journals, and 4 general magazines. The program was steadily expanded along these lines until it reached a cost of $450,000 in 1923.[2] In subsequent years the cost has been: 1924, $363,000; 1925, $370,000; 1926, $434,000; 1927, $451,000; 1928, $367,000.[3]

[1] Lesley, *op. cit.*, p. 226.

[2] *Ibid.*, pp. 231, 234, 235, 238, 242, 246.

[3] These data are for fiscal years ending October 31. For 1924-1928 they were supplied by Mr. Wm. M. Kinney of the Chicago office of the association.

To this point the Portland Cement Association seems "a very model of a modern trade association," if we may paraphrase Gilbert and Sullivan for such a purpose as the one in hand. In fact, there seems ground for the claim made by the association itself that it is a "great scientific and altruistic organization," as there certainly is for its further claim that it is "selling" the "use" of cement, not the "commodity." As a practical matter, however, this spirit of self-interested altruism seems not to extend beyond the continental boundaries of the United States. And this in spite of the fact that some of its members are located in Canada, Cuba, Mexico, and South America. At any rate, the association has in the recent past devoted a great deal of attention to the consideration of a protective tariff on cement and at the meetings of May and November, 1928, passed resolutions urging the enactment of such a tariff. Great prominence was given to the discussions and the resolutions in the July and December issues of *Concrete*. In the January, 1929, issue appeared a page article on the menace to American producers of the European cement cartel and an editorial favoring a protective tariff to combat this menace.[1] As we go to press there appears to be a strong probability that a substantial duty will be secured.

Finally, it should be noted that the Federal Trade Commission has filed a complaint against the association charging it with unfair methods of competition against the Vibrolithic Corporation. The association has adopted and promoted the use of a formula for concrete, and, according to the complaint, has sought to influence those who control the making, awarding, or approving of construction contracts by statements falsely disparaging and discrediting the Vibrolithic method—a formula requiring less cement. In its reply the association contends in general that the charges are not warranted, and specifically that since neither it nor its members compete with the Vibrolithic Corporation the Commission is without jurisdiction, and that certain published statements with reference to the Vibrolithic Corporation cited by the Commission

[1] Lesley, *op. cit.*, p. 196. *Concrete*, July, 1928, p. 108; December, 1928, p. 97; January, 1929, pp. 112, 113.

in support of its allegations were true in every particular and consequently not an unfair method of competition. The Commission has not yet determined the case, so that the association is entitled to be held innocent until proved otherwise.

The National Coal Association, like the Portland Cement Association, is only one of a number of such groups in the industry. It differs from the cement and other organizations, however, in covering a much smaller portion of the trade than its name suggests. Designed to include only operators in the bituminous field, it has never secured the adherence over any length of time of the producers of more than half of the commercial tonnage of the United States, and usually has had less than that. The fluctuating character of the membership is perhaps best illustrated by a committee report to the 1926 convention, showing that "Although 138 associations and individual members had been added to the rolls the past year the losses numerically had outrun these gains. . . ."[1]

The National Coal Association grew out of the emergencies resulting from the entrance of the United States into the war. Acting under the authority of the Act of Congress of August, 1916, the Council of National Defense appointed a Committee on Coal Production. In June, 1917, representatives of the coal industry met with this committee, agreed to appoint other committees for each of the coal-producing states with authority to fix prices f.o.b. mine, subject to approval by the Committee on Coal Production, and pledged themselves to observe these prices. Since it was believed that a national organization of coal operators would be necessary to make the price-fixing program effective, these representatives went ahead to form a tentative organization. Originally, then, the purposes of the group were coöperation with the federal government and advancement of the general interests of coal producers. For some months final consummation of the plans for the association were delayed, but about October 1, 1917, after changing its name from "The National Association of Coal Operators" to that now in use, it became a functioning reality. Since the first year of the association's history coincided almost

[1] *Coal Age,* vol. xxix, p. 859.

exactly with the last year of the war, its activities were concentrated during that period on the first of the objectives stated above. And to those activities should be ascribed in large measure the success of the industry in meeting the extraordinary demands for production of 1918. With the return of peace the association was able to turn its energies more directly to furthering the immediate ends of its members.

Critics within and without the trade have agreed for years that coal is "abominably inefficient." Speaking some years ago as an engineer, President Hoover characterized it as the worst conducted of all our industries.[1] And many of the critics, particularly those within, agreed that one of the most important reasons for chaotic conditions was inadequate cost-accounting, or no cost-accounting. As in many other lines there was, and is, reason to believe that an appreciable percentage of the producers for considerable periods of time sell at prices below their real costs. Consequently, we find strong emphasis placed on accurate cost-accounting from the beginning of the association to the present day.

The same reasons that underlie the advocacy of cost-accounting by association members explain their great interest in the collection and exchange of all sorts of coal statistics. At the convention of 1919 no trouble was spared to convince the delegates of the merits of open-price bureaus. Though many of the members were unwilling to agree with Fuel Administrator Garfield that production costs should be open and "as well known to the government as the cost of living," practically all seemed won over to the principle of open prices and a sufficiently large number had been reporting figures to enable the association to publish weekly summaries of prices from April to November of 1919.[2] At about this time, however, an unfortunate incident, the alleged removal by members of a United States Senate committee of "hundreds" of documents from the files of the National Coal Association without the permission of officials of the latter, caused some members to

[1] Hamilton and Wright, *Case of Bituminous Coal,* p. 1.
[2] *Coal Age,* vol. xv, pp. 1000, 1001; vol. xvii, p. 950.

discontinue their reports.[1] Others ceased reporting because of their uncertainty as to the legality of the practice. The program apparently remained in suspension for over two years, since in July, 1921, we find the association quoting the advice of its lawyers "to postpone the resumption of your statistical reporting system until the fall" when the Supreme Court would determine the Hardwood case.[2]

But as brought out later, the Hardwood decision went against that association and, consequently, the National Coal Association did not resume its activities in the collection and exchange of statistics until after the favorable trade association decisions of 1925. At the first convention subsequent to those decisions, however, they constituted the chief topic for discussion and were made the basis for plans for a comprehensive exchange of data. Though these plans have been pursued with vigor, the failure of the association to hold a larger percentage of the producers and its shifting constituency have rendered its figures less valuable than they might otherwise have been. On the other hand, the establishment by action of the association in December, 1919, of the Bureau of Coal Economics has provided the industry with a fact-finding body which has continued to the present time to provide both the industry and the public with much valuable information.

Other activities of the National Coal Association are supervised by its committees on marketing, safety, pool-buying, publicity, government relations, foreign trade and transportation.

The attitude of the association members toward safety work seems accurately reflected in the statements made at the annual conventions. Although the need for safety precautions is recognized, the burden of responsibility is usually shifted to the miners; almost invariably it is brought out and repeated that the main difficulty is in the carelessness of the men themselves.[3] Most of the operators still seem to be think-

[1] *Coal Age,* vol. xviii, p. 1295; vol. xix, p. 460.

[2] *Ibid.,* vol. xx. p. 110. But cf. vol. xx, p. 1021, where it is stated that the program was suspended because of the institution of the government's suit against the Hardwood Association.

[3] *Ibid.,* vol. xxvii, p. 933; vol. xix, p. 863.

ing in terms of accident frequencies rather than of accident severities. As is well demonstrated by this time, care on the part of workmen is the most satisfactory method of reducing frequencies, but "engineering revision," a responsibility of management, is most efficient in curtailing the severity rate.[1] Outstanding exceptions in which it has been realized that "a safety program could not be impressed on the minds of the individual workers unless the men responsible for it were fitted and sufficiently informed to pass along the information"[2] simply confirm the general impression. Particularly should it be noted that five years after the organization of the association the American Association for Labor Legislation was able to find only three bituminous coal-mining companies in the country's total of several thousands that rock-dusted their workings in order to prevent coal dust explosions. This notwithstanding the fact that rock-dusting has been standard practice in Great Britain for decades and is one of the reasons for her much lower fatality rate from mine accidents.

During the early years of the association its transportation committee was extremely busy with matters of car shortage, assigned cars, freight rates, etc. Recently, however, there has been much less need for such activity and the committee has functioned only intermittently.

Of such committees as those on marketing and pool-buying little need be said except that they appear to be functioning satisfactorily to the association and unexceptionably to the outsider. The foreign-trade committee began its work promptly with consideration of the possibilities of creating an export association under the terms of the Webb-Pomerene Act of 1918. Early in January, 1919, the committee recommended the incorporation of "American Coal Exporters, Inc.," and presented a carefully formulated and detailed plan for the new association. For various reasons, however, nothing permanent has been accomplished, so that as recently as January,

[1] Cf. *U. S. Bureau of Labor Statistics,* Bulletin No. 298, pp. 192-214.
[2] *Coal Age,* vol. xxix, p. 87.

1929, *Coal Age* carried an article urging the desirability of an export association.[1]

The most important activity of the government-relations committee to date seems to have been its work with the Federal Coal Commission of 1922. Acting through a smaller group designated as the "bituminous operators' special committee," this standing committee of the association filed thirty-one briefs with the Commission, aided in the preparation of five briefs submitted by local bituminous operators' associations, and carried on a number of studies upon which it spent approximately $500,000.[2] If one may judge from the temper of resolutions and speeches at conventions and meetings of the directors, the ideal situation from the point of view of the great majority of the members would be for this government-relations committee to have nothing to do. In an official statement the board of directors declared, ". . . the attitude of the industry . . . is that the law of supply and demand, if allowed to work, will adequately adjust any possible problem of overdevelopment. If the public will regularly place its orders for coal supply, the miners remain at work, and adequate transportation facilities are provided to haul the mine output, no difficulty ever will be experienced in meeting the public necessity for bituminous coal." [3]

Since the membership of the National Coal Association has always been drawn from producers in both union and non-union fields, it has during a good part of its existence scrupulously avoided any statements or actions that would indicate any "labor policy" for the association as such. During the investigations of the Coal Commission of 1922, however, the bituminous operators' special committee laid the responsibility for the ills of the industry at the door of the United Mine Workers and their officials, and reaffirmed these charges in the fall of 1923.[4] In May of 1924 the election of Mr. S. P. Hutchinson as president was hailed as strengthening "the be-

[1] Cf. *Coal Age,* vol. xv, p. 149, and vol. xxxiv, p. 25.

[2] *Trade Association Activities,* 1927, p. 184.

[3] *Coal Age,* vol. xxiii, p. 201. Cf. vol. xix, pp. 966, 1067; vol. xxvi, p. 554; vol. xxix, p. 853; vol. xxxi, p. 905.

[4] *Ibid.,* vol. xxiv, p. 603.

lief that the association is getting away from its original determination not to deal with labor matters and is becoming more and more the spokesman of the non-union branch of the industry."[1] In the following year, however, the president was taken from union territory and it was pointed out that half the offices and committee places were still awarded to representatives of union territory.[2] Subsequent events such as the abrogation of the Jacksonville agreement by certain powerful operators prior to the date to which they had agreed to maintain it, the increasing proportion of non-union mined bituminous in the total production, and the loss of the 1927-28 strike by the United Mine Workers, plus the comments upon these events by the leaders in the association and the change of some of them from a pro-union to an anti-union attitude, convince us that as a matter of fact the group has now and has had for some time a definite "labor policy," and that the core of that policy is "smash the union." And we are more than willing to grant that the United Mine Workers have at various times and places given ample provocation to the operators. We cannot agree, however, that the chief responsibility for the ills of coal is theirs. On the contrary, we are convinced that any permanent solution of those ills must embody the active coöperation of a strong union of the miners.

And this, in turn, brings us to the conclusion that in dealing with such a union and with the problems of the industry a stronger, more unified, and more forward-looking association must be brought about. Competition in bituminous has had ample time to demonstrate its effectiveness. It has failed. As an important cause of this failure we cannot improve upon the language of an operator speaking at the 1923 convention of the association: "Almost everything on the program [of the convention] sounded a warning against a continuance of the selfishness and backbiting between mining fields that has almost always marked operators' affairs."[3] But subsequent appeals by officers for additional members and the fluctuating

[1] *Coal Age,* vol. xxv, p. 781.
[2] *Ibid.,* vol. xxviii, p. 21.
[3] *Ibid.,* vol. xxiii, p. 1058.

personnel of the group go far to indicate that these warnings of 1923 were ineffective. During the period since that date the positive activities designed to bring a greater measure of order into coal that seem to have been uppermost in the minds of association members are: smash the union, consolidate, mechanize. Alongside these has been the negative, and almost panicky, opposition to any degree of governmental regulation. As previously indicated, we believe the attitude toward a union is unwise. The effect of mechanization to date apparently has been to aggravate the labor difficulties and, because of the pressure of fixed charges and the consequent desire for continuous production, to stimulate overdevelopment and periodic overproduction. These last have been the curse of coal for many years, but as a group the operators do not seem to realize the relation of mechanization to them.[1] That consolidations would be of benefit seems indisputable, but without provision for some measure of government regulation any relaxation of the antitrust laws to permit them is hardly to be expected.

Meanwhile, the most recent income-tax data available indicate that the financial position of the industry as a whole is extremely unsatisfactory.[2] No industry in the United States needs a forward-looking trade association more urgently than does bituminous coal. But the vital element is *bona fide* coöperation. Until and unless the operators advance from their present position as the "fundamentalists of *laissez-faire*" they cannot hope that their association will function in the satisfactory fashion so successfully demonstrated in other lines.

As this brief survey has indicated, trade associations through the twelve different lines of activity distinguished by the Department of Commerce are contributing in many branches of industry to efficiency, economy, and improved relations and standards among the groups affected. The demonstration they have afforded of the extent to which coöperation among competing business men may be carried to their advantage

[1] Cf. Hamilton and Wright, *The Case of Bituminous Coal,* chaps. vii, viii, and ix.

[2] *Coal Age,* vol. xxxiv, p. 9. The net loss for the industry was computed at $22,363,497 for 1925.

and without disadvantage to the public has contributed more than anything else to a better understanding of the combination and monopoly problem. If the antitrust laws are further modified along constructive lines, trade associations and their leaders will deserve chief credit for the change.

CHAPTER XVII

STATE ANTITRUST LEGISLATION AND ITS RESULTS

In bringing down to date the histories of the various trusts discussed in preceding chapters we have, of course, come far past the first legislative attempts to cope with undesirable aspects of the combination movement. Consequently it is necessary to retrace our steps to some extent for the purpose of developing the legal phases of the subject.

Long prior to the enactment of any statute in the United States, there had been built up in English jurisprudence a body of doctrine on restraints of trade. For centuries it had been the rule at common law that any restraint which an individual might lay upon himself by contract to refrain from any trade or labor was void and the contract unenforceable. About 1620, however, an exception was made to this general rule in a case upholding a contract not to engage in a particular trade in a designated town. At later periods other breaches were made in the original doctrine so that the courts came to recognize as enforceable agreements by which the vendor of a business agreed not to engage in that business in the immediate locality. Such an arrangement amounted to a sale of good will and enabled the vendor to secure a better price perhaps than he could otherwise have done. It also became possible for business partners to secure the enforcement against a former partner of an agreement not to compete with them. Such exceptions as these were designated as "reasonable" restraints of trade. The real meaning of the term reasonable here is that the contracts were viewed as subsidiary and ancillary to a major contract—*e.g.*, the sale of a business which was itself unquestionable. But if it could be demonstrated that the primary purpose of an agreement of the types suggested above was to restrict an individual's business or actually to get him out of it, then such an agreement would not be enforced. It was "unreasonable."

So far we have spoken only of contracts in which one of the parties to it was restrained. When the agreement restrained the trade of a third person, that is to say, one not a party to the contract, it was unenforceable at common law. In this doctrine there had been no change; there could be no issue of reasonableness or unreasonableness of contracts restraining a third party. At the time of the passage of our first state antitrust statutes these definitions and distinctions of the types of restraint of trade were thoroughly recognized and had been applied in scores of cases in both England and America.

But it must be noted that neither the unreasonable restraints affecting only the parties to the contract nor the restraint of third parties was at this time illegal; they were simply void and unenforceable. The change brought about by the state and federal statutes against trusts was to make such contracts positively illegal, actionable, and indictable. In other words, these statutes prohibited affirmatively and provided penalties for participation in certain contracts which the common law had previously only refused to support.[1] For a time it seemed that the Sherman Act had gone further than just indicated, but since 1911 this cannot be said. To this point we shall return later.[2]

The immediate background of the antitrust legislation, both state and federal, lay in the economic developments following the Civil War. Industrial overexpansion was a large factor in the panic of 1873. Combination seemed one method of at least partially avoiding overexpansion, so that, as has been previously brought out, business interests tried to relieve themselves of the wastes and restraints of competition by means of combination. The simple agreement and the pool were developed and utilized. Because of their unenforce-

[1] The best brief treatment of the status in 1890 of the common law on restraints of trade will be found in Taft, W. H., *The Anti-Trust Act and the Supreme Court,* Harper & Brothers, New York, 1914. We have relied upon it for the exposition in the text.

[2] Cf. chaps. xviii and xix, *infra.*

ability at common law, they were discarded in favor of the trustee device, which later, as explained in an earlier chapter, gave way to the holding company and the outright consolidation. Concentration was also in progress in the railroad business. Rate wars, discriminations, rebates and other abuses brought about a condition both chaotic and intolerable. After two years of investigation Congress in 1887 passed the Interstate Commerce Act. In the course of this investigation much information was brought to light concerning the character and tactics of industrial combinations, which in turn led to widespread demand for further governmental action. Tammany Hall in New York City appointed an antitrust committee which demanded that suitable action be taken by the people. Newspapers daily devoted columns to the dissemination of facts and near-facts about the trusts. The very secrecy of many of the most successful gave an added stimulus to muckraking. Anything that smelled of combination was frowned upon by the general public. Pamphleteers vied with the newspapers in denouncing trusts as the root of the economic disorders of the preceding few years and vigorous demands were made from a wide variety of sources for more severe legislation.

As a result of this agitation numberless bills were filed with the different legislatures during the next few years, three or more in every state. They aimed at forbidding every kind of combination or coalition for the purpose of checking competition, raising prices, etc. In response to this public demand many legislatures passed laws of some sort. The amount of constitutional and statutory prohibition by the states and territories of trusts and monopolies prior to the date of the passage of the federal law, July 2, 1890, is not generally recognized. Consequently, it is interesting to note that before this date at least fourteen states and territories had such prohibitions in their constitutions and at least thirteen had statutory prohibitions. The former group included: Arkansas, Connecticut, Georgia, Idaho, Kentucky, Maryland, Montana, North Carolina, North Dakota, South Dakota, Tennessee, Texas, Washington and Wyoming. The latter included: Iowa, Kansas, Kentucky, Maine, Michigan, Mississippi, Missouri, Nebraska, North Carolina, North Dakota, South Dakota, Tennessee, and Texas. States common to the two lists, that is, having both constitutional and statutory prohibitions prior to July 2, 1890, were Kentucky, North Carolina, North Dakota, South Dakota, Tennessee, and Texas.[1] The great majority of the states fell into line with

[1] Our list of constitutional prohibitions is longer than any we have found in previous attempts at such compilations. The differences rest partly on a broader interpretation of the language of the constitutions than our predecessors have seen fit to apply. The sections we consider to sustain us are as follows: Arkansas, Const. of 1874, Art. 2, §19; Connecticut, Const. of 1818, Art. 1, §1; Georgia, Const. of 1877, Art. 4, §2; Idaho, Const. of 1889, Art. 11, §18; Kentucky, Const. of 1850, Art. 13, §1; Maryland, Const. of 1867, Declaration of Rights, §41; Montana, Const. of 1889, Art. 15, §20; North Carolina, Const. of 1776, Declaration of Rights, §23, and Const. of 1868, Appendix 1, §31; North Dakota, Const. of 1889, Art. 7, §146; South Dakota, Const. of 1889, Art. 17, §20; Tennessee, Const. of 1870, Art. 1, §22; Texas, Const. of 1845, Art. 1, §18, and Const. of 1876, Art. 1, §26; Washington, Const. of 1889, Art. 12, §22; Wyoming, Const. of 1889, Art. 1, §30.

With respect to the prohibition of trusts by state enactment prior to July 2, 1890, we expected to find more agreement among investigators, but such has not proved to be the case. An exhaustive check of the codes and of court decisions has convinced us that most of the lists of such enactments in secondary sources are incomplete. (Cf. Van Hise, *Concentration and Control* [1912], p. 193, and Jenks and Clark, The *Trust Problem* [1929], p. 213.) The compilation in von Halle, *Trusts or Industrial Combinations in the United States,* pp. 17-18, is the longest we have found, but we believe it is incorrect in its inclusion of Idaho and Montana. Von Halle does not follow the writer he cites (F. H. Cooke in the *Annals of the American Academy of Political and Social Science,* vol. v, p. 569) and apparently confuses constitutional and statutory prohibitions. Probably the most frequently quoted list is that of Professors Jenks and Clark in their *Trust Problem.* The 1929 revision of this book at p. 213 repeats the statement of earlier editions that only eight states enacted laws condemning trusts prior to July 2, 1890. We include the same eight, but have added Iowa, Missouri, Nebraska, North Dakota, and Texas. The failure of Jenks and Clark to include the first two of these is extraordinarily difficult to understand, in view of the facts that Professor Jenks prepared Volume II of the report of the U. S. Industrial Commission dealing with trust statutes, that p. 100 of that volume gives the date of approval of the Iowa statute as May 6, 1890, and that p. 151 shows that the Missouri statute of 1891, which is reprinted therein, repealed the law of 1889. As a matter of fact, the first Iowa statute was passed two years earlier (cf. 102 Iowa 602, 607; 70 N. W. 107, 109 [1897] where it is construed) and the law cited by the Industrial Commission replaced it. On this point cf. *Code of Iowa, Annotated,* 1897, pp. 1968, xx, and xxiv-17. Further authority for our inclusion of Missouri will be found in 152 Mo. 1, 43 (1899). Nebraska began to legislate against "devices designed to restrain competition" as early as 1887, but her first general statute was not passed until two years later (laws of 1889, ch. 69). This statute was construed in 56 Neb. 386 (1898) and cited in 75 Neb. 637, 642 (1906). North Dakota's law of 1890 was ch. 174 of the

more or less rapidity, so that by the date of the report of the Industrial Commission in 1900 there were twenty-seven states and territories which prohibited trusts by law and fifteen by constitution. Eleven of the latter group had also passed laws. In 1929 all but eight states included antitrust regulations in their constitutions, statutes, or both. These eight were Colorado, Delaware, Nevada, New Jersey, Oregon, Pennsylvania, Rhode Island, and West Virginia.[1]

The objects of the state antitrust statutes were:

1. To make criminal many contracts and agreements which at the common law were unenforceable, but not positively illegal.

2. To condemn specifically certain practices which had in some cases already been held contrary to the principles of the common law or had been included under the general terms "monopoly" or "restraint of trade," thus meeting as far as practicable the demand for more definiteness in the law relating to this subject. Furthermore, a number of states have prohibited certain practices, such as local price-cutting and demands by manufacturers for exclusive dealing, which the lawmakers thought might possibly lead to restraint of trade or tend to monopoly if permitted.[2]

Although the antitrust laws of the various states differ so radically from one another in details that a practice strongly

---

laws of that year. The first statute of Texas of 1889 was cited in 275 S. W. 692, 696 (1894). Here again the report of Professor Jenks for the Industrial Commission is in error in leaving the impression that the first Texas statute was approved April 30, 1895 (cf. p. 235).

Since the antitrust laws of the various states have been frequently amended and since the codes frequently omit the date of the first passage of a statute we have found it extremely difficult to ascertain the facts. Consequently, though we believe our list is not too long, it may be found to be too short.

[1] The most convenient summary of the constitutional and statutory prohibitions of trusts by the states will be found in the current edition of J. S. Parker's *Corporation Manual.* We have used the 1929 volume in preparing the above summary. It should be noted, however, that this volume errs in including the antitrust statute of Colorado since it was declared unconstitutional by the U. S. Supreme Court on May 31, 1927 (cf. 274 U. S. 445, 453). As brought out later New Jersey passed antitrust laws in 1913, only to repeal them during the next seven years.

[2] Davies, J. E., *Trust Laws and Unfair Competition,* Government Printing Office, Washington, 1916, p. 143.

prohibited by one state may not even be mentioned in the statute of another, they necessarily cover the same ground to a considerable extent, so that the following brief review may fairly be said to indicate the general nature of the legislation:

1. Monopolies. The extent to which the states have acted against monopolies, using the term as narrower than "trusts," is largely a matter of interpretation of statutes and constitutions. Two standard works list seventeen and eighteen states, respectively, as prohibiting monopolies in their constitutions, but the Commissioner of Corporations included five not found in *Joyce on Monopolies,* and Joyce returns the compliment by listing six states not found in Davies's work.[1] The same confusion exists with reference to the interpretation of the language of statutes.

The constitutional prohibitions take a more or less sweeping form and make a very general statement of the prohibition. Maryland's constitution [2] states that monopolies are "odious, contrary to the spirit of a free government and the principles of commerce, and ought not to be suffered." In the constitution of North Carolina [3] it is declared that "perpetuities and monopolies are contrary to the genius of a free state, and ought not to be allowed." Many of the state antitrust statutes attempt to give definitions of monopolies. Typical examples of these will appear in the subsequent discussion of a few specific statutes.

2. Restraint of trade. Louisiana, Oklahoma, and New Mexico have constitutional prohibitions against restraint of trade. The latter two states direct the legislature to enact laws to prevent combinations in restraint of trade. Thirty-three states have passed statutory prohibitions.[4] In general they follow the words of the North Dakota statute which prohibits combinations of capital, skill, or acts by two or more persons, corporations, etc., "to create or carry out restrictions in trade." [5]

[1] Cf. *Joyce on Monopolies,* p. 268, and Davies, *op. cit.,* pp. 144 and 145.
[2] Art. 41. Reprinted in Bagley, *Annotated Code of Maryland,* 1924, p. 65.
[3] Art. I, sec. 31.
[4] Parker, *Corporation Manual* (1929).
[5] C. L., 1913, §9950.

3. Restraint of competition. Restraint of competition, as distinguished from restraint of trade, is prohibited in twenty-nine states. California, for example, prohibits combinations of capital, skill, or acts (a) which prevent competition in manufacturing, making, transporting, selling, or purchasing merchandise, produce, or any commodity, and (b) which make any agreement by which they shall establish or settle the price of any article, commodity, or transportation between them or themselves and others so as to preclude a free and unrestricted competition among themselves, or any purchasers and consumers in the sale or transportation of any such article or commodity.[1]

4. Pooling. Pools are prohibited in the constitutions of two states—Kentucky [2] and Louisiana [3]—and by the statutes of twenty-five, but are defined by only one—North Dakota—where the term is a synonym of "trust." The Kentucky and Louisiana constitutional prohibitions render pools illegal when interests are pooled for the purpose of forcing up or down the prices of articles of commerce. The general statutory prohibitions follow the form of the Alabama law, which prohibits any person or corporation from entering into any pool "to regulate or fix the price of any article or commodity to be sold or produced" within the state, or "to fix or limit the quantity of any article or commodity to be produced, manufactured, mined or sold" in the state.[4] In some states, pooling for special purposes only is declared illegal and still others supplement their general statutes by specific prohibitions. Kansas, Montana, and Nebraska prohibit combinations of grain dealers; Mississippi, pools for bidding on public work; Nebraska and Oklahoma, pools of bridge-builders; Washington, pools of commission men.

5. Price control. Twelve [5] states have constitutional pro-

[1] California Laws, 1907, chap. 530, sec. 1; G. L., 1920, Act. 5264 § 1.

[2] §198.

[3] Const., 1921, Art. XIX, §14.

[4] *Code,* 1923, §5212.

[5] Davies, apparently by a more strict construction of the language used, restricts this group to ten, omitting Alabama and Kentucky, which we have included. Cf. his pp. 168 and 169 with §103, Alabama constitution of 1901, and §198 of the Kentucky constitution.

visions either prohibiting price-fixing directly, or directing that laws be enacted to prevent corporations or associations from fixing prices. Thirty-five states prohibit control of prices by statutes. The Kansas law, a fair example, prohibits combinations of capital, skill, or acts by two or more corporations, firms, or persons to (a) increase or reduce the price of merchandise, produce, or commodities, or to control insurance rates; (b) fix any standard or figure whereby the price of any commodity, produce, etc., to the public or consumer shall be controlled; (c) make any agreement by which they shall bind themselves not to sell, manufacture, or transport any commodity below a common standard figure or to keep the price at a standard figure; (d) pool, combine, or unite any interests they may have in such a way as to affect the price in any fashion of any article, etc., they are making, selling, or transporting.[1]

6. Limitation of output. Seven states prohibit limitation of output by constitutional provision, Alabama limiting its prohibitions to articles of necessity, however. California and nine other states, through statutes, prohibit the issuance or ownership of trust certificates and combinations, contracts, or agreements, the purpose and/or effect of which shall be to place the management or control of such combination or the manufactured product thereof in the hands of any trustee with the intent to lessen the production or to prevent, restrict, or diminish the manufacture or output of any such article.[2] A total of thirty states prohibits limitation of output by statutory enactment.

7. Division of territory. In spite of the frequent use of the device of dividing territory by trusts it seems that only three states—North Carolina, Nebraska, and Texas—have prohibited such agreements. Moreover, the laws of Nebraska are restricted in their application to bridge-builders and bridge contractors.[3]

[1] *Revised Statutes,* 1923, §50-101.

[2] California G. L., 1915, Act 4166, §1.

[3] Nebraska, *Compiled Statutes,* 1922, §3440. North Carolina, L., 1911, c. 167, § 1 (f.) Texas, *Complete Statutes of 1920,* Art. 7796.

8. Competitive methods. In addition to prohibiting in general terms any business tactics designed to limit competition, restrain trade, etc., a number of the states have prohibited certain specific practices which were designed to secure these ends. The most common of such prohibitions is that against local price discrimination, found in the statutes of twenty-two states. The Massachusetts law, the language of which is closely followed in a number of states, provides that no person, firm, association or corporation dealing in a commodity in general use "shall maliciously, or for the purpose of destroying the business of a competitor and of creating a monopoly in any locality, discriminate between different sections, communities, towns or cities of the commonwealth or between purchasers by selling such commodity at a lower rate for such purpose in one section, community, town or city than is charged for such commodity by the vendor in another section, community, town or city in the commonwealth." Differences in prices resulting from differences in grade, quality, or cost of transportation are permitted.[1] A general prohibition of restraints on resales appears in the statutes of three states—Idaho,[2] Nebraska,[3] and North Dakota[4]—and a prohibition of resale price maintenance in the law of Virginia.[5] Exclusive contracts are prohibited by five states—Louisiana,[6] Massachusetts,[7] Michigan,[8] North Carolina,[9] and Virginia.[10] Combinations or agreements to refuse to deal with persons, firms, etc., are also prohibited by five states—Indiana,[11] Missouri,[12] Nebraska,[13] South Carolina,[14] and Texas.[15]

[1] G. L., c. 93, §8.

[2] *Compiled Statutes of Idaho*, 1919, §2534.

[3] *Revised Statutes*, 1913, §4050; *Compiled Statutes*, 1922, §3453.

[4] C. L., 1913, §9951, par. 3.

[5] Ex. Sess. L., 1919, c. 54, par. 4.

[6] L. 1915, Act No. 11, §4.

[7] G. L., c. 93, §1.

[8] C. L., §15028.

[9] L., 1911, c. 167, §1.

[10] Ex. Sess. L., 1919, c. 54, par. 4.

[11] Burns's *Annotated Statutes*, 1914, §3884.

[12] R. S., 1919, §9657.

[13] *Revised Statues*, 1913, §4018; *Compiled Statutes*, 1922, §3421. Limited to grain dealers.

[14] *Civil Code*, 1922, §3546.

[15] *Complete Statutes of 1920*, Art. 7798; *Penal Code*, Art. 1456.

9. Administration. The official most frequently responsible for the administration and enforcement of the state antitrust acts is, of course, the attorney general. In a number of states he is entirely responsible, but in others he shares this responsibility with county or district attorneys.

10. Penalties. The penalties provided for violations of the state antitrust laws present the widest variety of combinations. A total of thirty-seven states assess personal penalties against officers of trusts and all but five of these include prison sentences. All of the thirty-seven levy fines against the trust, its officers, or both.[1] In a number of states the corporate fines may run to high figures, since each day constitutes a separate offense and, in Texas for example, may be punished at the rate of $1,500 a day. The fines and prison sentences are heavier in some jurisdictions if the article monopolized is a necessity of life. Charters or permits to do business may be revoked for violation of the law in twenty-nine states. In twenty-six, any or all contracts made in furtherance of a restraint of trade or monopoly are void. Individuals or business concerns able to demonstrate injury at the hands of a trust may recover damages in twenty states. In some cases these are only actual damages, but in others they include costs, attorneys' fees, and double or treble damages.[2]

The foregoing summary is adequate as a generalized picture of state antitrust legislation, but it has the defect of all generalizations of omitting and obscuring details. Consequently it seems wise to supplement it with an analysis of a few of the laws and their results. Those of Texas and Missouri will be presented because those states made a more thoroughgoing attempt at enforcement than did other com-

[1] In addition to the eight states—Colorado, Delaware, Nevada, New Jersey, Oregon, Pennsylvania, Rhode Island, and West Virginia—which do not prohibit trusts either by constitution or by general statute, Georgia, Kentucky, Maryland, and Washington do not levy fines. Georgia has no general statute in spite of its constitutional prohibition of trusts, though the General Code (§4253) provides that contracts in restraint of trade cannot be enforced. Kentucky has repealed its law. Oregon's statute is limited to dairy products. Washington has two specific statutes, one applying to insurance rates, the other to dairy products, eggs, and poultry.

[2] Parker, *Corporation Manual,* 1929, pp. 1999-2158.

monwealths; those of New Jersey, though now repealed, are interesting because of the change of policy they represented.

The definition of trusts presented in the Texas statute may be condensed as follows: A trust is a combination of capital, skill, or acts by two or more persons, firms, corporations or associations of persons, or either two or more of them, for either, any, or all of the following purposes:

1. To restrain trade or commerce, or to restrain the free pursuit of any business authorized or permitted by the laws of this state.

2. To fix, maintain, increase, or reduce the price of merchandise, produce, or commodities, or the cost of insurance, or of the preparation of any product for market or transportation.

3. To prevent or lessen competition in the manufacture, making, transportation, sale, or purchase of merchandise, produce, or commodities, or the business of insurance, or to prevent or lessen competition in aids to commerce, or in the preparation of any product for market or transportation.

4. To fix or maintain any standard or figure whereby the price of any article or commodity of merchandise, produce, or commerce, or the cost of transportation or insurance, or the preparation of any product for market or transportation, shall be in any manner affected, controlled, or established.

5. To make contracts to keep prices of manufactured commodities, insurance, or transportation at a fixed or graded level or in any manner affect or maintain these prices, etc.

6. To regulate, fix, or limit the output of any article manufactured, mined, produced, or sold, or the amount of insurance which may be undertaken, or the amount of work which may be done in the preparation of any product for market or transportation.

7. To abstain from engaging in or continuing business or from the purchase and sale of merchandise, produce, or commodities partially or entirely within the state of Texas or any portion thereof.[1]

[1] *Revised Statutes*, 1925, Art. 7426.

The next article of the law defines a monopoly as a combination or consolidation of two or more corporations when effected by either of the following methods:

1. When the direction of the affairs of two or more corporations is in any manner brought under the same management or control for the purpose of producing, or where such common control tends to create a trust as just defined.

2. Where any corporation acquires shares or certificates of stock or bonds, franchises, or physical properties of any other corporation or corporations for the purpose of lessening competition.

Under Texas law the following acts are termed conspiracies in restraint of trade:

1. Where two or more persons, corporations, or firms enter into an agreement or understanding to refuse to buy from or sell to any person, firm, or corporation any article of merchandise, produce, or commodity.

2. Where any firms, persons, corporations, etc., shall agree to boycott or threaten to refuse to buy from or sell to any person, firm, or corporation buying from or selling to any other person, firm, corporation, or association.

Any and all trusts, monopolies, and conspiracies in restraint of trade, as defined above, are prohibited and declared to be illegal.

The penalties for violations of the statute are both drastic and comprehensive. Any corporation holding a charter under the laws of the state of Texas which violates any of the provisions of the statute forfeits its charter and franchise, and its corporate existence ceases.[1] When a corporation organized under the laws of Texas is convicted of a violation of any of the provisions of the act, and its charter and franchise forfeited, no other corporation to which the defaulting corporation may have transferred its property or business, or which has assumed the payment of its obligations, is permitted to incorporate or do business in Texas. Every foreign corporation

[1] That antitrust statutes have no application to interstate commerce is held not to affect the power of the courts to apply them to domestic commerce so as to forfeit the permit of a foreign corporation for violation. Waters-Pierce Oil Co. *v.* State, 44 S. W. 936 (1898).

violating the provisions of this statute is denied the right of and is prohibited from doing any business within the state of Texas. The fines assessable for violations range from $50 to $1,500 for each day the violation continues. The fee of the attorney prosecuting the case is 10 per cent of the fine on fines of $50,000 and less, and 5 per cent on any fine above $50,000.[1]

Any contract or agreement in violation of the provisions of the statute is void and not enforceable either in law or in equity.

Texas was one of the few states that made a sincere attempt to enforce its antitrust law rigidly. The most outstanding litigation resulting from this attempt was that against the Waters-Pierce Oil Company. This company had secured permission to do business in Texas in 1889. It was originally chartered in Missouri, but had become the largest concern in the petroleum business in Texas. Nine years after being admitted to the state the company was challenged as a violator of the state antitrust law, and accused of being a part of the Standard Oil combine. The purpose of the suit as brought was to cancel the permit to do business in the state. A judgment against the company in the Texas courts was affirmed by the Supreme Court of the United States.[2] By the terms of the judgment the permit of the Waters-Pierce Oil Company to do business in Texas, was revoked and cancelled, and it was perpetually enjoined from doing such business. This penalty was not as sweeping as it seems, for the court added that "Nothing herein contained shall be construed to in any way affect or apply to or prohibit said defendant's right to engage in interstate commerce within this state."[3] This clause was necessary, of course, to avoid the semblance of state control of interstate commerce. Moreover, it is interesting to note that in the Texas district court the jury had been in-

[1] In the case of Ft. Worth & D. C. Ry. *v.* State, 88 S. W. 370 (1905) it has been decided that the state has no right to penalties based on the grounds that the contract created a monopoly at common law or was in violation of the antitrust laws of the United States.

[2] 44 S. W. 936 (1898); 177 U. S. 28 (1900).

[3] 44 S. W. 936 (1898).

structed that the evidence on the alleged participation of the Waters-Pierce Company in the Standard Oil trust was to be disregarded as insufficient.

After this decision the old Waters-Pierce Oil Company went out of existence, but in May of 1900 the state of Texas gave a new Waters-Pierce Company a permit to do business within the state. The new company was identical in name, total amount of stock, and distribution of stock among the holders with the old one. Moreover, the new concern followed the same methods condemned in its predecessor. As time went on and knowledge of what had been done became more general a demand arose for another prosecution.

In the new suit, instituted in 1907, the state alleged that about January 1, 1870, John D. Rockefeller and his associates formed a conspiracy to monopolize the petroleum business of the United States and that this conspiracy had continued in force until the date of the institution of the suit. The state further claimed that a major part of the capital stock of the Waters-Pierce Company, although standing in the name of the president, H. C. Pierce, was in fact owned by the Standard Oil Company of New Jersey. Consequently, the dissolution of the old company in 1900 and the creation of the new company was held to have been in further pursuance of the conspiracy for the purpose of continuing the monopoly and control which had been acquired by the old company. The state alleged that as a result of this conspiracy:

1. The Waters-Pierce Company was dominated and controlled by and its business dictated by the Standard Oil of New Jersey.

2. A large number of corporations and individuals were excluded from doing business in Texas and competition was thus limited.

3. The price of oil was maintained at an exorbitant figure, being from 10 to 25 per cent higher than that of oil in territory not claimed by the Waters-Pierce Company.

4. Competition was suppressed and business destroyed in the state by unconscionable and unfair means.

5. A substantially complete monopoly in petroleum products was established, since the Waters-Pierce Company did at least 95 per cent of the petroleum business in the state.

6. The Waters-Pierce Company had taken over the Eagle Refining Company and the Texas Oil and Gasoline Company and had operated them from 1894 and 1896, respectively, as supposedly independent companies.

Because of the fact that the Texas antitrust act had been amended in 1903, that is, after the new Waters-Pierce Company had been chartered and before the second suit was begun, the company was charged with violating both the statutes: the earlier law of 1899 from May 31, 1900, to March 31, 1903, and the later law of 1903 from April 1, 1903, to April 29, 1907. Under both laws each day of violation constituted a separate offense, but under the former the fine per day might be assessed at any figure from $200 to $5,000, whereas under the latter it was set at $50.

In his charge to the jury the judge who presided in the state district court laid all the emphasis on the relationships between the Waters-Pierce Company and the Standard Oil of New Jersey and the results of those relationships in fixing prices, limiting trade, and preventing competition. The jury found for the state on all the issues submitted to it in the charge of the court, and assessed the penalties as loss of permission to do business in the state and a fine of $1,623,900. The latter was computed at the rate of $1,500 a day from May 31, 1900, to March 31, 1903, and $50 a day from April 1, 1903, to April 29, 1907.[1]

On appeal the decision of the district court was upheld by the Texas Court of Civil Appeals and the Supreme Court of the United States.[2] In the Texas court the most important points of interpretation were those in which it was held that the antitrust laws were valid and not indefinite or uncertain, that the Act of 1903 in diminishing the amount of fine that might be assessed per day did not affect the right of the state to collect the higher penalties of the law of 1899 for its viola-

[1] 106 S. W. 924 (1907).

[2] 106 S. W. 918, 930 (1907); 212 U. S. 86 (1909).

tion, that the penalties section of neither of the laws was indefinite, and that the fines assessed in this particular case were not excessive. Among the rulings of less import was the somewhat amusing one that "In construing written laws, courts are not bound by rules of grammar and may disregard them to give effect to manifest legislative intent!"[1]

Before the Supreme Court the chief claims of the Waters-Pierce Company were that since the agreement complained of was made outside the state the company was not liable in the state, that the statutes were so vague and indefinite as to deprive the company of due process of law, and that the fines assessed were so excessive as to amount to deprivation of property without due process. The court held the findings of the Texas courts conclusive on the facts and refused to accept the pleadings of the oil company on the issues of law. It held that even though the trust agreement had been made outside the state the state could prosecute if the parties to the agreement or their agents executed or attempted to execute said agreement within the state. It further held that the statutes were not vague or indefinite and that the fines were not excessive in view of the facts that the corporation had over $40,000,000 in assets and had declared dividends amounting to several hundred per cent per annum.[2]

The Waters-Pierce Company paid the fine but was allowed to continue to do business in the state. Other trusts avoided conflict with the law by going through the form of selling their products to new corporations created for that purpose.

The first paragraph of the Missouri law is a general condemnation of combinations in restraint of trade as conspiracies. It provides that "Any person who shall create, enter into, become a member of or participate in any pool, trust, agreement, combination, confederation or understanding with any person or persons in restraint of trade or competition in the importation, transportation, manufacture, purchase or sale of any product or commodity in this state, or any article or thing bought or sold whatsoever, shall be deemed and adjudged

[1] 106 S. W. 918, 919 (1907).

[2] 212 U. S. 86, 87 (1909).

guilty of a conspiracy in restraint of trade, and shall be punished as provided in this article." [1]

The next section states that any person who shall become a member of a pool, combination, etc., to regulate or control the price of any article of manufacture, merchandise, product of mining, etc., or the price or premium to be paid for insuring property, or to maintain such prices when so regulated or fixed, or becomes a member of a pool, trust, etc., to fix the amount or quantity of any article of manufacture, etc., shall be deemed and adjudged guilty of a conspiracy in restraint of trade, and be punished as provided for in this article. The courts by process of judicial interpretation, have extended the meaning of this section in certain particulars. It has been held that foreign and domestic corporations engaged in the violation of this section cannot defend themselves on the ground that they are governed by interstate commerce laws.[2] Also it is immaterial where the unlawful conspiracy was entered into, or by what means it was formed, if it concerns commodities which are sold in the state by the conspirators. In such case they are punishable in the state, whether the unlawful combination was formed in Missouri or not.[3] Moreover, the state has the power to oust the subsidiary company of a foreign corporation which violates this section.[4] Every direct restraint, great or small, no matter what the court thinks the effect is, is condemned by this section. A corporation which succeeds to the rights of another in an unlawful combination of trade is not relieved from liability.[5]

Subsequent sections declare that combinations to control or limit trade, to limit competition, or to boycott or threaten to boycott, and all sorts of combinations or agreements, entered into, designed, or made with a view to lessen or which tend to lessen full and free competition are conspiracies in restraint of trade. Moreover, the trustee type of trust is definitely banned by a section which makes it unlawful for any corpora-

[1] *Revised Statutes,* 1919, §9655.
[2] State *v.* Lumber Co., 260 Mo. 212; 169 S. W. 145 (1914).
[3] State *v.* Oil Co., 218 Mo. 1; 116 S. W. 902 (1908).
[4] State *v.* Harvester Co., 237 Mo. 369; 141 S. W. 672 (1911).
[5] State *v.* Ice Co., 246 Mo. 168; 151 S. W. 101 (1912).

tion to issue or to own trust certificates, or to enter into any combination, contract, or agreement the purpose and effect of which is to place the management or control of such combination or manufactured product thereof in the hands of any trustee with the intent to fix the price, or lessen the production, or to prevent, diminish, or restrict the manufacture or output of any such article.

Violators of the statute are to be adjudged guilty of a felony and upon conviction to be punished by imprisonment in the state penitentiary not exceeding five years, or by imprisonment in the county jail not exceeding one year or by a fine of from $500 to $5,000, or by both fine and imprisonment.

The circuit courts of Missouri are given jurisdiction over cases arising under the antitrust laws. The Attorney General of the state is empowered to institute proceedings in equity to prevent and restrain all such violations and to call upon the prosecuting or circuit attorney of the county in which proceedings are instituted for assistance. Upon proper proof that a corporation created under the laws of Missouri has violated the provisions of the antitrust law, the court may declare that it has forfeited its corporate rights and franchise. The court may also declare all or any part of the property of such corporation forfeited to the state, or simply levy a fine against it. In the case of State *v.* Harvester Company,[1] it has been decided that the court must pronounce judgment on a corporation if guilty, but may stay execution on terms fair to the welfare of the people and the corporation.

The law follows the federal model in providing that persons injured by a violation may recover triple damages and the costs of the suit, including a reasonable attorney's fee. The purchaser of any article or commodity from any concern operating in violation of the statute is not liable for the price or payment for such article. Local price discrimination is forbidden.

In Missouri a long series of cases marks its efforts to force adherence to its antitrust law. One of the most important suits was brought by Attorney General Hadley against the

[1] 237 Mo. 369; 141 S. W. 672 (1911).

Waters-Pierce Oil Company, the Standard Oil Company of Indiana, and the Republic Oil Company of New York [1] to forfeit the charter of the first concern and to revoke the licenses to do business in Missouri of the latter two. Hadley contended that they had forfeited their charters and licenses to do business in Missouri by forming and entering into a pool, trust, combination, or conspiracy in restraint of trade.

The Waters-Pierce Oil Company had been incorporated in Missouri in 1878 with a capital of $100,000, increased in 1882 to $400,000. At the time of its organization in 1879 the old Standard Oil Trust acquired 60 per cent of the stock of Waters-Pierce. In 1900 the latter corporation was rechartered as a result of the litigation in Texas discussed above and at that time the Standard Oil Company of New Jersey acquired 2,750 of the 4,000 shares and H. C. Pierce, the president, retained 1,250 shares. On the books of the company all of the stock except four shares stood in the name of H. C. Pierce, but in reality 2,750 shares were owned by the Standard Oil Company. The officers and directors of the Waters-Pierce Oil Company had a direct or indirect relation to the Standard Oil of New Jersey.

The Waters-Pierce Oil Company had built up a large business in a part of Missouri and in Arkansas, Texas, Louisiana, Indian Territory, Oklahoma, and Mexico. The refined products sold in the United States were obtained almost wholly from the Standard Oil Company of New Jersey or allied interests. Dividends on the stock ranged from 600 to 700 per cent per annum during the period from 1900 to 1905.[2]

The Republic Oil Company was organized under the laws of New York on June 3, 1901, and licensed to do business in Missouri on July 8, 1901. It was organized by the Standard Oil Company of New Jersey to take over the business of an independent firm by the name of Schofield, Shurmer, & Teagle of Cleveland, Ohio. It sold oil in the territory of both the Standard Oil of Indiana and the Waters-Pierce Oil Company

[1] State *ex. inf.* Hadley, Attorney General, *v.* Standard Oil Company, *et al.*, 116 S. W. 902 (1908).

[2] 116 S. W. 981, 982, 983 (1908).

of Missouri. All of its stock was held by the Standard Oil Company of New Jersey and its president was a clerk or assistant to Walter Jennings, a Standard Oil official. As a result of disclosures in this Missouri litigation all the properties of the Republic Company, except those in Missouri, were taken over by the Standard Oil of Indiana. In short, this company was what is known as a "bogus" independent organized for the purpose of facilitating the driving of competitors from business and preserving an outward form of competition in the sale of petroleum products in the state of Missouri.[1]

The Standard Oil Company of Indiana, organized in 1889 with a capital of $500,000, was licensed to do business in Missouri in 1897. The Standard Oil of New Jersey held practically all of its stock, either directly or indirectly, from 1889 to the time of the suit. Its field of operations was confined to the northern part of Missouri, the southern section being the sales territory of the Waters-Pierce Company. These territorial divisions were very strictly observed, but the Republic Oil Company, as explained above, operated in both sections for the purpose of simulating competition.

Prices were fixed by the Waters-Pierce Company and the Standard Oil of Indiana in their respective territories. The Republic followed their prices. Both the Standard Oil and Waters-Pierce Companies had a system of espionage by which they obtained reports from their agents and from railroad employees about competitors' shipments into this territory, with a view to prevent petroleum sales by independent dealers. By the use of these methods the defendants controlled and limited the trade in petroleum products in Missouri, prevented and destroyed competition in the purchase and sale of said products, and deceived and misled the public into the belief that they were separate and distinct companies.

By reason of the flagrant violation of the statutes of the state of Missouri the licenses of the Standard Oil Company of Indiana and the Republic Oil Company of New York were forfeited, annulled, and canceled, and these corporations were

[1] 116 S. W. 983, 984 (1908).

by the decree ousted of any and all rights and franchises granted to them under the laws of Missouri to do further business in the state. Moreover, they were fined $50,000 each, said fines to be paid by March 1, 1909. The Waters-Pierce Company was also fined $50,000. It was to have its franchises and charter revoked unless it immediately ceased all connection with the other two companies in maintaining the trust, and in the future refrained from all such pools to control the prices of petroleum. In case of sufficient evidence being shown that the decree of the court had been entirely complied with by January 15, 1909, the judgment would be suspended, and the corporation allowed to continue to do business. Otherwise the absolute ouster would apply. This decision was handed down by the Supreme Court of Missouri on December 23, 1908.[1]

The companies all paid the fines, but in the opinion of Attorney General Hadley no satisfactory evidence was submitted that the Waters-Pierce Company had complied with the court's decree. The court, however, ruled on a rehearing on March 9, 1909, that the company had sufficiently complied with its order and refused Hadley's request for an absolute ouster. By the terms of the decree as amended on rehearing the results of the litigation were then that the Waters-Pierce Oil Company continued to do business in Missouri with a simple fine of $50,000 and a suspended ouster; that the Republic Oil Company was fined $50,000, deprived of its license, and absolutely ousted from the state; and that the Standard Oil Company of Indiana was fined $50,000 and absolutely ousted. The last company appealed to the Missouri Supreme Court to have the ouster suspended. On June 28, 1913, more than four years later, the court agreed to a suspended ouster on the following conditions:

1. The court was to retain jurisdiction for the purpose of rendering necessary orders and judgments with respect to the stay and suspension of the writ of ouster.

2. Suspension of the ouster was granted upon condition that

[1] 116 S. W. 1048, 1049 (1908).

the Standard Oil Company of Indiana should faithfully obey all laws of the state, especially the antitrust laws.

3. In case such laws were again violated, the Attorney General should again move for a vacation of this suspended ouster.

4. The court reserved the right, independent of any action by the Attorney General, to make an investigation as to whether or not the defendants were faithfully complying with the laws of Missouri and to modify or vacate its order in conformity with the results of such investigation.

5. In order that the jurisdiction of the court should not be questioned, the case was to be kept open.

6. The company was to be responsible only for acts subsequent to the date of the suspended ouster.[1]

Another Missouri case was that brought by the Attorney General against the International Harvester Company of America, the sales agent of the International Harvester Company of New Jersey.[2] The Supreme Court of Missouri held the Harvester Company of New Jersey to be an unlawful combination, but it could not act directly against that corporation since it was not in Missouri in its own name. However, the America company was so obviously the agent and a part of the trust that it was possible to hold that it was not eligible to do business in the state; that is, an agent had no power to do what its principal could not. The court thereupon pronounced a judgment of ouster and fine. But it went on to point out that "It would be an injury to the people of this state to forbid the International Harvester Company to do business here,"[3] and consequently laid down a set of conditions under which the Harvester trust would be permitted to do business in its own name or through an agent. The chief of these were that it should pay a license tax proportionate to the part of its capital stock represented by its property and business in Missouri, that it should not use its power to force a competitor to sell out to it or to drive such com-

[1] 158 S. W. 601 (1913).

[2] State *ex. inf.* Attorney General *v.* International Harvester Company of America, 141 S. W. 672 (1911).

[3] 141 S. W. 679 (1911).

petitor from the market, and that it should not raise the prices of its commodities beyond a fair profit on their cost, including marketing expenses. A fine of $50,000 was assessed, but on rehearing was reduced to $25,000.[1]

That the state of Missouri has been one of the most active of the states in enforcing its antitrust law is attested by the large number of fines collected for violation. Among the more important cases in addition to those discussed were the following:

1. A suit against the packers,[2] in which it was held that a conspiracy existed to control prices of meat products, and each company participating was fined $5,000 with a suspended ouster.
2. A later case against the same group[3] in which $25,000 fines against each for restraint of trade, with suspended ouster, were imposed.
3. A decision against the Arkansas Lumber Company[4] held that certain members of the Yellow Pine Association had succeeded in restraining trade. Fines against twenty-five members of from $1,000 to $50,000 were imposed, with suspended ouster.

As is clearly demonstrated in the foregoing cases, the courts in Missouri have habitually used the suspended ouster rather than an absolute ouster (except where "dummy" companies which were mere agents to further unlawful plans existed) regardless of the size of the combination of capital, and however open, deliberate, avaricious, and flagrant the offense charged and proved, and however indubitable the proof. Bluntly stated, the power of absolute ouster has been used primarily as a club to facilitate the collection of fines.

New Jersey, unlike Missouri and Texas, has pursued a variable policy with regard to trusts. An amendment to her constitution in 1888, two years before the passage of the Sherman Act, gave corporations the right "to own and hold and dispose of shares [of stocks and bonds of other corporations]

[1] 141 S. W. 685 (1911).
[2] State *v.* Armour Packing Company *et al.*, 73 S. W. 645 (1903).
[3] State *v.* Armour, 176 S. W. 382 (1915).
[4] State *v.* Arkansas Lumber Company, 169 S. W. 145 (1913).

in the same manner and with the same privileges [as] individual owners," a provision made effective by legislation in 1889. From that time until 1913 New Jersey's lenient corporation laws facilitated the development of trusts.

In 1913, however, a radical change in her corporation law and her attitude toward trusts was made by the passage of the so-called Seven Sister Acts. The new laws were very rigid and took away the great advantages to trust incorporators that the state had previously afforded. The Seven Sister Acts were the direct outgrowth of the Presidential campaign of 1912. Mr. Wilson in that campaign emphasized the need of a more vigorous policy by the federal government against the trusts. Mr. Roosevelt retorted that it ill befitted the Governor of New Jersey to reproach the national authorities for their policy toward the trusts when it was notorious that New Jersey, through its wide-open corporation laws, was mainly responsible for the abuses from which the country suffered. The election which made Wilson President of the United States also returned a Democratic legislature in New Jersey. Wilson showed the sincerity of his desire to reform trust abuses by retaining the governorship of New Jersey until a special session of the legislature could be called in January and the antitrust laws drafted by his advisers could be adopted. These measures received little careful consideration and reflected not the wishes of the people of New Jersey, but the views of Governor Wilson.

The definition of a trust included in Chapter 13 of the laws may be summarized as follows: A trust is a combination or agreement between corporations, firms, or persons for the following purposes:

1. To create or carry out restrictions in trade or to acquire a monopoly in either interstate or intrastate commerce.

2. To limit or reduce the production or increase the price of merchandise or of any commodity.

3. To prevent competition in manufacturing, selling, transporting, etc., of merchandise, produce, or any commodity.

4. To fix the prices of goods to consumers.

5. To make pooling or other agreements restricting competition.

6. To make any secret oral agreements or arrive at any understanding without express agreement which shall preclude free competition.

Chapter 13 further declared trusts to be illegal and classed violations as misdemeanors. The directors of a corporation convicted of a violation were held individually liable. Upon proceedings by the Attorney General, the charter of an offending corporation could be revoked.

Chapter 14 made it unlawful for any person, firm, or corporation engaged in the production, manufacture, sale, or distribution of any commodity of general use to make discriminatory prices when the effect or intent of such discrimination was to secure or maintain a monopoly or to restrain trade.

Corporations were permitted by Chapter 15 to issue stock in payment for property, services, or other stock provided:

1. That when property was purchased, the purchasing corporation must receive in property or stock what the same was reasonably worth in money at a fair, *bona-fide* valuation.

2. That no fictitious stock should be issued.

3. That no stock should be issued for profits anticipated but not yet realized.

4. That when stock was issued by one corporation on the basis of the stock of any other corporation it might purchase, no stock should be issued thereon for an amount greater than the sum it actually paid for such stock in cash or its equivalent.

5. That the property purchased or the property owned by the corporation whose stock was purchased should be cognate in character and use to the property used or contemplated to be used by the purchasing corporation in the direct conduct of its own proper business, and that when stock was to be issued for property purchased or for other stock, a statement in writing should be filed by the directors of the purchasing corporation in the office of the Secretary of State setting forth the details of the transaction. Any corporation which should purchase the stock of any other corporation or any property

for the purpose of restraining trade, and the participating directors in such an action, were declared guilty of a misdemeanor.

Chapter 16 made it a misdemeanor to incorporate for fraudulent or unlawful purposes. Persons using their corporate powers unlawfully or for the promotion of a fraudulent object, or who had used the corporation in restraining trade or in acquiring a monopoly, were declared guilty of a misdemeanor.

Chapter 17 permitted consolidated corporations to mortgage property and to issue bonds, provided that such bonds should not bear a greater rate of interest than 6 per cent per annum.

Chapter 18 prohibited corporations from dealing in the securities of other corporations except that such securities might be received from non-competing corporations in the payment of a debt. Moreover, surpluses might be utilized for temporary investment purposes in non-competing corporations.

The final chapter of the Seven Sister Acts provided that no merger should impair the rights of creditors of either of the merged corporations, and that the approval of the Board of Public Utility Commissioners must be obtained for all mergers.

Because of a great falling off in revenues in the next few years [1] the legislature of New Jersey addressed itself to a repeal of the provisions of these Seven Sister Acts. In 1915 the prohibition on the purchase of the stocks of other corporations was substantially relaxed. In 1916 and 1917 other provisions were repealed or amended. Governor Edge in his message to the legislature in 1917 made a strong appeal for modification of the corporation laws. On the basis of his recommendations and those of a special commission appointed to investigate the matter, whatever was left of the Seven Sister Acts was repealed in 1920, since which time the

[1] During the five years 1911-15 the net annual revenue derived from franchise taxes on miscellaneous corporations never fell below $2,600,000. By 1918 it had fallen to $1,345,000, and in 1919 it was less than $1,153,000.

corporation law of New Jersey has been as sympathetic as that of any other state toward business combinations except that its fees and franchise tax are higher than those of Delaware and Nevada.

Under the present corporation law, three or more persons may organize a corporation, and no one of them need be a resident of New Jersey. Such organizers must hold at least one share of stock each. Although the minimum capital of a corporation is put at $2,000, a corporation may begin business after $1,000 has been subscribed and no part of this need be paid in cash. A convenient provision permits the amendment of the certificate of incorporation to an indefinite extent before the payment of any part of its capital. It is because of this provision that even such large organizations as the United States Steel Corporation may be incorporated by clerks of a New Jersey trust company with a very small initial capitalization and then enlarged in conformity with the developing plans of the promoters before any substantial payment is made to the state for the privilege of incorporation. Later changes in the provisions of the charter may be made to an indefinite extent by vote of a majority of the directors confirmed by a two-thirds vote of the stockholders at a meeting called together for the purpose.

A review of the records of the other states would add little to the above evidence of the inadequacy of state legislation as a remedy for trust abuses. The great majority did not take their laws seriously and made no particular effort to enforce them. Even in those states which were more active in prosecutions, the results achieved were more formal than real. The state of Texas collected one very large fine, but it did not by any means rid itself of the Oil Trust. Missouri was successful in collecting fines in cases of flagrant violations of her laws but in nearly every case her courts refused to oust the offending corporations from the state on the ground that their services or products were important to the public welfare. The following language used by Governor Edge in advocating the repeal of New Jersey's antitrust laws is particularly illuminating. He said: "These laws have been in force five years and that is sufficient time for a fair test. I am not in favor of letting down the bars, but I do want to get this revenue for New Jersey, if it can be gotten without fostering monopoly. . . . While my face is firmly set against the encouragement of unlawful combinations for the purposes of manipulation and extortion or undue restraint of trade, at the same time I am not committed to an idealist principle which costs the state a great deal in lost revenue and business prestige, if that principle is only idealist and not practical. I take the stand that while unlawful 'big business' is intolerable, all 'big business' is not unlawful and business is not unlawful because it is big."

The considerations that led Governor Edge to the conclusion that New Jersey was injuring herself, without benefiting the country, by her attempt, single-handed, to reform the corporation and trust situation in the United States, apply obviously with equal force to individual action by any other state. Although it has taken years to convince extreme advocates of state rights that the trust problem is national in its scope and can be dealt with effectively only through national action, Congress was not slow in placing a federal antitrust law on the statute books. The history and provisions of the Sherman law and the interpretation put upon it by the courts will now receive our attention.

CHAPTER XVIII

THE SHERMAN ANTITRUST ACT AND ITS INTERPRETATION: 1890-1903

As BROUGHT out in the preceding chapter, trusts and combinations had grown to such proportions by 1890 as to cause great concern to the people of the United States. Recognition of the fact that the problem was not limited by state boundary lines may be found as early as the 'eighties in the platforms of the political parties. In 1884, the minor party platforms contained denunciations of pools and monopolies in general and demands for legislation to correct the evil. The platform of the Democratic party for that year included a statement favoring the "prevention of monopoly," but in the same sentence declared that "the welfare of society depends upon a scrupulous regard for the rights of property as defined by law." By the next campaign popular apprehension of the dangers of monopoly had reached such a degree of intensity that both major party platforms were emphatic in their denunciation of it. The Democratic party stated that "Judged by Democratic principles, the interests of the people are betrayed when, by unnecessary taxation, trusts and combinations are permitted to exist, which, while unduly enriching the few that combine, rob the body of our citizens by depriving them of the benefits of natural competition." The Republican pledge read: "We declare our opposition to all combinations of capital, organized in trusts or otherwise, to control arbitrarily the condition of trade among our citizens; and we recommend to Congress and the state legislatures, in their respective jurisdictions, such legislation as will prevent the execution of all schemes to oppress the people by undue charges on their supplies, or by unjust rates for the transportation of their products to market. We approve the legislation by Congress to prevent alike unjust burdens and unfair discrimination between the states." [1]

As early as January 4, 1888, a resolution was introduced in the House by Mr. Mason of Illinois authorizing the Judiciary Committee to investigate charges that trusts and combinations were causing unreasonable increases in the prices of some necessaries of life and to recommend remedial measures if such charges were found to be warranted.[2]

Following this resolution there were innumerable others authorizing the investigation of specific trusts, and still others urging different committees to bring in bills upon the subject. Bills were introduced "to define trusts"; "to check and nullify the baleful operations of pernicious combinations commonly called trusts"; "for the punishment of persons connected with trusts"; "for the prevention of trusts"; [3] and other bills with various and sundry titles.

The Senate likewise had been considering legislation, offering resolutions, and authorizing investigations. The first general bill on the subject of trusts was introduced by Senator Reagan of Texas on August 14, 1888. The bill proposed to define trusts and to provide for the punishment of all persons connected with them.[4] On the same day Senator Sherman of Ohio introduced a bill even more drastic in its terms. Nothing tangible resulted in the Fiftieth Congress from either of these bills, but the discussions of them in committee and on the floor of the Senate were significant in forcing the attention of the legislators to the problems involved in drafting a measure which should be constitutionally sound but which should not hamper joint enterprises, such as the Farmers' Alliance, considered to be of a beneficial character.[5]

That the executive branch of the government also felt concern over the problem is demonstrated by the following extract from President Harrison's first annual message to Congress of December 3, 1889:

[1] McKee, Thomas H., *The National Conventions and Platforms of All Political Parties,* pp. 206, 235, 241.

[2] *Congressional Record,* vol. xix, p. 210.

[3] *Ibid.,* vol. xix, pp. 7740, 7998, 8228, 8459, 8460 *et al.*

[4] *Ibid.,* vol. xix, p. 7512.

[5] *Ibid.,* vol. xix, p. 7512; vol. xx, pp. 1167, 1457 *et seq.*

Earnest attention should be given by Congress to a consideration of the question how far the restraint of those combinations of capital commonly called "trusts" is matter of Federal jurisdiction. When organized, as they often are, to crush out all healthy competition and to monopolize the production or sale of an article of commerce and general necessity, they are dangerous conspiracies against the public good, and should be made the subject of prohibitory and even penal legislation.[1]

On the following day Senator Sherman introduced an antitrust measure which was referred to the Committee on Finance. In the debate on this bill, February 27, 1890, Senator George of Mississippi attacked it as "utterly unconstitutional, and even if constitutional, utterly worthless." In attacking its constitutionality he held that the bill attempted to regulate intrastate as well as interstate commerce; in criticizing its effectiveness he stated that, though the measure prohibited certain agreements and combinations, it was faulty in not extending the prohibition to acts done in pursuance of them and in failing to prohibit agreements made in foreign countries.[2] The convincing nature of George's presentation of his objections caused the Senate to recommit the bill to committee.

The substitute drafted by the committee was debated at length by the Senate between March 21 and March 27, 1890. The progress of the debates revealed a remarkable degree of agreement upon the necessity for some legislative action curbing trusts, the only opponent of such action being Stewart of Nevada, but upon the methods to be employed there was wide range of opinion. Hoar of Massachusetts criticized the proposals as not sufficiently comprehensive and as failing to provide proper remedies; Teller of Colorado feared that they would be used more to the detriment of farmers' and laborers' organizations than to that of the industrial combinations which Congress really intended to reach; and many Senators considered that in spite of the committee's efforts the substitute did not satisfactorily meet George's objections to the first bill that it was unconstitutional and ineffective.[3] During the course of the debates Reagan proposed a substitute for the

[1] Richardson, *Messages and Papers of the Presidents,* vol. xii, p. 5478.
[2] *Congressional Record,* vol. xxi, pp. 1765, 1766, 1768, 1769.
[3] *Ibid.,* vol. xxi, pp. 2567, 2561, *et al.*

substitute which was later adopted *in toto* as an addition to the committee's bill, and Sherman submitted a proviso to exempt labor, agricultural, and horticultural associations from the provisions of the act which was accepted without a record vote.[1] Numerous other changes of more or less importance were agreed upon, but on March 27 the bill with all amendments was referred to the judiciary committee.

Although the measure reported six days later became law in exactly the phraseology evolved in the committee as the "Sherman Antitrust Act," Senator Sherman had no part in the formulation of that phraseology. For years it was generally believed that Senator Hoar drafted the final form of the measure, but subsequently it was established that Senator Edmunds wrote Sections 1 (except seven words), 2, 3, 5, 6; Senator George, Section 4; Senator Hoar, Section 7; Senator Ingalls, Section 8; and Senator Evarts the seven words of Section 1 "in the form of trust or otherwise." [2] The importance of the precise terminology of the law warrants its reproduction in full at this point.

Section 1. Every contract, combination in the form of trust or otherwise, or conspiracy, in restraint of trade or commerce among the several States, or with foreign nations, is hereby declared to be illegal. Every person who shall make any such contract or engage in any such combination or conspiracy, shall be deemed guilty of a misdemeanor, and, on conviction thereof, shall be punished by fine not exceeding five thousand dollars, or by imprisonment not exceeding one year, or by both said punishments, in the discretion of the court.

Section 2. Every person who shall monopolize, or attempt to monopolize, or combine or conspire with any other person or persons, to monopolize any part of the trade or commerce among the several States, or with foreign nations, shall be deemed guilty of a misdemeanor, and, on conviction thereof, shall be punished by fine not exceeding five thousand dollars, or by imprisonment not exceeding one year, or by both said punishments, in the discretion of the court.

Section 3. Every contract, combination in the form of trust or otherwise, or conspiracy, in restraint of trade or commerce in any Territory of the United States or of the District of Columbia, or in restraint of trade or commerce between any such Territory and another, or between

[1] *Congressional Record,* vol. xxi, pp. 2456, 2611, 2612.

[2] Cf. Walker, A. H., *History of the Sherman Law,* p. 28, and *Congressional Record,* vol. xlvii, pp. 3485, 3486.

any such Territory or Territories and any State or States or the District of Columbia, or with foreign nations, or between the District of Columbia and any State or States or foreign nations, is hereby declared illegal. Every person who shall make any such contract or engage in any such combination or conspiracy, shall be deemed guilty of a misdemeanor, and, on conviction thereof, shall be punished by fine not exceeding five thousand dollars, or by imprisonment not exceeding one year, or by both said punishments, in the discretion of the court.

Section 4. The several circuit courts of the United States are hereby invested with jurisdiction to prevent and restrain violations of this act; and it shall be the duty of the several district attorneys of the United States, in their respective districts, under the direction of the Attorney-General, to institute proceedings in equity to prevent and restrain such violations. Such proceedings may be by way of petition setting forth the case and praying that such violation shall be enjoined or otherwise prohibited. When the parties complained of shall have been duly notified of such petition the court shall proceed, as soon as may be, to the hearing and determination of the case; and pending such petition and before final decree, the court may at any time make such temporary restraining order or prohibition as shall be deemed just in the premises.

Section 5. Whenever it shall appear to the court before which any proceeding under section four of this act may be pending, that the ends of justice require that other parties should be brought before the court, the court may cause them to be summoned, whether they reside in the district in which the court is held or not; and subpœnas to that end may be served in any district by the marshal thereof.

Section 6. Any property owned under any contract or by any combination, or pursuant to any conspiracy (and being the subject thereof) mentioned in section one of this act, and being in the course of transportation from one State to another, or to a foreign country, shall be forfeited to the United States, and may be seized and condemned by like proceedings as those provided by law for the forfeiture, seizure, and condemnation of property imported into the United States contrary to law.

Section 7. Any person who shall be injured in his business or property by any other person or corporation by reason of anything forbidden or declared to be unlawful by this act, may sue therefor in any circuit court of the United States in the district in which the defendant resides or is found, without respect to the amount in controversy, and shall recover three fold the damages by him sustained, and the costs of suit, including a reasonable attorney's fee.

Section 8. That the word "person," or "persons," wherever used in this act shall be deemed to include corporations and associations existing under or authorized by the laws of either the United States, the laws of any of the Territories, the laws of any State, or the laws of any foreign country.

The debates in the Senate on the final draft of the antitrust measure were unimportant except for two points. At one stage Senator Edmunds was asked by Senator Kenna the exact meaning of "monopolize" as used in Section 2 of the substitute, and, particularly, whether it covered the case of an individual who, because of his own superior energy and skill, received all the orders in his particular line of trade. Edmunds replied in the negative. Hoar came to his assistance by stating that after he had raised this identical question in the committee its members had convinced him that "monopoly" was a technical term known to the common law. He went on to define monopoly as "the sole engrossing to a man's self by means which prevent other men from engaging in fair competition with him." [1] This answer inevitably prompted the query from Kenna as to why, if monopoly were prohibited by common law, it was necessary to denounce it by statute. Hoar replied that, although the common law extended to subjects over which the individual states had jurisdiction, the United States as such had no common law, and that therefore the bill attempted to extend common-law principles to interstate and international commerce in this country.[2] In the opinion of many students the lack of what might be called "a common law of the United States" constitutes one of the most substantial justifications for the enactment of the Sherman law.

A number of amendments were proposed during the Senate debate, but, as previously indicated, they were all rejected, so that the bill passed as formulated by the committee. The vote was 52 to 1. The dissenting ballot was cast by Senator Blodgett of New Jersey, who had taken no part in the debates and who offered no explanation of his action.[3]

The debate in the House of Representatives on the bill was concentrated into one day, May 1, 1890. It revealed the fact that the members of that body were as thoroughly convinced

[1] *Congressional Record,* vol. xxi, pp. 3151, 3152.

[2] *Ibid.*

[3] *Ibid.,* p. 3153.

as the Senators of the necessity for some legislative action to curb trusts, although there was again evidence of a disagreement upon the most efficacious methods to be utilized. Wilson of West Virginia, for example, favored striking at the combinations through more stringent regulation by the states of the corporation charters. He also reiterated the view expressed many times in the Senate that the protective tariff was in large measure responsible for the organization and continuance of trusts. One amendment was adopted in the House, but after a series of conferences between the upper and lower branches of Congress it was eliminated, so that the bill became law on July 2, 1890, without the alteration of a word in it and with only one vote cast against it in both houses combined.

The explanation of this remarkable unanimity doubtless lay in the very general conviction that a measure of some sort must be passed. To say this is not to explain the conviction, however, for it may have represented a fear of constituents rather than a fear of trusts. In fact, the opinion is not rare that Congress was to a considerable extent intimidated by what amounted to a popular panic and some students go so far as to say that the statute was ambiguously drawn with the intent of pacifying the general disquietude without doing any serious damage to business interests. With these views we cannot agree. Universal perturbation there unquestionably was, and Congressmen doubtless shared it. The economic ideas of the day were in the best *laissez-faire* tradition except for those held by a few business men who had become convinced that it was entirely possible in certain lines or under certain circumstances for competition to be the "death of trade." Although Congress had been brought to a realization of the meaning of "cutthroat" competition in the railroad business, an overwhelming majority of both Senators and Representatives seemed unable or unwilling to recognize a similar possibility in industrial organizations. The speech of Senator Platt of Connecticut was an outstanding exception, but as indicated, he received no substantial support.[1] Trade

[1] *Congressional Record,* vol. xxi, pp. 2729-2731.

unions and farmers' alliances found their defenders in Congress; other combinations were practically without a spokesman. Since competition was conceived as the régime which should govern all industry, monopoly was considered to be necessarily an evil and all combinations were adjudged antisocial in character. With this prevalent economic doctrine in mind and the debates before us we see no reason to question the sincerity of the national legislators. They believed the country to be faced by a most serious problem. Although the action taken to meet it would have been characterized as perfect by few, an overwhelming majority was convinced that the job had been done in a thoroughgoing and, on the whole, satisfactory fashion.

However clear the intention of the legislature, the final determination of the meaning of a statute rests under our system with the courts. This makes necessary the detailed study of the judicial interpretation of the Sherman Act which follows. In the discussion of particular trusts we have already considered some aspects of important decisions applying the antitrust acts, therefore our survey in this and the immediately succeeding chapters is condensed. For the period prior to 1914 we shall consider the decisions in chronological order; for the period since 1914 we have adopted the topical method of presentation.

The first bill brought by the government under the new law was directed against a combination of coal-mining companies in Kentucky and Tennessee with a group of coal dealers in Nashville for the purpose of fixing prices and regulating output. In the opinion of the court "the purposes and intentions of the association could hardly have been more successfully framed to fall within the provisions of the act of July 2, 1890," and consequently it enjoined the further violation of the law.[1] The case was not appealed.

Other relatively minor cases which were decided by various federal courts during the next few years need not be considered here, but in 1894 the Circuit Court for the Northern District of Illinois announced a decision in a case destined to

[1] 46 Fed. 436, 437 (1891).

become famous—*viz.,* that of Eugene V. Debs. At the time Debs was president of the American Railway Union, an organization which attempted to win a strike of the employees of the Pullman Palace Car Company by declaring a boycott effective on June 26, 1894, against Pullman cars. The federal government subsequently charged that Debs and other officers of the union "had directed and ordered" all the members of the union employed on the railroads which were hauling Pullman cars to strike. The union officials contended that the strikes followed a vote taken by the men and the evidence seems to substantiate this claim, but whether the strikes were "ordered" from above or "voted" from below there is no doubt that every possible encouragement was given to the strikers by Debs and the other officers of the union. Since practically all the railroad companies were obligated by contract to haul Pullman cars, and since the American Railway Union was particularly strong in and west of Chicago, the refusal of its members to operate trains including Pullmans promptly resulted in a thoroughgoing demoralization of transportation, with attendant interference with the mails and interstate commerce. The federal government on July 2, 1894, sought and secured a preliminary restraining order from the Circuit Court in Chicago to prevent further interference. In bringing its petition the government alleged a "conspiracy in restraint of trade."

After the restraining order was issued the officers and members of the union continued to act about as they had before, insisting that they were doing nothing illegal. As a result of this attitude Debs and others were arrested on July 7 and held in $10,000 joint bail on a charge of contempt of court for violating the restraining order. The strike very shortly thereafter collapsed.

In its decision the District Court specifically held the Sherman Act applicable to the case and not restricted to combinations of capital. "Combinations are condemned, not only when they take the form of trusts, but in whatever form found, if they be in restraint of trade. That is the effect of the words 'or otherwise.'"[1] Furthermore, it refused to countenance the argument of the defendants that Section 4 of the law conferring on federal courts the power to prevent and restrain violations of the act was an unwarranted invasion of the right of trial by jury, and held that "it was competent for Congress to vest the courts with the jurisdiction granted by this section."[2] Finally, the court disposed of a relatively minor contention of the defendants by stating that the language of Section 6 of the law, providing for the forfeiture of any property owned under any combination, contract, or conspiracy and in the course of transportation at the time of the action, did not say or imply that only cases in which such property should be found subject to forfeiture should be deemed to be within the scope of the act.[3]

On the basis of the foregoing interpretation of the Sherman law and of the evidence, the court held the defendants guilty of contempt and sentenced them to six months in jail. When the case came before it on appeal the Supreme Court of the United States, on May 27, 1895, upheld the sentence on the ground that the acts enjoined interfered with interstate commerce and the carrying of the mails. It specifically added that "We enter into no examination of the act of July 2, 1890, . . . upon which the Circuit Court relied mainly to sustain its jurisdiction. It must not be understood from this that we dissent from the conclusions of that court . . . but simply that we prefer to rest our judgment on . . . broader ground."[4]

[1] 64 Fed. 747 (1894).

[2] *Ibid.*, p. 753.

[3] *Ibid.*, p. 752.

[4] 158 U. S. 600 (1895). We have included this discussion of the Debs case because of its priority, but we shall not consider the later labor cases, since this volume deals only with monopolistic industrial combinations. Combinations of labor are to our minds so essentially different from their industrial counterparts that they have no place in a discussion of "trusts" as we have defined that term. Also we wish, in passing, to record our conviction that our legislative attempts to deal with both sorts of combinations in one general statute have had only unfortunate results. The most important cases applying the antitrust acts to organized labor are:

1. Loewe *v.* Lawlor, 208 U. S. 274 (1908); 235 U. S. 522 (1915).
2. Duplex Printing Press Co. *v.* Deering *et al.*, 254 U. S. 443 (1921).
3. American Steel Foundries *v.* Tri-City Central Trades Council *et al.*, 257 U. S. 184 (1921).
4. United Mine Workers *v.* Coronado Coal Co., 259 U. S. 344 (1922).

Just five months previously, however, January 21, 1895, the first decision of the Supreme Court construing the act had been handed down in the E. C. Knight case.[1] The facts placed before the court demonstrated that by the acquisition of the Knight concern and three other competing Pennsylvania refineries in 1892 the Sugar Trust had secured for all practical purposes an absolute monopoly of the refining business. The point on which the case turned was whether or not a combination of *manufacturers* constituted an illegal restraint on *interstate commerce.* Without repeating the extracts from the majority opinion previously quoted [2] we restate our conclusion that the chief practical effect of the decision was to convince lawyers and business men that the Sherman Act had no "teeth" and that combinations in manufacturing and mining would be allowed to proceed unmolested.

From a strictly legal point of view the opinion may be criticized as embodying an unwarrantably narrow conception of "interstate commerce," and, in fact, was so criticized in the dissent of Justice Harlan. Though the decisions cited by the dissenter undoubtedly lend substantial support to his position, it seems that on the facts as presented in the government's brief the court took the only course open to it. The main question raised by the government was whether a New Jersey corporation, acting within the powers conferred by its charter, could acquire by purchase four sugar refineries located in Philadelphia, and the main relief asked for was a cancellation of this purchase, a return of the properties to their former owners, and an injunction preventing any similar purchases in the future. Since the prosecution failed to attack the trust because of its collective acts or because of its essential character as a monopolistic combination in restraint of commerce

5. Michaelson *v.* U. S. ex rel. C. St. P. M. and O. Ry. Co., 291 Fed. 940 (1924); 266 U. S. 42 (1924).

6. Bedford Cut Stone Co. *et al. v.* Journeyman Stone Cutters' Association of North America *et al.,* 274 U. S. 37 (1927).

A discussion of all but the last of these will be found in any standard treatise on the labor problem, among which may be mentioned W. B. Catlin, *The Labor Problem in the United States and Great Britain;* S. Blum, *Labor Economics;* and Commons and Andrews, *Principles of Labor Legislation.*

[1] 156 U. S. 1 (1895).

[2] Cf. pp. 58, 59, *supra.*

among the states, the disappointing outcome of the suit may more properly be blamed upon the Department of Justice than upon the courts. Had the same vigor and intelligence been shown in this prosecution as in the later oil and tobacco cases, there is reason for believing that the decision would have been different.

But if in its immediate and practical effects the result of the Knight decision was to narrow the meaning of the anti-trust act, the majority opinion in the next important case settled by the Supreme Court, on March 22, 1897, had the opposite effect, though in another aspect of interpretation. According to the evidence presented in this case, involving the Trans-Missouri Freight Association, a group of railroads operating in the territory south and west of the Missouri River had entered into an agreement effective April 1, 1889, "for the purpose of mutual protection by establishing and maintaining reasonable rates, rules and regulations on all freight traffic, both through and local," handled by these companies in the designated territory. As means to this end a committee was appointed to determine rates and rules, monthly meetings of the association were held to consider all matters of interest, and a system of fines was established for failure to attend meetings or for any violation of the agreement except one made in good faith to meet competition from some line not included in the association. The railroads contended that such an arrangement was necessary to prevent ruinous competition, and pointed out that a member might deviate from the rates or rules agreed upon over the objections of other members, provided that the member wishing to make the change brought the proposal before a meeting of the association for discussion prior to making the change, and in case of an adverse vote gave written notice immediately after the vote that it intended to disregard said vote.

The federal government filed suit January 6, 1892, alleging the plan to be in violation of the Sherman law. Before the case reached the Supreme Court, on November 19, 1892, to be precise, the association was dissolved; but in the next month a temporary agreement was reached by most of the members of the former association which effectively continued the same arrangement for some time. Partly for the reason that the "dissolution" seemed largely illusory the court refused to accede to the request of counsel for the association that the suit be dismissed. A more important reason was that such a device provided too easy a means of evading a final judgment upon the questions involved in the suit.

As a matter of fact, the court considered that there were two important questions: did the Sherman Act apply to railroads, and if so, did this agreement violate any section of that law? By that 5 to 4 vote which has become almost notorious in antitrust decisions, both these questions were answered affirmatively. In answering the first question the court laid down the proposition from which the case derives its chief significance—*viz.,* that "The language of the act includes *every* contract, combination in the form of trust or otherwise, or conspiracy, in restraint of trade or commerce. . . ."[1] In amplifying this deduction the court not only stated that "railroad companies are instruments of commerce, and their business is commerce itself," and, consequently, that they are included in the scope of the act; but went on to hold that both reasonable and unreasonable contracts in restraint of trade were condemned. The defendants had urged that Congress had intended to legislate against unreasonable contracts only. The court replied that this was contrary to what the language of the act "plainly imports," and that to accept the interpretation suggested by the railroads would be "to read into the act by way of judicial legislation an exception that is not placed there by the lawmaking branch of the government. . . ." From this view the minority dissented vigorously. Briefly stated, its argument was that the words "restraint of trade" had acquired by centuries of judicial interpretation a restricted meaning under which they embraced when applied to contracts "only contracts which unreasonably restrain trade." Therefore, when Congress embodied them in the Sherman Act they should be given the interpretation developed at common law, since any other interpretation would

[1] 166 U. S. 312 (1897). Italics in original.

frustrate the purpose of Congress. Attention was also called to the title of the law: "An act to protect trade and commerce against unlawful restraints and monopolies." In the opinion of the minority, "The word 'unlawful' clearly distinguishes between contracts in restraint of trade which are lawful and those which are not. In other words, between those which are unreasonably in restraint of trade, and consequently invalid, and those which are reasonable and hence lawful."[1] Finally, the minority characterized the majority opinion as "either arbitrary or unreasonable" for "insisting that the word 'every' is all-embracing," and immediately proceeding to make an exception of "covenants in restraint of trade which are collateral to a sale of property."[2]

Since this point of interpretation came up in a number of subsequent cases and since the minority opinion here finally secured the adherence of a majority of the court, it has been stressed at some length.

In considering the second question posed by itself, did the Trans-Missouri Freight Association agreement violate any section of the antitrust act, the court reviewed the purpose of the association as stated above, the nature of the agreement, the penalties provided against violations, and other pertinent facts. From these it concluded that the agreement's "direct, immediate and necessary effect is to put a restraint upon trade or commerce as described in the act." Moreover, it pointed out that since the "necessary effect" of the agreement was restraint, the government was not compelled to establish any intent on the part of the members to the agreement to restrain trade.[3]

The dissenting minority held it as an "elementary" principle that a general statute, such as the Sherman Act, will not be held to repeal a special statute, such as the Interstate Commerce Act, "unless there be a clear implication unavoidably resulting from the general law" that such was the intention. The dissenting judges considered that the nature of the

[1] 166 U. S. 352 (1897).
[2] *Ibid.*
[3] 166 U. S. 342 (1897).

two laws "clearly demonstrates that there was no such intention." Consequently, the first question for consideration in their view was whether or not such an agreement as that here presented was sanctioned by the Interstate Commerce Act. After reviewing the language of that law and the policy of the Interstate Commerce Commission, they concluded that the agreement was "covered by the law and embodied in its policy." [1]

In the following year, 1898, the Supreme Court was called upon to decide another railroad case, that of the so-called Joint Traffic Association, in which the facts were quite similar to those in the Trans-Missouri case. (At least the court held that there were no material differences sufficient to warrant a different decision in spite of strenuous efforts on the part of counsel for the association to demonstrate differences.) The court held that the agreement prevented, and was intended to prevent, not only secret competition, but any competition, and that it maintained rates above those which competition might have produced.[2]

But the major portion of the decision was devoted to a justification of the construction of the Sherman Act in the preceding railroad case, since it had been so vigorously attacked in the dissenting opinion there and in the arguments of counsel in the case at bar. The latter in particular insisted that if Congress had really intended to prohibit all contracts which in any degree restrained trade, it had exceeded its powers, and that the act so construed was unconstitutional in light of the guaranties of the Fifth Amendment. It was urged upon the court that its previous construction limited the freedom and destroyed the property of individuals to an extent which could scarcely be exaggerated, since the most ordinary sort of contracts, indispensable to the carrying on of business under modern conditions, frequently have the effect of somewhat restraining trade and commerce. In support of this contention a long list of contracts conceived to be illegal under the Trans-Missouri interpretation of the act were cited, all

[1] 166 U. S. 357, 361, 363, 370, 371 (1897).
[2] 171 U. S. 564, 567, 569 (1898).

of them obviously reasonable and more or less essential to the continuance of trade and commerce.

In replying to these contentions Justice Peckham, who wrote the majority opinion in both cases, repeated his exception of the sale of the good will of a business with an accompanying agreement not to enter into similar business as a contract not within the meaning of the act because it was collateral to the main contract of sale. In addition he quoted some five other types of contracts from the list of counsel for defendants with the comment that he was not aware it had ever been claimed that they restrained trade or commerce within any legal definition of that term. As a matter of fact, he considered most of the instances cited by counsel to be irrelevant, and quoted the statement in Hopkins *v.* United States, decided the same day, that the antitrust act "applies only to those contracts whose direct and immediate effect is a restraint upon interstate commerce." Furthermore, the Justice continued, the act must have a "reasonable" interpretation, and "To suppose, as is assumed by counsel, that the effect of the decision in the *Trans-Missouri case* is to render illegal most business contracts or combinations, however indispensable and necessary they may be, because, as they assert, they all restrain trade in some remote and indirect degree, is to make a most violent assumption and one not called for or justified by the decision mentioned, or by any other decision of this court."[1]

Three of the four justices who had dissented in the Trans-Missouri case again did so here but without filing an opinion. From the two cases one step in interpretation stands clearly revealed: the Sherman Act applied to railroads. The other step frequently stated as unqualifiedly true—*viz.,* that *every* contract in restraint of trade, whether reasonable or unreasonable, was illegal, seems to us definitely qualified by Justice Peckham's exceptions and by his reproof of counsel in the second case. To state the matter bluntly, it seems to us that he took away with one hand what he had given with the other. But from the point of view of most lawyers and busi-

[1] 171 U. S. 568 (1898).

ness men at the time the outstanding fact was the sweeping condemnation of *every* restraint; they discounted the exceptions for the fairly obvious reason that "every" seems all inclusive to most people.

The next important case, that of the Addyston Pipe Company, decided on December 4, 1899, has been fully discussed and its legal importance briefly stated in a previous chapter.[1] Our only task here is to amplify somewhat our statement of the court's reasoning and restate our conclusions. At the outset the court clearly and convincingly upheld the power of Congress to "enact such legislation as shall declare void and prohibit the performance of any contract between individuals or corporations where the natural and direct effect of such a contract will be, when carried out, to directly, and not as a mere incident to other and innocent purposes, regulate to any substantial extent interstate commerce."[2] In restating this principle the court considered at length the contentions of counsel for the pool that the power of Congress to regulate interstate commerce is limited to its protection from acts of interference by state legislation or by some political subdivision of a state, and that this power of Congress did not include the general power to interfere with or prohibit private contracts between citizens, even though such contracts have interstate commerce for their object and result in a direct and substantial obstruction to or regulation of that commerce. These contentions rested upon the claims that the purpose of giving Congress power to regulate interstate commerce was to secure uniformity and prevent conflicting and discriminatory state regulation, and that the constitutional guaranty of liberty of private contract operated as a limit upon Congress.

The court admitted that the prevention of conflicting state regulation was a primary reason for granting to Congress the power to control interstate commerce, but denied that this reason affected or limited the extent of the power itself. It disposed of the argument based on liberty of private contract by pointing out that, though the word "liberty" had been con-

[1] Cf. *supra*, pp. 94, 95.

[2] 175 U. S. 228 (1899).

strued to include not only liberty of person, but also a right to enter into certain types of contracts, it had not and should not be extended to cover a right of individuals to enter into any and all sorts of contracts wholly irrespective of the fact that they would, if performed, result in the regulation of interstate commerce and the violation of an act of Congress. Moreover, the position taken by counsel for the pool was illogical in the opinion of the court, for if Congress had the power to reach contracts in restraint of interstate commerce embodied in state legislation, why, asked the court, should this same power not apply to private contracts?

From these jurisdictional issues the opinion passed on to a review of the essential facts in the case to determine whether the "natural and direct effect" of the pipe pool was to restrain commerce among the states. On this point the members of the pool asserted that even if the agreement did affect interstate commerce it was only a reasonable restraint to prevent ruinous competition among themselves, but that as a matter of fact the agreement did not come within the meaning of the statute as interpreted in the Knight case. Consequently, they urged, on the authority of that decision, that the bill be dismissed.

The court replied that the facts "show conclusively that the effect of the combination was to enhance prices beyond a sum which was reasonable, and therefore the first objection above set forth need not be further noticed." It held further that "It is the sale and delivery of a certain kind and quality of pipe, and not the manufacture, which is the material portion of the contract, and a sale for delivery beyond the State makes the transaction a part of interstate commerce," and that, "the case is therefore not covered by that of *United States v. E. C. Knight Company*." [1]

From the facts presented here and in our survey of the trust movement in Chapter V the conclusion seems warranted that in its first decade the antitrust measure remained uncertain in meaning and largely ineffective in operation. The Knight decision was generally construed as negativing even

[1] 175 U. S. 227, 228, 229, 235, 238, 242 (1899).

the half-hearted attempts which the Department of Justice was making to enforce the act; the Addyston case, without overruling Knight expressly, seemed to do so practically. But between the dates of these two cases the most intensive period of combinations and mergers in the history of the country got under way. The railroad cases determined that the railroad business came within the scope of the law, but they raised more questions than they settled as to precisely what contracts "in restraint of trade" Congress had intended to legislate against. Business men and lawyers who held the statute to be of no consequence were confirmed in their opinion by the failure of the Attorney General, following the Knight decision, to initiate new prosecutions against notorious trusts, and by President Cleveland's statement that that decision made the trusts a state rather than a federal problem. In view of the general situation and of President McKinley's favorable attitude toward "big business," it was almost certain that his administration would not witness any extensive prosecution of trusts. And so it proved. With the accession of Roosevelt, however, and the creation on his recommendation of the Bureau of Corporations, whose chief function was to investigate large business organizations, governmental activity against the trusts was vigorously revived. To these events we turn in the next chapter.

CHAPTER XIX

DECISIONS APPLYING THE SHERMAN LAW, 1904-1914

CHRONOLOGICAL limits for the demarcation of periods in the history of the judicial interpretation of the Sherman Act are of necessity somewhat arbitrary, but for both 1904 and 1914 there seems a logical basis. 1903 marked the close of the second period of trust formation and was also the date of the organization of the Bureau of Corporations; 1904 witnessed the decision of the Supreme Court in the Northern Securities case, the most important in this field yet rendered by that body; 1914 was the date of the enactment of the Federal Trade Commission and Clayton Acts. Within these ten years investigating and prosecuting activities by Congressional committees, the Bureau of Corporations, and the Department of Justice assumed a prominence in national affairs never equaled before or since. Final decisions on many of the cases instituted during this period were not reached until subsequent to 1914, but the facts developed in reports or before courts were largely instrumental in creating the demand for the 1914 legislation. Moreover, among the cases which were finally determined there stand out a few which rank as the most important in the history of the Sherman Act.

The first important case in this period was Northern Securities Company *v.* U. S., decided March 14, 1904. Its significance to the minds of the Supreme Court justices is indicated by the facts that Justice Harlan wrote an opinion affirming the decree of the lower court, in which Justices Brown, McKenna, and Day concurred; that Justice Brewer wrote a separate opinion concurring in the result but raising some questions which will be discussed later; and that Justices White and Holmes both delivered dissenting opinions which secured the approval of each other, of the Chief Justice and of Justice Peckham. The significance of the case to the deve opment of the interpretation of the statute and to the trust movement lay in the fact that it was the first occasion on which the highest court had before it the question of the legality of the holding-company form of combination. As will be recalled, many concerns had adopted this type of organization after the trustee form had been declared illegal [1] and were operating under the impression that the holding-company charter guaranteed them immunity from prosecution under the Sherman Act. Since the outcome of the Northern Securities case demonstrated this guarantee to be entirely illusory, both the facts and the law in the case warrant fairly detailed treatment.

The Great Northern Railway Company, dominated by James J. Hill, and the Northern Pacific Railway Company, dominated by J. P. Morgan, owned and operated parallel lines of railroad connecting Duluth and St. Paul with Seattle and Portland. Prior to 1893 the Northern Pacific system had been operated by the Northern Pacific Railroad Company. When the latter concern became insolvent a majority of its bondholders effected an arrangement which provided for its virtual consolidation with the Great Northern, control resting with the latter company. In the case of Pearsall *v.* Great Northern Railway Company [2] this plan was held by the Supreme Court of the United States to violate the statutes of Minnesota forbidding just such an attempt at control by one railroad of a parallel or competing line.

Early in 1901 a new move was made toward placing the two roads under common control when they jointly acquired practically all the common stock of the Chicago, Burlington, and Quincy. This move brought forth strenuous opposition from the Harriman interests controlling the Union Pacific, since they too looked upon the Burlington as a feeder and feared a loss of traffic to them would result from its transfer to the joint control of the Northern Pacific and Great Northern. Consequently, Harriman proceeded to buy up a majority of the stock of the Northern Pacific. When the Hill-

[1] Cf. pp. 51-55, *supra*.
[2] 161 U. S. 646 (1896).

Morgan group realized what was happening they too began bidding for the stock and thus precipitated the famous Northern Pacific corner of May 7, 1901. The stock which Harriman had been able to acquire was largely preferred, and since it had been issued subject to a provision permitting its retirement prior to the time the Harriman group could vote it and both sides wished to avoid a contest, a compromise agreement was reached. Partly to prevent such a situation from again arising but primarily for other reasons, on November 13, 1901, a holding-corporation charter from New Jersey was secured for the Northern Securities Company. The new corporation proceeded to exchange its common stock for the stocks of the Great Northern and Northern Pacific, until at the time of the suit it held a controlling interest in the former and practically all of the latter. Since the total subscribed capital of the holding company was only $30,000, and since its authorized capital stock of $400,000,000 was just sufficient at the previously agreed upon exchange ratios to acquire all the stock of the two lines, there can be no doubt that the purpose of the holding company was to secure that unity of control over the two lines, inevitably resulting in the disappearance of competition, which had been prohibited by the decision in Pearsall *v.* Great Northern Railway Company.

But the new arrangement was at least in form quite different, and it had the sanction of the state of New Jersey. The reliance of counsel for the Northern Securities Company upon that sanction is brought out in Justice Harlan's statement that "Underlying the argument in behalf of the defendants is the idea that as the Northern Securities Company is a state corporation, and as its acquisition of the stock of the Great Northern and Northern Pacific Railway companies is not inconsistent with the powers conferred by its charter, the enforcement of the Act of Congress, as against those corporations, will be an unauthorized interference by the national government with the internal commerce of the States creating those corporations."[1] But this reasoning did not impress the majority of the Supreme Court as valid. It held that

[1] 193 U. S. 332 (1904).

the Sherman Act was a constitutional enactment, that the intent and result of the formation of the holding company was an illegal combination in restraint of interstate commerce, and that no state, merely by creating a corporation, could project its authority into other states in such a way as to prevent Congress from exerting its power of regulating interstate commerce or to exempt a corporation engaged in interstate commerce from obedience to a rule legally established by Congress for such commerce. Any other conclusion the majority considered would prostrate the federal government and its laws at the feet of local authorities.

Other contentions of counsel for the Securities Company were answered by showing that they had been previously decided by the court and that it saw no reason for reversing itself, and still others by holding them immaterial to the instant case. One point, however, deserves more than cursory attention since it received the support of Justice Holmes in his dissenting opinion. In his own words, "The question to be decided is whether, under the act of July 2, 1890 . . . it is unlawful at any stage of the process, if several men unite to form a corporation for the purpose of buying more than half the stock of each of two competing interstate railroad companies, if they form the corporation, and the corporation buys the stock."[1] Even under the assumption that every step in such a process was taken with the intent of ending competition, he still considered that the arrangement did not fall within the prohibitions of the statute. His reason was clear and simple: "there is no combination in restraint of trade until something is done with the intent to exclude strangers to the combination from competing with it. . . ." Since in this case the suppression of competition which he assumed was secured by a community of interest—a fusion rather than by an external restraint—it was not prohibited. Consequently, the defendants were within their rights in acquiring the stock of the two railways. Justice Holmes considered that the application of the majority opinion would "make eternal

[1] 193 U. S. 401 (1904).

the *bellum omnium contra omnes* and disintegrate society so far as it could into individual atoms." This he viewed as an effort to reconstruct society which was outside the constitutional powers of Congress and, in fact, beyond its intent in passing the statute.

With all due respect to one of the ablest intellects on the Supreme bench we must register our disagreement on this issue. As we understand the case the government did not deny or question the right of individuals or the Securities Company to acquire the stock of the competing railroads as a right; it did not contend that the acquisition or ownership of stock in a state railroad corporation was itself interstate commerce when that railroad did an interstate business. It did contend, however, that Congress had the power to protect the freedom of interstate commerce in any way that was appropriate and that the necessary result of the organization of the Securities Company was a combination which was illegal within the meaning of the statute. The validity of these contentions appears to us inescapable. Any other conclusion would have failed to distinguish substance from form and would have gone far toward vitiating the act.

The opinion of Justice Brewer, concurring in the affirmation of the lower court's order against the Securities Company, is noteworthy in that it marks his conversion to the point of view that only unreasonable contracts in restraint of interstate commerce were prohibited by the Sherman Act. He had been with the majority on the Trans-Missouri and Joint Traffic cases, which held that both reasonable and unreasonable restraints were included, but submitted his individual opinion in this case to declare that he was now convinced of the court's error in so ruling. However, it must not be understood that Brewer in 1904 believed the railroad combinations were legal, for he pointed out that in his opinion both of them effected unreasonable restraints and could have been dissolved without resorting to the more sweeping condemnation of all restraints to which he had agreed in 1897 and 1898.

But even though the decision in the Northern Securities case was a complete victory for the government in its legal aspects the practical consequences of the litigation were almost negligible. The decree enjoined the holding company from exercising further control over the two roads, but permitted it to restore the stocks of those companies to their former holders or to distribute them to its own stockholders. The former plan would have given control of the Northern Pacific to the Harriman interests. Since the latter was adopted, these interests instituted further litigation, which finally resulted in leaving the majority of the stocks of both the Great Northern and the Northern Pacific in the hands of the Hill-Morgan group.[1] In other words, the old community of interests was reëstablished and the restoration of competition, which was the avowed purpose of the decision, made more remote than it was before the Northern Securities Company was organized.

This community of interest among the Great Northern, the Northern Pacific, and the Burlington continued without material disturbance until the announcement by the Interstate Commerce Commission of its tentative proposals for the consolidation of the railroads of the country into nineteen systems under the provisions of the Transportation Act of 1920. These proposals called for the grouping of the Northern Pacific and the Burlington with some others in one system and the Great Northern, the St. Paul, and others in another system. The Northern roads objected and suggested that they, the Burlington, and the Colorado and Southern be placed in one system. Subsequently, on July 8, 1927, the Great Northern and the Northern Pacific made formal application for authority to unify the control of the two roads by exchanging their stock share for share with a new Great Northern Pacific Company. This last concern was also to take over the Spokane, Portland, and Seattle Railway, which had been jointly constructed in 1909 by the Great Northern and the Northern Pacific. Final testimony on this application was taken by the Interstate Commerce Commission on March 19,

[1] 197 U. S. 244 (1905).

20 and 21, 1928, but at the time of writing it had made no final disposition of the matter.[1]

On January 30, 1905, a unanimous Supreme Court affirmed, with some modifications, a decree of the Circuit Court for the Northern District of Illinois perpetually enjoining the members of the so-called Beef Trust from continuing certain practices which had resulted in the virtual disappearance of competition in the slaughtering and packing of fresh meat products in the Middle West and a great diminution of competition in the rest of the United States. The most important members of the trust were Swift & Company and Armour & Company. They with Nelson Morris & Company had organized in 1902 the National Packing Company for the purpose of acquiring control of the then independent packing houses in St. Louis, Omaha, Kansas City, and some other places. These concerns were frequently designated as the "Big Four." The joint ownership of the National by the other three indicates the lack of any real competition among them.

More definite indications of a purpose to escape the restraints and avoid the wastes of competition were cited by the government in 1902 in its request for an injunction against seven corporations, including the Big Four, a copartnership, and twenty-three individuals. Briefly stated, the bill charged a conspiracy among the packers not to bid against one another in the live-stock markets of the different states, to bid up prices for a few days in order to induce cattle men to ship their stock to the yards, to fix prices at which members of the combine would sell, and for that purpose to restrict shipments of meat when necessary, to establish a uniform rule of credit to dealers, to maintain a blacklist, to make uniform and improper charges for cartage, and to secure less than lawful rates from the railroads to the exclusion of competitors.

The opinion of Justice Holmes, after summarizing the facts alleged by the government, took up the objection of the defendants that the bill did not set forth sufficiently definite or

[1] Cf. *Railway Age,* vol. lxxiii, p. 1007; vol. lxxvi, p. 243; vol. lxxxiii, p. 105; and vol. lxxxiv, p. 683.

specific facts. He pointed out that this difficulty was inherent in the nature of the case, "The scheme alleged is so vast that it presents a new problem in pleading," but later in the opinion he demonstrated that the bill was adequately specific. He also showed that, even though the constituent elements of the scheme might be legal considered separately, they were, as a matter of fact, "bound together as the parts of a single plan," and that that plan was within the reach of the law. In the first place, the business carried on was distinctly interstate commerce. It was not analogous to that carried on by the defendants in the Hopkins case, for there the defendants were only commission merchants carrying on a local business of providing certain facilities for expediting actual sales. In this case the packers were buyers and sellers. Secondly, the packers' case was distinguished from that of E. C. Knight because in the latter the subject matter of the combination was manufacture, not commerce, whereas in the former the subject matter was sales "and the very point of the combination is to restrain and monopolize commerce among the States in respect of such sales."

In view of later decisions, particularly that in the Steel Corporation case, it is interesting to observe that the court in discussing the importance of the intent of the parties to such agreements as those alleged in the bill stated that "Where acts are not sufficient in themselves to produce a result which the law seeks to prevent—for instance, the monopoly—but require further acts in addition to the mere forces of nature to bring that result to pass, an intent to bring it to pass is necessary in order to produce a dangerous probability that it will happen. . . . But when that intent and the consequent dangerous probability exist, this statute, like many others and like the common law in some cases, directs itself against that dangerous probability as well as against the completed result." On the basis of the record the court had no difficulty in convincing itself that an intent to restrict competition motivated the packers. It did, however, agree with their contentions to the extent of ordering certain words and phrases stricken from the injunction on the ground that they were so general and vague as to put the whole conduct of the business at the peril of a summons for contempt.[1]

On the face of it the government had again won a sweeping victory. The muckrakers gloated over the restraints laid upon the "nefarious" combination which had been extending its "tentacles" over one of the necessities of life; the housewife who read the papers heaved a sigh of relief and expected a prompt decline in the price of steaks. But nothing happened. The decree had failed to order the dissolution of the National Packing Company, jointly owned by Swift, Armour, and Morris. The restoration of competitive conditions, without such action, was scarcely to be anticipated. That the packers completely disregarded the decree is evidenced by the fact that within less than sixty days of the date of the Supreme Court decision the government secured an indictment against the chief corporations and individuals in the packers' combination, charging that they were continuing to use methods prohibited in the decree. Their defense was that since they had been compelled to incriminate themselves in furnishing information to the Bureau of Corporations, they were immune from criminal prosecution. The district judge who presided at the trial directed the jury to bring in a verdict upholding the claim of immunity for the individuals concerned, but denying it for the corporations.[2] Though legally sound, of course, this outcome was such a preposterous travesty on justice that Congress took steps to limit more narrowly the possibility of the recurrence of an "immunity bath."

In the meantime both private and public investigations were being made of another aspect of the packing business. The sensational disclosures in Upton Sinclair's novel *The Jungle,* alleging sanitary conditions in the packing houses which were nothing short of nauseating, were substantiated by government investigators. The public protest against these conditions resulted in the enactment of the Pure Food and Drug and Meat Inspection Acts of 1906, requiring, among other things, rigid federal inspection of the packing business.

[1] 196 U. S. 394, 395, 396, 397, 401 (1905).

[2] 142 Fed. 808, 827 (1906).

Judicial action against the packers seemed about to be resumed in the closing months of 1906 when a federal grand jury began another investigation, but nothing was done until 1910, when a dissolution suit and a criminal indictment were brought against the National Packing Company and others. But the former was dropped and the latter quashed. Subsequently, another grand jury returned an indictment against ten of the leading packers. The charges were very similar to those made in 1902. But in this case the defendants were acquitted. Press comment at the time provides convincing proof of a nearly universal opinion that justice had again been defeated. The only bit of consolation available in the situation was that shortly after their acquittal the packers, under pressure of public opinion and another impending suit against the combine, dissolved the National Packing Company and distributed its assets. But again the weight of the evidence indicates that the relief was more illusory than real. Allegations that the packing interests were still employing illegal methods prompted President Wilson, on February 7, 1917, to direct the Federal Trade Commission to undertake a broad investigation of the production, storage, and distribution of foodstuffs. A part of the results of this study was embodied in a six-volume report on the meat-packing industry which appeared at intervals from 1918 to 1920. In a letter to the President transmitting its summary of the report the Commission stated that it had found "conclusive evidence" of the existence of "monopolies, controls, trusts, combinations, conspiracies [and] restraints of trade out of harmony with the law and the public interest." [1] The packers denied the validity of this conclusion and accused the Commission of making an unfair and biased investigation in which it suppressed and distorted evidence in every way in order to support previously formed judgments.[2] The Commission was equally free with its charges of "deliberate falsifications of returns," the establishment of "schools" in which packer witnesses were

[1] *Summary of the Report of the Federal Trade Commission on the Meat-packing Industry*, p. 3.

[2] Cf. American Institute of Meat Packers, *The Packing Industry*, p. 93, and Swift & Company's *Analysis and Criticism* of part ii of the *Report*.

"coached," destruction of documents, etc. Reproduction of the bases of these charges and countercharges has no place here. After examining them we are forced to the conclusion that as far as the methods of the two parties are concerned it was, in the homely phrase of the Negro mammy of the Southland, "a case of de pot callin' de kettle black"!

Regardless of the merits of these controversies, however, the report had two important results—the consent decree of 1920 and the Packers and Stockyards Act of 1921. The latter is discussed in our next chapter. By the terms of the former the "Big Five" packers, Swift, Armour, Morris, Cudahy, and Wilson, and nearly one hundred other smaller concerns, agreed to dispose of their holdings in public stockyards, stockyard railways and terminals, market newspapers, and public cold-storage warehouses, and forever to dissociate themselves from the retail meat business and all "unrelated lines" such as wholesale groceries, fresh, canned, or salt fish and over one hundred other enumerated commodities.[1] It should be noted that in signing this consent decree the packers specifically denied guilt and that the decree states in its first paragraph that it is not to be construed as a judgment of guilt. On May 1, 1925, the Supreme Court of the District of Columbia suspended the operation of the decree. The reason for the suspension was the damage done to the business of the California Coöperative Canneries. This group had a contract with Armour & Company under which the latter handled a large part of the canneries' products. Since the terms of the decree were drawn in such a way as to prohibit the continuance of the contract and since the Department of Justice had apparently ignored it in formulating the decree, the District of Columbia court ruled that the canneries were entitled to relief. But at the same time this court in a separate case denied the plea of Swift and Armour that the decree be entirely vacated. This denial was affirmed by the Supreme Court of the United States on March 19, 1928.[2] Thereupon, the United

[1] Cf. *Quarterly Journal of Economics,* vol. xxxiv, p. 678, and *The Federal Antitrust Laws with Amendments,* 1928, p. 155. The latter is a pamphlet prepared by the Department of Justice.

[2] 276 U. S. 311 (1928).

States instituted proceedings to determine the right of the California Canneries to intervene and to interfere with the enforcement of the decree. On May 20, 1929, the Supreme Court decided this case against the Canneries so that the decree is now in full force and effect.[1]

On February 1, 1909, the Supreme Court announced its determination of the Continental Wall Paper case. Though not precisely a leading case, it is interesting and significant as an illustration of a method by which a combination might be prevented from securing one of its primary objects—the extortion of unreasonable profits. The Continental was a selling company organized to control the wall-paper business of the United States. It actually controlled about 98 per cent of the wall-paper mills of the country. Lewis Voight & Sons Company, wholesalers of wall paper, were virtually compelled to sign a jobber's agreement with the combine which obligated them to buy all their paper from it and to sell at prices and terms not more favorable than those established by it. The Voight concern claimed that the prices it was charged were unreasonable, and refused to pay a balance of over $57,000 which the Continental claimed was due. Thereupon the latter company brought suit for this amount. The Supreme Court held that on the admissions of the Continental in the pleadings it was an illegal combination under the Sherman Act, that the contracts of sale were a part of the illegal combination and designed to maintain it, that the contract in this case was consequently illegal, that the courts could not lend their aid to a party seeking to secure the fruits of such an illegal contract, and that consequently it would not hold the Voight Company legally liable to pay the balance claimed.[2] The decision was surprising to many lawyers at the time, since it was rather generally considered that the decision in the case of Connolly *v.* Union Sewer Pipe Company [3] had settled this point in exactly the opposite fashion. The court, however, distinguished between the cases on the

[1] 49 Sup. Ct. 423 (1929), advance sheets.
[2] 212 U. S. 227 (1909).
[3] 184 U. S. 540 (1902).

ground that Connolly had no connection with the combination from which he had bought pipe and that his contract was not a "part of nor in execution of any general plan or scheme that the law condemned." In the Wall Paper case, on the contrary, the account sued on was admittedly made up in execution of the agreements which the court found illegal.[1]

The year 1911 proved to be extremely important in the interpretation and application of the Sherman law. A consent decree was entered against the General Electric Company, and Supreme Court decisions were announced in the Dr. Miles Medical, Standard Oil, and American Tobacco cases.

The Dr. Miles Medical Company case was chiefly concerned with the utilization of price maintenance contracts by the manufacturers of proprietary but not patented medicines. Since the Federal Trade Commission has devoted a great deal of time to the prosecution of such cases it will be more logical to include this case in our general treatment of the topic in Chapter XXII.[2]

The most important case determined during this period, and perhaps the most important case in the history of the interpretation of the statute, was that of the Standard Oil Company decided May 15, 1911. The facts presented to the courts have been sufficiently developed in Chapter VIII. On the basis of these facts the combination was declared illegal and its dissolution ordered. The opinion of the Supreme Court, prepared by Chief Justice White, after briefly summarizing the facts and the history of the litigation, noted that the prosecution and the defense were agreed on only one thing—*viz.,* that "the controversy in every respect is controlled by a correct conception of the meaning of the first and second sections of the Anti-Trust Act." [3] Thereupon the opinion traced the development of the meaning of the key words in those two sections, "restraint of trade" and "monopolize," and concluded that in 1890 the common law did not prohibit a restraint which was reasonable and only partial in its operation, and that attempts to monopolize included

[1] 212 U. S. 260, 261 (1909).
[2] Cf. particularly p. 507 *et seq.*
[3] 221 U. S. 48 (1911).

acts and contracts which unreasonably restricted competitive conditions, limited the rights of individuals, restrained the free flow of commerce, or brought about public evils such as an enhancement of prices. Finally, the opinion reiterated the principle that "where words are employed in a statute which had at the time a well-known meaning at common law or in the law of this country they are presumed to have been used in that sense unless the context compels to the contrary."

In the light of his historical résumé and the principle just stated, the Chief Justice proceeded to analyze the precise language of the first two sections of the statute. Because of their broad and general terms it seemed clear to him that their application "necessarily called for the exercise of judgment" and that this "required that some standard should be resorted to for the purpose of determining whether the prohibitions contained in the statute had or had not in any given case been violated." And because he had not changed his mind since writing his dissenting opinion in the Trans-Missouri Freight Association case he now held that "it was intended that the standard of reason" should be utilized in resolving the issue just stated.[1]

In the opinion of most students this "rule of reason" was a direct reversal of the position taken by the Supreme Court in the Trans-Missouri and Joint Traffic Association cases, but Chief Justice White did not admit this. On the contrary, in his Oil Trust opinion and in the American Tobacco opinion, which he handed down just two weeks later, he went to considerable pains to show that at the most the court had only "limited and qualified" those earlier decisions. The Trans-Missouri case, it will be recalled, drew a distinction between direct and indirect restraints and pointed out that the Anti-trust Act did not condemn the latter. Relying on this, the opinion in the Standard Oil case proceeds: "If the criterion by which it is to be determined in all cases whether every contract, combination, etc., is a restraint of trade within the intendment of the law, is the direct or indirect effect of the acts involved, then of course the rule of reason becomes the

[1] 221 U. S. 59-60 (1911).

guide, and the construction which we have given the statute, instead of being refuted by the cases relied upon [Trans-Missouri and Joint Traffic], is by those cases demonstrated to be correct." Even more positive language is found in the Chief Justice's opinion in the tobacco case: "In that case [Standard Oil] it was held, without departing from any previous decision of the court that as the statute had not defined the words restraint of trade, it became necessary to construe those words, a duty which could be discharged only by a resort to reason."[1] In another passage in the oil opinion he said: "As the cases [Trans-Missouri and Joint Traffic] cannot by any possible conception be treated as authoritative without the certitude that reason was resorted to for the purpose of deciding them, it follows as a matter of course that it must have been held by the light of reason, since the conclusion could not have been otherwise reached, that the assailed contracts or agreements were within the general enumeration of the statute, and that their operation and effect brought about the restraint of trade which the statute prohibited." In other words, the use by the members of the bench of their reasoning powers means that they were applying the "rule of reason"! We might go on, but the foregoing quotations are adequate. In an effort to reconcile two conflicting decisions the Chief Justice resorted to mere word juggling.

Justice Harlan, who concurred in the dissolution orders against both the oil and tobacco trusts, but submitted a dissenting opinion, was even more harsh in his criticism of the "rule of reason." In commenting on the decision in the tobacco case he said: "If I do not misapprehend the opinion just delivered, the court insists that what was said in the opinion in the *Standard Oil case,* was in accordance with our previous decisions in the *Trans-Missouri* and *Joint Traffic cases* . . . if we resort to *reason.* This statement surprises me quite as much as would a statement that black was white or white was black. . . . One thing is certain, the 'rule of reason,' to which the court refers, does not justify the per-

[1] Cf. 221 U. S. 66 and 178, 179 (1911).

version of the plain words of an act in order to defeat the will of Congress." [1]

Our own conclusion is that Justice White would have been better advised to admit that the new decisions departed from the rule laid down in the early railroad cases, while at the same time he maintained that they represented a true interpretation of the intention of Congress. His defense of the position now taken may carry conviction to some minds, but to us as economists a simpler way of justifying the result would seem to be through drawing a distinction between "restraints on competition" and "restraints on trade." The antitrust act forbids all "restraints of trade," but in the development of this conception of the common law the courts had long since recognized that many restraints on competition did not tend to restrain trade and therefore did not merit condemnation. The combination of two former competitors in a business partnership, while restraining and even extinguishing competition between them, might tend to enhance trade by increasing the scope and efficiency of their operations. On these grounds it is always necessary to consider the direct effect and tendency of combinations and agreements restraining competition to decide whether or not they are in a true sense restraints on trade. If deemed to be so they are violations of the Antitrust Act; if not they are advantageous, rather than inimical, to the trade interests of the country, and lawful.

The oil and tobacco decisions are important for other reasons than those discussed. In the first place, they made even more clear what some earlier decisions had indicated—*viz.*, that the doctrine of the E. C. Knight case was no longer controlling, and that manufacturing and mining corporations were within the scope of the Antitrust Act. Secondly, they reaffirmed the position taken in the Northern Securities case, that a holding-company charter was no guarantee of immunity from prosecution under the Sherman Act. Third, they clearly stated that the first and second sections of the statute were to be construed together, so that the tendency

[1] 221 U. S. 191, 192 (1911).

of a restraint to bring about a monopoly was one aspect to be considered in determining its lawfulness. Finally, the decision reaffirmed the power of the courts to order any sort of a dissolution which would break up the combination.

On the other hand, as pointed out in earlier chapters,[1] the plan of dissolution approved by the courts in the oil decree was entirely inadequate, and in the tobacco decree only slightly less so, to secure that restoration of competitive conditions which was the primary purpose of the suits.

Still another important result of these decisions was that they caused one large combination to abandon its original intention of fighting its case. The General Electric Company had in 1896 entered into an agreement with six other concerns which was of the nature of a pool. Among the purposes of the Incandescent Lamp Manufacturers Association, as the group styled itself, were the establishment of rules concerning the manufacture and sale of carbon lamps, on which the patents had expired two years earlier, the allotment of business, and the fixing of prices. In order to insure observance of the arrangements a system of deposits and fines was established. Subsequently ten other concerns became parties to the agreement. In 1901 the General Electric set up the National Electric Lamp Company to carry on the work of combining the lamp interests of the United States, though ostensibly the new concern was independent. Additional manufacturers of electric lamps were brought under its control by stock purchase and otherwise, and an agreement was effected with a number of other concerns, including the Westinghouse Electric Company to prevent deviation from the prices on carbon lamps fixed by the combination.

In the meantime German interests had developed tantalum and tungsten filament lamps which were superior to the carbon type and were rapidly displacing the latter. In 1906 the General Electric and the National Electric Lamp secured an exclusive selling agency in the United States for these German products and three years later acquired patents on them. Moreover, the combination used its new patents to tighten its

[1] Cf. pp. 123, 124 and 177 *et seq.*, *supra.*

grip on the carbon lamp business by compelling dealers to purchase all of such lamps needed from the combination as a condition of securing the newer types which popular demand required them to stock. Finally, manufacturers of bulbs, tubes, lamp machinery and other related products were more or less coerced into contracts which required them to sell exclusively to the trust or to sell at prices fixed by the latter. By the use of these methods the General Electric secured very nearly a 100-per-cent monopoly of the electric bulb business of the United States.

In view of the facts just summarized, the federal government filed suit against the combination. As stated above, the defendants chose to enter into a consent decree rather than fight. This decree was filed October 12, 1911. The defendants were adjudged to have been "engaged in unlawful agreements and combinations in restraint of trade" and to have been guilty of certain unlawful acts. The deception practiced by them in pretending that the National Electric Lamp and its large group of subsidiaries were independent of the General Electric was ordered discontinued, the National Electric and its subsidiaries dissolved, and the General Electric ordered to carry on all its business under its own name. Other practices summarized above, such as the exclusive contracts with bulb manufacturers, the use of the patented tungsten lamps as a bludgeon to compel dealers to purchase carbon lamps from the trust, and price-fixing, were perpetually enjoined. On the face of the decree, considerable success had been attained in securing the restoration of competitive conditions in the electric-lamp industry except as that was prevented by the legalized patent monopoly held by the General Electric on certain types of lamps.[1]

Although the General Electric desired to take full advantage of its rights under the patent law, it clearly evidenced its intent to observe the antitrust law by submitting its new plans for selling its products and licensing its patents to the

[1] Cf. on this section Stevens, W. H. S., "A Group of Trusts and Combinations," *Quarterly Journal of Economics,* vol. xxvi, p. 594 *et seq.* (August, 1912), and *Decrees and Judgments in Federal Anti-Trust Cases,* p. 267 *et seq.*

Attorney General of the United States. But, unfortunately, at least from the company's point of view, he would neither approve nor disapprove of its proposals, so that it had to rely on the advice of its own attorneys. The new methods became effective about March 1, 1912.[1]

The essential feature of the selling program on which the General Electric entered, as construed by it, was direct selling to consumers. By this it must not be understood that the company proposed to go into the mail-order business or that it intended to open a chain of retail stores. For the purposes of the plan the trade was divided into three classes. The first class consisted of sales to large consumers readily accessible to the company, so that sales could be negotiated by its salaried employees and deliveries made from its plants or warehouses. The second class was composed of sales to large consumers also, but these were negotiated by so-called class B agents who were appointed by the General Electric, who entered into yearly contracts to act as agents, and who made deliveries from stocks which the company obligated itself to maintain. The final group consisted of sales to general consumers by class A agents, who were also under contract. The lamps in the custody of both classes of agents remained the property of the General Electric until sold, although the agents were required to pay all expenses of storage, cartage, transportation, handling, sale, and distribution. On the other hand, the company has, since 1915, assumed all risk of fire, flood, obsolescence, and price decline, has carried whatever insurance is carried on stocks in the hands of its agents, and has paid whatever taxes are assessed.

The other feature of the new program of operations included a licensing system under which the General Electric authorized the Westinghouse interests and thirteen small concerns to manufacture and sell tungsten lamps on which it held the patents. The licensees agreed that such sales should be at prices fixed by the licensor and subject to change at the

[1] Although in accordance with our chronological arrangement, the story should be interrupted at this point, we have preferred to adopt the topical method and follow it to its conclusion in this chapter.

latter's discretion. Although the agency system was not a part of the license, it appears that at least the Westinghouse concern agreed to sell its lamps through agency arrangements similar to those just described.

In 1919 both the agency and license arrangements were called to the attention of the Federal Trade Commission with the purpose of securing an order from it to the General Electric that they be discontinued. On May 26, 1920, that body dismissed the case and specifically recognized the right of the company to prescribe the prices at which its agents and licensees might sell. The Commission further stated that "As to the charges of exclusive dealing (tying contracts and full-line forcing), and of refusal to sell, these were not supported by the evidence in the record." [1]

The Department of Justice, however, decided to bring suit against the General Electric, alleging that the agency system was simply a subterfuge, that the licenses were not protected by the patent law, and that the whole arrangement constituted a restraint of trade and a monopoly of the electric-lamp business in violation of the Sherman Act. These contentions did not receive the approval of either the District Court for the Northern District of Ohio or the Supreme Court. The latter court specifically held that "We find nothing in the form of the contracts and the practice under them which makes the so-called B and A agents anything more than genuine agents of the company. . . ." The Dr. Miles Medical Company and Standard Sanitary Manufacturing Company cases were distinguished on the ground that in both of them the contracts with dealers were contracts of sale, not of agency. Since they were contracts of sale, full title had passed to the purchasers and attempts to control their resale prices by vendors were illegal. After thus considering the facts and the precedents, the court concluded that there was nothing in either that required it to hold that "genuine contracts of agency like those before us, however comprehensive

[1] Quoted in the opinion of the District Court which subsequently considered the case: 15 Fed. (2d) 719 (1925).

as a mass or whole in their effect, are violations of the Anti-Trust Act." [1]

The decision on the license arrangements is even more significant, for after considering at length a number of its earlier decisions the court stated that the overruling of the Button-fastener and Dick cases in the Motion Picture Patents decision did not carry the overruling of the Bement *v.* National Harrow case, that the authority of this last had not been shaken, and consequently that the licenses were within the patent rights of the General Electric. A number of cases, such as the Boston Store *v.* American Graphophone Company and Straus *v.* Victor Talking Machine Company, were distinguished, again largely on the ground that they involved sales as distinguished from license agreements.[2]

One of the cases determined during this 1904 to 1914 period —that of the so-called Powder Trust—was not carried to the Supreme Court by the defendants, apparently because of a conviction of the futility of so doing. From the point of view of legal interpretation the case is not significant; as an application of the act to a major combination of many years' duration, however, it is important.

From the facts developed during the litigation instituted in 1907 by the federal government, it appears that as far back as 1872 seven of the largest manufacturers of explosives and powder in the country were working in harmonious co-operation through the instrumentality of a "Gunpowder Trade Association." This organization was in reality a pool which divided trade territory between its members, authorized price-cutting campaigns for the purpose of ruining outsiders or forcing them into the association, apportioned any losses resulting from these campaigns between the members, and fixed prices. The terms of the agreement were enforced by the levying of fines for violations. Approximately in this form the combination persisted until 1902, though as the result of the tactics described it had expanded to include sev-

[1] 272 U. S. 484, 488 (1926).

[2] *Ibid.*, pp. 493, 494. Cf. Chapter XXI for a discussion of a number of the cases cited above.

enteen members. Substantial control of the rifle powder, blasting powder, and dynamite business in the United States had been achieved by this time, and an agreement with European manufacturers had been reached under the terms of which the world trade in explosives had been parceled out to the members of the international combination. Early in 1902 the Powder Trust began to assume a corporate form as the result of a change in the management of its chief constituent: E. I. DuPont de Nemours & Company. Under the slightly altered name of E. I. DuPont de Nemours Company, a Delaware corporation, this concern began to acquire the assets and securities of other companies. In 1903 the E. I. DuPont de Nemours Powder Company of New Jersey was organized to hold the stock of the Delaware company and of the concerns it had by that time acquired. Other changes and rearrangements in financial structure were made, but for our purpose it is sufficient to note that by 1907 the holding-company trust had acquired the stock of and brought about the dissolution of sixty-four corporations and had secured a degree of control ranging from 64 to 100 per cent in the various types of explosives sold.

On the basis of these facts the Circuit Court of Delaware in its decision of June 21, 1911, held that the Du Pont Company constituted a combination in restraint of interstate commerce, with the purpose to monopolize a part of the same in violation of the Sherman Act.[1] The final decree was not filed until a year later, June, 1912. By its terms the Delaware corporation of 1902 was ordered dissolved and its property distributed among its stockholders. The New Jersey corporation of 1903 was ordered to divide its property and business into three parts, one to be retained by itself, in such a fashion that competitive conditions should be restored. The other two parts were to go to corporations which might be new creations or reorganizations of two members of the old pool. The Du Pont interests chose the former alternative and organized the

[1] 188 Fed. 127, 128 (1911). For an excellent discussion of this combination, see Stevens, W. H. S., "The Powder Trust, 1872-1912," *Quarterly Journal of Economics,* vol. xxvi, pp. 444-481 (May, 1912).

Hercules and Atlas powder companies. Finally, all the defendants and the new companies were enjoined from using any of an enumerated set of devices which would restore the old situation. Since the prohibitions laid down against the Powder Trust were in no material respects different from those previously discussed in the tobacco case, it is not necessary to repeat the criticisms there stated.[1]

Approximately a year after the oil and tobacco decisions the Supreme Court applied the rule of reason in the next case important for this discussion—the Terminal Railroad Association of St. Louis. The geographic and topographic location of St. Louis is such as to create there certain unique problems in railroad transportation. The city is located on some high hills on the west bank of the Mississippi. Railroads approaching from the east were faced with two difficulties in getting their lines into the city. First was the river itself, for its size made the cost and maintenance of railroad bridges by each of the railroads prohibitive. For a time the situation might be met by a system of railroad-car ferries, but with the growth of traffic this would become more and more inadequate and unsatisfactory. The obvious remedy was a toll bridge open to any and all lines on identical terms. But once across the river there was still the problem of the hills to be circumvented. Railroads approaching from the west had found the hills on that side something less of a problem because of the fact that they were penetrated by the narrow valley of Mill Creek, a little stream which traversed the city at about its center, but the possibilities there were restricted by the size of the valley, and long before the time of the suit it had been fully occupied. Railroads approaching from the north on the west bank of the Mississippi had the least difficulties of all because the hills were less precipitous on that side, but most of them had located their terminals in the northern edge of the city. As a result of these factors, of the twenty-four railroads which converged at St. Louis not a single one passed through the city. About half of them had their terminals on the Illinois side of the river. In order to

[1] Cf. p. 172 *et seq., supra.*

meet this situation a considerable number of different types of concerns developed. Among them were a ferry system, a toll bridge, and short rail lines connecting both of them with the railroad terminals. On the west side of the river it was necessary to tunnel the hills.

The Terminal Railroad Association of St. Louis, defendant in the suit now under consideration, was organized in 1889 by a number of the railroads having terminals in the St. Louis area for the purpose of combining and operating as a unitary system several then independent terminal concerns. The chief properties of the combination were the Union Depot of St. Louis, the Eads—or St. Louis—Bridge, and all of the connecting companies by which the bridge could be used by railroads terminating on either side of the river. The Eads Bridge was in 1889 the only one in existence. The only real competitor of the Terminal Railroad Association at this time was the Wiggins Ferry Company.

But in 1890 a third terminal system came into operation with the completion of a second railroad toll bridge known as the Merchants' Bridge. Two railway companies were organized to connect this bridge with terminals on either side of the river. Thus for a time there were three independent and competing terminal concerns: the Terminal Railroad Association, the Wiggins Ferry, and the Merchants' Bridge group. An attempt to guarantee the permanency of this competition had been made by the insertion in the Act of Congress, authorizing the Merchants' Bridge, of a provision that no other railway bridge company nor stockholder thereof should become a stockholder in the Merchants' Bridge Company. Part of the price paid for this competition was, of course, the maintenance of facilities which to some extent unnecessarily duplicated each other. The Terminal Association, however, had been organized for the purpose of controlling all the facilities connecting the railroad terminals in St. Louis. Apparently through its influence, Congress repealed the section of the act forbidding ownership of Merchants' Bridge shares by another railway bridge concern. Shortly thereafter the Terminal Association acquired control of the whole Merchants' Bridge system.

Meanwhile the Rock Island Railroad began taking steps in 1892 toward the acquisition of an independent entrance into the city by purchasing shares of the Wiggins Ferry Company. Since control of the Wiggins system by the Rock Island would prevent the Terminal Association from attaining the monopoly which it designed, the railroads which had organized it also began to buy Wiggins Ferry stock, with the result that prices for the latter reached extraordinary heights. A compromise was finally effected by which the Rock Island was admitted to joint ownership with the other railroads of all the terminal facilities controlled by the Terminal Association, and the shares of Wiggins Ferry stock owned by the Rock Island were purchased by the Terminal Association. The final result of the transactions was, of course, to put the control of all the terminal facilities into the hands of the Terminal Association; that is to say, into the hands of the railroads who jointly owned that association.

But of the twenty-four roads converging at St. Louis, only fourteen at the time the government filed suit enjoyed the privileges of participation in the association. Moreover, the agreement between the proprietary railroad companies in the association was so contrived that each one of them had an absolute power of veto over the joint use or control of any terminal facilities by a non-proprietary railroad. Manifestly, the Terminal Association or any one of its proprietary companies had the power to restrain trade and to interfere with the flow of interstate commerce. This situation, in view of all the attending circumstances, was sufficient to bring the arrangement within the prohibitions of the Sherman Act. The Supreme Court specifically held that "When, as here, the inherent conditions are such as to prohibit any other reasonable means of entering the city, the combination of every such facility under the exclusive ownership and control of less than all the companies under compulsion to use them violates both the first and second sections of the act, in that it constitutes a contract or combination in restraint of commerce among the states and an attempt to monopolize commerce among the states which must pass through the gateway at St. Louis."[1] In addition, the court held illegal certain specific practices of the association which operated "to the disadvantage of the commerce which must cross the river at St. Louis, and of non-proprietary railroad lines compelled to use its facilities."

The remedy considered adequate by the court was foreshadowed by the reference quoted above to the ownership of the association by "less than all the companies under compulsion" to use its facilities. In fact, the opinion pointed out that the combination would not have been held an illegal restraint had it acted as the "impartial agent" of all the companies. The restraint, the court stated, "grows out of administrative conditions which may be eliminated and the obvious advantages of unification preserved. . . ." Consequently, the Supreme Court remanded the case to the District Court with instructions to enter a decree requiring the defendants to submit a plan of reorganization of the Terminal Association which should provide that any existing or future railroad might acquire joint ownership and control of the terminal facilities upon just and reasonable terms or secure the use of these facilities without becoming a joint owner upon similar terms, that a number of specified objectionable practices should be discontinued, and that any subsequent disagreements between a railroad company desirous of becoming a joint owner or user of the terminal facilities and the association or any of the proprietary companies might be submitted to the District Court.

The actual form of the decree entered was such as to prevent the Terminal Association from doing some business which it apparently was not the intention of the Supreme Court to prevent, for in a subsequent opinion it ordered a modification of the decree "so as to recognize the right of the Terminal Company as an accessory to its strictly terminal business to carry on transportation as to business exclusively originating on its lines, exclusively moving thereon, and exclusively in-

[1] 224 U. S. 409 (1912).

tended for delivery on the same. . . ."[1] Extended comment on this case seems unnecessary. The facts show that a situation necessitating relief had arisen. In providing this relief in a fashion to retain certain benefits of combination in the terminal facilities at St. Louis the Supreme Court applied its newly formulated "rule of reason" in a manner which is unexceptionable. The progress which this decision registers from the negative and, so far as they were effective, destructive, decrees in the earlier railroad cases is striking.

[1] 236 U. S. 210 (1915).

CHAPTER XX

THE TRADE COMMISSION AND CLAYTON ACTS OF 1914 AND SUBSEQUENT LEGISLATION

PERHAPS the most important result of the oil and tobacco decisions of 1911 was to crystallize a sentiment, already strong in certain quarters and of many years' standing, that the Sherman Act needed amendment. The most convincing proof of this sentiment appears in the report of the committee on interstate commerce of the United States Senate, delegated on July 26, 1911, to investigate whether or not such amendment were necessary. After tracing the judicial interpretation of the statute of 1890 to the enunciation of the rule of reason, the report stated that in view of that rule "it has become imperative to enact additional legislation." The committee expressed full confidence in the intelligence, integrity, and patriotism of the Supreme Court, but found itself "unwilling to repose in that court, or any other court, the vast and undefined power which it must exercise in the administration of the statute under the rule which it has promulgated." Consequently, the committee suggested that Congress formulate a set of conditions upon which persons and corporations might engage in interstate and foreign commerce, that it prohibit certain known types of combinations, and that it create a commission to aid in the administration and enforcement of the existing antitrust act and any subsequent legislation.[1]

Although the committee had begun its hearings in November, 1911, its report was not presented until February 27, 1913. Meanwhile the election of 1912 had resulted in the choice of Woodrow Wilson for President and had given the Democrats control of both houses in the next Congress. As has been previously stated, the trust policy of the government

[1] Senate Report, No. 1326, 62d Congress, 3d Session.

had constituted an important issue in the campaign. The Democrats had roundly denounced the Republican Department of Justice for inadequately enforcing the Sherman Act and for acquiescing in the ineffective methods adopted for dissolving the oil and tobacco combinations; the Republicans had expressed satisfaction with their record, but had promised additional legislation prohibiting more clearly practices tending toward restraint and monopoly and creating a federal trade commission; the new Progressive party had emphasized the need for such a commission, but had carefully discriminated between combinations which had been organized by unfair means and others which it held were a natural economic growth and needed only regulation, not destruction. Although Wilson severely criticized Roosevelt's proposals for a commission as an "avowed partnership between the Government and the trusts,"[1] his message to Congress on trust legislation endorsed and advocated the creation of a commission. The President qualified his endorsement only to the extent of expressing the wish that it be not empowered to make terms with monopoly or to assume control of business in any way that would make the government responsible. His other recommendations called for legislation to prohibit specific undesirable practices leading toward monopoly, particularly interlocking directorates and holding companies; to make the individuals who violated the antitrust laws personally liable; to enable any person injured by a trust to base a suit for damages upon the facts proved in a government prosecution and thus facilitate the collection of those treble damages allowed by the Sherman Act; and, finally, to extend the powers of the Interstate Commerce Commission to include the regulation of the issuance of securities by the railroads.[2]

These recommendations were embodied in five bills, promptly christened the "Five Brother Bills," next of kin to the "Seven Sister Acts" of New Jersey.[3] After hearings extending over several weeks the portions of these bills relating to the trust problem which it was decided to retain were

[1] Wilson, W., *The New Freedom,* p. 202.

[2] *Congressional Record,* vol. li, pp. 1962-1964.

[3] Cf. Chap. xvii, p. 362 *et seq.*

fused together into the two bills which emerged as the Trade Commission and Clayton Acts. Since the final form of these laws represented compromises on a number of vital provisions, we will narrate briefly the legislative history of the two bills and point out certain significant features of the debates.

As has been suggested above, the proponents of a trade commission were sharply divided into two groups: first, those who held that monopoly was the ultimate result of industrial evolution, that it should be so recognized, declared vested with a public interest and regulated. Second, were those who considered monopoly in private hands to be intolerable and believed a commission would aid in preserving competition. It was to make effective the views of this second group that the original trade-commission bill was drafted and introduced into the House and Senate by Mr. Clayton and Senator Newlands, respectively.[1] During the consideration of the bill in the House committee it was so altered that when it went up to the Senate the committee on interstate commerce of that chamber substituted its own bill.

The outstanding difference between the two lay in the treatment of unfair competition. In the bill passed by the House the proposed commission was simply a slightly modified Bureau of Corporations with no quasi-judicial powers. If in the course of its investigations it obtained information of any unfair practice "not necessarily constituting a violation of law," it was to report the facts to the President to aid him in recommending additional legislation and was also to make the information public. The Senate bill was much more far-reaching. It declared unfair competition to be unlawful and vested the Commission with the power to prevent it by entering an order against it, said order to be enforced if violated by a district court on a suit in equity by the Commission. The conference report followed the model of the Senate bill except that it provided for a review of the Commission's

[1] On the legislative history of these acts, cf. the excellent articles by W. H. S. Stevens in *The American Economic Review* for December, 1914, and March, 1915.

order by petition of the respondent in the case as well as by the Commission, that it gave jurisdiction to the circuit courts of appeals, and that it prohibited unfair *methods* of competition rather than unfair competition.[1] In the opinion of Senator Cummins, a member of the committee, the two expressions meant exactly the same thing, but, as we shall show subsequently, the Federal Trade Commission and the courts have interpreted the phrase "unfair methods of competition" to include a somewhat wider range of activities than those encompassed by the common-law meaning of "unfair competition" as it stood in 1914.[2]

The debates on this unfair competition section (number 5 in the law) were the most spirited in the progress of the legislation. To those who desired an enumeration of illegal practices item by item the general phrase "unfair competition" was unsatisfactory. They argued that a primary purpose of the legislation was to clarify and define the law, and that "unfair competition" was as ambiguous as "unreasonable restraint." The reasons given by the conference managers for the House for retaining the general phraseology were that fixed definitions were too inflexible, and that it was practically impossible to formulate them in such a way as to include all unfair practices, to fit businesses of every sort in every part of the country, and to avoid presenting to the courts most difficult problems of construction.[3] It was also brought out in the debates that "unfair competition" had been the subject of numerous court decisions, and that in consequence it had a common-law meaning equally as definite as that of "restraint of trade" in 1890.

Another source of contention was the question of a judicial review of the orders of the proposed commission to a respondent to cease and desist from an illegal practice. In reply to a question, Senator Cummins stated that he was willing to confer upon the body the power to determine absolutely with-

[1] Cf. Senate Document, No. 573, 63d Congress, 2d Session, a comparative print showing the House, Senate, and conference forms of the bill.

[2] Cf. particularly the Winsted decision of the Supreme Court and the dissenting opinion of Justice Brandeis in the Gratz case, pp. 497-499 and 487, 488, *infra*.

[3] House Report, No. 1142, 63d Congress, 2d Session.

out appeal or review upon appeal the question of unfair competition in any given case, that he "tried to make it so that the courts would not have the power to review the discretion and the judgment exercised or the facts passed upon by the trade commission," and that he hoped an interference with the rights of property would be the only event in which the courts would be permitted to overrule the commission.[1] As stated above, the upshot of the discussions was to vest the power of review on the request of either party in the circuit courts of appeals (with further review by the Supreme Court on *certiorari*) with the proviso that the findings of fact of the commission were to be conclusive if supported by evidence. No penalties for a violation of an order were provided, but in case the violation continued after the order was affirmed the respondent was made liable for contempt of court.

An issue connected with Section 5, but really going back to the fundamental controversy over the nature and purpose of the commission, was that of the desirability of the issuance of advance opinions on the legality of proposed business practices. Business men were strongly in favor of a body to which they could take their plans for approval. They chafed under what they characterized as the uncertainty and confusion of the existing law. The language of the President's message encouraged them to believe that they would get from the new commission "the advice, the definite guidance and information," which they wanted. But when the bills were introduced into Congress the business interests were extremely dissatisfied. The New York *Journal of Commerce*, speaking editorially for the members of this group, went so far as to say that not only had there been no attempt made to aid them by creating a tribunal to pass upon questions of business procedure, but that on the contrary they would be hampered by a body whose powers were "needlessly inquisitorial and perniciously broad." In commenting upon this editorial, Representative Covington, chairman of the subcommittee which put the House bill in its final form, made it clear that it had been deemed unwise expressly to authorize

[1] *Congressional Record,* vol. li, pp. 11105, 11104.

advance opinions, but that the committee believed it had carried out the intentions of the President in Section 10 of the House bill providing that the commission might recommend readjustments of a business in such a manner as to bring its conduct within the law.[1]

The conference report, representing a series of compromises on the foregoing and other controversies, was finally agreed to on September 8 and September 10, 1914, by the Senate and House, respectively, and on September 26 the bill was signed by the President. The principal features of the act, in addition to the authority to prevent unfair methods of competition, may be summarized as follows:

(1) The Bureau of Corporations is replaced by the Federal Trade Commission of five members appointed by the President, with the advice and consent of the Senate, for terms of seven years at salaries of $10,000 each. No more than three commissioners are to be of the same political party. The records, papers, property, and employees of the Bureau of Corporations were transferred to the Commission and the latter was authorized to carry on all pending investigations of its predecessor.

(2) The Commission is given power to investigate corporations engaged in interstate commerce, other than banks and common carriers, and to require from them annual and special reports and other information.

(3) On its own motion, or at the request of the Attorney General, it may investigate the manner in which decrees affecting industrial combinations are being carried out and make public its findings, if it deems this wise.

(4) Upon the direction of the President or either house of Congress it is to investigate any alleged violation of the antitrust acts by any corporation.

(5) Upon the application of the Attorney General it is required to investigate corporate practices or arrangements not in conformity with the antitrust acts, and to recommend readjustments which will secure such conformity.

[1] *Congressional Record,* vol. li, pp. 8841, 8845. Section 10 of the House bill became Section 6 (e) of the present law. Cf. Chapter XXIII, pp. 532, 53

(6) It is to make annual and other reports, holding inviolate, however, trade secrets and customers' names.

(7) It is to classify corporations and to make rules and regulations for the carrying out of the act.

(8) It is to investigate trade relations with foreign countries.

(9) On the request of a federal court it is to act as master in chancery in advising as to the form which decrees of the court relating to industrial combinations should take, the acceptance of such advice being, of course, discretionary on the part of the court.

(10) To accomplish the foregoing objects the Commission is given full authority to secure by subpœna all necessary information, documents, testimony, etc., the penalty for failure to supply information or for destroying records being fines of from $1,000 to $5,000, and for delay in supplying information after thirty days' notice $100 a day for each day that the information is withheld.

(11) Penalties are provided for employees of the Commission who are guilty of giving out unauthorized information.

The details of the organization of the Commission, its procedure, and something of its accomplishments, will be discussed at length in the following chapters. At this point we shall proceed to a summary of the manner in which the remainder of the Democratic trust program was brought to fruition in the so-called Clayton Act.

In so far as the Clayton Act is an antitrust measure it represents a combination of three of the original "Five Brother Bills." In the course of its progress through Congress other sections, including those relating to matters of interest to organized labor, were engrafted upon it, so that the final result is as thoroughly disjointed and immiscible a law as could well be imagined. The bill reported by the House committee on the judiciary contained a number of proposals based directly upon the recommendations of the President's message, which were in turn, of course, a reflection of the current opinions of students of the trust problem. Although there were three minority reports filed by members of the

House committee opposing the passage of the bill for the contrary reasons that it would create doubt and uncertainty in the minds of business men, and that it was not a real anti-trust measure but an ineffective gesture; and although there was considerable opposition on the floor of the House, the committee report passed practically as it was submitted. In the Senate, however, the amendments were numerous and of a far-reaching character. Most of them were accepted by the House managers in the conference committee, so that the final form of the act corresponds more closely to the bill passed by the Senate.

In general terms the criticism of the bill centered upon the claim that its provisions were too lenient. The basis for this was the elimination of the criminal penalties provided in the bill as it came from the House for the violation of certain sections, and the addition of qualifying provisions to other sections which materially reduced their scope and effectiveness. As originally drafted, the measure contained sections prohibiting price discrimination, tying and exclusive contracts, intercorporate stockholding, and interlocking directorates, all but the second qualified to some extent and all carrying personal penalties of fine or imprisonment or both. The Senate struck out the sections prohibiting price discrimination and tying and exclusive contracts on the ground that they would be dealt with as unfair methods of competition under the Federal Trade Commission Act, but subsequently restored the second of them, including the criminal penalties, before sending the bill to conference. Its chief amendment to the intercorporate stockholding and interlocking directorates sections was the removal of the penalties. An important qualification of the former of these two sections in the House bill was the limitation of the prohibition to instances in which the effect of the ownership of one corporation's stock by another would be "to eliminate or substantially lessen competition" or "to create a monopoly." The interlocking directorate section was more complicated, but its most important limitation affecting industrial combinations was that, beginning two years from the date of the approval of the act, no person could at the same time be a director in any two or more industrial corporations which had a capital surplus and undivided profit aggregating more than $1,000,000, if the elimination of competition between these corporations would constitute a violation of any section of any of the antitrust laws.

In the conference committee the theory of the intercorporate stockholding section of the House bill requiring proof of an effect of lessening competition or creating monopoly was carried back to the price-discrimination and tying-contract sections, so that in the law all three contain this qualification. The language was modified so as to prohibit these practices where the effect "*may be* to substantially lessen competition or *tend* to create a monopoly." In the case of the tying and exclusive contracts section this qualification was in the nature of an addition to the original draft, but in that prohibiting price discriminations it was a substitute for a prohibition of such discrimination, "with the purpose or intent thereby to destroy or wrongfully injure the business of a competitor, of either such purchaser or seller. . . ."

When the conference report returned to the floor of the Senate the earlier attacks upon the measure were renewed. It was contended that the conferees had taken the inferior portions of both the House and Senate bills and omitted those which were valuable;[1] that the Democratic party had failed to carry out its platform pledges and the purport of the President's message, particularly with reference to "personal penalties";[2] that the injection of the phrase "substantially lessen competition" greatly weakened the force of the prohibitions it modified;[3] that the limitation of the use of court decrees in trust cases by private litigants in recovering damages to those "hereafter" issued showed the same solicitude for prominent and wealthy lawbreakers for which the Democrats had so roundly denounced the Republicans in the campaign of 1912;[4] and in more general terms that the law would make a dead

[1] *Congressional Record,* vol. li, p. 16042.
[2] *Ibid.,* pp. 15862, 16117.
[3] *Ibid.,* pp. 15857, 15935, 16047, 16117.
[4] *Ibid.,* pp. 16044, 16046, 16047.

letter of the Sherman Act,[1] and represented "the greatest victory of a legislative nature that has been won by the trusts and combinations within the lifetime of any man" in the Senate.[2] Despite these objections the conference report was agreed to by the Senate on October 5, 1914, and by the House on October 8, and the bill was signed by the President on October 15.

At the risk of some repetition we summarize the entire law:

(1) Price discriminations in connection with interstate commerce are declared to be unlawful, "where the effect of such discrimination may be to substantially lessen competition or tend to create a monopoly." Provisos permit differences based on grade, quality, or the quantity sold, on the cost of selling or transportation, or when "made in good faith to meet competition." Also the prohibition is declared not to prevent the selection of customers "in *bona fide* transactions, and not in restraint of trade."

(2) Exclusive selling or leasing contracts, whether of patented or unpatented articles, whose effect may be to "substantially lessen competition or tend to create a monopoly" are also declared unlawful.

(3) Damages due to acts in violation of these prohibitions, as well as the other prohibitions of the antitrust acts, may be sued for and recovered threefold.

(4) Final judgments or decrees in government suits under the antitrust acts are made, under certain limitations, *prima facie* evidence in private suits, exception being made of consent judgments or decrees.

(5) It is declared "that the labor of a human being is not a commodity or article of commerce" and that "nothing contained in the antitrust laws shall be construed to forbid the existence and operation of labor, agricultural or horticultural organizations, . . . nor shall such organizations or the members thereof be held or construed to be illegal combinations or conspiracies in restraint of trade under the antitrust laws."

(6) The acquisition of stock in one corporation by another,

[1] *Congressional Record,* vol. li, p. 15955.

[2] *Ibid.,* p. 16043.

or the combination of two or more corporations through stock ownership, where the effect "may be substantially to lessen competition . . . to restrain . . . commerce . . . or tend to create a monopoly," is prohibited. Provisos limit the application of this regulation in the case of common carriers developing branch lines, or subsidiary companies, etc., and exclude existing corporate relations.

(7) Somewhat complicated limitations are imposed upon interlocking directorates. The provision relating to industrial combinations prohibits any person, after two years from the approval of the act, from being a director in two or more corporations, any one of which has a capital of a million dollars or more, provided that the business carried on by such corporations be of such nature "that the elimination of competition by agreement between them would constitute a violation" of the antitrust laws.

(8) The same procedure created for the enforcement of the unfair-competition provision of the Trade Commission Act is prescribed for the enforcement of the above provisions (1), (2), (6), and (7) of the Clayton Act. It is also clearly indicated that Congress looks to the Trade Commission to serve the same purpose in connection with industrial combinations as does the Interstate Commerce Commission in connection with common carriers, and the Federal Reserve Board in connection with banks.

(9) Violation of any of the penal provisions of the antitrust acts by a corporation is declared to be also violation by the individual directors, officers or agents who have authorized, ordered, or done the acts constituting such violation, rendering them liable to the familiar penalties of the Sherman Act.

(10) In addition to enforcement through the Trade Commission, backed by a circuit court of appeals, provision is made for enforcement through the district courts at the instance of the district attorneys, acting under the direction of the Attorney General, as in the original antitrust act.

(11) Individuals are permitted to secure injunctions to

prevent the continued violation of the antitrust acts to their injury, exception being made of the common carriers.

(12) The conditions under which injunctions may be issued by the federal courts are laid down in great detail, as well as the procedure in contempt proceedings and the penalties that may be imposed. This was clearly designed to prevent the indiscriminate use of injunctions in connection with trade disputes, and to preserve to citizens enjoined from committing crimes the right to trial by jury, to which they would be entitled if proceeded against under the criminal law.

A comparison of the foregoing summaries of the Federal Trade Commission and Clayton Acts with the preëlection statements of Democratic leaders will convince anyone that not all their promises were fulfilled. But a further examination of the facts will also be convincing to most students that in certain respects the discrepancies between the platform planks and the legislative provisions were unavoidable, and that in others they are more to be commended than condemned. The postponed railroad securities bill has been since 1920 a part of the law, and it is probable that the delay led to no particularly pernicious results. The refusal of Congress to list the methods of competition included in the term "unfair" was undoubtedly wise if for no other reason than that it leaves the Trade Commission free to extend the scope of the law to meet the inventive genius of certain types of business men as rapidly as the courts will support it. The elimination of the criminal penalties from a number of the sections of the Clayton Act and the limitation of the authority of the Commission to the issuance of injunctions may have been a conscious or unconscious surrender to the pressure from "big business" as was charged in the Senate,[1] but there are other plausible explanations. Despite an appreciable degree of sympathy for the feeling of indignation aroused in some members of Congress by a review of the practices of the majority of our trusts, we are constrained to remember that a number of the business methods condemned by the orders of the Commission to date are still extremely widespread, so

[1] *Congressional Record,* vol. li, pp. 16054, 16056.

that any attempt to prevail upon juries to convict respondents in such cases might well be self-defeating. Our experience has demonstrated time and again that it is practically impossible to enforce criminal statutes under circumstances which make jurymen feel that a conviction would amount to singling out a few individuals for punishment for acts which dozens or hundreds of other business men are continuing to perform. Our two preceding chapters have presented considerable evidence to show that a penal statute such as the Sherman Act is a failure as a remedy for the undesirable concomitants of an industrial combination movement. The next chapter will present more of the same evidence. Consequently, it is entirely possible to construe the less drastic form of the law, as compared with the political platform, as an evidence of common sense on the part of the members of Congress rather than as a servile submission to the dictates of the "invisible government." Certainly we think it may safely be said that the legislation of 1914 dealt with the trust problem in a more realistic fashion than did that of 1890. The earlier act was formulated in the spirit of a crusade; Congressmen visualized themselves as knights in shining armor out to do battle with the hosts of Mammon. Although the majority of them were probably innocent of any extensive technical knowledge of the "laws" of economics as accepted at the time, they would doubtless have indorsed the pronouncements of the "Manchester school." Therefore they dealt in no halfway measures; they condemned *all* combinations in restraint of trade.[1] Competition was to be enforced.

But in the thirty-odd years which had passed before President Wilson went before Congress with his proposals for altering the policy of the government toward trusts, there had been a growing demonstration that the threat of penalties was not sufficient to deter promoters of combinations and that competitive conditions once destroyed, it was an exceedingly difficult matter to restore them. As indicated above, there were even some who had advanced to the position that combinations were not *per se* pernicious, that there were "good" as

[1] Cf. Senator Sherman's remarks, *Congressional Record,* vol. xxi, p. 2462.

well as "bad" trusts, but these notions found no place in the Democratic program. Competition remained the ideal. If its restoration proved difficult in certain cases, then all the more reason for preventing it from falling into such a state that it required restoration. And so prevention became the watchword; the new legislation was to be prophylactic rather than remedial. Moreover, since the Democratic philosophy held that the trusts were creatures of man's ingenuity, not the product of economic evolution, its adherents concluded that the preventive measures should be directed against those instrumentalities which had brought destruction to former competitors of the trusts. Thus such favorite weapons as local price discrimination, tying and exclusive contracts, and holding companies were to be specifically prohibited. To such a program of prevention the trade commission proposed by Republicans and Progressives was a logical adjunct, if not an outright necessity, and therefore we find it included in the Wilson recommendations.

In sum, then, the legislation of 1914 represents a new conception of the trust problem. The trust is no longer an ogre which is to be bludgeoned into submission with the club of a dissolution suit, but rather the result of a number of malignant growths each of which must be cauterized if the body upon which they have fastened is to be restored to health and vigor.

Postponing to later chapters consideration of the extent to which the purposes of the 1914 legislation have been realized, we turn attention next to the series of antitrust and related acts that have been enacted since that year. Chief among them was the Webb-Pomerene Act of 1918. At the time the House was debating the Trade Commission bill, a convention of foreign-trade interests met in Washington (May 27-28, 1914) to discuss the low estate to which that trade had fallen and measures for its revival. As is the common practice of such gatherings, the convention adopted a series of resolutions which were later transmitted to the executive and legislative branches of the federal government. Among them was one urging Congress to "take such action as will facilitate the development of American export trade by removing such disadvantages as may now be imposed by our antitrust laws. . . ."[1] Although a second convention, held in 1915, dispensed with the passage of formal resolutions on the subject, the proceedings show continued interest in it and a desire on the part of the delegates to see legislation enacted which would remove all ground for the existing differences of opinion on the applicability of the Sherman Act to export trade.[2]

Before this second convention took place, the United States Chamber of Commerce had received the report of its committee advocating the legalization of export associations; and the Trade Commission Act authorizing that body to investigate foreign-trade conditions, particularly as they might affect our own trade, had been passed. Some five months later, May, 1915, the Commission began its study. Its full report was not published until December, 1916, but on the basis of a summary of it presented to Congress on May 3, 1916, a bill was introduced by Mr. Webb of North Carolina on June 28 with the purpose of meeting the recommendations of the Commission and the wishes of the exporters.[3]

The primary findings of the Commission were:

"(1) That other nations have marked advantages in foreign trade from superior facilities and more effective organizations.

"(2) That doubt and fear as to legal restrictions prevent Americans from developing equally effective organizations for overseas business and that the foreign trade of American manufacturers and producers, particularly the smaller concerns, suffers in consequence."[4]

On the basis of its findings the Commission recommended that Congress enact declaratory and permissive legislation which would establish the legality of coöperation for export

[1] *Official Report of the National Foreign Trade Convention,* 1914, p. 452.

[2] *Official Report of the Second National Foreign Trade Convention,* 1915, pp. 53-75.

[3] *Congressional Record,* vol. liii, pp. 7285, 10186.

[4] Federal Trade Commission, *Coöperation in American Export Trade,* part i, p. 3.

trade. It recognized, however, the necessity for safeguarding domestic consumers and competing producers and suggested the features of the law as enacted which embody those purposes.

For reasons not made clear in the *Congressional Record* or in committee reports the original draft of the Webb bill (H. R. 16707) was not discussed in Congress. A second bill (H. R. 17350) was introduced on August 8, 1916, and passed on September 2,[1] but the Senate took no action at this session (the first of the 64th Congress). In the next session, although the President had urged its passage in his message and although it was reported out by the Senate committee on interstate commerce, the bill was not discussed in either house.[2] Again it failed to be considered in the short special session of March 5 to 16, 1917, but in the following session (the so-called "first session" of the 65th Congress) a bill (H. R. 2316) was introduced in the House on April 9, 1917, and passed on June 13.[3] The Senate, however, failed to vote on the measure before adjournment, so that it again became necessary for the President to urge its passage in his message of December 4, 1917. Eight days later the bill passed the Senate, but so amended that a conference was necessary. The report of the conference committee was accepted by both houses on April 6, 1918, and the bill was signed by President Wilson on April 10.[4]

Since the purpose of the legislation was to clarify the legal status of combinations for export trade, it was to be expected that it would take the form of a statement of the precise nature of the associations which should be permitted and of their exact relation to the antitrust statutes. And along these lines, with the addition of an introductory section defining the meaning of foreign and domestic trade for the purposes at hand, the bill was drafted. Interestingly enough, the definition of "export trade" as formulated and passed by the House in 1916 would have largely defeated those purposes,

[1] *Congressional Record,* vol. liii, pp. 12339, 13732.

[2] *Ibid.,* vol. liv, pp. 17,3406.

[3] *Ibid.,* vol. lv, pp. 502, 3585.

[4] *Ibid.,* vol. lvi, pp. 20, 186, 4698, 4724, 4999.

for it prohibited the associations organized under the act from "trading in or marketing within the United States or any Territory thereof" any goods, wares, or merchandise. As the friends of the measure pointed out, the language might logically be interpreted to prevent an association from buying the very commodities it was organized to export. The definition as finally phrased states that "the words 'export trade' shall not be deemed to include the production, manufacture, or selling for consumption or for resale, within the United States or any Territory thereof, of such goods, wares, or merchandise, or any act in the course of such production, manufacture, or selling for consumption or resale," thus effecting what was doubtless the original intent of Congress.

The second section of the bill as passed in 1916 was also so phrased as to defeat its own objectives. The section purported to free export associations from the restraints of the Sherman Act, but it concluded with the words "provided such association, agreement, or act is not in restraint of trade within the United States, *and does not restrain the export trade of the United States.*" Since the removal of the restraints which the law was believed to impose on export trade was the primary design of the measure, it was necessary to eliminate the words italicized above. As the law stands they have been supplanted by the expression "and is not in restraint of the export trade of any domestic competitor of such association," to which was added the proviso: "That such association does not, either in the United States or elsewhere, enter into any agreement, understanding, or conspiracy, or do any act which artificially or intentionally enhances or depresses prices within the United States of commodities of the class exported by such association or which substantially lessens competition within the United States or otherwise restrains trade therein." As is obvious from their phraseology these provisos were calculated to protect the interests which the Federal Trade Commission had insisted must be protected—*viz.,* those of domestic consumers and of competitors of the export associations.

Sections 3 and 4 of the law emerged from the legislative hopper in exactly the form in which they were first passed by the House in September of 1916. The former exempts export associations from the prohibitions of Section 7 of the Clayton Act on corporate stockownership "unless the effect of such ownership or acquisition [of stock or other capital] may be to restrain trade or substantially lessen competition within the United States." The fourth section extends the prohibition of unfair methods of competition contained in Section 5 of the Federal Trade Commission law "to unfair methods of competition used in export trade against competitors engaged in export trade, even though the acts constituting such unfair methods are done without the territorial jurisdiction of the United States."

The fifth and final section of the bill as first accepted by the House required associations to file with the Federal Trade Commission certain statements concerning their stockholders, officers, places of business, contracts, agreements, and understandings with any foreign or domestic associations in regard to the conduct of or practices in foreign trade, and to keep this information up to date by means of annual reports. Penalties of loss of privileges under Sections 2 and 3 and of $100 a day were provided for failure to file the reports on time. The amendments subsequently adopted slightly altered the phraseology requiring reports on business practices and relations to other associations, so that associations now report only "such information as the Commission may require" on these details, and added a lengthy paragraph authorizing the Commission to take steps against any association which it has "reason to believe" is violating the law.

On the face of it the Webb Act is a direct reversal for a large and growing part of American business of a policy of generations' standing. In terms the act specifically exempts export trade from the limitations of the Sherman law and a part of the Clayton law. Consequently, it may be interpreted as another aspect of that changing conception of the "trust problem" which we pointed out above, or as an application to export business by legislative action of the "rule of reason." An examination of the Congressional discussions of the bill fails to convince us, however, that either of these was the driving motive that secured for it such large majorities in both houses. All the emphasis was laid upon the alleged failure of our foreign trade to grow as rapidly as did that of some other countries, notably England and Germany, upon the passive and active encouragement by other governments of their foreign traders, and upon the handicaps which American exporters were consequently forced to overcome in meeting as individuals the combinations of their foreign competitors. It was freely granted that such combinations as those in the oil, steel, and harvester industries were not in need of the governmental aid proposed, since they had done very well for themselves in foreign marts, but there was much talk of the quite different status of the little fellows. The peruser of the *Congressional Record* finds his enthusiasm for these legislative defenders of the weak somewhat cooled, however, by the interchange between Morgan of Oklahoma and Webb, the author of the bill, on Morgan's proposed amendment limiting the provisions of the act to corporations with a capitalization of $1,000,000 or less. Webb objected that the amendment would "let the big fellows control." Morgan then asked if Webb would consent to any limitation, to which the latter replied: "I do not know that I would consent to any." [1]

In truth, the more the debates are studied the more clearly is revealed the fact that the dominating philosophy, if it may be called that, in the minds of most of the Congressmen who voted for the measure, was somewhat of a mixture of those of two groups supposedly long defunct: the mercantilists and the Know-Nothing party. Again we are indebted to the author of the bill for an outspoken presentation of this attitude. In discussing a possible combination of steel interests, including the United States Steel Corporation and the independents, he said: "If that combination will enable them to get a better price from foreigners than they get now, I want them to get it, just so it does not affect prices in the United States"; and a little later: "Would the gentleman object to the copper producers of this country getting as much from the foreign buyer as they get from our own people? I would like to see them

[1] *Congressional Record,* vol. liii, p. 13728.

get a little more as far as I am concerned."[1] The remarks of some of those opposed to the measure are equally illuminating. Representative Huddleston considered the bill dangerous since he held it just as pernicious for men to combine to purchase from producers as to sell to consumers. "It is true we care nothing about the exploitation of foreign peoples by our own people who have something to sell. However, we should have some regard for our producers. . . ."[2]

In the remarks of the few opponents of the measure we find some biting commentaries on the attitude just discussed. If combinations for private monopoly operating in the United States are "indefensible and intolerable," what, asked Representative Buchanan, is the justification for legalizing them to prey on foreigners? In his opinion a reason advanced in the committee report for the passage of the bill—*viz.*, that other governments encouraged and fostered such organizations as it proposed—was the finest reason for defeating it; he considered the policy the chief cause of the World War.[3] Representative Mondell of Wyoming pointed out that by the act of February 12, 1913, the Congress had made it "a felony for the foreigner to do the thing in our market which we now propose to allow the American to do in the foreign market," and insisted that the measure should be defeated so that American exporters might go into foreign markets "with clean hands."[4] Senator Reed of Missouri agreed with these sentiments when he stated that combinations involve moral issues, and that there are no geographical boundaries known to such issues. Senator Borah thought that if trusts were a good thing in foreign trade, they should be recognized as such at home.[5]

Other arguments, none of them of great importance, were advanced by the opponents of the bill, such as the contentions

[1] *Congressional Record,* vol. liii, pp. 13538, 13539.

[2] *Ibid.,* p. 13707.

[3] *Ibid.,* vol. liii, pp. 13681, 13685.

[4] *Ibid.,* p. 13703. The act referred to is an amendment to the Wilson tariff act of 1894, which made combinations of importers in restraint of trade illegal. The importance of the 1913 amendment lay really in the expansion of the power of the government to seize articles imported in violation of the act of 1894.

[5] *Ibid.,* vol. lvi, pp. 72, 71.

that the Democrats had "sold out" to "big business" in order to insure themselves another four years in power,[1] that the bill would make the Sherman law a piece of class legislation,[2] and that the figures on our foreign commerce did not, properly interpreted, lend themselves to the idea that our exporters were being crippled by the lack of such a law as that proposed.[3]

To our minds the most important issue presented by this legislation relates to its effect on our international relations. By enacting it we have permitted our business men to join forces, supported by the government, in the attempt to wrest foreign markets from similarly combined and similarly supported groups of foreign business men. No one can doubt that it was the suspicion and hostility resulting from such struggles for international markets among European countries that constituted one of the important causes of the World War. If the Webb-Pomerene Act is to cause our business men to become involved in new and more acrimonious struggles of this type, we may well hesitate to commend it as a progressive and useful piece of legislation. But there is another possible and we believe more probable result of the increased participation in foreign trade that is encouraged by this law. By bringing able representatives of the business groups of different countries together it may foster coöperation across national boundaries rather than intensify national hatreds. Signs are not lacking that business men are increasingly aware of the disastrous results of destructive international competition as they long have been as regards competition within each country. They are finding ways of avoiding the wastes and losses which this entails in the organization of international combinations or cartels, that control competition in the common interest and insure all participants a fair share in the world's trade. Some of the foreign trade associations authorized by the Webb-Pomerene Act appear already to have arrived at understandings with the international cartels

[1] *Congressional Record,* vol. liii, p. 13678.
[2] *Ibid.,* vol. lvi, p. 72.
[3] *Ibid.,* pp. 72, 111, 117.

in their fields. Along this line the measure may prove helpful to the promotion of that international understanding and good will indispensable to the maintenance of future world peace. It presents, however, the difficult problem of the regulation of international cartels for the protection of consumers, a topic considered in Chapter XXVI.

A second measure important in the history of our antitrust legislation that derived its immediate impetus from war emergencies was the Shipping Act of 1916. Although this law was approved before the Webb-Pomerene Act, we have deviated from our chronological treatment here in order to secure a more logical arrangement. In earlier periods, particularly in the days of the "clipper" ships, the American merchant marine had held its place with the best in the world, but for some time before the outbreak of war in 1914 we had been largely dependent upon ships of foreign registry to do our carrying. Since most of these vessels were owned by nationals of one of the belligerent powers, and since the extraordinary demands of war were sure to bring about a severe shortage in shipping, it was realized that the adequate protection of our interests required that shipbuilding be undertaken on a large scale. As early as August 24, 1914, a bill was introduced in the House of Representatives to authorize the United States, acting through a shipping board, to subscribe to the capital stock of a corporation which should purchase, equip, and maintain vessels to operate in foreign trade. This was the beginning of the measure that became law in 1916.

But for the section of the act of 1916 most important to us here, basic causes are to be found not in war emergencies, but in complaints by shippers against a so-called "shipping trust." The seriousness of these complaints may be judged from the fact that in several instances suits of a private character alleging violations of the Sherman Act had been filed, that the federal Department of Justice had instituted other suits of a similar nature, and that the House of Representatives began in 1912 an investigation of combinations of steamship companies. The cases involving the use of the usual type of conference, combination or agreement among water carriers brought by the Department of Justice against the Hamburg-American Packet Company, the Prince Line, the American-Asiatic Steamship Company, and others became moot because the arrangements were dissolved by the outbreak of the war. The lower federal court that heard them had as a matter of fact ruled that the use of "fighting ships" was illegal,[1] that a contract apportioning the steerage-passenger business among parties to the contract and pooling the receipts from such business was also illegal,[2] but that "an agreement between all the shipowners engaged in the same trade as to the number of vessels each should operate, the dates of sailings, exchange of freight between lines, and rates of freight, made for the purpose of assuring shippers regular sailings and affording them a fair rate so that they might meet the competition of trade from other countries, is not in itself an unreasonable restraint of trade contrary to the Sherman Anti-Trust Act."[3] Obviously, the net effect of these decisions was to permit many activities of a coöperative nature. The Supreme Court, however, refused to consider any of these cases on their merits, for the reason given above, so that it cannot be stated with certainty what the attitude of that tribunal was on such agreements.[4]

The Congressional investigation previously mentioned extended over a period of nearly two years. Its proceedings and report comprise a most detailed account of the operations of the alleged shipping trust in addition to information on market areas, trade routes, etc. In the judgment of the committee many of the provisions of the agreements under which the companies operated were unobjectionable, and consequently its report recommended regulation of the existing combinations rather than their destruction.[5] A bill to regulate carriers by water engaged in the foreign and interstate commerce of

[1] 216 Fed. 971 (1914).

[2] 200 Fed. 806 (1911).

[3] 220 Fed. 230 (1915).

[4] 239 U. S. 466 (1916); 242 U. S. 537 (1917).

[5] *Proceedings of the Committee on the Merchant Marine and Fisheries in the Investigation of Shipping Combinations, under House Resolution* 587, vol. iv, pp. 415-424. Reprinted in the *Annals of the American Academy of Political and Social Science,* September, 1914, p. 255 *et seq.*

the United States was introduced by J. W. Alexander, chairman of the investigating committee, on June 18, 1914.[1] Since the pressure of legislation prevented consideration of the bill in 1914, it was reintroduced on December 6, 1915. Meanwhile, on August 24 and September 4, 1914, there had been introduced shipping bills authorizing the United States to subscribe to the capital stock of a corporation which should purchase, construct, equip, maintain, and operate merchant vessels in the foreign trade of the United States. Immediately the emphasis of the discussions on shipping both in and out of Congress shifted from the regulation of the shipping combinations to the issue of "government ownership" of the merchant marine. During its consideration of the various proposals on shipping before it the House committee on the merchant marine and fisheries fused them into a single bill which finally became a law on September 7, as the Shipping Act of 1916.[2] The major provisions of the new law created a United States Shipping Board whose function was to encourage, develop, and create a naval auxiliary, a naval reserve, and a merchant marine for the United States; delegated to the Board powers deemed ample for attaining its purposes; and established a set of regulations for the control of carriers by water.

The principles of regulation adopted were obviously taken from those established in previous legislation. From the Interstate Commerce Act of 1887, with amendments, were borrowed prohibitions of discriminations against persons, localities, and commodities, and requirements of just and reasonable rates. As the Clayton Act included prohibitions of particularly notorious implements of oppression such as local price-cutting and tying contracts, so the Shipping Act prohibited the use of deferred rebates and fighting ships. But for our purposes the most important section is that relating to the antitrust laws. By the terms of this section all agreements among shipping lines concerning traffic, rates, earnings, number and character of sailings, etc., existing at the time of the creation of the Shipping Board were declared to be legal until

[1] H. R. 17328, 63d Congress, 2d Session.

[2] *Congressional Record,* vol. liii, pp. 8077, 8083.

such time as they might be disapproved by the board. Copies of such agreements were required to be filed with the board which might cancel, disapprove, or modify any it considered discriminatory or otherwise violative of the act of 1916. All agreements lawful under this section were specifically exempted from the Sherman Act and from the antitrust sections of the Wilson Tariff Act of 1894.[1] Here, too, then, the Congress saw fit to forswear in a degree its allegiance to the principles of *laissez faire* as so broadly proclaimed in 1890. And as time went on the developments in our foreign trade prompted yet another modification of those principles.

In the first place, the war-time demand for shipping amply justified the prophecies of its extent, in fact, it at times so greatly exceeded the supply that fabulous prices were paid for vessels that in the spring of 1914 were deemed ready for the scrap heap. But with the return of peace the reaction was, if anything, more violent. Ships were worth little or nothing because the demand for their services was relatively so meager. In this situation every effort was made to secure for American vessels as large a proportion of the business as possible. And in these efforts it was forcibly brought to the attention of all interested that one bar to the maintenance and further development of our merchant marine and our foreign trade was the state of our marine insurance companies. Before a Congressional investigating committee of 1919 it was demonstrated that foreign, and particularly British, concerns were doing the greater part of this business. The reasons for this situation, in addition to the advantages of an earlier beginning, were found to be broader reinsurance facilities, freedom to combine, permission to write various types of insurance, smaller overhead costs, lower taxes, and some others of less importance. The committee found an "appalling absence of such favorable factors" to American underwriters. On the contrary, the American companies were practically without reinsurance facilities, were prohibited from combining and from writing a number of types of business, and suffered from excessive taxes collected on gross premiums rather

[1] *U. S. Statutes at Large,* vol. xxxix, part 1, pp. 728-738.

than on net profits. Underlying the unfavorable conditions and fundamental to them were the facts that the insurance companies were chartered by the states, and that these tended to view marine insurance as a purely state matter rather than the national institution it is.[1]

Proposals for alleviating the ills of American marine insurance before the Congressional committee included government insurance, a model law for the District of Columbia which it was hoped other charter-granting bodies would be willing (or forced) to follow, and legislation permitting private concerns to operate in a pool or association. At this time nothing was done with respect to the first two proposals, but the last was included in the Merchant Marine Act of June 5, 1920. The primary purpose of this voluminous measure was to get the federal government out of the shipping business, but it likewise included some changes in the organization and functions of the Shipping Board, an amendment to the section of the law of 1916 dealing with unfair practices, and numerous detailed provisions on a wide variety of shipping matters. Section 29, the one of chief interest here, provides that nothing contained in the "antitrust laws" as designated in Section 1 of the Clayton Act "shall be construed as declaring illegal an association entered into by marine insurance companies for the following purposes: To transact a marine insurance and reinsurance business in the United States and in foreign countries and to reinsure or otherwise apportion among its membership the risks undertaken by such association or any of the component members." [2]

Under the permissive language just quoted there were created three merchant-marine syndicates designated A, B, and C. Syndicate A was purely a service syndicate which undertook to perform for the Shipping Board at cost and for others on "reasonable terms" a maintenance, inspection, and loss survey service. Syndicate B was to engage in hull insurance, but was confined in membership to American companies and in its operations to steel ships sold or to be sold by the Ship-

[1] *Economic World,* March 16, 1920, p. 344 *et seq.*

[2] *U. S. Statutes at Large,* vol. xli, part. 1, p. 1000.

ping Board. Syndicate C was also engaged in hull insurance, but was to the extent of a one-third underwriting interest open to foreign admitted insurance corporations and was to insure American steel ocean-going steamships owned privately.[1]

Apparently, however, these limitations on the principles of free competition were not adequate for the purposes in hand, for the House committee on the merchant marine and fisheries continued to investigate and to suggest further changes. In 1922 these recommendations bore fruit in the "Act to regulate marine insurance in the District of Columbia and for other purposes," described by its friends as the "model" law which all the states should hasten to copy. The chief features of the act were the substitution of taxation on net profits for taxation on premiums, the expansion of reinsurance facilities, the removal of certain limitations on the financial powers of marine insurance companies that had hampered their operations in foreign fields, and the permission to such companies to write practically any kind of insurance except life and corporate bonding.[2]

In describing the insurance measures supplementing the Shipping Act of 1916 we have passed over the more important railroad and telephone legislation of this same period. Section 5 of the Transportation Act of February 28, 1920, definitely authorized the railroads engaged in interstate commerce to combine, subject to the approval of the Interstate Commerce Commission. The Commission was directed to prepare a comprehensive plan for the consolidation of the railroad lines of the country into a limited number of systems, and, while it was not given power to require the railroads to consolidate, any railroad consolidation authorized by it was expressly "removed from the operation of the antitrust laws." Thus since 1920 the governmental policy toward the railroads has been unequivocally one of regulated combination rather than of enforced competition.

[1] *Economic World,* July 24, 1920, p. 129; February 19, 1921, p. 278.

[2] *U. S. Statutes at Large,* vol. xlii, part 1, p. 401 *et seq.* Cf. *Economic World,* May 27, 1922, p. 741.

An amendment added to the Interstate Commerce Act on June 10, 1921, similarly authorized, with the sanction of the Commission, the consolidation of telephone companies. The act expressly declares that "if the Commission finds that the proposed consolidation will be of advantage to the persons to whom service is to be rendered and in the public interest it shall certify to that effect, and thereafter any act or acts of Congress making the proposed transaction unlawful, shall not apply."

The next important federal legislation on trusts with which we are concerned is the Packers and Stockyards Act of 1921. For many years there had been agitation in and out of Congress for specific regulation of the packing industry, an agitation which received fresh impetus from the publication of the Federal Trade Commission's report on the packers in 1918-1920. Hearings and debates on proposed bills dragged along for more than three years. On August 15, 1921, the form of the measure finally agreed upon received the President's signature, but it bore little resemblance to earlier bills. The net effect of the alterations was to make the law less drastic than the original Sims bill of 1918 which had attempted to establish government ownership and operation of stockyards, storage facilities, branch houses, and refrigerator cars, and a federal license requirement for packers and livestock commission men.[1]

Title I of the law consists of definitions. Title II declares it unlawful for any packer to engage in unfair and deceptive practices, to apportion the supply of any article among other packers in restraint of commerce, to manipulate or control prices, to create a monopoly, and to conspire with others to do any of the aforementioned illegal acts. The administration of the law is vested in the Secretary of Agriculture. When he has "reason to believe" the law is being disregarded it is his duty to proceed against the offenders according to a procedure very similar to that laid down for the Federal Trade Commission—*i.e.*, by complaint, hearing, and cease-and-desist order. The packer may appeal to a circuit court of appeals

[1] *Congressional Record*, vol. lvii, p. 280; vol. lxi, p. 5864.

and the Supreme Court may subsequently grant *certiorari;* otherwise, the order of the Secretary of Agriculture is final. Title III is concerned with stockyards, market agencies for dealing in livestock or providing stockyard services, and dealers. By it persons engaged in operating stockyards or market agencies or as dealers are required to register with the Secretary of Agriculture and to furnish him with detailed statements of the services rendered and the charges therefor. These charges must be reasonable and non-discriminatory. The most significant section of Title IV is that by which the Federal Trade Commission is deprived of any jurisdiction over packers, stockyards, etc. The reason given for conferring this authority upon the Secretary of Agriculture was stated in the House committee report as resting upon a desire to prevent the "necessity of creating new commissions, bureaus, etc., duplicating existing machinery." [1] Mr. McLaughlin of Nebraska, a member of the committee, amplified this statement on the floor of the House: " . . . the Secretary of Agriculture was finally agreed upon mainly because of the fact that the department now has in the Bureau of Markets, the Bureau of Animal Husbandry, and the Pure Food Inspection Department scores of employees on the ground at the several market centers who can be of material assistance to the Secretary in gathering the information needed to insure intelligent action by him in exercising his supervisory relationship. In other words, it is the thought of the committee that the lodging of the supervisory power with the Secretary of Agriculture will make for both economy and efficiency." [2]

The last significant restriction upon the scope of the anti-trust acts was made in favor of a group for whom attempts to grant exemption from the Sherman law were made in 1890 —*viz.,* agricultural producers. It will be recalled that Senator Sherman's amendment to his own bill granting such exemption was rejected by the committee on the judiciary, and that Congress accepted the committee's report without change. These actions have been generally interpreted as indicating

[1] House Report, No. 77, 67th Congress, 1st Session.

[2] *Congressional Record,* vol. lxi, p. 1878.

the intent of Congress to grant no exceptions. In 1914, however, Section 6 of the Clayton Act provided that "nothing contained in the antitrust laws shall be construed to forbid the existence and operation of labor, agricultural, or horticultural organizations, instituted for the purposes of mutual help, and not having capital stock or conducted for profit, or to forbid or restrain individual members of such organizations from lawfully carrying out the legitimate objects thereof; nor shall such organizations, or the members thereof, be held or construed to be illegal combinations or conspiracies in restraint of trade, under the antitrust laws." Furthermore, since 1914 there has been included in the appropriation for the enforcement of the antitrust acts the proviso that no part of it should be used to prosecute "producers of farm products and associations of farmers who coöperate and organize in an effort to and for the purpose to obtain and maintain a fair and reasonable price for their products."

But the privileges granted by these enactments proved far from satisfactory either to trade unionists or to the farmers' organizations. Apparently the law went no further than to permit the existence of the organizations; many activities they wished to carry on were prohibited.[1] Consequently, there was renewed agitation by the farm bloc in Congress for clarification of the position of the agricultural associations, and although the attempts of Senator Capper and Representative Hersman in 1919 to secure the total exemption of such organizations died in committee, the agitation continued until the bloc secured a law which it considered satisfactory.

This new "act to authorize associations of producers of agricultural products," approved February 18, 1922, and commonly referred to as the Capper-Volstead Act, stands on the statute-books in almost the exact language in which it was introduced. It provides that agricultural producers such as farmers, dairymen, fruit-growers and others may act together in associations in "collectively processing, preparing for market, handling and marketing in interstate and foreign com-

[1] Cf. the decisions in Duplex *v.* Deering, 254 U. S. 443 (1921); and U. S. *v.* King, 229 Fed. 275 (1915); 250 Fed. 908 (1916).

merce," their products. These associations may be corporate or otherwise, with or without capital stock. They are permitted to have common marketing agencies and to make the necessary contracts and agreements to effect their purposes. Two qualifications of a restrictive character provide that associations must be conducted for the mutual benefit of their members and that they shall not deal in the products of non-members to an amount greater in value than that of members. It is further provided that associations must conform to one or both of the following requirements: first, that no member is allowed more than one vote because of the amount of his stock or membership capital; second, that there shall be no dividends on stock or membership capital in excess of 8 per cent per annum.

As in the Packers and Stockyards Act, the Secretary of Agriculture is given supervisory power. The only occasion for the exercise of this power, however, is that in which he has reason to believe that one of these associations is monopolizing or restraining trade "to such an extent that the price of any agricultural product is unduly enhanced by reason thereof." In such cases he is to issue a complaint and, if necessary, a cease-and-desist order. Appeals may be made to a district court which may affirm, modify, or set aside the order, or enter such other decree as the court may consider equitable.[1]

The only significant differences between the law as outlined and the original bill are the additions to the law providing that the associations may have marketing agencies in common and that they must not handle an excessive quantity of the products of non-members. Other amendments included were chiefly of a verbal character.[2] Two important amendments were rejected. One provided that the supervisory power over these associations be vested in the Federal Trade Commission; the other that nothing in the bill should be deemed to authorize the creation of or attempt to create a monopoly or to exempt a producers' association from proceedings under the unfair-methods-of-competition section of the Federal

[1] *U. S. Statutes at Large,* vol. xlii, part 1, pp. 388, 389.

[2] Cf. the original bill in *Congressional Record,* vol. lix, pp. 7849-7850.

Trade Commission Act. In both cases the action taken represented some distrust of the Trade Commission, but in the second it rested primarily on the feeling that the amendment "cut the heart out" of the legislation.[1]

Four years later the already broad powers granted to associations of agricultural producers were further amplified in the coöperative marketing act of 1926. Section 5 of this law provides that persons in such associations "may acquire, exchange, interpret, and disseminate past, present, and prospective crop, market, statistical, economic, and other similar information by direct exchange between such persons, and/or such associations or federation thereof, and/or by and through a common agent created or selected by them."[2] The language of the section was obviously drafted to permit activities similar to those of "open-price" associations which had been attacked as violative of the Sherman Act.[3]

The intent of the greater part of the special legislation described in this chapter is to permit group activities that without such legislation might be subject to antitrust-act penalties. In the Radio Act of 1927 (as amended in 1928), however, Congress in effect extended those penalties. Section 13 of that statute directs the Radio Commission to refuse a broadcasting station license or a permit for the construction of a station to any person, firm, or corporation which has been finally adjudged guilty by a federal court of unlawfully monopolizing or attempting to monopolize radio communication or of using unfair methods of competition. Section 15 provides that all federal laws relating to unlawful monopolies and restraints are applicable to the manufacture of and trade in radio apparatus and to interstate or foreign radio communication. Section 17 prohibits concerns engaged for hire in transmitting or receiving energy, communications, or signals by radio from in any way owning, controlling, or operating any cable, telegraph, or telephone system between any part of the United States and its possessions and a foreign country, and

[1] *Congressional Record,* vol. lxii, pp. 2120, 2121, 2172, 2218, 2225, 2270.

[2] *U. S. Statutes at Large,* vol. xliv, part 2, p. 803.

[3] Cf. p. 453 *et seq., infra,* for a discussion of these cases.

from owning or controlling any part of the stock or assets of such a system if in either case the purpose and/or effect is substantially to lessen competition or restrain commerce or tend to create monopoly in any line of commerce. The telephone or telegraph companies are likewise prohibited from acquiring, controlling, etc., any radio stations or radio transmission systems under similar qualifications.

As indicated in our discussions of the various laws, we are inclined to believe that in general the legislation of 1914 and subsequent years relating to trusts has been of a more realistic character than that of an earlier period. But in making final evaluations of such statutes the most important evidence is found in the interpretation of them by the courts and in the results of the attempts to enforce them. In preceding chapters we have presented a portion of this evidence; in those immediately following we continue it.

CHAPTER XXI

JUDICIAL INTERPRETATION OF THE ANTITRUST ACTS, 1915-1929

In the period covered in this and the following chapter we are dealing with more than one law. Partly for this reason we have abandoned the chronological order of treatment in favor of the topical method.

Of the Sherman Act cases, one of the most important concluded during this period was that involving the National Cash Register Company. As is true of a number of the cases since the enunciation of the rule of reason, it derives its significance from other factors than that of construction of the statute. The National Cash Register established a record in its methods of destroying competition which was even more reprehensible than those of the Standard Oil and American Tobacco trusts. Moreover, there can be no doubt that these devices were deliberately planned, since the Cash Register Company boasted of their success through the medium of lists of competitors forced out of business by them. One such list, published and distributed in January, 1910, claimed that "Within the past fifteen years, 158 cash register companies have been organized to compete with the National Cash Register Company. Of these, 153 have failed in business. Their combined capital was $5,735,000. Their combined loss was $1,970,000. According to the sworn affidavits of its officers the Boston Cash Register Company alone lost $192,750.08." [1] Further evidence of the plane upon which this trust carried on its business may be found in its maintenance at its Dayton, Ohio, factory of a room, referred to as the "Grave Yard," in which the registers of defunct competitors were displayed, each labeled with the name of the competitor, the date upon

[1] Quoted by W. H. S. Stevens, *Quarterly Journal of Economics*, vol. xxvi, p. 629.

which it had "died," the sum lost, and similar data. Visitors to the plant, particularly other manufacturers, were shown through this room.

Such practices, pursued unremittingly from the organization of the company in 1882, were a primary cause of the institution of a criminal suit under the Sherman Act in 1893, but this was allowed to lapse because the complaining witness became a member of the combination! [1]

For nearly twenty years the trust continued to pursue its course unmolested and built up its business so that by the time a second indictment was brought against its officers in 1912 it had for some time controlled 95 per cent of the trade in cash registers in the United States.[2] The federal grand jury charged the defendants with bribing employees of competitors, of common carriers, and of telegraph and telephone companies to reveal to them business secrets of competitors; with requiring all National sales agents to spy upon competitors and to obstruct and interfere with such competitors in every way, particularly by making false statements to prospective purchasers on the merits of competitors' machines, by inducing customers of competitors to break their contracts with them by the offer of National machines below cost, and by other means, and by secretly weakening, destroying, or removing parts of the mechanism of competitors' machines actually in use; with making "knocker" machines which closely imitated a competitor's, selling them for a time until their intentionally faulty mechanism had discredited said competing machine, and then withdrawing the "knocker"; with maintaining "bogus" independent concerns; with falsely threatening patent suits on foundationless claims of patent infringements; and with bribing employees and customers of competitors to leave the competitors for the employ of the National or to transfer their trade to it. Although the foregoing by no means exhausts the list of unfair methods, further detail seems unnecessary. If we may rely upon the

[1] 55 Fed. 605 (1893); 59 Fed. 280 (1894); *Decrees and Judgments in Federal Anti-Trust Cases,* p. 680.

[2] 201 Fed. 699 (1912).

grand jury which drew up the indictment, the compilation of a complete list is impossible, since the means used "were so numerous in kind and so shifting in character."[1]

A demurrer to this indictment was overruled, all of the defendants except one were convicted, sentence on one was deferred, and the other twenty-seven were sentenced to pay the cost of their trials and to serve nine months to one year in jail. The sentence of Mr. Patterson, the president, carried penalties of one year in jail and a fine of $5,000, plus costs.[2] The Sixth Circuit Court of Appeals, however, reversed the judgment on extremely technical grounds and remanded the case to the lower court for retrial.[3] The government applied to the Supreme Court for a review of the case, but was refused.[4]

In the meantime the National Cash Register Company had decided not to fight the civil action instituted against it at about the same time its officers had been indicted, and consequently entered into a consent decree on February 1, 1916. By the terms of that decree the company and its officers were adjudged guilty of violations of Sections 1 and 2 of the Sherman Act and were enjoined from the continued use of sixteen methods of unfair competition, including most of those listed above and some others. They were furthermore assessed the costs of the suit. The court retained jurisdiction of the case for the purpose of enforcing the decree.[5]

Comment upon such an outcome in this case is almost superfluous, but we cannot refrain from the statement that a more outrageously inadequate penalty is hard to conceive. If ever a group of lawbreakers richly deserved severe punishment for violating the antitrust acts, this one certainly did. Instead its members were left, on their promise to be good, in possession of 95 per cent of the trade in their product to

[1] 201 Fed. 704 (1912).

[2] 201 Fed. 697 (1912); 205 Fed. 292 (1913); *Decrees and Judgments in Federal Anti-Trust Cases*, p. 795.

[3] 222 Fed. 599 (1915).

[4] 238 U. S. 635 (1915).

[5] *Decrees and Judgments in Federal Anti-Trust Cases*, p. 315.

enjoy undisturbed the proceeds of thirty years of commercial piracy.

In justice to the company, however, it should be noted that the available evidence indicates that in the main the promise made in 1916 has been observed. Some years ago the Remington Cash Register Company complained that the National had reverted to its old methods, and at least partly on the basis of these representations the Federal Trade Commission instituted proceedings against the National.[1] Moreover, the Department of Justice brought suit in 1925, charging 92 sales agents of the company and others with violations of the decree of 1916. This suit dragged on until November 12, 1928, when *one* of the defendants was held guilty. On September 28, 1927, the charges against seventy defendants were dismissed; on September 24, 1928, charges against twenty others were dismissed, and on November 12, 1928, the ninety-first defendant went free.[2] The presiding judge made the following comment: "It seems highly reprehensible that any department of the Government should so needlessly and without that thorough investigation which the seriousness of the situation demanded, subject the defendants to groundless prosecution and thus jeopardize the positions, reputations, and good names of those individuals." [3] Since the complaint of the Trade Commission had been based on the same evidence, it was dismissed on December 15, 1928.

The case of the American Can Trust, determined by the District Court of Maryland about the time the consent decree in the Cash Register case was entered, is interesting as foreshadowing the policy which the Supreme Court subsequently adopted in the steel case. The American Can Company was a combination of ninety-five plants producing about 90 per

[1] *Annual Report,* 1926, pp. 144, 145. The period covered by these annual reports is the same as that of the federal government's fiscal year, July 1 to June 30. Hereafter references in the text to a report for any stated year will be understood to mean the year ending June 30 of that year.

[2] *The Federal Antitrust Laws with Amendments,* pp. 197, 198. This publication was issued by the Department of Justice as of November 30, 1928.

[3] *New York Times,* November 13, 1928. Cf. the conclusion in the National Industrial Conference's Board volume, *Mergers and the Law,* p. 59, that the company underwent "a change of heart."

cent of the tin cans being made in the United States in 1901. Since its promoters were largely interested in the sheet-steel combine, the source of "raw" material for cans, they were easily able to force former competitors into the trust. However, the efforts of the combine to extort too great profits resulted in the development of a degree of competition that by the time the government filed its suit had reduced the trust's control to about 50 per cent of the total. Moreover, certain unfair competitive methods used in the first years of the company's history had been abandoned.

On the record presented the court held "that the organization and early methods of defendant were intended and calculated to restrain competition in the manufacture and sale of cans, and to monopolize the same, and were clearly illegal as in violation of Sherman Anti-Trust Act . . . ; that while its large capital and business make it a potential instrument which may be used to restrain or monopolize a part of the commerce among the States, so long as no attempt is being made at present to so use them, and in view of the fact that former conditions cannot be restored, and that under its present methods by reason of its widespread business packers are enabled to make more beneficial contracts for the purchase of cans for future use, both from it and its competitors, than ever before, no public interest would be served by its dissolution, but that such interest would be better served by permitting the suit to stand open for such future action as changed conditions may require." [1]

The government was not satisfied with this judgment and requested a dissolution, but the court refused,[2] entered a decree in which it reiterated the opinion that a dissolution would be inexpedient, and retained jurisdiction of the case so that it might order dissolution later if it proved to be necessary.[3] The government's appeal to the Supreme Court was postponed until the termination of the war. On June 6

[1] 230 Fed. 859, 860 (1916). Quotation from syllabus of case.

[2] 234 Fed. 1019 (1916).

[3] *Decrees and Judgments in Federal Anti-Trust Cases,* p. 525.

1921, the case was dismissed on motion of the Solicitor General of the United States.[1] Though no reason was stated, it is highly probable that the decision in the steel case prompted this action.

In March, 1918, the Supreme Court applied the rule of reason to the so-called "Call" rule of the Chicago Board of Trade. As is well known, this organization is the center through which most of the trading in grain in the Chicago market is done. The standard forms of trading are:

1. "Spot" sales of grain already in Chicago in cars or in elevators and available for delivery by an order on the railroad company or by transfer of a warehouse receipt;
2. "Future" sales for delivery at some later date;
3. "To arrive" sales—that is, agreements to deliver on arrival grain already in transit to Chicago or to be shipped there within a specified time.

Dealing in "spots" and "futures" takes place during the regular sessions of the board between 9:30 A.M. and 1:15 P.M. "To arrive" sales are made at a special session termed the "Call" which begins immediately after the close of the regular session and usually lasts a half-hour or less. Purchases of grain "to arrive" are made chiefly from country dealers and farmers, by telegraph and telephone to some extent, but primarily by letters dispatched in the afternoon after the "Call" session. Such offers to buy must be accepted by 9:30 of the following morning.

In 1906 the Board of Trade adopted the "Call" rule, by which members were forbidden to offer between the close of the "Call" and the beginning of the next business day for grain "to arrive" any other price than the final bid made at the close of the "Call." Seven years later the federal government attacked this rule as an illegal restraint of trade. In the opinion of Justice Brandeis, speaking for the Supreme Court, the government's case "rested upon the bald proposition, that a rule or agreement by which men occupying positions of strength in any branch of trade, fixed prices at which they would buy or sell during an important part of the busi-

[1] 256 U. S. 706 (1921).

ness day, is an illegal restraint of trade under the Anti-Trust Law." But in the opinion of the court "the legality of an agreement or regulation cannot be determined by so simple a test, as whether it restrains competition. Every agreement concerning trade, every regulation of trade, restrains. To bind, to restrain, is of their very essence. The true test of legality is whether the restraint imposed is such as merely regulates and perhaps thereby promotes competition or whether it is such as may suppress or even destroy competition."[1] In order to determine into which of the suggested categories this particular restraint fell, the court emphasized the necessity of ascertaining all the pertinent facts. For this reason it criticized the district court for excluding certain evidence, but decided that "the evidence admitted makes it clear that the rule was a reasonable regulation of business consistent with the provisions of the Anti-Trust Law."[2] An examination of the list of improvements in grain-market conditions brought about by the rule as cited in the opinion convinces us that the operation of the rule was salutary.

Chronologically, the next Supreme Court decisions important for our purposes are those in the United Shoe Machinery and United States Steel Corporation cases. Since both the facts and the legal aspects of these cases have been previously discussed at length,[3] it is sufficient here to remind our readers of certain generalizations already drawn. In the former case the chief point at issue was the apparent inconsistency of the federal patent and antitrust laws which permitted the Shoe Machinery Company under its rights as a patentee to use leases on its machines which largely defeated the purposes of the Sherman Act. In order to remedy this situation Congress passed the Clayton Act, under which these leases were held illegal. The upshot of the steel decision was to broaden the "rule of reason" into the "rule of business expediency." Comment at the time indicated that the outcome was a profound surprise to many of those who had followed the litigation, and there is ground for the belief that

[1] 246 U. S. 238 (1918).

[2] *Ibid.*, p. 239.

[3] Cf. pp. 297 *et seq.* and 254 *et seq.*, *supra.*

this surprise was shared by Steel Corporation officials. Among the business fraternity this surprise was, of course, coupled with a high degree of satisfaction, for the decision seemed to give assurance of continued greater tolerance by the Supreme Court of arrangements of all sorts which sought to escape the wastes and restraints of competition. But in the very next year the decision of that court in the first of a group of open-price association cases materially dampened this feeling of elation, since it seemed to condemn a wide range of joint activities of these associations.

Before turning to the facts of these cases we wish to remind the reader that during and following the period of the war business men began to rely more and more upon the trade association as a device for escaping what they considered to be undesirable aspects of competition. Partly within and partly parallel to this development was that of the open-price or open-competition movement in which the members of industrial associations arranged to exchange data on their costs, sales, shipments, stocks on hand, prices, and other business facts. By its friends and advocates this movement was designated as "the new competition" and was hailed as the savior of business from ruinous competition. By others it was held that this "new competition" was not competition at all, but rather a new and insidious form of monopoly.[1] Since trade associations have become the most important contemporaneous form of combination in the United States, the leading decisions on this issue merit the most careful consideration.

For some years the judgment in Eastern States Retail Lumber Dealers' Association *v.* U. S.[2] was the ruling case in this field. Since 1921 to 1925, however, this decision has been overshadowed by four highly important decisions of the Supreme Court. The associations at bar were the American Hardwood Manufacturers' Association, the Linseed Crushers' Council, the Maple Flooring Manufacturers' Association, and the Cement Manufacturers' Protective Association. These cases are so intimately connected that we shall discuss them as a group.

[1] Cf. chap. XVI, p. 315 *et seq.*
[2] 234 U. S. 600 (1914). For discussion of this case cf. pp. 480, 481, *infra.*

The first named of the above organizations, the Hardwood Association, was a combination of the Hardwood Manufacturers' Association of the United States, organized in 1902, and the American Hardwood Manufacturers' Association, organized in 1917. The latter group was itself the result of a merger of the Gum Lumber Manufacturers' Association, organized in 1914, and the American Oak Manufacturers' Association, organized in 1916. The last of the combinations, retaining the name of the 1917 association, went into effect January 1, 1919. Its primary basis was the desire to obviate the duplication of work and expense involved in the partly joint membership of the two antecedent associations. At the time of the government's suit the association included 365 concerns controlling together one-third of the nation's business in hardwood lumber.[1]

The open-competition plan of the 1919 amalgamation was carried over from its 1917 forbear. Under it, it was the duty of the members to file six types of reports with the manager of statistics, which he tabulated and distributed in turn to the members. He was also supposed to send them monthly a market-report letter. Finally, frequent meetings were held for the discussion of the reports and other matters of joint interest. The members' reports provided information on production, sales, shipments, stocks, price lists, and inspections. Of these the monthly reports on production and the monthly price lists were abandoned as unrepresentative because too few of the members filed the information regularly. The contemplated daily reports of shipments were never put into effect.[2] The inspection reports were intended to check up the grading of their products by members, not necessarily to insist on uniform grading, but to provide information which would make the sales and price reports more intelligible. The stock reports were made monthly in considerable detail by the members, compiled into one report by the manager of statistics, and sent out in this form to the members.

[1] *Nelson, op. cit.*, pp. 124, 125.

[2] Cf. Nelson, *op. cit.*, pp. 129, 130, citing evidence in the hearing of the case. It is interesting to note that several other commentators on the case omit any reference to these changes from the original plan.

The daily sales reports were the backbone of the reporting system. At one time they included the names of purchasers, but this was discontinued because of the objections of some of the members. The items retained, however, covered practically every other conceivable detail. The members' reports to the manager of statistics were exact copies of the orders, including all agreements. The weekly summaries of these reports sent back to the members stated the name of the seller, and for each kind and grade of wood sold, the number of feet sold, the thickness, the date of sale, the destination of the order, and the delivered price paid by the purchaser. In order to make these delivered prices comparable, since they included varying quantities of freight, all prices were converted into their equivalent at a common "gateway"—Cairo, for example.

The market-report letter was sent out somewhat more irregularly than originally contemplated. Moreover, the manager of statistics often incorporated comments on the current situation with his weekly summaries of members' reports.

In February, 1920, the federal government brought suit against the American Column and Lumber Company and others, all members of the Hardwood Association, for a permanent injunction restraining the defendants from continuing their combination to enhance prices of hardwood lumber. The District Court for the Western District of Tennessee granted the injunction and was sustained by the Supreme Court.

The evidence convinced a majority of the court that the members of the association were guilty of coöperating "to suppress competition by restricting production" and "to raise prices regardless of cost or merit." [1] The extracts from the market letters and the minutes of association meetings quoted by Justice Clarke in the majority opinion fully support this position.

A contrary opinion of this evidence is expressed by Dr. M. N. Nelson, who goes so far as to say that "Isolated excerpts from letters or minutes of meetings were cited or quoted,

[1] 257 U. S. 402, 409 (1921).

and then strung together so as to fit in with the theory of the Government," with the result that "In many instances the evidence so presented is grossly distorted or misleading." [1] With this the present writers cannot agree. A considerable part of the evidence is just as baldly outspoken as the following communication from one of the members to the secretary. "The very first report which we received under this plan enabled us to increase our price $6 per thousand on a special item in oak. We had just taken a small order *at what we thought was a satisfactory price,* but discovered immediately that others were getting more money, and since that time we have booked orders for a number of these special items at an increase of $6 per thousand." [2] Such a statement needs no distortion and it certainly is not misleading. To its author the association was clearly an instrumentality for extorting from customers all the market would bear, regardless of his cost or what he had previously considered a "satisfactory" profit. Even if the minority opinion of the court that no convincing evidence of intent to restrict production was brought out be accepted as correct, though it does not seem so to us, the implied agreement to raise prices is so clear that it should stand condemned. We may go even further and admit that the economic forces at work during the period under survey would have resulted in greatly enhanced prices; our conclusion remains unchanged. The evidence impels us to agree with Justice Clarke that "the purpose of the organization and especially of the frequent meetings was to bring about a concerted effort to raise prices." [3]

The effect of the decision was in one respect most unfortunate, since it was rather widely interpreted as holding illegal all exchange of trade information by associations. Subsequent developments have demonstrated the error of this interpretation, but its adherents were strengthened in their opinion by the Linseed decision in 1923.

[1] Nelson. *op cit.,* p. 145.

[2] 257 U. S. 408 (1921). Italics not in original.

[3] *Ibid.,* p. 409.

Although the Linseed Crushers' Council was not, according to our definition, a trade association, its principal service was to connect its members with an open-price bureau. For this reason the decision affecting it belongs among those we are considering. The Council was composed of twelve independent corporations, ostensibly competitors in the business of manufacturing linseed oil, cake, and meal. They controlled together "a very large part" of the linseed products consumed in the United States.[1] These concerns entered into identical contracts with the Armstrong Bureau of Related Industries, agreeing to file complete price lists with the Bureau; to report by telegraph any deviation from these lists; to make elaborate reports of all sales, giving exact prices, terms and discounts, quantities sold and the function of the purchaser, that is, whether he was a jobber, dealer, or consumer; to deposit Liberty bonds subject to forfeiture for failure to keep any of the terms of the agreement; and to attend the monthly meetings supervised by an agent of the Bureau. The Bureau obligated itself to transmit all these details promptly to each subscriber. In case a prospective buyer failed to place an order the manufacturer might require the Bureau to secure from all the other subscribers any quotations they might have made to this buyer and distribute the information furnished. Every detail of the reports, communications, and meetings was kept as secret as any arrangements between thirteen parties could be. On the basis of these facts the following conclusion of the Supreme Court is unexceptionable:

> With intimate knowledge of the affairs of other producers and obligated as stated, but proclaiming themselves competitors, the subscribers went forth to deal with widely separated and unorganized customers necessarily ignorant of true conditions. Obviously they were not *bona fide* competitors; their claim in that regard is at war with common experience and hardly compatible with fair dealing.[2]

The opinion was unanimous.

[1] 262 U. S. 380 (1923).
[2] 262 U. S. 389, 390 (1923).

On June 1, 1925, the Supreme Court handed down the other two decisions mentioned above: those in the Maple Flooring and Cement cases. Both cases involved a system of "open competition." Both were decided favorably to the associations.

The activities on which the government based its complaint against the Maple Flooring manufacturers may be summarized in four counts:

(1) The computation and distribution to all members of their *average costs* of manufacturing all dimensions and grades of flooring.

(2) The distribution to members of a booklet showing the *freight rates* on flooring from Cadillac, Michigan, to between five and six thousand points in the United States.

(3) The reports made weekly by members to the secretary of the association showing dates of sales, quantities, the thickness, face, grade, and kind of wood, the delivery prices, average freight rate to destination, and rate of commission paid, if any; the monthly reports presenting the amount of production for the month, the amount of unfilled orders, the new orders booked for each variety of flooring, and the stocks on hand of each dimension and grade of flooring; and the compilation and redistribution of these data by the secretary.

(4) The meetings at which flooring-trade problems were discussed.

The simple enumeration of these points does not do justice to the government's case, however. The majority of the members of the Maple Flooring Association organized in March, 1922, had been members of similar organizations which preceded the defendant organization. One of these earlier groups had formulated in 1916 a minimum-price plan in accordance with which the members agreed not to sell below the minimum under pain of drastic penalties. This minimum was ascertained by adding a 10-per-cent-profit margin to the average cost to the members of manufacturing and selling flooring. Moreover, the antecedent association had incorporated in the freight-rate book it circulated a "delivered price" derived by adding the freight from Cadillac, Michigan, to the minimum price just described. The government conceded that the agreement concerning the minimum price and the practice of quoting delivered prices in the freight-rate book had been abandoned, but contended that in circulating the average costs of the members and the freight-rate book in which rates were quoted from Cadillac, Michigan, to upward of 5,000 delivery points the association was simply whipping the devil around the stump. Obviously, such a procedure was perfectly possible. Justice Stone's opinion stated, however, that "the record is barren of evidence that the published list of costs and the freight-rate book have been so used by the present Association." [1]

Since the reasoning of the court in the case of the Cement Manufacturers' Protective Association is practically identical with that in the Maple Flooring decision, they can be advantageously discussed together. Preliminary to that, however, we must present a brief summary of the activities constituting the basis of the complaint against the Cement Association. They may be classified as follows:

(1) The use of "specific-job contracts" for the future delivery of cement, enforced by a system of reports and espionage which would restrict deliveries on such contracts;

(2) The compilation and distribution to members of freight-rate books setting forth the rates from arbitrary basing points to a large number of delivery points;

(3) The exchange of credit information;

(4) The exchange of other information on production, shipments, stocks on hand and other matters;

(5) The meetings of the association.

In neither of these two cases did the government allege a definite agreement among the members to restrict production or fix prices; its charge was rather that the arrangements entered into were of such a nature that they justified the inference of an implied agreement to fix prices.

The bases upon which the Supreme Court justified its differentiation between the 1925 cases and the earlier ones in 1921 and 1923 were two: first, a difference in the facts, and

[1] Cf. on this section 268 U. S. 567, 571, 572, 576 (1925).

second, the failure of the government to bring the Maple Flooring and Cement cases within the rule laid down in the previous cases—*viz.,* that concerted action is prohibited "when the necessary tendency is to destroy the kind of competition to which the public has long looked for protection." [1] In examining these points it must always be held in mind that in no one of the four cases did the Supreme Court find a definite agreement or contract to restrict competition. In the first two cases it found sufficient evidentiary facts to justify the inference of an implied agreement to restrain commerce; in the second two it did not. Our question is, then, what facts did the Supreme Court find in the earlier cases which it did not find in the later ones?

From the decisions the most important items in answering the foregoing question seem to be:

(1) The exceedingly great increases in prices of lumber in the Hardwood case.

(2) The nature of the reports and letters sent out by the manager of statistics for the Hardwood Association. The court construed these as incitements to reduce production and raise prices.

(3) The nature of the meetings of the Hardwood Association which the court construed as it did the letters and reports just mentioned.

(4) The filing of price lists by members of the Linseed groups with the Armstrong Bureau and the obligation to report any deviation from list prices by telegraph.

(5) The "iron-clad" nature of the contracts in the Linseed case, involving the deposit of bonds as a guaranty of fulfillment of obligations, compulsory attendance at meetings, permission to the Bureau to audit members' books, etc.

(6) The nature of the meetings of the Linseed group where members were "put on the carpet" and rigorously questioned on their business dealings.

(7) The power of the Bureau in the Linseed case to investigate and report the details of any particular sale when requested to do so.

[1] Cf. 268 U. S. 578 (1925) with 262 U. S. 390 (1923).

Following this line of thought, the great majority of the commentaries which have come to our attention express the opinion that the differences in the facts justify the differences in the judgments. An outstanding exception is the view taken by Professor Myron W. Watkins, who believes that the court did not see "different things" in 1921 and 1925, "but that it saw things differently," and that "it is futile to attempt any rational reconciliation" of the two sets of decisions.[1] The real explanation he found in the differences in business conditions in the periods covered by the records. The earlier two were based on a time of prosperity and rapidly rising prices; the latter on a period of slack business and stable prices. The court concluded that price advances in hardwood lumber ranging from 33 to 343 per cent could not be solely "natural." Since there were no such price changes in the period under discussion in the Maple Flooring and Cement cases, "the Government was unable to paint a very terrifying picture of the predatory power of the defendants and the prosecution failed." In the Maple Flooring decision we find it stressed that prices were "fair and reasonable."

We do not fully agree with Professor Watkins's conclusion on the differences in the facts in the four cases, but the importance of his contention as to the "real explanation" is unquestionable. The change in the business situation coupled with the changes which had taken place in the membership of the court no doubt had great influence in determining the outcome of the last two cases.

But there remains for discussion the second ground on which the court itself justified its position: the rule of "necessary tendency" laid down in the earlier cases. The importance of this consideration is clear from the statement in the opinion in the Maple Flooring case that since it was not contended that there was an agreement restraining competition "the sole question . . . is whether the combination of the defendants in their existing association as actually conducted by them has a necessary tendency to cause direct and undue restraint of competition in commerce falling within the con-

[1] *American Economic Review,* Supplement, March, 1926, p. 231.

demnation of the act."[1] Moreover, the point was stated and restated time and again in the decision. Unfortunately for the purposes of clear analysis, however, the court was not consistent in its phraseology. Sometimes it speaks of "necessary tendency," sometimes of "necessary effect," and sometimes of "necessary result." For example, in contrasting the case at bar with the earlier Eastern States Retail Lumber Association, Hardwood, and Linseed cases the opinion three times uses "result" rather than "tendency."[2] Now it is extremely improbable that "tendency," "effect," and "result" all mean exactly the same thing to the justice who wrote the opinion, but there can be no doubt that he used them in such a way as to justify that conclusion.[3] And with no intention of quibbling over words we wish to insist that the exact meaning of the court is extremely important and that the confusion in phraseology may have most unfortunate results. In this connection the word "necessary" in the court's rule is more important than "tendency" or "result."

Since there was in no one of the cases a formal agreement to restrain trade, the prosecution was limited to the presentation of evidence from which the inference of such restraint might fairly be drawn. In tracing relationships between causes and effects in legal or economic controversies one is sure to find that those relationships are not as precise and clear as one would like. Usually it is not so difficult to locate the extremes. Some facts in the situation are of such a nature that it is all but impossible that they could cause a certain result; others are so closely related that the result is almost sure to follow. Thus a trade association may be subsidizing researches in some university laboratory. It is almost inconceivable that this in itself could result in an illegal restraint of trade. The same association may arrange frequent meet-

[1] 268 U. S. 578 (1925).

[2] *Ibid.*, pp. 584, 585, 586.

[3] In his suggestive article in the *Columbia Law Review*, April, 1926, p. 381, Professor H. Oliphant without discussion simply assumes that "tendency" and "result" are interchangeable terms in the opinion, and proceeds to criticize the court's rule of "necessary consequence," as he terms it. As will appear in the text, we are indebted to him for a good part of our own argument.

ings of its members in which prices, particularly future prices, are the chief topics of discussion. In this case it is almost inconceivable that the result could fail to be an illegal restraint. Between these extremes there are any number of joint activities the members of the association may be carrying on which seem more or less likely to result in price-fixing or some other illegal restraint. Practically no one will contend that competitors should be prohibited from contracting to carry on common activities which are all but incapable of bringing about an undue restraint of trade, and very few that they should not be prohibited from joint acts the necessary consequence of which is such restraint.

But the question remains as to exactly where the line which marks off the legal from the illegal should be drawn. If it includes as illegal all joint activities which may possibly result in limiting production or fixing prices, it is certain to prevent some coöperation that has only beneficial consequences. On the other hand, the limitation of the field of illegal joint activities to those of which the necessary result is, in Justice Stone's words, "to destroy the kind of competition to which the public has long looked for protection," would seem to render the prohibition of such activities almost futile. As Professor Oliphant points out in the article cited, a contract to pull the trigger of a loaded gun pointed at the head of a man ten feet distant whose back is turned does not have the necessary consequence of killing the man. The cartridge may fail to explode; the man may move. Of course, the natural and probable consequence of such a contract will be the death of the man, but the relationship is not one of necessity. If the court adheres to the strict logic of its ruling, evasion of the prohibition of contracts to fix price and limit production will be relatively easy to accomplish. The boundary of illegal activities should be erected at that point where it will include not only acts of which the *necessary* consequence is to destroy beneficial competition, but also all acts of which the *natural* and *probable* consequence is to destroy such competition. As a matter of fact this is the very standard of conduct now found in numerous places in our law; its workability is at least as well demonstrated as that of the "rule of reason." To the extent that the court really did intend to lay down a rule of "necessary consequence" or "necessary result," we are inclined to agree with Professor Oliphant's conclusions that, although that rule is valid as an *affirmative* test of illegality, it is not satisfactory as a *negative* test, and that when the situation is adequately presented to the Supreme Court (as it apparently was not in the Maple Flooring and Cement cases) the negative test of probability will be adopted.[1]

Furthermore, the present writers wish, in passing, to record their judgment that, had the court followed the rule suggested above, it would have sustained the lower court in its decision against the Maple Flooring Association. The changes in its program which were made from time to time and which Justice Stone construed as indicating "a purpose to keep within the boundaries of legality as rapidly as those boundaries were marked out by the decisions of the courts,"[2] seem to us to be changes of form rather than substance. The lower court and three justices of the Supreme Court went even further and held both Flooring and Cement groups within the rule of "necessary tendency" and consequently subject to dissolution.[3]

But in stating that different sets of facts would result in different decisions and in formulating its rule of "necessary tendency" the court seemed to feel that perhaps it had not been as definite as the business community might desire. Consequently, it concluded its opinion in the Maple Flooring case with the following paragraph, which was apparently designed to put a terminus to some misconceptions of its earlier decisions and at the same time to forestall a possible

[1] What Professor Oliphant means by "negative" and "positive" tests is made clear in his own example. If bodily injury is intentionally inflicted, liability follows. The obverse of this would be that if intention were not proved there would be no liability. Obviously this is not correct, for if it were, negligence could not be penalized. In other words, the "positive" test of liability for personal injury is *intention,* but it must be supplemented by the "negative" test of *negligence.*

[2] 268 U. S. 577 (1925).

[3] 294 Fed. 390 (1923); 268 U. S. 586, 587, 606 (1925). The decision of the lower court in the Maple Flooring case was apparently not reported.

misconception of this one, to wit, that the government had taken its hands off and that "the sky was the limit":

> We decide only that trade associations or combinations of persons or corporations which openly and fairly gather and disseminate information as to the cost of their product, the volume of production, the actual price which the product has brought in past transactions, stocks of merchandise on hand, approximate cost of transportation from the principal point of shipment to the points of consumption, as did these defendants, and who, as they did, meet and discuss such information and statistics without however reaching or attempting to reach any agreement or any concerted action with respect to prices or production or restraining competition, do not thereby engage in unlawful restraint of commerce.[1]

The only other trade association decision of any importance since those of 1925 is that concerning the Sanitary Potters' Association, but styled and generally referred to as the "Trenton Potteries" case. It differs from the four just discussed in that it was a criminal prosecution brought by the United States. The conviction of the defendants, twenty individuals and twenty-three corporations, in the District Court was reversed by the Second Circuit Court of Appeals, but reinstated by the Supreme Court. The Court of Appeals stated that the arrangements alleged by the Government, though differing in detail, were fairly analogous to those in the Eastern States Retail Lumber and Hardwood cases. The reversal was based chiefly on alleged errors of the trial judge, and the decision of the Supreme Court was primarily concerned with these errors. In fact, the opinion from the highest court stated that there was no contention by defendants that the verdict was not sustained by evidence showing that manufacturers producing 82 per cent of the sanitary pottery of the country combined to fix prices and to limit sales in interstate commerce to so-called "legitimate" dealers. The chief significance of the case for us lies in the fact that the Supreme Court held that the agreement on prices violated the Sherman Act whether the prices themselves were reasonable or unreasonable.[2]

[1] 268 U. S. 586 (1925).

[2] 300 Fed. 550 (1924); 273 U. S. 392 (1927).

Since the Hardwood and Linseed decisions and the consent decree in the Tile Manufacturers' Credit Association case[1] had checked the exchanging of trade statistics by associations, it was to be expected that the decisions of 1925 would revive these activities. This proved to be correct except for purely open-price operations.[2] And by and large this revival was desirable. While we fully appreciate the importance and usefulness of the exchange of trade information made possible by trade associations, we have failed in our purpose if this and the preceding chapters tracing the history of the trust movement have not also made abundantly clear the unwisdom of leaving the joint activities of business men absolutely without supervision. The almost universal distrust of combinations among the mass of the "common people" does not rest, as some of our corporation lawyers would have us believe, upon misconception and ignorance implanted by artful demagogues. It has a solid foundation in fact and experience. The gentlemen's agreement, the pool, the old Standard Oil type of "trust," the holding company, and the trade association, as they have been utilized by business men, have all too frequently deserved the censure they have received. It remains true, however, that there has been a rather steady shifting of emphasis from restrictive to constructive activities. In its usual form the gentlemen's agreement was largely pernicious. The same may be said of many pools, but in the railroad business they were frequently socially desirable. The holding-company device, essentially a legalization of the old "trust," has unquestionable merits. And of all of them the trade association seems to carry the most promise of securing the advantages of coöperation without losing those of competition, and consequently merits encouragement rather than suppression.

But encouragement does not require the withdrawal of supervision. In order to secure the maximum benefits from the most valuable constructive activity of trade associations

[1] Cf. p. 312, *supra*.

[2] Federal Trade Commission, *Open-Price Trade Associations*, pp. 15. 22.

the data collected must be really disseminated. The only guaranty of this is their circulation through some such agency as the "Survey of Current Business" now issued by the Department of Commerce. The oft-repeated claim that a private trade association is performing the functions of an organized exchange when it sets up the machinery for collecting and circulating trade data is extremely misleading. Prior to 1925, in fact, it is safe to say that in practically all cases such statements were untrue. The usual practice was for the information to be sent to all the sellers of a commodity who were in the association, but for no provision to be made for supplying it to buyers. Consequently, the latter were worse off than before. That there has been a change toward wider voluntary publicity of trade association data is indicated, however, in the *Open-Price Trade Associations* volume of the Trade Commission. But the evidence presented by the Commission and its own recommendation that the Census Bureau be given additional compulsory powers for collecting trade statistics support our contentions that there remains much room for improvement and that adequate publicity necessitates supervision by some governmental agency.[1]

In turning now to cases involving the application of the trust legislation of 1914 we wish to emphasize again the fact that the Federal Trade Commission was the chief agency for enforcing those laws. Consequently, we have centered the following discussion of cases on those initiated by the Commission, including only such others as bear directly on Commission cases or merit treatment because of their intrinsic importance.

Partly in both categories are certain cases defining the jurisdiction and powers of the Commission, such as the American Tobacco and P. Lorillard cases. They arose from the attempt of the Commission to investigate complaints against both corporations, alleging unfair methods of competition, and to carry out a Senate resolution of August 9, 1921, directing it to investigate a number of specified aspects of the tobacco

[1] Cf. pp. 12, 146-160, and xix of the Commission's report.

trade. The Commission demanded access to certain papers and records of the companies. Since these demands were refused in part, the Commission sought a mandamus to compel compliance, relying upon the Senate resolution and Sections 6 and 9 of its organic act. Both the District Court for the Southern District of New York and the Supreme Court disposed of the first basis for the request for a mandamus on the ground that the Senate resolution did not contain an allegation of a violation of the antitrust acts and hence did not fall within the requirements of Section 6 (d) of the Federal Trade Commission law. The Supreme Court construed the petition and argument of the Commission to claim under Section 9 "an unlimited right of access to the respondents' papers." To this contention the court replied that "Anyone who respects the spirit as well as the letter of the Fourth Amendment would be loath to believe that Congress intended to authorize one of its subordinate agencies to sweep all our traditions into the fire . . . and to direct fishing expeditions into private papers on the possibility that they may disclose evidence of crime. . . . It is contrary to the first principles of justice to allow a search through all the respondents' records, relevant or irrelevant, in the hope that something will turn up." [1]

In a subsequent case against three grain companies Judge Rose of the District Court of Maryland stated that the facts were "legally indistinguishable" from those in the tobacco cases, and, following the same line of reasoning as that just summarized, denied the petition of the Commission for writs of mandamus. The Supreme Court again affirmed [2] the decision of the lower court. In stating that the facts in these grain cases were "legally indistinguishable" from those in the tobacco cases, Judge Rose apparently did not mean to imply that complaints had been lodged against the former concerns for violating the antitrust acts, for he brought out later in the opinion that no such allegations had been made.

[1] 264 U. S. 305 (1924); 283 Fed. 999 (1922). In both courts both cases were argued and decided together.

[2] 284 Fed. 886 (1922); 267 U. S. 586 (1925). The respondents were the Baltimore Grain Co., the H. C. Jones Co., and the Hammond-Snyder Co.

The similarity of the cases lay in the reliance by the Commission upon Sections 6 and 9 of the statute creating it. On the basis of the decisions in these cases it seems clear that the courts are determined to require the Commission to specify precisely the information it is seeking and to permit no "fishing expeditions."

The decisions in two other important cases on the powers of the Commission were unfortunately such as to make it impossible to draw final conclusions from them, but they should be noted at this point. These two, the Maynard Coal and Claire Furnace cases, originated in a somewhat different fashion from those just described. The Congress, having become somewhat agitated by the increasing cost of living during and after the World War, was casting about for an appropriate expedient for convincing the electorate that action was being taken by it to meet the situation. In the course of these efforts the Commission was requested to suggest something it might do to help bring about the desired end. The proposal advanced was that the Commission collect and publish current information on the production, ownership, storage, and distribution of foodstuffs and other necessaries, as well as more or less similar data for certain basic industries such as steel and coal. The sum of $150,000 was appropriated by Congress to further these investigations and made available November 4, 1919.

A large number of corporations in both the steel and coal industries were requested to supply information of a most detailed character. The Claire Furnace Company and a number of other steel concerns chose to fight the Commission's requests and applied to the Supreme Court of the District of Columbia for a restraining order against any attempt to force them to supply the information. Both this group and the Maynard Coal Company were successful in the Supreme Court of the District of Columbia in securing the injunctions they desired. On appeal the Court of Appeals of the District of Columbia affirmed the decision of the lower court in the Claire Furnace case, but continued that of the Maynard Coal

Company pending a decision by the United States Supreme Court of the former case.

The decision of the Court of Appeals in the Claire Furnace case, if finally approved in principle by the United States Supreme Court, will be one of the most important, if not the most important, to date in construing the powers of the Commission. In the words of the court the contemplated investigation "seems to be more in the nature of a news-gathering expedition, in hope of securing something of public interest for publication, or possibly subject matter for future legislation by Congress. Common justice would seem to demand that before the business methods pursued by a corporation or by an individual should be investigated, the party should be appraised either by a formal charge or by a notice of the extent of the purposed investigation, in order that a day in court may be accorded." [1]

But the reason stated by the court for holding against the Commission was not that it had failed to bring a formal charge or notify the respondent of the extent of the proposed investigation; [2] the issue emphasized was that of interstate commerce. And this issue the court resolved by holding that, "since the manufacturing business of complainants is not commerce," it is "therefore not subject to regulation by Congress or investigation by the Commission." [3] The chief justice dissented from the opinion of his two associates in these words: "I am satisfied that the law requires that the information demanded be supplied, and therefore I think the decree of the lower court should be reversed, and the bill dismissed."[4]

The result of the United States Supreme Court's examination of this case was a pronounced disappointment to all interested. Instead of settling the issues presented, that court

[1] 285 Fed. 941 (1923).

[2] As a matter of fact, the sentence just quoted is extremely difficult to explain, except, perhaps, as an indication of the bias with which its author approached his task in this case. Far from failing to apprise the respondents of the "extent" of the proposed investigation the Commission had set forth its extent in such detail as to cause them to complain that the requests were unreasonable. Cf. *Annual Report* of the Commission for 1921, p. 56.

[3] 285 Fed. 944 (1923).

[4] *Ibid.*, p. 949.

remanded the case to the lower court after pointing out that the action of the Commission could be justified only under certain paragraphs of Sections 6 and 9 of the Federal Trade Commission Act, if at all, and that the only method of enforcing orders permitted under these paragraphs was by application to the Attorney General of the United States to institute an action for mandamus or proceedings to recover the penalties prescribed for failure to obey such orders. Furthermore, the court continued, "Until the Attorney General acts, the defendants cannot suffer, and, when he does act, they can promptly answer and have full opportunity to contest the legality of any prejudicial proceeding against them. That right being adequate, they were not in a position to ask relief by injunction. The bill should have been dismissed for want of equity."[1] In other words, after seven years of litigation the parties to it found themselves just where they started because of a petty error of the trial court. The Commission had, of course, followed the procedure laid down in the statute and insisted upon by the Supreme Court, but had been prevented from carrying the process through by the temporary restraining order and subsequent injunction of the District of Columbia courts.[2] As Justice McReynolds pointed out in a brief dissenting opinion, there was ample precedent for proceeding to a determination of the case.[3] In his opinion the Commission had gone beyond any power granted by Congress.

The Maynard case, held in abeyance until that of the Claire Furnace was decided, was resolved on November 7, 1927, by the Court of Appeals of the District of Columbia. The decision followed precisely that just discussed.[4] Since the appropriation with which the Commission was to make the investigation had long since lapsed, the outcome of the cases was unsatisfactory in every respect. The jurisdictional aspect is, of course, still in the balance. If and when this issue again comes before the Supreme Court, it is to be hoped that that

[1] 274 U. S. 174 (1927).
[2] F. T. C., *Annual Report*, 1920, p. 52.
[3] 274 U. S. 175 (1927).
[4] 22 Fed. (2d) 873 (1927).

body will decide it on its merits and not confuse it with the issue presented in the tobacco and grain cases already discussed. There is some prospect that it will, for otherwise it might simply have affirmed the Claire Furnace case as it did the grain cases in a three-line decision "upon the authority" of the tobacco cases. Without committing ourselves to an agreement with the court on the earlier cases, we wish to emphasize the vital difference between them and those of the Claire Furnace and Maynard Coal. The latter cannot by any possible contortion of the facts be construed as "fishing expeditions" begun with the hope of discovering something disadvantageous to the industries concerned. There seems no room to doubt that they were *bona-fide* attempts to make public certain facts which would in a degree stabilize those industries and, in the long run, perhaps aid in lowering the cost of living. As we brought out in discussing the open-price association cases, the value of collecting and disseminating business facts as a method of stabilizing business is generally accepted, but, to repeat, our experience seems to prove that if they are to be really disseminated that work must be done by, or under the supervision of, some governmental agency. For the court to hold that such activity is prohibited by the Fourth Amendment or any other provision of the Constitution would be most unfortunate.

Much less important than the foregoing cases, but significant as an interpretation of the intentions of Congress in distinguishing the jurisdictions of the Trade Commission and the Interstate Commerce Commission, was the case of the Fruit Growers' Express. The former administrative body issued an order to the Fruit Growers' Express to desist from the use of a contract with various railroads requiring exclusive use by the carriers of the refrigerator cars and refrigerating service of the express company. The Seventh Circuit Court of Appeals ruled that under Section 11 of the Clayton Act cases of this sort were in the sole jurisdiction of the Interstate Commerce Commission.[1]

[1] 2 F. T. C. D. 369 (1920); 274 Fed. 205 (1921); 261 U. S. 629 (1923). In the Supreme Court the case was "Dismissed with costs, per stipulation, on motion of *Mr. Solicitor General Beck* in that behalf."

The sections of the Clayton Act which the Federal Trade Commission was authorized to enforce, except in so far as they applied to banks and common carriers, were numbers 2, 3, 7, and 8. With the important qualifications and limitations previously discussed these sections prohibited, respectively, price discriminations, tying and exclusive contracts, stock acquisitions by corporations, and interlocking directorates. In its earlier years the Commission filed a large number of complaints alleging price discriminations and tying contracts (Sections 2 and 3), but of recent years there has been a marked decline in the number of such complaints. On the other hand, the records of these earlier cases show that in a considerable number of them the Commission failed to find as a fact that Sections 2 and 3 had been violated and either did not include a prohibition of price discrimination or the use of tying or exclusive contracts in its order, or dismissed the case without an order. Orders against violations of Section 7 on stock acquisitions by corporations had been issued in only seven instances prior to July 1, 1928, the date of the last report available.[1] Not a single order on Section 8, interlocking directorates, had been issued prior to that date. In a considerable number of the cases involving violations of the Clayton Act the Commission adopted the practice of also alleging a violation of Section 5 of the Federal Trade Commission Act prohibiting unfair methods of competition. Moreover, Volumes IV, V, VI, VII, VIII and IX of the *Decisions,* covering the period from July 1, 1921, to November 27, 1925, have only a half-dozen or less orders per volume concerning violations of the Clayton Act. In the period following the last published volume of *Decisions* but covered in the *Annual Reports* for 1926, 1927, and 1928, there was only one order on a Clayton Act case and that one was vacated in less than a year. In other words, the Commission has come more and

[1] This statement concerning orders under Section 7 does not agree with that in the Commission's *Annual Report,* 1927, p. 13. Subsequent figures in the text on orders on other sections likewise do not agree. In a letter of January 2, 1929, to one of the writers the secretary of the Commission admitted that the total figures for orders under Sections 2, 3 and 7 as published in the 1927 *Annual Report* were incorrect in each instance.

more to concentrate on the enforcement of the unfair competition section (5) of the law creating it. The reasons for this will appear in more detail as we proceed, but in general we may say that it has resulted from a less rigid differentiation by the Commission between Sections 2 and 3 of the Clayton Act, on the one hand, and Section 5 of the Commission Act on the other, the refusal of the courts to uphold the Commission in its interpretation of parts of the Clayton Act, and the more general avoidance of the use by business men of the devices prohibited in that act.

The price discriminations prohibited in Section 2 of the Clayton Act included a wider range of activities than the local price-cutting used so effectively by some of the trusts. As a matter of fact, in the eleven desist orders involving Section 2 which the Commission has issued between its organization and July 1, 1928, there is not a single example of local price-cutting.[1] This is particularly interesting in the light of the importance which was ascribed to this method in the Congressional debates and also serves to illustrate the difficulty of keeping legislation abreast of the ingenuity of those who wish to use unfair tactics.

Two [2] of the eleven orders were really directed against resale-price-maintenance schemes and forbade discrimination against dealers who refused to maintain prices and/or in favor of those who did, but since this practice has most frequently been handled as an unfair method of competition it will be treated in detail later. In its first order under Section 2 the Commission laid down the rather startling proposition that the Fleischmann Yeast Company should not discriminate in prices "where such discriminations in prices, if made, would be below the price or prices of a competitor or competitors.

[1] The cases will be found in the *Decisions*, vol. i, pp. 119, 199, 259; vol. ii, p. 446; vol. iv, pp. 258, 355; vol. v, p. 67; vol. vii, pp. 206, 218; and vol. viii, pp. 1, 480. A comparison of the dates of the issuance of these orders with the statistical summary of the Commission's work in the National Industrial Conference Board's volume, *Public Regulation of Competitive Practices*, pp. 240-244, makes it clear that the first three cases just cited were not included in that summary.

[2] 1 F. T. C. D. 199 (1918); 1 F. T. C. D. 442 (1919).

. . ."[1] Since the statute permits discriminations in price "made in good faith to meet competition," and since business conditions sometimes make it necessary to sell at almost any price rather than to continue to hold the commodity in question, it seems that this sweeping injunction is dubious law and worse economics. The same reasoning applies to the theory that any sale below cost is unfair and discriminatory, upon which the Commission was apparently relying in its complaint against the Sears, Roebuck Company,[2] which it charged with discriminating in favor of those purchasers of sugar who also purchased other commodities at the same time. The final order made no mention of price discrimination; a fact which may or may not reflect a change of viewpoint in the Commission. The Circuit Court of Appeals ruled that the Commission could not prevent a trader from selling articles below cost, but that it could prevent such sales when accompanied by misrepresentations which would injure other traders.[3]

An important group of cases among these eleven was concerned with discriminations which might arise from the long-established practices of giving trade or quantity discounts. Again it must be recalled that the statute specifically permitted certain types of discrimination, but in these cases the Commission issued orders against what it considered non-permissible arrangements. The first two, against the South Bend Bait Company and the Mennen Company, were entered in March, 1922. In the former case the respondent classified its customers into jobbers, wholesalers, retailers, and consumers, allowing the first three groups discounts from list prices of 50, 40, and 33 1/3 per cent, respectively, "wholly irrespective of the quantity purchased by a customer in any one of said groups." Since the Commission viewed the classification as purely arbitrary and not covered by any one of the exceptions listed in Section 2 of the Clayton Act, it held that the arrangements violated that section and Section 5

[1] 1 F. T. C. D. 138 (1918).
[2] 1 F. T. C. D. 163 (1918).
[3] 258 Fed. 307 (1919).

of the Trade Commission Act.[1] The respondents did not carry the case to the courts for review, but the order was subsequently rescinded because of the decision of the courts in the Mennen case.[2]

As just implied, the Mennen Company appealed its case and by a unanimous decision of the United States Circuit Court of Appeals for the Second Circuit secured a reversal of the Commission's order. The Supreme Court denied a petition for *certiorari.*[3] Prior to January 1, 1917, the respondent based its discounts strictly upon quantities purchased, but on that date it instituted a system by which all discounts were based upon a classification of its customers into "jobbers or wholesalers" and "retailers." Although a number of changes were subsequently made in details, the essential feature remained the distinction just stated. In the actual operation of the plan any dealer classed as a "retailer" got appreciably smaller discounts than one classed as a "wholesaler," even though he might purchase larger quantities in one shipment or over a period of time. Since by no means all the manufacturers of products similar to the Mennen's followed its practices, large retailers were able to secure discounts not available to smaller retailers from such companies. This situation was distasteful to both the small retailers and the old-line wholesalers. The former group attempted to improve the position of its members by organizing coöperative wholesale establishments which could buy in larger quantities and pass on to their organizers the benefits thus derived. Such organizations expected, of course, to be classified as "wholesalers" by companies which based their discounts on a classification of function rather than on quantities purchased. Such a plan, in the opinion of the established wholesalers, made a bad situation worse, for they stood to lose even more business if it proved successful. But the Mennen Company refused to classify these coöperative or mutual organizations as "wholesalers" and allowed them only the "retailers' " discount. In return

[1] 4 F. T. C. D. 355 (1922).

[2] *Annual Report,* 1924, p. 191.

[3] 4 F. T. C. D. 258 (1922); 288 Fed. 774 (1923); 262 U. S. 759 (1923).

for this discrimination against these new competitors it appears that the houses which it did classify as "jobbers or wholesalers" had an understanding with the Mennen Company to push its products; in other words, to discriminate against the manufacturers who refused to discriminate against the mutual corporations. The Commission held the whole arrangement to involve both unlawful discrimination in prices and an unfair method of competition.

In reviewing the order of the Commission the Circuit Court of Appeals ruled that nothing was alleged "which would justify the conclusion that the public suffered injury or that competitors had reasonable ground for complaint," and furthermore that the practices complained of did not lessen competition between the Mennen Company and its competitors. The court granted that the said practices might and probably did decrease competition among the customers of the Mennen Company or those who desired to become customers, but held that Congress had not intended to include the latter groups. In support of this contention the opinion quoted several paragraphs from the report of the judiciary committee of the House and went on to say that "There is nothing in the report of the committee which shows that in reporting the bill the committee had in mind anything more than the suppression of the evil . . ." of local price-cutting by a concern against its own competitors. Further, the court construed as supporting its position the elimination of the phrase which originally terminated Section 2—*viz.,* "with the purpose or intent thereby to destroy or wrongfully injure the business of a competitor of either such purchaser or seller," in favor of the present language prohibiting discriminations which tend to create a monopoly.[1] But as has been pointed out by other commentators, Congressman Webb in presenting the conference report to the House stated that the change in phraseology was made because the conference committee thought the original language was "probably too restricted" and that the change "would tend to give the section more elasticity and

[1] 288 Fed. 779, 778 (1923).

breadth."[1] From these facts it seems clear that a thorough investigation of the legislative history of the bill fails to sustain the interpretation placed upon it by the court.

In addition to presenting the faulty argument just discussed, the opinion is inaccurate on a matter of fact. It states that "The record filed in this court shows no contention by the Commission that the practices complained of have lessened competition between the Mennen Company and its competitors. . . ."[2] Paragraph nine of the findings of the Commission begins with this sentence: "That in the sale of its said products as wholesaler direct to retailers, in quantities of 1½ gross or more, respondent is in direct competition in interstate commerce with wholesalers engaged in selling said products to retailers." The paragraph goes on to show that retailers buying direct from the respondent received the same discounts as the coöperative wholesalers and concludes with the statement that "Respondent has used the situation thus created to take away from said coöperative or mutual corporations their retail customers for the products of respondent, or lessen the volume of such trade."[3] The court was at liberty, of course, to show that this finding was not supported by evidence, but its statement that there was "no contention" of a lessening of the competition between the Mennen Company and its own competitors reveals a surprising ignorance or disregard of the record.

As our criticisms of the decision in the Circuit Court of Appeals indicate, we consider it extremely unfortunate that the Supreme Court denied *certiorari* in this case. After six years, however, the highest court, in deciding a Clayton Act case to which the Commission was not a party, disposed of the chief point on which the lower court had rested its determination of the Mennen case. The litigants in the 1929 case were the American Can Company, the Van Camp Packing Company, and the George Van Camp & Sons Company, both of the latter packers of food products. In addition to

[1] Cf. Henderson, G., *The Federal Trade Commission,* pp. 276, 277, note.
[2] 288 Fed. 778 (1923).
[3] 4 F. T. C. D. 279 (1922).

making tin cans the American Can Company leased to purchasers of cans a machine for sealing them. The courts found that the George Van Camp concern paid the publicly announced standard prices for its cans and a rental on the machines, but that the Van Camp Packing Company paid 20 per cent less than the standard price, paid no rental on the machines, and was the recipient of large sums of money in bonuses, discounts, etc., from the can manufacturer. The George Van Camp Company applied to the Federal District Court of Indiana to enjoin these discriminations, but the bill was dismissed. When the case was carried to the Seventh Circuit Court of Appeals, that body certified the following two questions to the Supreme Court for instructions:

> Question 1. Does section 2 of the "Clayton Act" . . . have application to cases of price discrimination, the effect of which may be to substantially lessen competition, or tend to create a monopoly, not in the line of commerce wherein the discriminator is engaged, but in the line of commerce in which the vendee of the discriminator is engaged?
>
> Question 2. Where one who makes an article and sells it, interstate, to persons engaged, interstate, in a line of commerce different from that of the maker, discriminates in price between such buyers (said discrimination not being made on account of differences in the grade, quality or quantity of the commodity sold, nor being made as only due allowance for the difference in the cost of selling or transportation, nor being made in good faith to meet competition) and the effect of such discrimination may be to substantially lessen competition or tend to create a monopoly in the line of commerce wherein the buyers are engaged, does the maker and seller of the article, making such price discrimination, transgress section 2 of the "Clayton Act"? [1]

The court answered both of these questions in the affirmative, specifically rejecting the reasoning of the lower court in the Mennen case in these words:

> We have not failed carefully to consider *Mennen Co.* v. *Federal Trade Comm'n,* 288 Fed. 774 (followed in *National Biscuit Co.* v. *Federal Trade Comm'n,* 299 Fed. 733), cited as contrary to the conclusion we have reached. The decision in that case was based upon the premise that the statute was ambiguous and required the aid of committee reports, etc., to determine its meaning, a premise which we have rejected as unsound." [2]

[1] 278 U. S. 245, 249-250 (1929).

[2] *Ibid.,* at p. 254. For the National Biscuit case, cf. pp. 481, 482 *infra.*

But more important from an economic point of view were the *dicta* of the court in the Mennen case that the respondent had a "right" to decide whether it would sell to "retailers" or "jobbers" or both, and on what terms, and that it had a "right" to classify the coöperative purchasing corporations as "retailers." The unfortunate aspect of the latter part of this contention is that it lends the assistance of the courts to a system of discounts which stands in the way of possible improvements in the distribution of goods by making that distribution more direct. It is generally recognized that the technique of moving commodities from the producer to the consumer, as compared with the technique of producing them, has improved very little. Each group in the traditional line of manufacturer, wholesaler, retailer considers itself to have a vested interest in the maintenance of the "regular" procedure. In this case that maintenance was secured by a method which does not seem to us to fall within the exceptions permitted under Section 2 of the Clayton Act. The discounts were granted on a purely arbitrary basis and resulted in discriminations we believe to be illegal. Consequently, we are of the opinion that here again the decision defeated the purpose of the law and stands as a bar to progress in solving one of our most important economic problems: the high cost of distributing goods. Judicial support for our opinion may be found in the case of the Eastern States Retail Lumber Dealers' Association *v.* United States.[1] In this case the members of the association were shown to have reported to its secretary the names of wholesalers who sold directly to contractors and builders. If after investigation the fact of direct selling was established, the wholesaler's name was placed on a list of similar transgressors circulated by the association in its so-called "Official Report." This report was not in the form of an agreement to cease patronizing such wholesalers, but, as the opinion of the Supreme Court stated, "he is blind indeed who does not see the purpose in the predetermined and periodical circulation of this report to put the ban upon wholesale dealers whose names appear in the list." In other words, the purpose of the

[1] 234 U. S. 600 (1914).

arrangement was to force the lumber trade to continue to pass through channels which the retailers considered "legitimate." Although it is true that the court stressed the conspiracy element in this case, it equally emphasized the illegality of the purpose of the retailers.

The same purpose we think is clearly shown by the facts in the Mennen case. The court which decided that case did not consider it necessary to review the Commission's arguments that the costs of the coöperative wholesaler were lower than those of the old-line wholesaler, and that as a channel of distribution it was entitled to an unhindered opportunity to demonstrate its economic efficiency on equal terms with previously existing agencies of distribution. The failure of the court to consider these arguments appears to us to constitute a fatal imperfection in its reasoning. Had it not been for this deficiency it might have condemned the arrangement as an unfair method of competition, even though it were unable to find in it a violation of Section 2 of the Clayton Act.[1]

For the reasons just brought out in the Mennen case we consider it unfortunate that the courts have reversed the Commission's orders in the National Biscuit Company and Loose-Wiles Biscuit Company cases. Both these concerns gave discounts based on quantities purchased a month, both permitted the sales to chain stores in a given locality to be pooled for the purpose of computing the discount, but refused to grant discounts on the pooled orders of groups of independent grocers in the same locality. It must particularly be noticed that the sales to the chain stores were not made to a central office or depot of the system; each individual store of the chain was solicited for orders and deliveries made to it individually. Consequently, the costs of getting this business were identical with those incurred in dealing with independent stores similarly located and buying similar quantities. Moreover, it is amusing to note that though the Circuit Court of Appeals for the Second Circuit was able, in its own language, to "pierce the veil of corporate entity" and see that

[1] Cf. 9 *American Bar Association Journal* 210, an article in which Professor H. Oliphant makes a similar argument.

the coöperative purchasing companies in the Mennen case were not *bona-fide* "wholesalers," but "retailers" in disguise, it was not able to see that in their dealings with the biscuit companies the units of the chain systems were as independent as the privately owned groceries (except perhaps in paying their accounts), and solemnly announced that "it cannot be said that the branch store of the chain retailer is a separate or different purchaser as intended by Section 2." [1]

The most notable success achieved by the Trade Commission in the application of Section 2 was in compelling the United States Steel Corporation to desist from the Pittsburgh-plus practice discussed in an earlier chapter.[2] Although we cannot be positive what view the courts would have taken on the matter, there is no doubt in our minds that the practice had long outlived whatever usefulness it may have had at an earlier period and had become unfairly discriminatory in its operation.

The most recent court decision concerning price discrimination was rendered against the American Tobacco Company. From the evidence before the courts it appears that the Porto Rican American Tobacco Company of Porto Rico refused to coöperate with the American Tobacco Company in an attempt to prevent the passage (and later to secure a veto by the Governor) of an amendment to the tax laws of the island raising the tax on cigarettes. This amendment did not add to the taxes of the Porto Rican Company, since the increase was to be effective only upon cigarettes selling wholesale, exclusive of tax, at from $2 to $3 per thousand, whereas the Porto Rican Company's products sold at $1.75 exclusive of tax; but it did affect the "Lucky Strike" brand of the American Company. In fact, the American Tobacco Company claimed that the Porto Rican Company fostered the legislation with the idea of forcing a wider retail price difference between its own brands selling at the rate of 12 cents per package of 20 and the "Lucky Strikes" selling at 15 cents for 20. Therefore, the American Company called its sole customer in Porto Rico

[1] 299 Fed. 739 (1924).

[2] Cf. p. 246 *et seq., supra,* and 8 F. T. C. D. 1 (1924).

to New York, guaranteed this customer a $20,000 profit per year on his entire business, dispatched its export manager to Porto Rico to conduct a price war, sold its cigarettes to its Porto Rican jobber at lower prices than those charged to dealers in the United States, and cut its retail price on "Lucky Strikes" to 12 cents for 20. Since the Porto Rican Company's cigarette was admittedly of poorer quality, with total costs of production less than half of those of the American cigarette, there was a prompt shift of consumer demand to "Lucky Strikes" in spite of a reduction in prices by the Porto Rican Company. The losses of the two concerns were stated by the court to be running at the rate of an aggregate of $325,000 to $355,000 per year.

Other evidence was introduced, but the foregoing seems ample to sustain the judgment rendered that the American Tobacco Company had discriminated in prices in a manner not permitted under the Clayton Act. Moreover, we can find no ground to dissent from the view of the court that, however unjust the tax amendment and whatever the part played by the local concern in securing its enactment, "it could not be used as an excuse for unfair competition."[1]

[1] 30 Fed. (2d) 234, 237 (1929). Other cases on Section 2 not brought by the Commission and of relative unimportance will be found in 224 Fed. 566; 227 Fed. 46; 256 Fed. 571; and 3 Fed. (2d) 415.

CHAPTER XXII

JUDICIAL INTERPRETATION OF THE ANTITRUST ACTS, 1915-1929 (*Continued*)

ALTHOUGH violations of the exclusive dealing or tying contract provisions of Section 3 of the Clayton Act have constituted the basis for upward of one hundred formal complaints by the Commission, less than half of these have been carried on to a desist order, and up to the date of the last *Annual Report* only two of the twenty-odd of these orders which were protested had been sustained by a court.

The first order entered in a case of this character was against the A. B. Dick mimeograph concern, conspicuous for years for its use of tying contracts and victorious in a Sherman Act suit attacking them. The taking of testimony in the Federal Trade Commission proceedings was completed just prior to the decision of the United States Supreme Court in the Motion-picture Patents case. Upon the publication of this decision the respondent declined to defend the proceedings further and accepted the order.[1]

The most extensive and elaborate attempt of the Commission to enforce Section 3 was in a group of cases usually designated as the "tank-and-pump" cases. As is generally known, the most widespread method of dispensing gasoline to motorists is from an underground tank connected with an overground pump which is also a measuring device and an advertising medium. A number of gasoline producers had adopted the policy of leasing these tank-and-pump outfits to garage and filling-station proprietors at purely nominal sums on the condition that the lessee dispense from them only the lessor's products. Since in many cases a single tank was sufficient to meet the business secured, the proviso had the

[1] *Annual Report,* 1917, p. 9; 1 F. T. C. D. 20 (1917). For a brief statement of the earlier Sherman Act case involving the Dick Co. and for the Motion-picture Patents case cf. pp. 298 and 300 *supra.*

practical result in such cases of confining the purchases of petroleum products by the lessee to those of the lessor. The Commission, in fact, held that this result was deliberately sought by the various oil producers and that consequently the whole scheme was a violation of Section 5 of the Federal Trade Commission Act and Section 3 of the Clayton Act.[1] But with remarkable unanimity four circuit courts of appeals to which these cases were carried reversed the Commission, and in the cases which were carried to the Supreme Court these judgments were affirmed.[2] Moreover, the opinions took the Commission severely to task both for its methods of handling these cases and for its logic. In a decision involving the Canfield Oil Company and five other concerns the Circuit Court of Appeals for the Sixth Circuit objected to the adoption by the Commission of "one general form of findings" for a group of cases, since "in so far as these [six] particular cases are concerned, some of these findings are not only not supported by any evidence whatever, but are also in direct conflict with the only evidence on that particular issue, and they are also directly contrary to the stipulations and agreement of counsel in these cases in reference thereto."[3] In another circuit it was pointed out that since there was no contract preventing any dealer from selling any brand of oil or from leasing as many tanks as he pleased the arrangements were not illegal, and that on the contrary the affirmation of the Commission's order would result in unfairness and even dishonesty since the dealer might then be at liberty to sell from one producer's tank and pump the gasoline of a competitor.[4]

In affirming the decisions of the lower courts the Supreme Court held that the contracts did not obligate the lessees not to sell the goods of others than the lessor, that neither the findings nor the evidence brought the cases within the ruling of the Shoe Machinery case of 1922, and that no purpose or

[1] Orders in such cases will be found in the *Decisions,* vol. ii, pp. 26, 46, 127, 346, 357 (17 companies); vol. iii, pp. 68, 77, 78, 86 (13 companies).

[2] 273 Fed. 478 (1921); 274 Fed. 571 (1921); 276 Fed. 686 (1921); 282 Fed. 81 (1922); 261 U. S. 463 (1923).

[3] 274 Fed. 573 (1921).

[4] 273 Fed. 481 (1921).

power of monopoly had been disclosed.[1] On the basis of all the facts it is clear that the Commission misconstrued the statutes in instituting these cases and generally mishandled them.

The two individual cases which have assumed most prominence in connection with Section 3 are the Gratz and Curtis Publishing cases, although the former is, accurately speaking, not a Clayton Act case. In the original complaint the Gratz concern was charged with violating both Sections 5 of the Trade Commission law and 3 of the Clayton Act, but after hearings the Commission decided the latter charge was not sustained by the evidence. The facts developed before the Commission and the courts show that the firm of Warren, Jones & Gratz of St. Louis was the Carnegie Steel Company's sole agent for the distribution of steel ties used in baling cotton, that the latter concern manufactured such a large proportion of the ties made in the United States that it was able to dominate the market even to the extent of fixing and controlling prices, that the respondents were also sole agents west of the Mississippi for the largest manufacturer of jute bagging in the United States, and that they in many instances refused to sell ties unless the purchaser would also take a stipulated quantity of bagging with his ties. Since Warren, Jones & Gratz were sole distributors for the dominant manufacturer of ties, and since it frequently happened that purchasers of such ties could not secure them elsewhere, the Commission held that the combination sales were injurious to other manufacturers of jute bagging and other stuffs used in baling cotton, and that they constituted an unfair method of competition. As stated above, the allegation that the arrangements were tying contracts was dropped. It is clear that there were no agreements or understandings that the purchaser should not use or deal in the products of a competitor; he simply had to buy bagging to get the ties.

The Second Circuit Court of Appeals, however, reversed the order of the Commission on the ground that that body had based its conclusions on "exceptional and individual cases

[1] 261 U. S. 474 (1923).

which established no general practice affecting the public." It found that the only refusals to sell were those of refusals to sell at all to certain individuals with whom the respondents had had unsatisfactory dealings and refusals to sell ties without bagging at the opening of the market in 1916 and 1917 with the purpose of preventing speculation in ties which might endanger the marketing of the cotton crop.[1] The Supreme Court's affirmation of this decision is extremely unsatisfactory from the point of view of advancing our knowledge of how it would construe facts similar to these since the decision rested upon a technical point of pleading—*viz.*, that "the first count of the complaint is wholly insufficient to charge respondents with practicing 'unfair methods of competition in commerce' within the fair intendment of those words."[2]

In a vigorous dissenting opinion Justice Brandeis held that the complaint was sufficient to charge a violation and that the order of the Commission should be affirmed. In reaching these conclusions he pointed out that the nature of the proceeding under view should be considered in determining the adequacy of the complaint. To his mind the proceeding was neither punitive nor remedial, but preventive. Since it was preventive, the formal complaint needed to be only a plain statement of the thing claimed to be wrong. Under this conception of the Commission's function as prophylactic it is obvious that the reasoning of the lower court is entirely beside the point. One purpose of creating the Commission was to prevent unfair methods of competition from becoming "general." If the courts compel the Commission to establish as a fact that certain methods have become general before affirming an order to desist from such methods, they will go far toward defeating that purpose. Although conceding that circumstances alter cases, Justice Brandeis pointed out that an all-important circumstance was the relative strength of the competitors involved, so that a method of competition fair among equals might be very unfair in the hands of a dominating concern. Finally, he called attention to the facts that

[1] 258 Fed. 314, 317, 318 (1919).
[2] 253 U. S. 427 (1920).

Massachusetts by statute and judicial decision had declared this type of activity "unfair," that the Bureau of Corporations had condemned it in its study of the Harvester Trust, and that the Supreme Court in the dissolution decree in the Tobacco case of 1911 had enjoined an arrangement practically identical with that in question here.[1] Since we agree with Justice Brandeis's conception of the purpose of the 1914 legislation, and since we think the particular circumstances in this case bring it within his reasoning in general, we agree with his conclusion that the order of the Commission should have been sustained.

Furthermore, we are pleased to note that in the Fox Film and Chase and Sanborn cases it was specifically held that it was not necessary for a practice complained of to have become general in order that it be held unfair.[2]

The respondent in the Curtis Publishing Company case is the publisher of a number of magazines, the most important of which in circulation is *The Saturday Evening Post.* The Federal Trade Commission charged it with compelling a large number of established wholesale distributors of magazines to sign contracts which prevented them from acting as agents for any other periodicals than those published by it except with its written consent, and with uniformly refusing such permission for certain of its immediate competitors. In short, there was an elaborate system of exclusive dealing contracts.

When the Commission's order was carried to the Third Circuit Court of Appeals that court made an exhaustive review of the evidence, since it held that the Commission had made "no findings whatever . . . in reference to the greater part of the vast volume of testimony." From this testimony the opinion showed that the Curtis Publishing Company had gone to great trouble and expense to build up a sales organization of young schoolboys under the direction of local agents, that two of its competitors had in an underhanded fashion attempted to induce its agents to distribute their magazines through these schoolboys, and that the Curtis Com-

[1] 253 U. S. 429-442 (1920).

[2] 296 Fed. 353, 356 (1924); 12 Fed. (2d) 22, 27 (1926).

pany had actually utilized its exclusive contracts "solely to thwart the unfair plan" of these two competitors. Consequently, the court held that the Commission had not substantiated its contention that the contracts constituted an unfair method of competition in violation of Section 5 of the Trade Commission law. It disposed of the Clayton Act aspect of the case by showing that these contracts were contracts of agency, not of sale or lease, so that they were not covered by the language of Section 3.[1] The Supreme Court affirmed this decision,[2] and, in spite of some evidence to show that the contracts in question were really contracts of sale on condition, the result seems unexceptionable.

To this point the Trade Commission had uniformly failed in its attempts to state a violation of Section 3 which the courts would uphold. In two fairly recent cases, however, it has been sustained. The first of these involved an attempt on the part of the Butterick Company, by the use of contracts, to fix a resale price upon patterns for wearing apparel and to compel purchasers of its products not to deal in those of competitors. In an earlier case not brought by the Commission the Supreme Court had ruled on a practically identical set of facts that the Standard Fashion Company, a subsidiary of the Butterick Company, had violated Section 3.[3] The Butterick Company designated its contracts as contracts of agency, not of sale, but the Circuit Court of Appeals, Second Circuit, refused to accept this interpretation of them. *Certiorari* was denied by the Supreme Court.[4]

The other case likewise involved both resale-price maintenance and exclusive dealing contracts. The respondent was the Q. R. S. Music Company, a manufacturer of music rolls for player pianos which at the time covered by the Commission's investigation controlled well over 50 per cent of the industry. This fact, coupled with the high quality of its products and its national advertising, made it extremely advantageous, if not almost necessary, for dealers in music rolls

[1] 270 Fed. 881, 885, 911, 904-909 (1921).
[2] 260 U. S. 568 (1923).
[3] 258 U. S. 346 (1922).
[4] 4 Fed. (2d) 910 (1925); 267 U. S. 602 (1925).

to carry those of the Q. R. S. Company. In order further to improve its position and support its resale-price policy the respondent entered into exclusive dealing arrangements with nearly 500 dealers scattered throughout the country. The Seventh Circuit Court of Appeals accepted the Commission's findings of fact, including one that the respondent succeeded in destroying competition among the retailers. Consequently, the opinion closed with the statement, "The clerk will enter an order identical with the one entered by the Commission." [1] In both these cases the size and dominating position of the respondent seems to have been an important factor. Partly because of the lack of such a position, the Commission was reversed in the Pearsall Butter Company case, in which the respondent was doing about 1 per cent of the trade.[2]

The most important case turning on the interpretation of Section 3 of the Clayton Act is that involving the Radio Corporation of America. The Commission has filed a complaint which is still pending,[3] but meanwhile a number of independent manufacturers of radio tubes have brought suit under the Clayton Act.

As is generally known, the Radio Corporation of America owns a number of patents which it licenses to radio receiving-set manufacturers. As is not so well known, the basic patent covering the vacuum tubes used in such sets expired in 1922, throwing the tube-manufacturing industry open. Some time subsequently the Radio Corporation began to include in its license agreements with radio-set manufacturers a clause which required the licensees to purchase from it all the tubes used as initial equipment in sets. In 1927 the group of independent tube manufacturers previously mentioned brought suit against the Radio Corporation, alleging that the operation of "clause nine" in its licensing contract restricted competition in the tube business and tended to create a monopoly. In these contentions the independents were upheld by the Federal District Court of Delaware and the Third Circuit

[1] 12 Fed. (2d) 730, 733 (1926).

[2] 5 F. T. C. D. 127 (1922); 292 Fed. 720 (1923).

[3] *Annual Report,* 1928, pp. 48, 181.

Court of Appeals.[1] During the progress of the litigation the Radio Corporation had suspended the enforcement of the objectionable clause. The independent tube manufacturers, though granted a temporary injunction, did nct request its issuance, but subsequently applied for a permanent injunction. This question is still at issue.

Meanwhile counsel for the independents had secured from the Federal Radio Commission an opinion holding in the language of the Act of 1927 [2] that any concern finally adjudged guilty of violating the laws against monopoly or restraint of trade by attempting to monopolize broadcasting through the control or sale of radio products should be denied all broadcasting privileges. Because of the far-reaching consequences to tube manufacturers and others the outcome of the litigation is being awaited with great interest.[3]

As we have brought out in Chapter XX, the purpose of Congress in including Section 7 in the Clayton Act was to prevent further use by trust organizers of the holding-company device for lessening competition. Obviously this section covers only one of a number of possible methods of securing this object, so that the chief result of its passage has been, as Mr. Henderson neatly phrased it, that "Since the Clayton Act, consolidations in which the parties are well advised have been effected by some other means than by purchase of stock." [4] There were, however, seven instances between 1915 and July 1, 1928, in which a desist order was entered on a violation of this section. The respondents in these cases were the Aluminum Company of America, Armour & Company (two orders), Swift & Company, Western Meat Company, Thatcher Manufacturing Company, and International Shoe Company. All of these orders except the second against Armour were carried to the courts, but in the first Armour and the International Shoe litigations an agreement was made to hold them in abeyance until the decision of the Supreme Court in the Swift, Western Meat, and Thatcher cases.

[1] 24 Fed. (2d) 565 (1928); 28 Fed. (2d) 257 (1928).

[2] Cf. pp. 444, 445, *supra*.

[3] *Radio Retailing,* March, 1929, p. 52 *et seq.*

[4] *The Federal Trade Commission,* p. 321.

The first of the cases to be determined was that of the Aluminum Company. This company has for years had a monopoly of the production of aluminum ingots in the United States and has been the chief producer of rolled sheet aluminum. In 1912 the Cleveland Metal Products Company decided to enter the business of making aluminum kitchen utensils, subsequently perfected arrangements with European producers to provide it with aluminum ingots, and erected and operated an aluminum rolling-mill. Only 27 per cent of the sheets rolled in this mill, however, were used in making kitchen utensils; the remainder was sold in competition with the Aluminum Company of America. With the outbreak of the World War the foreign supply of ingots was cut off, so that the Cleveland Company was compelled to purchase them from the Aluminum Company of America. The market situation was such that the Cleveland Company made excellent profits for a time, but with the entrance of the United States into the war and the intention of the government, carried out in March, 1918, to fix prices of sheet aluminum, it found that the prices which it had contracted to pay the Aluminum Company were too high to permit a profit under the new fixed prices for sheets. Although the Aluminum Company refused to abrogate the contracts, a solution was found in the creation of a new company, the Aluminum Rolling Mills Company, of which the Cleveland was to take one-third of the stock and the Aluminum Company two-thirds. The new concern was to acquire the rolling-mill and sheet business of the Cleveland Company.

The Federal Trade Commission held that the transaction was a mere subterfuge and that realistically viewed it was a violation of Section 7. Since the defenses of the respondent were unsatisfactory to the Circuit Court of Appeals, Third Circuit, it affirmed the Commission's order directing said respondent to divest itself of the stock of the Aluminum Rolling Mills Company. The Supreme Court refused *certiorari.*[1] The practical results of this litigation in preventing the acquisition of the former property and business of the

[1] 3 F. T. C. D 302 (1921); 284 Fed. 401 (1922); 261 U. S. 616 (1923).

Cleveland Company by the Aluminum Trust were exactly nil, however. As the final outcome of a somewhat complicated series of transactions the Aluminum Trust regained the physical assets of the Aluminum Rolling Mills Company to satisfy an unpaid balance due it on purchases of aluminum ingots and pig. The Federal Trade Commission claimed that this debt was entirely fictitious, created only for the purpose of acquiring these assets, and that to permit the transaction to go through would be to sanction an evasion of its order and the court's decree. Since it was not able to convince the court that the debt was fraudulent, the Aluminum Company apparently remains in possession of the field.[1]

The Commission, however, does not seem willing to concede defeat and has instituted a new set of proceedings against the Aluminum Company alleging violations of Sections 2 of the Clayton Act and 5 of the Federal Trade Commission Act.[2] Since at this time (July, 1929), the Commission has not yet issued its final order and since the case will certainly be carried to the courts in the event an order is issued, there seems no point in detailing the charges.

The Western Meat, Thatcher, and Swift cases differ from the Aluminum case in the important particular that the stock of their competitors was purchased directly. The second and third of these differ from the Western Meat in that prior to the issuance of a complaint by the Commission they had dissolved their former competitors and acquired title to and possession of their physical properties. On the basis of this latter distinction the Supreme Court in one decision covering all three cases held that the order of the Commission in the Western Meat case should be affirmed, but that in the others it should be reversed. In all three the Commission had ordered the respondents to divest themselves of all properties and business of their former competitors as well as the illegally acquired stock. The Court stated that "The act [Clayton §7] has no application to ownership of a competitor's property and business obtained prior to any action by the Commis-

[1] 299 Fed. 361 (1924).

[2] *Annual Report,* 1926, pp. 10, 11.

sion, *even though this was brought about through stock unlawfully held.* The purpose of the act was to prevent continued holding of stock and the peculiar evils incident thereto." [1]

Chief Justice Taft, Justice Holmes, and Justice Stone joined Justice Brandeis in the following dissenting opinion:

In my opinion, the purpose of §7 of the Clayton Act was not, as stated by the court, merely "to prevent continued holding of the stock and the peculiar evils incident thereto." It was also to prevent the peculiar evils resulting therefrom. The institution of a proceeding before the Commission under §7 does not operate, like an injunction, to restrain a company from acquiring the assets of the controlled corporation by means of the stock held in violation of that section. If, in spite of the commencement of such a proceeding, the company took a transfer of the assets, the Commission could, I assume, require a retransfer of the assets, so as to render effective the order of divestiture of the stock. I see no reason why it should not, likewise, do this although the company succeeded in securing the assets of the controlled corporation before the Commission instituted a proceeding. Support for this conclusion may be found in §11, which provides for action by the Commission whenever it "shall have reason to believe that any person is violating *or has violated* any of the provisions" of the earlier sections.[2]

Here again we find ourselves with the minority of the Supreme Court on the Thatcher and Swift cases, but add no further comment since we consider it impossible to improve upon that of Mr. Brandeis. We shall say, however, that we consider it unfortunate that the doctrine of these cases has been applied to an order issued under Section 5 of the Commission law directing the Eastman Kodak Company to desist from an agreement with the Allied Laboratories by which the latter obligated itself to use American-made films only in return for an obligation by the Eastman Company not to operate laboratories which it had acquired for the purpose of compelling said agreement and further directing the Eastman Company to divest itself of these laboratories. The first part of the order was sustained; the latter reversed as in the Thatcher and Swift cases because of the Commission's lack of equity powers. But as Justices Stone and Brandeis pointed

[1] 272 U. S. 554, 561 (1926). Italics ours.
[2] *Ibid.,* pp. 563, 564. Italics in the opinion.

out in their dissent, Section 5 of the Commission law is broad and comprehensive in its language, not restricted as are the sections of the Clayton Act, and "To make its want of equity powers ground for limiting those expressly conferred by the statute is to condemn all the orders ever made by the Commission." [1]

As stated above, the first of the Armour cases and the International Shoe case under Section 7 had been held in abeyance until the decisions in the Western Meat, Swift, and Thatcher cases were announced. Meanwhile, however, the Commission on July 14, 1926, issued another order against Armour for violating this section on a set of facts involving entirely different companies. Following the decisions just discussed, the first order against Armour was rescinded on March 11, 1927, and the second vacated on April 13, 1927,[2] but the Commission interpreted these decisions as justifying its order in the International Shoe case. In this judgment it was upheld by the First Circuit Court of Appeals.[3]

The opinion of the court shows that in May, 1921, the International acquired a controlling interest in the stock of the W. H. McElwain Company; that it "refused to have anything to do with the merger on the basis of purchasing assets," but insisted on getting the stock; that the Trade Commission filed a complaint alleging a violation of Section 7 of the Clayton Act in May, 1923; and that subsequent to the complaint the International Company divested itself of the stock but absorbed the assets of the McElwain concern. The court agreed with the Commission that this transaction was "a mere artifice and subterfuge to avoid said act of Congress," [4] and consequently affirmed the order of the Commission without change.

The only other instances of the application of Section 7 of the Clayton Act which have come to our attention have not been included in our discussion, for reasons stated earlier.[5]

[1] 274 U. S. 627 (1927).

[2] *Annual Report*, 1927, pp. 76, 131.

[3] 29 Fed. (2d) 518 (1928).

[4] 29 Fed. (2d) 522 (1928).

[5] Among these may be mentioned, U. S. *v.* New England Fish Exchange,

In a large majority of the cases which we have treated as applications of the Clayton Act a violation of Section 5 of the Federal Trade Commission Act prohibiting unfair methods of competition was also alleged, and, as we have previously stated, the Commission has tended to concentrate its activities more and more upon that section. In the remainder of this chapter we purpose to state the facts and conclusions of certain of the more important cases on unfair methods of competition, reserving for the next chapter a presentation of the philosophy and policies which underlie them.

But before passing to a discussion of these cases we wish to emphasize the fact that it is out of Section 5 that the chief importance of the Commission as a regulating body has grown. There seems to be a tendency on the part of many lawyers and students to view the Commission as a body primarily engaged in making economic investigations and in attempting to enforce the Sherman and Clayton Acts. Both of these acts were directed against monopolies and certain types of restraints of trade. The tests of illegality of such restraints as price discrimination, tying, and exclusive contracts, etc., were a tendency materially to lessen competition or to create a monopoly. There is no such test in Section 5 of the Trade Commission law; it declares unfair methods of competition illegal without requiring proof of a tendency to monopoly. And in so doing it obviously marks a still further departure from the traditional doctrines of *laissez-faire* and *caveat emptor*. By it an instrumentality of the federal government is created for the purpose of aiding the business community to

---

258 Fed. 732 (1919); an investigation by the Interstate Commerce Commission of the acquisition of a large block of the shares of the Wabash and Lehigh Valley railroads by the Pennsylvania, *New York Times,* July 29, 1928, section ii, p. 13; a complaint filed by the I. C. C. against the Kansas City Southern for acquiring and holding a large part of the capital stock of the Missouri, Kansas, and Texas, and of the St. Louis Southwestern, *Railway Age,* March 3, 1928, p. 547; a subsidiary complaint against the Missouri, Kansas, and Texas for acquiring stock of the St. Louis Southwestern, *Railway Age,* April 7, 1928, p. 822; and the order of the Interstate Commerce Commission to the Baltimore and Ohio, the New York Central and the New York, Chicago, and St. Louis railroads to divest themselves of portions of the stock of the Wheeling and Lake Erie, *Railway Age,* March 16, 1929, p. 629.

bring the standards of all its members up to the level attained by its better elements.

In dealing with the hundreds of desist orders issued under Section 5 it is imperative that some attempt should be made at their classification.[1] But since many of the cases illustrate a number of different types of unfair competition, and since any possible classification involves a considerable degree of overlapping, it will be necessary to draw somewhat arbitrary lines, and then, at times, to disregard them. The largest single group may be designated as misrepresentations, including false advertising, false statements on the character of a product, false claims of government endorsement or adoption, passing off, and similar practices. Other important types of unfair methods are attempts to direct the channels of commerce by boycotts and other devices, commercial bribery, and resale-price maintenance.

The leading case in our general category of misrepresentations is that of the Winsted Hosiery Company, involving both false statements as to the character of product and false advertising. Briefly stated, the charge in this case was that the Winsted Hosiery Company had labeled, advertised, and sold as "merino," "natural wool," "gray wool," etc., knit underwear which was in fact composed partly of cotton. The Commission held that a substantial part of the consuming public understood these terms to designate an all-wool product, that some buyers for retailers and some salespeople interpreted the terms in the same way, that some retailers and their salespeople relied on such labels and used them to sell this underwear as all-wool, and that the result of this set of circumstances was to encourage misrepresentation by dealers and actually to mislead and deceive a substantial portion of the consuming public. Consequently, it ordered the respondent to cease using such labels except when the products were all wool.[2]

[1] The Commission has published lists of practices condemned by it as "unfair." For the most recent of these see pp. 535-537, *infra*. As will be noticed, they are in no sense a classification.

[2] 2 F. T. C. D. 202 (1920).

On appeal this order was reversed by the Second Circuit Court of Appeals because it was proved that "the trade was not misled in any respect by the label complained of." The comments in the opinion upon the practice are extremely interesting as reflecting a refusal by the court to see in Section 5 of the Commission law any alteration in the existing common-law doctrine of unfair competition. Among other things it said:

The Commission is not made a censor of commercial morals generally. . . . In this case there was obviously no unfair method of competition as against other manufacturers of underwear. The labels were thoroughly established and understood in the trade. . . . There was no combination in restraint of trade nor any attempt to establish a monopoly. Manifestly no other manufacturer of underwear could have maintained a suit against the petitioner for unfair competition or for an injunction or damages under the antitrust acts. Assuming that some consumers are misled because they do not understand the trade signification of the labels, or because some retailers deliberately deceive them as to its meaning, the result is in no way connected with unfair competition, but is like any other misdescription or misbranding of products. . . . It may be that it will be desirable to prevent the use of the particular labels, but it is, in our opinion, not within the province of the Federal Trade Commission to do so.[1]

With but one dissenting vote the Supreme Court reversed this decision. The opinion stated flatly that the arguments which had prevailed with the Court of Appeals were "unsound." It held that the labels in question were "literally false," that they were calculated to and did deceive a substantial part of the public, that it was to the interest of the public that a proceeding be brought to stop the practice, and that said practice constituted "an unfair method of competition as against manufacturers of all-wool knit underwear and as against those manufacturers of mixed wool and cotton underwear who brand their product truthfully," since customers were attracted from the honestly branded goods to those fraudulently misbranded. The Court specifically repudiated the idea that a general knowledge in the trade of the practice of misbranding saved it from condemnation as unfair: "A method inherently unfair does not cease to be so because

[1] 272 Fed. 960 (1921).

those competed against have become aware of the unlawful practice." [1] The final outcome of this litigation will ultimately receive the approval of all interested parties. The decision of the lower court was directly in line with established precedents, but those precedents reflected an unfortunate hiatus in the law which it was one purpose of the Federal Trade Commission Act to close. The Supreme Court's decision certifies the authority of the Commission in such cases and has aided it in rectifying some undesirable if not pernicious practices.

It must be noted, however, that some cases have arisen since the Winsted decision in which the courts have found it necessary to modify an order against false and misleading advertising because of a conflict in the evidence not reflected in the findings of the Commission or for other reasons. Perhaps the most representative case of this sort was that of the L. B. Silver Company, a breeder and shipper of thoroughbred hogs. The charge of the Commission included a number of items, among them being allegations that the Ohio Improved Chester hogs bred by the Silver Company were really not a separate and distinct breed from the Chester Whites as claimed by it, that the respondent falsely claimed its hogs were more resistant to disease than other breeds, and that it also falsely claimed to secure lower rates for transportation from express companies than those received by its competitors. The court which reviewed the case found that there was a sharp difference of opinion among experts on the question of the difference, if any, between the Ohio Improved Chester and the Chester White breeds, so that a claim in an advertisement that they were different could not be construed as an unfair method of competition. The other parts of the order were sustained, except for an unimportant item on the weight of two hogs once owned by the respondent.[2]

An interesting group of cases has arisen in the automobile tire, typewriter, and adding-machine industries. As is well known, it is possible to take from partially worn tires fabric

[1] 258 U. S. 493, 494 (1922).
[2] 4 F. T. C. D. 73 (1921); 289 Fed. 985 (1923).

which is still sound and by the use of vulcanizing and other processes reconstruct or rebuild tires which superficially appear to be new. Obviously there is no objection to these salvaging operations unless the resulting product is misrepresented. The Commission has found such misrepresentation, and in a number of instances ordered concerns in this business to cease from representing such tires as new and from offering them for sale unless it is plainly and prominently indicated on them that they are rebuilt or reconstructed.[1] This misrepresentation was in some instances aggravated by the additional offense of attempting to pass off such rebuilt tires as the product of a nationally known manufacturer by simulating its name, as in the cases of the Good Wear Tire and Tube Company and the Racine Tire Sales Company.[2]

Misrepresentations in the rebuilt typewriter business are obviously more closely akin to the second aspect of those in tires, since it is practically impossible to "reconstruct" a typewriter so that it would not be instantly recognized as the product of one of the half-dozen established manufacturers. The same is true of adding machines. Because the good will of the public based on performance is so vitally important to these manufacturers it is clear that the Commission's orders insisting that rebuilt machines be so labeled are well taken from their point of view as well as from that of the public.[3]

The termination of the World War gave rise to a group of misrepresentation cases of a particularly pernicious sort. The government had, of course, accumulated extremely large stocks of numerous articles ranging from saddles to canned beans, for which it had no use after demobilization. These stocks were sold at auction at prices which were frequently well below what the government had paid for them. Many retailers took advantage of these sales and so-called "Army and Navy" stores sprang up all over the country. Some dealers, however, utilized the situation to pass off as former government stores articles which had never been its property,

[1] 1 F. T. C. D. 380 (1919); 2 F. T. C. D. 119 (1919).
[2] 2 F. T. C. D. 216 (1920); 5 F. T. C. D. 327 (1922).
[3] 1 F. T. C. D. 105, 109 (1918).

which could not meet its specifications, and in some instances articles which had actually been rejected as not up to requirements.[1] Other false claims of government indorsement not resulting from the sales of surplus war stocks have also been made.[2] There can be no disagreement that such cases constitute unfair methods of competition and that the Commission is to be commended for its vigorous work in prosecuting them. As a result of its efforts these practices have been materially checked, though occasional orders against them appear in the more recent summaries of the Commission's work.[3]

Attempts to direct or control the channels of commerce by the use of trade discounts have already been discussed in our treatment of the Mennen case. Since our reasons have been set forth there for believing that such tactics are extremely unfortunate in that they hamper the development of more efficient methods of distributing goods, it is necessary here only to supplement that argument by reference to a few cases in which the methods used were different, though the object was the same. As a matter of fact, the method most frequently attacked by the Commission is that condemned by the Supreme Court in the Eastern States Retail Lumber Dealers' Association case—*viz.*, the boycott.

The most important of these cases are those of the Wholesale Saddlery Association of the United States and the National Harness Manufacturers' Association of the United States,[4] the Western Sugar Refinery *et al.*,[5] Wholesale Grocers' Association of El Paso, Texas, *et al.*,[6] the Chamber of Commerce of Minneapolis *et al.*,[7] the Arkansas Wholesale Grocers' Association *et al.*,[8] and the Pacific States Paper Trade Asso-

[1] 4 F. T. C. D. 102 (1921); 5 F. T. C. D. 112 (1922); 5 F. T. C. D. 253 (1922).

[2] 4 F. T. C. D. 41 (1921); 4 F. T. C. D. 144 (1921); 285 Fed. 853 (1922); 4 F. T. C. D. 387 (1922).

[3] *Annual Report,* 1925, pp. 172, 174; *Annual Report,* 1926, p. 107; *Annual Report,* 1927, p. 135.

[4] 1 F. T. C. D. 335 (1919).

[5] 2 F. T. C. D. 151 (1919).

[6] 3 F. T. C. D. 109 (1920).

[7] 7 F. T. C. D. 115 (1923).

[8] *Annual Report,* 1926, p. 106.

ciation *et al.*[1] Each of these cases was taken to the courts and in all but the last the charge of the Commission on this particular point was affirmed, though in some of them it was reversed on other parts of its order.[2] The Pacific States Paper Trade Association did not contest this part of the Commission's order.[3] Reinforced by these decisions, the Commission has proceeded to carry on vigorously its campaign against these boycotting activities.[4] The essential difference between these cases and that of the Mennen Company is that in them the courts found a conspiracy or agreement to direct and control the channels of commerce. Since the result of that company's discount plan was to erect the same barrier to the free flow of commerce as that found in these boycotting cases, we reiterate our conclusion that the plan should have been condemned by the courts.

The investigations of the Federal Trade Commission in the field of commercial bribery have revealed in a number of industries a situation repellent to even the most rudimentary concept of fair play. Despite the wishes of a considerable portion of the concerns in these industries, whole groups had been forced to the competitive practices of their meanest members. The Commission quotes a statement from "one man of prominence in an industry who welcomed the proceedings of the Commission destined to destroy the practice," as follows: "From an experience of thirty years in the industry I don't believe that there is a single house in it that has not had to pay bribes to hold old business or to obtain new business."[5]

Though sporadic offenses have been disclosed in a wide range of businesses, those worst afflicted were ship chandlery, dye, road machinery, and paint and varnish. The housecleaning in these lines has been of a thoroughgoing character

[1] 7 F. T. C. D. 155 (1923).

[2] 268 Fed. 705 (1920); 275 Fed. 725 (1921); 277 Fed. 657 (1922); 13 Fed. (2d) 673 (1926); 18 Fed. (2d) 866 (1927).

[3] 273 U. S. 52, 66 (1927).

[4] Cf. *Annual Report,* 1925, pp. 30, 31, 157, and *Annual Report,* 1926, pp. 14, 102, 103.

[5] *Annual Report,* 1920, p. 53.

and highly satisfactory results have been secured[1] within the limited scope of the Commission's activities. But it is clear that cease-and-desist orders are not the most satisfactory method of meeting such a situation. In fact, the Commission has recognized this, and as long ago as May 15, 1918, submitted a special report to Congress explaining its limitations and requesting additional legislation. Among other things the report pointed out that bribery was criminal *per se* and should be punished as a crime and that the Commission was able to reach only the giver of the bribe, whereas the recipient was equally guilty.[2] To these should be added the obvious limitation upon the Commission of proving interstate commerce, a limitation to which it has not adhered as strictly as the courts deemed necessary in reversing its orders against two ship-chandlery concerns.[3] In other cases the courts have ruled that the Commission had exceeded its authority in ordering a manufacturer to desist from giving to employees of customers or prospective customers gratuities such as cigars, liquor, meals, theater tickets, or entertainment of any kind, and in ordering another manufacturer to desist from giving premiums to salesmen of retailers, with the knowledge and consent of the retailers, to induce the salesmen to push the products of the manufacturer. In neither case did the final order of the Commission allege the use of money as a bribe.[4] The first of these cases raises the undoubtedly difficult question as to where ordinary business courtesy ceases and bribery begins. In instances at or near the boundary line it may prove wiser for the Commission to refuse to act. Since almost all of the Commission's orders in cases of this type have been accepted without protest, its procedural and other handicaps have not prevented it from accomplishing a

[1] Cf. *Decisions,* vol. i, pp. 60, 71, 77, 78, 81, 82, 107, 112; vol. iii, pp. 20, 205, 208, 209, 213, 217, 222, 223, 227, 235, 239, 242, 313, 316, 320, 323, 353, 357, 418, 421, 425, 430; vol. iv, pp. 65, 69, 97, 108, 129, 220, 225, 230, 243, 248, 253, 292, 313, 316, for cases involving the crudest form of bribery—*viz.,* by the use of money.

[2] Reprinted in *Annual Report,* 1920, pp. 52-54.

[3] D. A. Winslow & Co. and Norden Ship Supply Co., Inc. 277 Fed. 206 (1921). *Certiorari* denied by Supreme Court, 258 U. S. 618 (1922).

[4] New Jersey Asbestos Co. case, 264 Fed. 509 (1920); Kinney-Rome Co. case, 275 Fed. 665 (1921).

substantial reform in reducing bribery in certain industries. On the other hand, the Commission believed in 1918 that in general there was a tendency for the practice to become more widespread. Even if this tendency has now been checked to some extent by the Commission's work, there is no doubt that its recommendation for action by Congress has been too long ignored.

The fourth and last of our general categories of unfair methods of competition was resale-price maintenance. In this field the Commission has not only issued cease-and-desist orders, but also has undertaken a general study of the economic and legal aspects of the problem. As we go to press only part of the report has been published, and, unfortunately from our point of view, it does not include any appreciable amount of the "facts of a quantitative or statistical nature based on actual business results of dealing in trade-marked or otherwise identified products" which are promised in part two.[1] The greater part of the report now available consists of a summary and tabulation of the answers recorded on questionnaires sent out by the Commission. There is in addition an excellent brief summary of the court decisions on resale-price maintenance in the United States and of the status of the practice in several foreign countries. The questionnaires just mentioned were directed to five groups: consumers, professional men, manufacturers, wholesalers, and retailers. Most of the questions called for an expression of opinion, with the reasons or facts upon which the opinion rested. As the most cursory examination of the report will show, however, there was a practically uniform failure on the part of those answering the questions to be specific or to cite instances of events supporting their generalizations. Moreover, the Commission notes instances in which some generalizations of the manufacturers contradict others made by the same group and concludes that the wholesalers of barbers' supplies had in most cases set down "canned" answers prepared by some central

[1] Federal Trade Commission, *Resale Price Maintenance*, part i, p. xi; printed as House Document, No. 546, part i, 70th Congress, 2d Session, 1929.

agency.[1] The case of the manufacturers is particularly amusing. In reply to one question a heavy majority of those answering claimed that when dealers cut prices on their own products their volume of sales was reduced. In replying to the next question, however, an even heavier majority of those answering contended that the cutting of prices by dealers on competitors' products also resulted in a decrease in the sales of their own goods. The inference in the second case is that the business went to the competitor, but as the Commission says, "Obviously both of these conclusions cannot in general be true." To this we would add that for all these reasons it seems probable that the first part of the report is of more value to psychologists than to economists. Certainly it provides them with ample illustrations of the inability of most of us to treat objectively any proposition of close and immediate importance to us.

But regardless of their lack of logic and of objective data to support their opinions, the business men are in favor of legalizing price maintenance. This is true of manufacturers, wholesalers, and retailers, and in each group by large majorities. On the other hand, a small majority of the professional classes oppose it and an overwhelming majority of consumers likewise oppose it. The most common objections of consumers were the fear of higher prices, of the elimination of competition, and of monopoly and monopoly profit. The professional groups (lawyers, economists, and statisticians) objected primarily on the grounds that the practice interferes with the dealer's right to conduct his own business, that it restricts or eliminates competition, and that it tends toward monopoly and higher prices.[2]

Price-cutting appears obnoxious to the manufacturer for a number of reasons. In the first place he knows that it is frequently a device used by dealers to attract trade and feels that such dealers are capitalizing the good will for which he has paid. Now if the result of this use of his product as a "leader" were simply to increase his total sales volume, he

[1] F. T. C., *Resale Price Maintenance,* part i, pp. 52, 59-61.
[2] *Ibid.,* pp. 14 and 25.

would have little ground for protest and probably would not protest, but, as previously stated, he is generally convinced that the practice is more likely to reduce his total sales. His argument is that the consuming public, seeing his product offered at a price below that he set, will not only become suspicious of the quality of the product, but also will reason that the established price includes an exorbitant amount of profits. Consequently, he contends, purchasers will drift away from him. Moreover, the dealers who have maintained his prices may become disgruntled if accused by their customers of exacting unreasonable profits and refuse to continue to handle the product.

In addition to eliminating the alleged evils of dealers' competition, legalized price maintenance would also, in the opinion of the manufacturers who replied to the Trade Commission's inquiries, remove certain evils of manufacturers' competition such as unprofitable business, price instability, loss of advertising benefit, and price competition. These claims are particularly interesting in view of the contentions of advocates of price maintenance that it will not restrict or reduce competition among manufacturers.[1]

Although 84.4 per cent of the 2,334 retailers whose questionnaires were tabulated by the Commission favored legalizing price maintenance, this group contains the chief opponents of such a plan—*viz.,* the department and chain stores. The spokesmen of these organizations feel that to allow the manufacturers of an appreciable part of the articles they sell to determine their prices for them would be to reduce themselves to little more than agencies of those manufacturers. They prefer to determine their own sales policies. They contend that their price-cutting policy and their enormous turnover are mutually complementary and that neither would be possible without the other. Moreover, they point out that the public secures an appreciable advantage from that policy, and that the manufacturer receives from them the prices he asks.

In the light of these facts it was inevitable that producers should attempt to secure adherence to their established prices

[1] F. T. C., *Resale Price Maintenance,* part i, p. 39.

and that these attempts should be resisted. Long prior to the creation of the Federal Trade Commission such controversies had been taken to the courts so that there was by 1915 a considerable body of judicial precedent on the legality of resale-price maintenance. Before proceeding to the Commission's activities in this field it will be necessary to review briefly some of the leading cases previously adjudicated.

Early cases in the lower courts had sustained price maintenance arrangements when they could be brought within the privileges of the patent or copyright laws,[1] but the Supreme Court has a practically consistent record of ruling against price maintenance.

The leading price-maintenance case was for years that of the Dr. Miles Medical Company *v.* Park & Sons Company.[2] The former concern manufactured proprietary though unpatented medicines, upon which it set a price. Dealers in these medicines were required to sign contracts to sell only at the established prices, and, in the case of wholesalers, only to retailers who agreed to maintain prices. Park & Sons Company secured a supply of the medicines from dealers in spite of refusing to sign the standard contract, and proceeded to cut prices on them. The manufacturers sought an injunction to restrain this activity, but were refused in the Circuit Court of Appeals and the Supreme Court. The last court construed the contracts as falling within that prohibited class whose sole purpose is the destruction of competition and the fixing of prices. It specifically pointed out that "The present case is not analogous to that of a sale of good will, or of an interest in a business, or of the grant of a right to use a process of manufacture,"[3] and refused the contention of the Miles Company that it was entitled to rights analogous to those granted a patentee by stating that since it had not seen fit to take out letters patent the "case lies outside the policy of the patent

[1] Victor Talking Machine Co. *v.* The Fair, 123 Fed. 424 (1903); Edison Phonograph Co. *v.* Kaufmann, 105 Fed. 960 (1901).

[2] 220 U. S. 373 (1911).

[3] *Ibid.*, p. 407.

law, and the extent of the right which that law secures is not here involved or determined."[1]

In a subsequent case, however, just this right was considered. Bauer & Cie, copartners, of Berlin, Germany, were the assignees of letters patent from the United States covering the product Sanatogen. On the sealed packages containing the bottles of this product was printed a statement to the effect that they were not to be sold at less than one dollar each and that any such sale or use after such sale would be construed as an infringement of the patent and would render an infringer liable to injunction and damages. The defendant, a retail druggist of Washington, D. C., named O'Donnell, sold Sanatogen at less than one dollar. The Supreme Court held that these sales were not an infringement of the patent since they fell within the established rule that "a patentee who has parted with a patented machine by passing title to a purchaser has placed the article beyond the limits of the monopoly secured by the patent act."[2] The opinion distinguished this case from that of the Dick mimeograph concern by pointing out that in the latter the evidence showed that the machines were sold at cost or less, that the manufacturer of them expected to secure his profits from the ink, stencils, etc., which the purchaser was required by the license restriction to use with them, that there were no analogous facts in the Bauer case, and that the attempt to designate the sales of Sanatogen as a license to use was a "mere play upon words."[3]

The Federal Trade Commission instituted a number of proceedings in price-maintenance cases shortly after its organization, but before any of them had been carried to the Supreme Court that body had determined in favor of the defendants the case of the Colgate Company which had been criminally prosecuted under the Sherman Act because of its price-maintenance policy. The Colgate Company did not require its customers to sign contracts binding themselves to maintain its resale prices, but did distribute letters, telegrams, circulars, etc., showing uniform prices to be charged, urging dealers

[1] 220 U. S. 402.
[2] 229 U. S. 1, 17 (1913).
[3] *Ibid.*, p. 16.

to adhere to such prices, announcing that no sales would be made to price-cutters and requesting information on price-cutters. It also investigated alleged cases of price-cutting, placed offenders on "suspended lists," requested such offenders to give assurances of price maintenance as a condition of resumption of business relations and refused to sell to all who would not give such assurances, although it sold freely to all who did. In spite of this rather formidable list the District Court for the Eastern District of Virginia which first heard the case ruled that the indictment failed to charge any offense under the Sherman Act or any other law of the United States, chiefly because there were no allegations of monopoly or attempt to monopolize or contracts in restraint of trade, and quashed the indictment. The Supreme Court accepted the interpretation of the indictment made by the lower court, agreed that it did not charge the Colgate Company "with selling its products to dealers under agreements which obligated the latter not to resell except at prices fixed by the company," and consequently affirmed the previous decision. The Miles Medical case was distinguished because of the use by that company of a series of uniform contracts.[1]

In the following year the Supreme Court reaffirmed the importance of the distinction between the use or non-use of contracts for maintaining resale prices and held as violative of the Sherman Act the contracts used by A. Schrader's Son, Inc. When they were used the decision in Dr. Miles Medical Company was still controlling, since there was in the opinion of the court an "obvious difference" between them and the situation in the Colgate case where "a manufacturer merely indicates his wishes concerning prices and declines further dealings with all who fail to observe them." [2]

The leading case in which the Federal Trade Commission attempted to restrain a system of resale-price maintenance as an unfair method of competition is that of the Beech-Nut Packing Company, manufacturer of food products and chewing-gum. In selling its products the respondent had formu-

[1] 253 Fed. 522, 524, 528 (1918); 250 U. S. 300, 303, 307, 308 (1919).
[2] 252 U. S. 85, 99, 100 (1920).

lated what it designated as the "Beech-Nut policy," the essential feature of which was resale-price maintenance. In the furtherance of this policy the company worked out an elaborate system of regulations and of checks upon its customers. All of them, wholesalers, jobbers, and retailers, were informed that they were expected to maintain the established prices, that no sales would be made to any concern which deviated from these prices or which, in the case of a wholesaler, sold to another which had so deviated, and that they were expected to report price-cutters. The company pointed out to dealers the advantage of the liberal profit margins established by the fixed prices. To secure the results desired the Beech-Nut Company maintained card records of thousands of distributors, marking upon the cards of those who had cut prices a notation of some sort indicating that they were "undesirable" and were not to be supplied, developed a system of numbers or symbols on the containers of its products for the purpose of tracing them, and carried out its threat to refuse to sell to price-cutters. The Beech-Nut Company did not require its customers to sign contracts obligating themselves to carry out its plans, but it was established that these customers, both wholesale and retail, regularly coöperated with the company by reporting cases of price-cutting.

The language of the opinion of the lower court clearly shows that this coöperation between producer and distributors was to these judges sufficient ground for bringing the case within the rule of the Dr. Miles case; the purpose was the same in both, and whether that purpose was attained by "acquiescence and coöperation" or by "express agreement" seemed to them immaterial. Despite this reasoning, on the authority of the Colgate case, the order of the Commission was reversed.[1]

But as in the Schrader case the Supreme Court ruled here that its decision in the Colgate case had been "misapprehended" by the lower court, and reiterated its statement that in that decision it "had no intention to overrule or modify the doctrine of *Dr. Miles Medical Co.* v. *Park & Sons Co.*" The majority of the court held that "The facts found show

[1] 264 Fed. 889 (1920).

that the Beech-Nut system goes far beyond the simple refusal to sell goods to persons who will not sell at stated prices, which in the Colgate Case was held to be within the legal right of the producer." After outlining certain of the features of that "system," the court went on to say that it might infer, indeed could not escape the conclusion, "that competition among retail distributors is practically suppressed." It specifically dealt with the matter of contracts by pointing out that the inference just stated was not overcome " . . . by the conclusion stated in the Commission's findings that the merchandising conduct of the company does not constitute a contract or contracts whereby resale prices are fixed, maintained, or enforced. The specific facts found show suppression of the freedom of competition by methods in which the company secures the coöperation of its distributors and customers, which are quite as effectual as agreements expressed or implied intended to accomplish the same purpose." Although thus affirming the principle of the Commission's order, the court expressed the opinion that in form it was too broad and directed a modification of its terms, making them more specific.[1] Four justices dissented, one of them basing his dissent on the authority of the Colgate case.

It must be admitted that a review of these cases leaves the student somewhat confused as to the exact state of the law on this important issue. In our judgment the cause of this uncertainty and bewilderment is that the Colgate case was incorrectly decided. In the light of the Supreme Court's own summary of the methods used by that concern,[2] we are unable to comprehend how that body could have referred to its actions as a "simple refusal to sell goods to persons who will not sell at stated prices."[3] The trial court reduced the question which it posed to itself to these simple terms and the Supreme Court accepted its formulation, but in so doing it seems to us that it entirely disregarded just the sort of facts which it held all-important in the Beech-Nut case. More-

[1] 257 U. S. 441, 452, 454, 455, 456 (1922).
[2] Cf. 250 U. S. 303 or our pp. 508, 509, *supra*.
[3] 257 U. S. 454 (1922).

over, we do not believe our conclusions can be refuted by insistence upon the difference between the Sherman and Federal Trade Commission Acts; in other words, that a practice might be condemned as "unfair" under the latter without bringing it within the prohibitions of the former. As a general proposition this distinction is incontrovertible, but in two of the quotations made above from the opinion of the court, reference is made to the "suppression of competition" as a basis for the decision. To these we may add the following: "The system here disclosed necessarily constitutes a scheme which restrains the natural flow of commerce and the freedom of competition in the channels of interstate trade *which it has been the purpose of all the antitrust acts to maintain.*"[1] If we understand this language correctly, the practices of the Beech-Nut Company were illegal under the Sherman Act as well as under the Federal Trade Commission Act. And if we understand the facts in the Colgate case, its practices were illegal under the former.

Subsequent to the Beech-Nut decision a number of orders on resale-price maintenance have been upheld in the form issued or with only slight modifications.[2] The most interesting of these was that to the Cream of Wheat Company in which the court did not stop with affirming the prohibition of certain practices but, for the first time in such cases, went on to enumerate a list of activities tending toward price maintenance which were positively permitted. This list took the form of a proviso to paragraph six of the Commission's order in the following words:

> *Provided, however,* That nothing herein shall prevent the respondent from performing the following acts:
>
> (a) Requesting its customers not to resell Cream of Wheat at less than a stated minimum price.

[1] 257 U. S. 454 (1922). Italics ours.

[2] Among these are the Butterick Co., 4 Fed. (2d) 910 (1925); Sealpax Co., 5 Fed. (2d) 574 (1925); Hills Bros., 9 Fed. (2d) 481 (1926); Toledo Pipe, 11 Fed. (2d) 337 (1926); Chase and Sanborn, 12 Fed. (2d) 22 (1926); Q. R. S. Music Co., 12 Fed. (2d) 730 (1926); Cream of Wheat Co., 14 Fed. (2d) 40 (1926); J. W. Kobi Co., 23 Fed. (2d) 41 (1927).

(b) Refusing to sell to a customer, because he resells below such requested minimum price, or because of other reasons.

(c) Announcing in advance its intention thus to refuse.

(d) Informing itself, through its soliciting agents, and through publicly circulated advertisements of customers which come to its attention, and through other legitimate means, without any coöperative action with its other customers or other persons, as to the prices at which Cream of Wheat is being sold.[1]

Although not a pronouncement of the Supreme Court, the above summary indicates accurately, we believe, the prevailing view in that body. While it makes no attempt to enumerate the things that manufacturers *may not* do in their effort to control the prices of their products, it is clear and definite as to things that they *may* do and to that extent clarifies the legal situation.

In two cases the Second Circuit Court of Appeals has reversed price-maintenance orders. The first, directed against the American Tobacco Company and practically all the wholesale tobacco dealers in and around Philadelphia, was discussed in Chapter XI.[2]

The second reversal was in the case of Harriet Hubbard Ayer, Incorporated, a manufacturer of perfumes and cosmetics. The controlling factor in the decision was the opinion of the court that the respondent had urged or solicited price maintenance by its customers in only occasional instances and that it had not adopted the elaborate system of follow-ups disclosed in the Beech-Nut record. The Supreme Court denied *certiorari*.[3]

In this treatise we are, of course, more interested in the economic than in the legal aspects of this problem. Fundamentally it resolves itself into another phase of the question discussed in the review of the Mennen case, namely the controversy in regard to the merits of two competing methods of distributing goods. The rival methods are those of the cut-price department store, chain store, and mail-order organizations, on the one hand, and of the established hierarchy of

[1] 14 Fed. (2d) 50 (1926).

[2] Cf. pp. 187, 188, *supra*.

[3] 15 Fed. (2d) 274 (1926); 273 U. S. 759 (1927).

manufacturers, wholesalers, and retailers, on the other. Among business men the most incisive critics of plans of price maintenance are the executives of the cut-price stores. Manufacturers and the representatives of the established order of wholesalers and retailers for the distribution of their goods, whom they largely dominate, are the chief supporters of such plans. In this controversy the interests which we are most concerned to promote are those of the purchasing public. From the public's viewpoint the arguments of the manufacturers seem decidedly weak. The defense they sometimes offer that only a limited group of articles is affected by price-maintenance plans will not bear scrutiny. Common knowledge to the contrary is supported by investigations of the Federal Trade Commission. Moreover, there is good reason to believe that if such plans were given legal support they would be rapidly extended to embrace an even larger proportion of the commodities offered for sale. For the purchasing public the problem presented is not only which of these methods of distribution is likely in the long run to prove most efficient, but by which method will the gains of efficiency be most widely diffused. A basic principle of the cut-price department and chain stores and of the mail-order houses is, as was pointed out earlier,[1] large turnover on a narrow margin of profit. The advocates of resale-price maintenance propose that manufacturers shall be allowed to determine not only their own prices, but the prices to be charged by dealers; in other words, to dictate the margin of profit which dealers are to receive. To the extent that this would establish profit margins higher than the cut-price stores require for the successful conduct of their businesses, and it is difficult to see how otherwise the less economically administered hierarchy of wholesale and retail establishments could afford to handle the products concerned, the plan clearly seems economically unsound and a bar to progress. Believing as we do that it is in connection with our distributive system that there is the greatest need for the promotion of economy and efficiency, and believing also that the most hopeful development in that

[1] P. 506, *supra*.

field, next to the coöperative movement, is the multiplication of cut-price stores and mail-order houses, we would consider any modification of the present condemnation of price maintenance plans as undesirable.

On the other hand, we appreciate thoroughly the necessity for protecting manufacturers from certain types of price-cutting, which are as unfair and uneconomic as would be an all-pervasive system of resale price maintenance. When the managers of cut-price stores or mail-order houses deliberately and persistently use the widely advertised products of a particular manufacturer as a means, not primarily of extending the sale of such products, but falsely to create the impression in the minds of their customers that because they are offering these products at prices below those advertised by the manufacturer, therefore their prices for goods generally are correspondingly low, the manufacturer is himself the victim of unfair competition. We believe that it is the duty of the Federal Trade Commission to be as alert to such unfair methods on the part of distributors as they have shown themselves to be to unfair practices of manufacturers. Discriminating between fair and unfair methods in this as in other border-line situations will undoubtedly prove difficult, but we think that criteria for such discrimination can be developed and that the extension of the concept of unfair methods into this field is urgently called for.

The review of decisions presented in the foregoing pages provides a basis for conclusions in reference to the work and accomplishments of the Federal Trade Commission, and with these the next chapter is concerned.

CHAPTER XXIII

THE FEDERAL TRADE COMMISSION

In the preceding chapters the reasons for the creation of the Federal Trade Commission, its powers and functions as provided in the various acts affecting it, and the interpretation of those powers and functions by the courts have been discussed. In this chapter the organization, procedure, policies, and accomplishments of the Commission will be treated in more detail. We omit reference to the special activities assumed by the Commission at the behest of the President or of Congress during the Great War as having now only an historical interest.

The organization of the Commission has undergone some important changes from time to time, but fundamentally it has rested upon the division of functions provided for in the original act—that is, the functions of investigation and of regulation. Investigation has been the chief task of the economic division, regulation that of the legal division. Although the separation has been maintained, it has never prevented one division from calling upon the other for aid. Since its first organization, the Commission has had a third division, administrative, which was at first under the direction of the secretary of the Commission. It includes such units as personnel, fiscal affairs, publications, docket, mail and files, and supplies, and has continued to the present time practically without change except that it is now supervised by the assistant secretary of the Commission. The fourth division of the Commission, which has continued to function since its first organization, is the export trade division, created to carry out the powers delegated to the Commission by the Webb-Pomerene Act of 1918. As the most important of the four, the economic and legal divisions merit somewhat more detailed treatment.

The economic division was originally under the direction of a chief economist, to whom were subordinated an assistant chief economist and the chief of the division of corporation reports. Very shortly an economic advisory board was substituted for the first arrangement, but since it did not function satisfactorily, the earlier plan was restored. To the chief economist, three assistant chief economists, a chief accountant, and a number of clerks and assistants are now subordinated.

For something over ten years the legal division was organized in two sections, but during the fiscal year 1925-26 these were increased to five: the chief counsel's division, legal investigating division, board of review, trial examiner's division, and trade practice conferences division, each of which is now separate and independent and responsible only to the Commission. The functions of these legal divisions will become apparent in the discussion of procedure below.

The procedure of the Federal Trade Commission in handling alleged violations of the various statutes with which it is concerned has been from time to time subjected to severe attacks. Since certain changes, designed to meet criticisms, were put into effect in March, 1925, it is necessary occasionally, in the discussion which follows, to indicate divergences between the "old" and the "new" rules.

The formal machinery of the Commission as a regulating agency is not put in motion until a complaint is issued. Prior to this, however, a great deal of preliminary work must be done. The Commission cannot issue a complaint until it has "reason to believe" that the law has been violated. The method by which the body acquires its belief that action is necessary is not prescribed. As a matter of practice, nearly all the cases considered arise because of a representation to the Commission by some interested person that the law is being violated. This representation must be in writing, must be signed by the complainant, and must contain a brief statement of the case, but otherwise is without formality. This stage of the proceedings is called a "preliminary inquiry," as is the written statement just described. Such preliminary inquiries are referred to the chief examiner, the head of the legal investigating division, to decide whether or not the Commission has jurisdiction in the case, and, since March, 1925, to attempt to settle the matter by conference or correspondence without the formality of either a stipulation [1] or a complaint. Literally hundreds of inquiries have been thrown out at this stage because of lack of jurisdiction or because the facts stated clearly did not warrant formal action. Many others have been disposed of by conferences or correspondence. But there is a remainder of cases in which the jurisdictional elements are present that cannot be settled by the chief examiner, and in which the inquiry warrants further investigation. Such an inquiry is docketed as an application for a complaint.

Each such application is assigned to an examiner (a lawyer) for investigation. And at this point the controversy over procedure begins. The Commission states that "The first step in the investigation is to present to the party complained against a complete statement of [the] matter, without identifying the applicant, and to request the party complained against to submit such statements, evidence, and documents in defense or explanation of his position as he may desire to be brought to the attention of the commission." [2] On the other hand, there have been protests from business men that complaints have been issued without opportunity to the respondent of stating his defense. A committee of the Chamber of Commerce of the United States reported in 1918 that "There seem to be indisputable instances in which a defendant has had his first intimation through service of a formal complaint that any of his business methods were in question." The committee found an even worse situation in cases in which the Commission had given to the newspapers

[1] Technically, a stipulation is an agreed statement of facts. Since the spring of 1925 the Commission seems to have used the word in two somewhat different senses. In one it is simply an agreed statement of facts upon which a cease-and-desist order is issued; in the other the stipulation includes, in addition to a statement of facts, agreements by the respondent to cease and desist from the objectionable practice and to permit the use of the agreed facts against it in case it should later resort to such practice. In such cases no formal cease-and-desist order need be issued by the Commission. Cf. *Annual Report,* 1925, p. 21; *Annual Report,* 1926, pp. 4, 7, 154-165.

[2] Cf. the Commission's *Annual Report,* 1924, p. 22.

details of the charges which were not included in the formal complaint received by the defendant.[1] As recently as May, 1925, an interviewer for *The Nation's Business,* a periodical published by the Chamber of Commerce of the United States, charged that the Commission had "totally without warrant or justification" condemned and maligned innocent business men.[2] On the same page Commissioner Humphrey was quoted as stating that as a result of some new rules of procedure "no complaint shall issue against the parties complained of until they have had an opportunity, if they so desire, to be heard." The interviewer comments that "This is directly opposite to the policy that has dominated the Commission for many years. The crux of it is that the party complained of shall have his day in court and shall no longer be condemned unheard." The unmistakable inference is that star-chamber condemnations were for "many years" the regular practice of the Commission. In the opinion of the writers this condemnation is far too sweeping. Individual cases of such injustice have undoubtedly occurred and are inexcusable, but so far as we have been able to ascertain the critics of the Commission have cited only isolated cases. To base upon these cases attacks of the sweeping sort cited appears to us as inexcusable and unfair as was the Commission's action in those cases. On the other hand, we are convinced that some of the protests against the "complaint" system as a method of procedure rest upon a more solid foundation, a matter to which we shall return.[3]

After the investigating attorney has developed the facts he summarizes his work in a final report to the chief examiner with a recommendation that the application for complaint be dismissed or that a formal complaint be issued. Under the old rules the chief examiner endorsed his approval or disapproval of this report and in the event that a formal complaint appeared necessary referred the file to the board of review. Otherwise the file was sent directly to the commissioner in

[1] *The Nation's Business,* October, 1918, p. 10.
[2] *Ibid.,* May, 1925, p. 30.
[3] Cf. p. 522 *et seq.*

charge of the particular case. The board of review, after examining the file, summarized the evidence, stated the law applicable, and made a recommendation for Commission action. Under the rules adopted in 1925 important changes were made in the powers of both the chief examiner and the board of review, particularly with reference to the settlement of cases by conferences, stipulations, or informal hearings.

After the board of review concluded its work, under both sets of rules, the case was referred to the commissioner in charge of the particular case for another review and recommendation to the entire body for dismissal or the issuance of a complaint. In deciding this a majority vote rules. If a complaint is decided upon the chief counsel drafts it, but it must be approved by the Commission. Thus the Commission has reviewed the facts twice before they come before it in its judicial capacity.

The original complainant is not a party to the case; it is now the Federal Trade Commission *versus* the respondent. The complaint may be served upon the respondent in person (upon any one of certain officers in the case of a corporation), by leaving it at the principal office of the respondent, or by registered mail. The last method is usually followed. Thirty days are allowed for the filing of an answer. Both the Trade Commission and Clayton acts require that the complaint shall include a notice of a hearing at a fixed place and time, the time to be at least thirty days after service of the complaint. In practice a supplementary notice is inclosed stating that because of the pressure of work the hearing will not be held until a later date, of which notice will be given.

When the case comes to trial the chief counsel is responsible for the presentation of the Commission's charges before the trial examiner. After the testimony is concluded the trial examiner is supposed to prepare a statement of facts to which either side may file exceptions.[1] Briefs are then filed and the case comes up for final argument before the full Com-

[1] In practice the findings of the trial seem to have been frequently dictated by the counsel for the Commission rather than by the trial examiner. Such a procedure is obviously unfair and should be abolished. Cf. Henderson, G. C., *The Federal Trade Commission,* p. 85.

mission. If the complaint is sustained an order to "cease and desist" from the practices condemned is issued. On the other hand, the case may be dismissed because of lack of proof, an intervening court decision, the discontinuance of the practice, or other reasons.

The foregoing summary has assumed that the complaint was contested. A considerable number of cases are settled without a trial, even after the complaint has been issued, by the entrance of a stipulation of agreed facts upon which an order to cease and desist is issued.[1] But this settlement by stipulation must be distinguished from that under the "new" rule on stipulations adopted in March, 1925, since in the latter case no cease-and-desist order is issued; the respondent simply agrees to discontinue the practice. Moreover, it should be noted that the "new" rule on stipulations is to a considerable extent simply a reversion to the method of "conference rulings" followed by the Commission during the first few years of its existence and again, though not under the name of conference rulings, during the period February to October, 1923.[2]

Criticisms have been directed against a number of relatively minor details of the procedure not brought out above. We have pointed out the undesirable nature of the practice of permitting the prosecuting counsel rather than the trial examiner to prepare the "findings" after the trial. Another item to which the legal fraternity particularly objects is that practically without exception no demurrer or motion to dismiss will be entertained either on the basis that the facts alleged do not constitute an offense under the law or on jurisdictional grounds. The adoption of the principle of receiving such motions might accelerate the disposition of cases. If so, the change should be made. A third rule of practice of the Commission which is at least dubious is its refusal to reveal the identity of the person who called attention to the alleged illegal practice. The defense of this procedure, that it would cause many persons to refrain from making complaints be-

[1] *Annual Report,* 1925, p. 24.

[2] For a further discussion of the 1925 rule on stipulations cf. pp. 523-526.

cause of fear of retaliation from the respondent, has some merit, but so has the counter claim that the present scheme may encourage malicious attacks which will hamper a business competitor at no cost to the complainant. Even more unfortunate is the refusal of the Commission to entertain motions for bills of particulars, or for orders that complaints be made more specific. Common justice demands that such requests, when reasonable, should be granted.

But underlying complaints against the procedure and most important of them all is the general one that the Commission is unfair and partial and cannot be anything else because of the fact that it is prosecuting attorney, jury, and judge all rolled into one. Now a part of this situation is inherent in administrative as distinguished from judicial procedure. Congress realized that the work which it was delegating to this new body was of a technical nature and consequently included in its organic statute the provision that its findings of fact should be conclusive "if supported by testimony." Nearly thirty years' experience with the Interstate Commerce Commission had demonstrated the practicability of such a form of organization. But in laying down the general lines of the procedure to which the Commission was to conform, Congress adopted as its central and pivotal point the issuance of a formal complaint. In other words, the judges who were to pass on the merits of the case were compelled under the law to act as their own grand jury and draw up the indictment. As if this were not enough of a handicap to complete impartiality the Supreme Court in the Gratz case magnified the already top-heavy importance of the complaint by ruling that unless the complaint sets forth sufficient facts to show on its face a violation of law an order based upon it will be set aside, even though the evidence justifies the order.[1] Such a holding practically compels a prejudgment of the case, not only before the trial, but before the complaint is formulated. Furthermore, the Commission early adopted the practice of giving to the press at the time of the filing of a complaint a detailed statement of the charges against the

[1] Cf. p. 486 *et seq., supra.*

respondent. Since it fell steadily behind its docket for the first ten years, a particular case did not come up for hearing for months after the charges had been broadcast over the country. During all this time the respondent stood under the shadow of charges of illegal and unfair practices. When this period of suspended judgment was added to the issuance of a complaint without giving the respondent any opportunity to present his side of the issue, as in the cases found by the committee of the Chamber of Commerce of the United States, there can be no question that the procedure resulted in injustice. Even without this combination of circumstances it is equally beyond question that the publicity policy of the Commission was for a number of years of such a nature as to antagonize the very group to which it was intended that the new body should extend aid and guidance. Thus instead of being the helpful brother of business the Commission threatened for a time to become the wicked uncle.

With the intention of meeting at least some of the objections to its procedure a majority of the Commission, over the protests of two members, adopted in the spring of 1925 the new rules of procedure mentioned before. Among these alterations one defines more narrowly the class of complaint the Commission will consider and another encourages settlement of a wider proportion of cases through stipulations without resort to formal complaints. The limitation of complaints that will hereafter be handled excludes alleged unfair practices where "the alleged violation of law is a purely private controversy redressable in the courts except where said practices substantially tend to suppress competition as affecting the public." In reference to the wider use of stipulations the new rule is that "all cases shall be settled by stipulation except when the public interest requires otherwise." [1]

While these changes may be abused by a Commission indifferent to the purposes which inspired the Trade Commission Act, and while there seemed to be ground for charging such indifference to the majority of the members of the Commission during the reactionary period which followed the over-

[1] *Annual Report,* 1925, p. 111.

extension of governmental activities in connection with the Great War, they are in the interest of economy of the Commission's time and of an increase of its efficiency in safeguarding the public interests where they are really in jeopardy. Even neglect of some cases that might properly engage the attention of the Commission will be better than failure to handle adequately and promptly cases over which the Commission assumes jurisdiction.

With regard to the publicity to be given complaints a number of important changes were made. First, there are to be no more statements of the charges against a respondent issued to the press when a complaint is filed; second, no statement for publication in regard to a case will be made after the complaint is filed until after the final determination of the case; but, third, "after a complaint has been issued and the answer of the respondent has been filed or in case the respondent fails to file an answer by the rules provided, the papers in the case shall be open to the public for inspection, under such rules and regulations as the secretary may prescribe."[1] These changes in the rules certainly meet the objection of undue publicity so frequently brought against the Trade Commission. As a matter of fact they go so far as to raise a serious question as to their wisdom. No one approves of publicity on a complaint which is subsequently proved to be unwarranted, but the remedy would seem to be greater care in the issuance of the complaints.

The opposition of Commissioners Thompson and Nugent to the changes in procedure was based primarily upon the conviction that in limiting the publicity given to the Commission's complaints and orders the majority had seriously restricted the value of its activities. They particularly objected to the majority's application of its rule on stipulations, and during the period covered by the annual reports for 1925 and 1926 one or both of them registered scores of dissenting opinions. Although these cases cannot be treated *in extenso* here, a few facts from the most important of them

[1] *Annual Report,* 1925, p. 111.

provide a basis for certain generalizations on the merits of the conflict within the Commission.

An important group of cases in which such dissents were recorded involved the dismissal of a case because the practices complained of had been discontinued. It may seem that, the purpose of the proceeding having been accomplished, further action was unnecessary, but an examination of specific cases makes it clear that the minority's objections were not without merit. In a complaint against the Mack, Miller Candle Company the Commission charged that it had sold as "altar" candles a product containing less than the fifty per cent beeswax required by the rules of the Roman Catholic Church for such "altar" candles. The respondent entered a formal reply denying the allegations of the complaint, but subsequently admitted that it had been guilty of just the practices charged prior to a given date on which it claimed they were discontinued. Upon a stipulation in which the respondent admitted its former unfair and deceptive practices and agreed not to reëngage in them the case was dismissed. Commissioner Thompson contended that since the competitors who initiated the complaint had seen the public denial of the charges, subsequently admitted to be false, and that since they had been damaged by the tactics of the respondent, they had a right to know the facts subsequently developed and to expect the Commission "to give to honesty and square dealing some measure of recognition and reward by publicly condemning unfair practices and those pursuing them." Moreover, he believed that the public was entitled to a knowledge of the facts as a basis for placing future business. If this were not done he held that the "prophylactic" function of the Commission would be largely destroyed. In support of his position he quoted the statement of the "unfair competition bureau of the paint and varnish industry" that, "The commission should give greater weight to the welfare of the industry affected and the purchasing public, than the interests of the single respondent who has been guilty of fraudulent conduct." [1]

[1] *Annual Report,* 1925, pp. 209-211.

In the case of H. R. Mallinson & Company, silk manufacturers, it was demonstrated that in spite of a series of conference rulings, the wide publicity given to them and to the decision in the Winsted Hosiery case, a score of orders in similar cases, and a resolution of the National Association of Hosiery and Underwear Manufacturers establishing standards for their advertising, the respondent continued to misbrand and falsely advertise its products. In view of the facts the claim of its vice-president that it had "never dawned" upon him that the company was doing anything wrong or different from the remainder of the industry appeared to Commissioner Thompson to be ridiculous. He considered it "utterly illogical and unfair" to discriminate in favor of this large concern by not issuing an order. Only by the issuance of findings of fact and a desist order, in his opinion, could the ends of justice be secured.[1]

In another group of cases the minority members of the Commission dissented because they held that the facts established proved a violation of some part of the laws they were appointed to enforce. Among these may be mentioned those of Fels & Company, Douglas Fir Exploitation and Export Company *et al.*, Michigan Wholesale Grocers' Association, Corn Products Refining Company, and Chicago Retail Lumber Dealers' Association.[2] The first of these is representative of a group of cases in which the Commission issued complaints against the practice of manufacturers of guaranteeing stocks of their products in the hands of wholesalers and jobbers against price declines. There is no doubt that these practices increased the difficulties of small competitors, but on the other hand the majority was not without justification for refusing to condemn them as unfair. The handling of the Douglas Fir and Chicago Retail Lumber Dealers' cases by the majority seemed even more open to criticism, and appears to us to justify the statement that from being unduly harsh in its interpretation of "unfair methods of competition," the Commission became in this period unduly lenient.

[1] *Annual Report,* 1925, pp. 214-218.

[2] *Annual Report,* 1925, pp. 188, 193, 198, 201; 1926, p. 121.

As might have been expected, the struggle within the Commission was paralleled by a struggle in Congress, one group demanding the abolition of the Commission because it had become too sympathetic with "Big Business," another trying to cut off its appropriations on the ground that business needed to be let alone and that a suspension of the Commission's inquisitorial activity was very much to be desired. In spite of considerable oratory Congress took no action.

From the foregoing discussion it is clear that the procedural changes of 1925 did not solve the Commission's difficulties; in fact, there is considerable evidence that because of the way in which it was administered the remedy proved for a time almost as bad as the disease. And this, of course, brings us back to the real cause of the recent difficulties. There is general agreement that in establishing the particular procedure which it did Congress handicapped the Commission, but on the other hand it is self-evident that the efficacy of any procedure rests upon the manner of its administration. Shortly after the changes of 1925 were made it was charged that Mr. W. E. Humphrey had "packed" the board of review by enlarging its membership from three to five and appointing to it men whom he could dominate. Subsequently he was asked to comment on the charge by the Washington correspondent of the *St. Louis Post-Dispatch.* His answer as quoted in the Senate was as follows:

"What of it? . . . Do you think I would have a body of men working here under me that did not share my ideas about these matters? Not on your life. I would not hesitate a minute to cut their heads off if they disagreed with me. What in hell do you think I am here for?" [1]

There is rather general agreement that one reason for the ineffectiveness of the Sherman Act during the early 'nineties was the lack of sympathy with its purposes on the part of some of those responsible for its enforcement. If we have correctly interpreted the purposes of the 1914 legislation, then

[1] *Congressional Record,* vol. lxix, p. 2956; Senator Norris quoting the interview as published by the correspondent, Mr. Paul Anderson.

the conclusion is inescapable that after 1925 a majority of the Commission was for some time out of sympathy with those purposes. Appointment of commissioners who believe that the spirit of the Act should be carried out with discretion and fairness, but also with firmness, rather than changes in methods of procedure, is obviously the only effective remedy for this situation.

A final item in procedure, reserved to this point because of its extra-legal character and because of its significance, is the trade practice conference, or, as it was formerly called, the trade practice submittal. The submittals were begun in 1919 with the purpose of securing the coöperation of an industry in establishing its own set of standards. They were conceived to be a more practicable plan for meeting a widespread unfair practice than a number of actions against individuals. Originally there was nothing formal or binding about the procedure. On invitation of the Commission, on its own initiative or at the suggestion of some members of an industry, representatives of the industry met with a member of the Commission to discuss the practices complained of and any others which might be brought before the meeting. After discussion each practice was submitted to a vote of the representatives of the industry for their judgment on its fairness or unfairness, usefulness or harmfulness. The Commission was not bound to observe such a vote, but agreed to give it careful attention in evaluating the practices voted upon.

But as the possibilities of the plan became more apparent the Commission found itself without any orderly method of meeting the increasing number of requests that came in for such submittals. Consequently, on April 19, 1926, it ordered the creation of a new legal division to be called the division of trade practice conferences. Fundamentally, the conference is the same thing as the submittal, a method by which business men in one industry may meet with a government official and formulate their own standards of competition, but the text of the order creating the new division makes it clear that it is the purpose of the Commission to make the results of the conference more formal and more binding both upon itself and upon the industry. In the first place the action taken by the conference is to be approved or disapproved by the Commission. Next, the director of the division of trade practice conferences is instructed to communicate or confer with concerns not represented at the conference for the purpose of securing their assent to and compliance with the action taken and approved. Moreover, he is to "keep informed as to how the action taken at the conference and approved by the Commission is being conformed to by the members of the industry" and to "investigate and report directly to the Commission any violation thereof, *irrespective of whether the person violating the rules has subscribed thereto.*"[1] A report "showing such violation shall be the basis upon which the Commission may issue its complaint."

In carrying out the new policy embodied in the foregoing summary the Commission has in the opinion of some business men again gone too far. A specific example may be cited in the controversy which has arisen over a trade practice conference in the furniture business. The furniture manufacturers in some instances have claimed that they were not given a fair opportunity to be heard before the rules for their industry had been drawn up. Furthermore, they objected to the attempt on the part of the Commission to secure a definite acceptance or refusal of acceptance of these rules. They objected even more strenuously to a press release of July 4, 1926, containing a list of furniture manufacturers who had refused to describe their goods in accordance with the formulæ drawn up at the conference.

However, the Commission has issued a large number of complaints and cease-and-desist orders.[2] One of the latter was selected by agreement and carried to the courts, where the order of the Commission was affirmed. The Supreme Court denied *certiorari*.[3] The outcome of this case will undoubtedly aid the Commission in carrying on the trade practice conference work. Moreover, the Chamber of Commerce

[1] *Annual Report,* 1926, p. 49. Italics ours.

[2] Cf. *Annual Report,* 1927, pp. 50-52; 1928, p. 141.

[3] Indiana Quartered Oak Co. case. 26 Fed. (2d) 340 (1928); 278 U. S. 623 (1928).

of the United States has formally approved the conferences and the state of California has amended its general dairy law by providing that the license of any dairy produce exchange may be revoked when the holder thereof has been proved guilty of violation of any of the "rules of the Federal Trade Commission governing unfair trade practices in the handling of butter, cheese, and/or eggs." [1]

There can be no doubt that these conferences are a much more logical method of meeting a dubious practice which has become widespread than a number of complaints against individual organizations. They have usually tended to reduce the combative, resentful attitude which formal complaints too often engender, and in the long run probably secure better results. The trade practice conference has done more in aiding the business community to work out its problems than perhaps any other single activity of the Commission, it is one of the most useful devices which the Commission could have hit upon, and it should continue to be used extensively.

Before proceeding to a discussion of the policies of the Commission it is necessary to note the manner in which it has carried out the injunction of Congress "to provide for the publication of its reports and decisions in such form and manner as may be best adapted for public information and use." [2] Although the Commission decided against giving advice in advance on proposed business practices, it expressed the hope in the preface to the first volume of its *Decisions* that "this publication may aid in furnishing that 'definite guidance and information' which the President and the Congress had in view in the establishment of the Federal Trade Commission, by the gradual working out of a code of business law." In the nine volumes now available which bring the records down to November 27, 1925, this hope has been only partially fulfilled, although the later volumes are superior in this respect. The chief difficulty with the reports is that only one side is stated. This results from the facts that in cases where the

[1] F. T. C. *Trade Practice Conferences* (March 15, 1928), p. 3.
[2] Federal Trade Commission Act, section six, paragraph (f).

"findings" are not in support of the "complaint" the complaint is simply dismissed, often without assigning reasons, and that even in the cases in which the Commission issues a cease-and-desist order, and states that the case is "reported in full," the report consists only of the full text of the complaint, the findings of fact, and the final order without including the reply of the respondent or any adequate indication of his evidence. Consequently, unless the respondent carries his case to the courts, that evidence remains more or less buried in the files of the Commission. However, the author of the most careful and thorough study of the Commission recorded his conviction that 90 per cent of the "replies" of respondents were not worth printing, since they consisted of little or nothing more than a categorical denial or admission or profession of ignorance on each of the items in the Commission's complaint.[1]

When the printed "findings" are examined they present a striking contrast to such documents as the reports of decisions of the federal Supreme Court. We agree with Mr. Henderson in the majority of the criticisms which he brought against the form of the findings. Too often the background of the case is omitted or inadequately treated. Presentation of the findings in a series of numbered paragraphs and in legal phraseology usually detracts from rather than adds to clearness. But even more unfortunate defects are revealed in a number of cases in which it is possible to compare the findings with the evidence subsequently disclosed in the courts or in which Mr. Henderson compared them with the stipulations of facts upon which they rest. These comparisons show that in some cases the language of the findings has been phrased with the apparent purpose of concealing conflicts in the evidence, that in others evidence has been actually suppressed, and that in still others the phraseology is unfair and unjust. The most astonishing conclusions reached by Mr. Henderson were those in regard to fifty-seven cases settled on stipulated facts. On comparing the findings as published with the stipulations in the Commission's files, he found fifteen instances

[1] Henderson, *op. cit.*, p. 106.

in which they corresponded word for word, fifteen in which there were minor changes of no importance, but twenty-seven in which the findings differed materially from the stipulations and in all cases to the disadvantage of the respondent.[1]

As pointed out by Mr. Henderson, the sample of cases analyzed is only a small minority of the total cases settled in this way, but even so the twenty-seven altered as they were constitute a serious reflection on the impartiality of the procedure. On the other hand, the later volumes of *Decisions,* particularly the last five, are definitely superior in a number of the matters criticized, although we have not undertaken to make a comparison of findings and stipulations.

Against the background of the foregoing details of the changes in the organization and procedure of the Federal Trade Commission, its policies and accomplishments may be seen in more accurate perspective. But equally a part of that background and in some ways of more importance are certain other elements. One of them, the altered conception of the nature of the problem with a change of emphasis from "trust-busting" to controlling methods and practices of competition, has been discussed above.[2] Another is the failure for several months of the original members of the Commission to agree on certain questions of policy, three of which were: Should the Commission undertake to give advice in advance on the legality of proposed business arrangements? Did the Commission have jurisdiction over combinations in violation of the Sherman law? Did the phrase "unfair methods of competition" in Section 5 of the Trade Commission Act include fraudulent practices? The Commission finally decided not to attempt to give advance advice on legal points in spite of numerous requests so to do and in spite of its avowed purpose of giving "definite guidance and information" to the business community. This conclusion confirmed that of the House committee, which put the bill in final form.[3] More-

[1] Henderson, *op. cit.,* pp. 158-159.
[2] P. 424 *et seq., supra.*
[3] Cf. pp. 417, 418, *supra.*

over, since there could be no guaranty that the courts would pay any attention to such action by the Commission, there can be no question that its decision was wise.[1] Both the other questions were decided in the affirmative, a position which the United States Supreme Court has upheld in the Beech-Nut and Winsted cases discussed above.[2] A third element is the status of the doctrine of unfair competition, both as a part of the common law and as interpretation of such statutes as the Sherman Act and various state anti-trust laws. The final element in our background consists of previous attempts in legal and economic treatises to formulate lists of methods of "unfair" competition.

As pointed out in a preceding chapter, Congress refused to draw up such a list for the guidance of the Commission and contented itself with the prohibition of certain specific practices in Sections 2, 3, 7, and 8 of the Clayton Act and the general statement in Section 5 of the Federal Trade Commission Act that "unfair methods of competition in commerce are hereby declared unlawful." Our central problem in discussing policies then may be stated as follows: How has the Commission interpreted "unfair methods of competition," and how far has it been successful in securing recognition of its interpretation from the courts and the business community?

The evidence upon which our answer rests has to a considerable extent been presented in preceding chapters, but before summarizing and interpreting it, we must amplify it by certain statements from the annual reports of the Commission. The first report, because of the delays incident to organization, was little more than a statement that organiza-

[1] Cf. an address by George Rublee, one of the ablest of the original members of the Commission whose appointment the Senate persistently refused to confirm because of the opposition, on purely political grounds, of the senior Senator from his state, New Hampshire, "The Original Plan and Early History of the Federal Trade Commission," published in the *Proceedings of the Academy of Political Science,* January, 1926, pp. 114-120.

[2] Pp. 509 *et seq.* and 497 *et seq., supra.*

tion had been achieved. In the second, for the year ending June 30, 1916, this statement appears:

> The Commission has made no attempt to define in general terms what methods of competition are "unfair" so that a "proceeding by it in respect thereof would be to the interest of the public." Unfair competition, like "fraud," "due care," "unjust discrimination," and many other familiar concepts in the law, is incapable of exact definition, but its underlying principle is clear—a principle sufficiently elastic to cover all future unconscionable competitive practices in whatever form they may appear, provided they sufficiently affect the public interest.[1]

The Commission goes on to say that "unfair" covers at least methods which restrain trade, substantially lessen competition, or tend to create monopoly, and that it is of the opinion that it covers misbranding and false advertising where the public is likely to be misled.

In its 1919 report, after noting the fact of a common-law concept of "unfair competition," the Commission expressed the opinion that "upon the creation of the Commission it was empowered to leave the shores defined by the common law and, taking the knowledge of these decisions with it, to embark on an uncharted sea, using common sense plus the common law for its compass."[2] The origin of the phraseology was the decision in the Sears, Roebuck case,[3] which the Commission construed as expressing the opinion that the Commission had the power—using common sense—to declare whether an act complained of came within the language of the statute. In this same opinion the court held that the phrase "unfair competition" is not void for indefiniteness, "quite irrespective of whether the specific practices in question have yet been denounced in common-law cases."[4] But it must not be inferred that the decision in the Sears, Roebuck case gave to the Commission the final authority of determining what acts constituted "unfair" methods, for the Circuit Court of Appeals specifically pointed out that the restraining orders of the Commission are "merely provisional" and that the respond-

[1] *Annual Report,* 1916, p. 6.
[2] *Ibid.,* 1919, p. 45.
[3] Cf. pp. 475, *supra,* and 542, *infra.*
[4] 258 Fed. 311 (1919).

ent "is entitled to his day in court" where common law and statutory principles and tests previously formulated were to control.

The Supreme Court in the Gratz case the following year (1920) was even more definite, stating that the meaning of the words "unfair method of competition . . . is for the courts, not the commission, ultimately to determine."[1] Although the Court did not attempt a definition of the term, it did express the view that it was "clearly inapplicable to practices never heretofore regarded as opposed to good morals because characterized by deception, bad faith, fraud or oppression, or as against public policy because of their dangerous tendency unduly to hinder competition or create monopoly."[2] In passing we must note our conviction that a more unfortunate phraseology would be difficult to imagine. The static conception of business morals embodied in the words "never heretofore" if rigidly adhered to, would have defeated the clear purpose of Congress.

Meanwhile the Commission's annual report for 1917 had presented a list of methods of competition drawn from complaints issued prior to June 30, 1917, with the statement that these methods were "alleged" in the complaints to be "unfair." A similar list appeared in the 1918 report, but not in that for 1919. The 1920 report lists the "methods of competition condemned" by that time. The reports for 1921, 1922, and 1923 do not contain such lists, but they appear in those for 1924 to 1928, inclusive. The list for 1928 covers three and one-half closely printed pages.[3] Among the practices condemned are:

(1) Misbranding of fabrics and other commodities respecting the materials or ingredients of which they are composed, their quality, origin, or source.

(2) Adulteration of commodities, misrepresenting them as pure or selling them under such names and circumstances that the purchaser would be misled into believing them to be pure.

(3) Bribery of buyers or other employees of customers and

[1] 253 U. S. 427 (1920).

[2] *Ibid.*

[3] *Annual Report,* 1928, pp. 59-62.

prospective customers to secure new customers or induce continuation of patronage.

(4) Making false or disparaging statements respecting competitors' products, their business, financial credit, etc.

(5) The use of false or misleading advertisements.

(6) False claims to patent, trade-mark, or other rights or misrepresenting the scope thereof; appropriating and using trade-marks wrongfully.

(7) Trade boycotts or combinations of traders to prevent certain wholesale or retail dealers or certain classes of such dealers from procuring goods on the same terms accorded to the boycotters or conspirators, or to coerce the trade policy of their competitors or of manufacturers from whom they buy.

(8) Passing off of products, facilities, or business of one manufacturer or dealer for those of another by imitation of product, dress of goods, or by simulation or appropriation of advertising or of corporate or trade names, or of places of business, and passing off by a manufacturer of an inferior product for a superior product theretofore made, advertised, and sold by him.

(9) Misrepresentation in the sale of stock of corporations.

(10) Selling rebuilt machines of various descriptions, rebuilt automobile tires, and old motion-picture films slightly changed and renamed as and for new products.

(11) Sales of goods at cost, coupled with statements misleading the public into the belief that they are sold at a profit.

(12) The use by monopolistic concerns of concealed subsidiaries for carrying on their business, such concerns being held out as not connected with the controlling company.

(13) Schemes and devices for compelling wholesalers and retailers to maintain resale prices on products fixed by the manufacturer.

(14) Combinations of competitors to enhance prices, maintain prices, bring about substantial uniformity in prices, or to divide territory or business, or to put a competitor out of business, or to close a market to competitors.

(15) Acquiring stock of another corporation or corporations

where the effect may be to substantially lessen competition, restrain commerce, or tend to create a monopoly.

(16) Various schemes to create the impression in the mind of the prospective customer that he is being offered an opportunity to make a purchase under unusually favorable conditions, when such is not the case.

(17) Discriminating in price, with the effect of substantially lessening competition.

(18) Imitating or using standard containers, customarily associated in the minds of the general purchasing public with standard weights of the product therein contained, to sell to said public such commodity in weights less than the aforementioned standard weights.

(19) Misrepresenting in various ways the advantages to the prospective customer of dealing with the seller.

(20) Tying or exclusive contracts, leases, or dealings, in which, in consideration of the granting of certain rebates or refunds to the customer, or the right to use certain patented equipment, etc., the customer binds himself to deal only in the products of the seller or lessor.

(21) Direct misrepresentation of the composition, nature, or qualities of the product offered and sold.

(22) Use by business concerns associated as trade organizations or otherwise of methods which result or are calculated to result in the observance of uniform prices or practices for the products dealt in by them, with consequent restraint or elimination of competition, such as use of various kinds of so-called standard cost systems, price lists or guides, exchange of trade information, etc.

(23) Securing business through undertakings not carried out and through dishonest and oppressive devices calculated to entrap and coerce the customer or prospective customer.

(24) Giving products misleading names so as to give them a value to the purchasing public or to a part thereof which they would not otherwise possess.

The tendency has been, of course, for the Commission's list to grow longer, and this in spite of a few deletions from earlier lists as the result of adverse court decisions. From time to time there have been changes in the emphasis laid upon these various methods by the Commission, but it seems safe to say that the most important types, either because of their great frequency or their seriousness in obstructing fair competition, have been misbranding, false and misleading advertising, misrepresentations of various sorts, commercial bribery, passing off, and resale price maintenance.

Among the numerous controverted points in the development of the concept of unfair methods of competition, perhaps none is more significant than that of the character of the public interest involved in that clause which directs the Commission to take up a case "if it shall appear to the commission that a proceeding by it in respect thereof would be to the interest of the public." The major portion of the discussion of public interest has centered on the point as to whether Congress intended the phrase to limit action to a certain kind of unfair competition viewed as affected with public interest or whether it intended simply to provide the Commission with a degree of discretion in determining what cases it should handle. In accepting the former alternative the Circuit Court of Appeals, Second Circuit, in the New Jersey Asbestos Company case restated its conclusions in the Gratz case in even more unmistakable form than it had originally put them: " . . . only unfair practices which affect the public as distinguished from individuals, are within the jurisdiction of the commission." [1]

Now the language of the statute appears to the writers to give more support to the contrary view that Congress intended to convey discretionary power here, not to lay down a principle of law. The first sentence of Section 5 does not contain any qualifications. It declares unlawful "unfair methods of competition." Subsequently, when detailing the Commission's procedure, the phrase concerning public interest is introduced. The conclusion seems inescapable that though all unfair methods are illegal under the statute, the Commission is to select for prosecution only those of sufficient general importance to warrant such action. A court may consider that poor judgment was used in the selections,

[1] 264 Fed. 510 (1920).

but in our opinion it should not be able to reverse an order to cease and desist because it considered the public interest was not involved. That the courts have this power to substitute their judgment for the Commission's on public interest was definitely held by the Second Circuit Court of Appeals in the case of John Bene & Sons, Inc., *v.* Federal Trade Commission:

> As a conclusion of law, we hold that, there being no proof of a public interest herein, or of its being to the interest of the public that this proceeding should have been begun, or the order complained of made, said order must be reversed; and it is reversed accordingly.[1]

But as a matter of fact the foregoing argument is only incidental to the more fundamental question previously posed: What is the nature of the public interest with which the Commission is concerned? Since that "phantom public" which Mr. Lippmann exposed so well is incapable of initiating a preliminary inquiry before the Commission, even though it may more or less definitely realize its interests are being disregarded or abused, it comes about that actual allegations of unfair competition must originate with certain individuals or groups who consider themselves injured and who are articulate. It is of course necessary, particularly since March, 1925, for such injured parties to convince the Commission that action by it in the circumstances presented would be in the public interest. By this means we come to a conception of public interest which holds that it is in the public interest for the Commission in some situations to forestall or alleviate a private injury expected from, or the result of the use of, unfair methods of competition. Since it is possible that our preceding conclusion that it was the intention of Congress to invest the Commission with discretionary power to decide whether it was in the public interest to investigate a particular allegation of unfair methods may lead our readers to believe that we agree with the concept of public interest just stated, we hasten to add that we do not so agree.

Our reasons for disagreeing rest upon the conviction that the real interest of the public under the foregoing interpretation of it becomes subordinate to private interests; in the

[1] 299 Fed. 473 (1924).

actual working of this interpretation the main objective is lost sight of in the consideration of *minutiæ*. Cases are brought up because some individuals have been injured. If redress is granted they receive some benefit, and possibly the public does also, but it is more than likely to be insignificant. In certain respects the situation is analogous to that which existed in the United States prior to 1911 with reference to employers' liability laws. They were conceived as instruments to aid a workman who had been injured (in a physical sense) in securing redress. But in practice the employers' common-law defenses and the astuteness of casualty company attorneys all too frequently prevented that redress from being adequate to the individuals who needed it. Much more important, however, was the demonstration that the organism we call society had failed to meet the responsibilities engendered by the development of a new type of economic organization; that, at least in a certain field, it had come dangerously near to the position of subserviency to the machine which we all prefer to be confined to the state of "Erewhon." The realization of this failure resulted in the adoption of a program of social legislation, inadequate though it is as yet. The policy underlying this program is not confined to redressing injuries. Of course when we pass safety laws and workmen's compensation acts we are interested in preventing injury to individuals or alleviating its results for them or their dependents, but more fundamentally we are desirous of erecting a system of controls which will insure to society the maximum benefits of the machine process with a minimum of its ills. The abolition of dueling and the present efforts to outlaw war rest upon the same conception of public interest. We are not concerned so much with the preservation of individual lives, important though that may be, as with the resolution of private and national disputes in a rational and ordered fashion involving the least possible interruption of social life and progress. Following this line of reasoning, we have shifted the emphasis from individual injury in extending the social control of business over industrial accidents. We need to make the same shift with reference to the public interest in the restraint of unfair methods of competition.

The real nature of the public interest in the elimination of unfair methods of competition is to be found in the necessity in such a complex society as ours for securing universal adherence to fair methods. To repeat, we are not so much concerned with the injury done to particular individuals as with the most efficient functioning of the economic order. Such functioning is hampered if not destroyed by unfair business practices.

With these alternative concepts in mind we return to the work of the Commission and to the consideration of certain questions raised by the statement of the alternatives. Which one of the foregoing interpretations has controlled the Federal Trade Commission in construing the public interest in unfair methods of competition? In working toward a realization of its conception of public interest what tests have been applied by the Commission? To what extent have the courts followed the Commission in its interpretation of public interest and in its tests of it?

A direct answer to the first of these questions seems to be found in the annual report of the Commission for 1922: "The public interest which is made the test for the Commission's consideration in all cases is therefore an interest in the preservation of free and fair competition." But as a matter of fact this statement does no more than restate the problem. An examination of the complaints and cease-and-desist orders which have been published lends support to the opinion of a former member of the Commission [1] that that body has never faced the alternatives suggested, but has rather assumed the validity of the first, *viz.*, that some private injuries are so affected with a public interest as to warrant redress by a federal administrative tribunal.[2]

[1] Mr. N. B. Gaskill in the *Proceedings* of the Academy of Political Science, vol. xi, pp. 124, 125 (January, 1926). We are indebted to Mr. Gaskill for suggesting parts of the argument in the text.

[2] Among the complaints and orders which seem most certainly to embody this conception of public interest may be listed the following: in vol. i of the *Federal Trade Commission Decisions*, pp. 13, 16, 44, 60, 139, 144, 235, 259, 272, 325; in vol. ii, pp. 27, 58, 67, 72, 96, 152; in vol. iii, pp. 1, 36, 53, 68,

In an additional large number of cases it is difficult to determine whether private injury is being used as a test of the public interest in the case or as a test of the unfairness of the method of competition. In still other cases there can be no doubt that injury is used solely as a test of unfairness, an inevitable situation, of course, since injury has been a central feature of the common-law doctrine of unfair competition for generations.

In the decisions of the federal courts on cease-and-desist orders which have been carried to them there seems no doubt that injury has been a test both of public interest and of unfairness. In a number of these cases the phrase "public injury" is used; in others it is clear that "private injury" is the basis of the opinion. Moreover, sentences can be selected from certain of the cases which seem definitely to contradict the generalization that the test of public interest is found in a private injury of such a nature as to warrant action by the Federal Trade Commission. As an example may be cited the following from the opinion of the Seventh Circuit Court of Appeals in the Sears, Roebuck case: [1] "The Commissioners are not required to aver and prove that any competitor has been damaged or that any purchaser has been deceived." But in the very next sentence the court goes on to say that the Commission is expected to ". . . stop all those trade practices that have a capacity or a tendency to injure competitors directly or through deception of purchasers, quite irrespective of whether the specific practices in question have yet been denounced in common law cases." [2] In other words, the Commission is not limited to the list of practices previously condemned at common law, but the basic test is still injury, and moreover the court here reverts to "injury to competitors." Later this same circuit court in the Kinney-Rome case, after citing the Sears, Roebuck and other cases said: "We con-

109, 246, 253, 259, 265, 272, 284; in vol. iv, pp. 1, 23, 41, 55, 92; in vol. v, pp. 24, 77, 82, 87, 92, 105, 424, 451, 473; in vol. vi, pp. 11, 79, 84, 92, 107, 159, 184, 259; in vol. vii, pp. 1, 54, 73, 115, 279, 296, 301, 375, 461, 477, 490, 503, 510.

[1] For the facts in this case see p. 475, *supra*.

[2] 258 Fed. 311 (1919).

clude . . . that there must be some fraud in trade that injures a competitor, or lessens competition, before it can be said that there has been used an 'unfair method of competition.'"[1] In a later case, although admitting that the sales methods of the Chicago Portrait Company involved the use of a "falsehood about the usual sale price" which was "reprehensible, and an unworthy device to be used in trade," this court vacated the Commission's order because there were "no facts, nor findings of fact supported by evidence, that any one was in any way injured, or could have been."[2]

The opinions of the Second Circuit Court of Appeals are particularly interesting here, both because it has handled more cases than any other federal court and because it seems to have made some important modifications of the position it took in the earlier Gratz and New Jersey Asbestos cases, where it held that "unfair methods of competition between individuals are not contemplated by the act."[3] These cases were determined in May, 1919, and February, 1920, and do not include any more definite test of the public interest than the loose phrase that the cases brought must affect the public generally. But in April, 1921, this court reversed the Commission's order to the Winsted Hosiery Company to cease advertising and labeling as "wool" underwear which was partly some other material, because, since this was a common practice "thoroughly established and understood in the trade, . . . there was obviously no unfair method of competition as against other manufacturers of underwear." The court went on to say that even "Assuming that some consumers are misled, . . . the result is in no way connected with unfair competition."[4] The test applied here is unmistakable: the order was reversed notwithstanding an admitted tendency toward misleading the public because, in spite of the facts that other manufacturers were cognizant of, and in some cases utilized, the same false labels, they were not injured. But as brought out in a preced-

[1] 275 Fed. 668 (1921).
[2] 4 Fed. (2d) 762, 763 (1924).
[3] 258 Fed. 316 (1919); 264 Fed. 511 (1920).
[4] 272 Fed. 960 (1921).

ing chapter,[1] the Supreme Court reversed this decision. Consequently, in cases since that reversal the Second Circuit Court of Appeals has usually considered both injury to competitors and to the "general public" in deciding whether methods of competition were unfair and whether the public interest was involved in the particular case. This is particularly noticeable in the Royal Baking Powder decision very shortly after the Winsted reversal, in which it was held that "The method of advertising adopted by the Royal Baking Powder Co." when it changed from a cream of tartar to a phosphate powder in 1919 "was unfair alike to the public and to the competitors in the baking powder business." Elsewhere the court stated that "The interest of the act is the prevention of injury to the general public."[2] The same tendency is presented in the Mennen case settled in 1923, and in the National Biscuit and Loose-Wiles Biscuit cases determined in 1924.[3] In the Fox Film case, in which this Second Circuit Court of Appeals affirmed an order of the Commission directing the company to cease from issuing old motion-picture films under new names, it emphasized injury to competitors, treating the public aspect more as a case of deception than of injury. Finally, among this court's decisions should be mentioned that of John Bene & Sons, Inc., *v.* Federal Trade Commission. The respondent was a manufacturer of hydrogen peroxide who bought samples of a competitor's product called Daxol, advertised as superior to peroxide as an antiseptic, submitted the samples to two commercial chemists, and circulated the unfavorable reports on the analyses, together with some adverse comments of his own, to several chain-store purchasers of Daxol. The Commission ordered Bene to cease circulating these analyses and statements, resting its case clearly on the injury to the maker of Daxol. The court reversed the order making the "findings of fact" that "Daxol is a product of varying composition, and misbranded, in that the public is by its label requested to use it for purposes for which it is

[1] Cf. p. 497 *et seq., supra.*

[2] 281 Fed. 753, 745 (1922).

[3] 288 Fed. 774 (1923); 299 Fed. 733 (1924). Cf. pp. 475 *et seq.*, 481, *supra.*

medically unfit," and that "The public has no interest in the protection of such an article." [1]

In the decisions of the Supreme Court on Federal Trade Commission orders there is to date only one direct reference to the nature of the public interest in the control of unfair methods of competition. In the Winsted Hosiery case that court said: "The facts show that it is to the interest of the public that a proceeding to stop the practice be brought." In the opinion of the court "a substantial portion of the purchasing public" was deceived and misled by the false labels used.[2] But the precise nature of the test of public interest used by the court is not clear. Here, as so frequently, it is difficult to be positive as to whether the tests applied are for public interest or for unfair competition. But at least it is certain that the Supreme Court's conception of public interest was more inclusive than that of the lower court which it reversed in this case.

As pointed out above the Supreme Court, though holding that the meaning of "unfair methods of competition" is for the final determination of the courts, attempted no more of a definition than the negative statement that the term was "clearly inapplicable to practices never heretofore regarded as opposed to good morals because characterized by deception, bad faith, fraud or oppression, or as against public policy because of their dangerous tendency unduly to hinder competition or create monopoly." [3] This statement has been reiterated in practically every subsequent opinion of the Supreme Court involving Section 5 of the Federal Trade Commission Act. But it should not be interpreted as restricting the meaning of unfair competition to the old common-law idea; the Winsted case is sufficient refutation of that.

From the foregoing sections of this chapter and from the discussion of Trade Commission cases in other chapters it must be clear that it is impossible to state in precise terms just what the policies of the Commission have been. Changes in

[1] 299 Fed. 473 (1924).
[2] 258 U. S. 493 (1922).
[3] 253 U. S. 427 (1920).

personnel, the influence of such criticisms as those by the United States Chamber of Commerce, the incidence of court decisions, have all affected those policies. To the extent to which it is possible to trace one guiding principle through the unquestionable vacillations and fluctuations in the Commission's record, it seems to us that that principle is found in the body's own interpretation of the purposes of the 1914 legislation—"the preservation of the competitive system." In attempting to preserve this system the Commission has usually placed emphasis upon prophylactic measures rather than upon prosecution. And this brings us to the final and most important aspect of this chapter—What has the Federal Trade Commission accomplished?

As was expected and contemplated, the Commission has carried on the valuable series of reports on various industries commenced by the Bureau of Corporations. A simple list of these reports fills half a dozen pages. Consequently, we confine ourselves to an enumeration of only a few of the most important, including a group of reports on the coal industry issued between 1917 and 1925; the *Report on the Causes of High Prices of Farm Implements,* 1920; the *Report on the Meat Packing Industry* in six parts, 1918-20; the *Report on the Grain Trade* in six volumes, 1920-25; the *Report on Coöperation in American Export Trade,* 1916; a group of reports on the petroleum industry issued from 1915 to 1928; a report on the Pittsburgh-plus practice and on war-time profits and costs in the steel industry, 1919 and 1925; three reports on the tobacco industry, 1921, 1922, and 1926; a report on taxation and tax-exempt income, 1924; a report on national wealth and income, 1926; two reports on the power industry, 1927 and 1928; a series of monthly reports on utility corporations, 1928; a report on *Coöperative Marketing,* 1928; a report on *Resale Price Maintenance,* 1929; and a report on *Open Price Associations,* 1929. Against some of the reports valid criticisms of inaccuracies and even injustices to the subjects of the reports have been brought. In discussing the International Harvester Company we noted certain points in the *Report on the Causes of High Prices of Farm Implements* on which the Harvester Company's criticisms convinced us the Commission was wrong.[1] The committee of the Chamber of Commerce of the United States which published a report on the work of the Commission in 1918 concluded that the results shown at that time in the lumber, resale-price maintenance, and bituminous-coal investigations did not justify the expense they had entailed; that prominent features of the food investigation were "subversive of common justice," reference being had chiefly to the methods of carrying on the investigation; and that in the report on profiteering made to the Senate June 28, 1918, general charges of a calumnious nature had been made without supporting data.[2] In view of these facts it is impossible to credit all of the Commission's reports with the degree of scholarly accuracy and impartiality which we have a right to expect from a governmental agency. On the other hand, they should be credited as a group with providing to students and business men a body of facts whose general educational value it is difficult to overestimate.

On the foundation of these reports rest certain other noteworthy accomplishments of the Commission. In the field of legislation there are two outstanding results: the Webb-Pomerene Act following the *Report on Coöperation in American Export Trade,* and the Packers and Stockyards Act following the reports on the meat industry.

The former of these, it will be recalled, amplified the scope of the Commission's work; the latter restricted it. In carrying out the duties laid upon it by the Webb-Pomerene Act the Commission has acted chiefly as a dispenser of information to concerns interested in organizing export associations and as a depository for the various reports the latter are required to make. In the first capacity it has, of course, materially aided in the development and stabilization of our export business since the war. In the first year or two after the passage of the Act it found that a number of concerns which had filed papers with it were not entitled to the protection of the statute because they were not engaged solely in export business. As

[1] Cf. p. 272 *et seq., supra.*
[2] *Nation's Business,* October, 1918, pp. 10, 11.

the law became better understood, however, this difficulty more or less automatically corrected itself. From April 10, 1918, to July 1, 1928, a total of 156 associations filed papers with the Commission, and of these 56 were still in existence at the latter date.[1] The 100 which were discontinued have as a rule been replaced by stronger organizations, so there has been a steady growth in quality if not in numbers. Their total reported exports amounted in 1927 to $371,500,000, and there is good reason to believe, because of the activity of the Copper Exporters Association and of the Steel Export Association of America organized in that year to handle the exports of the U. S. Steel Corporation and the Bethlehem Steel Company, that the total for 1928 was substantially higher.

The 56 active associations represent a great variety of industries and as many as 800 different firms. Naturally, industries concerned with raw or partially finished materials (*e.g.*, lumber, copper, zinc, and naval stores) and with foodstuffs (*e.g.*, meat, lard, flour, sugar, rice, milk, canned salmon, sardines, and dried fruits) predominate. At the same time manufactured products are well represented, especially different forms of iron and steel, wooden ware and chemicals. During the first few years there was uncertainty whether it was necessary for an association, in order to operate under the law, actually to handle the exports of its members or whether it might act merely as an agency for fixing export prices and allocating orders on some agreed plan among them. This issue was settled by a decision by the Commission rendered July 31, 1924, extending the privileges of the Act to associations which did not actually handle exports. The same ruling opened the door for agreements between export associations organized under the law and foreign groups of business men engaged in the same lines of business. The Commission said: "There seems to be no reason why a Webb-Pomerene Association . . . might not adopt a trade arrangement with non-nationals reaching the same market, providing

[1] Cf. the excellent article on "Ten Years' Operation of the Webb Law," by William Notz, in the *American Economic Review* for March, 1929, from which a good deal of the information which follows has been derived.

this market was not the domestic market of the United States and the action of this organization did not reflect unlawfully upon domestic conditions." Since this opinion was expressed, several of the export associations representing all or a substantial proportion of the industry with which they are concerned have entered into agreements with foreign cartels, and at least one of them, the Copper Exporters Association, has been under investigation by the Federal Trade Commission to determine whether by its operations it "substantially lessens competition within the United States or otherwise restrains trade therein," as prohibited by the Act. Since the Commission has made no report of findings, it appears probable that the outcome was favorable to this Association. In fact, up to the time of writing (June, 1929), no association has been found guilty under the provisions of the law cited, though the inevitable reaction of a concerted move between organized American exporters and foreign producers to advance the price in the world market of a particular product on the domestic price of that product makes this a difficult borderland in which the Commission will be required at some time to indicate more clearly than does the law at what point unlawful "restraint" begins. We return to this subject in Chapter XXVI.[1]

The advantages to American industry of the Webb-Pomerene Act as liberally administered by the Commission have proved substantial, and while complaints have been raised against this breach in our antitrust legislation the evidence that small business men have benefited from it as much as or more than large corporations is convincing. It has fostered a more coöperative spirit and proved the possibility of realizing the advantages of combination without suffering the disadvantages of monopoly. The only serious attempts to amend the law have been in the direction of extending it to permit combinations in the importing as well as in the exporting field as regards materials not produced in substantial quantities in the United States. This is further evidence of

[1] Pp. 624 *et seq., infra.*

the general approval with which the operation of the law has been observed.

In connection with its foreign trade activities it is important to note the work of the Commission in handling complaints against American exporters and importers by foreign business interests. This is not done under any section of the Webb-Pomerene Act, but under section six (h) of the Commission law. The complaints usually come first to an American consulate and are referred to the Commission, which makes an investigation informally, without publicity, and reports to the interested foreigner through the Departments of State and of Commerce. Though many of the controversies are in themselves relatively insignificant, there is no doubt that the Commission's work in this field is aiding materially in establishing good will and confidence in foreign markets.[1] In some cases it has been necessary to take more formal action. Recent examples are the issuance of cease-and-desist orders against seven respondents engaged in exporting automobiles, trucks, and automobile parts, and the issuance of a complaint against an exporter of apples and pears.[2]

During the war the Commission was authorized to carry on two important items in the augmented list of government activities. One of these was the administration of the leasing to citizens of the United States of enemy patents; the other was the determination of the costs of producing a wide range of commodities as an aid to government purchasing, price-fixing, etc. In pursuance of the latter authority the economic division prepared and submitted to the President, the Food and Fuel Administrations, the War Industries Board, and other governmental agencies over 250 cost reports.

Deserving of particular commendation is the Commission's work in securing the abolition of the Pittsburgh-plus practice in selling steel.[3] The Commission found that the farmers alone in eleven Middle Western states paid approximately $30,000,000 "imaginary freight" every year in buying steel

[1] Cf. *Annual Reports,* 1921, pp. 60, 63, 64; 1923, p. 84; 1926, pp. 66, 71, 72; 1928, p. 95.

[2] *Annual Report,* 1928, pp. 58, 141, 46.

[3] Cf. p. 246 *et seq., supra.*

products under this scheme. In view of some of the current criticisms of the high cost of government by boards and commissions, it is interesting to compare this figure, discounted to allow for possible exaggeration, with the modest average annual budget of less than $1,000,000 on which the Commission has operated to date.

The foregoing record provides a basis for evaluating the work of the Federal Trade Commission in "solving" or "remedying" the trust problem. Although our own valuation has been to a considerable extent made clear in passing, we have formulated it more concretely in Chapter XXVII. Meanwhile we turn to the experiences and policies of Germany and other countries before presenting our conclusions.

CHAPTER XXIV

THE TRUST PROBLEM IN GERMANY

Industrial combinations have played a more prominent rôle in the economic life of Germany than in that of any other country. This has been due in part to two characteristics of her legal system that are in striking contrast with the system of the United States. The first and less important relates to the restrictions imposed on corporations. Germany has one corporation law applying to the whole country, which, unlike our loose state laws, is quite strict in its provisions and which has been successful since its enactment in 1884 in preventing serious corporate abuses. German business men have been restrained by it from seeking profits through stock-watering, deception as to earnings, and the similar practices that have been all too common in the United States. Consequently the hostility toward big business that has played no inconsiderable part in shaping opinion and policy toward trusts here has shown itself much less in Germany.

The second and more important difference is the absence from German law of any condemnation of combinations in restraint of trade and monopolies. An oft-quoted decision of the German imperial supreme court (*Reichsgericht*) rendered in 1897 in a case involving a combination of wood-pulp manufacturers [1] shows its tolerant attitude toward monopolistic combinations. The court said:

> When the prices of the products of an industry fall to an unreasonably low level, and the successful operation of the industry is thereby endangered or made impossible, the resulting crisis is detrimental not only to the individuals affected but to society at large. Therefore, it is to the interest of society that prices in any given industry should not remain long at a level that is below the cost of production. . . . Therefore it cannot be simply and generally considered contrary to the public welfare that producers interested in a given branch of industry should unite in order

[1] *Entscheidung des Reichsgerichts in Civilsachen,* vol. xxxviii, pp. 156-158.

to prevent or to moderate price-cutting and the consequent general decline in the prices of their products. On the contrary, when prices are for a long time so low that financial ruin threatens the producers, their combination appears to be not merely a legitimate means of self-preservation, but also a measure serving the interests of society.

Thus, instead of operating under the shadow of a legal system which made their restrictive contracts not only unenforceable but even criminal, German combinations have been encouraged by one which interprets freedom to carry on business enterprise to include freedom to combine as well as freedom to compete. The only restrictions on the action of combinations, before the enactment of the cartel law of 1923, resulted from government intervention, which was rarely resorted to, or the application of the provision of the Civil Code making business men liable for "intentionally" inflicting injury on others "in a manner repugnant to good morals," [1] or of the supplementary law prohibiting certain enumerated forms of unfair competition.[2]

With what was thus virtually a free field for development, combinations began to be organized in the coal and potash mining fields in the late 'seventies, and from these spread in varied forms to other industries, to the number, by 1905, according to an official estimate, of 385. Most of these combinations were what in German nomenclature are called "cartels."

Professor Robert Liefmann, long a recognized authority on the subject, defines a cartel as "a voluntary combination of business enterprises engaged in the same line of business and each retaining its independence, for the purpose of establishing monopolistic control of the market." This definition properly emphasizes as the chief characteristic of the cartel that it is made up of enterprises which retain their independence. As the term is commonly employed, however, it includes all kinds of pools and not merely those which aim at monopolistic control of the branches of production affected. Furthermore, this definition goes too far in stating that the agreement

[1] *Bürgerliches Gesetzbuch,* Art. 826.

[2] *Gesetz gegen den unlauteren Wettbewerb,* June 7, 1909. Cf. pp. 584, 585, *infra.*

must be "voluntary." During and since the war the German government, finding it easier to deal with an organized group than with individuals, has several times required cartels about to dissolve to re-form, whether the members desired to continue the arrangement or not.[1]

Along with cartels, or monopolistic pools, as defined above, Germany has developed also the other familiar forms of combinations. According to German nomenclature, vertical combinations (combines) are called *Konzerne* while outright consolidations into giant, all-embracing, single corporations or holding companies are called *Fusionen* or simply *Truste.* Up to the time of the conclusion of the war cartels were the commoner form of German combination. During the period of inflation cartels, except the special type known as "condition-cartels" (*Konditionen-kartelle*), which determined the conditions of sale and payment for the protection of the producer, lost their importance, and instead *Konzerne,* like the well-known Stinnes' combine, came forward prominently. Their organizers owed a part of their capital to the indemnities paid to former owners for the 26 per cent of the country's coal resources, 74 per cent of her iron-ore resources, and other property, which were lost to Germany through the Treaty of Versailles. They were men who realized that huge profits might be made by securing tangible property in exchange for promises to pay in marks during the period when the mark was depreciating. Stinnes and his imitators thus bought not only sources of raw material and plants turning out semi-finished products to combine with the finished branches of manufacturing they were also acquiring, but newspapers, hotels, and other forms of property, which for convenience they placed under one management, although they had little in common except common ownership. With the stabilization of the mark in November, 1923, the advantage enjoyed by these combines disappeared. Already greatly extended, some of them, like the Stinnes' combine itself, became overextended by force of their own momentum, and in the summer of 1925, when competition was severe and extensions of credit were

[1] The German term for such "forced cartels" is *Zwangskartelle.*

difficult to obtain, fell to pieces even more rapidly than they had been pieced together. In the period of stable prices that has followed, cartels have again become the commoner form of combination, but with a more marked tendency to give place to "trusts," in the German sense of the term, especially in industries where the rapid introduction all along the line of more efficient methods of production has been deemed essential to success in international competition.

The legal forms of organization of cartels have been varied. The simplest type is the civil law association without legal entity or registered name (*Gesellschaft des bürgerlichen Rechts*). The most complicated is the combination of such an association with a private limited liability company (*Gesellschaft mit beschränkter Haftung,* usually written *G. m. b. H.*) or a corporation (*Aktiengesellschaft,* usually written *A. G.*).[1] In these "double-company" (*Doppelgesellschaft*) organizations the same individuals, or firms, constitute the membership of the underlying association and of the partnership or corporation which acts for it in its dealings with outsiders. If the second organization is a corporation, all of its stock is held by the members of the association, holdings being in proportion to the agreed productive capacity of their respective plants or mines. To give a clearer picture of these different types of combination in action we will describe in some detail the Rhenish-Westphalian coal cartel, combinations in the steel industry culminating in the Steel Trust (*Vereinigte Stahlwerke, A.G.,* organized in 1926), and the potash cartel.[2]

The German coal industry is divided into about a dozen different branches, depending on the districts in which coal is found and the kinds of coal mined. Of these the principal are "stone" (coking) coal and "brown" coal, a form of lignites. For industrial purposes, and especially for use in the iron and steel industry, stone coal is most important. In 1927

[1] The differences between these two forms are discussed in the next chapter, p. 582 *et seq.*

[2] In the sections on combinations in the coal, steel, and potash industries which follow, we have drawn freely from the valuable book by Dr. Rudolf K. Michels on *Cartels, Combines, and Trusts,* submitted as a doctor's dissertation at Columbia University and published by the University Press in 1928.

over 75 per cent of Germany's stone coal was produced in the Rhenish-Westphalian field known also as the Ruhr district. Combination among the coal producers in this field began with the formation of an export association in 1877, but did not result in a well-organized cartel until 1893, three years after the successful launching of a reorganized coke cartel, with which the coal cartel has always maintained close relations.

The *Rheinish-Westfählisches Kohlensyndikat* adopted the double company form of organization, a civil-law association of mine-owners and operators, and a corporation whose stock was owned by these same mine-owners and operators. These organizations mutually bind themselves through a purchase-and-sales contract which makes the corporation the selling agent for all of the coal produced by the members and not used in their own plants; and through a second contract in which they agree to obey the decisions of the authorities set up in the association or in the corporation to decide upon allotments or quotas, percentage reductions in output, minimum prices (*Richtpreise*), sales and accounting prices, assessments, etc. The original members accepted, on entering the cartel, a production rating which might be increased by the allotment committee on proof that they had opened new shafts or acquired the production rights of other members, or decreased as their mines showed signs of exhaustion. The same committee determined the production rating to be given new members. Since a chief reason for the formation of the cartel in 1893, and for its maintenance ever since, except during the war years when it was for a time a *Zwangskartell* has been to check overproduction and maintain remunerative prices, the quotas represent not the amount a mine or group of mines is authorized to produce but the basis to which the production-curtailment percentage of the given period is to be applied, to determine the mines' authorized production. For example, in July, 1925, production was curtailed 55 per cent of the quota tonnage, or, to express it differently, the mines were allowed to produce for sale only 45 per cent of their quotas. The business of the sales corporation, after the production tonnage and minimum price for the period were determined, was to fix the actual selling prices for the different grades of coal in different markets so that the entire output would be disposed of. The so-called settlement prices—that is, the prices that the corporation was to pay the members, were adjusted by reference to the minimum prices. It often, if not usually, happened, however that to sell surplus coal in outside markets, the corporation would have to lower its prices below the settlement prices. The resulting loss could be made up only through assessments upon the members, and the manner in which these assessments should be apportioned was long a cause of controversy and friction.

When the cartel was first organized, it was thought that the interests of all the members would be best promoted if the agreement was confined to coal to be offered for sale, the coal used in iron and steel furnaces and mills or other plants owned by the members not being included. As the cartel succeeded in its purpose of advancing prices to more remunerative levels, large industrial coal-consumers were given a strong incentive to acquire mines of their own, and thus a movement was started which threatened to deprive the cartel of some of its chief customers. The dissatisfaction this caused owners of commercial mines was allayed for a time by concessions secured through the coke cartel, but it was still a serious cause of difference when by the so-called Coal Industry Law (*Kohlenwirtschaftsgesetz*) of March 23, 1919, the socialist government, which came into power after the revolution of 1918, assumed control in the public interest of the whole coal industry. The program which the sponsors of this law contemplated was the nationalization or "socialization" of coal and other basic industries. As a step in this direction the law provided for the creation of a National Coal Council (*Reichskohlenrat*) to be made up of representatives of employers, employees, dealers, consumers, and certain of the German states. It also provided that the coal mines of the country should be combined into some twelve regional syndicates, and that each coal property must, whether its owners so desired or not, join the syndicate of its particular district. To work out the administrative details it created a committee of fifty members made up of representatives of the same interests as were to compose the Coal Council to report a plan to a special legislative committee of twenty-eight members as a basis for further legislation. Through the work of these committees a supplementary bill was prepared and passed by the Reichstag on August 21, 1919.[1] Since there was complaint that these measures did not go far enough, the special committee on socialization of industry was reconvened the following year. By this time more conservative views as to the desirable relation between the government and industry had become dominant, and the majority report of the committee opposed the proposal for immediate nationalization of the coal mines urged by the minority, and recommended instead modifications of the plan embodied in the Coal Industry Acts that it thought would promote economy and efficiency, but by which ownership and management would be left in private hands, while distribution and sales would be subject to government regulation. The net result of the coal-industry legislation was to make the coal cartels, most of which had been organized voluntarily before the war, all-embracing for their respective areas and kinds of coal produced, since membership was now obligatory, and to make the National Coal Council, with the concurrence of the Minister of Economic Affairs, final authority in regard to price and sales policies. The representation given to employees and to customers on the Council has proved an effective check on any desire for unreasonably high profits which owners and operators may evince, and at the same time has given all parties a clearer understanding of the difficulties with which management is confronted in its task of developing the industry to meet the expanding needs of the community.

The new Rhenish-Westphalian coal cartel agreement entered into in 1920 and all subsequent agreements have required, before they became effective, the approval of the Coal Council and the Minister of Economic Affairs. The changed situation was brought home to mine owners by a special decree issued

[1] For a fuller account of the provisions of these acts, cf. Stockder, *German Trade Associations: The Coal Kartell,* pp. 178-220.

by the government, declaring the *Stahlwerke Becker, A.G.*, which had delayed in attaching its signature to the agreement, a member whether it signed or not. Thus for the first time all coal operators in the region became members of the cartel. When this agreement expired in 1922 and no new agreement was reached, the government again intervened by declaring that the old agreement should remain in full force and that the old members should continue members, its decree taking the place of express agreement on their part. Under these auspices the cartel was continued through the troublous period of the French occupation of the Ruhr, the collapse of the mark, and the year 1924 following stabilization. After prolonged negotiations, in which members of the Coal Council took a leading part, a voluntary agreement was reached on May 1, 1925, by all the mine owners and operators, the owners of one large mine, *Westfalen,* being induced to sign by the payment to them of a special indemnity of nearly $100,000. This agreement attempted among other things to solve the two problems referred to above—the apportionment among the members of the losses on coal sold in outside markets and the application of the production-curtailment percentage to company-used coal.

The solution of the first question was found in a new method of handling sales in uncontrolled markets. Under the new agreement the selling company every month informs the members interested in foreign sales of the prices that may be obtained for different kinds of coal. The members then decide whether they wish to participate in these sales and to what extent, and the losses incurred are divided among those who actually do participate in proportion to the tonnage they respectively supply.

The solution, perhaps only temporary, of the more difficult problem presented by company-used coal was to make it subject to a limited extent to the production-curtailment percentage. Instead of continuing to allow integrated concerns to mine all the coal they wished for use in their own plants or subjecting them to the same percentage curtailment as applied to the purely commercial mines, they were required to curtail production for their own use by 35 per cent of the curtailment percentage decided upon for the commercial mines. Concretely, the application of this rule, when as in July, 1925, the curtailment percentage was 55 per cent, resulted in a curtailment percentage for coal produced for use of 19¼ per cent. Integrated concerns are thus required under this plan to buy roughly one-fifth of the coal, which under the old arrangement they might have produced from their own mines, from the cartel to the benefit of the members whose entire output is turned over to the selling company for disposition.

Under the new cartel agreement Germany's coal industry has enjoyed great activity and a fair measure of prosperity in the last three years. It was, of course, stimulated by the British coal strike in 1926. Atlantic coast markets, which had depended on English coal, were forced to buy from the German cartel, and in some cases were induced to enter into long-time contracts which extended the benefit to German coal producers many months after the strike was called off. The managers of the cartel resisted the temptation to increase coal prices at this period, and instead directed their efforts to increasing the output of member mines. The average monthly production, which had been 8,300,000 tons during the year preceding the strike, was increased to over 10,000,000 tons during the six months the struggle continued, and was still 9,800,000 tons in the fall of 1927. The increased profit from this larger tonnage was seriously cut into on May 1, 1927, when an order of the Minister of Labor became effective requiring the mine operators to grant in part the demand of the miners for an increase in wages. The operators sought to pass on the higher wage bill to consumers by increasing their prices for coal 7½ per cent, but this proposal was vetoed by the National Coal Council during the summer of 1927, mainly on the grounds that such increase would cause price increases in all the industries making large use of coal, and that the proof submitted by the mine owners that their profits were inadequate was unconvincing. Subsequently the cartel members submitted more conclusive evidence that they were doing their utmost to increase the efficiency of their mines and that unless prices were advanced some of them would be forced into bankruptcy. On this basis, after several months' further consideration, the Coal Council, with the assent of the Minister of Economic Affairs, authorized a moderate price increase effective May 1, 1928.[1] As these incidents illustrate, while permitting and even fostering monopolistic combinations to manage the country's coal resources, the German government now exercises a large measure of control in the public interest over both their wage and price policies.

The combination movement in the German iron and steel industry presents a much more complicated story than in coal. Records of rail and tin-plate combinations go back to the 'fifties and 'sixties. The movement was stimulated by the depression in the middle 'seventies, but no general combination in the industry was launched prior to that of rolling mills in 1886, which before its dissolution in 1893 embraced the whole country. The organization of a firm coke cartel in 1890 and of the Rhenish-Westphalian coal cartel in 1893 afforded a basis for a thoroughgoing cartellization of the iron and steel industry in the late 'nineties and early nineteen hundreds, which culminated in the *Stahlwerks-Verband, A.G.*, organized in 1904 to manage sub-cartels, of which the principal were concerned with crude steel (*Rohstahlgemeinschaft*), rails, structural steel, etc., called "A-products" (*A-Produkten-Verband*), bar iron (*Stabeisen-Verband*), band iron (*Bandeisen-Vereinigung*), thick sheets (*Grobblech-Verband*), rolled wire (*Walzdraht-Verband*), and drawn wire (*Draht-Verband*). Since no socialization law has been enacted for the iron and steel industry and since combination has continued to follow the lines entered upon before the war, we may pass at once to a description of the present situation.[2]

The iron and steel industry of Germany suffered even more than coal in consequence of the territorial provisions of the

[1] The increase averaged 2 RM. per ton, which was about 13 per cent of the prices maintained in 1926 and 1927.

[2] A full account in English of the movement prior to 1906 is given in Francis Walker's article on "The German Steel Syndicate," reprinted in Ripley's *Trusts, Pools and Corporations,* pp. 833-868.

Versailles Treaty. Even before the war Germany was an importer of iron ore. The loss of 74 per cent of her known iron-ore resources, through the Treaty, and of the iron and steel plants of Lorraine and Luxemburg, seriously disturbed relations in the industry. It was necessary for German plants to depend more largely on foreign mines for the iron ore they required and to protect themselves through the tariff and other measures from competition in the domestic markets from plants that were no longer German. Readjustments were greatly assisted by two circumstances—the concentration of the industry in the Ruhr district and its virtual control by the ten large integrated concerns which also control the stone coal industry. According to official returns for 1926 four-fifths of Germany's iron and the same proportion of her steel products were manufactured in the Ruhr district. A government investigation of the degree of control in the coal, iron and steel industries exercised by the ten largest integrated concerns in 1924 credited them with 88 per cent of the own-consumption quota of the coal cartel, 49 per cent of its coal-for-sale quota, 65 per cent of the total production of pig iron of the pig-iron cartel and 59 per cent of the total production of steel of the steel cartel. While more or less coöperation among the largest producers continued during the war and the inflation period which followed, only the pig-iron cartel (*Roheisen-Verband, G.m.b.H.*) maintained its existence. The stability of the latter was due in part to the fact that the blast furnaces of Lorraine and Luxemburg had never been members and in part to the fact that it was controlled by the steel-mill owners, who had a strong motive for stabilizing the price of their chief raw material. This control by steel-mill owners has resulted in the recent past in making fully four-fifths of the output of pig iron by members of the cartel production for own-consumption, only one-fifth being production for sale. Competition in Germany has therefore centered upon steel products rather than upon pig iron.

Stabilization found the steel industry in a highly disorganized and demoralized condition, but the strong conviction of German industrialists in favor of combination caused them to lose no time after November, 1923, in starting conferences which at length bore fruit in the formation of a crude steel cartel (*Rohstahl-Gemeinschaft*) on November 1, 1924. This was followed in 1925 by the reorganization of all of the important pre-war cartels headed, as before, by the *Stahlwerks-Verband, A.G.*, which had retained its charter during the war and inflation periods, although its activity had been largely suspended.

The steel-ingot cartel, which expires October 31, 1929, has limited itself to the attempt to control production. Prices and other details of marketing are left entirely to its individual members. The quotas assigned to different firms were based on the maximum monthly output prior to November, 1924, the total being 13,400,000 tons per year. Curtailments decided upon during the first year were 20 per cent or more of the quotas, but the steel boom which Germany began to enjoy late in 1926 required an average curtailment for the first seven months of 1927 of only 1.4 per cent and has permitted an increase in the total quota since, based on plant expansions and improved methods of production. The complicated arrangements made for differentiating between steel-for-use and steel-for-sale, when the quota limitation exceeded 25 per cent, have under these favorable conditions become superfluous. For curtailments below 25 per cent the simple plan was adopted of having the limitation apply to the entire output, whatever its destination. More important practically has been the penalty for exceeding the allotment. There is no penalty for exceeding the quota for a single month, but when the quota is exceeded for two consecutive months, the member concerned must pay the cartel 25 RM. for every ton in excess. At the end of each year the proceeds from these penalties are distributed, up to but not exceeding 25 RM. per ton of the deficiency, to members who during the year have produced less than their quotas.

The cartel for half-finished steel products (*Halbzeug-Verband*), which next became effective (January 1, 1925), is a complete cartel—that is, it controls not only output, but sales. In a few months it became part of the revived A-products cartel (*A-Produkten-Verband*), which in turn is under the control of the general steel cartel (*Stahlwerks-Verband, A.G.*). The other special steel cartels, which were organized in 1925 and 1926, took the half-finished steel cartel as their model. Under its plan of organization, the cartel is the exclusive selling agent, a penalty of 100 RM. being imposed for every ton sold directly by a member. The cartel secures the orders and distributes them among the members, who are obliged to fill those assigned to them. It receives payment for all sales and distributes to the members monthly their proportionate shares, its own expenses being met through assessments. Thus, instead of making a profit from the sales it handles, it always operates at a loss. Several large steel enterprises, which did not wish to become members of the cartel, were yet willing to agree not to sell any half-finished products in the open market. Since the members bound themselves not to sell their plants except on condition that the new owner should become a member, the cartel's control over the domestic market for the products with which it is concerned has been fairly complete.

The reëstablishment of the *Stahlwerks-Verband, A. G.*, in its old position of directing head of the special steel cartels was brought about in April, to become effective May 1, 1925. The agreements continue operative until April 30, 1930. The first task was to establish satisfactory relations with competitors in Lorraine, Luxemburg, and other near-by regions, and after prolonged negotiation it succeeded in forming the International Steel Cartel in October, 1926.[1]

The greater concentration which resulted from the organization of large integrated combines (*Konzerne*) in the inflation period was favorable, upon the break-up of some of these combines, to the organization of an outright steel trust. Forward-looking steel manufacturers organized on January 14, 1926, the *Vereinigte Stahlwerke, A.G.*, with an initial capitalization of 60,000 RM., to serve as a nucleus of a trust, provided

[1] Cf. chap. XXVI, pp. 622-624.

satisfactory terms could be worked out which would be acceptable to the principal steel producers. Among the motives was desire to facilitate a remodeling of plants to effect every possible economy in preparation for the intensified competition that was foreseen and to command more readily the capital that this would require. Within a few months all details were satisfactorily arranged, and on May 5, 1926, the trust increased its capital to 800,000,000 RM. in common stock and 50,000,000 RM. and 75,000,000 RM. in participating "A" and "B" warrants respectively. The American firm of Dillon, Read & Company shared in the necessary underwriting, and American capital has since been repeatedly drawn upon to assist in the further expansion of the German steel industry. The German Steel Trust, like the U. S. Steel Corporation, is a great holding company, the constituent firms and corporations being for the most part kept in existence as administrative units.

The seven interests that were combined at the outset were: (1) *Gelsenkirchener Bergwerks, A.G.;* (2) *Deutsch-Luxemburgische Bergwerks und Hütten, A.G.;* (3) *Bochumer Verein für Bergbau und Gusstahlfabrikation;* (4) The *Thyssen* group; (5) *Phönix A.G. für Bergbau und Hüttenbetrieb;* (6) *Vereinigte Stahlwerke von der Zypen und Wissener Eisenhütte, A.G.;* and (7) *Rheinische Stahlwerke.* Of these the first three had been combined earlier into the *Rhein-Elbe Union, G.m.b.H.*, which when first organized was largely controlled by Hugo Stinnes. The Thyssen group consisted of six nominally independent concerns, which were controlled by the powerful Thyssen family, and fifteen additional enterprises controlled in part through stock ownership. Numbers five and six constituted the Phönix combine, while number seven was controlled by the German dye trust (*Interessen-Gemeinschaft Farbenindustrie, A.G.*), organized November 28, 1925, as another great holding company *Trust.* The proportionate shares of these seven groups in the Steel Trust and the division of the common stock among them are shown in the following table:

TABLE XVIII

PERCENTAGE PARTICIPATION OF CONSTITUENT COMPANIES IN THE STEEL TRUST

Gelsenberg	15.1 %		
Deutsch-Lux	15.1 %	Rheinelbe-Union	39.5 %
Bochumer Guss	9.3 %		
Thyssen	26.0 %	Thyssen group	26.0 %
Phönix	23.65%		
von der Zypen	2.25%	Phönix combine	26.0 %
Rheinstahl	8.5 %	Rheinstahl	8.5 %
	100.00%		100.00%

In exchange for the cash and securities received the owners of these different companies turned over to the trust some thirty-three large coal properties, twenty-nine iron and steel mills, and supplies valued at 203,200,000 RM. Through ownership of these properties and later acquisitions the Steel Trust controls more than 50 per cent of the production allotments in the crude steel cartel (*Rohstahl-Gemeinschaft*), in the other important steel cartels mentioned above and in still others since organized.

The only large steel companies which have thus far declined to sell out to the trust are the three integrated combines which have long operated successfully as family concerns: the *Fried. Krupp, A. G., Klöckner Werke, A.G.,* and *Eisen und Stahlwerke Hoesch, A.G.* These combines have shown no hostility to the trust, in fact have coöperated with it on numerous occasions, but they have preferred to preserve their separate identities and the good will which attaches to their well-known names.

Notwithstanding the great activity of the German steel industry since the trust was organized, its success as a business enterprise has not been striking. According to its annual reports, its net profits above all charges in 1927 were 59,940,000 RM. and in 1928, 52,500,000 RM., barely permitting the maintenance in both years of a dividend of 6 per cent on its common stock.[1] These comparatively low net earnings were

[1] The fiscal year of this, as of most other German corporations, ends September 30.

doubtless due in part to the heavy appropriations to cover depreciation on plants that were either closed down as obsolete or modernized by the substitution of efficient, up-to-date equipment for that in use when the trust was formed. Only experts thoroughly familiar with the operation of the trust's plants can estimate to what extent such appropriations are likely to be reflected in higher profits in coming years. That the management has been more interested in future than in immediate profits is indicated by the fact that whereas net profits were lower in 1928 than in 1927, gross profits were larger, the amounts for the two years being, respectively, 289,-170,000,000 RM. and 270,400,000 RM. It is perhaps not altogether fanciful to think that German industrialists have preferred to make a modest showing as regards profits until the amount of reparations payments to which they will be required to contribute has been definitely determined. However, another factor of importance has been the low scale of prices for steel products that it has been deemed wise to maintain to enable German producers to regain a foothold in the world market.

Like the United States Steel Corporation, the German Steel Trust has confined itself to the cruder forms of steel products. According to a careful calculation of Dr. Metzner [1] there were in operation in 1926 seventy-three cartels in the iron fashioning industry with many of which the steel trust was concerned. The number of cartels he found in related industries was even more striking. Engaged in different kinds of machine manufacturing were 147, and in the iron and steel ware industries, 234. As these figures illustrate, German industrialists in this field, where large fixed investments of capital are necessary, are convinced believers in the usefulness, if not the necessity, of combination as a means of promoting efficient production and stabilizing output and prices.

The potash industry differs from the coal and iron and steel industries in being based upon a natural resource, of which Germany, before the war, enjoyed a monopoly. The war altered this situation by causing the transfer to France of

[1] *Kartelle und Kartellpolitik* (1926), p. 13.

Alsace, in which a new potash field was in process of development. Under the new circumstances German and French producers had a strong motive for combining to control supplies and prices of potash in the international market and this they did through an agreement entered into on August 15, 1924, by the German and French potash cartels (*Deutsches Kalisyndikat, G.m.b.H.* and *Société Commerciale des Potasses d'Alsace*).[1] As long as German and French producers act in concert and until sources of supply have been developed in other countries, the industry will be a German-French natural monopoly.

Another peculiarity of the potash industry has been its subjection from its inception to an amount of governmental regulation that has been extreme even for Germany. This came about because the first mines opened and the first experiments proving the value of potash salts were enterprises fostered by the German states, Prussia and Anhalt. With the development of the industry four varieties of potash salts have proved commercially important—carnallite, kainite, hard salts, and sylvinite.[2] While the crude salts are used for some commercial purposes (e.g., kainite as a fertilizer), most of the product is concentrated or manufactured before it is marketed. The most important commercial forms of potash are muriate of potash, used as a fertilizer for cotton and other crops, and sulphate of potash, used in tobacco-growing in the United States. The use of potash for a fertilizer soon far surpassed all other uses. By 1880 over 42 per cent of the total product was used in agriculture. By 1905 the proportion had increased to over 84 per cent. Combination in the industry began in the late 'seventies and it is significant that the mines owned and operated by the states of Prussia and Anhalt not only joined in the first restrictive agreements but played a leading part in securing their adoption. In 1888 a full-fledged

[1] For later developments, cf. chap. xxvi, pp. 621, 622.

[2] Cf. article by H. R. Tosdal on "The German Potash Syndicate: A Typical Kartell," in *Quarterly Journal of Economics,* vol. xxiii (1913), pp. 140 *et seq.,* (reprinted in Ripley, *Trusts, Pools and Corporations,* pp. 799-832). Much of the information in regard to pre-war developments which follows has been derived from this article.

cartel with a central selling agency was organized. Continuously since that date, though with mounting difficulties owing to the overexpansion of the industry, some form of cartel has been maintained, and has included most of the time among its members the mines and factories owned and operated by Prussia and Anhalt.

One consequence of the unwillingness or inability of the cartels to check the opening up of new mines was that the aggregate production capacity was constantly growing more rapidly than the demand for potash products. This resulted in an increase in the curtailment percentage and rising costs, due to the fact that none of the mines were permitted to operate at capacity. A crisis arose on the expiration of the cartel agreement then in operation on June 30, 1909. Although through special concessions the cartel had succeeded in inducing all of the forty-nine mines in operation in 1908 to become members before the close of that year, there were at that time in addition sixty-five companies which had begun borings or the construction of shafts. The aggressive newer companies chafed at the cartel restrictions. If permitted to operate their properties at capacity they knew that they could make large profits even at substantially lower prices, and they objected to being held back for the benefit of the older or less efficiently operated mines. On the other hand, the public authorities concerned with the state mines and the owners of the older mines urged a policy which would maintain high export prices and thus give Germany the full benefit of its natural monopoly at the same time that its potash resources were conserved for future generations. Outside of Germany the United States had by this time become the largest user of potash. It was the bold tactics followed by a combination of German and American capitalists, when the cartel expired, that precipitated the drastic government interference with a nominally private industry that ensued. On June 14 the International Agricultural Corporation was opportunely organized under the laws of New York. Sometime after midnight on June 30, it acquired the important Sollstedt mine from its owner, Mr. Schmidmann, who in turn became president of the International Corporation. Similar developments affecting other important potash properties resulted within the next few days in contracts to supply American importers with 120,000 tons of pure potash at prices 40 per cent lower than those that had been fixed by the cartel. This was said to be fully four-fifths of their requirements for an entire year. This "American invasion" was resented by other potash producers and by German citizens generally, and led the government, after several months of official and unofficial negotiation, to enact the potash law (*Kaligesetz*) of May 25, 1910, which was to remain in effect until December 31, 1925.

The potash law checkmated the efforts of American capitalists to get control of German potash mines and operate them for the exclusive benefit of American fertilizer factories by empowering a government commission (*Verteilungstelle*) to determine allotments, imposing heavy penalties for production in excess of allotments, and requiring each mine to divide its permitted output in the same proportion between domestic and export sales as every other mine. The chairman and two other members of the allotment commission were appointed by the Imperial Chancellor subject to confirmation by the Federal Council, while other members were chosen by the mine-owners. The official scale of prices for potash products, which for the first years was embodied in the law, was declared to be the maximum that might be charged domestic users but the minimum for export sales.[1] The expense of administering the new policy was imposed on mine-owners through a tax of approximately seven cents for every hundred pounds of potash salts produced. The penalty for producing in excess of quota, on the other hand, was from, approximately, $1.25 to $2.25 per hundred pounds of excess.

The potash law was shrewdly devised to retain for Germany the advantages of her natural monopoly, but it had one fatal weakness. It placed no adequate check upon the

[1] The future regulation of prices was a task assigned to the upper house of Parliament (*Bundesrat*). Beginning January 1, 1914, it was to fix prices for five-year periods on the basis of a hearing at which producers and consumers were to present their views.

opening up of new mines and shafts. The regulations in regard to this vital matter were that new mines, though at the outset given allotments below their rated capacity, should, after the third year of operation, receive the same treatment as old mines. The increase in allotment for the construction of a new shaft was to be 10 per cent of the former allotment. Allotments might be freely transferred as theretofore, with the sole restriction that when a transfer affected more than 50 per cent of a given quota it must receive the approval of the government to be valid. In practice these limitations checked little, if at all, the tendency to expand the already overexpanded industry. Investments in new shafts and new mines merely to obtain larger quotas continued, and the organization prescribed by considerations of economy and efficiency—that is, a limitation of operating mines to the number required to produce, when operating at full capacity, the amount of potash needed to supply the world demand at the prices fixed—remained as far from realization as ever. The failure of the cartel law to check expansion is shown by the fact that the number of quota mines increased from the 49 in operation in 1908 to 68 in 1910, 167 in 1913, and 207 by the middle of 1916.

The law did not make the renewal of the cartel agreement obligatory, but since essential conditions were henceforth regulated through governmental agencies there was nothing to be gained by staying out of the cartel. A new cartel agreement was, therefore, entered into by all the potash mine-owners on June 7, 1910.

The new law gave little satisfaction to any group, but the outbreak of the war intervened before further legislation had been formulated, so that it was not until after the revolution in 1918 that another potash law was enacted, this time a socialization law, similar to that adopted at the same period for the coal industry.

The potash socialization laws of April 24 and July 18, 1919, created somewhat elaborate machinery for the regulation of the potash industry in the public interest. All potash producers were required to combine in a sales cartel (*Kalisyndikat*) by

October 31, 1919, and if they failed to do so by voluntary agreement such a sales cartel to continue in operation indefinitely was to be created by governmental decree. For the determination of important issues concerning the industry a Federal Potash Council (*Reichskalirat*) was created composed of thirty members, five representing the producers, three the cartel, eight wage-earners in the industry, two clerical and technical employees, eleven consumers and dealers, and one an expert. The council must ratify agreements and by-laws, fix potash sales prices, and, through a committee, regulate quotas for five-year periods. At all its meetings a representative of the government is to be present with power to object to any proposed resolution or agreement, subject to appeal to the Minister of Economic Affairs. Owing to the dominant position given to owners and their employees in the council, and their tendency to disregard the interests of consumers, control of prices has been largely taken from that body and is exercised by the Minister of Economic Affairs. Section 74 of the law requires that all potash products be turned over for sale to the cartel, which has exclusive control over this branch of the business. The provisions of the law for the regulation of new mines and shafts proved ineffective, and this led to the enactment two years later (October 22, 1921) of the "potash mine-closing law" (*Stillegungsverordnung*), under which the long over-due contraction of this industry has since occurred.

The mine-closing law was drastic. It declared prevailing quotas fixed until December 31, 1934, prohibited the opening of new mines or new shafts, unless the public welfare was deemed to require it, and empowered the government to order mines producing at exceptionally high costs to close down. At the same time it permits mines which close down voluntarily or in deference to governmental decree, and which remain closed until 1935, to retain their quota until that year, while it requires the scaling down of the quotas of other mines, as they become unable to maintain their outputs. This law, unlike its predecessors, has been followed by a rapid decrease in the number of producing mines. By 1924, out of

211 potash mines only 130 were producing their quotas. More than half of these have since discontinued. The monthly average number of producing mines in 1926 was officially reported as only 66.[1]

An important contributing factor to the concentration of production in the lower-cost mines has undoubtedly been the intensified competition among the large producers to expand their quotas by buying up additional mines, in order to permit the operation at capacity of the better of their controlled mines while the poorer were closed down until market conditions had become more favorable. As a result of this competition Dr. Michels reports that the largest combine in the industry, the Wintershall combination, controlled in 1926 about 40 per cent of the German potash production, while it was opposed by a less closely organized defensive alliance of the other private producers, controlling almost an equal share of the production.

The mines owned by Prussia and Anhalt have not entered these alliances, but have become relatively such an unimportant factor in the situation that they now play a very minor rôle. The struggle is not yet ended, but it seems likely from the step taken by the Wintershall combination, in September, 1926, of reducing the capitalization of its producing branch, the *Kali-Industrie, A.G.*, from 320,000,000 to 120,000,000 RM., that further concentration will be coupled with "rationalization" until the excessive overcapitalization by which the industry is handicapped has been corrected. The consensus of opinion among students of the matter appears to be that the German potash industry affords a striking example of the abuses that are too apt to develop when a combination is released from the restraints of even potential competition. In this instance Germany enjoyed a natural monopoly of a commodity whose importance to industry and particularly to agriculture was steadily expanding. The eagerness of private producers to reap the largest advantage from this situation was reinforced by the desire of the Prussian and Anhalt fiscal authorities to derive maximum revenues from the state

[1] *Statistisches Jahrbuch,* 1928.

mines. This cupidity was restrained by the insistence of the government that preferential treatment should be accorded German consumers, particularly farmers, but as regards export prices it was limited only by consideration of what the traffic would bear. When in 1909 American fertilizer interests sought to break through and get the potash they required at prices corresponding more nearly to reasonable costs, the government came to the support of the monopoly and subjected it to restrictions that increased rather than decreased temptation to continue the development of the industry along uneconomical lines. The loss of the Alsatian potash deposits to France and the potential competition which this has introduced into the situation, together with the bitter lessons of past experience, are causing German producers and German officials to seek to bring the industry back to an efficient basis. This is likely to be assisted by the development of valuable potash deposits in other parts of the world.[1] This perhaps justifies the expectation that the future will cause combination in the German potash industry to follow similar lines to that displayed in the coal industry, where price policies have been held in restraint by potential when not by actual competition and the economies of combination have been effected while the wastes of monopoly have been largely avoided.

The three examples of monopolistic combinations in German industry that have been selected typify the combination movement that has played such a rôle in that country. Any general statement about the number of cartels in existence is rendered difficult because of the very different senses in which that term may be employed. One of the latest attempts to estimate the number in operation was made by Dr. Max Metzner[2] in 1926. He starts with the official governmental estimate, made about the middle of 1925, of 3,050. Of these, 2,500 were credited to industry, 400 to wholesale trade, and 150 to retail trade. These figures he considers seriously exaggerated. As regards wholesale trade, he believes the num-

[1] The potash deposits that have been discovered in Texas and New Mexico are said to be not only extensive, but of high quality. Cf. p. 622, *infra*.

[2] *Kartelle und Kartellpolitik,* 1926, pp. 16-18.

ber of cartels that are at all significant does not exceed 30 to 35. In retail trade he knows of no cartel of any importance. He thinks the official figures more nearly accurate as regards cartels in industry, but would estimate a total under 2,000, or a grand total for industry and trade together of just about that number. Of these, more than one-half are cartels regulating conditions of sale rather than outputs or prices (*Konditionenkartelle*), which have little monopolistic ambition or influence. Actual price cartels he estimates at only between 500 and 600. On the other hand, Dr. Metzner goes on to say that if we consider the effect of combinations on the buying and selling of products in present-day Germany we will find "almost every branch of business intercourse enmeshed in a net of cartels or cartel-like silent agreements and free competition in the determination of prices much more restricted than it has ever been supposed to be." We thus seem justified in concluding that combination rather than unrestrained competition is the accepted condition under which German industry is now carried on. This does not mean that German business men do not chafe at the restraints which the combinations to which they so commonly belong impose upon them. In a recent discussion one of the speakers said, "I would like to see a cartel member who likes to be in a cartel." The oft-repeated declaration of German commentators is that "cartels are the children of necessity." Subjected as they are to the pressure of outside competition, German business men have found protection and strength in combining to advance their common interests, and this has caused them to accept the restraints which effective combination necessarily imposes in somewhat the same way that wage-earners accept the restraints imposed by their trade unions. In order to understand why the German public and the German government have on the whole supported this movement toward combination we must now turn to a consideration of the governmental policies which have accompanied and to a certain extent controlled it, the subject of the next chapter.

CHAPTER XXV

GERMANY'S POLICIES TOWARD CORPORATIONS AND TRUSTS

THE American policy in reference to the organization of corporations has become that of permitting the incorporators to arrange pretty nearly everything, except the fees and taxes they must pay to the government, as may suit their purposes. Germany, on the other hand, in the law enacted for the whole country in 1884, rigidly limits what the incorporators may do, especially as regards the relation between capitalization and *bona-fide* assets, and holds promoters, incorporators, and boards of directors strictly responsible for compliance with its provisions. This law was not hastily adopted. The country had experienced the ill effects of a lax corporation law in the early 'seventies after the Franco-Prussian war. An unusually representative and competent commission was then created to study the subject, and every aspect was carefully considered before it submitted the recommendations to the Reichstag which were embodied in the statute. Since 1884 numerous occasions for reconsidering the law have arisen. The subject was discussed preceding the enactment of the German Stock Exchange law in 1896 and the adoption of the revised commercial code in 1897. After the war the modification of this as of other laws to conform to the views of the socialist government which came into power was considered, but it, with the whole commercial code, was continued in full force in accordance with Article 178 of the Constitution adopted in 1919. The uncertainties of the period of inflation made necessary the temporary suspension of some of the provisions in regard to the compulsory liquidation of a company which had become insolvent, but the only change of importance that has resulted from the substitution of a liberal republican for the earlier monarchical form of government has been the requirement that wage-earners shall have representation on the supervising boards of directors of the corporations which employ them. This would seem to indicate a conviction on the part of all classes interested in German corporations that the law is in essentials wise and that it has not unduly hampered the expansion of German business. That it has had much to do with the absence in Germany of the distrust and hostility toward large corporations with which we are familiar is beyond question.

The German law permits the organization of a business corporation (*Aktiengesellschaft*) in either of two ways. The *simultaneous* method requires that all of the capital be subscribed and paid for at not less than par before the corporation is launched; the *successive* method permits incorporation after all of the capital has been subscribed for at par, and not less than 25 per cent has been paid in. So many restrictions hamper incorporation by the successive method that the simultaneous plan is that usually adopted. Since under this all stock must be taken at par and full value in cash or property given for it, the only opportunities for profit which are left to the promoters of German corporations are through sales of the stock at a premium at the outset or sharing in the success of the corporation through retaining large blocks of the stock until that success has been demonstrated. Only business men or bankers of established reputation for integrity and sound judgment can hope to induce purchasers to pay premiums for the stock of a new corporation, and only those with large means can afford to await the demonstrated success of a new business before they realize on their investment. In consequence the German law eliminates from the beginning the unscrupulous and financially irresponsible type of corporation promoter who has been too much in evidence in this country and confines the task of planning and launching new corporations to careful, constructive business men and bankers, who prosper and can only prosper, not at the expense of those who trust them, but with those who trust them.

In Germany, as in the United States, the principal privilege attaching to incorporation of a business enterprise is the limited liability, or more accurately the exemption from liability except for money actually paid in or subscribed for stock, of the shareholders. Since the federal government alone can issue charters of incorporation, there has been no wavering in German governmental policy from the principle that the privilege shall be extended only under conditions that clearly benefit the public. Before the War few thought that granting limited liability to small business enterprises, the capital for which can easily be supplied by individuals or partners, would benefit the public. Regarding the privilege as justified only when the size of the enterprise called for substantial investments of capital, German lawmakers imposed restrictions which made incorporation attractive only to businesses of some magnitude. Among these were the requirements that the shares of stock must have a par value of not less than 1,000 M. ($240)[1] and that when shares were issued for property instead of cash elaborate measures must be taken to insure that the property was actually worth at least as much as the par value of the shares issued in exchange for it. Under the German law every corporation must have two boards of directors, a supervising board (*Aufsichtsrat*) and a managing board (*Vorstand*). No one may be at the same time a member of both of these boards. Before a corporation can be admitted to registry the members of these boards must be chosen and they must examine and report under oath upon all the organization proceedings, becoming personally liable if they make statements which are untrue and which result in subsequent loss to others which cannot be recovered from those principally responsible. Such liability attaches even when the deception was not deliberate, unless the offender can prove that he exercised the diligence of a prudent business man in verifying the accuracy of the statements to which he has subscribed. When one of the directors is also one of the organizers (*Gründer*) of the corporation, interested in

[1] Following the period of inflation modifications were made in regard to the minimum par value of shares, which may now be as low as 100 RM. This has encouraged small corporations, but the rigid requirements still applying to them have prevented their undue multiplication.

property acquired in exchange for stock, special outside auditors must investigate and report on the transaction. The application for registry must be made by all of the organizers of the corporation and by all of the members of both the supervising and the managing boards. To it must be attached the proposed articles of association, the minutes of the organization meeting showing the election of the members of the two boards and other business transacted, and the reports of the boards, the organizers, and the outside auditors, when required, in regard to the terms and considerations for which all the shares of stock were issued, and the names of the stockholders. When stock is issued for property, the organizers have to include in this sworn written statement the basis for the valuation put upon such property, including the price paid for such property in any transactions in which it has figured during the preceding two years, or if it is a going business, its net earnings during such years.. For the accuracy of such statement they are civilly and, in case of fraud, criminally liable, the penalty being a fine up to 20,000 RM. and imprisonment up to five years or both together. As a result of these requirements three and, in case a director is also an organizer, four independent investigations must be made and reported upon under oath to establish the parity between the value of property acquired by the corporation and the stock issued for such property, and the danger that a German corporation will begin business with nominal capitalization exceeding its *bona-fide* assets is reduced to the vanishing point. The requirements described are supplemented by regulations imposing special liability on those offering the stocks of corporations for sale during the first two years of their existence and by the denial of the privilege of admission to the stock exchanges of the securities of new corporations until they have filed their first annual balance sheets.

Preventing overcapitalization on the launching of a new corporation cannot, of course, prevent impairment of its capital through losses incurred after organization. But the German law goes very far to insure that such losses shall not be hidden from stockholders, creditors, and investors and to protect creditors from the losses that might fall upon them if the entire capital were dissipated. The central feature in Germany's policy of enforced and effective publicity in regard to the financial operations of her corporations is the requirement of an annual balance sheet which must be reported to the stockholders within three months after the close of each business year on the authority of both boards of directors, and which must be formally accepted by them before the boards are discharged. If stockholders controlling 10 per cent of the capital question any points in the balance sheet, outside auditors may be called in to verify its accuracy. The balance sheet must be drawn up on a most conservative basis and must show as a separate item the profit or loss surplus, or the difference between the total liabilities and total assets. Dividends may legally be paid only when a positive surplus is shown, so that a German corporation which incurs a loss which impairs its capital must not only suspend dividends during the year in which the loss occurs but must make up such a loss out of subsequent earnings before dividends may be resumed. Moreover, there is a general requirement that 5 per cent of net earnings must be added to a legal reserve until this reserve, which must appear in the balance sheet as a liability, equals 10 per cent of the capital. In consequence, after a few years a successful German corporation should have net assets equal to at least 110 per cent of its nominal capitalization. In valuing assets for purposes of the balance sheet all items are to be entered at cost, unless they have depreciated in value, when they must be entered at their current value. As this implies, the valuation put on buildings and similar wasting assets must allow for depreciation. Since, on the other hand, land and other items that are likely to appreciate must be carried at cost, the aggregate assets reported by a German corporation usually understate rather than overstate the value of its property, especially since no item for good will can be included except where it has been bought and paid for in connection with the absorption of a going business.

When, notwithstanding these requirements, the net assets of a corporation have been so impaired that they equal less than 50 per cent of the capital liability, the law imposes the duty upon the managing board to call a special meeting of the stockholders to lay the facts before them and submit for consideration the question whether a reorganization scaling down the capitalization to correspond with the reduced assets would be desirable. Further, when, and if, the net assets against the capital liability are entirely wiped out, the managing board must immediately file a petition in bankruptcy for the protection of the creditors.

It should not be inferred from these statements that stockholders in Germany are any more alert in following the details of the operation of the corporations in which they are interested than they are in this country. There, as here, reliance is placed by the rank and file of stockholders in the integrity and capacity of the management, and annual meetings are, as a rule, as perfunctory as though the presentation and voting of the balance sheet were a mere matter of routine. The difference is that behind the balance sheet is the personal liability of the directors, that the information it presents is brought to the attention of all investors through the financial press, and that it thus affords a basis for intelligent discussion and criticism, which determines the standing of corporations and the reputations of all of those connected with them. This all contributes to caution and conservatism in corporate financial operations and has spared German investors the continual drain upon their savings which fraudulent and near-fraudulent corporate promotions and operation cause in the United States. After what has been said it is hardly necessary to add that no-par stock is not tolerated by the German law. On the other hand, the law allows great latitude to organizers in creating different classes of stock as regards preferences in dividends or assets on liquidation and as regards voting privileges. Also German companies are permitted to acquire and hold the stock of other corporations, and the resulting holding companies are in some fields as involved and complicated as they have become in this country.

Although the German law contains no prescription in regard to the minimum capital a corporation must have, its practical effect has been to make the corporate form of organization especially attractive to large business enterprises. German business men do not complain that the restrictions on corporations hamper enterprise or industry. On the contrary, all available evidence indicates that prior to the war German industry was expanding more rapidly than that of any other European country. Similarly, since the stabilization of the mark in November, 1923, German industry has recovered with truly surprising rapidity.

No doubt one reason why German business men find little or no fault with the restrictions of the corporation law is that another form of organization is open to small enterprisers, the private limited liability company (*Gesellschaft mit beschränkter Haftung*), which better meets their legitimate requirements. The organization of a *G. m. b. H.*, to use the customary German designation, is effected quite easily by agreement among the parties attested by a notary. The capital, according to an Act passed in 1898 as amended in 1924, must be at least 5,000 RM. and the shares (*Anteile*) taken by each member must be at least 50 RM. The shares need not be of equal value. Their transfer is made as difficult as the transfer of shares (*Aktien*) in a corporation is made easy. In general such transfer is valid only when attested by a notary, approved by the officers of the *G. m. b. H.*, and entered in its registry. These regulations and others effectively prevent sales of shares to the public and preserve the character of the *G. m. b. H.* as private, conservatively managed enterprises. The members of the *G. m. b. H.* are liable not only for the full amount they have subscribed for their shares, but also, in case one of their number fails to meet his liability, *pro rata* for the amount of his deficiency. As regards their operation, *G. m. b. H.* are not required to have a supervising board, but they must present an annual balance sheet. Their management may be vested in a single person and they may be dissolved through appropriate action before a notary public by a three-fourths vote as easily and inexpensively as they are organized.

The following statistics about corporations and *G. m. b. H.* in operation in Germany at the end of 1913 and 1927 indicate that there are about five times as many private limited liability companies as corporations, though the aggregate capital of the latter is, of course, very much greater.

TABLE XVIII

NUMBER AND TOTAL CAPITAL OF CORPORATIONS AND NUMBER OF *G. m. b. H.* IN OPERATION IN GERMANY

	December 31, 1913			December 31, 1927		
	No.	Total capital in 1,000,000 RM.	Av. capital in 1,000 RM.	No.	Total capital in 1,000,000 RM.	Av. capital in 1,000 RM.
Corporations	5,139	16,527	3,215	11,966	21,542	1,800
G. m. b. H.	26,790			50,288		

The fact that exact records are kept of the total number of these "legal persons" permitted to carry on business and of the capital of the corporations illustrates the difference between the German and the American attitude toward this problem. Though the average capital of corporations is less than before the war, the average shown for 1927 of 1,800,000 RM. bears out the assertion that corporate business in Germany is predominantly big business.

The statement made in the last chapter,[1] that under German law combinations have enjoyed "virtually a free field for development," did not mean, as was later brought out, that their practices and policies have not been continuously subject to governmental supervision. The provision of the Civil Code (Article 826) making anyone liable for damages who "intentionally inflicts injury upon another in a manner repugnant to good morals" might always be appealed to against a combination whose policies were grossly unfair or oppressive.

[1] Cf. *supra*, p. 553.

Applying this in a case where the boycott was used to force independents to maintain cartel prices, the Supreme Court, in an important decision rendered December 14, 1902, made the determining consideration whether the very existence of the competitor was imperiled by the methods used by the combination. Quoting Dr. Michels's summary of this decision,[1] "If a plan adopted by a cartel threatened the existence of another's business to the extent of weakening or undermining it and of substantially injuring his credit or his standing in the business world, it was repugnant to good morals and fell under Section 826 of the Civil Code."

The general condemnation of unethical business conduct of the civil law was made more precise and effective by the statute against unfair competition enacted May 27, 1896, and amended June 7, 1909. The first section of the amended act declares expressly that "whoever in business affairs, for the purpose of competition, commits acts which are repugnant to good morals may be subject to an action to desist therefrom and to pay damages." It will be observed that the language of this provision is more general than that of the Civil Code, omitting the word "intentionally" (*vorsätzlich*), and that it authorizes injunctive relief as well as damages. The courts have interpreted "business affairs" broadly to include artistic, scientific, legal, and medical activities for profit, as well as business in the ordinary sense, and have taken the standards and practices of honest and upright citizens as their test of "good morals."

Later sections of the law deal specifically with fraudulent and deceptive advertising (Sections 3, 4, and 5), bankrupt and closing out sales (Sections 6-10), bribing the employees of competitors (Section 12), divulging trade secrets (Sections 17-20) and other practices that are considered unfair. For some of these offenses imprisonment for not more than one year and fines of not more than 5,000 RM. may be imposed. In general, little use is said to have been made of

[1] *Cartels, Combines and Trusts in Post-War Germany,* pp. 60, 61. The authors have found the careful analysis of the German laws relating to combinations in this book most helpful and commend it to the reader who desires a fuller discussion of the subject.

these criminal penalties, reliance for enforcement being placed on the resort to damage suits by injured parties, and the issue of injunctions where continued violations are threatened. Like the unfair competition provision of the Federal Trade Commission Act, the German law appears to have put a stop to many deceptive and unfair practices and thus raised the standards of business conduct.

As the cartels multiplied in the 'nineties the reasons for their organization and their relation to the general welfare received more and more attention. In Germany as in the United States in the same period a connection was traced between the protective tariff and the combinations, and attempts were made to have duties on products controlled by the cartels lowered or abolished but without success. The first serious study of the subject was through a representative governmental commission created in 1902, which made a careful investigation during the next three years and published an exhaustive report entitled, significantly, "Contradictory Proceedings About German Cartels." [1] In the course of this investigation many of the charges that had been brought against cartels were disproved, while the grounds for others were removed by the voluntary discontinuance by the cartels of the practices objected to. Meantime the agitation for cartel regulation had subsided and the government was glad to be guided by the decision of the Commission that the time was not yet ripe for interference with the free development of the combination movement.

The only important legislation prior to the outbreak of the war was the Potash law of 1910, which, as brought out in the last chapter,[2] was due less to a desire to regulate the cartel than to prevent foreign interests from gaining control of German potash mines and from exploiting them for their own rather than Germany's advantage.

The war caused the German government to make use of the cartels to effect the rapid and complete coördination of German industry which contributed so greatly to that country's

[1] *Kontradiktorische Verhandlungen über deutsche Kartelle.* Berlin, 1906.
[2] Cf. *supra,* p. 570 *et seq.*

initial successes in the struggle. From permitting cartels, the government changed its policy to that of making their continuance obligatory and at the same time directing their policies as to output, prices, etc., as conditions made desirable.

With the revolution which followed the war, control of the German government passed to the Socialist party. A definite plan, known as the Wissel-Möllendorf program, was presented to the country for combining all of the business enterprises in each important branch of industry into public corporations and organizing an industrial parliament to be made up of representatives of the different business groups and to determine important questions of economic policy under the guidance of a Minister of Economic Affairs. In accordance with this program "socialization" laws were passed during the year 1919 applying to the coal, potash, and electrical industries. Before these had been pushed to the point of nationalizing these industries a reaction set in. The three industries mentioned were subjected to special governmental supervision through national councils on which wage-earners and consumers as well as owners were represented, but without any change as regards their private ownership. Nor was the socialization program extended to other industries. While they were strongly opposed to bureaucratic control of industry, German industrialists recognized the need for some plan by which the misuse of their economic power by the cartels could be prevented and the public interest in reasonable prices, etc., safeguarded. They therefore assured the Minister of Economic Affairs of their desire to coöperate, and at his suggestion through their powerful national associations [1] organized in 1921 a cartel mediation board (*Kartelleinigungstelle*). This has been an important agency in adjusting disputes among the cartels and their organized customers ever since.

[1] The principal associations (called *Spitzenverbände*) are the National Association of German Industry (*Reichsverband der deutschen Industrie*), the National Association of German Wholesale and Foreign Trade (*Reichsverband des deutschen Gross—und Überseehandels*) and the Central Association of German Retail Trade (*Hauptgemeinschaft des deutschen Einzelhandels*).

But for the special hardships which were inflicted upon consumers by the cartels during the inflation period, the policy of regulation through voluntary negotiation might have been continued. However, the temptation to the organized producers to insist on terms of sale which would impose the losses resulting from the decline of the mark upon their customers was too strong to be resisted. By requiring full payment with orders or at prices readjusted to current conditions when payment was made, they transferred to the buyer the entire risk resulting from what came to be called "the dance of the mark." The big coöperative societies, which were the principal sufferers, demanded protection from the government. In the memorable crisis year 1923 Herr Stresemann, the rising strong man of Germany who later became chancellor, promised relief to German consumers through some sort of cartel supervision law. To avert the crisis that threatened, the Reichstag enacted on October 13, 1923, a statute giving, at the demand of the new chancellor, the full force of law to decrees formally issued by the government, unless and until their abrogation should be ordered by the Reichstag. It was on the basis of this extraordinary authority that Herr Stresemann promulgated the so-called cartel law (*Decree against the Misuse of Economic Power* [1]) on November 2, 1923. Since it has been accepted by the Reichstag, its position as part of the law of the land, though at first challenged on technical grounds, is now unquestioned. The same month in which this decree was issued witnessed the stabilization of the currency, an achievement for which Dr. Schacht, head of the Reichsbank, is given chief credit. A new form of mark, the *Rentenmark,* with the same gold exchange value as the pre-war mark, was put out and made exchangeable for the paper marks in circulation in the ratio of one *RM.* = one trillion (1,000,000,000,000) *PM.* By judicious control of the foreign exchanges the German government has succeeded in maintaining the stability of this new mark, now styled the *Reichsmark,* ever since. November, 1923, thus stands as the turning-point in

[1] *Verordnung gegen Missbrauch wirtschaftlicher Machtstellungen vom 2. November, 1923.*

the economic history of post-war Germany, comparable in importance with September, 1924, when the Dawes Plan became operative, and August, 1929, when the Young Plan was finally agreed to in its stead by the allied powers and Germany.

The central feature of the cartel law, about which nearly all of the provisions in its twenty-three sections revolve, is the creation of a special court (*Kartelgericht*). Germany had already developed a special federal economic court (*Reichswirtschaftsgericht*) to pass on business issues. Section 11 of the new act makes it the duty of this court to organize the cartel court. The president of the Republic appoints the president of the cartel court and two assistants or alternates to sit in his place when necessary. They must have the qualifications of federal judges. In addition the law provides for four associate judges, one of whom must be a member of the federal Economic Court. Two additional associates must be qualified experts representing the two sides in the economic issues in dispute. Finally, the fourth is an economist qualified to represent the general welfare in connection with these issues. As its composition indicates, this unique court of five members is rather a board of qualified experts to determine when and how administrative control should be exercised over cartels and other monopolistic combinations, than a judicial body to decide cases. Section 12 makes its jurisdiction exclusive and its decisions final and binding upon courts of justice and courts of arbitration, even as regards its own jurisdiction. The law links the activities of the court closely to those of the federal Minister of Economic Affairs (*Reichswirtschaftsminister*), whose powers over combinations are made broader and upon whose initiative most of the issues which may arise under the law are brought before the court.

In deciding upon the jurisdiction to be given to the cartel court and the enlarged powers to be conferred on the Minister of Economic Affairs the Stresemann government had to choose between the demands of the spokesmen for the cooperatives, who wished the cartels, especially as regards their price policies, to be subjected to rigid governmental control, including a registry of all such combinations, complete publicity in regard to all their agreements, etc., and the spokesmen of the cartels themselves, who wished to be let alone. The fact that the provisions of the decree have not yet been altered by later legislation indicates that the middle course steered by the government has satisfied in reasonable measure both sides. As a step toward publicity, clarity, and simplification Section 1 of the act requires that "all contracts and agreements involving obligations in regard to the manipulation of production or sales, the conditions to be observed in business transactions, the methods of fixing prices or price demands (syndicates, cartels, conventions, and similar agreements) must be in written form." Section 2 reinforces this by declaring such contracts or agreements based on "word of honor or similar solemn assurance" null and void. To prevent possible confusion Section 21 gives parties to verbal agreements already in force three weeks of grace, within which time they must embody such agreements in written form in order to maintain their validity. The language of Section 1, at the same time that it minimizes controversies as to whether or not an agreement was entered into and what were its terms, indicates with sufficient clearness the kind of activities to which the law applies and the jurisdiction of the cartel court. Combinations of employees are clearly not included, nor employers' associations as regards their activities concerned with labor relations. Also complete consolidations would not be affected except as they belonged to cartels. Section 19 further exempts from the operation of the law combinations created by law and agreements or prices which have been ordered or approved by a duly constituted governmental authority. This exempts among others the coal and potash cartels.

The principal powers conferred upon the federal Minister of Economic Affairs (*Reichswirtschaftsminister*) are specified in Section 4. When he believes that contracts or agreements of the kind described in Section 1 have been entered into or a specified manner of carrying them out adopted which endangers the national economy or common welfare (*Gesamtwirtschaft oder Gemeinwohl*) he may: (1) appeal to the cartel court to have them declared null and void or to have the specified manner of carrying them out prohibited; (2) order that any party to such contracts may, at any time and without notice, withdraw from them; (3) order that copies of such agreements and of the regulations made for carrying them out shall be delivered to him and shall take effect only after he has received them. As examples of dangers to the national economy and common welfare the act goes on to specify the economically unjustified raising of prices or maintaining them at a high level, the unfair restriction of freedom of action by boycotts in connection with sales and purchases, and the fixing of discriminatory prices or conditions. It is noticeable here and in other provisions how far reliance is placed upon publicity and the free play of self-interest, if members are released from their cartel agreements, to protect the public from abuses. The minister is given the further power in Section 5 to require the persons who have been proceeded against in accordance with Section 4 to deliver to him future contracts with certain limitations to enable him to exercise the same supervision over them. This requirement has been made operative against the steel cartel following an official condemnation of a proposed increase in prices.

Correlative with the power given the Minister of Economic Affairs, the cartel court by Section 7 is expressly empowered when appealed to by him and "when it deems the national economy or the common welfare to be endangered, to declare the contract or agreement in whole or in part null and void or to prohibit the specified manner of carrying it out." Further, Section 9 prescribes that in connection with the contracts and agreements covered by the act, bonds may not be forfeited or other penalties imposed on members charged with breaches of the agreement without the consent of the president of the cartel court, who must withhold his consent when he deems that the measure threatens the national economy or common welfare or unfairly restricts the economic freedom of the party concerned.

Even more sweeping is the power given to the Minister of Economic Affairs and the cartel court by Section 10. This declares that: "Whenever the business agreements or the methods by which producers or combinations of producers (trusts, community of interest combines, syndicates, cartels, conventions, or similar combinations) fix prices are calculated to endanger the national economy or common welfare through the misuse of an economically powerful position, the cartel court may, on the proposal of the federal Minister of Economic Affairs, declare that all injured parties may withdraw from all contracts, which have been concluded under the conditions objected to." The section requires the court to publish its decision as soon as it has formulated it and protects the combination by adding that unless the right to withdraw granted by the court is exercised within two weeks such right lapses. The power given by this provision appears rarely if ever to have been exercised, and it is significant chiefly as showing the determination of the government to give the cartel court, acting at the behest of the Minister of Economic Affairs, full power to curb the "misuse of economic power."

While the president of the court may, in appropriate cases, decide without consulting his associates, Section 13 gives interested parties the right to appeal from his decisions within three days to the cartel court. Thus quick action is insured at the same time that arbitrary decisions based on the judgment of a single judge are prevented.

In actual practice the provision of the law that has proved most important is Section 8. Under it "any participant may without previous notice withdraw from contracts and agreements of the kinds described in Section 1, for reason of weight." Such a reason, the section adds, may be that "the freedom of economic activity of the withdrawing party, especially in connection with production, sale, or the fixing of prices, is unfairly restricted." When this right is exercised, appeal may be made by other parties to the agreement within two weeks to the cartel court, which must decide whether the withdrawal was justified. If no such appeal is made within two weeks the withdrawal is deemed valid.

It will be observed that this provision seriously impairs the binding force of cartel agreements. Vigorous objection is brought against it and the grounds for such objection seem well founded. Under other provisions of the law, on appeal to the Minister of Economic Affairs, parties to an agreement may be released from it when he deems this in the public interest. Also he may request the cartel court to abrogate such agreement when this is thought to be in the public interest. Finally the cartels are prohibited from taking extreme measures against unwilling members until such measures have been approved by the president of the cartel court. Assuming that cartels, when properly administered, are in the general interest—and few in Germany question this assumption—why permit members who enter into cartel agreements voluntarily to withdraw at will without first securing authority from the governmental agencies provided for that purpose? Business men are not allowed to withdraw at will from other contracts when this appears to be to their personal advantage. Why should cartel agreements be weakened by the addition of this provision when other means are provided for safeguarding the public interest in any situation that may arise? While convincing to the writers, this objection in practice has less force than might appear because of the unwillingness which the cartel court has shown to sanction withdrawals. The majority of the cases that come before the cartel court concern attempted withdrawals under this section of the law, and the overwhelming majority of decisions appear to have been against the withdrawing member on the ground that no reason of sufficient weight to justify breach of his agreement has been shown. At the same time decisions on this issue have established pretty clearly what reasons for withdrawal will be accepted as valid by the court, and this checks the number of attempted withdrawals on unsubstantial grounds. Dr. Michels [1] enumerates the following reasons for withdrawal that have received the sanction of the court:

(1) A decrease in the number of members of the cartel which seriously endangers the aims of the cartel or makes their achievement altogether impossible.

[1] Cf. *Cartels, Combines, and Trusts,* p. 54.

(2) A permanent decrease of the percentage of the total production combined in the cartel. An increase of outsiders from 5 per cent to 20 per cent of the total production has been considered sufficient reason for withdrawal.

(3) Mergers within the cartel. Upon entering the cartel every member figures on a certain influence he is going to have on the affairs of the cartel. If later on one member of the cartel succeeds in absorbing other members to such an extent as to dominate the cartel, members who have lost their power of influencing the policies of the cartel may withdraw.

(4) A radical change in the aims and purposes of the cartel may be a reason for withdrawal.

(5) If the cartel fails to adapt itself to changing conditions to such an extent as to affect seriously the interests of some of its members, these members may have a right to withdraw.

(6) The establishment of a community of interest between some members and outsiders may be a reason of weight.

(7) If the cartel discipline has broken down or been stiffened to an unreasonable extent, those suffering have a right tò withdraw.

As this enumeration implies, hardship to the party wishing to withdraw, short of threatened financial ruin, is not considered a reason of weight. On the other hand, evidence that the cartel has lost its control of the market for the benefit of its members, or that the withdrawing member is at the mercy of some stronger faction that has developed since he entered the cartel, is so considered.

While Section 8 seems inconsistent with the attitude of approval and coöperation which the German government has usually assumed toward cartels, it should be noted that its tendency is to place combinations in restraint of trade in Germany in a situation not unlike that which they have come to have under the English common law. As will be brought out in the next chapter, in applying the principle that "unreasonable" restraints on trade are unlawful in the sense that the courts will not enforce them, English judges have become more and more liberal in their views of what is "reasonable." Under English law the courts will enforce restrictions unless they are deemed "unreasonable" as between the parties or the public interest is thought to be injured by them. Under Section 8 the cartel court will sanction withdrawal from restrictive agreements only when it can foresee no serious injury to the public interest from their breach and the consequent weakening of the cartel. The approach is different, the criteria applied are to some extent different, but the outcome is similar. Under both systems restrictive agreements that are clearly opposed to the public interest become unenforceable.

The somewhat formal analysis of the provisions of the cartel law that has been given, like any formal description of the text of a law that is in actual operation, may easily mislead the reader. As has already been stated, the cartel court is more an administrative than a judicial body. Its sessions are private and its procedure informal. While created to check abuses on the part of combinations, its attitude is cooperative and constructive rather than hostile and obstructive. One of its leading members is Dr. Siegfried Tschierschky, the accomplished and indefatigable editor, almost from its inception twenty-seven years ago, of the leading periodical on the cartel problem, the well known *Kartell-Rundschau.* With his associates he regards it as the function of the court less to decide cases by the issue of formal decisions than to attempt to conciliate the members of the cartels as differences arise and thus to assist them to carry out their legitimate business objects—the test of legitimacy always being *die Gesamtwirtschaft oder das Gemeinwohl* so frequently referred to in the act. Under these conditions it was as inevitable as it is desirable that the important work of the court should be accomplished not in its formal sessions but in the informal conferences held with litigants, where issues are threshed out and adjustments affected with a minimum of publicity and a maximum of benefit to all concerned. There is, of course, criticism of the court for not carrying on all its activities in the full light of publicity, but thus far such criticism has been free from any charge of bias or self-interest on the part of the judges and is far outweighed by the recognition that the presence of a gallery does not aid in the solution of issues requiring patient conference and thoughtful deliberation.

Under the law the more important issues that come before the court require the initiative of the federal Minister of Economic Affairs. Here, as in the constitution of the court itself, the personal equation is all-important. The German Republic since 1923 has been fortunate in its Ministers of Economic Affairs and the successful operation of the cartel law has been due in large measure to the moderation and judgment shown in bringing it into operation. Large industrialists object to many features of the law, but seem to agree that in practice it has worked better than might have been expected.

One of the writers attended the sessions of the convention of German and Austrian jurists (*Deutscher Juristentag*) in Salzburg in September, 1928, at which a whole day was devoted to a discussion of the question, "Is it desirable that the German and Austrian cartel laws be altered and simplified?" There seemed a strong preponderance of opinion that the German law should be altered and simplified, but except for the demand that Section 8 be repealed, the meeting of minds in regard to just what should be done was not conspicuous. That a determined effort will be made to amend the law when the more vital issue of reparation payments is settled was clearly indicated by the addresses at this conference. That the law will be repealed or the power given the Minister of Economic Affairs and the cartel court to check cartel abuses abridged, appear, however, unlikely. Some regulatory law had long been advocated by important sections of public opinion, and now that it has embarked on this course the German government is not likely to recede from it.

The problem that has engaged the interest of German industrialists and of the German government since 1923 much more than the new cartel law is that of "rationalizing" German industry. As this term has come to be used in Europe it signifies all that is connoted by "scientific management" in this country—standardization, simplification, efficient plant organization, job analysis, systems of wage payment that enlist the interest of the workers in increased production, etc.—plus the correlation on a national, when not international, scale of production and market requirements that is necessary to stabilization. The cartels contribute to such a correlation but they have shown one serious disadvantage. They tend to aid high-cost producers to survive at the expense of industrial efficiency. German industrialists and government officials have come to realize that along these lines German industry cannot win back the foreign markets she lost during the war, pay reparations, and recover the leading place she held in 1914. Forms of combination are, therefore, being sought which will not only permit the adjustment of output to market requirements, but will make possible the concentration of production in the best located and most up-to-date plants and the scrapping of poorly located and poorly equipped plants in the interest of economy and efficiency. Combinations which merely control markets and prices no longer command approval or support. They must also control methods of production and insure improvements in efficiency and a sharing of the benefits of such improvements with consumers on the one hand and wage-earners on the other to satisfy the democratic aspirations of present-day thought. These are the considerations that lie behind the rationalization movement which has transformed many German industries (*e.g.*, coal, iron and steel, potash) in the last five years and given rise to what is beginning to be styled "the New Industrial Revolution."[1] But before we can judge of the full significance of this latest phase of the combination movement we must review briefly the policies in this field that are being tried by other countries.

[1] Cf. Walter Meakin's book with this title, further described as *A Study . . . of Rationalization and Post-War Tendencies of Capitalism and Labour,* published in May, 1928.

CHAPTER XXVI

TRUST POLICIES OF OTHER COUNTRIES: INTERNATIONAL CARTELS

It is not our purpose to attempt a complete survey of the policies of other countries. Instead, we have limited ourselves to a consideration of those of the leading English-speaking countries, which in so many respects are like our own, and to a brief account of the policy of the Russian Soviet Government, which is so fundamentally different.

Until the wave of antitrust legislation swept over the country in the late 'eighties and early 'nineties, the law of the United States in reference to combinations in restraint of trade and monopolies was the English common law, as modified by the decisions of American courts. The United Kingdom has continued to this day to rely on the common law to impose whatever restrictions are considered necessary in this field. Three reasons go far to account for this contrast. First the United Kingdom has had one corporation law for the whole country and has sought through its repeated amendment to protect investors from the crasser abuses from which American investors under our loose corporation laws have suffered. Second, the United Kingdom has enjoyed a monopoly in no form of natural wealth. Third, before combinations had developed in other countries, she had come to depend for her prosperity largely upon the foreign market, and, in consequence, had repealed her protective tariff. For these last reasons monopolistic combinations have been rare in the United Kingdom, and since they have been curbed by the free admission to English markets of foreign-made goods, their practices have as a rule aroused little or no opposition. An added consequence of the comparative immunity from oppressive monopolies which the United Kingdom has enjoyed has been that English courts have applied common-law restrictions with greater and greater liberality at the very period when in this country the common law was being reenforced by antitrust statutes.

The present corporation law of the United Kingdom is the Companies (Consolidation) Act of 1908 as amended by subsequent legislation, particularly by the carefully framed Companies Act Amendment Act of August 3, 1928. The central principles of this legislation are publicity and personal responsibility of promoters and directors for the accuracy of their published statements, whether in prospectuses or in the annual reports they are required to make to their shareholders. The law is much more liberal than the German law as regards the permitted relationship between assets and liabilities at the time a company is launched and thereafter. But it is equally stringent in requiring every corporation to keep full and accurate books of account and to lay before its shareholders at their general meeting each year a profit and loss statement and a balance sheet, which will acquaint them with the financial condition of their company. The English law further makes obligatory a check on the accuracy of these annual financial statements which is not found in the German law. Every English company must have an auditor who must certify to the accuracy and adequacy of the financial reports or explain his reasons for questioning their accuracy or adequacy. As the profession of certified public accountant has attained great prestige in the United Kingdom, the responsibility of these company auditors is no light one. They run the risk not only of punishment, but, what is more serious, of loss of their professional standing if they fail to perform their duties conscientiously. This, with the special penalties applying to promoters who issue false or misleading prospectuses, goes far to check both fraudulent promotions[1] and the circulation of untrue and misleading statements about the financial standing and prospects of corporations after they have been launched as going concerns. It is, of course, not true

[1] Companies whose securities are offered to the public are called "public companies" and are subject to more stringent regulations than private companies.

that these measures prevent any and all corporate abuses, but it seems to be true that such abuses are much less common in the United Kingdom than in the United States, and that there is correspondingly less suspicion and hostility toward large business corporations there than here.

The development of the English law in reference to contracts and combinations in restraint of trade is a standard illustration of the advantages of the English common-law system. Under it general principles can be modified by court decisions and adapted to changing economic conditions to an almost indefinite extent. As already pointed out [1] the view that *all* contracts in restraint of trade were unlawful early gave place to the view that only *unreasonable* contracts in restraint of trade are unlawful. Also, as already pointed out, unlawful in this connection means not criminal but unenforceable or valid ground for an action for damages or for a demand for an injunction on the part of a third party suffering injury. In broadening the concept of *reasonable* as contrasted with *unreasonable* as applied to restrictive contracts, English judges have sought to strike a balance between the advantages of complete freedom of trade unhampered by any restrictive contracts whatever and complete freedom of contract, which might, if upheld without limit, lead even to the reintroduction of human slavery. The restrictive contracts which are most important in connection with the trust problem are those by which an individual in parting with an established business agrees not to engage in such business again either absolutely or in a particular locality or for a specified period of years. For some time the courts held that absolute or general restrictions caused a contract to be unlawful, whereas a special restriction, limited as regards either the area to which it was to apply or the period of time during which it was to be observed, was lawful provided it was reasonable as between the parties concerned and not opposed to the public interest. But the view even that a general restriction was necessarily and always unlawful was given up in the early 'nineties, since which time the "rule of reason" has been applied in all cases. As Lord

[1] Cf. *supra*, pp. 339, 340.

Macnaghten formulated the present rule in a case[1] decided in 1894: "All interference with individual liberty of action in trading, and all restraints of themselves, if there is nothing more, are contrary to public policy, and therefore void. That is the general rule. But there are exceptions: restraints of trade and interference with individual liberty of action may be justified by the special circumstances of a particular case. It is a sufficient justification . . . if the restriction is reasonable, that is, in reference to the interests of the parties concerned and reasonable in reference to the interests of the public, so framed and so guarded as to afford adequate protection to the party in whose favour it is imposed, while at the same time it is in no way injurious to the public."

In applying the principles laid down by Lord Macnaghten the English judges have gone very far to validate all contracts that are justified by considerations of self-interest as regards the contracting parties. The reasoning as regards the public interest in the sale of the good will of a business was well stated in the decision of the case of Morris *v.* Saxelby by the Judiciary Committee in 1916. In upholding the terms of a sale under which the vendor agreed not to compete, Lord Shaw said:[2]

"When a business is sold, the vendor who, it may be, has inherited it or built it up, seeks to realize this piece of property, and obtains a purchaser upon a condition without which the whole transaction would be valueless. He sells, he himself agreeing not to compete; and the law upholds such a bargain and declines to permit a vendor to derogate from his own grant. Public interest cannot be involved to render such a bargain nugatory: to do so would be to use public interest for the destruction of property. Nothing could be a more sure deterrent to commercial energy and activity than a principle that its accumulated results could not be transferred

[1] Nordenfelt *v.* Maxim-Nordenfelt Guns and Ammunition Co,. A. C. 565. Quoted by W. A. Sanderson in *Restraint of Trade in English Law* (1926) pp. 5-6. The authors desire to record their indebtedness to Dr. Sanderson, whose clear treatment of this much-discussed topic is commended to students who wish a fuller analysis of the important decisions.

[2] 1916 A. C. 713, 714.

save under conditions which would make its buyer insecure." Lord Atkinson went even further in this case [1] saying: "All those restrictions on trading are permissible which are necessary at once to secure that the vendor shall get the highest price for what he has to sell and that the purchaser shall get all that he has paid for."

Another type of case illustrates even better the lengths to which the English courts now go in upholding restrictive contracts. A Motor Trade Association had an arrangement with automobile and accessory dealers by which they agreed to maintain a schedule of prices. The means of enforcement adopted by the association was to put on the "stop list" the name of any dealer who sold at lower or higher prices than those listed. A dealer sold a car at a higher price and appealed to the courts for protection when he was put on the "stop list" and could no longer secure cars or parts from other members of the association, on the ground that this involved a combination in unreasonable restraint of trade. His plea was denied, the court holding that the agreement was a reasonable and legitimate means of stabilizing prices. One of the judges even declared that he found the agreements "both reasonable and indeed necessary, for I do not know how the object could otherwise be obtained." [2] As this decision makes clear, resale-price maintenance agreements are considered reasonable under English law, and those entering into them are upheld in imposing agreed penalties on parties who do not live up to such contracts. With such liberal views as to what the public interest requires, it is not surprising to read the assertion in connection with a famous Australian case that will receive later attention, that "their Lordships are not aware of any case in which a restraint though reasonable in the interests of the parties has been held unenforceable because it involved some injury to the public." [3] This should not be interpreted,

[1] Sanderson, *op. cit.*, p. 701.

[2] Ware *v.* Motor Trade Association *et al.* (1912) 3KB40. 19 A. L. B. 893. Cf. address by Felix H. Levy on *Amendments to U. S. Anti-Trust Law*, May 23, 1927.

[3] Att'y-Gen. of Commonwealth of Australia *v.* Adelaide Steamship Co. (1913) A. C. 795.

of course, to mean that the public interest is not always considered, but merely that the public interest in the efficient promotion of business and the upholding of contracts is deemed supreme.

In regard to combinations in restraint of trade, the general trend of English law has been quite as favorable as in regard to contracts in restraint of trade. Monopolies at law were long understood to be only those based on some legal grant. As a result of the famous struggle between Parliament and Elizabeth and the Stuarts, the Statute of Monopolies was passed in 1624 denying to the Crown the right to issue patents of monopoly. The struggle continued through the century, but the Bill of Rights adopted in connection with the Revolution of 1689 forever deprived British sovereigns of this prerogative and vested control over patents, copyrights, and exclusive trading or other charters in Parliament. There remained the offenses of engrossing, forestalling, and regrating, which were condemned by statute in 1552, but any legal restriction on such practices was formally withdrawn in 1844 by an act which declared that no suit should thereafter be entertained "against any person for or by reason of any of the said offenses or supposed offenses." The Defence of the Realm Act ("Dora") was the basis for the same sort of regulation of industry in the United Kingdom during the late war that was found necessary in other countries, but such regulation has been largely suspended since the signing of the Armistice.

In February, 1918, a representative parliamentary committee was appointed to make a study of trade organizations and combinations and report a program for action if any were deemed necessary. This "Committee on Trusts," as it came to be called, submitted both a general report concurred in by all the members and a supplementary minority report, voicing the opinions of E. Bevan, J. A. Hobson, W. H. Watkins, and Sidney Webb, who thought more drastic measures should be taken than the majority were prepared to support.

The principal recommendation of the committee was summed up in the statement,[1] "We are unanimously of the opinion that it would be desirable to institute in the United Kingdom machinery for the investigation of the operation of monopolies, trusts, and combines similar to the Commissions and other tribunals created for that purpose in the United States of America and the British Colonies." It adds: "We are satisfied that Trade Associations and Combines are rapidly increasing in this country and may within no distant period exercise a paramount control over all important branches of the British Trade." The investigating authority it recommends was to function under the Board of Trade and through its findings of fact and recommendations preface the way for more constructive policies later.

The minority report [2] thought that more drastic action was immediately called for. Among other things it declares: "The fact is that Free Competition no longer governs the business world. We find that capitalist combination, in one or other form, and at one or other stage of production, transportation, and distribution, now loads in varying degrees the price of practically everything that we purchase." Starting with these convictions, the minority naturally proceed to the advocacy of price regulation, to be followed, where monopolistic combinations have completely superseded competition, by co-operative or government ownership and operation. They do not, however, advocate any form of antitrust legislation. "Apart from the experience that no such interference can be made effective," they declare, "we have to recognize that association and combination in production and distribution are steps in the greater efficiency, the increased economy, and the better organization of industry. We regard this evolution as both inevitable and desirable. It is, however, plain that the change from competitive rivalry to combination calls for corresponding developments to secure for the community both

[1] Cf. *Report of the Committee on Trusts,* April 24, 1919 (Cd 9236, reprinted in 1924.)

[2] Reprinted as Appendix IV in Levy's *Monopolies, Cartels, and Trusts in British Industry,* second edition, 1927.

safeguards against the evils of monopoly, and at least a large share of the economic benefits of the better organization of industry which it promotes."

Seemingly the views of the minority carried more weight with the parliament of the period than those of the general report. On August 19, 1919, a Profiteering Act was passed. Following a preamble stating that "it appears that the prices of articles are, to the detriment of the people, being enhanced . . . by the charging of prices yielding an unreasonable profit," the act empowers the Board of Trade to investigate the prices, costs, and profits of articles which it thinks should come under the act, to determine what would be reasonable prices and to take steps to establish such prices. Though passed originally for only six months, the law with amendments was continued until May 19, 1921, when it was allowed to lapse. Since that date the governmental policy towards monopolistic combinations has again been that of *laissez-faire.* Though its success in accomplishing the purposes aimed at was not conspicuous, the Profiteering Act may serve the Labor Government, returned to power in May, 1929, as a precedent for further legislation designed to control monopolistic combinations in the public interest and to promote government ownership and operation. It is significant that Mr. Sidney Webb was chosen by Premier MacDonald as one of the members of his Cabinet and may thus have an opportunity to contribute to the shaping of legislation intended to put in practice some of the proposals of the minority members of the Trust Committee. Meanwhile, the law of the United Kingdom allows great freedom to the combination movement and is especially tolerant of the organization of monopolistic trusts, although it may, even though it seldom does, withdraw the protection of the courts for restrictive contracts on the ground that they are in unreasonable restraint of trade.

Oddly enough, Australia was led to enact antitrust legislation less from fear of combinations within that country than from dread of the injuries which foreign and especially American trusts might inflict upon her industries if left unrestrained. Under the Australian constitution the powers of the Commonwealth government are limited very much as are those of Congress under the federal Constitution. The Australian Parliament has power to pass laws regulating "(1) Trade and Commerce with other countries and among the states"; and "(2) Foreign corporations and trading or financial corporations formed within the limits of the Commonwealth." On the basis of these and other provisions of the constitution the Parliament enacted in 1906 the Australian Industries Preservation Act, which, as amended in 1908, 1909, and 1910, is still in force. The act is a composite measure dealing with three evils which in most other countries have been treated separately—*viz.,* monopolies, unfair competition, and, as a special form of the latter, "dumping." In the account which follows we describe the act as amended, noting the time when the most important changes were introduced. In the definition section, the law includes under the term "commercial trusts" combinations of persons or corporations, whether limited to Australia or extending into the foreign field, and defines "person" to include "corporation and firm and a commercial trust."

Section 4 of the act, as amended in 1910, declares that:

"(1) Any person who, either as principal or as agent, makes or enters into any contract, or is or continues to be a member of or engages in any combination, in relation to trade or commerce with other countries or among the States—

"(a) in restraint of or with intent to restrain trade or commerce: or

"(b) to the destruction or injury of or with intent to destroy or injure by means of unfair competition any Australian industry the preservation of which is advantageous to the Commonwealth, having due regard to the interests of producers, workers and consumers, is guilty of an offence.

"(2) Every contract made or entered into in contravention of this section shall be absolutely illegal and void.

"(3) It shall be a defense to a proceeding for an offense under paragraph (a) of sub-section 1 of this section and an answer to an allegation that a contract was made or entered into in restraint of or with intent to restrain trade or commerce if the party alleged to have contravened this section proves:

(a) that the matter or thing alleged to have been done in restraint or with intent to restrain trade or commerce was not to the detriment of the public and (b) that the restraint of trade or commerce effected or intended was not unreasonable."

Section 7 as amended in 1910 provides that:

"(1) Any person who monopolizes or attempts to monopolize or combines or conspires with any other person to monopolize any part of the trade or commerce with other countries or among the states is guilty of an indictable offense.

"(2) Every contract made or entered into in contravention of this section shall be absolutely illegal and void."

The close resemblance which this legislation bears to the Sherman Act is evident, and also the important exceptions which it in express terms includes, that is, that the restraint of trade charged shall not be deemed unlawful if the defendant can show that it was "not to the detriment of the public" and "not unreasonable." Australia thus from the outset qualified its antitrust law by the "rule of reason" which the U. S. Supreme Court in 1911 accepted as its guide in applying the Sherman law and by the "rule of public interest," which, though perhaps not so definitely formulated, clearly influenced that court in its decisions in the Steel Corporation case in 1920 and in several later cases. These qualifications were deemed so important by the Australian lawmakers that the original act of 1906 was so phrased as to impose the burden of proof that the restraint was detrimental to the public upon the prosecution. Since 1910, however, the burden of proving the contrary has rested upon the defendant.

The test of "unfair competition" set up by the amended act (Section 6) is "competition which is unfair in the circumstances." "In the following cases," the section adds, "the competition shall be deemed unfair unless the contrary is proved:—(a) If the defendant is a commercial trust; (b) If the competition would probably or does in fact result in an inadequate remuneration for labour in the Australian industry; (c) If the competition would probably or does in fact result in creating substantial disorganization in Australian industry or throwing workers out of employment; (d) If the defendant with respect to any goods or services which are the subject of the competition gives, offers, or promises to any person any rebate, refund, discount or reward upon condition that that person deals or in consideration of that person having dealt with the defendant to the exclusion of other persons dealing in similar goods or services."

In addition to the provisions quoted there are others prohibiting and penalizing exclusive or tying contracts with "commercial trusts," regulating the use of injunctions to curb unlawful contracts and monopolies, and prohibiting dumping. The penalties for violation of the penal clauses of the law are limited to fines, but the maximum fine of £500 may be applied to every day during which the violation is continued.

The principal case which has arisen under the sections of the act quoted above and according to Dr. Sanderson [1] "practically the only case" is that of the Commonwealth of Australia *v.* Adelaide Steamship Company, usually referred to as the Coal-vend Case, decided on appeal by the Judiciary Committee of the House of Lords in 1913,[2] but begun on June 4, 1910, before the amendments added to the law in November of that year became effective. This case was decided against the defendants in the lower Australian court, December 22, 1911. The judgment was on appeal reversed by the High Court of Australia, September 30, 1912, and the position then taken was affirmed by the Law Lords in an able and exhaustive opinion presented by Lord Parker and concurred in by all of his associates. As the application of the common law as well as of the Australian statutes was involved, the decision has been frequently cited as a precedent in later cases in all parts of the British Empire.

The issues before the court in this case were whether an elaborate series of agreements between the coal producers in the Newcastle and Maitland fields in New South Wales and the shipping companies, which not only conveyed this coal to market in the different Australian states and abroad but

[1] Sanderson, *op. cit.*, p. 162.
[2] A. C. 781.

sold it at retail, did not give rise to an unlawful combination in restraint of trade. By these agreements the f. o. b. wholesale prices, the maximum retail prices, and the distribution of orders among the coal-producers were regulated for the avowed purpose of putting a stop to the ruinous competition that had previously prevailed, stabilizing prices and production and assuring adequate wages to coal-miners and adequate profits to those engaged in the industry. The two sets of agreements, one among the coal-producers, called the "vend" agreement, and the other among the shipping companies, were, as held by all the judges who considered the case, in restraint of trade and the basis of a combination in restraint of trade. On the other hand, it was admitted that as regards the foreign market, at least, they did not result in a monopoly, since coal was drawn from other fields, and that no effort was made to fix a higher price for coal in the domestic market than prevailed in the foreign market. Underlying the decision of the court was an interpretation of the conditions out of which the agreements had developed and which they were intended to remedy, that largely influenced the opinion of the judges. After explaining how the wages of coal miners had by agreement been made for many years to depend on the price of coal, 6½*d.* out of every shilling added to the price of coal above a minimum price going to the employees in the mines, Lord Parker describes these conditions as follows:

"In the first years of the present century a new coal-field situated about twenty miles from Newcastle, and sometimes called the Maitland coal-field, began to be developed, and Maitland coal gradually forced its way into the market in competition with Newcastle coal. The competition was so fierce that it became impossible to maintain any 'vend' among the colliery proprietors in the Newcastle field. These proprietors accordingly entered on a course of ruinous competition with each other and with the colliery proprietors in the Maitland field, until in the spring of 1906, though the declared price of the best coal was for the purpose of the hewing rate 9*s.*, such coal was being actually sold f. o. b. at Newcastle at 7*s.* 6*d.*

only. The collieries in the Newcastle coal-field were ceasing to pay dividends and falling into the hands of the banks who had financed them; the miners had little chance of an advance in wages, though there had been a general advance in prices; and the prosperity of Newcastle, which is dependent on the coal industry and the shipping industry in connection therewith, was seriously threatened.

"Further the coal output of the Newcastle field was in the spring of 1906 about equally divided between the home trade, the inter-State trade, and the foreign trade. For the purpose of the inter-State trade and foreign trade the colliery proprietors sold their coal f. o. b. at Newcastle. In the case of the inter-State trade such coal was for the most part bought by shipping companies who owned coal vessels in which they carried it to the various ports of disembarkation in the States and there sold it wholesale or retail. In some cases the coal sold was delivered to the purchasers straight from the vessel itself. In other cases it was landed and stored by the shipping companies and subsequently sold. The shipping companies, in fact, carried on the business of coal merchants as well as the business of shippers. Under these circumstances it was essential in the interest of the colliery owners that there should be a sufficient number of shipping companies always ready to purchase and ship their coal, and it was essential in the interest of the shipping companies that they should always be able to purchase and ship coal as soon as their vessels arrived at Newcastle; otherwise the colliery proprietors might be put to expense in storing coal pending the arrival of a vessel in which it could be shipped, and the shippers might incur expense in the nature of demurrage. J. & A. Brown & Co., who owned the chief colliery in the Maitland field, had vessels of their own and were themselves exporting coal to Melbourne and Adelaide, and selling it there through their own agents. The shipping companies were already suffering from the low prices at which J. & A. Brown & Co. sold their coal in those towns. Moreover, some of the shipping companies had controlling interests in companies owning collieries in the Newcastle and Maitland fields, and were suffering from the reduction due to the competition of J. & A. Brown & Co. in the f. o. b. prices at Newcastle as well as the c. i. f. prices at Melbourne and Adelaide.

"It was under these circumstances that on January 5, 1906, there was a meeting of some of the proprietors of collieries in the Newcastle and Maitland fields. The chairman pointed out the necessity of forming an association of all the collieries if the present very unsatisfactory state of the coal trade was to be improved. The meeting thereupon passed a resolution that it was desirable to form an association to raise and maintain the price of coal, and a committee was appointed to draft a scheme. The idea obviously was to reconstitute the 'vend,' admitting the colliery owners in the Maitland field, whose competition has proved so disastrous. The necessity of obtaining the concurrence of those shipping companies who had interests in the Newcastle and Maitland fields was expressly recognized. Lengthy negotiations followed, of which a record was preserved and put in evidence at the trial. Ultimately a draft agreement hereinafter called 'the vend agreement,' was prepared, and in April, 1906, assented to by a number of the colliery proprietors, including Messrs. J. & A. Brown & Co., and, though never actually executed, was no doubt acted on and considered binding by the assenting parties."

After describing in detail the agreements that resulted, the court considered the question whether the resulting restraints on trade manifested an intent to injure the public. It did not find evidence of such intent in the fact that one purpose of the agreement was to advance the price of coal. On the contrary, it declared: "It can never, in their Lordships' opinion, be of real benefit to the consumers of coal that colliery proprietors should carry on their business at a loss, or that any profit they make should depend on the miners' wages being reduced to a minimum. When those conditions prevail the less remunerative collieries will be closed down, there will be great loss of capital, miners will be thrown out of employment, less coal will be produced, and prices will consequently rise until it becomes possible to reopen the closed collieries or open other seams. The consumer of coal will lose in the long run if the colliery proprietors do not make fair profits or the miners do not receive fair wages. There is in this respect a solidarity of interest between all members of the public. The Crown cannot, therefore, in their Lordships' opinion, rely on the mere intention to raise prices as proving an intention to injure the public."

But, the Court next inquired, did not the extent to which prices were raised in this case prove such intention? The evidence showed that the f. o. b. price of the best Newcastle coal was advanced by successive steps from 7*s.* 6*d.* a ton, the price prevailing early in 1906, to 9*s.* before the end of that year, to 10*s.* for the year 1907, and to 11*s.* for 1908 and subsequent years. The lower court had held prices above 9*s.* 8*d.* for 1910 excessive, but the Court of Appeals had dissented from the view on grounds that seemed to the Law Lords convincing. Lord Parker says: "The onus of proving that the prices charged were unreasonable clearly lay with the Crown, and the Crown tendered no satisfactory evidence in this respect. There was no evidence whatever as to the profits made by the colliery proprietors when the prices in question prevailed. On the other hand, there was evidence that with the hewing rate at 4*s.* 2*d.*, which was admitted to be the lowest hewing rate consistent with a fair remuneration to the miners, and which corresponds to a declared price of 11*s.*, the colliery proprietors could not afford to sell the best coal f. o. b. at less than 11*s.* Further, there is evidence that the prices actually charged inter-State were also obtained in the foreign market, where at any rate free competition prevailed."

Since combining to raise prices and the higher prices actually fixed by the combination were held to show no intention to injure the public, even less were the measures by which the combination sought to correlate the production, distribution, and consumption of coal and stabilize the industry believed to indicate such intention. Finding in the mass of evidence presented "no evidence (at any rate no satisfactory evidence) of any sinister intention on the part of either colliery proprietors or shipping companies" and "no evidence (at any rate no sufficient evidence) of injury to the public," the Law Lords concurred in the opinion of the Australian Court of Appeals and dismissed the suit. While reference is frequently made in this decision to the fact that by the act of 1906 the burden of proving intent to injure the public or injury to the public rests on the government, whereas the amendment added in 1910 requires the defendant to disprove such intent or injury, there is reason to believe that the outcome in this case would have been the same under the new requirement as under the old. The reasoning of the judges brings out clearly the interest of the public in adequate and stable prices, and shows that they regarded the coal combination and its essential, if not all of its policies, as reasonable and conducing to the public welfare. As thus interpreted, the Australian legislation has the merit of prohibiting unfair and oppressive policies and combinations which result in unreasonably high prices, while it permits combination for the legitimate purpose of preventing the wastes and losses that may result from unbridled competition.

Since this decision was rendered, repeated efforts have been made (the last in 1919) to amend the Australian constitution to give parliament control over intrastate as well as interstate trade and to promote the nationalization of industries, but these have all been unsuccessful.

In this situation the different Australian states, with one exception, have been content to rely on the common law to prevent unreasonable combinations in restraint of trade within their boundaries. Two reasons for this are suggested. The states have been conservative in the corporation laws which they have enacted, and the railroads of the country are practically all owned and operated by the state governments, so that there has been no discriminating in rates in favor of big business. The exception referred to is New South Wales, which in 1923 passed a Monopoly Act. This prohibits monopolies or attempts to monopolize along the familiar lines of antitrust legislation in this country, empowers the Board of Trade to investigate combinations suspected of violating or intending to violate the law, and provides criminal and civil penalties as well as injunctive relief.

During and after the war there was special legislation increasing the power of the government over industries and penalizing profiteering in the Australian states, as in other countries, but these have been repealed with the restoration of normal peace-time conditions.

Legislating in reference to corporations and trusts has been a simpler task in New Zealand than in Australia, since exclusive power to legislate for the whole country is there lodged in the national legislature. The regulations in regard to corporations are rigid like those of the Australian states, and as in Australia the railroads are owned and operated by the government with the result that no discrimination in favor of large shippers has been practiced. Another resemblance is that the earliest reason for legislation was fear of foreign rather than of native trusts. In 1905 the Agricultural Implement Manufacturers Importation and Sale Act was passed to prevent the dumping on the New Zealand market of certain foreign-made agricultural implements. A similar act applying to flour and other products was passed in 1907, and in 1908 the two were combined in the Monopoly Prevention Act. These measures were at first temporary, but by the Finance Act of 1922 were continued in force until they should be repealed. Following the example of Australia, New Zealand passed in 1910 a comprehensive antitrust or "Commercial Trusts Act" to take effect November 1, 1911. Section 2 of this act defines a "commercial trust" as any association or combination of persons (including firms and corporations) (a) having as its object (1) the controlling, determining, or influencing the supply or demand price of any goods in New Zealand or elsewhere or (2) the creating or maintaining in New Zealand or elsewhere of a monopoly, whether complete or partial, in the supply or demand of any goods; or (b) acting in New Zealand or elsewhere with any such object. Sections 3 and 4 deal with exclusive or tying contracts and discrimination in sales policies. Section 5 declares that "Any person who conspires with any other person to monopolize wholly or partially the demand or supply in New Zealand or any part thereof of any goods or to control wholly or partially the demand or supply or price in New Zealand or any part thereof of any goods, is guilty of an offence if such monopoly or control is of such nature as to be contrary to the public interest."

To sell goods at prices that are "unreasonably high," if such prices are in any manner controlled or determined by a commercial trust, is a punishable offence according to Sections 6 and 7. Section 8 declares that the price of any goods is to be deemed unreasonably high "if it produces or is calculated to produce more than a fair and reasonable rate of commercial profit to the person selling or supplying such goods."

In practice this act appears to have been successfully enforced in only a few instances, one of which involved a local sugar trust. Its weakness in application, or perhaps its wise moderation, was illustrated by a case brought against a combination of millers (Crown Milling Co. *et al. v.* The King). This combination was organized after the government relaxed its control of grain and flour prices following the Armistice, its purpose being to prevent a return to the demoralized conditions that had prevailed before the outbreak of the war. The millers of the country through a selling company, "Distributers Limited," whose stock they held, fixed uniform prices for different grades of flour and distributed orders so that each firm would be able to produce its allotted quota. Attacked as a monopoly "contrary to the public interest" in accordance with Section 5 of the act, the trial judge upheld it as reasonable and not opposed to the public interest.

The New Zealand Court of Appeals by a three-to-two vote took the opposite view, but on appeal to the Judicial Committee of the Privy Council the lower court was sustained by a Scotch verdict "not proven."[1] It thus appears that under the New Zealand law, as under the Australian law and the English common law, in consequence of the liberal view taken by the courts of what is compatible with the public interest, combinations in restraint of trade, even when exerting a considerable measure of monopoly power, may be upheld as lawful.

New Zealand has also had her troubles attempting to regulate the meat industry. By a series of measures culminating in

[1] 1927 A. C. 394.

the Meat Export Control Act passed in 1921, the control of the whole export trade in meat is lodged in a special board representative of both the government and the meat-packers. The general attitude of the government toward combinations is constructive rather than destructive, and by the Board of Trade Amendment Act passed in 1923 the powers formerly exercised by the Board are vested in the Minister of Industries and Commerce, one of whose duties is to advise the governor how the industries of the country can best be encouraged, developed, and protected. Investigation and publicity are thus relied upon more than suppression to safeguard the public interest.

Canadian legislation in regard to trusts presents an interesting blending of the antitrust viewpoint that has shaped American legislation, and of the appreciation of the potential advantages of combination that has guided the policies of the mother country. Even before the United States Congress, the Canadian Parliament in 1889 passed "An Act for the Prevention and Suppression of Combinations formed in Restraint of Trade." As reproduced in the Criminal Code of 1906 the central provision of this law declares that:

"(1) Every one is guilty of an indictable offence and liable to a penalty not exceeding $4,000 and not less than $200 or to two years' imprisonment, or if a corporation is liable to a penalty not exceeding $10,000, who conspires, combines, agrees or arranges with any other person or with any railway, steamship, steamboat or transportation company—(a) to unduly limit the facilities for transporting, producing, manufacturing, supplying, storing, or dealing in any article or commodity which may be a subject of trade or commerce; or (b) to restrain or injure trade or commerce in relation to any such article or commodity; or (c) to unduly prevent, limit, or lessen the manufacture or production of any such article or commodity or to unreasonably enhance the price thereof, or (d) to unduly prevent or lessen competition in the production, manufacture, purchase, barter, sale, transportation, or supply of any such article or commodity or in the price of insurance upon person or property."

This law served as the basis of several prosecutions against trusts, but Canada, like the United States, felt the need of more adequate machinery for the investigation of combinations charged with violation of the law as a preliminary to prosecutions. This led in 1910 to the enactment of the Combines Investigation Act, which, as amended in 1923, is the basis of the country's present trust policy. Section 2 of this act defines a "combination" in the comprehensive fashion that "trust" is defined in American legislation, its essence being the concerted raising or fixing of the price of any article of commerce or service. Administration of the law is given to the Minister of Labour, who is to be assisted by a Registrar of Boards of Investigation, which may be organized under the act. In considerable detail the act then provides that on the complaint of any six citizens presented in a prescribed form to a competent judge that a combine exists which has increased prices or restricted competition "to the detriment of consumers or producers," and that an investigation of it will serve the public interest, he shall within thirty days hold a hearing to which the complainants and those complained against shall be invited. If the judge is satisfied by the evidence brought out at such hearing that a combine exists as alleged, he is required to transmit to the Registrar an order for the organization of a Board of Investigation of three members. These are formally appointed by the Minister of Labour, one on the nomination of the complainants, one on that of those complained against, and the third on the nomination of these two, or if they cannot agree, by the Minister independently. The board so constituted is required to make an investigation and to report its findings to the Minister of Labour for publication in the *Gazette*. If the board is convinced by its investigation that a combine as defined by the statute exists, it is to report the fact, "including such findings and recommendations as, in [its] opinion, are in accordance with the merits and requirements of the case." One or all of three remedies may then be applied by the government: (1) If the report shows that the article enhanced in price enjoys protection under the tariff law, the import duty upon it may be, by the Governor in

Council, lowered or completely abolished; (2) If the combine is shown to have taken advantage of some patent it controls to build up its unlawful monopoly, by appropriate procedure the patent may be revoked; (3) Any person found guilty of maintaining or participating in the combine is guilty of an indictable offence and may be fined not more than $1,000 for each day he continues such participation after the expiration of ten days from the date the board's adverse report is published in the *Gazette.*

The principal change made in the act in 1923 was the substitution of permanent commissioners of investigation for the temporary boards originally relied upon. An illustration of the way in which this Canadian policy operates was afforded in 1927, when a final report was submitted by the commissioner who had been appointed to investigate the Canadian Proprietary Articles Trade Association. He found that the association controlled the entire Canadian trade in nationally advertised proprietary medicines and toilet articles and that it had "operated and [was] likely to operate to the detriment of and against the interest of the public." The association is said to have withdrawn its "stop" list and ceased to operate in the ways objected to immediately after the publication of this report.[1]

While the powers lodged in the Canadian Parliament are somewhat broader than those given to the United States Congress, it too is debarred from proceeding very far in the regulation of intrastate as distinguished from interstate commerce. A Board of Commerce Act and a Combines and Fair Prices Act, passed in 1919, were held to exceed the Parliament's constitutional powers and therefore to be invalid.

The operation of the qualification in the Combines Investigation Act that to be unlawful combines must be proved to operate "to the detriment of consumers or producers" was illustrated in a recent decision applying to retail coal-dealers in Winnipeg. Through a Retail Coal Dealers Association, they had combined to stabilize the price of coal. A dealer sold coal below the fixed scale and the association took steps to cut off

[1] Cf. *Annual Report of Federal Trade Commission for 1928,* p. 100.

his supply from wholesalers with which the association had an exclusive agreement. In denying this dealer the injunction and damages he claimed on the ground that he was the victim of an unlawful conspiracy, the judge held:[1] "Having regard to these abuses [of cut throat competition] which have been a real menace to the coal trade and a loss to producers for many years, one can scarcely find fault with the efforts of the association or others, to suppress such activities. The small gain to those who happened to buy at the reduced price is more than offset by the probable failure to obtain well-prepared coal and the absence of these dealers carrying their fair share of the burden of necessary reserve supplies, together with the injury they inflict upon bona fide dealers with large investments. . . . Upon these grounds I have come to the conclusion that, in its activities in endeavoring to limit or prevent this unfair competition, it has not operated to the detriment or against the best interests of the public."

From this brief review of the operation of the Canadian legislation, the conclusion seems warranted that that country, too, relies mainly upon investigation and publicity to protect the interests of consumers and producers, but that it stands ready to deal with monopolistic combinations which exact unreasonable prices or use oppressive or unfair methods either by imposing heavy fines upon those responsible, or by lowering the tariff to expose them to the pressure of foreign competition, or by abrogating patents under whose cover their monopoly may be maintained. A more extended review of the judicial decisions would show that in actual practice the Canadian courts are less liberal than those of the United Kingdom in deciding what is reasonable from the point of view of the public interest (refusing, for example, to uphold resale-price-maintenance agreements) but more liberal than the courts of the United States in applying our antitrust laws.

The policy of Russia or of the Union of Soviet Socialist Republics toward trusts is unique among contemporary governments. While 98 per cent of agricultural production in

[1] Cited by Felix H. Levy in an address on *Amendments to the U. S. Antitrust Acts,* delivered on March 23, 1927.

Russia is still through individual farmers, 90 per cent of the industrial output comes from the state trusts, responsible to the Supreme Economic Council for efficiency, quality of product, and profitable operation, but enjoying since 1927 a certain degree of autonomy. In 1928 there were, according to official figures,[1] 8,750 large enterprises operated through these state trusts. In addition, many small establishments were operated by coöperatives or as private enterprises. There were also in operation June 1, 1928, 97 concessions to foreign firms, 40 of them for mining and manufacturing undertakings. The state trusts are organized usually on the horizontal principle, but concentration and mergers are encouraged and vertical trusts are created when it is thought that they will make for economy and efficiency. Since the administration is through the government and for the government, there is opportunity through the State Planning Commission *(Gosplan)* to attempt to coördinate production, distribution, and consumption on a scale that has never before been attempted. Some of the state trusts control the industry assigned to them for the whole country; others control it for particular geographical regions only. The government seems fully alive to the difficulty of securing efficient administration through monopolistic trusts and is bending every effort to show results, with what degree of success it is difficult for those not in intimate touch with what is going on to judge. As regards oil and coal production, the official returns appear to leave no doubt that the total output of the country is now substantially above the pre-war figures. On the other hand, there appears to be still a marked shortage in manufactures for ordinary use. Without venturing an opinion as to the probable success or failure of the Russian experiment, the authors recommend it as a profitable field of study for the light it may throw on the advantages and disadvantages of coördinated production as contrasted with the disorganized competitive production which still dominates most branches of industry in Western countries. Russia, through her state-directed industries,

[1] Cf. *The Soviet Union—Facts, Descriptions, Statistics.* Published by Soviet Union Information Bureau, Washington, 1929.

is striving to secure the advantages of unified control and stabilized industry which in Western countries are sought through cartels and other forms of combination "rationalized" so as to distribute the benefits equitably between producers and consumers.

The last topic we shall consider briefly in this chapter is international cartels. These are the inevitable results of the successful development of national cartels or other forms of combination in potentially competing countries, as the latter are the necessary condition to their organization. As national cartels owe their creation in part to the desire to eliminate wasteful competition within the country concerned, so international cartels are an obvious device for eliminating wasteful competition among countries. Tariff barriers and the practice of dumping surplus products on the foreign market afford added incentives. Domestic producers always covet control of the domestic market. Protective tariffs assist to this end, but where producers are organized in a cartel or trust or production is so concentrated that a few firms can control the national policy for a given industry, another and more effective method is to enter into an international agreement with the organized producers of other countries, reserving to the producers of each country their domestic markets, and curbing somewhat the intensity of competition in the free territory left for exploitation.

Before the war, there were said to be as many as 114 international cartels in operation.[1] As many as 26 of them were in the coal, iron and steel and other metal industries. The chemical and allied industries were credited with 19. Transportation was given 18, most of them shipping conferences, and the remainder were widely scattered among different branches of manufacturing. The war disrupted most of these international arrangements, but as belligerent countries have gradually recovered following the Armistice, the movement to form international cartels has been resumed more actively than ever. Germany, as the country in which national cartels

[1] *Journal of Political Economy,* October, 1920. Cf. Liefmann, R., *International Cartels, Combines and Trusts,* p. 19.

are most numerous, has resumed her leadership in the international agreement field. For our purpose a brief account of the three international cartels that are perhaps of greatest interest to American business men will serve to illustrate the more striking aspects of the movement.

Germany's loss to France of Alsace and Lorraine seriously crippled her iron and steel industry and deprived her of the monopoly she had previously enjoyed of the potash industry. Her experience of the advantages of unified management in connection with the sale in the world's markets, and particularly in the American market, of potash products gave her strong reasons for wishing to come to some understanding with her new competitor, and this was facilitated by the fact that most of the Alsatian mines were controlled by the French government. After prolonged negotiations the *Deutsches Kalisyndikat, G. m. b. H.* and the *Société Commerciale des Potasses d'Alsace* entered into an agreement in regard to sales to the United States on August 15, 1924. This included a division of the American market for the ensuing three years on a basis which gave Germany somewhat less than two-thirds and France somewhat more than one-third of the total sales, and the organization in the United States of a common selling agency, the Potash Importing Corporation. In the following year the German and French potash producers substituted a modified and more comprehensive agreement in accordance with which:

(1) The producers in each country retained exclusive control of the markets of the respective countries, France in this connection including the French colonies.

(2) Distribution outside of the two countries was to be divided on the basis of 70 per cent to Germany and 30 per cent to France up to a total sale of 8,400,000 tons, with the proviso that sales in excess of this volume should be divided on a fifty-fifty basis.[1]

(3) As regards sales in the American market, the ratios were to be, Germany 66 2/3 per cent and France 33 1/3 per cent.

[1] The total volume of sales in 1925 was only 5,500,000 tons, so that this proviso is of no immediate significance.

This arrangement appeared to be operating to the general satisfaction of German and French potash-producers, but in April, 1927, the Attorney General of the United States began a suit against the Potash Importing Corporation and its French and German organizers and stockholders as an unlawful trust. The plea advanced that it was really an agency of the French government, and therefore privileged, having been dismissed as without merit under our law, a consent decree was entered under which the corporation gave up its place of business in New York and went into liquidation. This did not cause the dissolution of the cartel whose members will in future handle their export business to the United States through a common agent with headquarters in Europe. It is believed that this arrangement will not be held to violate our antitrust laws. A significant aspect of the situation is the stimulus which the continuance of this European monopoly gives to efforts to develop the potash resources of the United States. Congress has appropriated $100,000 for the exploration of potash beds in Texas and New Mexico, and the reports available indicate that in these states extensive deposits exist which compare favorably in every way with those of Germany and Alsace.[1]

The situation as regards the German iron and steel industry was complicated by the fact that under the Treaty of Versailles Germany was required, until January 1, 1925, to admit up to 1,780,000 tons of steel annually from Lorraine free of duty.[2] This greatly increased competition in the German market and hastened the reorganization of the German Crude Steel Cartel *(Rohstahlgemeinschaft)*, which had lapsed during the war, in November, 1924. With their own industry organized and the currency stabilized, German crude-steel producers proceeded vigorously to push the project of an international cartel as a means of protecting the domestic market. At the outset French producers, the principal invaders of the

[1] Cf. Michels, *Cartels, Combines, and Trusts in Post-War Germany*, pp. 168-169, and Stocking, *The Potash Industry, passim.*

[2] The account of the "Continental Steel Cartel" which follows is based in part on an unpublished monograph on the subject by Gilbert Goodman, to whom the authors' acknowledgment is made.

German market, were indifferent, but when, immediately after January, 1925, Germany took advantage of her restored liberty of action to erect a high tariff wall against Lorraine steel, the conditions were more favorable to some agreement. As always in connection with international cartels attempting to regulate production, the greatest stumbling-block was the determination of the quotas of the participating countries. France was ready to agree to base quotas on the respective tonnages of the contracting countries in the last quarter of 1926. Belgium, whose adhesion was deemed necessary to success, objected. Finally, in order to bring about an agreement, Germany, although her quota was relatively smaller than she considered herself entitled to, assented to a further cut for the benefit of Belgium, which cut was to be restored if the total production rose to 29,250,000 metric tons, 4,000,000 tons above the figures then prevailing. On this basis the agreement was signed on September 30, 1926, by Germany, France, Belgium, Luxemburg, and the Saar. The percentages for the first year for an estimated total production of 25,250,000 metric tons of steel were: Germany 40.45 per cent; France, 31.89 per cent; Belgium, 12.57 per cent; and Luxemburg, 8.55 per cent. From the outset Germany was penalized in consequence of her eager desire to have the cartel formed. Under the usual system of penalties for exceeding quotas and premiums for falling below, which was part of the agreement, she was liable in the second quarter of 1927 to pay into the common fund $4 a ton on 833,000 excess, or over $3,000,000, while France was entitled, for producing less than her quota, to a premium of about $225,000. It was estimated that France was receiving premiums amounting to about 4 RM on every ton she produced and sold in this period, while Germany was taxed 2.5 RM on every ton of her production. Under these conditions, it is not surprising that Germany's enthusiasm for the continuance of the cartel agreement waned, while that of France increased.

Under a provision of the agreement which permitted the steel-producers in other countries to join, if willing to comply with the same terms, Austria, Hungary, and Czechoslovakia became members on January 1, 1927, at first jointly, but after June, 1928, as separate individual members. Negotiations were entered into with Poland about the same time, and there were rumors that Great Britain might join, but apparently the producers of neither country have been greatly impressed with the advantages of sharing the responsibilities and possible penalties of membership when they can enjoy most of the benefits from the resulting regularization of the industry while holding aloof.

One striking feature of the agreement was the provision for its easy termination. Its final suspension was to take place on April 1, 1931, but several grounds might be given for its earlier dissolution and at the time of writing (June, 1929) the one that seems likely to be effective is announcement before May 1, 1929, by any member country of an intention of withdrawing October 31, 1929. At the meeting of the cartel held in March of this year Germany announced that she proposed to withdraw and it was agreed by all the signatories that unless the cartel was renewed in revised form by that date it would go out of existence. There is difference of opinion whether a renewal will be effected, but it seems clear that Germany will not continue unless there is a substantial readjustment of quotas. Also it happens that the present *Rohstahlgemeinschaft* expires on that same date and her further participation depends on the continuance of that cartel on which her membership has depended.

The international copper cartel is unique in that its operation is through an American Webb Law export association, Copper Exporters, Inc.[1] Preceding the organization of this association, October 12, 1926, the copper producers of the world passed through a long and painful period of business depression. This prepared the minds of leaders of the industry to support a coöperative effort to control the market for their product and such effort was greatly facilitated by the high degree of concentration which copper-mining had at-

[1] The authors have derived a good deal of the information which follows from an unpublished M. A. essay on *Price Control through Combination in the Copper Industry* by H. B. Kirshen, to whom they wish to express their indebtedness.

tained, less than a score of giant companies controlling the bulk of the world's output. During the war the American price of the metal was fixed through the War Industries Board at 23.5 cents and later at 26 cents per pound. To handle the difficult task of liquidating the surplus stocks of copper left in the hands of the United States and other governments, the Copper Export Association was organized in 1918 under the recently enacted Webb-Pomerene Act. In spite of its efforts to maintain the price it fell to 19 cents in 1919 and as low as 12¾ cents at the end of 1920. In 1921 the Association, which as selling agent had taken over the government's surplus stock in 1919, resorted to the expedient of borrowing $40,000,000 on 8-per-cent notes secured by 400,000,000 pounds of copper, the sale of which it was by this means enabled to spread out over the next four years. The form of organization of this association was not entirely satisfactory to all of its members. Some of the largest American producers (*e.g.*, Kennecott, Phelps-Dodge, and the American Smelting and Refining Co.) withdrew in 1923, and after prolonged negotiations the new export association (Copper Exporters, Inc.) was organized three years later to act as selling agent not only for nearly all of the large American companies, but also for nearly all of the large foreign companies, who became associate members. At the time of writing (June, 1929) the combination is said to control through its membership over 90 per cent of the total production. The association has 100 no-par non-dividend paying shares of stock, of which each member may hold one and only one. The nine directors are given unusually broad powers, including the right to recall and cancel the share held by any member who has broken the agreement into which each firm or corporation must enter upon becoming a member. Among the avowed purposes of the association was that of eliminating speculation in copper through middlemen, which for many years had centered in the London Metal Exchange, and substituting, so far as possible, direct sales to *bona-fide* consumers of copper. To this end the association established at Brussels its central office in Europe under the name of the Copper

Export Trading Company. It also maintains six branch selling agencies in Germany, and five each in the United Kingdom and France. Shortly after its organization, owing, no doubt, in large measure to more favorable relations that had developed between demand for copper and the current volume of production, the price of the metal began to advance. Theretofore the American price had exceeded the European price. In this advance movement the European price took the lead, though, of course, the American price was not slow to follow. By April, 1929, the price which had long hung below 14 cents had advanced above 24 cents. This was generally regarded as out of line with the cost of production for the volume of copper required by the world market, and in the week beginning April 7 it fell back to 18¼ cents, at which point, with slight variations, it was stabilized during the succeeding months. While Copper Exporters, Inc., has no direct control over outputs, limiting its operations to the sale of the metal abroad, its members showed a willingness to coöperate in the efforts to stabilize the price by voluntarily curtailing production about the time the April recession in price occurred. The inevitable readjustments of American prices for a world commodity like copper to the foreign price raises the question whether Copper Exporters, Inc., by controlling the foreign price, is not tending to restrain domestic trade as prohibited by the Webb Act. The policies of the association were investigated by the Federal Trade Commission during the closing months of 1928 and the early months of 1929, when the advance in price was proceeding so rapidly, but as no action was taken and the price has been stabilized at a level which is considered at least by the producers as fair and reasonable, it seems unlikely that any charge of unlawfulness will result. Without suggesting that in this case the international combination has taken advantage of its position to exact from the consumers of the world a higher price for the product it so largely controls than costs and diminishing world reserves justify, the authors wish to emphasize that as regards this product, machinery exists that, though thus far used in ways that promote economy and efficiency, might easily be misused, and that prosecuting Copper Exporters, Inc., as an unlawful trust under our laws would afford no adequate remedy, though the danger of such prosecution may act as a means of deterring this association from adopting extreme or socially undesirable policies. In this case the international cartel has not been influenced by tariff policies, as copper mining has long ceased to be an object of tariff protection in any of the important producing countries.

The conclusions that seem warranted from this brief survey of international cartels are:

(1) The progress taking place all over the world toward concentration in manufacturing and mining industries and the organization of national combinations to stabilize industry within national boundaries facilitate the organization of international cartels.

(2) Such international combinations, if administered with due regard to the public interest, are not only more effective but are less objectionable means of giving national producers advantages in their respective domestic markets than protective tariffs.

(3) They also may serve to promote better understanding among the business men of different countries and to substitute international coöperation for the hostility-breeding competition for markets that was one of the factors which brought about the World War.

(4) No country has yet developed an adequate system for protecting its citizens against the exploitation that may result from misuse of the monopolistic powers of international cartels, and this problem, therefore, calls for serious consideration.

CHAPTER XXVII

FEDERAL INCORPORATION, PUBLICITY, AND PREVENTION OF UNFAIR METHODS OF COMPETITION AS REMEDIES

To a considerable extent the foregoing chapters constitute a bill of indictment. To be sure, they contain only secondary counts as compared with that embodied in the failure of the competitive system to hold the engines of economic enterprise on the track; a failure which at increasingly frequent intervals has piled those engines in the ditch and closed factory doors while millions of workmen were clamoring for jobs. But these secondary counts are of the same character as the primary one, for they are not only or even primarily directed against particular individuals, combinations, or practices. They charge the "invisible hand" with a failure to accomplish those beneficent results of which Adam Smith and his followers down to the present time were so certain. *Laissez-faire* is moribund: strangled by the hands of those who are the most determined opponents of any type of collectivism. The explanation of the paradox has been suggested by the claims of the organizers of the trusts we have reviewed, that the particular industry with which they were concerned was "different"; that competition in that industry always tended to be "ruinous." With the same logic, or lack of it, the Senator from Massachusetts has been an ardent protectionist, *except* on hides; and the Senator from Louisiana, at least until 1928, has been relatively a free-trader, *except* on sugar. Luncheon clubs, manufacturers' associations, and chambers of commerce, with an enthusiasm unequaled outside the "rooting" section of a football stadium, rally behind the slogan, "less government in business," at the same time that they proceed to push tariff legislation of the 1922 and 1929 variety, beside whose towering exactions the "tariff of abominations" of 1828 reminds one of the building blocks of a three-year-old.

But we have failed in our purpose if our chapters have not been less an indictment than a record of the methods by which business operations have been and are "controlled." Moreover, the record shows that control has all too frequently been exercised with an almost complete disregard of the interests of those entitled to the last degree of consideration. The liberalization of the state incorporation laws and the combination of businesses have in different degrees secured a number of salutary results, but shareholders, creditors, and consumers have not been adequately protected. Consequently, the most valuable use to which we can put the record we have built is to base upon it additional outposts in the campaign to secure adequate "social" control of business.

Among the abuses of charter-mongering detailed in our fourth chapter the most conspicuous were: the failure of many of the states to impose adequate personal liability on promoters, incorporators, and directors; the lack of effort to cause nominal and actual capital of a corporation to correspond; the failure to require adequate annual reports; and the chartering of holding companies with their inevitable tendencies to diffuse responsibility and confuse the interests to be protected. The foregoing abuses are of long standing. They have been aggravated by certain results of the issuance of non-voting and no-par stock and by the intensified activities of such states as Delaware, Florida, South Dakota, and Nevada in selling charters. And this aggravation has taken place in spite of numerous attempts by leaders in various professions to bring about much-needed changes and in spite of notorious examples of the results of the lax policies of our states.

Writing in 1891, W. W. Cook, author of a work on corporations which has been a standard treatise for more than a generation, made the following statement concerning the corporations of that time: "These companies have been found to be efficient instruments of fraud, speculation, plunder and illegal gain. In these latter days the spoliation of corporations and stockholders by the corporate directors and managers has been systematized into well-known methods of proceeding, and the carrying out of such plans has become a profession and an accomplishment." [1]

Twenty-odd years later Justice Louis Brandeis, then a practicing lawyer, contributed to *Harper's Weekly* a series of articles later published in book form as *Other People's Money.* Of all these brilliant essays there is perhaps none more pregnant with meaning for the situation in which we find ourselves today than "The Failure of Banker-Management." The text for Brandeis' discourse was the collapse of the New York, New Haven, and Hartford Railroad. From the vantage-point of the sixteen years which have elapsed since he wrote, it is even more clear that his criticisms were justified. Although the attempt at monopolization was important in this case, the failure of banker management was primarily the result of confusing the functions of banker and business man. The president of the road indicated before the Interstate Commerce Commission that his judgment had been overruled by the bankers, particularly with reference to the acquisition of the New York, Westchester, and Boston. As is well known, moreover, banker management not only wrecked the finances of the New Haven, with resultant hardships among hundreds of New England folk who had considered its securities as among the safest of investments for generations, but also disregarded the well-being of the road in other respects to such an extent as to precipitate a series of disastrous wrecks of a physical character. In its report on one of these the Interstate Commerce Commission said: "On this directorate were and are men whom the confiding public recognize as magicians in the art of finance, and wizards in the construction, operation, and consolidation of great systems of railroads. The public therefore rested secure that with the knowledge of the railroad art possessed by such men investments and travel should both be safe. Experience has shown that this reliance of the public was not justified as to either finance or safety." [2]

Of recent years the exploits of banker managers have been concerned more with new organizations and reorganizations

[1] *The Corporation Problem,* p. 81.

[2] Quoted in Brandeis, *Other People's Money,* p. 201.

than with attempts at monopolization, though in the electric-light-and-power field many of the holding company developments have gone further than the "natural" monopoly elements of the situation seem to warrant. In some of the recent transactions the chief end seems to have been the realization of quick profits on so-called "organization capital," but in many cases the organization, or reorganization, has left in control a banking group whose *bona-fide* investment is negligible. A conspicuous case in point was the reorganization of Dodge Brothers in 1925 by Dillon, Read & Company of New York. For property whose value was certified by Haskins and Sells to be $102,766,494.38 the bankers paid $146,000,000 in cash. "Dodge Brothers" of Michigan was reincorporated in Maryland as "Dodge Brothers, Incorporated." A $75,000,000 issue of 6-per-cent gold debentures due in 1940 was sold at par; 850,000 preferred shares of no-par value were sold at $100 each, and with each share was given as a bonus one share of Class A common stock. Of this Class A stock, which was without par value and without voting power, 1,500,000 shares were issued of which the 650,000 shares not needed as bonus were retained by Dillon, Read. The control of the new corporation was vested in 500,000 voting shares of no-par Class B common which were also retained by the bankers. As Professor Ripley suggested, it seems a perfect demonstration of that supposedly impossible feat of eating one's cake and having it, too.[1]

In addition to the complete divorce of management from ownership effected in the Dodge deal through the instrumentality of non-voting stock, the bankers utilized the no-par provision now common in our state corporation laws, to convert $15,002,000 of the debentures into 434,563 and 17/21 shares of Class A no-par shares, enter these shares among the liabilities at ten cents each, and transfer the difference, $14,958,543, to surplus account.[2] Since the publicly stated surplus as of December 31, 1925, was only $31,477,234, it is readily seen that approximately half of it was simply created by the ac-

[1] Ripley, W. Z., *Main Street and Wall Street,* p. 87.

[2] For the details of this transaction cf. Ripley, *Main Street and Wall Street,* p. 200, and Poor's *Industrials,* 1926, pp. 1321, 1322.

counting device just described. To many financiers and some accountants there seems no objection to such a procedure; to paraphrase Kipling they apparently hold that there are "nine and sixty ways" of computing surplus, "and every single one of them is right." In the Dodge case there is no intimation of misrepresentation, since the method by which the surplus figure was derived is clearly stated, but the possibilities are obvious. Since no-par stock in most states does not have to be entered on the balance sheet at any definite figure, any desired portion of the proceeds from the sale of such stock may be entered as "surplus." To an actual or prospective shareholder this surplus item may convey an impression of substantial earnings, whereas as a matter of fact it too frequently represents little more than figure-juggling.[1]

Another objectionable result of the possibility of transferring a large part of the proceeds of stock sales to surplus is that it may be used to defeat the purpose of the statutory prohibitions against the payment of unearned dividends. The general rule is, of course, aimed at the impairment of capital by such payments. But with no-par stock and the crediting of money received therefor to surplus it can be claimed that "capital" was not impaired. The possible injustices to *bona-fide* investors or to creditors in cases of liquidation are apparent.[2] In the judgment of one of the outstanding recent writers on these matters, ". . . only a very clear prohibition will prevent the express intent of the parties from governing whether or not their payments are capital or paid-in surplus. . . ."[3]

Numerous other objections against non-voting stock and no-par stock have been advanced during the vigorous controversy that has been going on concerning them in the past five years. Without further detailing them we may note certain conclusions reached by prominent writers. Bonbright holds that the Delaware no-par stock law, followed in most

[1] Cf. *Main Street and Wall Street,* pp. 194-201, for other examples of this practice.

[2] Cf. an excellent treatment of this problem by Professor J. C. Bonbright in the *Quarterly Journal of Economics,* vol. xxxviii, pp. 440-465 (May, 1924).

[3] Berle, A. A., *Studies in the Law of Corporation Finance,* p. 71 (note).

of the states, "apparently makes it possible for promoters to perpetrate all the customary frauds of overvaluation while escaping the liabilities that they were formerly under as long as shares had a par value" and that it would not be a serious exaggeration to say that it makes the outstanding feature of the corporation type of business "not *limited* liability but *no* liability."[1] Ripley considers that in accepting non-voting shares investors have sold out their birthright of control for a mess of pottage, and that though no-par stock "is not altogether bad" it is "overflowing with possibilities of fraud and deception."[2] Berle views no-par stock as "Probably the greatest single step in transferring control of property rights from stockholders to corporate management. . . ."[3] Cook considers that "The whole plan is to avoid the common law and the statutory liability on stock. Investors and creditors are sacrificed for the promoter."[4]

But far-reaching as the possibilities just recounted seem to be in permitting irresponsible management a free hand in the use of "other people's money," they are entirely eclipsed by certain more recent developments in the art of charter-writing. As we have pointed out, a charter is theoretically a grant of privilege in which the most significant concession is that of limited liability. In the days when most shareholders had a vote their chief function in relation to management was to elect a board of directors who were responsible for the proper conduct of the business. With the almost total relaxation of adequate supervision by the states it has become the practice for the lawyers who draft charters for the promoters of new corporations to include in the charters clauses which go far toward a total destruction of the responsibility and liability of directors. Previously, common decency had become crystallized in the legal principle that corporate managements could not deal with themselves; that is, the law intended to prevent a director or directors as individuals from selling property to themselves as a corporate management. Now

[1] *Quarterly Journal of Economics,* vol. xxxviii, pp. 455, 460 (May, 1924).
[2] *Main Street and Wall Street,* pp. 49, 50, 78.
[3] Berle, *op. cit.,* p. 64.
[4] Cook, *Principles of Corporation Law,* p. 154.

the charters issued by a number of states specifically grant the power to directors to vote upon transactions in which they are interested. In some instances the interest must be disclosed to fellow directors, but frequently this is not true. The charter of the Pennsylvania-Dixie Cement Corporation from New Jersey provides that no contract or transaction in which an officer or director may have an interest adverse to the cement company's shall be invalidated or in any way affected by such interest "even though the vote of such director might have been necessary to obligate the corporation upon such contract or transaction, and even though the fact of such interest was not disclosed to other directors or stockholders of the corporation acting upon or with reference to such contract or transaction. No director having such adverse interest shall be liable to the corporation or to any stockholder thereof, or to any other person, for any loss which may be incurred by the corporation . . . and no such director shall be accountable for any gains or profits realized therefrom."[1] Language can go no further in permitting the legal looting of a corporation by its directors, unless it may be in that of the charter of the Central and Southwest Utilities Company, according to which each stockholder of the concern, by reason of becoming such, waives all objections to such thievery! The charters of Dodge Brothers, Standard Oil of California, Tide Water Oil, and Interstate Power all contain similar provisions except that with the last three the language is less sweeping.[2] Berle is of the opinion that such provisions ". . . would more likely be taken by a court as a badge of fraud than as a contract of protection," but points out a real danger in the general inclusion of such clauses whereby ". . . the idea may be accepted and the standard of good faith previously required may be broken down."[3] There is, of course, no excuse for forcing upon the courts the duty of "mopping up" after a group of careless or corrupt legislators. Since there is no indication of any tendency to house-cleaning among the

[1] Quoted in Ripley, *Main Street and Wall Street*, p. 58.

[2] Berle, *op. cit.*, pp. 31-32.

[3] *Ibid.*, p. 36.

charter-peddling states, it becomes necessary to review the merits of federal control of large-scale corporations.

The various proposals made from time to time for meeting by federal action the situation described above may be roughly classified as federal regulation, federal license, and federal incorporation, though these categories are not entirely satisfactory in that they are not mutually exclusive. By the first is usually meant federal action along the lines already adopted by some of our states or along those applied to the railroads (not including such features as price regulation). Of the federal license plans those suggested by the late W. J. Bryan and by the Commissioner of Corporations in his report for 1904 are among the most significant. Bryan's proposal was that any corporation wishing to do business outside the state in which it was chartered must secure from a federal body to be created by Congress a license to do such business. Furthermore, the law was to require as conditions for the issuance of a license:

1. That the evidence should show that there was "no water" in the stock of the corporation;

2. That the evidence should show that the corporation was not at the time of applying for the license nor at any previous time attempting to monopolize any branch of industry or any article of commerce;

3. Full publicity of the corporation's affairs.[1]

The Commissioner of Corporations was somewhat more willing to rely on the discretion of Congress for the details of the statute which he recommended, but favored the compulsory requirement of a federal license for conducting interstate business and "the requirement of such reports and returns as may be desired as a condition of the retention of such franchise or license." [2] By 1910, however, partly as a result of the reports of the Bureau of Corporations, President Taft was willing to recommend to Congress the enactment of a statute providing for federal incorporation of such corpora-

[1] *Chicago Conference on Trusts*, 1899, p. 584.

[2] *Report of the Commissioner of Corporations*, 1904, pp. 47, 56.

tions engaged in interstate commerce as wished to avail themselves of that privilege. The purpose of the recommendation was not so much the remedy of corporate abuses *per se* as the establishment of "such limitations as will secure a compliance with the antitrust law." Nevertheless, the specific suggestions of the message were designed to eliminate stock watering and holding companies and to secure full and complete reports of corporate operations at regular intervals.[1] Though the proposed legislation failed of enactment, the evidence has continued to accumulate that nothing can be expected from the states, evidence which fully warrants the statement of the president of the National Conference on Uniform State Laws of 1924 that "It will never be possible to get all of the states to agree upon the theory of an incorporation act, as some of the states will always adhere to the conservative policy of encouraging corporate management, other states will always incline toward a strict regulation of corporations, while a third group will regard incorporations as a mere revenue-producing procedure."

Among the wide divergencies in the remedial measures suggested there is one proposal upon which there seems practically unanimous agreement *viz.*, greater publicity of corporate affairs. Though the Chicago Conference on Trusts of 1899 disclosed the utmost diversity of opinion, so much so that the committee on resolutions refused "to adopt resolutions purporting to declare the sense of the conference upon any aspect of the subject of discussion," no reader of the speeches made at that conference would take exception to Bryan's reference to "that publicity which everybody has spoken of and about which everybody agrees." [2] Even before this time individual writers such as W. W. Cook had been advocating publicity, and since 1899 the conclusions of numberless investigators, both public and private, from the Industrial Commission's report of 1902 to Ripley's magazine articles in 1926 have struck the same note. Nor has it been only "outsiders" who have taken part in the chorus; in the *World's*

[1] *Messages and Papers of the Presidents,* vol. xvii, pp. 7834, 7835.

[2] Cf. pp. 626 and 584 of the proceedings of the conference.

Work for December, 1926, Judge Gary restated his well-known opinions in an article called "The Public Be Informed!"

During the intervening years since these demands for publicity first became general much has been done, but that a great deal remains to be accomplished cannot be doubted when such a conservative sheet as the *Wall Street Journal* can refer to a large part of corporate reports as "a mess of tripe." Specifically, the reports are faulty in their failure to show clearly and simply the condition of the corporation at a given time by means of a properly drawn balance sheet or to provide shareholders with an adequate income account which will reveal the progress of the concern through a period of time. A balance sheet which lumps together in one figure the items of "plant, property, equipment, machines, patents, and good will" or "property, equipment, good will, etc.," as the most cursory examination of the financial manuals will demonstrate that numberless corporations do, is worse than useless. When to this is added a total disregard in the published statements of depreciation, replacement, and obsolescence, and the entry of no-par shares on the balance sheet at one dollar each, with an accompanying promise to pay seven-dollars dividends a year on each of the shares, the "investment" of funds in the enterprise partakes of the nature of "bucking" the old-time "shell game." Consequently, we are compelled to agree with our predecessors that more complete publicity is imperative.

For the purpose of securing such publicity we believe that the most desirable procedure would be to require all corporations except railroads capitalized at $10,000,000 or more and engaged in interstate commerce to make to the Federal Trade Commission full and complete annual reports of their operations. The fundamental features of such reports would be a balance sheet, income account and statement of earnings. As is generally known, a considerable number of our largest corporations now make such reports and give them the widest publicity through newspapers and financial journals. But even with the very best of these voluntary reports, those of the United States Steel Corporation, various investigators from the Bureau of Corporations to the present writers have found certain difficulties which prompt a further suggestion that the prescribed reports should be prepared upon some uniform basis worked out with and agreed to by the corporations interested. Since the certified public accountants of the country have been for years insisting upon the crying need for a standardization of accounting terms and methods, and since the trade associations have already accomplished a great deal in establishing uniform accounting systems among their members, we do not believe our suggestion is out of line with what is now being sought by a large part of the business interests. Even if it is, our experience with the railroads establishes the wisdom of uniformity.

The figure of $10,000,000 for the capitalization of companies required to make reports to the Trade Commission may be considered to set too high a minimum, but in view of the rising tide of mergers and reorganizations of the past few years it seems that a smaller figure would affect such a large number of corporations that it would prevent the most effective administration of the proposed measure. Moreover, there is some indication that such a minimum would receive support among business men in the recommendation several years ago by Judge Gary of a federal license system for corporations of this size.

There is reason to believe that the Federal Trade Commission has power under the act creating it to require the reports advocated, but because of the uncertainties raised by some of the court decisions previously discussed we further advocate an amendment to that act clearly imposing upon the Commission the obligation of establishing the reporting system. This would involve, of course, appropriate prescriptions by the Commission insuring that assets and liabilities are fully and accurately stated in the reports, that surplus is distinguished from net earnings, etc. And as a corollary to these changes it would be necessary to abolish no-par stock. For reasons already made clear real publicity and the prevention of payment of dividends from capital are made difficult, if not impossible, of accomplishment when such stock is authorized.

A further reason for abolishing no-par stock exists in the desirability of compelling all corporations, regardless of size, to conform to regulations similar to those established in Germany for the purpose of making sure that the assets are equal to the nominal capitalization. The evils attendant upon the issuance of inflated securities have been recognized at least since the days of the British South Sea Bubble, but they still persist. As just suggested, we believe the most practicable method for preventing them is that adopted by Germany more than forty years ago and still retained. It will be recalled [1] that in the organization of a corporation the features of the German system here in point were those that required promoters to make a detailed report of all transactions involved in the issuance of stock for property, including the prices paid during the preceding two years for the purchase or construction of property; that made promoters civilly and criminally liable for the accuracy and completeness of the report; that required both the managing and supervising boards to examine the circumstances attending the formation of the corporation, particularly the prices at which property is to be taken over; and that required in many cases an examination by an independent board of auditors. These safeguards at the time of organization are supplemented by others designed to continue the close relation of actual assets to capitalization. Among these latter are the requirements that securities and goods having a stock-exchange or market value are to be entered in the balance sheet at that value as of the date of said balance sheet in case such value is below the cost price, but otherwise at cost price; that promotion or administration expenses cannot be included among assets; and that the amount of the capital and of all reserves and depreciation funds must be included among liabilities. At some points these requirements may appear less well adapted to American conditions than those embodied in the British Companies Act, as amended in August, 1928.[2] The important thing is to prescribe full and adequate annual reports and to empower the Federal Trade

[1] Cf. particularly pp. 578-581.
[2] Cf. pp. 598, 599.

Commission through conference with the auditors of the corporations affected to work out and prescribe uniform systems of accounting which will give stockholders and others interested the information which they are entitled to have.

To the members of that large group who still do lip-service to the ideal of "no government interference in business" the foregoing proposals will doubtless seem more than sufficient, but for those measures in which we have advocated the adoption of the principles of the German model it is obvious that we can expect no action from the states within the next millennium. It is equally obvious, however, that federal action relating to all interstate business corporations with a capitalization of $10,000,000 or more cannot be expected until Congress clears up the anomalous situation existing with regard to our interstate public utilities. For more than forty years now the federal government has been "regulating" the railroads. As is well known, the first statute of 1887 was an incomplete, inadequate, highly unsatisfactory effort to deal with a situation that railroads and shippers alike found intolerable. Successive Congresses have pruned and grafted, tinkered and patched, renovated and revised the original law until in some respects it now proclaims a policy exactly the reverse of that with which it started. Not until 1906 was the Interstate Commerce Commission given the power to compel the railroads to keep their accounts in a uniform fashion, and not until 1920 was it given the control over new issues of railway securities that it is reasonable to expect might have prevented such disgraceful episodes as the New Haven crash. The whole system of regulation has rested, of course, on the patently interstate nature of the business, coupled with the demonstration in the so-called "granger laws" of the 'seventies that state regulation was nothing short of ridiculous. But in 1929 the Southern Pacific Company still operates under a charter from Kentucky in which it has not a mile of track! The logical first step in a comprehensive program for meeting the difficulties clearly recognized in the 'eighties was the requirement of federal incorporation. The nature of many of the amendments we have made to the original statute simply reinforces that judgment.

Meanwhile, the growth of holding-company control of the electric light and power and allied utilities has gone far to undermine the effectiveness of state regulation of them. In addition to the incredibly and needlessly complex character of many of these holding-company structures, making the placing of responsibility difficult if not impossible, there have been the usual concomitants of a period of combinations: the issuance of huge quantities of highly inflated securities and reckless speculation in them by "insiders" and others. Since the holding companies have been held by the courts not to be public utilities, the state commissions are powerless. During 1924 and 1925 the activities of more or less irresponsible promoters of utility holding companies provoked numerous warnings from such leaders in the industry as Samuel Insull, H. A. Wagner of Baltimore, M. S. Sloan of Brooklyn, Alex. Dow of Detroit, and Samuel Ferguson of Hartford. All of these gentlemen are thoroughly cognizant of the advantages in financing and operating which the holding company possesses as compared with the local more or less isolated operating company. They are not so positive of these economies, however, when the comparison is made between the far-flung holding company, operating in nineteen states and the Philippines, and the large operating companies of many of our cities. Particularly are the advantages questionable when one considers the fierce competition between holding companies for operating properties and the consequent overvaluation of those properties. As President Ferguson of the Hartford Electric Light Company asks, "What is the value of the economies to the communities if in order to effect them it has been necessary to capitalize the savings for years to come, and in their capitalized forms to donate them either to the former stockholders or to the speculative banker who has brought the parties together?" And he answers his own question in these words: "Obviously, the advantages are not mutual in such a case, and as the public-utility business is in effect a partnership between capital and the public, I view such action in exactly the same light as I would a transaction in any other line of business partnership in case one partner should take all the profits from a joint transaction." The disclosures attending the collapse of the securities of United Light and Power in the spring of 1926 and the precipitous drops in the prices of other utility securities attested the truth of the warnings just mentioned. State control had again demonstrated its weaknesses. And if further evidence be wanted of the necessity of additional control over the power interests, we believe it is provided in plenty by the hearings before the Federal Trade Commission relative to the propaganda by these interests directed toward subverting our schools and newspapers.

Consequently, it seems to us that both for the railroads and for other interstate public service companies immediate and compulsory federal incorporation is necessary. Included herein should be, of course, the holding companies just described. We have tinkered and patched, procrastinated and delayed; now the evidence demands the action that logic long ago indicated.

At the same time that it makes federal incorporation mandatory for these interstate public service companies Congress should also enact a statute providing for federal incorporation of all interstate concerns capitalized at $10,000,000 or more that wish to avail themselves of the privilege. As indicated above, we believe such a voluntary federal incorporation law should embody the essential principles of the German and British models with the modifications and adaptations suggested by American experience. The vital features of a satisfactory statute would include machinery to insure that the original capitalization of a corporation was represented by actual assets and that subsequent issues of securities did not destroy this relation; that promoters, original subscribers to stock, and directors were held responsible for the accuracy of all representations made during the flotation of the corporation; and that the relation of directors to shareholders should definitely be established as a fiduciary one. Among the detailed provisions necessary for the accomplishment of these objectives would be included requirement of the publicity previously discussed, the abolition of no-par stock, and the investiture of all securities, including bonds, with voting rights, though in the case of bonds and possibly preferred stock it might be wiser to confer only limited voting rights contingent upon the development of certain clearly defined emergencies. Though it is probable that at the outset the only corporations which would apply for federal charters would be some of those already conforming in most respects to the standards of the proposed legislation, there is reason to believe that in order to escape so far as possible from the hampering restraints of forty-eight sets of requirements and to secure the prestige which would redound to holders of federal charters, the number of concerns applying would tend to increase. The advantages from the administrative point of view of beginning the process with a small number of corporations each sympathizing with the new methods and coöperating to facilitate their improvement are obvious. Gradually a body of experience and precedent would be fabricated from which we might proceed to the last step to which the authors are prepared to commit themselves, the compulsory federal incorporation of all interstate concerns with a capital of $10,000,000 or more.

Now it goes without saying that no such action can be expected from Congress until after it develops a sufficiently national viewpoint to require federal incorporation of the railroads and probably not until after we have had some experience with a voluntary law, but the merits of a mandatory federal law so far outweigh certain disadvantages which any thoughtful person will admit that sooner or later its adoption must be secured.

The conclusive advantage of a compulsory federal statute is that it removes once and for all the fundamental cause of the evils now existing: the competitive selling of charters by half a hundred different authorities. The alternatives of further regulation or a federal license plan represent more "tinkering"; they could scarcely fail to leave untouched many of the difficulties we have discussed. In fact, one writer has expressed the judgment that "Nothing could be more to the liking of these industrial combinations than to have their present charter powers validated by a Federal license against present possible state and federal assault."[1] Federal incorporation, on the contrary, stands on a clear-cut legal theory, brings the entire matter under one jurisdiction and reduces the friction between federal and state authorities to a minimum.

With reference to the legal theory involved it should be recalled that the power of Congress to create federal corporations to engage in interstate commerce is beyond dispute. Although the Constitution does not specifically invest Congress with such authority, the Supreme Court has upheld the legislative arm in creating corporations to carry on banking, railway, and interstate bridge businesses. In all cases of this sort the court has ruled that the corporations were a legitimate means to the end of accomplishing some power clearly reserved to Congress in the Constitution, such as the regulation of interstate commerce, and that their creation was within the discretion of Congress. To trace in detail the successive decisions by which the principle was established seems unnecessary, but it is important to note the language of the court in the North River Bridge case of 1894 which not only substantiates the generalization just made, but also opens the way for an extension of the principle established earlier. "Congress, therefore, may create corporations as appropriate means of executing the powers of government, as, for instance, a bank for the purpose of carrying on the fiscal operations of the United States, or a railroad corporation for the purpose of promoting commerce among the states."[2] Throughout the opinion strong emphasis is laid upon the comprehensive doctrine that Congress had authorized the bridge as a means "to facilitate commerce." And although bank, railroad, and interstate bridge enterprises are all public utilities, the broad test of "promoting commerce among the states" certainly should cover the creation of interstate corporations of a general business character whenever Congress chooses to act.

[1] H. L. Wilgus in 3 *Michigan Law Review* 279.
[2] 153 U. S. 525, 529 (1894).

In addition to supporting the creation of the types of corporations just mentioned, the Supreme Court has held that they may exercise the right of eminent domain within a state, if so authorized, without the consent of the state,[1] that they are exempt from state control and/or taxation in so far as the same might impair their efficiency as instruments for carrying on the purposes for which they were organized,[2] and that they have a right to sue in the Federal courts.[3]

Objections to a federal incorporation system include complaints from the states that they would lose the revenue from incorporation fees and that their powers of taxation would be interfered with; that federal corporations would be hampered by the inability of Congress to empower them to produce or to carry on business within the several states; that the proposed system is unnecessarily drastic; and that it would produce even more of that centralization of governmental functions of which it is claimed we already have too much. Since the scramble for incorporation fees has been primarily responsible for the lax state laws to which we object, the removal of this source of temptation seems to us a merit, not a defect. And since these fees come from the citizens in the long run, the essential point is not which government receives them, but which can give the best service for the least money. Moreover, there is no insurmountable obstacle to a modification of the method of taxing national banks or the Pacific railroads—the states to tax the real and personal property within their borders—while the federal government collects a reasonable franchise tax. Here again is an opportunity for a simplification and clarification of a situation which many business groups declare has become intolerable in its complexity and uncertainty.

The power of Congress to give to federal corporations the right to produce, manufacture, or mine commodities within a state is a constitutional question on which we have found no positive statements from the courts. The inferences drawn by

[1] 153 U. S. 525 (1894).

[2] 9 Wall. 353 (1869); 18 Wall. 5 (1873); 91 U. S. 29 (1875); 188 U. S. 220 (1903).

[3] 166 U. S. 606 (1897).

various commentators from decisions that skirt the problem without resolving it differ materially.[1] The Commissioner of Corporations, for example, in his report for 1904 expressed the view that in the famous case of McCulloch *v.* Maryland the language of Chief Justice Marshall "seems to cover completely the power to produce and the right to grant a franchise for that purpose—'Let the end be legitimate, let it be within the scope of the Constitution, and all means which are appropriate, which are plainly adapted to that end, which are not prohibited, but consist with the letter and spirit of the Constitution, are constitutional.'"[2] The Commissioner argued that conferring the power to produce upon federal corporations was not only an appropriate incidental to the Congressional power of regulating interstate commerce, but also that it was an absolutely essential means for carrying out the object of regulating such commerce. In support of his contentions he called attention to the language of the statutes according to the national banks "all such incidental powers as shall be necessary to carry on the business of banking."

After an exhaustive analysis of the Commissioner's arguments, Professor H. L. Wilgus of the University of Michigan concluded that the federal government could not under the power to regulate commerce give to its own corporation, or one of any state, the legal right to produce within any state without its consent. He insisted, however, that there was no legal or actual necessity for conferring the power to produce upon the federal interstate corporations. In his judgment it is sufficient to give them the "corporate capacity to produce, if the state where production is undertaken does not object," for the probability that the various states will extend to federal corporations the same privileges of producing within their borders that they have heretofore accorded to corporations of other states amounts almost to a certainty. Further-

[1] Cf. *Report of the Commissioner of Corporations,* 1904, p. 51; Wilgus, H. L., in 2 *Michigan Law Review* 382-384 and in 3 *Michigan Law Review* 273-278; Heisler, R. C., *Federal Incorporation,* p. 20; Morawetz, V., in 26 *Harvard Law Review* 667-683; Keasbey, E. Q., in 32 *Harvard Law Review* 689-708; Goodnow, F. J., *Social Reform and the Constitution,* p. 120 *et seq.*

[2] Report, p. 51; 4 Wheat. 315, 420 (1819).

more, Professor Wilgus elsewhere expressed the view that an attempt by the federal government to authorize a corporation organized for private business purposes to go into a state and against its consent to establish and operate a manufacturing plant there "would and ought to be resented by every state." [1]

Among the other commentators we have found none who supports the sweeping conclusions of the Commissioner of Corporations. Practically all of them, however, agree with Wilgus that the decisions indicate very strongly that the Supreme Court would sustain an act authorizing federal interstate corporations to manufacture and mine within a state if the state permitted. Partly because of his present position the most significant concurrence with this opinion is that of the then President Taft in the message of January 7, 1910, recommending a voluntary federal incorporation law.[2]

As a negative expression of the policy outlined above it would probably be necessary to prohibit corporations of $10,000,000 or more capitalization from carrying on an interstate business without a federal charter. There appears to be no reason to doubt that Congress can make such a prohibition and that the Supreme Court will sustain it. In Crutcher *v.* Kentucky the Court said: "To carry on interstate commerce is not a franchise or a privilege granted by the State; it is a right which every citizen of the United States is entitled to exercise under the Constitution and laws of the United States; and the accession of mere corporate facilities, as a matter of convenience in carrying on their business, cannot have the effect of depriving them of such right, unless Congress should see fit to interpose some contrary regulations on the subject." [3] And in the Northern Securities case the Court refused to permit the state of New Jersey to "project its authority into other States, and across the continent, so as to prevent Congress from exerting the power it possesses under the Constitution over interstate and international commerce. . . ." [4]

[1] 2 *Michigan Law Review* 383.
[2] *Messages and Papers of the Presidents,* vol. xvii, p. 7837.
[3] 141 U. S. 47, 57 (1891).
[4] 193 U. S. 197, 345 (1904). Cf. also Hale *v.* Henkel, 201 U. S. 43 (1906).

But in all these proposals we have only indirectly touched one problem resulting from the diversity of state laws which is perhaps of more immediate interest to the directors and executive officers of corporations than those we have treated *in extenso*. The laws relating to "foreign" corporations differ among the states just as do those relating to "domestic" concerns. As long as a Delaware corporation, for example, carefully restricts its dealings with customers in the other states so that they are strictly interstate commerce, it does not have to conform to the laws of those states relating to "foreign" corporations doing business within them. Just what constitutes "doing business in other states" seems upon the face of it a not too difficult problem, but a recent writer on the subject has found several hundred decisions whose net result is confusion worse confounded.[1] A large group of state cases holds that a single intrastate transaction constitutes doing business in the state; another group almost as large holds that it does not. The maintenance of an office in a state for the sole purpose of effecting interstate business does not subject a corporation to the laws on "foreign" corporations, but the greatest care must be exercised, for the sale of a sample, confirmation of a contract, or the acceptance of a payment on an account in that office may bring the corporation within the penalties of doing business in the state without a license. Consequently, it is most desirable that some uniform and reasonable method of "domesticating" corporations should be established. Just as we have had to restrict greatly the powers of state railroad commissions on the ground that their activities constituted an interference with and a regulation of interstate commerce, so we may have to restrict the state legislatures in their indiscriminate regulation of "foreign" corporations on the same ground. As previously pointed out the Supreme Court has at least opened the way to sustaining such restriction in the broad language of the North River Bridge case. Until cases involving the disputed points treated above come before it we can only speculate.

[1] Haring, H. A., *Corporations Doing Business in other States*. Cf. particularly chaps. i and iii.

To the other objections to a federal incorporation law—that it is too drastic and would result in unwarranted centralization—we feel no necessity for devoting much space. A condition of the gravity of that in which we find ourselves is not to be remedied by "pink pills for pale people." Moreover, for the benefit of those who must hark back to the founding fathers for direction and guidance, we might recall that on five different occasions the convention which drafted the Constitution unanimously resolved that Congress should be given power "to legislate in all cases to which the states are incompetent, or in which the harmony of the United States may be interrupted by the exercise of individual legislation." The states have demonstrated their incompetence; the resulting disharmony is spread over thousands of pages of court records. The federal government must act. And in taking action we believe it will find support from many corporation executives who have been harassed by the multiplicity and complexity of the laws relating to "foreign" corporations.

Additional support for the extension of the "social control" of business which we have advocated in the foregoing pages is found in the application of that principle to unfair competition. As previously brought out, the common law limitations on such competition were greatly strengthened by the statutory prohibition of unfair "methods" of competition in the Federal Trade Commission Act of 1914. The change in phraseology from "unfair competition" to "unfair methods of competition" and the creation of a federal administrative body whose chief function has become the enforcement of the prohibitions of the statute have shortened the distance by which the law usually lags behind social progress. Much more important, of course, is the fact that the burden of fighting unfair competition is no longer left to the initiative of injured individuals, but is placed squarely upon the shoulders of an agency of government. The business men and corporations who have suffered most from unfair methods employed by their competitors in the past have been just those who were financially least able to fight such competitors in the courts. And the position of the public, inarticulate and incohesive, has been even more unfortunate. To correct this situation Congress prescribed that the guiding principle for the Commission in proceedings against those who employed unfair methods should be the "public" interest. As we endeavored to show in Chapter XXIII, the Commission's conception of the nature of that public interest has vacillated in an unfortunate manner, but the principle is in the law, and sooner or later we hope to see it applied more consistently than has heretofore been true. The necessity for a firm application of the principle is particularly important in a period of mergers and combinations such as that in which we now are. There is basis for the opinion that had there existed a body similar to the Trade Commission in the early days of the trust movement we might have been spared some of the most objectionable features of that movement and might have avoided some of the futilities of our "trust-busting" ebullitions.

But before proceeding from the importance of the prevention of the use of unfair methods of competition as a remedy for certain of the trust and corporation problems we have raised to the effectiveness of the prohibition, it is significant to note briefly the extensive adoption of the principle in other countries. At the time of the survey made by the Bureau of Corporations [1] there were at least twenty-five nations which in their general codes or by specific statute, or both, had taken action to prevent unfair competition. In a number of them, however, it must be said that the action taken had not been of particular consequence. In most of western Europe and in the British colonies, on the other hand, there had been a considerable volume of legislation as well as a veritable mass of judicial treatment. The tendency in the former was toward a broad general provision of the civil law applicable to the ever-varying forms of unfair practices, supplemented by special provisions prohibiting certain more easily defined or more obnoxious practices.

Since 1914 there has been a steady growth in the appreciation of the need of such legislation and a tendency to follow the example of the United States in establishing an official

[1] Published in 1916 as chap. x of *Trust Laws and Unfair Competition*.

government agency for more effective control. Conspicuous among the countries representing this latter tendency are Germany and Canada.

Judgments of the effectiveness of preventing unfair methods of competition as a remedy for trust and corporate ills will vary, of course, with the estimates placed upon the record of the Federal Trade Commission in this field. Speaking more generally of the work of the Commission in building up a body of administrative law for the guidance of business men, Henderson concluded that its success had been discouragingly small. The chief cause of this failure he found in the nature of the reports of cases presented in the Commission's decisions. Certainly the earlier volumes were not comparable to the reports of important cases adjudicated in Federal courts in which the student usually finds a summary of the basic facts, the nature of the defendant's case, and the reasoning on fact and law which brought the court to its determination of the issues. But there has been marked improvement here and the shift in emphasis to a greater use of the trade practice conference method can prove useful. Unfortunately, there is substantial ground for the opinion of a distinguished New York lawyer [1] that some of the resolutions passed at trade practice conferences and subsequently adopted by the Commission as rules for the guidance of the industry themselves border on illegality, as violations of the Sherman Act. As stated before, we believe the remedy for this situation is the appointment of commissioners who are more fully in sympathy with the purposes of the 1914 legislation.

As suggested in Chapter XXIII, perhaps the most important contribution of the Federal Trade Commission has been its influence in raising the general level of business ethics. This influence has frequently taken the form of compulsion; at other times that of assistance. And in spite of the previously quoted dictum of the Supreme Court,[2] this influence has been exerted in both forms in the direction of extending the con-

[1] Felix H. Levy in an interview in the *Journal of Commerce*, March 23, 1929.

[2] Cf. p. 535, *supra*.

cept of "unfair" to cover business practices not generally so regarded prior to 1914. In fact, this extension is shown in the Supreme Court's own decision in the Winsted Hosiery case as well as in subsequent decisions of other courts such as that of the Second Circuit Court of Appeals in the Royal Baking Powder case. But of course, it must be admitted that the Commission has done less to map out new areas of prohibited practices than to provide a central agency specifically designated by Congress to work toward that end. The situation prior to 1914 provided an excellent illustration of the old adage that "everybody's business is nobody's business." Moreover, the more unscrupulous traders tended to set the standard for the group. Consequently, the Commission found ample opportunity for the exercise of its powers in bringing into line the groups, constituting in most industries only a small minority, that really desired to use unfair methods, by issuing desist orders—that is, by compulsion. Its assistance in raising standards has been chiefly through the trade practice conference (formerly "submittal") in which the industry itself has an opportunity to put pressure more effectively on its less conscientious members.

The facts presented in this and earlier chapters make unnecessary a detailed statement of the fields in which the Commission has been most successful in elevating commercial morals, but a brief recapitulation and evaluation of its achievements are not amiss. In the field of commercial bribery the results secured, both in revealing its widespread prevalence and in limiting it, have been highly satisfactory. During 1918, 1919, 1920, and 1921 there were issued 206 complaints against this practice, but since then there have been only about a half-dozen a year. In practically 100 per cent of such cases the respondent has accepted the desist order without appeal to the courts. Of the other types of prohibited practices we find that of recent years nearly three-fourths of the applications for complaints docketed fall into one of five general classes: misbranding, passing off, false and misleading advertising, resale price maintenance, and misrepresentations of various sorts. And in all five of these classes desist orders have been upheld by the courts.[1]

Some adverse critics of the Commission have attempted to prove that its work has been largely futile because of the facts that prior to June 30, 1928 (the date of the last *Annual Report*), of 68 cases involving a desist order decided by the circuit courts of appeals, 35 decisions have gone against the Commission and that in 16 decisions the Supreme Court has 10 times reversed the Commission. On the other hand, it must be noted that 5 of the adverse decisions in the lower courts were reversed by the Supreme Court, and that of 851 (net) orders issued by the Commission prior to June 30, 1928, only 75 were taken to the courts by the respondents.[2] Moreover, there can be no question that the cases so contested were probably those in which the respondents had the best chance of succeeding. Finally, the argument assumes that an adverse court decision proves the Commission wrong, but no one who has followed the opinions of the courts on Sherman Act cases, or even on Federal Trade Commission cases, can admit the validity of that assumption. To conclude from such arguments, or from criticisms of the Commission's procedure and its findings, that the body is simply "another commission" wasting the taxpayers' money in work which might better be either left undone or handled by private litigation in the courts is to betray a lack of perspective. On the record of the Commission which we have presented we are quite willing to agree that some of its actions have been unfortunate, that others have been unwise, and even that there are a few which have been nothing short of shameful; but we cannot agree that it should be abolished or emasculated until it is no more than a decadent scion of the old Bureau of Corporations. The principles upon which it rests are sound and in time we are confident that it will demonstrate itself to be an indispensable part of the machinery for the "social control of business."

[1] Cf. Stevens, *American Economic Review,* vol. xv, p. 640. (December, 1925.)

[2] *Annual Report,* 1928, pp. 62, 89-91.

CHAPTER XXVIII

CONCLUSIONS

IN RECONSIDERING the many topics discussed in the preceding chapters, the authors are impressed by two developments that appear to be worldwide. First, in all progressive countries there has been an increased tendency to organize industrial combinations. Second, this movement, instead of arousing the antagonism that greeted American trusts forty years ago, has been viewed with tolerance if not approbation by nearly all governmental authorities. That there has been a decided revival of the combination movement in the United States is shown convincingly in the review of developments in *Industry* contributed by Dr. W. L. Thorp to the report of the Hoover Committee on *Recent Economic Changes in the United States.*[1] In the fields of manufacturing and mining he found records of a steadily increasing number of mergers from 1923, when 67 were recorded, until 1928, when 221 were listed. The number of merged or acquired firms increased correspondingly, rising from 311 in 1923 to as many as 1,038 in 1928.

No country has greater reason at the present time to review carefully all of its industrial policies than the United Kingdom. This gives special significance to the series of reports of the representative British Committee on Industry and Trade (the "Balfour Committee"), which was appointed by the Labor Government during its first short lease of power (July 28, 1924) and whose *Final Report*[2] was presented shortly before the Labor Government again assumed direction of British national policy in May, 1929. This Committee declares: "The information available shows a strong tendency, both in this and other industrial countries, for enterprises engaged in production to increase in average size, a tendency which shows no

[1] Published by McGraw-Hill Co., May, 1929, p. 181 *et seq.*
[2] March, 1929. Cmd 3282. London: H. M. Stationery Office.

sign of reaching its limit. There is also a tendency for separate productive undertakings to associate themselves with other similar enterprises with a view to regulating output, price, marketing, or other matters."[1] In regard to governmental policies to cope with this combination movement, the Committee states: "We certainly could not recommend the enactment of any such measures for the suppression of combination as have been attempted, with very doubtful success, during the past forty years by the Anti-Trust laws of the United States."[2] Instead it contents itself with proposing that "the Board of Trade should include among its general duties the watching of the movement toward consolidation and agreement in industry, and the continuous collection of data in regard to various forms of combination" with a view to making periodical reports on the subject to Parliament.

In advocating a continuance of the *laissez-faire* policy toward trusts, supplemented by increased attention to collecting information about the movement, the Balfour Committee echoes the more balanced conclusions in regard to the advantages of "rationalization" and of international trade agreements, to which the World Economic Conference had come at Geneva in May, 1927.[3]

For the more favorable trend of world opinion in reference to industrial combinations there have been at least three good reasons. First and most important was the demonstration that was afforded in all countries during the war of the advantages of the unified control of important industries. When compelled to marshal every national resource to the single end of winning the war, combination and the elimination of the friction and rivalries of competition were entered upon as a matter of course by all the belligerent countries. To secure unified control, vital agencies like railroads and ocean

[1] Final Report, *op. cit.*, p. 176.

[2] This and the following quotations are taken from *ibid.*, pp. 191-193.

[3] An amusing indication of how far these departed from the antitrust viewpoint to which our government has been committed is afforded by the note appended to this part of the report: "The members of the U. S. A. Delegation, while not opposing, did not feel able to participate in the vote on this subject." The full Report is reprinted in the *Annals of the American Academy of Political and Social Science* for November, 1927, pp. 174-206.

shipping were even taken over and operated directly by governments. Many mistakes were made. An amount of governmental regulation was developed that was felt to be intolerable when peace conditions had been reëstablished, and there followed a strong reaction toward private ownership and operation. But the experience of the advantages of coördinated industry left a lasting impression on the minds of thoughtful leaders of public opinion in every country.

A second reason is the clearer realization of the limitations to the combination movement. An excellent restatement of these limitations is presented in Dr. Thorp's account of recent changes in American industry, to which reference has just been made.[1] He points out that small scale production must continue to predominate in:

> (1) Industries in which products cannot be standardized and establishments which make products to suit the different tastes of consumers. Such industries produce tailored suits, high-grade furniture, art goods and finely bound books.
>
> (2) Industries producing for a small market, such as those manufacturing artists' materials.
>
> (3) Industries in which the local market is small and whose product has a high transportation cost.
>
> (4) Industries in which the material used is widely scattered and cannot be concentrated because of high transportation costs or perishability. Cheese factories and cider mills may be included in this class.
>
> (5) Industries in which skilled labor is the chief element, such as engraving and job printing, whose products are really services rather than commodities.

And, we are moved to add:

(6) Industries whose operations must be spread out over a wide area, so that much of the labor performed must be by scattered, self-directed workers. Most branches of farming belong in this group.

The third reason is the change in the attitude and policies of the directors and managers of big business enterprises. No one who has studied the trust movement can fail to be impressed by the extent to which the old "public be damned" attitude has given place to the new "public be served" atti-

[1] Cf. *Recent Economic Changes in the United States,* p. 188.

tude. No doubt self-interest, the desire for profit, is still the guiding motive of private business enterprise, but it is tempered by the conviction, born of experience and of a growing sense of social solidarity, that the road to profit is through better and cheaper service to satisfied patrons, rather than through the exploitation of disgruntled customers. It is this new point of view which inspires the rationalization movement, which is receiving so much attention in Europe.[1]

Before we attempt to summarize the policies toward trusts which leading countries are pursuing and to formulate our own conclusions about American policy, we should speak briefly of three aspects of the combination movement that we may seem to have neglected. These are the relation between the tariff and the trusts, "dumping," and the statistical evidence as to the influence of the trusts on prices and their success or failure as business enterprises.

We have given only incidental attention to the relation between the tariff and the trusts because our views on the subject can be stated in a few words and require little illustration or argument. Undoubtedly the tariff has had an important influence on the combination movement in most countries. Without their protective tariffs the United States and Germany would not have had several of their most important combinations. When Mr. H. O. Havemeyer, president of the Sugar Trust at the time of its organization, said "the tariff is the mother of trusts" he no doubt told the truth about his own combination. Similarly, without the McKinley Act there could hardly have developed a Tin-plate Trust, perhaps not a tin-plate industry, in the United States.[2] On the other hand, more important combinations like the Standard Oil Trust and the American Tobacco Trust owed little or nothing to the tariff.

While there has been and still is this connection between the tariff and the trusts, the tariff-made and tariff-supported trusts are those which are most easily controlled in the public

[1] Cf. *supra,* pp. 595, 596, and *infra,* p. 670.

[2] Also, as has been pointed out (*supra,* p. 597), the tardy development of combinations in the United Kingdom was in part due to her free-trade policy.

interest. In principle all that is needed is the adoption of the policy which Canada introduced in 1910. Empower the administration to lower or withdraw entirely the protective duties on the products of trusts which impose unreasonably high prices on domestic consumers. This is easier said than done, no doubt, but provision in the Tariff Act for some revision of duties, even if rarely exercised, may serve as an effective means of checking extortionate policies on the part of trust managers.

In regard to dumping we have had little to say because it is a rather special topic, is ably dealt with in easily accessible books,[1] and the means of curbing it are now not only well understood but actually practiced by most countries. Again what is required is that authority be given to the administration to change tariff rates, this time to advance them, if necessary to prohibitive levels, when the producers or dealers of another country make a practice of unloading their products at prices below those charged their own nationals to wrest the coveted market from native producers. In this case the remedy is so obvious and easy that its application may well prove worse than the disease. As was pointed out in one of the resolutions of the World Economic Conference in 1927 already referred to, while "dumping must be reduced to a minimum . . . importing countries which find themselves compelled to take defensive measures against [it] should not resort to excessive, indirect or vexatious measures which would leave a more far-reaching effect than is intended."

More serious, perhaps, is our failure to present in more detail available statistical evidence in regard to the effect of trusts on prices and their success as business enterprises. Excellent reviews of the facts in regard to prices have been given by other writers on the trust problem[2] and as regards certain aspects they are undoubtedly conclusive. There appears to be no question, for example, that the usual first effect of the organization of a strong combination is an advance in prices.

[1] Cf. Viner, J., *Dumping: A Problem in International Trade*, 1923.

[2] We commend especially on this topic Jenks and Clark, *The Trust Problem*, fifth edition, 1929, chap. vii, and Jones, *The Trust Problem in the United States*, 1921, chap. xi.

Professor Jenks shows this quite convincingly for sugar at different periods in the history of the Sugar Trust. A more recent example is the substantial advance in the price of copper which followed the organization of Copper Exporters, Inc. The difficulty is to determine whether this rise of prices has been carried to unreasonable heights and maintained there through the control a strong combination is able to exercise over the supply. There are so many complicating factors that a study of prices alone throws no convincing light on this question. Each trust presents an individual problem calling for an elaborate comparison of prices, costs, and profits, and even when the data for such comparison are available, which is not usually the case, the question yet remains: were costs reduced by the combination so that it enjoyed its relatively large earnings, not at the expense of consumers, who might have had to pay even higher prices had not wasteful methods of production and marketing been eliminated, but as the reward of its superior industrial efficiency? This is one of the points where exact statistical information still fails to reinforce the more or less speculative conclusions of economic analysis.

It would seem as though there should be much less difficulty in ascertaining with a fair degree of certainty how many of the trusts have been successful as business enterprises and what has been the degree of that success. A few years ago one of the authors made a careful study of the twenty largest trusts that were organized in the United States before 1904. He found to his own satisfaction, though some of his tests were open to question, that of the sixteen trusts which were still in operation, eight had been quite successful and the remaining eight unsuccessful or only barely successful. But when he considered the causes of success he was so impressed with the importance of efficient management to the result—that is, of the personal equation—that he would be reluctant to base any generalization on his findings. How difficult it is to decide on a proper criterion of success when the initial capitalization is heavily watered and the method of accounting followed includes no uniform principle in regard to allowances for depreciation, was amusingly illustrated by the experience of another investigator, who on applying his carefully-thought-out criterion of success to the United States Steel Corporation found that it must be numbered among the failures!

The latest attempt to determine the degree of success of big business, as contrasted with moderate-sized and small business enterprises in the United States, is reported by Dr. Thorp in connection with the study of *Recent Economic Changes.*[1] Comparing the changes in value of products and number of wage-earners employed for identical establishments in nine representative manufacturing industries from 1923 to 1925, he found that in eight of the nine industries the large concerns gained more than the middle-sized establishments. It is significant of the persistence of competition that he found also that in only three did the large establishments increase more rapidly than the small establishments. Applying the test of the valuation the stock market places upon the securities of large, medium-sized, and small enterprises in four industries over the longer period 1918 to 1928, his assistant, Mr. Albert Abrahamson, found that the securities of large enterprises increased most rapidly in three industries and were second in the fourth. It seems quite clear that stock-market wise big business has been viewed with growing favor during the last ten years, and, of course, underlying this favorable reaction in most instances have been favorable showings as to earnings. The author's warning that this investigation was hedged about "so tightly by assumptions as to bring it near to strangulation" illustrates again the difficulty of applying the statistical method to the problem.

About all that we can say with certainty is that the idea once so widely held, that when the scale of corporate enterprise is enlarged beyond a certain point slackened efficiency is almost sure to result is beginning to be challenged on the basis of contemporary experience. In spite of the fact that it has the added temptation to relaxed efficiency of being a monopoly, the American Telephone and Telegraph Company is fa-

[1] Pp. 195, 196, and 199.

mous for its alert and progressive management. Nor are the United States Steel Corporation, the General Motors Company, or the Standard Oil companies usually criticized for failure to manage their affairs in accordance with the highest efficiency standards. The reasons for the current efficiency of these and other large corporations are suggested in a note which Colonel M. C. Rorty appended to the concluding chapter of the report on *Recent Economic Changes*.[1] He says:

> One of the most significant results arising from improvements in the science of management has been an increasing ability to secure from large units or "chains" the type of individual efficiency that a few years ago could be secured only in the small organization working under the direct supervision of a competent employer-owner. Under the older type of organization there was a gain in efficiency with size, up to the point where the reductions in costs, through ability to specialize and functionalize the work of a larger group of workers and the increases in process, purchasing and selling efficiency under larger scale operation, began to be more than offset by a reduced general efficiency due to the inability of the employer-owner to maintain close contacts with the members of the enlarged organization. Recent developments in management methods, and in accounting and statistical control, have apparently broken down these former economic limitations on the size of the individual organization or "chain," with the result that practically all types of business and industry are now open to efficient large-scale corporate control. If this tendency persists, it may represent a fundamental economic change having very far-reaching consequences.

We are not quite prepared to agree that these changes have opened "practically all types of . . . industry" to successful large corporate enterprise, but that they permit a great enlargement of the scale of operations for industries adapted to large-scale production without apparent slackening in their efficiency will hardly be denied. It remains true, of course, that as the scale of operations increases the losses that may result from poor management increase, but management itself has become a profession. The methods by which the armies of employees of vast business enterprises may be stimulated each to make his maximum contribution to the success of "*our*" company are becoming every year better understood and more widely practiced.

[1] P. 864.

In the preceding chapters we have described the changing policies toward trusts of some of the leading countries of the world. Our state and federal governments in the late 'eighties and early 'nineties placed drastic antitrust laws on their statute books, but when the enforcement of these laws was seriously undertaken some years later, the courts interpreted them in conformity with the distinction which the common law had come to draw between reasonable and unreasonable restraints of trade. Definite agreements in regard to prices and outright monopolies are prohibited, but the executive branches of the government, which are relied upon to enforce these prohibitions, have during the last decade shown less interest in opposing than in promoting coöperation among business men. The place of dissolution suits has been taken by such prophylactic measures as consent decrees, trade practice conference rules and stipulations, so that attempts to apply the criminal penalties of the law have been infrequent and unimportant.

Germany's policy has from the beginning differed fundamentally from that embodied in Anglo-American law. German law has never prohibited contracts and combinations in restraint of trade and monopolies. So long as the methods of such combinations do no violence to German legal standards of good morals, they are allowed to flourish freely. There, freedom of contract has been interpreted to include freedom to combine as well as freedom to compete, and restrictive contracts, with the exceptions embodied in the Cartel Law of 1923, have been enforced without question by German courts. The government has not only permitted monopolistic combinations, but it has at times made them obligatory and through state owned industries itself has been a party to them.

Between these extremes lie the policies of the other great English-speaking countries, the United Kingdom, Australia, New Zealand, and Canada. In them the common law, reinforced outside of the United Kingdom by statutes, has prohibited contracts and combinations in unreasonable restraint of trade, making the criterion more and more their effect upon the common welfare. Under this system, monopolistic combinations run the risk of being held to be unlawful, but if their policies are fair toward their actual or potential competitors and the prices they charge are reasonable, this risk is small because of the increasingly liberal attitude of the courts, especially the highest court of all, the Judiciary Committee of the Privy Council.

Finally, Russia has entered upon the policy, never before attempted on so gigantic a scale, of having all important mining and manufacturing industries operated by state trusts or under exclusive concessions subject to rather strict regulation.

Space has not permitted an examination of the policies of other countries, but that has been less necessary because they have shown a liberality toward monopolistic combinations, subject, when the public interest required, to governmental regulation, similar to that displayed by the United Kingdom and Germany. That Mussolini favors the organization of trusts as a measure that facilitates governmental regulation when deemed necessary, has been repeatedly shown. The French government is so tolerant toward monopolistic combinations that it has itself joined the German potash cartel in perfecting an international organization for harmonizing the interests of the two countries in the industry over which they have at least a temporary monopoly. Through its selling agency in Brussels, Copper Exporters, Inc., controlling through its American and associate members the sale of 90 per cent of the world's output of copper, distributes the product to European consumers. Neither Belgium nor any other European country has taken steps to attack it as a monopoly, though during the months when the European price of copper was being rapidly advanced its policies were severely criticized. Tolerance of the international steel cartel and of many others of which no mention has been made attest the willingness of the countries concerned to accept such monopolistic combinations as inevitable and even desirable and to condemn them only when their policies are clearly opposed to the public interest.

In a world already so largely committed to national and international industrial combinations, what policy will serve best to promote the long-run interests of the people of these United States? Current opinion on this question may be distinguished into four groups:

(1) There are some who still believe that our antitrust laws should be maintained in spirit and in letter and that our mistake has been in exempting export associations and special branches of industry like farming and ocean shipping from their prohibitions. This is a dwindling minority still articulate on the political platform before election day, but with little influence even in Congress, where baiting the trusts, so long a favorite pastime, has now largely gone out of fashion.

(2) A second group urges that the United States is prospering under its present laws, illogical and haphazard in enforcement as they notoriously are, and that we should therefore leave them unchanged. In this group are, among others, extreme opponents of governmental regulation who prefer statutes which appear to curb combinations but in reality are almost inoperative to milder measures which might be enforced. Such a policy of opportunism makes little appeal to the growing body of thoughtful citizens who consider the multiplicity of statutory prohibitions which are openly and continuously violated as the greatest defect in our governmental system, and believe that no effort should be spared to bring about conformity between law and practice, in this instance by liberalizing the law to correspond with the increasing practice of coöperation among business men all over the world.

(3) A third group approves of the exceptions that have been made in the application of the antitrust laws and thinks that this policy should be cautiously extended by permitting combination under suitable regulation among industries concerned with our dwindling natural resources, particularly petroleum, coal and forest products.

(4) Finally, a fourth group would go even further and amend our antitrust laws so that they would conform with those of Australia—that is, by introducing along with the qualification that only unreasonable contracts and combinations are prohibited, which has come through judicial interpretation, the further qualification that the prohibition applies

only when such contracts and combinations are opposed to the public interest.

The trend of the discussion in the preceding pages indicates pretty clearly where the authors' sympathies lie. We cannot believe that any useful purpose would be served by reviving our extreme antitrust policies. Historically they rendered a highly important service by reasserting the dominance of the interests of the nation in connection with our business development over any group of private interests. But we believe Congress has been well advised to exempt the railroads, export associations and coöperative farmers' organizations and shipping conferences from the prohibitions of these laws.

The program of the second group appeals to us even less. To support our existing statutory system not because we believe in it in principle, but because it is so feebly enforced, is too like the attitude of the bootlegger toward our even better known prohibition laws to command approval.

We are persuaded by our study of the combination movement at home and abroad that it is essentially a movement making for economy, efficiency, and better relations in business. The contribution which it might make under wise guidance to the conservation of our limited oil and forestry resources and to the more efficient management of our bituminous coal industry makes us particularly responsive to the proposal of the third group as a program to be urged upon Congress at this time. In Chapter IX we discussed the present situation in the American Petroleum Industry. Since that chapter was written the outcome that might have been foreseen, the inability of the leading oil-producing states to agree on a wise program of conservation without federal leadership unhampered by the prohibitions of the antitrust acts, has been experienced. President Hoover has gone as far as he is permitted under present laws by withholding the public oil lands from registry. Since the adjournment on June 12, 1929, without definite action or prospect of action of the representatives of the leading oil states who were called together on the initiative of the federal government, the country's production of crude oil has mounted to new heights. The measures for conservation that might so easily be enforced by joint action will almost certainly again be weakened by interstate competition, and the long-run best interests of the country be sacrificed to a legal system which business men engaged in this particular field of endeavor almost unanimously condemn.

The arguments against permitting combination in the oil industry subject to governmental supervision and regulation are of course not lightly to be disregarded. It is feared that the grave abuses of which the Standard Oil Trust was guilty [1] would recur if another giant combination were permitted to organize, this time not a billion-dollar trust, but if all the capital controlled by all the large American oil companies were now combined, more nearly a twenty-billion-dollar trust. It is believed that an aggregation of capital so vast and a business so widespread and ramified would result that there would be a serious deterioration in efficiency. Finally it is thought that advantage would be taken of consumers by advancing the prices charged for petroleum products to unreasonable levels and that whatever conservation of oil resources resulted would be for the benefit not of the nation, but of the stockholders of the trust. Rejoinders to these arguments readily suggest themselves. The abuses formerly committed occurred before there was an efficient Interstate Commerce Commission and before unfair methods of competition were prohibited or a Federal Trade Commission to prevent them created. These government commissions still leave much to be desired, but that any such unfair and oppressive policies as were practiced as recently as twenty-five years ago would now be attempted or tolerated is highly improbable. In regard to the possible resulting inefficiency we have already indicated our belief that modern methods of management are able to cope as effectively with a twenty-billion-dollar business as a billion-dollar unit, and we already have several billion-dollar enterprises in this field. Finally the fear of unreasonable price policies overlooks the extent to which competition already fails to protect us adequately against unduly high prices. Where a business has come to be controlled by ten or a dozen

[1] Cf. chap. viii, *supra*.

giant corporations, common action in regard to prices, if deemed to be in the interest of those concerned, cannot, we believe, be avoided.[1] If we would need machinery for ultimate price regulation under the new policy, we submit that there are strong reasons for believing that we need it already. Germany meets this problem not by clothing any governmental authority with power to fix prices, but merely by giving the Minister of Economic Affairs power to veto prices proposed by monopolistic cartels. Perhaps the existence of such authority as regards petroleum products would lead to the development of machinery for conference between producers and representatives of the government before changes were put into effect that would make its actual exercise unnecessary. Then there is the probability that not all producers would be drawn into the trust, or at any rate that foreign competition would still persist and exercise a measure of restraint. These suggestions, we agree, are highly speculative. Our controlling reason for favoring the change is that through this policy, and so far as we can see only through this policy, could we place the federal government in a position to outline and secure the adoption of a wise program for conserving this limited natural resource. The huge wastes of competition could be eliminated. Enormous savings could be effected in connection with the marketing of the product. Higher standards of business morality could be developed. Finally, our oil-producers could be put in a position to deal on more equal terms with foreign combinations and to insure our consumers some share of the world's petroleum resources outside of the United States after our supplies become exhausted.

[1] We do not mean to imply a belief that the executives of the big oil companies enter into secret agreements in violation of law in regard to the prices of petroleum products. Why should they? Experience has taught them that their interests are much better served by stable prices. Their policy appears to be, therefore, to maintain the prices established in the principal markets of the country for weeks and even months at a time. When conditions of demand and supply call for a change some one company takes the lead in announcing it and the others follow. There is very active, wastefully active, competition for customers, but the whole industry is benefited by relative stability of prices for finished products. This relative stability will not be lessened by the organization of a Petroleum Export Association on the model of Copper Exporters, Inc., to which all the leading producers belong and which at the time of writing (July, 1929) is just beginning to function.

The case for permitting combination under suitable regulation in the bituminous coal industry seems to us equally convincing, though there the chief end to be sought is not conservation but regularization. This is still a highly competitive industry and therefore outside the field covered by this book, but we have been impressed by the remarkable progress Germany has made through the coöperative efforts of her giant cartels to a better coördination of the coal, iron and steel, and chemical industries and the neglected opportunities for similar improvements in this country.[1] Regularization of the coal industry would benefit operators and consumers, but most of all the coal-miners, who have suffered more than any other group of American wage-earners from persistent irregularity of employment.

The argument that permitting the organization of industrial combinations, under suitable regulation, would contribute to stabilization supports strongly the proposal of group four, viz., that combinations whose policies do not run counter to the interests of the public be permitted. On purely economic grounds we would be disposed to favor their program, also, but our experience of the difficulties presented under our form of government to the development of adequate regulative machinery for the railroad industry, serves as a warning that we should proceed cautiously in imposing new regulative tasks on the authorities at Washington. While we consider the first part of the slogan of the late President Harding, "less government in business," both impossible and undesirable, we recognize the need of the second part, "more business in government," and that its realization, though immensely advanced in recent years, must continue to be a slow and painful process.

The most serious objection to our present policy of prohibiting agreements or combinations in regard to prices is that it prevents, so far as it is effective, coöperation among business men at the very point where it might most benefit them and the public. We could not have stronger testimony in regard to the advantages of stable prices than from the members of President Hoover's own committee on *Recent Economic*

[1] Cf. Meakin, W., *The New Industrial Revolution,* chaps. i-viii. 1928.

Changes. In the forefront of the reasons for the almost uninterrupted prosperity enjoyed by the United States from 1922 to 1929 they place "Relative Price Stability". They say:[1] "The increasing tendency toward price stability, both as between classes of commodities and in the price experience of individual commodities, was a characteristic of the period under review, tending toward a more equitable basis of exchange of products among the various groups." And they add: "Whether the [stable] price relationships of recent years prove to be transitory or permanent, they represent today a huge gain which is reflected in all parts of the economic organism." It is the contention of advocates of stabilization through combination that national policy should be definitely directed toward preserving and perpetuating this "huge gain." Believing that important factors in the price stability of recent years have been the conviction of the executives of big business organizations that continuous price competition was disadvantageous for all concerned and the conduct which this conviction has suggested, these advocates urge that reasonable price agreements should be legalized and maintain that the open discussion of them that would thereafter occur would more fully protect the interests of consumers than does our present policy.[2] As we have indicated above, we believe that the measures advocated in the last chapter should be put into effect before we proceed to legalize reasonable price agreements, but once they are in operation it seems probable that the definite legalization of the open-competition or open-price plans discussed in Chapters XVI and XXI would be to the advantage not only of the business groups interested but of the whole community.

The Hoover committee concludes its survey by pointing out that the problem of perpetuating prosperity is a problem of maintaining the "Economic Balance": "Once an intermittent starting and stopping of production-consumption was char-

[1] *Recent Economic Changes in the United States,* pp. xiii and xiv.

[2] The most persistent and enthusiastic spokesman of the fourth group is Mr. B. A. Javits, whose book, *Make Everybody Rich—Industry's New Goal,* 1929, is commended for its sincerity, idealism, and eloquence.

acteristic of the economic situation," it says.[1] "It was jerky and unpredictable, and overproduction was followed by a pause for consumption to catch up. For the seven years under survey, a more marked balance of production-consumption is evident. With greater knowledge of consuming habits, with more accurate records of the goods consumed, a sensitive contact has been established between factors of production and consumption which formerly were so often out of balance." And looking forward, the committee declares: "To maintain the dynamic equilibrium of recent years is, indeed, a problem of leadership which more and more demands deliberate public attention and control. Research and study, the orderly classification of knowledge, joined to increasing skill, well may make complete control of the economic system a possibility."

It is this "complete control of the economic system" that is visualized in Europe under the term "rationalization." Russia is attempting to attain it through state trusts, Italy through her benevolent dictatorship. Germany, and, to an increasing extent, the United Kingdom, realize that to attain the "economic balance" and at the same time retain freedom of industrial enterprise, business men must be permitted to coöperate all along the line, even as regards prices, with the sole limitations that their policies must have constant regard to the public interest and that unfair methods of competition must not be resorted to. It is not merely the economies of standardization, simplification, etc., that may be attained through large-scale production that are at stake. The problem is that of adjusting production to consumption for a whole industry and even related industries, and not merely for a given period but over a series of years. Nor will the reward be merely the "huge gain" that will come from stabilizing prices, but the larger gain that will result if the irregularities in the employment of labor and capital that occur with the swings of the business cycle can be ironed out, a gain not only to business men in larger profits, but even more to wage-earners in more continuous earnings and to the whole community in ampler supplies of goods and services.

[1] *Recent Economic Changes in the United States,* pp. xx and xxi.

Our survey of the combination movement convinces us that the time has come when American national policy must be consciously directed toward the attainment of these larger ends. During the war emergency all classes put aside their purely personal interests and devoted themselves to advancing what they believed to be the public good. We are optimistic enough to think that a change in the attitude of the government toward the combination movement, not suddenly introduced, but applied first to our limited natural-resource industries, and then extended to industries generally, as we develop the necessary regulative machinery to prevent abuses of monopoly power, would meet with a similar response. Business men will continue to strive to advance. Incentives to do so will persist and multiply even though the severities of competition are tempered by combination. American business men have demonstrated by their success in stabilizing industry in so many directions during the last seven years, in spite of a hostile legal system, that they are ready to grapple with the larger problems which call for nation-wide coöperation. If the country will modify its policy from one of prohibition and restriction to one of guidance and leadership, that "complete control of the economic system" which is so obviously essential to our material welfare may become not merely a "possibility," but a reality.

TABLE OF CASES

BIBLIOGRAPHY

A. Corporations

Berle, Adolph A., Jr., *Studies in the Law of Corporation Finance.* Chicago. Callaghan & Co., 1928.

Burton, T. E., *Corporations and the State.* New York, D. Appleton & Co., 1911.

Cook, W. W., *A Treatise on the Law of Corporations Having a Capital Stock.* 5 vols. 7th ed., 1913.

Cook, W. W., *The Corporation Problem.* New York, G. P. Putnam's Sons, 1891.

Davis, J. P., *Corporations: Their Origin and Development.* 2 vols. New York, G. P. Putnam's Sons, 1905.

Dewing, A. S., *Corporate Promotions and Reorganizations.* (Harvard Economic Studies, vol. X.) Cambridge, Harvard University Press, 1914.

——— *The Financial Policy of Corporations.* 5 vols. New York, Ronald Press, 1920.

Gerstenberg, C. W., *Materials of Corporation Finance.* 2nd ed. New York, Prentice-Hall, 1915.

Gillette, K. C., *The People's Corporation.* New York, Boni & Liveright, 1924.

——— *World Corporation.* Boston, New England News Co., 1910.

Greene, T. L., *Corporation Finance.* New York, G. P. Putnam's Sons, 1897.

Haring, H. A., *Corporations Doing Business in Other States: State Regulations and Requirements Regarding Foreign Corporations.* New York, Ronald Press, 1927.

Heisler, R. C., *Federal Incorporation,* 1913.

Hendrick, F., *The Power to Regulate Corporations and Commerce.* New York, G. P. Putnam's Sons, 1906.

Lownhaupt, F., *Investment Bonds.* New York, G. P. Putnam's Sons, 1908.

Mead, E. S., *Corporation Finance.* 6th ed. 2 vols. Vol. I. New York, D. Appleton & Co., 1928.

Morawetz, V., *A Treatise on the Law of Private Corporations.* 2nd ed. 2 vols., 1886.

Parker, J. S., *Corporation Manual: Statutes, Forms, Precedents.* 30th ed. U. S. Corporation Co., 1929.

Reed, H. L., *Principles of Corporation Finance.* New York, Houghton, Mifflin Co., 1925.

Reynolds, G. G., *The Distribution of Power to Regulate Interstate Carriers between the Nation and the State.* New York, Columbia University Press, 1928.

Ripley, W. Z., *Main Street and Wall Street.* Boston, Little, Brown & Co., 1927.

Sullivan, J. J., *American Corporations.* New York, D. Appleton & Co., 1910.

U. S. Bureau of Corporations. *Laws Relating to Business Corporations.* Prepared under the direction of the Commissioner of Corporations. Boston, Wright & Potter Co., 1915.

WALKER, W. H., *Corporation Finance.* New York, Alexander Hamilton Institute, 1924.

WILDMAN, J. R. and POWELL, W., *Capital Stock without Par Value.* Chicago and New York, A. W. Shaw Co., 1928.

WILGUS, H. L., "A Proposed National Incorporation Law," *Michigan Law Review,* Vol. II, pp. 501–596 (April, 1904).

——— "Federal License or National Incorporation?" *Michigan Law Review,* Vol. III, pp. 264–281 (February, 1905).

——— "Need of a National Incorporation Law," *Michigan Law Review,* Vol. II, pp. 358–395 (February, 1904).

——— "Should There Be a Federal Incorporation Law for Commercial Corporations?" *Reports of the American Bar Association,* Vol. XXVII, pp. 694–753 (1904).

B. TRUSTS

ADAMS, H. C., *Relation of the State to Industrial Action.* Publications of the American Economic Association, 1887.

ARMOUR, J. OGDEN, *The Packers, the Private Car Lines and the People.* Philadelphia, H. Altemus & Co., 1906.

BAKER, C. W., *Monopolies and the People.* 3rd ed., rev. and enl. New York, G. P. Putnam's Sons, 1899.

BAUMGARTEN, F. and MERZLÈNY, A., *Kartelle und Trusts.* Berlin, Otto Liebmann, 1906.

BEACH, C. F., *Monopolies and Industrial Trusts.* St. Louis, 1898.

BERGLUND, A., "The United States Steel Corporation." *Columbia University Studies in History, Economics and Public Law,* Vol. XXVII, No. 2, 1907. New York, Columbia University Press, 1907.

BLATCHLEY, R. S., *Waste of Oil and Gas in the Mid-continent Fields.* U. S. Bureau of Mines, Technical Paper No. 45. Washington, Government Printing Office, 1913.

BOLEN, G. L., *The Plain Facts as to the Trusts and the Tariff.* New York, Macmillan, 1903.

BRANDEIS, L. D., "An Illegal Trust Legalized." *The World Today,* Vol. XXI, pp. 1440–1441 (December, 1911).

——— "Shall We Abandon the Policy of Competition?" *Case and Comment,* Vol. XVIII, pp. 494–496 (February, 1912).

BRIDGE, J. H., ed., *The Trust: Its Book.* New York, Doubleday, Page & Co., 1902.

BROOKINGS, R. S., *Industrial Ownership: Its Economic and Social Significance.* New York, Macmillan, 1925.

BROWN, W. J., *The Prevention and Control of Monopolies.* New York, Dutton & Co., 1914.

BUTLER, R. C. and LYNDE, C., *The Federal Trade Commission and the Regulation of Business under the Federal Trade Commission and Clayton Laws; Explanatory Comments.* Chicago, Callaghan & Co., 1915.

CARTER, G. R., *The Tendency Towards Industrial Combination.* London, Constable, 1913.

CARVER, T. N. "The Possibilities of Price Fixing in Time of Peace." *American Economic Review*, Vol. IX, pp. 246–251 (March, 1919, Supplement).

Chicago Conferences on Trusts. Chicago, The Civic Federation of Chicago, 1899, 1907.

CLARK, J. B. and J. M., *The Control of Trusts.* Rev. and enl. New York, Macmillan, 1914.

CLARK, J. M., *Economics of Overhead Costs.* Chicago, University of Chicago Press, 1923.

——— *Social Control of Business.* Chicago, University of Chicago Press, 1926.

CLEMEN, R. A., *American Livestock and Meat Industry.* New York, Ronald Press, 1923.

COLLIER, W. M., *The Trusts.* New York, Baker & Taylor Co., 1900.

CONANT, L., *Industrial Consolidations in the United States.* American Statistical Association, Vol. VII, No. 53, pp. 209–226 (March, 1901).

COOK, W. W., *"Trusts": The Recent Combinations in Trade.* 2nd ed. New York, L. K. Strouse & Co., 1888.

CROWELL, J. F., *Trusts and Competition.* Chicago, A. C. McClurg & Co., 1915.

CURTIS, E. N., *Manual of the Sherman Law: A Digest of the Law under the Federal Anti-trust Acts.* New York, Baker, Voorhis & Co., 1915.

DEWING, A. S., *A History of the National Cordage Company.* Cambridge, Harvard University Press, 1913.

——— "Statistical Test of the Success of Consolidations." *Quarterly Journal of Economics*, Vol. XXXVI, pp. 84–101 (November, 1921).

DOMERATSKY, L., *The International Cartel Movement.* U. S. Dept. of Labor Bulletin No. 556. Washington, Government Printing Office, 1928.

DURAND, E. D., *The Trust Problem.* Cambridge, Harvard University Press, 1915.

EDDY, A. J., *The Law of Combinations.* 2 vols. Chicago, Callaghan & Co., 1901.

——— The New Competition. Chicago, A. C. McClurg Co., 1916.

ELY, R. T., *Monopolies and Trusts.*, 2nd ed. New York, Macmillan, 1906.

FAY, C. N., *Big Business and Government.* New York, Moffat, Yard & Co., 1912.

Federal Anti-trust Decisions, 1890–1927. 10 vols. Lott, J. L. and Benton, T. G., compilers under the direction of the Attorney-General. Washington, Government Printing Office.

FEDERAL TRADE INFORMATION SERVICE. *A General Charter for Trade Associations. Correspondence between the Attorney-General and the Secretary of Commerce.* New York and Washington, Federal Trade Information Service, 1922.

Final Report of the Committee on Industry and Trade. Cmd 3282, 1929. London, H. M. Stationery Office, 1929.

FITZGERALD, P., *Industrial Combination in England.* London & New York, Sir I. Pitman & Sons, Ltd., 1927.

FLECHTHEIM, J., *Die rechtliche Organisation der Kartelle.* Berlin, J. Bensheimer, 1923.

FORBES, R., *Governmental Purchasing.* New York, Harper & Brothers, 1929.

FOREMAN, C. J., "Theories and Tests of Monopoly Control." *American Economic Review*, Vol. IX, pp. 482–501 (September, 1919).

FRIEDLÄNDER, H., *Konzernrecht: Das Recht der Betriebs- und Unternehmens-Zusammenfassungen.* Berlin, J. Bensheimer, 1927.

GOLDBAUM, W., *Kartellrecht und Kartellgericht.* Berlin, Georg Stille, 1926.

GORDON, A. P. L., *Problem of Trust and Monopoly Control.* London, Routledge & Sons, Ltd., 1928.

GUNTON, G., *Trusts and the Public.* New York, D. Appleton & Co., 1899.

HALLE, E. VON, *Trusts or Industrial Combinations and Coalitions in the United States.* New York, Macmillan, 1899.

HAMILTON, W. H. and WRIGHT, H. R., *The Case of Bituminous Coal.* New York, Macmillan, 1926.

Handelsgesetzbuch mit Einführungsgezetz vom 10 Mai, 1897. München, Becksche, 1925.

HANEY, L. H., *Business Organization and Combination.* Rev. ed. New York, Macmillan, 1914.

——— "Price Fixing in the United States During the War." *Political Science Quarterly*, Vol. XXXIV, pp. 104–126 (March, 1919); pp. 262–289 (June, 1919); pp. 434–453 (September, 1919).

HARLAN, J. M. and MCCANDLESS, L. W., *The Federal Trade Commission: Its Nature and Powers; an Interpretation of the Trade Law and Related Statutes.* Chicago, Callaghan & Co., 1916.

HARVEY, G. B., *Henry Clay Frick, the Man.* New York and London, Charles Scribner's Sons, 1928.

HARVEY, R. S. and BRADFORD, E. W., *A Manual of the Federal Trade Commission, Presenting the Origin, Development and Construction of the Anti-trust Laws, with Decisions upon the Constitutional and Unfair Trade Questions Involved, Together with the Rules of Practice, Forms, Texts of Statutes, Debates in Congress, and Complete Memoranda of Anti-trust Cases instituted by the United States.* Washington, D. C., J. Byrne & Co., 1916.

HAUSSMANN, F., *Grundlegung des Rechts der Unternehmens-Zusammenfassungen.* Berlin, J. Bensheimer, 1926.

HENDERSON, G. C., *The Federal Trade Commission.* New Haven, Yale University Press, 1924.

HIRST, F. W., *Monopolies, Trusts and Kartells.* New York, Dutton & Co., 1905.

HOBSON, J. A. *The Evolution of Modern Capitalism.* Rev. ed. London, Scott, 1926.

HOOVER, H., et al., *Recent Economic Changes in the United States*, 2 vols. New York, McGraw-Hill Book Co., 1929.

HUDSON, S. D. M., "Federal Incorporation." *Political Science Quarterly*, Vol. XXVI, pp. 63–97 (March, 1911).

INSTITUTE OF AMERICAN MEAT PACKERS, *The Packing Industry.* Chicago, University of Chicago Press, 1924.

ISAY, R., *Studien in offentlichen und privaten Kartellrecht*, 1922.

ISAY, R. TSCHIERSCHKY, S., Kartellverordnung, 1925.

JACOBSTEIN, M., "The Tobacco Industry in the United States." *Columbia University Studies in History, Economics and Public Law*, Vol. XXVI, No. 3, 1907. New York, Columbia University Press, 1907.

JEANS, J. S., *Trusts, Pools and Corners as Affecting Commerce and Industry.* (Social Questions of Today; H. de B. Gibbons, ed., No. 11) London, 1894.

JENKS, J. W. and CLARK, W. E., *The Trust Problem.* 5th ed., rev. and enl. Garden City, N. Y. Doubleday, Doran & Co., 1929.

JONES, ELIOT, *The Anthracite Coal Combination in the United States.* Cambridge, Harvard University Press, 1914.

——— "Is Competition Ruinous in Industry?" *Quarterly Journal of Economics,* Vol. XXXIV, pp. 473–519 (May, 1920).

——— *The Trust Problem in the United States.* New York, Macmillan, 1921.

JONES, F. D., *Trade Association Activities and the Law.* 1st ed. New York, McGraw-Hill Book Co., 1922.

KALES, A. M., ed., *Cases on Contracts and Combinations in Restraint of Trade, Selected from the Decisions of English and American Courts.* 2 vols. Chicago, Callaghan & Co., 1916.

Kartell-Rundschau. Edited by S. Tschierschky. 1902–1929. Berlin, Carl Heymann.

Kartellstelle des Reichsverbandes der deutschen Industrie, Sammlung von Entscheidungen und Gutachten des Kartellgerichts. Current publications, 1923 to date.

KELLOGG, F. B., "Federal Incorporation and Control." *Yale Law Journal,* Vol. XX, pp. 177–190 (January, 1911).

KESTNER, F. and LEHNICH, O., *Der Organisationszwang,* 2nd edition, 1927.

KING, W. L. MACKENZIE, "The Canadian Combines Investigation Act," *Annals of the American Academy of Political and Social Science,* Vol. XLII, pp. 149–155 (July 1912).

KIRSCH, B. J., *Trade Associations: The Legal Aspects.* New York, Central Book Co., 1928.

KNAUTH, O. W., "The Policy of the United States Toward Industrial Monopoly." *Columbia University Studies in History, Economics and Public Law,* Vol. LVI, No. 2, 1914. New York, Columbia University Press, 1914.

Kontradiktorische Verhandlungen üfer deutsche Kartelle, 5 vols. Berlin, Siemenroth, 1903–06.

KRÜGER, O., *Die Moderne Kartellorganisation der Deutschen Stahlindustrie* 1927.

LEROSSIGNOL, J. E., *Monopolies Past and Present.* New York, Crowell & Co., 1901.

LESLEY, R. W., et al., "History of the Portland Cement Industry in the United States." Reprint from the *Franklin Institute Journal,* November, 1928.

LEVY, F. H., "Amendments to the United States Anti-trust Laws." Address before the Committee on Commerce of the American Bar Association at a Public Hearing held at the Chamber of Commerce in New York City, March 23, 1927.

——— "The Anti-trust Laws with Special Reference to the Mennen Co. Decision, the Hardwood Lumber Decision and the Edge Resolution." Address Delivered at Atlantic City, N. J., May 9, 1922. New York, The Beacon Press, 1922.

——— "Sherman Law and the Australian Statute." *Virginia Law Register,* n.s. Vol. VIII, pp. 882–896 (April, 1923).

——— "Sherman Law and the English Doctrine." *Cornell Law Quarterly,* Vol. VI, pp. 36–55 (November, 1920).

——— "Should the Sherman Law Be Revised?" *Virginia Law Review* Vol. VI, pp. 1–19, (October, 1919).

LEVY, H., *Monopolies, Cartels and Trusts in British Industry.* London, Macmillan & Co., Ltd., 1927.

——— *Monopoly and Competition.* London, Macmillan & Co., Ltd., 1911.

LEWIS, J. O., *Methods for Increasing the Delivery from Oil Sands.* Bureau of Mines Bulletin No. 148; Petroleum Technology 37. 1st ed. Washington, Government Printing Office, 1917.

LIEFMANN, R., *Die Unternehmungen und ihre Zusammenschlüsse;* Vol. I, *Die Unternehmungsformen mit Einschluss der Genossenschaften und Sozialisierung,* 4th ed., 1927. Vol. II, *Kartelle, Konzerne und Trusts,* 7th ed., 1927.

——— *International Cartels, Combines and Trusts.* London, Europa Publishing Co., 1928.

——— *Kartelle und Trusts.* Stuttgart, E. H. Moritz, 1924.

——— "Monopoly or Competition as the Basis of Government Trust Policy." *Quarterly Journal of Economics,* Vol. XXIX, pp. 235–261 (February, 1915).

LITMAN, S., *Prices and Price Control in Great Britain and the United States during the World War.* New York, Oxford University Press, 1920.

LLOYD, H. D., *Wealth against Commonwealth.* New York, Harper & Brothers, 1898.

LÖFFLER, D., *Die Moderne Konzerniernung.* Frankenstein i. Schles. E. Phillips' Buchhandlung, 1926.

MACROSTY, H. W., *The Trust Movement in British Industry.* London, Longmans, Green & Co., 1907.

——— Trusts and the State: A Sketch of Competition. (Fabian Series, Vol. I.) New York, 1901.

MACGREGOR, D. H., *Industrial Combination.* London, George Bell & Co., 1906.

——— *International Cartels.* 1927.

MCKEE, T. H., *The National Conventions and Platforms of All Political Parties, 1789–1905.* 6th ed., rev. and enl. Baltimore, Friedenwald Co., 1906.

MARSHALL, A., *Industry and Trade.* London, Macmillan & Co., Ltd., 1920.

MEAKIN, W., *The New Industrial Revolution.* New York, Brentano, 1928.

METZNER, M., *Kartelle und Kartellpolitik.* Berlin, Heymann, 1926.

MEYER, B. H., *A History of the Northern Securities Case.* Madison, Wis. Bulletin of the University of Wisconsin, 1906.

MICHELS, R. K., "Cartels, Combines and Trusts in Post-War Germany." *Columbia University Studies in History, Economics and Public Law,* New York, Columbia University Press, 1928.

MITCHELL, W. C., *Business Cycles, the Problem and Its Setting.* New York, National Bureau of Economic Research, Inc., 1927.

MONTAGUE, G. H. *Business Competition and the Law.* New York, G. P. Putnam's Sons, 1917.

——— *The Rise and Progress of the Standard Oil Company.* New York, Harper & Brothers, 1903.

——— *Trusts of Today.* New York, McClure, Phillips & Co., 1904.

——— "Webb Bill and the Anti-trust Laws." *American Bar Association Journal,* Vol. III, pp. 145–164 (April, 1917).

MOODY, J., *The Truth About the Trusts.* New York & Chicago, Moody Publishing Co., 1904.

MUSSEY, H. R., "Combination in the Mining Industry: A Study of Concentration in Lake Superior Iron Ore Production." *Columbia University Studies in History, Economics and Public Law,* Vol. XXIII, No. 3, 1905. New York, Columbia University Press, 1905.

NATIONAL CIVIC FEDERATION, *The Trust Problem* (Replies of 16,000 representative Americans to a questionnaire). New York, M. B. Brown Printing and Binding Co., 1912.

NATIONAL INDUSTRIAL CONFERENCE BOARD, *Industrial Standardization.* New York, National Industrial Conference Board, Inc., 1929.

——— *Mergers and the Law.* New York, National Industrial Conference Board, Inc., 1929.

——— *Public Regulation of Competitive Practices.* New York, National Industrial Conference Board, Inc., 1925.

——— *Trade Associations: Their Economic Significance and Legal Status.* New York, National Industrial Conference Board, Inc., 1925.

NAYLOR, E. H., *Trade Associations.* New York, Ronald Press, 1921.

NELSON, M. N., "Open Price Associations." *University of Illinois Studies in the Social Sciences,* Vol. X, No. 2. Urbana, University of Illinois, 1923.

NETTLETON, A. B., ed., *Trusts or Competition? Both Sides of the Great Question in Business, Law and Politics.* Chicago, Leon Publishing Co., 1900.

New York, Report and Proceedings of the Joint Committee of the Senate and Assembly Appointed to Investigate Trusts (Lexow Report). Transmitted to the Legislature on March 9, 1897. Albany and New York, Wynkoop, Hallenbeck, Crawford Co., 1897.

NIMS, H. D., *The Law of Unfair Competition and Trade Marks.* 2nd ed. New York, Baker, Voorhis & Co., 1917.

NOTZ, W. F. and HARVEY, R. S. *American Foreign Trade, as Promoted by the Webb-Pomerene and Edge Acts, with Historical References to the Origin and Enforcement of the Anti-trust Laws.* Indianapolis, The Bobbs-Merrill Co., 1921.

NOYES, A. D., *Forty Years of American Finance.* New York, G. P. Putnam's Sons, 1909.

Ohio Supreme Court, State of Ohio *v.* Standard Oil Co., *Brief of the Relator in Contempt Proceedings.*

——— State of Ohio *v.* the Akron Underwriters' Association. *Brief for the State of Ohio,* Frank S. Monnett, Attorney-General.

——— State of Ohio (*ex rel.* F. S. Monnett, Attorney-General) *v.* the Buckeye Pipe Line Co. *Points in Oral Argument.*

——— State of Ohio (*ex. rel.* F. S. Monnett, Attorney-General) *v.* the Pittsburgh, Cincinnati, Chicago & St. Louis Railway Co. and the Cincinnati, Hamilton and Dayton Railway Co. Record.

OHIO, *Trust Investigation of Ohio Senate.* Columbus, Ohio, 1898.

OLIPHANT, H., *Cases on Trade Regulation, Selected from Decisions of English and American Courts.* St. Paul, West Publishing Co., 1923.

Passow, R., *Die Aktiengesellschaft, eine Wirtschaftwissenschaftliche Studie.* Jena, Gustav Fischer, 1922.

——— ed., *Materialien für das Wirtschafts-wissenschaftliche Studium.* Vol. I. *Kartelle des Bergbaues.* Leipzig, Berlin, B. G. Teubner, 1911.

Phelps, E. M., compiler, *Selected Articles on Federal Control of Interstate Corporations.* 2nd ed., rev. and enl. White Plains, N. Y., and New York City, H. W. Wilson Co., 1915.

Pierce, F., *The Tariff and the Trusts.* New York, Macmillan, 1907.

Powell, T. R., "Supreme Court Decisions on Federal Power Over Commerce, 1910–1914." *Minnesota Law Review,* Vol. VI, pp. 123–139, 194–218 (January, 1922).

Proceedings of the Committee on Merchant Marine and Fisheries in the Investigation of Shipping Combinations under Resolution 587. Report on Steamship Agreements and Affiliations in the American Foreign and Domestic Trade, including the Recommendations of the Committee. Washington, Government Printing Office, 1914.

Raffalovitch, A., *Trusts, Cartels et Syndicats.* Paris, Guillaumin, 1903.

Reed, H. B., *The Morals of Monopoly and Competition.* Menasha, Wis., Banta Publishing Co., 1916.

Refined Sugar Contract Litigation. Opinions, Orders, Decrees and Charges to Juries in Suits Instituted against Buyers for Breach of 1920 Refined Sugar Contracts. Issued by the American Sugar Refining Co., and the Franklin Sugar Refining Co., 1923.

Reichswirtschaftsminister, Konzerne, Interessengemeinschaften und ähnliche Zusammenschlüsse im Deutschen Reich, Ende 1927.

Report of the (British) Committee on Trusts. H. M. Stationery Office, London, Cd. 9236, 1919. Reprinted 1924.

Richardson, J. D., *A Compilation of the Messages and Papers of the Presidents.* 12 vols. New York, Bureau of National Literature and Art, 1917.

Ripley, W. Z., ed., *Trusts, Pools and Corporations.* Rev. ed. Boston, New York, Ginn, 1916.

Robinson, M. H., "The Distribution of Securities in the Formation of the United States Steel Corporation." *Political Science Quarterly,* Vol. XXX, pp. 277–300 (June, 1915).

Rousiers, P. de, *Cartels and Trusts and Their Development.* League of Nations Publ. of 1927, Economic and Financial Section, II, 21.

——— *Les Industries Monopolisées aux Etats Unis.* Paris, Bibliothèque du Musée Social, 1898.

Sanderson, W. A., *Restraint of Trade in English Law.* London, Sweet and Maxwell, Ltd., 1926.

Seager, H. R., *Principles of Economics.* 3rd ed., rev. and enl. New York, Henry Holt & Co., 1923.

——— "The Anti-trust Acts." *Political Science Quarterly,* Vol. XXX, pp. 448-462 (September, 1915).

——— "The Recent Trust Decisions." *Political Science Quarterly,* Vol. XXVI, pp. 581–614 (December, 1911).

Sherwood, S., *Influence of the Trust in the Development of Undertaking Genius.* Publications of the American Economic Association, 3rd series, Vol. I, pp. 163–176 (1900).

Smith, E. J., *The New Trades Combination Movement.* 1899.

STAFFEL, W., *Missbrauch wirtschaftlicher Machtstellungen.* Berlin, Walter de Grunter & Co., 1926.

Statisches Jahrbuch für das Deutsche Reich, 1928.

STEVENS, W. H. S., "A Classification of Pools and Associations Based on American Experience," *American Economic Review*, Vol. III, pp. 545–575 (September, 1913).

——— "A Group of Trusts and Combinations." *Quarterly Journal of Economics*, Vol. XXVI, pp. 593–643 (August, 1912).

——— ed., Industrial Combinations and Trusts. New York, Macmillan, 1913.

——— "The Clayton Act." *American Economic Review*, Vol. V, pp. 38–54, (March, 1915).

——— "The Powder Trust, 1872–1912." *Quarterly Journal of Economics*, Vol. XXVI, pp. 444–481 (May, 1912); "The Dissolution of the Powder Trust." *Quarterly Journal of Economics*, Vol. XXVII, pp. 593–643 (August, 1912).

——— *Unfair Competition: A Study of Certain Practices with Some Reference to the Trust Problem in the United States of America.* Chicago, University of Chicago Press, 1917.

STOCKDER, A. H., *Business Ownership Organization.* New York, Henry Holt & Co., 1922.

——— *German Trade Associations: The Coal Kartells.* New York, Henry Holt & Co., 1924.

STOCKING, G. W., *The Oil Industry and the Competitive System.* Boston, New York, Houghton, Mifflin Co., 1925..

SWIFT AND COMPANY, *An Analysis and Criticism of Part II of the Federal Trade Commission Report on the Meat Packing Industry of Nov. 25, 1918.* Issued April 5, 1919, by Swift & Co.

TAFT, W. H., *The Anti-trust Act and the Supreme Court.* New York & London, Harper & Brothers, 1914.

TARBELL, I. M., *History of the Standard Oil Company.* 2 vols. New York, McClure, Phillips & Co., 1904.

——— *Life of Elbert H. Gary.* New York, D. Appleton & Co., 1925.

THORNTON, W. W., *Treatise on the Sherman Anti-Trust Law.* 1913.

THORP, W. L. and MITCHELL, W. C., *Business Annals.* New York, National Bureau of Economic Research Publication No. 8, 1926.

THORP, W. L., *The Integration of Industrial Operation.* Washington, Government Printing Office, 1924.

TSCHIERSCHKY, S., *Kartell-Organisation.* Berlin, Industrieverlag Spaeth & Linde, 1928.

——— *Kartell und Trust.* Leipzig, Göschensche Verlagshandlung, 1911.

TUGWELL, R. G., *Industry's Coming of Age.* New York, Harcourt, Brace & Co., 1927.

——— *The Economic Basis of Public Interest.* Menasha, Wis., Geo. Banta Publishing Co., 1922.

UFERMANN, *Der deutsche Stahltrust*, Berlin, *Verlagsgesellschaft des allgemeinen deutschen Gewerkschaftsbundes, G. m. b. H.*, 1927.

U. S. BUREAU OF CORPORATIONS, *Report of the Commissioner of Corporations on the Beef Industry, March 3, 1905.* Washington, Government Printing Office, 1905.

——— *Report of the Commissioner of Corporations on the International Harvester Co., March 3, 1913.* Washington, Government Printing Office, 1913.

——— *Report of the Commissioner of Corporations on the Petroleum Industry.* 2 vols. Washington, Government Printing Office, 1907.

——— *Report of Commissioner of Corporations to the President on Prices of Tobacco,* Senate Document No. 78, 61st Congress, 1st Session, 1909. Washington, Government Printing Office, 1909.

——— *Report of Commissioner of Corporations on the Steel Industry.* 3 vols. Washington, Government Printing Office, 1911–13.

——— *Report of Commissioner of Corporations on the Tobacco Industry.* 3 vols. Washington, Government Printing Office. 1909–15.

——— *Report of Commissioner of Corporations on Transportation and Freight Rates in Connection with the Oil Industry.* Washington, Government Printing Office, 1906.

——— *Report of Commissioner of Corporations on Trust Laws and Unfair Competition, March 15, 1915.* Washington, Government Printing Office, 1916.

U. S. Committee Reports. *Report from Special Committee on the American Sugar Refining Co.* House Report No. 331, 62nd Congress, 2nd Session, 1912. Washington, Government Printing Office.

——— *Export Trade.* Senate Reports: No. 1056, 64th Congress, 2nd Session, 1917; No. 9, 65th Congress, 1st Session, 1917; No. 109, 65th Congress, 1st Session, 1917. Washington, Government Printing Office, 1917.

——— *Promotion of Export Trade.* House Report No. 1118, 64th Congress, 1st Session, 1916; House Report No. 50, 65th Congress, 1st Session, 1917. Washington, Government Printing Office, 1916, 1917.

——— *Report from Committee on Interstate Commerce on the Federal Trade Commission.* Senate Report No. 597, 63rd Congress, 2nd Session, 1913–14.

U. S. Committee Reports. *Report from Committee on Judiciary on Joint Resolution Proposing an Amendment to the Constitution of the United States Conferring Power on Congress to Define, Regulate, Prohibit and Dissolve Trusts.* House Report No. 1501, 56th Congress, 1st Session, 1899–1900.

——— *Report from the Committee on Judiciary to Accompany House Report No. 10539, a bill to amend the Sherman Act.* House Report No. 1506, 56th Congress, 1st Session, 1899–1900.

——— *Report from Committee on Judiciary on Unlawful Restraints and Monopolies.* Senate Report No. 698, 63rd Congress, 2nd Session, 1913–14.

U. S. Congress. *Hearings before Committee on Agriculture and Forestry.* Senate, 67th Congress, 4th Session, January 8, 9, and 10, 1923. *Proposed Merger of Meat Packing Corporations (Armour & Co.)* Washington, Government Printing Office, 1923.

——— *Hearings before Committee on Agriculture and Forestry.* Senate, 67th Congress, 4th Session, February 14, 1923. *A Bill to Amend the Packers and Stockyards Act of 1921.* Washington, Government Printing Office, 1923.

——— *Hearings before Committee on Banking and Currency.* Senate, 63rd Congress, 2nd Session. *The Regulation of the Stock Exchange.* Washington, Government Printing Office, 1914.

——— *Hearings before Committee on Interstate Commerce.* Senate, 62nd

Congress, 2nd Session, 1911–12. 3 vols. Pp. 315–322, and Vol. II, *On the Control of Corporations, Persons and Firms Engaged in Interstate Commerce.* Washington, Government Printing Office, 1912.

——— *Hearings before Committee on Interstate Commerce.* Senate, 65th Congress, 1st Session, 1917. *On Price Regulation of Steel.* Washington, Government Printing Office, 1917.

——— *Hearings before Committee on Interstate and Foreign Commerce.* House, February 11, 1921. *Amendment to Section 10 of the Clayton Act.* Washington, Government Printing Office, 1921.

——— *Hearings before Committee on Interstate and Foreign Commerce.* House, 63rd Congress, 2nd Session, 1914. *The Interstate Trade Commission.* Washington, Government Printing Office, 1914.

——— *Hearings before Committee on Investigation of U. S. Steel Corporation.* House Report No. 1127, 62 Congress, 2nd Session, 1911.

——— *Hearings before Committee on Judiciary.* House, 66th Congress, 1st Session, 1919. *High Cost of Living as Affected by Trusts and Monopolies: Statement of Federal Trade Commissioners.* Washington, Government Printing Office, 1919.

——— *Hearings before Committee on Judiciary.* House, 63rd Congress, 2nd Session, 1914. 2 vols. *On Trust Legislation.* Washington, Government Printing Office, 1914.

——— *Hearings before Committee on Judiciary.* House, 64th Congress, 1st Session, July 19, 1916. *To Amend Clayton Anti-trust Act.* Washington, Government Printing Office, 1916.

——— *Hearings before Sub-committee on Judiciary.* Senate, 60th Congress, 1st Session, 1908. *On the Amendment of the Sherman Anti-trust Law.* Washington, Government Printing Office, 1908.

——— *Pulp and Paper Investigation Hearings.* House Document No. 1502, 60th Congress, 2nd Session, 1908–09. 5 vols. Washington, Government Printing Office, 1909.

——— *Report on Investigation of Trusts.* H. R. No. 3112, Vol. IX, 50th Congress, 1st Session, 1887–88. Washington, Government Printing Office, 1888.

——— *Transportation and Sale of Meat Products.* Senate Report No. 829, Vol. III, 51st Congress, 1st Session, 1889–90. Washington, Government Printing Office, 1890.

U. S. Courts. *Decrees and Judgments in Federal Anti-trust Cases: July 2, 1890–January 1, 1918.* Washington, Government Printing Office, 1918.

U. S. Court Papers. International Harvester Co. *v.* United States. *Brief for International Harvester Co.* In the District Court of the U. S., District of Minnesota, 3rd Division.

——— International Harvester Co. *v.* United States. *Defendant's Statement of the Case.* In the District Court of the U. S., District of Minnesota, 3rd Division.

——— International Harvester Co. of New Jersey *et al. v.* United States. *Brief for the United States.* In the Supreme Court of the United States, October term, 1914. No. 757.

——— International Harvester Co. of New Jersey *et al. v.* United States. *Brief for the International Harvester Co.* In the Supreme Court of the United States, October term, 1914. No. 757.

——— International Harvester Co. of New Jersey *et al. v.* United States. *Reply Brief for the Appellants.* In the Supreme Court of the United States, October term, 1916.

——— International Harvester Co. of New Jersey *et al. v.* United States. *Brief for the United States (Reargument).* In the Supreme Court of the United States, October term, 1916.

——— International Harvester Co. of New Jersey *et al. v.* United States. *Reply Brief for International Harvester Co. (Reargument).* In the Supreme Court of the United States, October term, 1916.

——— Standard Oil Co. *v.* United States. *Brief for the United States.* In the U. S. Circuit Court of Appeals for the 7th Circuit, October term, 1907.

——— Standard Oil Co. *v.* United States. *Brief for the Standard Oil Co.* 2 vols. In the Supreme Court of the United States, October term, 1909.

——— Standard Oil Co. *v.* United States. *Summary of Facts and Brief of the Law. Brief for the United States.* 2 vols. In the Supreme Court of the United States, October term, 1909.

——— Standard Oil Co. *v.* United States. *Reply Brief for the United States.* In the Supreme Court of the United States, October term, 1910.

——— United Shoe Machinery Corporation *et al. v.* United States. *Brief for the United States (Reargument).* In the Supreme Court of the United States, October term, 1921.

——— United States *v.* Aluminum Co. of America. *Petition.* In the District Court of the U. S. for the Western District of Pennsylvania.

——— United States *v.* Aluminum Co. of America. *Decree.* In the District Court of the U. S. for the Western District of Pennsylvania.

——— United States *v.* American Can Co. *et al. Brief for the United States.* In the District Court of the U. S. for the District Court of Maryland. No. 40.

——— United States *v.* American Can Co. *et al. Petitioner's Summary of Evidence.* In the District Court of the U. S. for the District of Maryland. No. 40.

——— United States *v.* American Can Co. *Brief for American Can Co.* In the District Court of the U. S. for the District of Maryland. No. 40.

——— United States *v.* American Sugar Refining Co. *Petition.* In the Circuit Court of the U. S. for the Southern District of New York.

——— United States *v.* American Tobacco Co. *et al. Original Petition.* In the Circuit Court of the U. S. for the Southern District of New York.

——— United States *v.* American Tobacco Co. *et al.* (No. 660), and American Tobacco Co. *et al. v.* U. S. (No. 661). *Transcript of Record.* 5 vols. In the Supreme Court of the United States, October term, 1908.

——— United States *v.* American Tobacco Co. *et al.* (No. 118), and American Tobacco Co. *et al. v.* U. S. (No. 119). *Brief for the United States.* In the Supreme Court of the United States, October term, 1910.

——— United States *v.* E. I. du Pont de Nemours and Co. *et al. Transcript of Record.* 13 vols. In the Circuit Court of the U. S. for the District of Delaware. No. 280.

——— United States *v.* E. I. du Pont de Nemours and Co. *et al. Brief for the United States.* 2 vols. In the Circuit Court of the U. S. for the District of Delaware.

——— United States *v.* E. I. du Pont de Nemours and Co. *et al. Breif for E. I. du Pont de Nemours and Co. and various other defendants, with Appendix to Brief.* In the Circuit Court of the U. S. for the District of Delaware. No. 280.

——— United States *v.* Eastman Kodak Co., *et al. Petition.* In the District Court of the U. S. for the Western District of New York.

——— United States *v.* General Electric Co. *et al. Petition.* In the Circuit Court of the U. S. for the Northern District of Ohio.

——— United States *v.* International Harvester Co. *Brief for the International Harvester Co. in answer to Supplemental Petition.* In the District Court of the U. S., District of Minnesota, 3rd Division.

——— United States *v.* International Harvester Co. *et al. Appendix to Defendants' Brief.* In the District Court of the U. S. for the District of Minnesota. No. 624.

——— United States *v.* International Harvester Co. *et al. Brief for the United States (Supplemental Petition).* In the District Court of the U. S., District of Minnesota, 3rd Division.

——— United States *v.* National Cash Register Co. *et al. Petition.* In the Circuit Court of the U. S. for the Southern Judicial District of Ohio, Western Division. No. 6802.

——— United States *v.* Standard Oil Co. of New Jersey *et al. Original Petition.* In the Circuit Court of the U. S. for the Eastern Division of the Eastern Judicial District of Missouri.

——— United States *v.* Standard Oil Co. *et al. Answer of the Standard Oil Co. et al.* In the Circuit Court of the U. S. for the Eastern Division of the Eastern Judicial District of Missouri. No. 5371.

——— United States *v.* Standard Oil Co. *et al. Additional Answer of the Standard Oil Co. et al.* In the Circuit Court of the U. S. for the Eastern Division of the Eastern Judicial District of Missouri. No. 5371.

——— United States *v.* Standard Oil Co. *et al. Brief for the United States.* In the District Court of the U. S. for the Northern District of Illinois, Eastern Division.

——— United States *v.* Swift & Co. *et al. Decree and Consents, Answers and Stipulation.* In the Supreme Court of the District of Columbia. No. 37623.

——— United States *v.* Swift & Co. *et al. Brief for the United States.* In the Supreme Court of the United States, October term, 1904. No. 103.

——— United States *v.* United Shoe Machinery Co. *et al. Original Petition.* In the District Court of the U. S. for the Eastern District of Missouri.

——— United States *v.* United Shoe Machinery Co. *Brief for the United States (Reargument).* In the Supreme Court of the United States, October term, 1917, No. 207.

——— United States *v.* United States Steel Corporation *et al. Petition.* In the Circuit Court of the U. S. for the District of New Jersey.

——— United States *v.* U. S. Steel Corporation *et al. Brief for the United States* (in two parts). In the District Court of the U. S. for the District of New Jersey, October term, 1914. No. 6214.

——— United States *v.* U. S. Steel Corporation. *Brief for the United*

States. 2 vols. In the Supreme Court of the United States, October term, 1916. No. 481.

——— United States *v.* U. S. Steel Corporation. *Brief for the U. S. Steel Corporation*. In the Supreme Court of the United States, October term, 1916. No. 481.

U. S. DEPARTMENT OF COMMERCE. *Trade Association Activities*. Rev. ed. Washington, Government Printing Office, 1927.

U. S. DEPARTMENT OF JUSTICE. *Annual Reports of the Attorney-General*, 1890–1928.

——— *The Federal Anti-trust Laws with Amendments*. Washington, Government Printing Office, 1928.

——— *Proposed Merger of Iron and Steel Corporation: Letter transmitting information*. 67th Congress, 2nd Session, 1922. Washington, Government Printing Office, 1922.

U. S. FEDERAL OIL CONSERVATION BOARD. *Reports 1925, 1928, and 1929*.

——— *Report of the Committee of Nine to Federal Oil Conservation Board, January 28, 1928*. Washington, Government Printing Office, 1928.

U. S. FEDERAL TRADE COMMISSION, Publications of:

Annual Reports, 1915–1928.

Bakery Combines and Profits, February 9, 1927.

Book Paper Industry, August 15, 1917.

Coal—Anthracite and Bituminous, June 20, 1917.

Coal—Investment and Profits in Soft-coal Mining, May 31, 1922.

Coal, Nos. 1–7, June 30, 1919.

Coal—Premium Prices of Anthracite, July 6, 1925.

Combed Cotton Yarns, April 14, 1921.

Commercial Bribery, March 18, 1920.

Commercial Feeds, March 29, 1921.

Commercial Wheat-flour Milling, September 15, 1920.

Competition and Profits in Bread and Flour, January 11, 1928.

Co-operation in American Export Trade, Parts I and II, June 30, 1916.

Co-operation in Foreign Countries, December 2, 1924.

Co-operative Marketing, May 2, 1928.

Cottonseed Industry, March 5, 1928.

Cotton Merchandising Practices, June 7, 1924.

Cotton Trade, Parts I and II, April 28, 1924.

Cotton Trade, Preliminary, February 26, 1923.

Decisions, 9 vols. 1920–1927.

Electric Power Industry—Control of Power Companies, February 22, 1927.

——— *Supply of Electrical Equipment and Competitive Conditions*, January 12, 1928.

Export Grain, 2 vols., May 16, 1922; June 18, 1923.

Farm Implements, Causes of High Prices of, May 4, 1920.

Fertilizer Industry, 2 vols., August 19, 1916; March 3, 1923.

Flour Milling and Jobbing, April 4, 1918.

Flour Milling—Competitive Conditions in, May 3, 1926.

Foreign Trade Series, No. 1, 1919.

Functions of Federal Trade Commission, July 1, 1922.

Fundamentals of a Cost System for Manufacturers, July, 1916.

Grain Trade, 7 vols., September 15, 1920—June 25, 1926.

Guarantee Against Price Decline, May 27, 1920.
High Cost of Living, April 30–May 1, 1917.
House Furnishings, 3 vols., January 17, 1923–October 6, 1924.
Index Digest of Decisions, Vol. 1, 2, 3.
Lumber Manufacturers Trade Associations, March 29, 1922.
Lumber—Southern Pine Lumber Manufacturers, May 1, 1922.
Meat-packing Industry, Maximum Profit Limitations on, September 25, 1919.
——— *Summary and 6 parts*, June 24, 1919 to December, 1919.
Milk and Milk Products, June 6, 1921.
National Wealth and Income, May 25, 1926.
Newsprint Paper Industry, June 13, 1917.
Northern Hemlock and Hardwood Manufacturers, May 7, 1923.
Open-price Trade Associations, February 13, 1929.
Packers' Consent Decree, December 8, 1924.
Petroleum Industry, Foreign Ownership in, February 12, 1923.
——— *of Wyoming*, January 3, 1921.
——— *Pacific Coast*, Part I, April 7, 1921; Part II, November 28, 1921.
——— *Prices, Profits and Competition*, December 12, 1927.
Petroleum, Panhandle Crude, February 3, 1928.
——— *Pipe Line Transportation of*, February 28, 1916.
——— *Products, Advance in Prices of*, June 1, 1920.
——— *Trade in Wyoming and Montana*, July 13, 1922.
Price Associations, Letter to President, 1921.
Private Car Lines, June 27, 1919.
Profiteering, June 29, 1918.
Radio Industry, December 1, 1923.
Resale Price Maintenance, June 30, 1919; January 30, 1929 (Part I).
Rules of Practice and Procedure, with Amendments, February 1, 1924–October 1, 1928.
Shoe and Leather Costs and Prices, June 10, 1921.
Southern Livestock Prices, February 2, 1920.
Steel—Pittsburgh Basing Point for, October 15, 1919.
——— *War-time Costs and Profits*, February 18, 1925.
Stock Dividends, December 5, 1927.
Sugar Supply and Prices, November 15, 1920.
Taxation and Tax Exempt Income, June 6, 1924.
Tobacco Industry, December 11, 1920.
Tobacco—Prices of Tobacco Products, January 17, 1922.
——— *Report on American Tobacco Co. and Imperial Tobacco Co.*, (Sen. Doc. 34, December 23, 1925.)
Trade and Tariffs in South American Countries, June 30, 1916.
Trade Marks, Patents, etc., 1918.
Trade Practice Conferences, September 15, 1927; March 15, 1928.
Trade Practice Submittals, July 1, 1925.
Trust Laws and Unfair Competition, March 15, 1915.
Unfair Competition at Common Law.
Uniform Contracts and Cost Accounting Definitions, July, 1917.
Utility Corporations (Testimony) Nos. 1–14, March 15, 1928—May 15, 1929.

Western Red Cedar Association, January 24, 1923.

Wheat Flour Milling Industry, May 16, 1924.

Wholesale Marketing of Food, June 30, 1919.

U. S. FUEL ADMINISTRATION REPORT. *Prices and Marketing Practices Covering the Distribution of Gasoline and Kerosene Throughout the United States.* (A. G. Maguire). Washington, Government Printing Office, 1919.

U. S. INDUSTRIAL COMMISSION. *Report.* Vols. 1, 2, 13, 18, 19, 1900–1902.

U. S. INTERSTATE COMMERCE COMMISSION. *Report of Investigation of Conditions Affecting the Production, Transportation, and Marketing of Crude Petroleum. October 11, 1915.* 361, I. C. C. Reports, pp. 425–510.

U. S. LAWS, STATUTES, ETC. *Anti-trust Laws with Amendments*, 1890–1923. Compiled by Elmer A. Lewis. Washington, Government Printing Office, 1924.

U. S. LIBRARY OF CONGRESS. *Select List of References on Unfair Competition. August 7, 1924.*

VAN HISE, C. R., *Concentration and Control: A Solution of the Trust Problem in the United States.* Rev. New York, Macmillan Co., 1914.

Verhandlungen der vom K. K. Handelministerium veranstalten Kartellenquete. Wien, Druck und Kommissionsverlag der K. K. Hof- und Staatsdruckerei, 1912.

VINER, J., *Dumping: A Problem in International Trade.* Chicago, University of Chicago Press, 1923.

VIRTUE, G. O., "The Meat Packing Investigation." *Quarterly Journal of Economics*, Vol. XXXIV, pp. 626–685 (August 1920).

VOGT, P. L., *The Sugar Refining Industry in the United States.* Publications of the University of Pennsylvania, Series in Political Economy and Public Law, No. 21, 1908.

WALKER, A. H., *History of the Sherman Law of the United States of America.* New York, The Equity Press, 1910.

WALKER, F., "Policies of Germany, England, Canada and the United States towards Combinations." *Annals of American Academy of Political and Social Science*, Vol. XLII, pp. 183–201 (July, 1912).

——— "The Beef Trust and the United States Government." *Economic Journal*, Vol. XVI, pp. 491–514 (December, 1906).

——— "The German Steel Syndicate." *Quarterly Journal of Economics*, Vol. XX, pp. 353–398 (May, 1906).

——— "The Law Concerning Monopolistic Combinations in Continental Europe." *Political Science Quarterly*, Vol. XX, pp. 13–41 (March, 1905).

——— "The Oil Trust and the Government." *Political Science Quarterly*, Vol. XXIII, pp. 18–46 (March, 1908).

WATKINS, M. W., *Industrial Combinations and Public Policy.* New York, Houghton Mifflin Co., 1927.

WHITE and KEMBLE, compilers, *Map of the U. S. Steel Corporation Properties, with Statistics, Earnings, and Documents.* New York, *The Wall Street Journal* (Dow, Jones & Co., publishers), 1903.

WHITNEY, E. B., *Governmental Interference with Industrial Combinations.* Publications of the American Economic Association, 3rd Series, 6, pp. 231–249 (1905).

WIBAUT, F. M., *The Margarine Trust.* Amsterdam, The International Federation of General Factory Workers, 1929.

WICKERSHAM, G. W., *The Relation of the Federal Government to Industrial Combinations.* An Address at Philadelphia, Pa., February 26, 1914. Washington, Government Printing Office.

WIEDENFELD, K., *Kartelle und Konzerne, 1927.*

——— *Cartels and Combines* (English translation). Geneva, Imp. Kundig, 1927.

——— *Das Rheinisch-Westfälische Kohlensyndikat.*

WILGUS, H. L., *A Study of the U. S. Steel Corporation in its Industrial and Legal Aspects.* Chicago, Callaghan & Co., 1901.

WILSON, W., *The New Freedom.* New York and Garden City, Doubleday, Page & Co., 1913.

WOLL, M., "Anti-combination Laws: Ruin." *Forum,* Vol. LXVI, pp. 64–72, (July, 1921).

WYMAN, B., *Control of the Market: A Legal Solution of the Trust Problem.* New York, Moffat, Yard & Co., 1911.

YOUNG, A. A., "The Sherman Act and the New Anti-trust Legislation." *Journal of Political Economy,* Vol. XXXII, pp. 201–220 (March, 1915); pp. 305–326 (April, 1915); pp. 417–436 (May, 1915).

YOUNGMAN, A., "The Tendency of Modern Combination." *Journal of Political Economy,* Vol. XV, pp. 193–208 (April, 1907); pp. 284–298 (May, 1907).

ADDITIONAL TITLES

FREUND, E., *Legal Nature of Corporations.* Thesis, Ph.D., Columbia University, 1896.

JAVITS, B. A., in collaboration with C. W. WOOD, *Make Everybody Rich: Industry's New Goal.* New York, B. C. Forbes Publishing Co., 1929.

JOYCE, J. A., *A Treatise on Monopolies and Unlawful Combinations or Restraints.* New York, The Banks Law Publishing Co., 1911.

MACHEN, A. W., *Treatise on Modern Law of Corporations.* Boston, Little, Brown & Co., 1908.

INDEX

Big Business

Economic Power in a Free Society

An Arno Press Collection

Alsberg, Carl L. **Combination in the American Bread-Baking Industry:** With Some Observations on the Mergers of 1924-25. 1926

Armes, Ethel. **The Story of Coal and Iron in Alabama.** 1910

Atkinson, Edward. **The Industrial Progress of the Nation:** Consumption Limited, Production Unlimited. 1889

Baker, John Calhoun. **Directors and Their Functions:** A Preliminary Study. 1945

Barron, Clarence W. **More They Told Barron:** Conversations and Revelations of an American Pepys in Wall Street. 1931

Bossard, James H. S. and J. Frederic Dewhurst. **University Education For Business:** A Study of Existing Needs and Practices. 1931

Bridge, James H., editor. **The Trust:** Its Book. Being a Presentation of the Several Aspects of the Latest Form of Industrial Evolution. 1902

Civic Federation of Chicago. **Chicago Conference on Trusts.** 1900

Clews, Henry. **Fifty Years in Wall Street.** 1908

Coman, Katharine. **The Industrial History of the United States.** 1910

Crafts, Wilbur F. **Successful Men of To-Day:** And What They Say of Success. 1883

Davis, John P. **The Union Pacific Railway:** A Study in Railway Politics, History, and Economics. 1894

Economics and Social Justice. 1973

Edie, Lionel D., editor. **The Stabilization of Business.** 1923

Edwards, Richard, editor. **New York's Great Industries.** 1884

Ely, Richard T. **Monopolies and Trusts.** 1912

Ford, Henry. **My Life and Work.** 1922

Freedley, Edwin T. **A Practical Treatise on Business.** 1853

Hadley, Arthur Twining. **Standards of Public Morality.** 1907

Hamilton, Walton, et al. **Price and Price Policies.** 1938

Haney, Lewis H. **Business Organization and Combination.** 1914

Hill, James J. **Highways of Progress.** 1910

Jenks, Jeremiah Whipple and Walter E. Clark. **The Trust Problem.** Fifth Edition. 1929

Keezer, Dexter Merriam and Stacy May. **The Public Control of Business.** 1930

La Follette, Robert Marion, editor. **The Making of America:** Industry and Finance. 1905

Lilienthal, David E. **Big Business:** A New Era. 1952

Lippincott, Isaac. **A History of Manufactures in the Ohio Valley to the Year 1860.** 1914

Lloyd, Henry Demarest. **Lords of Industry.** 1910

McConnell, Donald. **Economic Virtues in the United States.** 1930

Mellon, Andrew W. **Taxation:** The People's Business. 1924

Meyer, Balthasar Henry. **Railway Legislation in the United States.** 1909

Mills, James D. **The Art of Money Making.** 1872

Montague, Gilbert Holland. **The Rise and Progress of the Standard Oil Company.** 1904

Mosely Industrial Commission. **Reports of the Delegates of the Mosely Industrial Commission to the United States of America, Oct.-Dec., 1902.** 1903

Orth, Samuel P., compiler. **Readings on the Relation of Government to Property and Industry.** 1915

Patten, Simon N[elson]. **The Economic Basis of Protection.** 1890

Peto, Sir S[amuel] Morton. **Resources and Prospects of America.** 1866

Ripley, William Z[ebina]. **Main Street and Wall Street.** 1929

Ripley, William Z[ebina]. **Railroads:** Rates and Regulation. 1912

Rockefeller, John D. **Random Reminiscences of Men and Events.** 1909

Seager, Henry R. and Charles A. Gulick, Jr. **Trust and Corporation Problems.** 1929

Taeusch, Carl F. **Policy and Ethics in Business.** 1931

Taylor, Albion Guilford. **Labor Policies of the National Association of Manufacturers.** 1928

Vanderlip, Frank A. **Business and Education.** 1907

Van Hise, Charles R. **Concentration and Control:** A Solution of the Trust Problem in the United States. 1912

The Wealthy Citizens of New York. 1973

White, Bouck. **The Book of Daniel Drew.** 1910

Wile, Frederic William, editor. **A Century of Industrial Progress.** 1928

Wilgus, Horace L. **A Study of the United States Steel Corporation in Its Industrial and Legal Aspects.** 1901

[Youmans, Edward L., compiler] **Herbert Spencer on the Americans.** 1883

Youngman, Anna. **The Economic Causes of Great Fortunes.** 1909